SOCIAL PROBLEMS IN A DIVERSE SOCIETY

Diana Kendall
Baylor University

Edward G. Thompson
McMaster University

Vicki L. Nygaard
University of
British Columbia

FOURTH CANADIAN EDITION

PEARSON

Toronto

Editorial Director: Claudine O'Donnell
Acquisitions Editor: Matthew Christian
Marketing Manager: Christine Cozens
Program Manager: Madhu Ranadive
Project Manager: Pippa Kennard
Developmental Editor: Rachel Stuckey
Production Services: Cenveo Publisher® Services
Permissions Project Manager: Kathryn O'Handley
Photo Permissions Research: Nazveena Syed, Lumina
Text Permissions Research: Tom Wilcox, Lumina
Interior Designer: Anthony Leung
Cover Designer: Anthony Leung
Cover Image: Karavai/Shutterstock

Vice-President, Cross Media and Publishing Services: Gary Bennett

Credits and acknowledgments for material borrowed from other sources and reproduced, with permission, in this textbook appear on the appropriate page within the text.

Original edition published by Pearson Education, Inc., Upper Saddle River, New Jersey, USA. Copyright © 2016 Pearson Education, Inc. This edition is authorized for sale only in Canada.

If you purchased this book outside the United States or Canada, you should be aware that it has been imported without the approval of the publisher or the author.

2 17

Library and Archives Canada Cataloguing in Publication

Kendall, Diana Elizabeth, author
    Social problems in a diverse society / Diana Kendall, Edward G. Thompson, Vicki L. Nygaard.—Fourth Canadian edition.

Includes bibliographical references and index.
ISBN 978-0-205-88575-6 (paperback)

    1. Social problems—Textbooks. 2. Social problems—Canada—Textbooks. I. Thompson, Edward G., 1945-, author II. Nygaard, Vicki Leanne, 1964-, author III. Title.

HN17.5.K45 2015   361.1   C2015-905658-6

ISBN 978-0-205-88575-6

Dedication

To my dear partner, Helen.

Edward G. Thompson

To the memory of Dr. Paul Morgan Baker (1949–2009), close friend and mentor, who taught me to be a sociologist.

Vicki L. Nygaard

Brief Contents

Contents

* 21 pages

31 pages

21 pages

Preface

Learning about social problems can be a highly rewarding experience. Although we live in challenging times, a course on social problems provides an excellent avenue for developing critical thinking skills and for learning how to use sociological concepts and perspectives to analyze specific social concerns ranging from war and terrorism, media concentration, drug addiction, and violence to the inequalities of racism, sexism, classism, ageism, homophobia, and ableism.

Our first and foremost goal in writing this book is to make the study of social problems interesting and relevant for students. To stimulate interest in reading the chapters and participation in class discussions, we have used lived experiences (personal narratives of real people) and statements from a wide variety of analysts to show how social problems impinge on people at the individual, group, and societal levels. Moreover, we have applied the sociological imagination and relevant sociological concepts and perspectives to all the topics in a systematic manner.

The fourth Canadian edition of *Social Problems in a Diverse Society* focuses on the significance of racialization and ethnicity, age, sexual orientation, class, ability, and gender in understanding social problems in Canada and around the globe. Throughout the text, people—especially those from marginalized groups—are shown not merely as "victims" of social problems, but also as individual actors with agency who resist discrimination and inequality and seek to bring about change in families, schools, workplaces, and the larger society. To facilitate the inclusion of previously excluded perspectives, Chapters 2 through 6 examine wealth and poverty, racialized/ethnic inequality, gender inequality, and inequalities based on age and sexual orientation. Thereafter, in Chapters 10 through 16, concepts and perspectives are intertwined in the discussion of specific social institutions, such as education, health care, and the environment.

This fourth Canadian edition is balanced in its approach to examining social problems. However, it includes a more comprehensive view of feminist and postmodern perspectives and global perspectives on a vast array of subjects than other social problems texts. As sociologists who integrate social theory into our lectures, we were disheartened by the minimal use of sociological theory in most social problems texts. Those that discuss theory typically do so in early chapters but then fail to use these theories as a systematic framework for examining specific social issues in subsequent chapters. Similarly, many texts give the impression that social problems can be solved if people reach a consensus on what should be done. But *Social Problems in a Diverse Society*, fourth Canadian edition, emphasizes that how people view a social problem is related to how they believe the problem should be reduced or solved. Consider poverty, for example: people who focus on individual causes of poverty typically believe that individual solutions (such as teaching people a work ethic and reforming welfare) are necessary to reduce the problem, whereas those who focus on structural causes of poverty (such as chronic unemployment and inadequate educational opportunities) typically believe that solutions must come from and through the larger society. Moreover, what some people see as a problem, others see as a solution for a problem (e.g., the sex trade as a source of income, or abortion to terminate a pregnancy). The epilogue allows students to explore further the question, "How can social problems be solved?"

Finally, we wrote *Social Problems in a Diverse Society* to provide students and instructors with a text that covers all the major social concerns we must deal with today, but does not leave students believing that the text—and perhaps the course—was a "depressing litany of social problems that nobody can do anything about anyway," as many students have stated about different texts. We have written this text in hopes of resolving those students' concerns, because we believe the sociological perspective has much to add to our individual, local, national, and global dialogues on a host of issues, such as environmental degradation; Canadian involvement in overseas military missions; discrimination based on racialization and ethnicity, class, gender, age, sexual orientation, or other attributes; and problems in media and education. Welcome to an innovative examination of social problems—one of the most stimulating and engrossing fields of study in sociology! We welcome your engagement in the effort to make the world a better place.

ORGANIZATION OF THIS TEXT

Social Problems in a Diverse Society, fourth Canadian edition, has been organized with the specific plan of introducing disparities in wealth and poverty, racialization and ethnicity, gender, age, and sexual orientation early on so that the concepts and perspectives developed in these chapters may be applied throughout the text. All chapters offer theoretical analyses from structural functionalism, conflict or Marxist perspectives, symbolic interactionism, and feminist theories. In addition, other theories are introduced where most relevant.

Chapter 1 explains the sociological perspective, several of the central methods of analysis, and provides an analysis of attempts at problem solving at the micro, mid-range, and macro levels of society.

Chapter 2 looks at wealth and poverty in Canada and around the world. Students will gain new insights into disparities between the wealthy and the poor and into problems such as workfare, homelessness, food insecurity, and poverty. The chapter concludes with a thematic question, "Can class-based inequality be reduced?" This question will be asked throughout the text as new topics are discussed.

Chapter 3 integrates the previous discussion of class-based inequalities with an examination of racialized and ethnic inequality. The chapter looks at issues of democratic racism and White privilege in Canada, and at the ways that racism manifests throughout Canadian institutions and practices.

Chapter 4 highlights factors such as mainstream gender socialization and social barriers that contribute to the unequal treatment of women in the workplace, in the family, at school, and at other social institutions. Transgender issues and global gender issues are also introduced for discussion.

Chapter 5 explores ageism and inequality based on age, and problems like employment, retirement, health and health care, housing, and death and dying are discussed.

Chapter 6 highlights inequality based on sexual orientation, placing these important topics in a context similar to the studies of prejudice and discrimination rooted in racism and sexism in contemporary societies. In addition, feminist intersectionality theories and queer theories are highlighted as ways of analyzing issues and inequalities around sexual orientation.

Chapter 7 links previous discussions of racialization and ethnicity, class, and gender to an analysis of the sex trade. The discussion of pornography has also been reintroduced to this chapter. The chapter provides up-to-date information on the globalization of sex work and gives students insight into the rationales of both sex workers themselves and their clients. New information on global sex tourism is presented, with a specific focus on differences and similarities between female and male sex tourists. Finally, controversies and legal challenges regarding the legalities of sex work in Canada are presented as important issues to consider in the 21st century.

In Chapter 8, social problems caused by addictions—alcohol, tobacco, other drugs, and gambling—are discussed in depth, and students are provided with information about the drug commonly called the "date rape" drug; the abuse of prescription drugs, over-the-counter drugs, and caffeine; as well as the characteristics of problem gambling.

Chapter 9 discusses crime and criminal justice and takes an incisive look at sociological explanations of crime.

Chapter 10 highlights health and health care and its problems, disability, mental illness, and our health care system.

Chapter 11 explores the changing family, emphasizing diversity in intimate relationships and families, and child-related family issues. It also explores the dark side of family life.

Chapter 12 presents contemporary problems in education, tracing the problems to such issues as what schools are supposed to accomplish, how they are financed, and why higher education may become less widely accessible with increasing tuition fees.

Chapter 13 explores current issues in the global economy and politics, such as Canada's economic report card, the recent global recession, politics in Canada, as well as globally comparing voter participation and confidence in parliament.

Chapter 14 discusses ongoing concerns regarding the Canadian and global media, such as media concentration, new media technology, and consequences of exposure to violent, racist, and sexist media.

Chapter 15 provides a survey of problems associated with population and the environmental crisis, focusing particularly on the causes and consequences of high rates of global migration and certain types of pollution. It also includes a look at urban problems, detailing the powerful impact of urbanization on both high-income and low-income nations of the world.

Chapter 16 presents an overview of Canada's roles in the ongoing U.S. "war on terror," examining the consequences of war and terrorism for people and the environment. The politics of war, as well as global and domestic terrorism, are highlighted.

The epilogue asks, "How can social problems be solved?" and includes a review of the four main sociological theories used to explain social problems, plus some thought-provoking questions about everyone's role in creating solutions to social problems.

DISTINCTIVE FEATURES

A number of special features have been designed to incorporate racialization and ethnicity, class, sexual orientation, and gender into our analysis of social problems and to provide students with new insights on the social problems that they learn about in the news. The following sections discuss the text's distinctive features.

NEW TO THIS EDITION

The most substantial new feature of *Social Problems in a Diverse Society,* fourth Canadian edition, is the inclusion of multiple international comparisons, both with our peer high-income countries and with the global community as a whole. In previous editions, Social Problems in Global Perspective boxes showed some comparisons between Canada and other countries. This edition shows international comparisons both in these boxes and throughout the chapters to illustrate how Canada is doing relative to other countries, as measured by international organizations like the United Nations (UN), the World Economic Forum (WEF), and the Organisation for Economic Co-operation and Development (OECD); Canadian institutions like the Conference Board of Canada and Statistics Canada; and peace, democratic, and environmental groups at home and abroad. When you see how Canada is doing relative to other countries, it may inspire ideas for how you and your peers can get involved in advocacy and problem solving. Examples of such comparisons include the following:

- Canada's relative performance in income, crime, acceptance of diverse groups, voter turnout, etc. (Chapter 1)
- Canada's disadvantaged groups (e.g., disabled, elderly, and children) and rates of poverty (Chapter 2)
- Canada's position in the Gender Inequality Index (Chapter 4)
- Canadians' level of alcohol consumption relative to those in other countries (Chapter 8)
- Organized crime in Canada and on the international level (Chapter 9)
- The Global Health Burden (Chapter 10)
- The well-being of Canada's children (Chapter 11)
- Canada's report card on education and skills (Chapter 12)
- Canada's economic report card, and Canada's quality of democracy ranking (Chapter 13)
- Canada's ranking in the Global Peace Index (Chapter 16)

The text also explores many international comparisons with our high-income peer countries, including the following:

- Canadians' acceptance of diversity (Chapter 3)
- Canada's gap in wages between men and women (Chapter 4)
- Poverty among Canada's elderly (Chapter 5)
- Canada's health report card (Chapter 10)
- Canada's voting participation and confidence in parliament (Chapter 13)
- Canada's environmental report card (Chapter 15)

In addition to this major improvement, we have created two new types of boxes for several chapters. First, Critical Thinking and You boxes invite you to think carefully about what constitutes a social problem in Chapter 1, how to choose a university in Chapter 12, and whether we should have a two-tiered Internet (Net neutrality) in Chapter 14. Second, Social Problems and Social Statistics boxes invite you consider how to measure what we call social problems, such as how to measure poverty, in Chapter 2.

BUILT-IN STUDY FEATURES

These pedagogical aids promote students' mastery of sociological concepts and perspectives:

- Chapter outlines: A concise outline at the beginning of each chapter gives students an overview of major topics.

- What Can You Do? sections: This section gives students suggestions about how they can tackle social problems on their own, as individuals, or collectively in a group.
- Key terms: Major concepts and key terms are defined and highlighted in bold print within the text. Definitions are also available in the glossary at the back of the text.
- Summaries in question-and-answer format: Each chapter concludes with a concise summary in a convenient question-and-answer format to help students master the key concepts and main ideas in each chapter.
- Questions for Critical Thinking: End-of-chapter questions provide opportunities for students to develop important critical-thinking skills about the issues raised in each chapter.

SUPPLEMENTS

Instructors can download the following supplements specific to this text from a password-protected location of Pearson Education Canada's online catalogue. Contact your local sales representative for further information.

- Instructor's Manual—a comprehensive resource that provides you with tools for classroom discussion, assignments, and recommendations for related films and readings.
- PowerPoint Presentations—highlight the key concepts in each chapter of the text.
- Test Item File—contains multiple choice, true/false, and essay type questions. Each question is classified to difficulty level and includes the appropriate page reference.
- Computerized Test Bank—Pearson's computerized test banks allow instructors to filter and select questions to create quizzes, tests or homework. Instructors can revise questions or add their own, and may be able to choose print or online options. These questions are also available in Microsoft Word format.

COURSESMART

CourseSmart goes beyond traditional expectations, providing instant, online access to the texts and course materials you need at a lower cost for students. And even as students save money, you can save time and hassle with a digital eTextbook that allows you to search for the most relevant content at the very moment you need it.

Whether it's evaluating texts or creating lecture notes to help students with difficult concepts, CourseSmart can make life a little easier.

See how when you visit www.coursesmart.com/instructors.

ACKNOWLEDGMENTS

We wish to personally thank the many people who have made this new edition a reality. First, we offer our profound thanks to the following reviewers who provided valuable comments and suggestions on how to make this text outstanding. Whenever possible, we have incorporated their suggestions into the text.

Helene A. Cummins	*Univeristy of Western Ontario, Brescia University College*
Augie Fleras	*University of Waterloo*
J. David Flint	*Saint Mary's University*
Kierstin C. Hatt	*University of Albert, Augustana Campus*
Charles Quist-Adade	*Kwantlen Polytechnic University*
Erin Steuter	*Mount Allison University*

The fourth Canadian edition of *Social Problems in a Diverse Society* has benefited from the expertise and excellence of Madhu Ranadive, program manager and Rachel Stuckey, developmental editor. We sincerely appreciate all the support and encouragement they provided throughout this revision.

I could not have written this book without the assistance of my partner, Helen Barron, who has not only provided continuing support, but also edited each of my original chapters. I also wish to acknowledge the help of Lama Hamdanieh, a former student, who ably reviewed and commented on several chapters.

—*Edward G. Thompson*

With overwhelming gratitude, love and appreciation I wish to acknowledge Freja Nygaard and Phoenix Nygaard, for continuing to inspire me and bring me joy every single day; Marilyn Hardy, for her unwavering love, Stephen Kayer for "the beautiful love"; Anni Torikka and Tabitha Steager, for their ongoing encouragement and support; Logan MacNair and Jes Hovanes, for excellent research assistance; and last, but certainly not least, my co-author Ed Thompson, for stepping in when things went a little sideways during the revision process of this edition. "*Let us be grateful to the people who make us happy; they are the charming gardeners who make our souls blossom.*" (Marcel Proust)

—*Vicki L. Nygaard*

To each of you reading this preface, we wish you the best in teaching or studying social problems and hope that you will share with us any comments or suggestions you have about *Social Problems in a Diverse Society,* fourth Canadian edition. The text was written with you in mind, and your suggestions (with appropriate attribution) will be included whenever possible in future editions. Let's hope that our enthusiasm for "taking a new look at social problems" will spread to others so that together we may resolve some of the pressing social problems we encounter during our lifetime.

—*Diana Kendall*
—*Edward G. Thompson*
—*Vicki L. Nygaard*

4001

Ryan Remiorz/CP Images

Studying Social Problems in the Twenty-First Century

Whether it takes place in a small-town school or on a busy city street, homicide—the intentional killing of one human being by another—leaves shock and anguish behind. It is also considered a standard setter for overall violent crime. Around the world, homicide is a major social problem. On a daily basis, the Internet and television news channels quickly spread word of the latest bombing, the latest massacre, and the latest homicide. In Canada, a place not known for the level of violence reported daily in the United States, murders of authority figures by youth or lone-terrorists, or youth by other youth, have made sensational headlines. Among the recent murders of note were the killing of five young people by another young person in Calgary in May 2014, the killing of three RCMP officers in June 2014, and the killing of military personnel by lone terrorists in October 2014.

Many of us condemn drive-by shootings and cold-blooded homicides, yet we enjoy watching action movies with lots of "blood and guts" or potentially violent sports such as wrestling, hockey, football, and boxing. Despite these contradictory attitudes, homicide certainly counts as a social problem.

WHAT IS A SOCIAL PROBLEM?

Although not all sociologists agree about what constitutes a social problem, most would agree with this general definition: a *social problem* **is a social condition (such as poverty) or a pattern of behaviour (such as violence against women) that people believe warrants public concern and collective action to bring about change.** Social conditions or certain patterns of behaviour are defined as social problems when they systematically disadvantage or harm a significant number of people (or a number of "significant" people?), or when they are seen as harmful by many of the people who wield power, wealth, and influence in a group or society. To put it another way, social problems are social in their causes, consequences, and possible sources of resolution.

The study of social problems is one area of inquiry within *sociology*—**the academic and scholarly discipline that engages in systematic study of human society and social interactions.** A sociological examination of social problems focuses primarily on issues that affect an entire *society*—**a large number of individuals who share the same geographical territory and are subject to the same political authority and dominant cultural expectations**—and the groups and organizations that make up that society. Because social problems are social in their causes, public perception of what constitutes a social problem can remain the same or change. What are the major social problems facing Canadians? Over the last 35 years, Canadians have reported to pollsters that their greatest concerns have been unemployment and the economy (Ibbitson 2013). But when does something become serious enough to be considered a social problem?

As the Conference Board indicates (see Box 1.1), homicide is a major social problem affecting Canada's social performance, even though it is not directly related to the economy. The following box provides information on worldwide rates of homicide. Later we will use sociological perspectives to help better understand the causes of homicide.

Sociologists apply theoretical perspectives and use a variety of research methods to examine social problems. Some social problems—such as homicide—are commonly viewed as conditions that affect all members of a population (see Box 1.2). Other social problems—such as racialized discrimination and sexual harassment—may be viewed (correctly or incorrectly) as conditions that affect some members of a population more than others. However, all social problems may be harmful to all members in a society whether they realize it or not. Sociological research, for example, has documented the extent to which White racism wastes the energies and resources of people who engage in racist actions as well as those of the targets of the actions (see Feagin and Sikes 1994; Feagin and Vera 1995).

Social problems often involve significant discrepancies between the ideals of a society and their actual achievement. For example, in Canada, the rights of individuals are guaranteed by the *Charter*

Critical Thinking and You
Box 1.1

Determining What Constitutes a Social Problem and How Well Canada Deals with Social Problems

Which of the following is defined as a major social problem in Canada?

- Driving a motor vehicle, which resulted in over 2000 deaths in 2011 in Canada (Transport Canada 2013)
- Playing contact sports in school, which results in many injuries among young people
- Hunting for wild game, which results in numerous injuries and deaths among hunters and bystanders

If you answered "None of the above," you are correct. Although driving a motor vehicle, playing contact sports, and hunting may have hazardous potential consequences, few people view these actions in and of themselves as being a social problem. In other words, not all behaviour that may result in violence or even death is classified as a social problem.

What questions should we ask to determine if something is a social problem? Here are a few suggestions:

1. Is there a public outcry about this conduct or this condition? Are people actively discussing the issue and demanding that a resolution be found?
2. Does the conduct or condition reflect a gap between social ideals and social reality? What social ideals are involved? What is the social reality about the situation?
3. Are a large number of people involved in defining the problem and demanding that a solution be found? Does the matter have national attention? If not, is a special-interest group the primary source of demands that something be done about the condition?

4. Can a solution be found for the problem? If not, can we reduce the problem or alleviate the suffering of some victims of the problem?

How does Canada rank relative to other similar countries regarding dealing with social problems?

The Conference Board of Canada has devised a report card on how Canada compares with other high-income countries regarding the participation of citizens, the minimizing of inequalities, and the cohesion of society. They chose 16 variables ranging from "acceptance of diversity" to "homicide" to "voter turnout," and found that overall, Canada ranked 7 of 17 high-income countries for a grade of "B." The Scandanavian countries ranked highest, usually with "As," and Japan and the United States ranked at the bottom with "Ds." Since most of these problems will be discussed in the following chapters, they will not be identified here (for the full list, see http://www.conferenceboard.ca/hcp/details/society.aspx).

Questions for Consideration

1. Based on these questions and excluding the problems identified by the Conference Board, what pressing social issues are we overlooking in our nation that should be considered as social problems requiring immediate action?
2. What issues receive too much attention from the media and the public?
3. How do culture, religion, and politics influence our definition of what constitutes a social problem?

---

of Rights and Freedoms, which also provides the legal basis for remedying injustices. One such discrepancy is **discrimination—actions or practices of dominant-group members (or their representatives) that have a harmful impact on members of subordinate groups.** Sociologists define the **dominant group** as the group whose members are disproportionately at the top of the hierarchy, "with maximal access to the society's power resources, particularly political authority and control of the means of economic production"** (Marger 1999:273). *Subordinate groups* are those whose members, in relation to the dominant group (or groups), do not occupy such positions of power. The term usually used for a subordinate group is *minority group* (see Chapter 3).

Discrimination may be directed along a number of lines—class, race, gender, and age. It also may be directed against subordinate group members whose sexual orientation, religion, nationality, disability, or other attributes or characteristics are devalued by those who discriminate against them. Sometimes, discrimination is acted out in the form of violence. This type of violent act is referred to as a *hate crime*—**an act of violence motivated by prejudice against people on the basis of racialized identity, ethnicity, religion, gender, or sexual orientation.** This can include the dissemination of materials intended to

Social Problems in Global Perspective

Box 1.2

Worldwide Homicide

The United Nations Office on Drugs and Crime (UNOCDC) released a report, *Global Study on Homicide*, in 2013. The report seeks to shed light on the worst of crimes: the unlawful, intentional killing of one person by another. The global average homicide rate stands at 6.2 per 100 000 population. As might be expected, some regions have much higher rates, such as Central America and South Africa, which have rates four or five times the worldwide average. In contrast, some regions, such as Europe and eastern Asia, have rates a quarter or less than the worldwide average. High homicide rates occur in countries that have just over a tenth of the world's population (UNODC 2013:12).

There are also great differences in rates in terms of gender. Men are much more likely to be killed than are women (79 vs. 21 percent), and men are much more likely than women to be killers (95 vs. 5 percent) (UNODC 2013:13). However, in family and intimate relations, the reverse is the case: about two-thirds of victims of this kind of violence are women and one-third are men. In other words, women are more likely to be killed by someone they know, and men are more likely to be killed by a stranger (UNODC 2013:13). Homicide victims are also more likely to be young, with more than half the victims 29 years of age or younger (UNODC 2013:13)

UNODC identified three types of homicides: those related to criminal activities, those related to interpersonal conflict, and those related to socio-political agendas (UNODC 2013:13). In the Americas, about 30 percent of the killings are related to criminal activities, especially drugs. In some places, such as Sweden, Costa Rica, and India, interpersonal conflict accounts for about half of the killings (UNODC 2013:14). It is very difficult to identify homicides related to socio-political agendas, but most terrorist killings would fit into that category (see Chapter 16).

Several factors are related to a lower homicide rate. One factor is a well-organized criminal justice system that is able to do rigorous investigation and fair adjudication. This contributes both to justice for victims (and families) and ensures that potential perpetrators know they could be caught. Such organization can be measured in terms of cases solved and convictions. A great difference exists among countries in conviction rates, ranging from 81 percent in Europe to 48 percent in Asia and 24 percent in the Americas (UNODC 2013:18). These conviction rates are inversely correlated with the homicide rates: people are more likely to commit a crime when there is little chance of them being punished.

Interestingly, development factors were not studied in the 2013 edition of the UNODC report. They were mentioned in the 2011 edition, where researchers found that higher levels of homicide are associated with lower scores on the Human Development Index (HDI). First, using the HDI (an index combining life expectancy, educational level of the population, and per capita income), countries high on the index had homicide rates of less than 5 per 100 000 population, those in the middle had homicide rates of 10, and those lower on the index had rates of 20 per 100 000 population. In addition, using the Gini Index (a measure of inequality in a country where 0 is perfect equality and 1 is perfect inequality), countries high on the Index had a homicide rate of over 20 per 100 000 population, those in the middle of the Index had a rate of 15 to 20, and those low on the Index had a rate of below15 (UNODC 2011:4).

Another factor that the earlier study included was the likelihood of gang-related or organized crime-related homicides. The researchers found that in the Americas, there was a much higher rate of homicides (25+) compared to other areas like Asia (7) and Europe (less than 5). In addition, South and Central America and the Caribbean had a much higher percentage of deaths by firearms than other regions did (UNODC 2011:5).

Later in this chapter we will show how these perspectives help us to understand this data in a more comprehensive and complete manner.

Questions for Consideration

1. Explain why homicide rates are related to inequality. What consequences do you think this has for growing inequality in Western countries?

2. Homicide in Western countries is generally declining (see Canada's data in Chapter 9). Why do you think that might be the case?

Independent research

This text stresses the large number of social problems that are related to inequalities. Begin itemizing the number of problems caused by inequalities, starting with homicide.

Sources: *United Nations Office on Drugs and Crime (UNODC), 2011*, Global Study on Homicide 2011 – Key Findings. *United Nations Publication. Retrieved June 6, 2014 (https://www.unodc.org/unodc/en/data-and-analysis/statistics/crime/global-study-on-homicide-2011.html); UNODC, 2013*, Global Study on Homicide 2013. *United Nations Publication. Retrieved June 6, 2014 (http://www.unodc.org/documents/gsh/pdfs/2014_GLOBAL_HOMICIDE_BOOK_web.pdf)*.

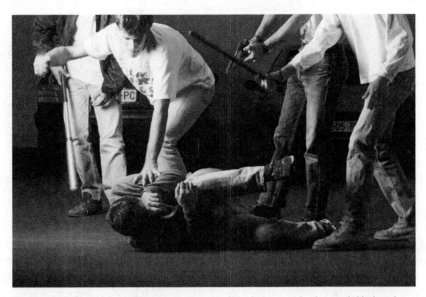

What does this photo show us about the discrepancies that exist between the democratic ideals and the social realities of our society? Does discrimination against subordinate group members take place in other societies as well?

Cesar Lucas Abreu/The Image Bank/Getty Images

incite hatred. Although hate crimes were added to the *Criminal Code* only quite recently, the crimes themselves date back hundreds of years (see Chapters 3, 6, and 9 for further discussion of hate crimes).

WHY STUDY SOCIAL PROBLEMS?

Studying social problems helps us understand the social forces that shape our lives on both personal and societal levels. In our daily lives, we rely on common sense— "what everybody knows"—to guide our conduct and make sense of human behaviour. But many common-sense notions about why people behave the way they do, who makes the rules, and why some people break rules and others follow them are *myths*—beliefs that persist even when the actual truth is different. Myths about social problems frequently garner widespread acceptance and sometimes extensive media coverage.

A sociological examination of social problems enables us to move beyond common-sense notions, to gain new insights into ourselves, and to develop an awareness of the connection between our own world and the worlds of other people. According to sociologist Peter Berger (1963:23), a sociological examination allows us to realize that "things are not what they seem." Indeed, most social problems are multifaceted. When we recognize this, we can approach pressing local, national, and global concerns in new ways and make more effective decisions about those concerns. In taking a global perspective on social problems, we soon realize that the

lives of all people are closely intertwined, and that any one nation's problems are part of a larger global web of interrelated problems.

THE SOCIOLOGICAL IMAGINATION AND SOCIAL PROBLEMS

Just like other people, sociologists usually have strong opinions about what is "good" and "bad" in society and what might be done to improve conditions. However, sociologists know their opinions are subjective. Thus, they use systematic research techniques and report their findings to other social scientists for consideration. In other words, sociologists strive to view social problems *objectively*. Of course, complete objectivity may not be an attainable—or desirable—goal in studying human behaviour. Max Weber (1864–1920), an early German sociologist, acknowledged that complete objectivity might be impossible and pointed out that *verstehen* ("understanding," or "insight") was critical to any analysis of social problems. According to Weber, *verstehen* enables individuals to see the world as others see it and to empathize with them. *Verstehen*, in turn, enables us to develop what is called the sociological imagination.

According to sociologist C. Wright Mills (1959b), the ***sociological imagination* is the ability to see the relationship between an individual's experiences and the larger society in which they are contextualized.** The sociological imagination enables us to connect the private troubles of individuals to the public issues of a society. Public issues (or social problems) are matters beyond a person's control that originate at the regional or national level and can be resolved only by collective action. In *The Sociological Imagination*, Mills used unemployment as an example of how people may erroneously separate personal troubles from public issues in their thinking. The unemployed individual may view his or her unemployment as a personal trouble concerning only the individual, other family members, and friends. However, widespread unemployment resulting from economic changes, corporate decisions (downsizing or relocating a plant abroad), or technological innovations (computers and advanced telecommunications systems displacing workers) is a public issue. The sociological imagination helps us to shift our focus to the larger social context and see how personal troubles may be related to public issues.

Sociologists make connections between personal and public issues in society through microlevel and macrolevel analysis. ***Microlevel analysis* focuses on small-group relations and social interaction among individuals.** Using microlevel analysis, a sociologist might investigate how fear of unemployment affects workers and their immediate families. In contrast, ***macrolevel analysis* focuses on social processes occurring at the societal level, especially in large-scale organizations and major social institutions such as politics, government, and the economy.** Using macrolevel analysis, a sociologist might examine how globalization and the attendant labour market restructuring have impacted Canadian workers and their families.

As Mills suggested, a systematic study of a social problem such as unemployment gives us a clearer picture of the relationship between macrolevel structures such as the Canadian economy and microlevel social interactions among people in their homes, workplaces, and communities. It does not get the individual his or her job back, but it provides a better understanding of how the situation happened. With a clearer understanding of how we find ourselves in the situations we do, we may be able to develop more effective levels of prevention and intervention.

USING SOCIAL THEORY TO ANALYZE SOCIAL PROBLEMS

To determine how social life is organized, sociologists develop theories and conduct research. A ***theory* is a set of logically related statements that attempt to describe, explain, and occasionally predict social events.** Theories are useful for explaining relationships between social concepts or phenomena, such as "ethnicity and unemployment" or "gender and poverty." They also help us interpret social reality in a distinct way by providing a framework for organizing our observations. Sociologists refer to this theoretical framework as a ***perspective*—an overall approach or viewpoint toward some subject.** Four major theoretical perspectives have emerged in sociology: the functionalist perspective, which views society as a basically stable and orderly entity; the conflict perspective, which views society as an arena of competition and conflict; the interactionist perspective, which focuses on the everyday, routine interactions among individuals; and the feminist perspective, which focuses on the gendered (and racialized and classed) inequalities between groups and on strategies for positive social change. The functionalist and conflict perspectives are based on macrolevel analysis because they focus on social processes occurring at the societal level. The interactionist perspective is based on microlevel analysis because it focuses on small-group relations and social interaction. The feminist perspective involves both macro- and microlevel analysis by looking at the ways, for example, that the dominant gender ideology (macro) impacts the specific interactions (micro) between woman X and man Y within a capitalist and patriarchal White-dominant culture.

The Functionalist Perspective

The functionalist perspective grew from the works of early social thinkers such as Auguste Comte (1798–1857), who is thought to be the founder of sociology. Comte compared society to a living organism. Just as muscles, tissues, and organs of the human body perform specific functions that maintain the body as a whole, the various parts of society contribute to its maintenance and preservation. According to the ***functionalist perspective*, society is a stable, orderly system composed of several interrelated parts, each of which performs a function that contributes to the overall stability of society (Parsons 1951).** These interrelated parts are social institutions (such as families, the economy, education, and the government) that a society develops to organize its main concerns and activities so that it meets social needs. Each institution performs a unique function, contributing to the overall stability of society and the well-being of individuals (Merton 1968). For example, the functions of the economy are producing and distributing goods (such as food, clothing, and shelter) and services (such as tourism services and dry-cleaning), whereas the government is responsible for coordinating the activities of other institutions directed to such ends as health care, education, maintaining law and order, dealing with unmet social needs, and handling international relations and peace.

Manifest and Latent Functions

Though the functions of the economy and the government seem fairly clear-cut, functionalists suggest that not all the functions of social institutions are intended and overtly recognized. In fact, according to the functionalist perspective, social institutions perform two different types of societal functions: manifest and latent. *Manifest functions* are intended and recognized consequences of an activity or social process. A manifest function of education, for example, is to provide students with knowledge, skills, and cultural values. In contrast, *latent functions* are the unintended consequences of an activity or social process that are hidden and remain unacknowledged by participants (Merton 1968). The latent functions of education include the babysitter function of keeping young people off the street and out of the full-time job market while their parents work, and the matchmaking function whereby schools provide opportunities for students to meet and socialize with potential marriage partners. These functions are latent because schools were not created for babysitting or matchmaking, and most organizational participants do not acknowledge that these activities take place.

Dysfunctions and Social Disorganization

From the functionalist perspective, social problems arise when social institutions do not fulfill their functions or when dysfunctions occur. *Dysfunctions* are the undesirable consequences of an activity or social process that inhibits a society's ability to adapt or adjust (Merton 1968). For example, a function of education is to prepare students for jobs, but if schools fail to do so, then students have problems finding jobs, employers or governments have to spend millions of dollars on employee training programs, and consumers have to pay higher prices for goods and services to offset worker-training costs. In other words, dysfunctions in education threaten other social institutions, especially families and the economy.

Dysfunctions can occur in society as a whole or in a part of society (a social institution). According to functionalists, dysfunctions in social institutions create social disorganization in the entire society. *Social disorganization refers to the conditions in society that undermine the ability of traditional social institutions to govern human behaviour.* Early in the 20th century, sociologists Robert E. Park (1864–1944) and Ernest W. Burgess (1886–1966) developed a social disorganization theory to explain why some urban areas had higher rates of *social deviance*, which they defined as a pattern of rule violation, than other areas had. Social disorganization causes a breakdown in the traditional values and norms that serve as social control mechanisms, which,

under normal circumstances, keep people from engaging in nonconforming behaviour. *Values are collective ideas about what is right or wrong, good or bad, and desirable or undesirable in a specific society* (Williams 1970). Although values provide ideas about behaviour, they do not state explicitly how we should behave. Norms, on the other hand, have specific behavioural expectations. *Norms are established rules of behaviour or standards of conduct.* French sociologist Emile Durkheim (1858–1917) suggested that social problems arise when people no longer agree on societal values and norms. According to Durkheim, periods of rapid social change produce *anomie*—a loss of shared values and sense of purpose in society. During these periods, social bonds grow weaker, social control is diminished, and people are more likely to engage in nonconforming patterns of behaviour, such as crime.

While examining the relationship between social problems and rapid industrialization and urbanization in Britain, Western Europe, and the United States in the late 19th and early 20th centuries, early sociologists noted that rapid social change intensifies social disorganization. *Industrialization is the process by which societies are transformed from a dependence on agriculture and handmade products to an emphasis on manufacturing and related industries.* At the beginning of the Industrial Revolution, thousands of people migrated from rural communities to large urban centres to find employment in factories and offices. New social problems emerged as a result of industrialization and *urbanization, the process by which an increasing proportion of a population lives in cities rather than in rural areas.* During this period of rapid technological and social change, urban social problems such as poverty, crime, child labour, inadequate housing, unsanitary conditions, overcrowding, and environmental pollution increased sharply.

Applying the Functionalist Perspective to the Problem of Homicide

Some functionalists believe that homicide arises from a condition of anomie, in which many individuals have a feeling of helplessness, normlessness, or alienation. These feelings can lead to seeking attachments in organized deviant behaviour, especially among the young. The 2013 United Nations (UN) study discussed earlier (see Box 1.2) found that many victims of homicide were involved in drug gangs and organized crime in the Americas, and that most of these victims were under 30 years of age. Others believe that homicide increases when social institutions such as the family, schools, and religious organizations weaken, and the main mechanisms of social control in people's everyday lives are external (i.e., law enforcement agencies and the criminal justice system) and weak or non-existent. The 2013 UN study found that homicide occurs more frequently when the rates of conviction for homicides are low.

Other functionalist explanations of violence focus on how changes in social institutions put some people at greater risk than others of being victims of violent crime. According to the *lifestyle–routine activity approach*, **the patterns and timing of people's daily movements and activities as they go about obtaining such necessities of life as food, shelter, companionship, and entertainment are the keys to understanding violent personal crimes and other types of crime in our society** (Cohen and Felson 1979). Several changes over the past 50 years may have put people at increased risk for violent crime victimization. The 2011 UN study found that the increase of gangs and organized crime in the Americas involved in the drug trade was related to high rates of homicide. The lifestyle–routine activity approach suggests that people who willingly put themselves in situations that expose them to the potential for homicide should modify their behaviour, or that society should provide greater protection for people whose lifestyle routine leaves them vulnerable to attackers. The lifestyle–routine activity approach offers some insight, but does not address the issue of homicide in the home and other supposedly safe havens. Further, it does not explain the homicide itself; it simply points out that people are at risk, which tells us nothing that would assist in eliminating violence.

How would functionalists approach the problem of homicide? Most emphasize shared moral values and social bonds. They believe that when rapid social change or other "disruptions" occur, moral values may erode, and problems such as school violence or hate crimes are likely to occur more frequently. Functionalists believe that to reduce homicide, families, schools, religious organizations, and other social institutions should be strengthened so that they can regenerate shared values and morality. Most functionalists also believe that those who engage in homicidal behaviour should be prosecuted to the full extent of the law.

The Conflict Perspective

The *conflict perspective* **is based on the assumption that groups in society are engaged in a continuous power struggle for control of scarce resources.** Unlike functionalist theorists, who emphasize the degree to which society is held together by a consensus on values, conflict theorists emphasize the degree to which society is characterized by conflict and discrimination. According

to some conflict theorists, certain groups of people are privileged while others are disadvantaged through the inequitable use of political, economic, or social power. Not all conflict theorists hold the same views about what constitutes the most important form of conflict. We will examine two principal perspectives: the value conflict perspective and the critical-conflict perspective.

The Value Conflict Perspective

According to value conflict theorists, social problems are conditions that are incompatible with group values. From this perspective, value clashes are ordinary occurrences in families, communities, and the larger society, in which individuals commonly hold many divergent values. Although individuals may share certain core beliefs, they do not share all values or a common culture. *Culture* refers to the knowledge, language, values, customs, and material objects that are passed from person to person and from one generation to the next in a human group or society.

Discrepancies between ideal and real culture are a source of social problems in all societies. *Ideal culture* refers to the values and beliefs that people claim they hold; *real culture* refers to the values and beliefs they actually follow. In Canada, members of such diverse groups as the Heritage Front, the Aryan Nations, and the Urban Alliance on Race Relations all claim to adhere to ideal cultural values of equality, freedom, and liberty; however, these ideal cultural values come into direct conflict with real cultural values when issues of racialized/ethnic relations arise.

The value conflict perspective has been criticized by critical-conflict theorists, who argue that it overlooks the deeper social problems of inequality and oppression based on class, racialization, and gender.

Critical-Conflict Perspective

Unlike the value conflict approach, critical-conflict theorists suggest that social problems arise out of the major contradictions inherent in the way societies are organized. Some critical-conflict perspectives focus on class inequalities in the capitalist economic system; others focus on inequalities based on "race"/ethnicity or gender.

Most class perspectives on inequality have been strongly influenced by Karl Marx (1818–1883), a German economist and activist who recognized that the emergence of capitalism produced dramatic and irreversible changes in social life. *Capitalism* **is an economic system characterized by private ownership of the means of production, from which personal profits can be derived through market competition and without government intervention.** According to Marx, members of the *capitalist class* (the *bourgeoisie*), who own and control the means of production (e.g., the land, tools, factories, and money for investment), are at the top of a system of social stratification that affords them different lifestyles and life chances from those of the members of the *working class* (the *proletariat*), who must sell their labour power (their potential ability to work) to capitalists. In selling their labour power, members of the working class forfeit control over their work, and the capitalists derive profits from the workers' labour.

Marx believed that capitalism leads workers to experience increased levels of impoverishment and *alienation*—a feeling of powerlessness and estrangement from other people and from oneself (Marx and Engels 1847/1971:96). He predicted that the working class would eventually overthrow the capitalist economic system. Although Marx's prediction has not come about, Erik Olin Wright (1997) and other social scientists have modified and adapted his perspective to apply to contemporary capitalist nations. In today's capitalist nations, according to Wright (1997), ownership of the means of production is only one way in which people gain the ability to exploit others. Two other ways in which individuals gain control are through control of property and control over other people's labour. In this view, upper-level managers and others in positions of authority gain control over societal resources and other individuals' time, knowledge, and skills in such a manner that members of the upper classes are able to maintain their dominance.

Some critical-conflict perspectives focus on racialized and gender subordination instead of class-based inequalities. Critical-conflict theorists who emphasize discrimination and inequality based on "race" or ethnicity note that many social problems are rooted in the continuing exploitation and subordination of people of colour and Indigenous people by White people, or, more accurately, by institutions and systems set up by and for White people. For example, the Canadian Human Rights Commission report, entitled "Equality Rights of Aboriginal People," found Indigenous peoples continue to experience conditions of persistent disadvantage, including a greater likelihood of suffering violent crimes and physical, emotional, or sexual abuse (Canadian Human Rights Commission 2013). Throughout this text, where we discuss conflict theory, we will use critical-conflict theory (rather than the value conflict approach) to highlight the power relations that result in social problems.

Applying the Conflict Perspective to the Problem of Homicide

Conflict theorists who focus on class-based inequalities believe that the potential for homicide is inherent in capitalist societies. In fact, say these theorists, the wealthy

engage in one form of violence, and the poor engage in another. They note that the wealthy often use third parties to protect themselves and their families from bodily harm, as well as to secure their property and investments in this country and elsewhere in the world. For example, the wealthy who live in Canada or other high-income nations and who own factories (or own stock in factories) in middle- and low-income nations use the governments and police of those nations—third parties—to control workers who threaten to strike. The wealthy also influence Canadian government policy by supporting or not supporting political parties that deploy peacekeeping or military intervention in nations where they may have investments or desire to have investments.

In contrast, these theorists say, when the poor engage in violence, the violence is typically committed by the individual and may be a reaction to the unjust social and economic conditions he or she experiences daily on the bottom rung of a capitalist society. In fact, the 2011 UN study found that higher rates of homicide occur in countries with greater inequality and in countries low on the Human Development Index. The economic exploitation of the poor, conflict theorists note, dramatically affects all aspects of the individual's life, including how the person reacts to daily injustices, stress, and other threatening situations. In gang-related homicide, the vast majority of offenders—as well as victims—are poor, young, and unemployed, or working in low-level, low-paying jobs. In fact, most violent street crime is an intra-class phenomenon. Arrest and conviction data suggest that poor and working-class people typically victimize others who are like themselves. In part, this is due to the fact that violence committed by middle- and upper-class individuals is not investigated and/or prosecuted to the same degree as that committed by poor and working-class people. Moreover, middle- and upper-class individuals often enlist the services of people from lower classes when they wish to commit homicide. Another factor that could be included in the conflict perspective is age stratification (older people are usually more powerful than younger people). The 2013 UN study found that over half the victims of homicide were under 30 years of age.

The conflict perspective argues that the criminal justice system is biased in favour of the middle and upper classes. Because of this, its definition of violence depends on where a person's ethnicity, class, and gender locate him or her in the system of stratification. In this way, violent crimes are but one part of a larger system of inequality and oppression. Sexism and racism are also reinforced by the overarching class structure that benefits the powerful at the expense of the powerless. The conflict perspective that focuses on racialized/ethnic inequalities points out that racism is an important factor in explaining such violent acts as hate crimes.

No matter what approach conflict theorists take, they all agree on one thing: homicide around the world is unlikely to diminish significantly unless inequalities based on class and ethnicity are reduced at the macro-level in society.

The Interactionist Perspective

Unlike the conflict perspective, which focuses on macro-level inequalities in society, the interactionist perspective focuses on microlevel analyses of how people act toward one another and how they make sense of their daily lives. The *interactionist perspective* **views society as the sum of the interactions of individuals and groups.** Most inter-actionists study social problems by analyzing how certain behaviour comes to be defined as a social problem and how individuals and groups come to engage in activities that a significant number of people view as a major social concern.

German sociologist Georg Simmel (1858–1918), a founder of the interactionist approach, investigated the impact of industrialization and urbanization on people's values and behaviour within small social units. Simmel (1902/1950) noted that rapid changes in technology and dramatic urban growth produced new social problems by breaking up the "geometry of social life," which he described as the web of patterned social interactions among the people who constitute a society. According to Simmel, alienation is brought about by a decline in personal and emotional contacts. How people *interpret* the subjective messages they receive from others and the situations they encounter in their daily life greatly influence their behaviour and perceptions of what constitutes a social problem.

Labelling Theory and the Social Construction of Reality

While Simmel focused on how people interpret their own situations, other interactionists have examined how people impose their shared meanings on others. According to sociologist Howard Becker (1963), *moral entrepreneurs* are people who use their own views of right and wrong to establish rules and label others as deviant (nonconforming). *Labelling theory*, as this perspective is called, suggests that behaviour that deviates from estab-lished norms is deviant *because* it has been labelled as such by others. According to this theory, deviants (noncon-formists) are people who have been successfully labelled as such by others. Labelling theory raises questions about why certain individuals and certain types of behaviour are labelled as deviant but others are not. The answer is

suggestive of an analysis of power, which this theory has no real view of.

According to some interaction theorists, many social problems can be linked to the *social construction of reality*—the process by which people's perception of reality is shaped largely by the subjective meaning that they give to an experience (Berger and Luckmann 1967). From this perspective, little shared reality exists beyond that which people socially create. It is, however, this social construc-tion of reality that influences people's beliefs and actions. Other interactionists suggest that how we define a situa-tion affects our reactions to it. According to sociologists William I. Thomas (1863–1947) and Dorothy S. Thomas (1899–1977), when people define situations as real, the situations become real in their consequences. Elaborating on the Thomas Theorem (1928), as it has come to be called, sociologist Robert Merton (1968) suggested that when people perceive a situation in a certain way and act according to their perceptions, the end result may be a *self-fulfilling prophecy*—**a false definition of a situa-tion that evokes a new behaviour that makes the original false conception become true.** For example, a teenager who is labelled a "juvenile delinquent" may accept the label and adopt the full-blown image of a juve-nile delinquent as portrayed in television programs and films: wearing "gang" colours, dropping out of school, and participating in violence or other behaviour that is labelled as deviant. If the teenager is subsequently arrested, the initial label becomes a self-fulfilling prophecy.

Applying Interactionist Perspectives to the Problem of Homicide

Interactionist explanations of homicide begin by noting that human behaviour is learned through social interac-tion. Violence, interactionists state, is a learned response, not an inherent characteristic in the individual. Some of the most interesting support for this point of view comes from studies done by social psychologist Albert Bandura (1973), who studied aggression in children. Showing children a film of a person beating, kicking, and hacking an inflatable doll produced a violent response in the chil-dren, who, when they were placed in a room with a simi-lar doll, duplicated the behaviour shown in the film and engaged in additional aggressive behaviour. Others have noted that people tend to repeat their behaviour if they feel rewarded for it. Thus, when people learn that they can get their way by inflicting homicide or the threat of homicide on others, their aggressive behaviour is rein-forced. It is important to point out that the "reward" may only be perceived as a reward in the eyes of that person.

Interactionists also look at the types of social interac-tions that commonly lead to violence. According to the *situational approach*, **violence results from a specific interaction process, termed a "situational transaction."** Criminologist David Luckenbill (1977) has identified six stages in the situational transaction between victim and offender. In the first stage, the future victim does something behavioural or verbal that is considered an affront by the other (e.g., a glare or an insult). In the second, the offended individual verifies that the action was directed at him or her personally. In the third, the offended individual decides how to respond to the affront and may issue a verbal or behavioural challenge (e.g., a verbal threat or a raised fist). If the problem escalates at this point, injury or death may occur in this stage; if not, the participants enter into the fourth stage. In this stage, the future victim further escalates the transaction, often prodded by onlookers siding with one party or the other. In the fifth stage, actual violence occurs when neither party is able to back down without losing face. At this point, one or both parties produce weapons (if they have not already appeared), which may range from guns and knives to bottles, pool cues, or other bludgeoning devices, and the offender kills the victim. The sixth and final stage involves the offender's actions after the crime: some flee the scene, others are detained by onlookers, and still others call the police themselves. Homicide due to interpersonal conflict could be better understood with this situational approach. Wrong steps at these stages could readily lead to an attack of one person on another and a subsequent homicide. The 2013 UN study mentioned that the young were more likely than the old to be killed. It is likely that the young are less experienced in social interactions. Because of their lack of understanding of how to remove themselves from these situations, they are more likely to be trapped in these stages.

The situational approach is based first on the assumption that many victims are active participants in the homicide perpetrated against them, and second on the idea that confrontation does not inevitably lead to violence or death. As Robert Nash Parker (1995) has noted, in the first four stages of the transaction, either the victim or the offender can decide to pursue another course of action, and most often does.

According to interactionists, reducing homicide requires changing those societal values that encourage excessive competition and violence. These changes must occur at the microlevel, which means agents of socialization must transmit different attitudes and values toward violence. The next generation must learn that it is an individual's right—regardless of gender, racialized status, class, religion, or other attributes or characteristics—to live free from violence and the devastating impact it has on individuals, groups, and the social fabric of society.

Feminist Perspectives

Feminist theorists begin their analysis by pointing out that mainstream sociological thought and theory is both androcentric and Eurocentric (Alvi, DeKeseredy, and Ellis 2000:19). This means most sociological theory is based on the experiences, ideas, and issues of concern for males of European and Western extraction. European and male perspectives are valid, of course, but they are partial. All perspectives are partial, but in the past, these perspectives were treated as though they were representative of the experiences, ideas, and issues of all people. Today, we know this is impossible; hence feminist theories, anti-racist theories, post-colonial theories, Indigenous theories, and so on have been created and employed to account for more of social life, in addition to maintaining the mainstream theories previously discussed.

There are no "feminist issues" per se. Every issue is a feminist issue. Basically, when feminist theorists engage in analysis, they "gender" the issues under study. This means that theorists look at the differential impacts of social phenomena for men and women, and more recently for transgendered or non-gendered people as well. This does not mean that feminists study only gender, although in the past that may have been more true. Feminist theories typically examine dynamics of power in relationships between individuals, roles, structures, and so on. The focus on power differentials is shared with conflict and Marxist theories, but feminist theories add a focus on gendered power and patriarchy. A final defining feature of feminist theories is the idea of beginning one's analysis from a particular "standpoint." This is to say that social life is examined from the situated vantage points of the individuals and/or groups involved.

Since there is no one feminist perspective, there is no one feminist perspective on social problems. Many authors put forth summaries of numerous variations of feminist theory (liberal, Marxist, radical, socialist, anti-racist, lesbian, cultural, and so on); however, it may be more useful to distinguish between the types of theories instead of the specific variants. Lengermann and Niebrugge-Brantley (1992:319) provide a classification system that categorizes various feminist theories as (a) theories of difference, (b) theories of inequality, or (c) theories of oppression. Theories are distinguished from one another by the approach taken to answering the question, Why are women's situations as they are? Theories of difference are premised on the idea that men and women experience different realities based on their differential locations in most situations. Theories of inequality assert that women's situations are not only different from men's, but are also less privileged or are disadvantaged relative to men's. Theories of oppression suggest that not only are women's situations different from and unequal to men's, but that women are actively subordinated and kept disadvantaged, both by patriarchal structures and by individuals reinforcing sexist socialization and ideologies.

Feminist theories and the people who advance them have been appropriately criticized for perpetuating the same kinds of injustice based on "difference" that mainstream sociological theories perpetuated because of their androcentrism and Eurocentricity. Most feminist theory in the past (and today) comes from a White, middle-class, heterosexual, educated women's bias. The issues assumed to be central by these theories, then, are the issues of interest and concern to these groups of people. Criticism arose, for example, because where White and educated feminists saw men and patriarchy as denying them reproductive freedom (e.g., access to birth control and abortion), Indigenous women and women of colour saw racism and acts of discrimination (e.g., in employment or housing) affecting both the men and the women of racialized groups as *the* issue of importance. Poor feminists saw academic elitism and poverty as *the* issue of importance for men and women. Lesbians and women with disabilities saw their perspectives silenced or marginalized. So, the locations or situations of the particular theorists determine what issues are defined as the most important feminist issues to be taken up.

Modern-day feminist theories, if they are reflexive, turn the lenses back upon themselves. If one is supporting a particular theory, is it sexist? Is it racist? Is it homophobic? Is it classist? Is it ableist? Many contemporary feminists spend a good deal of time deconstructing the theories they favour—the underlying assumptions, exclusions, inclusiveness, impacts of the analysis, and dissemination of the analysis. While this exercise may seem academic—and it is, in some senses—it is also important to know where the theory is weak, where it cannot be used to see an issue clearly, what the bias is, whose voice is missing, and so on. Several feminist theorists today call for simultaneous analyses of interlocking oppressions (see Chapter 3). These feminist theorists view the social world as a matrix of domination where sexism, racism, heterosexism, classism, and other marginalized statuses meet in myriad ways over issues. Theoretical analysis focuses on how these interlocking oppressions play out in different contexts. Other concepts important to contemporary feminist theorists are "public and private spheres, ideology [and] relations of ruling" (Swingewood 2000:240). Focusing on these concepts allows us to analyze macro and micro issues and the interplay between the two, an important feature if we are to have the ability

to understand social life from a broader perspective. This leads to a final defining feature of feminist theory—a propensity to propel its adherents toward engaged social action.

Applying Feminist Perspectives to the Problem of Homicide

Feminist perspectives of homicide highlight issues of dominance and power. Inequalities between groups can result in violence. People who enjoy power and privilege likely commit as many acts of violence as those who are disenfranchised. The main difference between groups is that those without power are disproportionately targeted. The 2013 UN study explored earlier showed that in intimate partner violence, two-thirds of the victims are women and only one-third are men. This is also true in Canada (see Chapter 11). Since men are usually more dominant in relationships, women are more likely to be victimized.

Feminists also add social class oppression as a location of domination. For example, in Chapter 4, the fact that the 1989 Montreal Massacre at École Polytechnique gained such notoriety is contrasted with the comparatively little stir created by the murders of many poor women from the downtown East Side of Vancouver.

Finally, one feminist perspective suggests that violence against women is a means of reinforcing patriarchy. According to this analysis, in a patriarchal system, the sexual marketplace is characterized by unequal bargaining power, making transactions between men and women potentially coercive in nature. Gender stratification is reinforced by powerful physical, psychological, and social mechanisms of control, including force or the threat of force. Fear of violence forces women to adapt their ways of being in the world—living, acting, and dressing—to ensure they are not in a position to be victimized by men, and thus they are deprived of many basic freedoms (see Gardner 1995).

USING SOCIAL RESEARCH METHODS TO STUDY SOCIAL PROBLEMS

Sociologists use a variety of research methods to study social problems such as homicide and violence generally. Research methods are strategies or techniques for systematically collecting data. Some methods produce *quantitative data* that can be measured numerically and lend themselves to statistical analysis. For example, the Uniform Crime Reports (UCRs), published annually by the Canadian Centre for Justice Statistics (CCJS), provide crime statistics that sociologists and others can use to learn more about the nature and extent of violent crime in the Canada. Other research methods produce *qualitative data* that are reported in the form of interpretive descriptions (words) rather than numbers. For example, *qualitative data* on homicide in Canada might provide new insights on how the victims or their families and friends cope in the aftermath of a violent attack such as school shootings or terrorist bombings. Sociologists use three major types of research methods: field research, survey research, and secondary analysis of existing data. Although our discussion focuses on each separately, many researchers use a combination of methods to enhance their understanding of social issues.

Field Research

Field research is the study of social life in its natural setting: observing and interviewing people where they live, work, and play. When sociologists want firsthand information about a social problem, they often use participant observation—field research in which researchers collect systematic observations while participating in the activities of the group they are studying. Field research on social problems can take place in many settings, ranging from schools and neighbourhoods to universities, prisons, and large corporations.

Field research is valuable because some kinds of behaviour and social problems can be studied best by being there and developing a more complete understanding through observations, face-to-face discussions, and participation in events. For example, over the past 40 years in the United States, field research examining the effects of violence in the media on children has indicated that some children behave more aggressively after viewing violence. Children were shown episodes of either *Batman* and *Spiderman* or *Mister Rogers' Neighborhood* (a children's show featuring "Mr. Rogers" who encourages children to be kind and to share with others) for several weeks, after which they were observed for an additional two weeks to see how they behaved. Children who watched the violent cartoons were more likely to interact aggressively with other children, while those who watched *Mr. Rogers' Neighborhood* were more willing to share their toys and cooperate with others. Other studies exposed children to shows such as *Mighty Morphin Power Rangers* and the results were similar: children who watched episodes containing violence were more prone to aggressive behaviour such as hitting, kicking, shoving, and insulting others than were children who did not watch the episode (Kaiser Family Foundation 2003).

Sociologists who use field research must have good interpersonal skills so they can gain and keep the trust of the people they want to observe or interview. They also must be skilled interviewers who can keep systematic notes on their observations and conversations. Above all, they must treat research subjects fairly and ethically. The Code of Ethics of the Canadian Sociological Association provides professional standards for sociologists to follow when conducting social science field research.

Survey Research

Survey research is probably the most frequently used research method by social scientists. Survey research is a poll in which researchers ask respondents a series of questions about a specific topic and record their responses. Survey research is based on the use of a sample of people who are thought to represent the attributes of the larger population from which they are selected. Survey data are collected by using self-administered questionnaires or by interviewers who ask questions of people in person or by mail, telephone, or the Internet.

Statistics Canada conducts the General Social Survey (GSS) every five years. This survey includes questions about victimization to fill in the gaps of the Uniform Crime Reports (UCR) of crimes reported to police. These surveys indicate that the number of crimes committed is substantially higher than the number reported in the UCR.

Survey research allows sociologists to study a large population without having to interview everyone in that population. Surveys yield numerical data that may be compared between groups and over periods of time. However, this type of research does have certain limitations. The use of standardized questions limits the types of information researchers can obtain from respondents. Also, because data can be reported numerically, survey research may be misused to overestimate or underestimate the extent of a specific problem, such as violence.

Secondary Analysis of Existing Data

Whereas the GSS provides primary data—data that researchers collected specifically for that study—sociologists often rely on secondary analysis of existing data—a research method in which investigators analyze data that originally were collected by others for some other purpose. This method is also known as *unobtrusive research* because data can be gathered without the researcher having to interview or observe research subjects. Data used for secondary analysis include public records such as birth and death records, official reports of organizations or governmental agencies such as Statistics Canada, and information from large databases such as the GSS (mentioned above).

Secondary analysis often involves *content analysis*, a systematic examination of cultural artifacts or written documents to extract thematic data and draw conclusions about some aspect of social life. Although it is a number of years old, the National Television Violence Study (NTVS) is the most definitive study of violence on television in the United States. During a nine-month period each year from October 1994 to June 1997, researchers at several universities selected a variety of programs, including dramas, comedies, movies, music videos, reality programs, and children's shows, on 23 television channels, thus creating a composite of the content in a week of television viewing. The viewing hours were from 6:00 a.m. until 11:00 p.m., for a total of 17 hours a day over the course of a week (NTVS 1998). Although the study's findings are too numerous to list them all, here are a few (NTVS 1998:26–31):

- Much of television violence is glamorized, sanitized, and trivialized. Characters seldom show remorse for their actions, and there is no criticism or penalty for the violence at the time that it occurs.
- Across the three years of the study, violence was found in 60 percent of the television programs taped—only a few of which carried antiviolence themes—and the networks and basic cable stations increased the proportion of programs containing violence during prime time (the three-hour period each night that draws the most viewers).
- "High-risk" depictions (those that may encourage aggressive attitudes and behaviours) often involve (1) "a perpetrator who is an attractive role model," (2) "violence that seems justified," (3) "violence that goes unpunished," (4) "minimal consequences to the victim," and (5) "violence that seems realistic to the viewer."
- The typical preschool child who watches cartoons regularly will come into contact with more than 500 high-risk portrayals of violence each year. For preschoolers who watch television for two to three hours a day, there will be, on average, about one high-risk portrayal of violence per hour in cartoons.

Clearly, researchers can learn much from content analysis that they could not learn through other research methods because it allows them to look in more depth at a specific topic of concern and to systematically analyze what they find. A strength of secondary analysis is its unobtrusive nature and the fact that it can be used when subjects refuse to be interviewed or the researcher does not have the opportunity to observe research subjects firsthand. However, secondary analysis also has inherent problems. Because the data originally were gathered for some other purpose, they might not fit the exact needs of the researcher, and they might be incomplete or inaccurate.

SOCIAL CHANGE AND REDUCING SOCIAL PROBLEMS

The concept of social change is important to any discussion of reducing social problems. *Social change* **is the alteration, modification, or transformation of public policy, culture, or social institutions over time** (Kendall 2000). Notice that this definition states that social change occurs "over time"; social change has a temporal dimension. Some efforts to deal with social problems are *short-term* strategies, whereas others are *middle-term* remedies, and still others constitute *long-term* efforts to alleviate the root causes of a social problem. In other words, efforts to alleviate individual unemployment or 5 reduce unemployment rates in a community have a different temporal dimension than do efforts to change the political economy in such a manner that high levels of employment and greater wage equity are brought about throughout a nation or nations. Clearly, efforts to alleviate individual unemployment are a short-term solution to the problem of unemployment, while efforts to reduce unemployment in a community or to change the entire political economy are middle-term and long-term solutions, respectively. Sometimes discussions of social change sound idealistic or utopian because they are middle-term or long-term strategies that attempt to target the root causes of a social problem. For most social problems, however, a combination of strategies is required to eliminate or reduce them.

Microlevel Attempts to Solve Social Problems

Earlier in this chapter , we described sociologist C. Wright Mills's (1959b) belief that we should apply the sociological imagination to gain a better understanding of social problems. According to Mills, the sociological imagination is the ability to see the relationship between an individual's experiences and the larger society. For Mills, social problems could not be *solved* at the individual level because they are more than personal troubles or private problems. However, sometimes social institutions cannot deal with a problem effectively, and political and business leaders are unwilling, or unable, to allocate the resources necessary to deal with the issue. In these situations, we typically begin to deal with the problem in an individualized way.

Seeking Individual Solutions to Personal Problems

Microlevel solutions to social problems focus on how individuals operate within small groups to try to remedy a problem that affects them, their family, or their friends.

Usually, when individuals have personal problems, they turn to their *primary groups*—**small, less-specialized groups in which members engage in face-to-face, emotion-based interactions over an extended period of time.** Primary groups include one's family, close friends, and other peers with whom one routinely shares the more personal experiences in life.

How can participation in primary groups help us reduce personal problems? According to sociologists, members of our primary groups usually support us even when others do not. For example, some analysts believe that there are many more people without a domicile (technically homeless) than current statistics suggest, but whenever possible, these people live with relatives or friends, many of whom already live in overcrowded and sometimes substandard housing. Many people who seek individualized solutions to personal troubles believe the situation will be temporary. However, if the problem is widespread or embedded in the larger society, it may stretch out for months or years without resolution. At best, individualized efforts to reduce a problem are short-term measures that some refer to as a "Band-Aid™ approach" to a problem because they do not eliminate the causes of the problem: they merely ameliorate the effects of it for a few, for a while.

Some microlevel approaches to reducing social problems focus on how individuals can do something about the problems they face. For example, a person who is unemployed or among the "working poor" because of low wages, seasonal employment, or other factors may be urged to get more education or training and work experience in order to find a "better" job and have the opportunity for upward mobility. Individuals who appear to have eliminated problems in their own lives through such efforts are applauded for their "determination," and are often held up (sometimes unwillingly or unknowingly) as examples that others are supposed to follow.

Mid-Range Attempts to Solve Social Problems

Mid-range solutions to social problems focus on how secondary groups and formal organizations can help individuals to overcome issues such as drug addiction or domestic violence. Some groups help people cope with their own problems, and some groups attempt to bring about community change.

Groups That Help People Cope with Their Problems

Most mid-range solutions to social problems are based on two assumptions: (1) some social problems can best be reduced by reaching one person at a time; and (2) prevention and intervention are most effective at the personal and community levels. Groups that attempt to reduce a social problem by helping individuals cope with it, or eliminate it from their own lives, are common in our society. Among the best known are Alcoholics Anonymous (AA) and Narcotics Anonymous (NA); however, a broad range of "self-help" organizations exists in most Canadian communities. Typically, self-help groups bring together individuals who have experienced the same problem and have the same goals. For example, a shared goal may be quitting a particular behaviour that has caused the problem, which can be anything from abuse of alcohol, tobacco, and other drugs to overeating, gambling, and chronic worrying. Volunteers who have had similar problems (and believe they are on the road to overcoming them) often act as role models for newer members. For example, AA and NA are operated by recovered alcoholics and/or other recovered substance abusers who try to provide new members with the support they need to overcome their alcohol addiction or drug dependency. According to some analysts, AA is a subculture with distinct rules and values that alcoholics learn through their face-to-face encounters with other AA members (Maxwell 1981). Social interaction is viewed as central for individual success in the programs. Confessing one's behavioural problems to others in an organizational setting is believed to have therapeutic value to those who are seeking help.

Like other mid-range approaches, organizations such as AA and NA may bring changes in the individual's life; however, they usually do not systematically address the structural factors (such as unemployment, work-related stress, and aggressive advertising campaigns) that may contribute to the problems. For example, AA typically does not lobby for more stringent laws pertaining to drunk driving or the ready sale and consumption of alcoholic beverages. In British Columbia, for example, fairly recent legal changes have made the purchase of alcohol easier by expanding the hours it can be made available to consumers and expanding the kinds of outlets where it can be sold. As a result, larger societal intervention is necessary to reduce the problems that contribute to individual behaviours.

Grassroots Groups That Work for Community-Based Change

Some grassroots organizations focus on bringing about a change that may reduce or eliminate a social problem in a specific community or region. *Grassroots groups* **are organizations started by ordinary people who work in concert to deal with a perceived problem in their neighbourhood, city, province or territory, or nation.** Using this approach, people learn how to empower themselves against local, provincial, territorial, and national government officials, as well as corporate executives and media figures who determine what constitutes the news in their area.

A central concern of those who attempt to reduce a social problem through grassroots groups is the extent to which other people are apathetic about the problem. Some analysts suggest that even when people are aware of problems, they do not think that they can do anything to change them or they do not know how to work with other people to alleviate them.

According to social analysts, more community dialogue is needed on social issues, and more people need to become involved in grassroots social movements. A *social movement* **is an organized group that acts collectively to promote or resist change through collective action** (Goldberg 1991). Because social movements are not institutionalized and are outside the political mainstream when they begin, they empower outsiders by offering them an opportunity to have their voices heard.

An example of a mid-range group is Pollution Probe, a Canadian environmental organization, whose purposes are

- to define environmental problems through research;
- to promote understanding through education; and
- to press for practical solutions through advocacy.

Pollution Probe started in 1969 when a few University of Toronto students began working with faculty members such as Donald Chant, then chair of the Department of Zoology. Early concerns were dangers of pesticides for birds, high levels of phosphates in detergents for freshwater lakes, and smog in cities. To help deal with these concerns, Pollution Probe undertook a variety of programs. For example, in 1970, a community development project was devised to send people (including one of the co-authors (EGT)) to different parts of southern Ontario's cottage country to encourage summer camp participants, cottage association members, and townspeople to look into problems of water pollution and waste management in their area. Over its 40-year history, Pollution Probe has had a wide variety of accomplishments, including limiting the phosphate content of detergents, encouraging household recycling, helping to launch the Coalition on Acid Rain, contributing to an Ontario act that guarantees the right of residents to participate in environmental decisions, and being instrumental in the passage of an act for mandatory emissions testing of vehicles in Ontario. An example of a recent Pollution Probe action is the Energy Exchange, which encourages people to participate in an energy literacy initiative and stresses the three "3 Es" of responsible energy use: energy efficiency, energy from renewables, and emissions reductions during energy production. Pollution Probe has an enviable combination of accomplishments and trust that should ensure its continued effectiveness.

Many social movements, such as Mothers Against Drunk Driving (MADD), begin as community-based grassroots efforts. Over time, many mid-range organizations evolve into national groups; however, their organization and focus often change in the process (Adams 1991). Table 1.1 provides examples of activist organizations that seek to reduce specific social problems in communities.

Grassroots organizations and other local structures are crucial to national social movements because these movements must recruit members and gain the economic resources that are necessary for nationwide or global social activism. Numerous sociological studies have shown that the local level constitutes a necessary microfoundation for larger-scale social movement activism. Such movements, as they multiply and spread, represent a different sort of globalization, one tantamount to a "globalization from below."

To understand how grassroots organizations help national social movements, consider the problem of environmental degradation. Leaders of national environmental organizations often participate in local or regional rallies, protests, and letter-writing or email campaigns, particularly when politicians are making decisions that environmentalists believe will have a negative effect on the environment. By working with local and regional activists and seeking to influence local and regional power structures—city councils, provincial and territorial planning commissions, and legislatures—national organizations assert the need for their existence and attempt to garner additional supporters and revenue for their efforts nationwide or around the globe. By intertwining local, regional, and national organizational structures, these groups create a powerful voice for social change. In this sense, then, many social movement groups participate in what well-known Canadian sociologist William Carroll (1997:29) has defined as counter-hegemonic practice—"a coherent practical and ethical alternative" to prevailing hegemony. The danger of creating counter-hegemonies is one that social movement groups need to be aware of: by defining a group's issues as "the" issues of the day, thereby relegating other groups' issues to the back burner, a group risks the possibility of creating new injustices (Carroll 1997). However, a paradigm shift that moves people away from notions and practices of competition is one way of ensuring this does not happen. If social movements are truly counter-hegemonic, then they leave us with a "hopeful prognosis for social and political transformation" (Carroll 1997:25).

TABLE 1.1 Selected Organizations That Seek to Reduce a Social Problem

Category	Organization	Website Address
Environment	Earth First	http://www.earthfirst.org
	Greenpeace	http://www.greenpeace.org/canada/en
	Sierra Club	http://www.sierraclub.org
	Pollution Probe	http://www.pollutionprobe.org/
	Western Canada Wilderness Committee	http://www.wildernesscommittee.org
Drunk driving	Mothers Against Drunk Driving	http://www.madd.ca.madd2/
Wages and working conditions	Canadian Labour Congress	http://canadianlabour.ca
	Industrial Workers of the World	http://iww.org
Poverty, hunger, and homelessness	Food Banks Canada	http://foodbankscanada.ca/
	Canada Without Poverty	http://www.cwp-csp.ca/
	PovNet	http://www.povnet.org
	Raising the Roof (Homelessness)	http://www.raisingtheroof.org
Violence and war	Food Not Bombs	http://www.foodnotbombs.net
	I Wage Peace.org	http://www.iwagepeace.org
	Canadian Peace Congress	http://www.canadianpeacecongress.ca/

Note: Web addresses often change. Those given here were accurate at the time of publication.

Macrolevel Attempts to Solve Social Problems

Macrolevel solutions to social problems focus on how large-scale social institutions such as the government and the media may be persuaded to become involved in remedying social problems. Sometimes individuals who view themselves as individually powerless bind together in organizations to make demands on those who make decisions at the national or global level.

For example, when Canadian workers organize to support the rights of workers in low-income nations and are able to bring about changes that keep them from competing with these workers, they not only help workers abroad, they also help themselves.

Working through Special-Interest Groups for Political Change

At the national level, people seeking macrolevel solutions to social problems may become members of a *special-interest group*—a political coalition composed of individuals or groups sharing a specific interest they wish to protect or advance with the help of the political system. Examples of special-interest groups include the Canadian Labour Congress, the Reform Party, and REAL Women.

Through special-interest groups, which are sometimes called *pressure groups* or *lobbies*, people seek to change social situations by exerting pressure on political leaders. These groups may be categorized on the basis of four factors:

1. *Issue focus:* Some groups focus on single issues, such as abortion, gun control, or teaching acceptance for family diversity in Canadian schools; others focus on multiple issues, such as equal access to education, employment, and health care.

2. *View of the present system of wealth and power:* Some groups make radical demands that would involve the end of patriarchy, capitalism, governmental bureaucracy, or other existing power structures; others do not attack the legitimacy of the present system of wealth and power, but insist on specific social reforms.

3. *Beliefs about elites:* Some groups want to influence elites or incorporate movement leaders into the elite; others want to replace existing elites with persons whom they believe share their own interests and concerns.

4. *Type of political action:* In recent decades, many special-interest groups have been single-issue groups that focus on electing and endorsing politicians who support their views. There may be more than one single-interest group working to reduce or eliminate a specific social problem. Usually, however, these groups do not agree on the nature and extent of the problem or on proposed solutions. For this reason, competing single-interest groups may aggressively place their demands in front of elected officials and bureaucratic policymakers.

Working through National Social Movements to Reduce Problems

Collective behaviour and national social movements are significant ways in which people seek to resolve social problems. **Collective behaviour is voluntary, often spontaneous activity of a large number of people that typically violates dominant-group norms and values.** Public demonstrations and riots are examples of collective behaviour. Since it was first used in the 1919 Egyptian Revolution against British occupation, one popular form of public demonstration has been **civil disobedience—non-violent action that seeks to change a policy or law by refusing to comply with it.** People often use civil disobedience in the form of sit-ins, marches, boycotts, and strikes to bring about change. When people refuse to abide by a policy or law and challenge authorities to do something about it, they are demanding social change with some sense of urgency. Since Thoreau first wrote about it in 1849 in his essay "Civil Disobedience," it has been implemented by many mass movements seeking change through non-violent means. Protestors at the 1999 World Trade Organization (WTO) meeting in Seattle used civil disobedience strategies by sitting on the street, linking arms together, and chanting over and over the words "non-violent protest" in response to the advancing lines of the National Guard in full riot gear. This strategy has also been used to great effect in India, East Germany, South Africa, and Czechoslovakia since the early 1900s.

Groups that engage in activities that they hope will achieve specific political goals are sometimes referred to as *protest crowds*. For example, in June 2010, Torontonians and others protested the G20 (high-income countries plus emerging powers like China and Brazil) meeting in Toronto and many were arrested during a non-violent vigil (about 1200 people, setting a Canadian record for civil disobedience arrests).

Several types of national and international social movements may be used to reduce social problems.

Collective behaviour is a powerful form of social protest against perceived injustices. Numerous protests have been staged in Canada against environmental degradation caused by logging, pollution, hunting, and other activities.

Graham Hughes/THE CANADIAN PRESS

National social movements may be divided into five major categories: reform, revolutionary, religious, alternative, and resistance movements. *Reform movements* seek to improve society by changing some specific aspect of the social structure. Environmental groups and disability rights groups are examples of groups that seek to change (reform) some specific aspect of the social structure. Reform movements typically seek to bring about change by working within the existing organizational structures of society, whereas *revolutionary movements* seek to bring about a total change in society. Examples of revolutionary movements include utopian groups and radical terrorist groups that use fear tactics to intimidate and gain—at least briefly—concessions from those with whom they disagree ideologically. For example, some radical terrorists may kill people in their pursuit of a society that more closely conforms to their worldview.

Religious movements (also referred to as *expressive movements*) seek to rejuvenate people through inner change. Because they emphasize inner change, religious movements are often linked to local and regional organizations that seek to bring about changes in the individual's life. National religious movements often attempt to persuade political officials to enact laws that will reduce or eliminate what they perceive to be a social problem.

Maude Barlow was instrumental in the formation of the not-for-profit group Council of Canadians.

Jeff McIntosh/CP Images

For example, some national religious movements view abortion as a social problem and thus lobby for a ban on abortions. In contrast, *alternative movements* seek limited change in some aspects of people's behaviour. Currently, alternative movements include a variety of so-called New Age movements that emphasize such things as the development of a collective spiritual consciousness.

Finally, *resistance movements* seek to prevent change or to undo change that has already occurred. In public debates over social policies, most social movements advocating change face resistance from reactive movements, which hold opposing viewpoints and want social policy to reflect their own beliefs and values. Examples of resistance movements include groups opposing same-sex marriage initiatives for gay or lesbian couples; anti-abortion groups, such as "Operation Rescue," which seek to close abortion clinics and make abortion illegal; and anti-immigrant groups seeking to close Canadian borders to outsiders or place harsher demands on immigrant workers.

Can national activism and social movements bring about the changes that are necessary to reduce social problems? Some analysts believe that certain social problems can be reduced through sustained efforts by organizations committed to change. An example of national social movements is the Council of Canadians. The not-for-profit council was formed in 1985 by a group of prominent Canadians and has become Canada's pre-eminent citizen watchdog organization.

The Council of Canadians is sustained by volunteers and financed by its members. The organization helps people take action through more than 70 chapters across the country. As a public interest organization, it does not take money from corporations or governments. Past campaigns include combatting bank mergers, control of newspapers by conglomerates, changes in public and unfair trade deals, and water policies. Recently, the Council has focused its work on protecting Canadian values by promoting progressive, independent, national policies on fair trade, clean water, safe food, public health care, and other issues of social and economic concern to Canadians.

A major successful campaign was the fight against the Multilateral Agreement on Investments (MAI) in 1998. The Council of Canadians called it a charter of rights and freedoms for global corporations. As part of the campaign to free up the movement of capital and protect investors, the MAI was criticized for wanting standardized pan-national policies that could potentially erode environmental legislation, culture, and sovereignty and bring in a two-tiered health system. The Council sent a letter to then Prime Minister Chrétien, supported by prominent Canadians such as

Carol Shields, David Suzuki, Judy Rebick, and Buzz Hargrove, emphasizing five principles that should govern all international trade and investment agreements. The principles included:

1. Upholding the rights of citizens;
2. Protecting the common good;
3. Promoting the development of sustainable communities;
4. Guaranteeing the sovereignty of democratically elected governments over corporations; and
5. Ensuring effective citizen participation in the development of trade and investment policies. (Council of Canadians 1999).

The Council of Canadians called on Canada to pull out of MAI negotiations. The MAI was defeated because, in 1998, France, and later Australia—also concerned about the MAI's encroachment on their national sovereignty—pulled out of the negotiations. One of its major campaigns now is to end fracking to extract shale gas (see Chapter 15).

What about global activism? Once again, we turn to the environmental movement for an example. According to Jared Diamond (2000), a geography professor and director of the World Wildlife Fund, some transnational corporations are becoming aware that they have a responsibility for the environment. A Canadian publication, *Corporate Knights* (a magazine for clean capitalism), recently identified the 2014 Global 100. These are companies that rank high on a number of metrics ranging from revenue per gigajoule of energy consumption, to revenue per cubic metre of water withdrawn, to percent of women senior executives and CEO-to-average pay. They found well-known companies from two dozen countries who were working hard to meet sustainability standards, including Canadian companies like Bombardier, Tim Hortons, Bank of Montreal, and Suncor Energy. Companies from Australia, the United States, Finland, Norway, and France made up the top five positions (Morrow 2014:38). Of course, consumers have also demanded that corporations become more accountable for their actions. For example, growing consumer awareness has led some companies that buy and retail forest products to no longer sell wood products from environmentally sensitive areas of the world and instead give preference to certified wood—that is, lumber that has been derived from forests where guidelines for environmentally sound logging practices have been met. Consumer power should not be underestimated when it comes to impacting corporations' profits. Indeed, consumer power is so great that many companies have rushed to assure the public that their products and services are environmentally friendly, even when they are not—a new practice called "greenwashing."

According to some analysts, what is needed is the "globalization from below" mentioned previously. In other words, people cannot rely on corporations to solve environmental problems. Indeed, it is necessary to develop a human agenda that will offset the corporate agenda that has produced many of the problems in the first place. Social activists Brecher and Costello (1998) suggested these criteria for any proposed human agenda some time ago, but they are still relevant today:

- Improve the lives of the great majority of the world's people over the long run.
- Correspond to widely held common interests and should integrate the interests of people around the world.
- Provide handles for action at a variety of levels.
- Include elements that can be at least partially implemented independently but that are compatible or mutually reinforcing.
- Make it easier, not harder, to solve social problems such as environmental degradation and war.
- Grow organically out of social movements and coalitions that have developed in response to the needs of diverse peoples.

To achieve these guidelines, it is obvious that a drastic redirection of our energies be undertaken.

Do you believe such human co-operation is possible? Will it be possible for a new generation of political leaders to separate *politics* from *policy* and focus on discovering the best courses of action for Canada and the world? Where do ideas regarding possible social policies come from? Some of the ideas and policies of tomorrow are being developed today in public policy organizations and think tanks like the right-wing Fraser Institute or the left-leaning Canadian Centre for Policy Alternatives. If, as some analysts believe, these think tanks are increasingly setting the Canadian government's agenda, how much do we know about these groups, their spokespersons, and the causes they advocate?

Perhaps gaining more information about the current state of Canadian and global affairs is the first step toward individual efforts to be part of the solution rather than part of the problem in the future. At the end of each chapter we make several suggestions to help you get involved with solving social problems.

SUMMARY

How Do Sociologists Define a Social Problem?

According to sociologists, a social problem is a social condition (such as poverty) or a pattern of behaviour (such as substance abuse) that people believe warrants public concern and collective action to bring about change.

How Do Sociologists View Violence/Homicide?

Sociologists view violence as a social problem that involves both subjective awareness and objective reality. We have a subjective awareness that violence can occur in such public settings as schools, daycare centres, businesses, and churches. Our subjective awareness becomes an objective reality when we can measure and experience the effects of violent criminal behaviour.

How Do Sociologists Examine Social Life?

Sociologists use both microlevel and macrolevel analyses to examine social life. Microlevel analysis focuses on small-group relations and social interaction among individuals; macrolevel analysis focuses on social processes occurring at the societal level, especially in large-scale organizations and major social institutions.

How Does the Functionalist Perspective View Society and Social Problems?

In the functionalist perspective, society is a stable, orderly system composed of interrelated parts, each of which performs a function that contributes to the overall stability of society. According to functionalists, social problems such as violence arise when social institutions do not fulfill the functions that they are supposed to perform or when dysfunctions occur.

How Does the Conflict Perspective View Society and Social Problems?

The conflict perspective asserts that groups in society are engaged in a continuous power struggle for control of scarce resources. This perspective views violence as a response to inequalities based on "race," class, gender, and other power differentials.

How Does the Value Conflict Perspective Differ from the Critical-Conflict Perspective?

According to value conflict theorists, social problems are conditions that are incompatible with group values. From this perspective, value clashes are ordinary occurrences in families, communities, and the larger society, where people commonly hold many divergent values. In contrast, critical-conflict theorists suggest that social problems arise out of major contradictions inherent in the way societies are organized.

Why Are There So Many Different Approaches in the Conflict Perspective?

Different conflict theorists focus on different aspects of power relations and inequality in society. Perspectives based on the works of Karl Marx emphasize class-based inequalities arising from the capitalist economic system.

How Does the Interactionist Perspective View Society and Social Problems?

Unlike the functionalist and conflict perspectives, which focus on society at the macrolevel, the interactionist perspective views society as the sum of the interactions of individuals and groups. For interactionists, social problems occur when social interaction is disrupted and people are dehumanized, when people are labelled deviant, or when the individual's definition of a situation causes him or her to act in a way that produces a detrimental outcome.

What Is the Feminist Perspective?

Feminist perspectives focus on patriarchy—a system of male dominance in which males are privileged and women are oppressed. Other perspectives emphasize that "race," class, and gender are interlocking systems of privilege and oppression that result in social problems. However, these perspectives are based on the assumption that inequality and exploitation, rather than social harmony and stability, characterize contemporary societies.

What Are Three Research Methods that Sociologists Use to Study Social Problems?

In field research, sociologists observe and interview people where they live, work, and play. In survey research, sociologists use written questionnaires or structured interviews to ask respondents a series of questions about a specific topic. In secondary analysis of existing data, sociologists analyze data that originally were collected for some other purpose.

What Is Social Change? Why Is It Important in Reducing Social Problems?

Social change refers to the alteration, modification, or transformation of public policy, culture, or social institutions over time. Social change is important in reducing social problems because a combination of strategies, some previously untried, are usually required to reduce major social problems.

What Are Microlevel Solutions to Social Problems? What Are the Limitations of This Approach?

Microlevel solutions to social problems focus on how individuals operate within small groups to try to remedy a problem that affects them, their family, or their friends. Most people turn to their primary groups for help in dealing with a problem. However, solving social problems one person at a time does not take into account the fact that secondary groups and societal institutions play a significant part in creating, maintaining, and exacerbating many social problems.

What Are Mid-Range Attempts to Deal with Social Problems? What Are the Limitations of This Approach?

Mid-range attempts to deal with social problems focus on how secondary groups and formal organizations deal with problems or seek to assist individuals in overcoming problems, such as addiction to drugs or alcohol. Grassroots groups often work to change a perceived wrong in their neighbourhood, city, province or territory, or nation. Although local efforts to reduce problems affecting individuals and collectivities in a specific city or region have brought about many improvements in the social life of individuals and small groups, they usually lack the sustained capacity to produce the larger systemic changes needed at the national or international levels to reduce or eliminate the problems.

What Are Macrolevel Attempts to Deal with Social Problems? What Are the Limitations of This Approach?

Macrolevel solutions to social problems focus on how large-scale social institutions such as the government and the media may become involved in remedying social problems. Some people work through social movements, others through special-interest groups, and still others through various forms of collective behaviour. While macrolevel approaches are necessary for reducing or eliminating many social problems, some analysts believe that these approaches overemphasize structural barriers in society and give people the impression that these barriers constitute insurmountable walls that preclude social change. Macrolevel approaches may also de-emphasize the importance of individual responsibility.

What Are Four Key Factors That Differentiate Special-Interest Groups?

The four factors by which special-interest groups may be categorized are (1) issue focus (single-issue vs. multiple demands); (2) view of the present system of wealth and power (positive vs. negative); (3) beliefs about elites (whether to try to influence elites or seek to replace them); and (4) type of political action.

What Is Collective Behaviour? How Does Civil Disobedience Occur?

Collective behaviour is voluntary, often spontaneous activity of a large number of people that may violate dominant-group norms and values. As a form of collective behaviour, civil disobedience refers to non-violent action that seeks to change a policy or law by refusing to comply with it. In 1999, in Seattle, many WTO protestors engaged in this form of direct action by linking arms, sitting in the streets, and chanting.

What Are the Key Characteristics of the Five Major Categories of National Social Movements?

National social movements are divided into five major categories: reform, revolutionary, religious, alternative, and resistance movements. Reform movements seek to improve society by changing some specific aspect of the social structure. Revolutionary movements seek to bring about a total change in society. Religious movements seek to renovate or renew people through "inner change." Alternative movements seek limited change in some aspects of people's behaviour and currently include a variety of so-called New Age movements. Resistance movements seek to prevent change or undo change that has already occurred.

KEY TERMS

capitalism, p. 8
civil disobedience, p. 18
collective behaviour, p. 18
conflict perspective, p. 8
discrimination, p. 3
dominant group, p. 3
functionalist perspective, p. 6
grassroots groups, p. 15
hate crime, p. 3
industrialization, p. 7
interactionist perspective, p. 10

lifestyle–routine activity approach, p. 8
macrolevel analysis, p. 6
microlevel analysis, p. 6
norms, p. 7
perspective, p. 6
primary groups, p. 15
self-fulfilling prophecy, p. 10
situational approach, p. 11
social change, p. 14
social disorganization, p. 7

social movement, p. 16
social problem, p. 2
society, p. 2
sociological imagination, p. 5
sociology, p. 2
subordinate groups, p. 3
theory, p. 6
urbanization, p. 7
values, p. 7

QUESTIONS FOR CRITICAL THINKING

1. What are some of the impacts on a nation when high levels of violence exist within its borders?

2. Value conflict theorists suggest that social problems are conditions that are incompatible with group values. How would value conflict theorists view debates over gun control laws?

3. Some critical-conflict theorists believe that social problems arise from the major contradictions inherent in capitalist economies. What role does violence play in a capitalist economy?

4. Using feminist and interactionist perspectives, what kind of arguments can you make to explain why males are more frequently involved in acts of physical violence than females are? What do your own observations tell you about the relationship between social norms and violent behaviour?

5. Do you believe that corporations can be trusted to "do the right thing" when it comes to reducing or eliminating existing social problems? Is good corporate citizenship a possibility in the global economy today? Why or why not?

6. Suppose you were given the economic resources and political clout to reduce a major social problem. Which problem would you choose? What steps would you take to alleviate this problem? How would you measure your success or failure in reducing or eliminating the problem?

Wealth and Poverty: Canadian and Global Economic Inequities

Don Ryan/AP Photo/CP Images

Since the 1970s in Canada, social programs have increasingly ended up on the chopping block. A great deal of research has focused on looking at the impacts of social program cuts and the concomitant governmental focus on "fraud." Despite the ongoing shredding of Canada's safety net, needs for services among Canada's population have increased, not decreased. Decreases in real wages, as well as unemployment and underemployment, mean that cuts to services not only impact those people who are on income assistance, but also lead to increased poverty for those who work full- and part-time. This chapter examines these issues as well as some of the impacts of poverty and the ways we deal with poverty and income inequalities as a nation.

For decades, Canada has been described as a "land of opportunity"— a place where the so-called "American dream" can be realized. Simply stated, the *American dream* is the belief that the members of each generation can have a higher standard of living than that of their parents (Danziger and Gottschalk 1995). Implicit in the American dream is the belief that all people—regardless of ethnicity, colour, national origin, gender, ability, age, sexual orientation, or religion—should have an equal opportunity for success. This is the same as saying that Canadians view themselves as living in a *meritocracy*, **a nation where the best person can rise to the top in any situation, despite his or her antecedents.** Sociologists John Macionis and Linda Gerber (2002:257) define meritocracy as a "system of social stratification based on personal merit." But do all the people in this nation really have an equal opportunity for success? How equally divided are national and global resources? What kinds of inequalities exist in the world and Canada today?

WEALTH AND POVERTY IN GLOBAL PERSPECTIVE

When sociologists conduct research on wealth and poverty around the world, they frequently analyze secondary data that were originally collected by organizations such as the World Bank and the United Nations. These data focus on quality-of-life indicators such as wealth, income, life expectancy, health, sanitation, the treatment of women, and education for high-income, middle-income, and low-income nations.

- *High-income nations* are countries with highly industrialized economies; technologically advanced industrial, administrative, and service occupations; and relatively high levels of national and per capita (per person) income.
- *Middle-income nations* are countries changing from agrarian to industrial economies. Recently, the World Bank subdivided middle-income nations into two categories: upper-middle-income economies and lower-middle-income economies.
- *Low-income nations* are primarily agrarian countries that have little industrialization and low levels of national and personal income.

Table 2.1 shows the four levels of income and total population, average income, and secondary school attendance for a range of countries.

Over the past 30 years, despite the great changes in China and India, the people in the high-income countries have been increasing their incomes much more than those in the other groups (see Figure 2.1). Whereas the average income of those in low-income to upper-middle countries has increased, the average income of those in high-income has increased even more.

Today, more than 800 million people live in *absolute poverty*, **a condition that exists when people do not have the means to secure the most basic necessities of life (food, clothing, and shelter).** Absolute poverty is life threatening. People living in absolute poverty may suffer from chronic malnutrition or die from hunger-related diseases. Current estimates suggest that more than 600 million people suffer from chronic malnutrition and more than 40 million people die each year from hunger-related diseases. To put this figure in perspective, the number of people worldwide dying from hunger-related diseases each year is the equivalent of more than 300 jumbo jet crashes a day with no survivors, and with half the passengers being children. Even those who do not live in absolute poverty often experience hardships based on *relative poverty*, **a condition that exists when**

TABLE 2.1 Countries by Level of Income, Population, and Education

Income categories	Income classification criterial: gross national income per capita in 2009 (US$)	Number of countries	Country examples	Total population	Average income in 2010 (constant PPP 2005 international $)	Secondary school enrolment rate, 2010
High-income countries (rich countries)	Higher than $12 276	70	Canada Poland, U.S.	1.1 billion	$33 232	100%
Upper-middle-income countries	$3976 to $12 275	54	Brazil, China, Russia	2.5 billion	$8731	90%
Lower-middle-income countries	$1006 to $3975	56	Guatemala, India, Nigeria	2.5 billion	$3287	64%
Low-income countries (poor countries)	$1005 or less	35	Bangladesh, Cambodia, Kenya	817 million	$1099	39%

Source: *Conference Board, 2014*, World Inequality. *Retrieved September 6, 2014 (www.conferenceboard.ca/hcp/hot-topics/worldinequality.aspx).*

PPP is a monetary tool used to eliminate the fluctuation in currencies. It allows a comparison of the cost of purchasing a basket of goods in different countries and thus, a comparison of wages.

people can afford basic necessities such as food, clothing, and shelter but cannot maintain an average standard of living in comparison to that of other members of their society or group. An example would be individuals who live in an extremely hot or cold region but cannot afford adequate protection from environmental conditions, while others in their community enjoy heated or air-conditioned residences and wear clothing appropriate to current weather conditions.

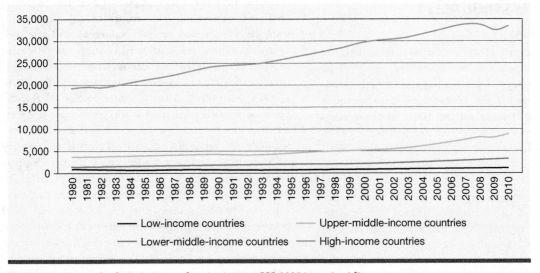

Figure 2.1   Income Per Capita by Income Grouping (constant PPP 2005 International $).

Source: *Conference Board, 2014*, World Inequality. *Retrieved September 6, 2014 (www.conferenceboard.ca/hcp/hot-topics/worldinequality.aspx).*

Despite the disparity in life chances and the prevalence of poverty, experts project that the populations of middle- and low-income nations will increase by almost 60 percent by the year 2025, while the populations of high-income nations will increase by about 11 percent. Because half of the world's population of more than 7 billion people already lives in lower-middle and low-income nations, this rapid increase in population can only compound existing problems and increase inequality on a global basis (see also Chapter 15 about population concerns).

How do social scientists explain the disparity between wealth and poverty in high-income and low-income nations? According to the "new international division of labour" perspective, the answer lies in the global organization of manufacturing production. Today, workers in a number of low-income nations primarily produce goods such as clothing, electrical machinery, and consumer electronics for export to the United States and other high-income nations. Using this global assembly line, transnational corporations find that they have an abundant supply of low-cost (primarily female) labour, no corporate taxes, and no labour unions or strikes to interfere with their profits (for a fuller explanation, see Chapter 13). Owners and shareholders of transnational corporations—along with subcontractors and managers in middle- and low-income nations—thus benefit, while workers remain in poverty despite long hours in sweatshop conditions. What has taken place among the world's countries has also occurred among social groups within these countries, including Canada.

ANALYZING INEQUALITY IN CANADA

Despite the notion that anyone can get ahead if she or he tries hard enough, one of this country's most persistent social problems is that it is a highly stratified society. *Social stratification* **is the hierarchical arrangement of large social groups on the basis of their control over basic resources** (Feagin and Feagin 1999). Today, the gap between the rich and the poor in Canada is wider than it has been for decades.

This widening gap, which is linked with global systems of stratification, has a dramatic impact on everyone's life chances and opportunities. Affluent people—the higher classes—typically have better life chances than the less affluent lower classes because the affluent have greater access to quality education, safe neighbourhoods, high-quality nutrition and health care, police and private

security protection, and an extensive array of other goods and services. In contrast, people who have low and poverty-level incomes tend to have limited access to these resources.

How are social classes determined in Canada? Most contemporary research on class has been influenced by either Karl Marx's means of production model or Max Weber's multidimensional model. In Marx's model, class position is determined by people's relationship to the means of production. Chapter 1 described Marx's division of capitalist societies into two classes: the bourgeoisie or capitalist class, which owns the means of production; and the proletariat or working class, which sells its labour power to the capitalists to survive. According to Marx, inequality and poverty are inevitable by-products of the exploitation of workers by capitalists.

Like Karl Marx, German sociologist Max Weber (1864–1920) believed that economic factors were important in determining class location and studying social inequality, but he also believed that other factors were important. Weber was interested in people's *life chances*—**the extent to which individuals have access to important societal resources such as food, clothing, shelter, education, and health care.** He developed a multidimensional class model that focused on the interplay of wealth, power, and prestige as determinants of people's class position. *Wealth* **is the value of all economic assets, including income and savings, personal property, and income-producing property, minus one's liabilities or debts.** While some people have great wealth and are able to live off their investments, others must work for wages. Wealth should be differentiated from income. *Income* **refers to the economic gain derived from wages, salaries, and income transfers (governmental aid such as income assistance [welfare] or ownership of property).** Like wealth, income is extremely unevenly divided in Canada. According to the Conference Board's Report Card on Canada, Canada has higher income inequality than Europe and lower inequality than the United States (Conference Board 2014). *Power* **is the ability of people to achieve their goals despite opposition from others.** People who hold positions of power can achieve their goals because they can control other people; on the other hand, people who hold positions that lack power must carry out the wishes of others. *Prestige* **is the respect, esteem, or regard accorded to an individual or group by others.** Individuals who have high levels of prestige tend to receive deferential and respectful treatment from those with lower levels of prestige.

Recent theorists have modified Marx's and Weber's theories of economic inequality. According to sociologist Erik O. Wright (1997), neither Weber's multidimensional model of wealth, power, and prestige nor Marx's two-class system fully defines classes in modern capitalist societies or explains economic inequality. Wright sets forth four criteria for placement in the class structure: (1) ownership of the means of production; (2) purchase of the labour of others (employing others); (3) control of the labour of others (supervising others on the job); and (4) sale of one's own labour (being employed by someone else). Based on these criteria, Wright (1979, 1985) identified four classes: the capitalist class, the managerial class, the small-business class, and the working class.

Although most people are aware of the wide disparity in lifestyles and life chances between the rich and the poor, far fewer of us stop to analyze the differences between middle-class and poverty-level living arrangements in Canada. Should social policies be implemented to equalize opportunities for people? Why or why not?

Wealth and Income Inequality

According to Forbes.com, a U.S. business e-publication, Bill Gates is the richest person in the world, worth US$76 billion. Carlos Slim Helu and family are the second richest people on earth, worth $72 billion (Forbes 2014). Down 23 ranks from Gates is the richest Canadian, David Thomson, whose total net worth in 2014 was US$24.6 billion, or approximately CDN$27 billion.

Galen Weston placed second in Canada, worth US$9 billion or CDN$10 billion. No other Canadian comes close to owning that kind of wealth, although Canada has a number of billionaires, including the Westons, the Bronfmans, and the Irvings, and even British Columbia's own "rags to riches" story maker, Jimmy Pattison. The vast majority of Canadians will never amass even a fraction of the wealth these people possess. Overall in the world, in 2014, there were 1645 billionaires, compared with 1125 in 2008 (Forbes.com 2014). While the net worth of many of Canada's millionaires and billionaires has declined since before the recession of 2008, they are still a long way from experiencing the economic recession the way people with low incomes or those who are impoverished do. The face of poverty is increasingly diverse with regard to family type, as more Canadians experience layoffs, lack of real wage gains, and reduced work hours.

Wealth and income are clearly correlated with life chances. Overall, when we talk about income, it is helpful to divide the population into fifths, or quintiles. If there was no inequality in income in Canada, each fifth of the population would receive 20 percent of the available income. Of course, we know that is far from the case. What is particularly interesting is that the distribution of income for each quintile of the Canadian population has remained amazingly stable from 1976 until the mid-1990s. Figure 2.2 shows how inequality has risen since then, but has remained constant since 2000. Inequality is measured by the Gini Index, which rises from 0.0 for perfect equality to 1.0 for perfect inequality.

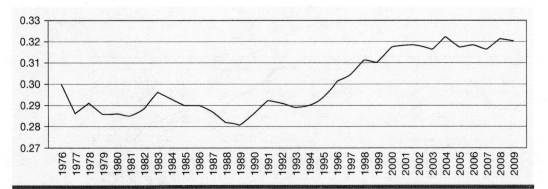

Figure 2.2   Income Inequality in Canada, 1976–2009 (Gini Index using adjusted after-tax income, where 0 represents exact equality and 1 represents total inequality).

Source: *Conference Board, 2014,* Income Inequality. *Retrieved September 6, 2014 (http://www.conferenceboard.ca/hcp/details/society/income-inequality.aspx).*

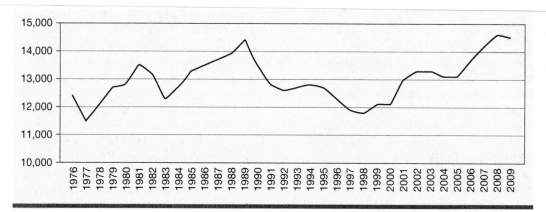

Figure 2.3   Average Income of Poorest 20 Percent of Canadians, 1976–2009 (average after-tax income, 2009 $).
Source: *Conference Board, 2014*, Income Inequality. *Retrieved September 6, 2014* (*http://www.conferenceboard.ca/hcp/details/society/income-inequality.aspx*).

The Canadian Lower Class

The lower class in Canada makes up approximately 20 percent of the population and comprises the working poor and the chronically poor. The working poor are those who work full-time in (often) unskilled positions, such as seasonal or migrant agricultural workers or the lowest-paid service sector workers, but still remain at the edge of poverty. Minimum wages in this country no longer keep people out of poverty, although that is what they were intended to do. Figure 2.3 shows how in 2008, the income of the bottom 20 percent of the population was only at late 1980s levels, and that income likely declined again after 2008 during the recession.

When the minimum wage was introduced in Canada in 1974, an individual with full-time, full-year employment earning minimum wage could expect to live 10 percent above the poverty line. Today, an individual needs to earn considerably more than $10 per hour, full-time, full-year, to even escape poverty. It is easy, therefore, to see why so many Canadians fall into this class, despite the overall wealth of the nation.

Although the poor constitute between 9 and 14 percent of our population, depending on the measure used (see Figure 2.4), they receive only about 5 percent of the overall Canadian income. Individuals who are chronically poor include people of working age who are unemployed or outside the labour force, and children who live in poor families caught in long-term deprivation. Overrepresented among low-income and poverty-level individuals are those who are unable to work because of age or disability and lone-parent mothers who are

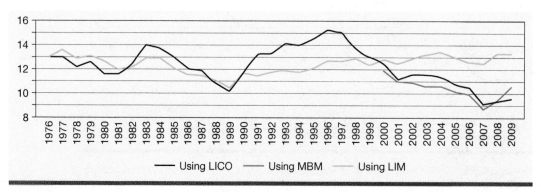

Figure 2.4   Percent of Canadian Population in Low Income, 1976–2009.
Source: *Conference Board, 2014*, Income Inequality. *Retrieved September 6, 2014* (*http://www.conferenceboard.ca/hcp/details/society/income-inequality.aspx*).

heads of households, along with their children. The term *underclass* is sometimes used to refer to people who are chronically poor, but this term not only negatively labels poor people, it also puts them outside the mainstream of society.

POVERTY IN CANADA

The fact that Canada is a high-income nation, but one in which such a high proportion of the population lives in low-income and poverty situations, has made it the target of international criticism, particularly from the United Nations. Many Canadians do not suffer from absolute poverty, as the homeless do, but they do experience relative poverty on the basis of what is available to other people in Canada. Box 2.1 shows the different ways of measuring poverty in Canada.

Age, Family Structure, Sex, Immigration, and Indigenous Status

The chances of being in poverty vary dramatically by major demographic variables. As shown in the above figures, As shown in Box 2.2, age is an important variable in determining poverty. Children have a much greater likelihood of being poor than seniors.

Figure 11.5, which uses different age categories, shows that working-age people 18–64 years have the greatest likelihood of having a low income (10.1 percent), young people under 18 years are next (8.2 percent), and seniors 65+ years have the least likelihood of having a low income (5.3 percent). In terms of family structure, Figure 11.5 shows that people in families, except for female lone-parent families, are much less likely to have a low income (measured by LICO after taxes) than unattached individuals of any age (5.9 vs. 26.9 percent respectively).

In addition, unattached senior females (15.4 percent) and female lone-parents (21.8 percent) have a greater likelihood of having a low-income than unattached single males (11.5 percent) and all people in families (5.9 percent) have. Recent immigrants have a greater likelihood of having a low income than does the Canadian-born population and immigrants who have been in Canada for longer time periods (though no percentages are mentioned) (Statistics Canada 2013s). Finally, since Canada's Indigenous population earned about $10 000/year less than the non-Indigenous population in 1996, 2001, and 2006 (income was not asked in the 2011 Census), there is a greater likelihood that a higher percentage of them will have a low income compared to the non-Indigenous population (Wilson and Macdonald

---

Social Problems and Statistics   Box 2.1

Measuring Poverty

How do we measure poverty in Canada? Unlike the United States, we do not have a poverty line. Instead, we have three ways of measuring poverty:

- **Low-income measure** (LIM) is half the median family income. Those below that level have a low-income. The LIM is adjusted for family size.
- **Low-income cut-off** (LICO) is the income level below which a family would devote 50+ percent of their income to food, clothing, and shelter. The LICO is also adjusted for family and community size and before or after taxes. In 2009, the threshold for a person living in Toronto was $18 421 (see Figure 11.5).
- **Market basket measure** (MBM) is the income a family would need to be able to purchase a basket of goods that includes food, clothing, shelter, transportation, and other basic needs. Like the other measures, MBM varies by family size and composition, and community size

and location. MBM data have only recently been compiled (Conference Board 2014).

The three measures produce somewhat different results. In 2009, the percent of Canadians living in low income ranged from almost 9 to almost 14 percent, as shown in Figure 2.4.

Questions for Consideration

1. Is one kind of measure better than the others for illustrating different problems of poverty? Which one helps in analyzing which type of problem?
2. How would you choose one of these methods to use in analyzing poverty and why?
3. Do you think Canada should have a poverty line? If so, how would you calculate it?

Social Problems in Global Perspective

Box 2.2

Poverty of Some Vulnerable Groups in Canada Relative to Those in Other High-Income Countries

The Conference Board of Canada has compared the poverty levels of some potentially vulnerable groups of Canadians (e.g., children, disabled people, working age people, and the elderly) with those in other high-income countries. The following figures show the results of those comparisons. Overall, Canada has a very uneven record: two "A's," a "C," and a "D."

Figure 2.5 shows that Canada ranks 15th of 17 countries and gets a "C" rating. Canada has had a "C" rating since the 1980s. Children are a very vulnerable group, since poor nutrition as well as other poverty variables can cause behaviour problems, development delays, and other health problems.

In November 1989, Ed Broadbent, then-leader of the NDP, put forward a motion in the House of Commons to end child poverty by the year 2000. It was passed unanimously, but was derailed by free trade agreements, deregulation, and deficit cutting during the 1990s. Since the mid-1990s, our child poverty rate has actually increased a few percentage points.

Figure 2.6 shows that our disabled population fares well economically. For this group, Canada ranks 8th of 16 countries and earns an "A." Disabled people earn over 80 percent of what non-disabled people earn. Canada relies on integrating disabled people into the workforce rather than direct benefits.

Figure 2.7 shows that Canada ranks very low relative to other high-income countries in terms of poverty among working-aged people. Canada ranks 15th of 17 countries and earns a "D." In the mid-1990s, Canada earned a "C." Although just about every other country's grade declined with the recession, it is still a great waste of human resources and consuming opportunities.

Figure 2.8 shows that the ranking of Canada regarding the elderly is excellent, ranking 3rd of 17 and earning an "A." Pension benefits, including old-age security, Canada Pension Plan, RRSPs, private pensions, and other savings have helped elderly Canadians attain a high ranking in this area. Some, like Ontario Premier Kathleen Wynne, think that not enough money is being saved for retirement. As a result, Ontario is considering setting up an additional provincial pension plan. While Canada's record is currently excellent, it is difficult to know what will happen when a quarter of our population is 65+ years, likely in 2030. Will resources be present to keep them out of poverty? In fact, Figure 5.3 in Chapter 5 shows that the poverty curve is starting to edge up for this age group.

Canada's overall scores for the four vulnerable groups studied indicate that these results are better than for the United States, but not very distinguished relative to the Scandanavian countries.

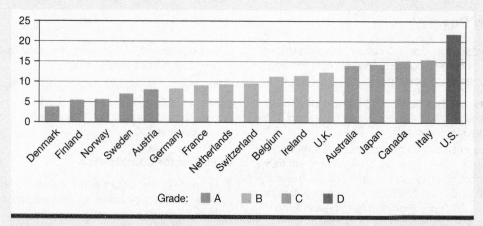

Figure 2.5   Child Poverty Rate, Late 2000s (percent).

Source: *Conference Board, 2014, Child Poverty. Retrieved September 5, 2014 (www.conferenceboard.ca/hcp/details/society/child-poverty.aspx).*

Social Problems in Global Perspective

Box 2.2 continued

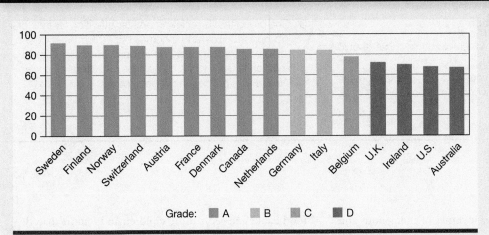

Figure 2.6   Income of People with Disabilites, Mid-2000s (income of people with disabilities as a share of income of people without disabilities).

Source: *Conference Board of Canada, 2014, Disabled Income. Retrieved September 5, 2014 (www.conferenceboard.ca/hcp/details/society/disabled-income.aspx).*

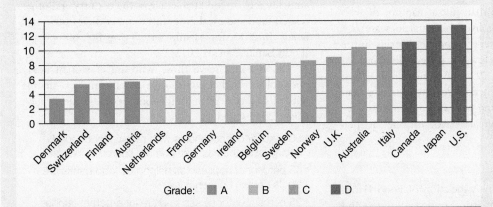

Figure 2.7   Working-Age Poverty Rate, Late 2000s (percent).

Source: *Conference Board of Canada, 2014, Working Age Poverty. Retrieved September 5, 2014 (http://www.conferenceboard.ca/hcp/details/society/working-age-poverty.aspx).*

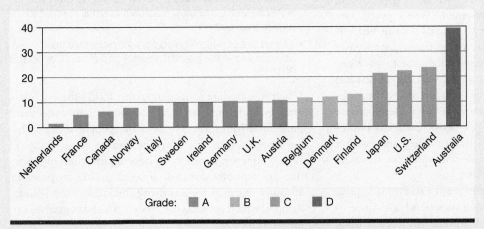

Figure 2.8   Elderly Poverty Rate, Late 2000s (percent).

Source: *Conference Board of Canada, 2014, Elderly Poverty. Retrieved September 5, 2014 (www.conferenceboard.ca/hcp/details/society/elderly-poverty.aspx).*

Social Problems in Global Perspective

Box 2.2 continued

Questions for Consideration

1. Can you think of other vulnerable groups that should be included on this list?
2. What social policies do you think would help increase our ranking in child and working age poverty?
3. One group that is receiving greater attention for lack of job opportunities and income, but which has not yet received international comparisons, is university graduates, particularly in the humanities and social sciences. What social policies might help them?

2010:8). (See Figure 3.1 for incomes of Indigenous and non-Indigenous peoples.)

Consequences of Poverty

Poverty statistics are more than just a snapshot of who is poor and how the poor live: these statistics are also predictors. As such, they tend to predict a grim future for individuals who live below the poverty line and for the entire nation (Gleick 1996). As one social analyst (Ropers 1991:25) has noted, "Poverty narrows and closes life chances. . . . Being poor not only means economic insecurity, it also wreaks havoc on one's mental and physical health."

Health and Nutrition

According to the Canadian Association of Food Banks (2002:5), "[w]ithin a domestic context, hunger and food insecurity are best understood as consequences of extreme poverty."

Good nutrition, which is essential to good health, depends on the food consumed. When people are poor, they are more likely to purchase cheap but filling foods such as beans, rice, and potatoes that may not meet all daily nutritional requirements, or to go without food altogether. Using data from the 2005 Canadian Community Health Survey conducted by Statistics Canada, the Canadian Council on Social Development (CCSD) reported that 3.3 percent of Canadian households were food insecure without hunger, and another 1.8 percent were food insecure with moderate to severe levels of hunger (CCSD 2009b).

Poor children particularly are at risk for inadequate nutrition and hunger. Emergency food assistance is especially pronounced in urban areas, but recently there has been greater need in rural communities as well. Rural food banks make up almost half of the nation's food banks and serve more children and seniors than do urban food banks.

Since the first food bank opened its doors in Edmonton, Alberta, in 1981, high numbers of people annually rely on food banks across the country and other related food and meal programs to meet their nutritional needs. In 2013, food banks served over 800 000 people (Food Banks Canada 2013:2).

Food banks serve those who are at risk of being poor, older single people, lone-parent families, people with disabilities, and Indigenous people. The *Hunger Count 2013* stated:

- 50 percent of households who receive food report social assistance as their primary source of income;
- 43 percent of households helped by food banks are single person households;
- 25 percent of those assisted are lone-parent families;
- 16 percent of households assisted are living primarily on disability-related income supports;
- 11 percent of individuals assisted self-identify as First Nations, Métis, or Inuit (25 percent in small towns and rural areas); and
- 11 percent of people helped are immigrants who have arrived in the past 10 years (Food Banks Canada 2013: 5).

It is important to recognize that food hampers generally provide only enough food for five days, and that most food banks are able to allow people access only once per month. The nutritional value of most food-bank hampers is dubious, considering the kinds of foods that are typically donated. Imagine trying to provide adequate nutrition for a growing child from a food-bank hamper, which contains few fresh fruits and vegetables or high-quality foods.

When these hampers are used in emergency situations, as they were originally intended, this does not present many problems. However, when people rely on food-bank hampers over the long term, the consequences are detrimental and severe. Prolonged malnutrition can contribute to or result in such medical problems as rickets, scurvy, parasitic worms, and developmental disabilities. The long-term health care costs of cuts to income assistance should be clear.

Problems associated with food and shelter are intricately linked. When parents are forced to decide between paying the rent and putting food on the table, many choose to pay the rent in hopes of keeping a roof over their children's heads. Sometimes, however, they cannot afford to do either.

Housing

The lack of affordable housing in many regions in Canada has become a crisis. Over the past three decades, low-cost housing units in many areas have been replaced by expensive condominiums or single-family residences for affluent residents in a process known as "gentrification." This shift to condominiums and single-family residences has made finding housing even more difficult for individuals and families living in poverty. When low-income housing is available, it may be located in high-density, often overcrowded areas. The housing often has inadequate heating and plumbing facilities, infestations of insects or rodents, and dangerous structural problems due to faulty construction or lack of adequate maintenance. Homelessness will be discussed later in Chapter 15, but a recent report on homelessness in Canada, *The State of Homelessness in Canada: 2013*, the first extensive Canadian report card on homelessness, highlights that:

- As many as 1.3 million Canadians have experienced homelessness or extremely insecure housing during the last five years;
- At least 200 000 Canadians experience homelessness in a year;
- 30 000 people are homeless on a given night in shelters, special institutions, or without shelter;
- 8.2 percent experience moderate or severe food insecurity;
- 4000 to 8000 people are chronically homeless;
- 50 days is the median length of stay in shelters; and
- Single males, youth, and Indigenous people are overrepresented (Gaetz, Stephen et al. 2013).

Education

As will be seen in Chapter 12 (Education Report Card), Canada does a good job in elevating the performance of disadvantaged schools, as shown by the small difference in reading scores between advantaged and disadvantaged schools. But one group, Indigenous peoples, who have a much lower income than non-Indigenous peoples, have a much lower rate of completing secondary and post-secondary school (see also Chapter 3). In 2011, 89 percent of the non-Indigenous population, aged 18–44 years, had a high school diploma or equivalent, while only 72 percent of First Nations, 77 percent of Métis, and 42 percent of Inuit had this level of education (Statistics Canada 2014a).

How Canada Deals with Poverty

As part of an overall retrenchment of government programs and services in Canada, structural poverty is dealt with as though it is an individual problem. Rather than examining ways of eliminating poverty or dealing with poverty at a societal level, we offer temporary assistance. More often than not, that temporary assistance is through charity—both individual charities, such as serving a meal at a soup kitchen or making a donation of money or goods, and charitable organizations, such as soup kitchens, sandwich trucks, and food banks, which almost always rely on volunteer labour and community donations, and which rarely receive base year-to-year funding from the government.

Following a great deal of lobbying by Canadian activists and non-governmental organizations (NGOs) in the late 1990s and early 2000s, including the delivery of a "State of Emergency Declaration" to the United Nations, the federal government began taking baby steps toward looking at the problem of poverty. During the early 2000s, several agreements were signed between the federal government and the provincial, territorial, and municipal governments to cost-share expenses for some infrastructure spending (Crowe 2007). While it was thought that the agreements would mainly focus on funding new social housing, it became quickly evident that most of the money would be spent on sewers and water supply. While sewers and water are terribly important, and while the funding agreements are a welcome shift away from funding cuts, this does nothing to address poverty and homelessness in Canada.

So our national "non-strategy," so far, is to temporarily fund shelters and food banks in Canada as though poverty and its attendant problems are fleeting aberrations. Yet poverty did not significantly decrease, despite strong overall economic growth over the past decade, and state welfare programs, such as Employment Insurance (EI) and Income Assistance (IA), continue to be retrenched, resulting in heightened risks of poverty for income-insecure individuals.

By way of example, revisions to the employee- and employer-funded EI program have resulted in drastically narrowed eligibility criteria and shorter benefit periods, even though the program has always run at a surplus. Most recent data demonstrate that a mere 37 percent of the applicants meet new criteria, compared to more than 74 percent one decade ago (Canadian Labour Congress 2006), and it has remained at this level during the Conservative government. The government of 2011 changed the rules. Additionally, waiting periods for benefit receipt have been lengthened, and individuals who need income assistance while waiting for a decision about their EI claim must agree to pay that money back when they receive EI benefits. In the past, unemployed workers were able to achieve EI benefits of up to 75 percent of their previous earnings; however, today workers are only able to receive *up to* 55 percent of their previous earnings, and often for only a few short weeks.

Since its inception, the EI program has run at a surplus. Employers and employees both continue to pay into the EI fund, so why have there been so many cuts? The EI money has been used to pay off the deficit, pay for tax cuts, and pay down government debt. If you are laid off tomorrow, your chances of accessing any of the surplus you and your employer helped create are very low. Think about what you would do to survive for six weeks or more while your eligibility was being determined. *If* you were successful in getting EI, how well could you make ends meet on half your current monthly income? How long do you think it would take you to find another job at your current salary? What about your parents, if they are still in the labour force?

SOCIAL WELFARE IN CANADA

Canada, like many other advanced capitalist nations, is a *welfare state*—**a nation in which the government intervenes in the welfare of its citizens through various social policies, programs, standards, and regulations.** Most Canadians are so accustomed to the benefits of the Canadian welfare state that we take them for granted. All of our social programs, such as universal health care, education, pension plans, worker's compensation, minimum wage, employment standards, environmental regulations, health and safety standards, social or income assistance, child tax benefits, and so on, are subsumed under the mantle of the welfare state.

One of the unintended, but useful, consequences of the welfare state has been to ameliorate the worst contradictions created by capitalism's normal boom and bust business cycles; therefore, as Teeple (2000:442) points out, the welfare state soothes "the worst effects of economic inequality and . . . placate[s] resistance to all political and social implications of such inequality."

In 1966, the federal government brought into effect the Canada Assistance Plan (CAP). The purpose of the plan was to outline the ways the federal government would cost-share income assistance with the provinces and territories and to establish national social assistance standards. The criterion upon which people could access CAP was need, based on the idea that all Canadian citizens had certain basic human rights. These rights, enshrined in the CAP, were (a) the right to income assistance when in need; (b) the right to an amount of income assistance that meets basic requirements; (c) the right to appeal decisions if the person disagrees; (d) the right not to have to work or train in order to collect income assistance; and (e) the right to collect income assistance, regardless of the province of origin (Swanson 2001:108). Historically derived from a charity model, income assistance based upon need became a right for all citizens in Canada. Unemployment had to be kept low. Business cycles needed to be stabilized. All of this protected corporations and citizens from the worst of the cyclical nature of capitalism (Shragge 1997). The CAP was just one of many social programs that were part of the welfare state, along with universal health care and education, pension plans, and unemployment insurance.

In the early 1970s, capitalism shifted from a national to an international economic system—in short, capitalism became global. Capitalist enterprises were no longer reliant on the purchasing power of any particular nation-state when the whole world was now the market. Additionally, workers in any particular nation no longer had to be placated when capitalist enterprises could easily move production from nation to nation—one reason why cuts to social programs like EI have been so devastating. Under various trade agreements, capitalists sought to level ("harmonize") social and economic policies between nations to facilitate easier and more profitable trade.

A newly internationalized capitalism put increased pressure on governments to enact new neo-liberal policies that would have the effect of reducing government interventions such as income assistance, EI, and so on, called "barriers to trade" by neo-liberals. These "interventions," in the form of social programs and public protections, are being retrenched or cut back more each year, using a variety of justifications, from the "deficit-mania" hysteria in the 1990s to the superficially convincing arguments that Canadian health care is "just too expensive," when the facts underlying these sophisticated advertising campaigns demonstrate much different realities.

In July 1995, the Liberal government passed Bill C-76, which signalled the end of the CAP. On April 1, 1996, the government replaced the CAP with the *Canada Health and Social Transfer Act* (CHST) and turned it into a block grant. Where the federal government had covered 50 percent of provincial program costs in the past, in 2014–15, provinces and territories will receive $65 billion in major transfers, like health, social programs, and equilization (among provinces) transfers. These transfers are estimated to account for 19 percent of provincial and territorial revenues in that year. The health transfer is $35 billion, about three times the social programs transfer. In addition, this has meant reduced spending for postsecondary education, which has caused student tuition to rise and students to accumulate much debt.

Replacing the CAP with the CHST was part of a broader strategy of retrenchment by the government, decreasing its responsibilities in general for the welfare of citizens through the reduction of various social services (Morel 2002). Sociologist Gregg M. Olsen (2002), in a comparative analysis of Canada, the United States, and Sweden, states that while all three are advanced capitalist nations, Canada has always existed somewhere between the other two with regard to policies and programs and their effects. With globalization expanding, Canada has become increasingly similar to the United States in terms of social policies, cost-cutting measures, and cutbacks in social services and programs. Welfare state retrenchment in Canada has had farther-reaching and more "acute, punitive, and brutal" changes, because we are becoming more like the United States than like Sweden (Olsen 2002:3). Political scientist Sylvie Morel (2002:19) notes that one of the distinctive features of Canadian welfare-policy reform is the classification of social assistance recipients according to a criterion of fitness for work. One of the major effects of replacing the CAP with the CHST was that it ended our participation in the United Nations Covenant of Social, Economic, and Cultural Rights, which Canada signed in 1976. Among other things, the covenant declared that all citizens have the right to "freely chosen" employment and to "an adequate standard of living . . . including adequate food, clothing and housing and . . . the continuous improvement of living conditions" (UN 1992, in Swanson 1997:158). Every five years, each nation that has signed the covenant must report to the UN how it is complying. In the past, Canada used the CAP to demonstrate its commitment to the covenant. No more.

Another and a related effect of the CHST was to end the citizen's right to financial assistance and make

workfare legal in Canada. The term *workfare* is generally used to describe a particular direction taken by governments as they reform social assistance, with a particular focus on the shift from income assistance based on need to some type of mandatory employment activity in exchange for benefits (Morel 2002; Shragge 1997). Workfare programs are based on the assumption that there are two groups of poor: the deserving and the undeserving. The deserving poor are those who, for reasons completely beyond their control (for example, extreme old age or extreme disability) are unable to work. The undeserving poor, rated as the vast majority of people on income assistance, are those who suffer from the "damaging consequences of dependence on the welfare system" (Shragge 1997:17). According to proponents of workfare schemes, the undeserving poor need the "tough love of workfare" to give them "a hand up and not merely a hand out" (Shragge 1997:19). Ideally, this tough love would improve the moral conduct of the undeserving poor, who, it is supposed, must be taught "appropriate sexual conduct" and a "life of thrift and humility," rather than squandering their meagre incomes on alcohol, tobacco, bingo, and other luxuries Shragge 1997; Swanson 2001).

The official rationale for retrenchment and for workfare was to save money and reduce welfare dependency. Initially both caseloads and costs declined. It was believed by many that "the poor" were unmotivated, or did not value work, or had no work ethic, or had, through a "culture of poverty," "cultural values and attitudes which precluded a commitment to work." Anti-poverty activist Jean Swanson (1997) calls this "Newspeak," based on the language made up by government officials in George Orwell's famous novel *1984*. In Orwell's novel, new terms are created in order to shape and direct citizens' understandings of social and political life in particular ways. Swanson (1997:151) argues that "social policy 'experts,' corporate lobby groups, and right-wing politicians" have devised a new language of blame that serves to obscure the truth about welfare and workfare programs and to create a climate where cuts can be justified. Newspeak about workfare was based on two myths: (1) that people on welfare need to be forced to take employment because they are lazy; and (2) that enough employment, paying living wages, exists. A coalition of social justice groups concerned with poverty, End Legislated Poverty (ELP), catalogued at least 15 Newspeak terms currently in use and their meanings (Swanson 1997). The following reflects a sampling of these terms. Have you heard these expressions before?

Social Problems and Social Policy

Box 2.3

Income Splitting—Benefits for High-Income Canadians

In October 2014, the Harper government announced its plan for couples with children under 18 years of age to split their incomes and pay taxes at reduced rates. This is obviously not a universal program like universal child daycare (as found in Quebec); it targets families where one earner makes much more than the other earner or who supports the family on one income. This program does not help families where the earners make identical salaries or lone-parent families. According to this plan, the higher earner can transfer up to $50 000 in income from the higher to lower earner and save a maximum of $2000 in taxes. Although the Universal Child Care Benefit will increase for all who have children under age 18, it is expected that the beneficiaries of this package will be high earners. The rationale given is that it transfers money directly to people and does not create a large bureaucracy. The past and late Finance Minister, Joe Flaherty, opposed the plan in 2013 because mostly high earners benefit and as a result he did not include this plan in his budget. The C.D. Howe Institute (a conservative think tank) said something similar about a more generous plan proposed in 2011.

Questions for consideration

1. Should social programs be universal or targeted?
2. If targeted, who should be the recipients, the people with lowest or highest earnings?
3. Because of spending cuts, the federal government is expected to have a surplus in 2016. The Conservatives think that much of this surplus should be devoted to tax cuts. How would you apportion the surplus?

Breaking the Cycle of Poverty: This phrase implies that children are taught to be poor by poor adults who pass their preference for poverty onto their children. ELP notes that "no one is exhorted to 'break the cycle of wealth' where rich people pass their wealth on to children who pass it on to their children, perpetuating inequality of income distribution" (Swanson 1997:152–153).

Bring Social Programs into the 21st Century: This phrase typically means to "cut and slash social programs so that people will have to work at low-wage jobs [if they can find them] so they can compete with people in Mexico making $5 a day" (Swanson 1997:153).

Self-Esteem: This phrase is most often used in conjunction with the idea that people need employment to build and maintain their self-esteem. "It implies that a single parent must build her self-esteem at a low-wage, exploitative paid job, rather than by staying home to raise her children to be good citizens" (Swanson 1997:154).

Training for the Jobs of the Future: This phrase is used to describe the plan to get the unemployed training in high-tech jobs like computer programming and air-traffic control to get them off welfare or EI. But of course, even if the 6.8 percent of the labour force that were unemployed in 2015 were able to do those jobs, Canada does not need that many high-tech workers now (Swanson 1997:154–155).

Canadian economist Lars Osberg (2009:15), in his research on cuts to EI and other social programs, points out that the only thing that has ever worked to move people off income assistance is employment. This fact, along with changes to the CHST, will spell trouble ahead for the provinces and territories in the years to come.

Speaking about so-called welfare dependency, Swanson (1997:150), citing 40 years of research in British Columbia, makes the further point that "welfare benefits are so low, the welfare system so controlling and demeaning, that the vast majority of people engineer their own escapes from it as soon as they can." Her comments are based on provincial governmental research showing that only 10 percent of assistance recipients stay on it for more than two years. Income assistance programs in Canada cost taxpayers as much money as tax breaks to RRSP holders do, and yet the latter group of citizens is not held to blame for the Canadian deficit problem. Further, tax breaks to corporations (see Chapter 13) far outweigh the amount of money spent on social programs, yet few people lobby for an end to the corporate dole. If it is true that most people only use income assistance as a safety net in times of real need, as was intended, and if forced work programs have not been shown to be effective for their stated purpose (to save money and reduce the numbers on income assistance), and if these social programs do not cost Canadian taxpayers much money, why do governments persist in moving ahead with workfare programs and the like?

The main social policy initiative of the Harper Conservatives has been their social justice and crime agenda. Their view of federalism is that governments operate in compartments. They do not wish to see national standards throughout the country, not in education, and not even in the area of health delivery. Their future major transfers, like health and social programs (mentioned above), will permit provinces to make their own plans. The government does believe in income transfers to the middle class, their usual supporters (see Box 2.3).

PERSPECTIVES ON POVERTY AND CLASS INEQUALITY

Social-class inequality and poverty can be understood from various perspectives. The framework that is applied influences people's beliefs about how poverty might be reduced.

The Symbolic Interactionist Perspective

Symbolic interactionists examine poverty from the perspective of meanings, definitions, and labels. How is poverty defined? How are people who are poor viewed by non-poor society members? How do people who are poor define themselves and their situations? What stigma is attached to poverty, or homelessness, and how do people live with, or manage, that stigma? What are the consequences of being labelled as "poor" or "low income" or "homeless"?

Canada is a meritocracy, and much of contemporary rhetoric suggests, then, that if people wish to succeed, they can. Definitions of *success* are rarely explicitly discussed; instead, a common understanding of the term is assumed and taken for granted. If someone fails to succeed, it follows that the fault lies with the individual, who is "irresponsible," "lazy," "immoral," "lacking in motivation," and so on. This is the "land of opportunity," and people who do not succeed have no one but themselves to blame for their lacks and flaws (Feagin 1975). Workfare programs for social assistance recipients are based on individualistic explanations for poverty. To many sociologists, however, individual explanations of poverty amount to **blaming the victim—a practice suggesting that the cause of a social problem emanates from within the individual or group who exhibits the problem, by virtue of some inherent lack or flaw on the part of the individual or group.** Conversely, symbolic interactionists also examine what it means to be wealthy. How are those with wealth viewed by others? While impoverished people tend to be negatively stigmatized, wealthy individuals tend to be seen as hard working and deserving of their

wealth. Where do we get information about the relative merits of whole groups of people? As author and journalist Jeremy Seabrook (2002:129) points out, "while it is easy to find a table of the 20 richest people in the world, it would be impossible to do the same with the 20 poorest." Further, since wealthy people have the means to avoid being observed and investigated in ways that poor people do not, sociologists know relatively little about them. In the absence of evidence about the hardworking (or other) practices of wealthy people, we must rely simply on ideology.

Symbolic interactionists are also interested in what it means to people to be poor and what impact stigma has on people's self-concepts. Some researchers have focused on how cultural background affects people's values and behaviour. Among the earliest of these explanations is the "culture of poverty" thesis by anthropologist Oscar Lewis (1966). According to Lewis, poor people have different values and beliefs than people from the middle and upper classes, and so develop a separate and self-perpetuating system of attitudes and behaviours that keeps them trapped in poverty. Among these attitudes and behaviours are the inability to defer gratification or plan for the future; feelings of apathy, hostility, and suspicion toward others; deficient speech and communication patterns; female-headed households; and a decided lack of participation in major societal institutions. People trapped in the "culture of poverty" socialize their children into this cycle of poverty, and hence the culture supposedly perpetuates. The "culture of poverty" thesis has provided political leaders, social analysts, and many other Canadian citizens with a reasonable-sounding rationale for blaming the situations endured by poor people on the poor themselves. The "culture of poverty" thesis, while popular, has been soundly criticized. Critics point out that people who are poor, just like people who are not poor, develop attitudes and behaviours as *responses* and ways of coping with stigma and other limitations and barriers placed on their participation. The "culture of poverty" thesis has also been critiqued for suggesting that poor people both enjoy their impoverished situations and do not know any better. Besides being incorrect, these notions are paternalistic and based on stereotypes.

More recent cultural explanations of poverty have focused on the lack of *cultural capital***—social assets, such as values, beliefs, attitudes, and competencies in language and culture that are learned at home and required for success and social advancement** (Bourdieu and Passeron 1990). From this perspective, low-income people do not have adequate cultural capital to function in a competitive global economy. According to most sociologists, cultural explanations again deflect attention from the true structural sources of poverty (unemployment, racism, sexism, and so on) and shift blame from the affluent and powerful to the poor and powerless (Sidel 1996:xvii–xviii).

The Structural Functionalist Perspective

Unlike individual and cultural explanations of poverty, which operate at the microlevel, structural explanations of poverty focus on the macrolevel, the level of social organization that is beyond an individual's ability to change. One structural explanation of poverty (Wilson 1996) points to changes in the economy that have dramatically altered employment opportunities for people, particularly those who have the least wealth, power, and prestige. According to the functionalists who espouse this explanation, social inequality serves an important function in society because it motivates people to work hard to acquire scarce resources. In 1945, sociologists Kingsley Davis and Wilbert Moore published a paper explaining that social stratification exists in every society in some form and must, therefore, be functional. Davis and Moore asserted that some occupations require more training and investment than others, or are difficult or unpleasant to do, and so should be compensated more, through prestige and pay. This explains, they felt, why doctors and judges have high prestige and pay, while restaurant servers and truck drivers do not. This thesis has been criticized for several reasons, among them the idea that inequities in pay and prestige are functional for society. Why are women paid less than men? For whom is this functional? Is the work of a child-care provider really worth millions of dollars less per year than the work of an NHL star? Why are occupations that are overly dirty or dangerous not rewarded with high salaries? Functionalists also assert that it is functional to maintain a pool of more desperate workers in order to fill the occupations that no one wants to do. This is deemed "functional" but is likely problematic for those "desperate few" who are forced to work in unfavourable conditions, often for low wages. This is a main criticism of functionalist perspectives generally— we must always ask the question, Functional for whom? Lastly, poverty may be seen as functional for those who work in the "poverty industry" (for example, financial assistance workers) and for those who need a market for second-rate or inferior-quality items.

The Conflict Perspective

Another structural explanation for poverty is based on a conflict perspective that suggests poverty is a side effect of the capitalist system. Using this explanation, analysts note that workers are increasingly impoverished by the wage squeeze and high rates of unemployment and underemployment. The *wage squeeze* is the steady downward pressure on the real take-home pay of workers that has occurred over the past three decades. During these decades, shareholders in major corporations have had substantial increases in dividends, and chief executive officers have received extremely lucrative salaries and compensation packages. In a few decades after the 1950s, executive pay has risen from tens of times the average worker's salary to hundreds of times the average worker's salary. Corporate downsizing and new technologies that replace workers have further enhanced capitalists' profits and contributed to the impoverishment of middle- and low-income workers by creating a reserve army of unemployed people whom the capitalists use for casual labour and as a means to keep other workers' wages low. Corporations' intense quest for profit results in low wages for workers, a wide disparity in the life chances of affluent people and poor people, and the unemployment and impoverishment of many. Sociologist Harley D. Dickinson (2000) notes that unemployment is a normal consequence of capitalism and, in fact, is necessary. Conflict between the capitalists (Marx's bourgeoisie) and the workers (Marx's proletariat) has in part been ameliorated in past decades by welfare state programs like EI or income assistance (Dickinson 2000). What effect will continued retrenchment have on class conflict in Canada? Although some analysts suggest that high rates of poverty will always exist in advanced capitalist societies, others believe that inequality and poverty can be reduced, and even eliminated, if the political will exists.

Feminist Perspectives

Many feminist perspectives on poverty or class inequality focus on the gendered character of stratification and poverty. Most of the people living in poverty are women and their children. This **trend of women being disproportionately represented among individuals living in poverty has been called the *feminization of poverty*.** Feminist theorists look at the differential valuing of occupations and roles within Canadian society, noting who has power and prestige, which occupations are deemed more or less valuable, and so on. Feminist theorists examine what factors propel women into poverty and keep them there, looking, for instance, at women's economic positions following divorce or marital dissolution. The fact that women are more likely than men to have children living with them after marital breakup disproportionately burdens them, particularly if fathers are not contributing to the new household financially. This can be especially problematic as women make lower wages in nearly every occupation in Canada. Further, women are more likely to be widowed than men, and older women's pensions are often negligible because many were not in the paid labour force for long. Lastly, work that is considered to be "women's work" (i.e., any paid work that mimics that done in the home—cleaning, caregiving, and so on) is compensated poorly as it is deemed more a "labour of love" than real "work" requiring proper compensation.

In work that later became the foundation of a socialist–feminist analysis of the intersection of gender and class, or patriarchy and capitalism, Engels theorized that the fact of private property was at the heart of patriarchy. With capitalism came the private ownership of the means of producing goods and services. With private property came the desire to pass it on along with the wealth it generated to the children of the bourgeoisie. This then made knowing one's genetic offspring very important to the bourgeoisie, which made the establishment of a system for ensuring paternity very important. In order to ensure a man's children were indeed his own, monogamy and the subjugation of women became necessary. Engels (1884/1972:120) referred to this, in a famous phrase, as "the world-historical defeat of women." One of the criticisms of a socialist–feminist perspective is that it is deterministic; it lacks an explanation of why capitalism must unfold this way (Muszynski 2000). More recently, instead of seeing women and men as oppositional classes, scholars have analyzed the variety of ways that gender, racialization, and class intersect within a capitalist economic system, recognizing the complexities in an analysis of who is poor and who is wealthy, who is an oppressor and who is oppressed.

If we are going to understand poverty, if indeed this is a necessary precursor to ending it, our explanations will need to become more comprehensive. Is it possible to reduce or eliminate class inequality and poverty without a theoretical understanding?

HOW CAN POVERTY BE REDUCED?

Chapter 1 made the point that how people view a social problem is related to how they believe the problem should be reduced or solved. Poverty and social inequality are no exception. Analysts who focus on individualistic explanations of poverty typically suggest individual solutions: Low-income and poverty-level people should change their attitudes, beliefs, and work habits.

Similarly, people who use cultural explanations seek cultural solutions; they suggest that poverty can be reduced by the enhancement of people's cultural capital. They urge the development of more job training and school enrichment programs to enhance people's cultural capital and counteract negative familial and neighbourhood influences. Seeking cultural solutions, the federal government developed job training and young entrepreneur programs to provide children and adolescents from low-income families with the cultural capital (White, middle-class values, really) they need to succeed in the White, middle-class world.

Although some analysts seeking structural solutions suggest that poverty can be eliminated only if capitalism is abolished and a new means of distributing valued goods and services is established, others state that poverty can be reduced by the creation of "a truly open society—a society where the life chances of those at the bottom are not radically different from those at the top and where wealth is distributed more equitably" (MacLeod 1995:260). The latter analysts feel that federal, territorial, and provincial governments can and should play a vital role in reducing poverty and lessening people's need for social assistance.

Canadians of every political persuasion (poll results were remarkably similar for all political affiliations) are ready for action on poverty, and they want all levels of government to take leadership. What is particularly interesting about this poll is that the majority of people indicated that that they would be more likely to support a political party that pledged to make poverty reduction a priority (CCPA 2008).

Dr. David Hay, a research and information management consultant, also believes that Canadians "feel that their current social reality is disconnected from long standing, essential and shared Canadian values" (2009:9). So how might we get back on track and become more aligned with our social values?

Taking concrete and immediate action on poverty reduction is one way. According to Hay (2009), who reviewed performance on poverty reduction in Canada and other nations, the development of effective programs and benefits can work to reduce poverty. However, what might a poverty reduction strategy look like? The Canadian Centre for Policy Alternatives (CCPA) published a poverty reduction strategy in December 2008 that still seems very timely in 2015. Based on research of other jurisdictions that have successfully reduced poverty, the report (CCPA BC 2008) described the following common characteristics of the most effective poverty reduction plans:

- *Targets and timelines:* The plan must have clear targets and timelines, using multiple and widely accepted measures of progress. The benchmarks for the timelines must be concrete enough, and frequent enough, that a government can be held accountable for progress within its mandate. The targets and timelines should be legislated.

- *Accountability:* Accountability mechanisms are key to an effective and credible plan. The plan should lay out overarching goals for the whole of government and include the development of implementation plans within key ministries. The lead minister responsible should be required by legislation to submit an annual progress report to the legislature.
- *Comprehensiveness:* The plan must deal comprehensively with the multiple dimensions and causes of poverty and homelessness. Policy measures put in place must aid those in the low-wage workforce and those who cannot work in paid labour (either temporarily or long term); they must also enhance the social programs/public goods (such as housing, child care, and accessible post-secondary education) that are relied upon by everyone, and in particular, low- and middle-income households.
- *Focus on marginalized groups:* The plan must include measures that focus specifically on populations where poverty and marginalization are most acute—namely Indigenous people, recent immigrants, lone mothers, single senior women, people with disabilities, and people with severe mental illness, addictions, and other health problems.
- *Community involvement:* An official government strategy should be the product of a meaningful province-wide consultation process—one that hears in particular from those most affected by poverty. That said, there are policy actions that require immediate implementation and should not wait for further consultation.

Hay (2009:18) cites the National Council of Welfare following a national consultation on "solving poverty" in 2007, stating that "the Council concluded that 'if there is no long term vision, no plan, no one accountable for carrying out the plan, no resources assigned, and no accepted measure of result, we will continue to be mired in poverty for generations.'" According to the CCPA Office (2008b:8–9), an effective poverty reduction plan should include the following, each with targeted priority actions and timelines, and with clear channels of accountability specific to the province or territory in question (as appropriate today as when recommended in 2008):

1. Provide adequate and accessible income support for the unemployed.
2. Improve earnings and working conditions for low-wage workers.
3. Address the needs of those most likely to be living in poverty.
4. Address homelessness and the lack of affordable housing.
5. Provide universal, publicly funded child care.
6. Provide support for training and education.
7. Promote the health of all citizens.

Although poverty reduction plans like the one presented here will not "solve" the problem of poverty overnight, they will temper and reduce the price poor people pay for living in the "land of opportunity."

WHAT CAN YOU DO?

- Lobby politicians to support real job-creation strategies, higher minimum wages, universal child care, and affordable housing.
- Volunteer at a local food bank, shelter, or soup kitchen.
- Donate money, food, or time to an organization such as a food bank or an anti-poverty organization.
- Write a letter to the local newspaper or your university or college paper outlining some little-known facts about poverty, welfare, "wealthfare," workfare, or hunger in your region. Send a copy of your letter to Food Banks Canada (www.foodbankscanada.ca).
- Participate in alternative economies such as food-share programs and car-share programs.
- Grow a garden and donate some of your efforts to a local food program.
- Bookmark some of the websites for organizations that keep up-to-date statistics on hunger and homelessness in Canada on your computer.
- Engage a homeless person in conversation and find out about his or her life.
- Bake cookies and hand them out to homeless people.
- Make a phone call to your city hall and ask what programs and services the municipality has in place for homeless people. Use your voice as a housed person!
- Become a member of Food Banks Canada or a local anti-poverty organization.
- Attend demonstrations and protests on poverty issues to gain information about local issues. For example, in Victoria, BC, a group of temporary shelters made of cardboard, erected in an out-of-the-way place, was torn down by police at the directive of the municipality. Taking away people's belongings and a semi-dry place to sleep did not stop the problem of homelessness in that city. Use your privilege as a literate person with more media access than most homeless people have to get these issues heard.
- Organize a food drive for your local food bank. For example, at Christmas time in some urban centres, municipal garbage collection workers, organized through the Canadian Union of Public Employees (CUPE), ask citizens to leave wrapped, non-perishable food donations outside on garbage collection days and then ensure they get to the local food bank. Some university campuses organize an annual "Trick or Eat" campaign and go door to door on Halloween collecting food for the local food bank. Remember, good advance publicity is the key to a successful campaign.
- Visit a local grocery store, deli, or bakery and ask if they donate leftover food to the local food bank or soup

kitchens. Call places that do and thank the managers of those stores. This encourages people to continue to operate with their civic responsibilities in mind.

- Send a donation to Food Banks Canada (an organization whose member food banks and agencies feed over 85 percent of Canada's hungry). For every dollar you donate, Food Banks Canada can move $75 worth of food.

- Attend all-candidates forums and ask political hopefuls what they and their party are doing to reduce homelessness, hunger, and poverty in Canada. Ask to see their poverty reduction strategies.

- Intervene when you hear someone poor-bashing or negatively stereotyping poor people. Educate friends, family members, and classmates or professors who are not as knowledgeable about the issues. Keep up to date about the facts so you are comfortable educating others.

- In the words of Toronto street nurse Cathy Crowe (2007:170), "be angry that our governments are not working together to fund the right to safe and truly affordable housing. Your anger is vital to the momentum needed to create the wind for social change." Get angry about the injustice of poverty in Canada.

SUMMARY

Why Is Social Stratification a Social Problem?
Social stratification refers to the hierarchical arrangement of large social groups based on their control over basic resources. In highly stratified societies, low-income and poor people have limited access to food, clothing, shelter, education, health care, and other necessities of life.

Who Makes Up the Lower Classes In Canada?
The Canadian population is divided into several classes. Members of the lower class include the working class and the poor. The working class holds occupations such as semi-skilled machine operator or counter help in a fast-food restaurant. The poor include the working poor and the chronically poor. The working poor are those who are attached to the labour market but whose wages are not sufficient to provide them with the necessities. The chronically poor include individuals of working age who are outside the labour force, some with disabilities, and children who live in poor families. Relative to other high-income countries, Canada provides good financial support to the elderly and disabled, but poor support to those who are children and those of working age.

How Does the "New International Division Of Labour" Perspective Explain Global Inequality?
According to this perspective, transnational corporations have established global assembly lines of production in which workers in middle- and low-income nations, earning extremely low wages, produce goods for export to high-income nations such as the United States and Japan.

Consequences of Poverty
1. Poor health and insecure nutrition
2. Homelessness
3. Poor educational opportunities

Social Welfare in Canada
After WWII, Canada created a welfare system consisting of pensions, health care, and educational support that lasted until the mid-1970s. Since that time, Successive governments have been cutting back their support for universal programs like child care and using targeted funding to support, for example, people raising young children. For example, the Conservative government initiated income supports and income splitting in 2014 for those with children under 18 years of age. While this has led to reduced deficits by government, it has also brought about the decline of the value of universality and increasing inequality in contrast to the programs implemented after WWII.

What Are Individual and Cultural Explanations of Poverty?
Individual explanations of poverty focus on the attitudinal and motivational problems of individuals or the amount of human capital a person possesses. Cultural explanations of poverty focus on how cultural background affects people's values and behaviour. These explanations focus on the microlevel, and most sociologists view them as attempts to blame the victim for the problem.

What Are Structural Explanations of Poverty?
Structural explanations of poverty focus on the macrolevel, the level of social organization that is beyond an individual's ability to change. These explanations consider how changes in the economy have altered employment opportunities or how inequality and exploitation are inherent in the structure of class and gender relations in a capitalist economy.

What Solutions Have Been Suggested for Poverty?
Most individual and cultural solutions focus on the importance of work. Individual perspectives suggest that people should work harder. Cultural perspectives suggest enhancing people's cultural capital to make them better prepared for employment. Structural perspectives are based on the assumption that society can reduce poverty by creating real jobs and by investing in people through the provision of child care, health care, and affordable housing. For the chronically unemployed, a guaranteed annual income could be necessary.

KEY TERMS

absolute poverty, p. 24
blaming the victim, p. 37
cultural capital, p. 37
feminization of poverty, p. 38
income, p. 26

life chances, p. 26
meritocracy, p. 24
power, p. 26
prestige, p. 26
relative poverty, p. 24

social stratification, p. 26
wealth, p. 26
welfare state, p. 34

QUESTIONS FOR CRITICAL THINKING

1. What would happen if the wealth in Canada were redistributed so that all adults had the same amount? Some analysts suggest that within five years most of the wealth would be back in the possession of the people who hold it today. What arguments can you give to support this idea? What arguments can you give to refute it?

2. Forcese (1997:215) states that "employers can, if obliged, produce jobs as well as products. Educational institutions, if obliged, can generate mobility. Political parties, if obliged, can legislate benefits." Assess the implications of "obliging" employers, educational institutions, and political parties to do these things.

3. Assess the implications of Canada's immediate adoption of a poverty reduction strategy like the one introduced at the end of this chapter.

Jeff McIntosh/CP Images

CHAPTER

3

Racism and Ethnic Inequality

While many in Canada know that racism is unacceptable, their privileged positions blind them to ways they participate in and perpetuate it. Non-White Canadians, regardless of class position, gender, sexual orientation, ability, age, size, educational level, or occupation, may experience prejudice and discrimination on any given day in what is supposed to be a multicultural society. We know from experience that right now many of you suspect that we are non-White people writing this, because our socialization in Canada teaches us that issues of racialized prejudice and discrimination (racism) are not White issues, that they are only issues for Indigenous people or so-called visible minorities. We are White people, and therefore are every bit as implicated in the racism we are speaking about in this chapter as most of the readers. This chapter will not only discuss many of the manifestations of racist discrimination in Canada, but will also raise issues of privilege and dominance and examine possibilities for change.

As described in Chapter 1, *discrimination* is the actions or practices of dominant group members that have a harmful impact on members of subordinate groups (Feagin and Feagin 2011). Like many other social problems, racialized and ethnic discrimination signals a discrepancy between the ideals and realities of Canadian society today. While equality and freedom for all—regardless of country of origin, skin colour, creed, or language—are stated ideals of this country, many subordinate group members experience oppression based on racializing factors, regardless of their other statuses.

RACISM AND ETHNIC INEQUALITY AS A SOCIAL PROBLEM

A decade and a half into the 21st century, racism is still among the most divisive social problems facing Canada and the one that creates most hate crimes (see Figure 3.4 and Chapter 9). At the same time, sociologists suggest that we all—regardless of racialized or ethnic background—share certain common interests and concerns that cross "race" and class boundaries. Some of the problems are unemployment and job insecurity, declining real wages, escalating medical and housing costs, a scarcity of good-quality child-care programs, worries about the quality of public education, and violence in many neighbourhoods. From this perspective, racialized and ethnic inequality is a problem for everyone, not only for people "of colour." Additionally, all people can be allies in working toward the elimination of racism. While the anti-racism torch has been lit and carried by non-White people for many years in Canada, it is time for White people to exercise some of their considerable privilege to join this campaign. Who better to speak out against racism than those who benefit most from it? Who better than those who are viewed as credible sources (as opposed to those viewed as "whining special-interest groups") to take up this discussion publicly and to press for the necessary changes? Changes for the better have already been made, and there is no doubt, despite backlash, that they will continue. The process of change can, however, move more quickly when alliances across difference are forged.

What Are Ethnicity, "Race," and Racialization?

In Canada, the terms *ethnicity* and *"race"* are often used interchangeably, while *racialization* is a term many people have never heard of. It is useful, therefore, to define these concepts at the outset. In this country, we talk mainly of "ethnicity," and Statistics Canada censuses have historically collected data based primarily on ethnic group. An **ethnic group is a category of people who are distinguished, by others or by themselves, on the basis of cultural or nationality characteristics** (Feagin and Feagin 2011). These can include language, country of origin, and adherence to a culture. Briefly stated, members of an ethnic group share five main characteristics: (1) unique cultural traits; (2) a sense of community; (3) a feeling that one's own group is distinct; (4) membership from birth; and (5) a tendency, at least initially, to occupy a distinct geographic area (such as a Chinatown, Little Italy, or Greektown). "White ethnics," such as Norwegian Canadians, Ukrainian Canadians, and Jewish Canadians, are also examples of ethnic groups. Ethnicity can be, and often is, used as a basis to judge an individual or group as inferior or superior. Ethnicity is a contested issue. Some, like sociologist J. Milton Yinger (1994), support a more narrow definition of ethnicity based on three criteria: (1)

members of a group must view themselves as distinct; (2) others must view the group as distinct; and (3) group members must participate in collective "activities that have the intent or the effect of affirming their distinctiveness" (Fleras and Elliott 1999:104). Sociologists Augie Fleras and Jean Leonard Elliott (1999) point out, however, that these criteria render invisible the most dominant group in Canada—White Canadians—a conclusion they find problematic. It is problematic to assert that most members of the dominant group have no ethnicity. It presents White existence as a neutral standard and masks the ethnicized nature of our institutions, practices, and beliefs (see Box 3.2 on page 53). Moreover, it suggests that ethnicity is really a euphemism for "minority group," which again puts White experience at the centre, a standard against which "others" (e.g., non-White ethnics) are measured. Fleras and Elliott (1999:104) caution, "To ignore white ethnicity is to redouble its hegemony by naturalizing whiteness."

Where ethnic groups are defined on the basis of cultural or nationality characteristics, sociologists note that racialized groups are usually defined on the basis of alleged physical characteristics. As with ethnicity and gender, sociologists view "race" as a *social construct*—**the classification of people based on social and political values—rather than as a biological given** (see Omi and Winant 1994). However, because physical features such as skin colour, hair texture, or eye shape are often used to determine "race," many people believe that "race" stems from real and immutable genetic differences, as opposed to subjective and arbitrary perceptions of differences—an important distinction. As the Thomas Theorum so aptly reminds us, "if a situation is perceived as real, it *is* real in its consequences." In humans, genetic differences by population do not exist—we share a generalized gene pool. The only "race" that exists with regard to humans is the "human race," or human species. Socio-culturally, however, the concept of race has been and continues to be salient. European, Chinese, and Arab people were active in attempting to classify humans into racialized groups as early as the 15th century, although Europeans became the first to use "science" to legitimate and popularize race as a classification system (Fleras and Elliott 1999). Several authors suggest that popular use of the concept of race stems from the need to justify slavery and/or capitalist exploitation (Johnson 2006). Canadian political scientist Grace-Edward Galabuzi notes that while arguments like these are compelling, and while the definitions of "races" have been fluid (for example, the Irish, along with several other European ethnic groups, were often described as "Black" or "Negro" by writers like John Beddoe and Robert Knox in the middle and late 1800s), the use of

"race" as a means to differentiate some "other" dates back to ancient times, pre-dating both capitalism anywhere and the slave trade in the United States (2006).

In contrast to an attempted biological definition of "race," sociologists define a *racialized group* **as a category of people who have been singled out, by others or themselves, as inferior or superior on the basis of subjectively selected physical characteristics such as skin colour, hair texture, and eye shape.** Blacks, Whites, Asians, and Indigenous peoples are all examples of categories of people who have been racialized. Racialization is therefore a process that occurs to or with a group in that it becomes "racialized," or comes to be seen as having certain distinct traits that are supposed to mean something. In addition to persistent efforts to classify people along "racial" lines, despite the continued lack of biological substantiation, it is in the definition and ranking of traits where racism can be seen, because definitions applied to certain features or characteristics are completely arbitrary: they vary across cultures and change over time. This is not the same as saying "race" doesn't matter. Race does matter, not because of innate differences between people, but because racialized individuals and groups have been treated as though certain characteristics matter in certain ways (discussed in Box 3.2). As Grace-Edward Galabuzi explains, "The process of racialization therefore involves the construction of racial categories as real, but also unequal, for purposes that impact the economic, social and political composition of a society . . . and has led to differential treatment and outcomes in Canada [for racialized groups]" (2006:34).

Historical and Political Roots of "Race"

Fleras and Elliott (1999:47) define "race" as the classification of people into categories on the basis of preconceived attributes; each group is defined as different by virtue of predetermined properties that are seen as fixed and permanent because of real or alleged characteristics.

Several classification schemes were developed from the 1700s onward, beginning with Swedish naturalist Carl von Linne's (Linnaeus') four-category scheme from 1735. Others since have come up, with anywhere from 30 to 150 categories (Fleras and Elliott 1999). The best known of these typologies is the one still often employed today: Mongoloid (for Yellow people), Caucasoid (for White people), and Negroid (for Black people). It is curious that this three-category typology has remained so stubbornly in our lexicon when there are such serious flaws with its use, not the least of which is, under which category do we classify Red people or Brown people? Several other arguments against the use of "racial" typologies deserve mention. Discrete boundaries between "races" are indefinable and, hence, arbitrary. "Racial" purity is a myth. The selection of traits defined as meaningful in some way is completely arbitrary. Why skin colour, for example, and not eye colour or length of big toe or shape of ear? It is important to understand that there is more variation on any criterion within a supposed race than between "races"; for example, there are more variations in skin tone within any racialized grouping than between two racialized groupings.

The politics of race are hotly debated and highly divisive because people who are attached to racial classifications often attempt to "rank diversity along an ascending/descending order," with implicit and explicit messages about concomitant superiority or inferiority (Fleras and Elliott 1999:49). Others acknowledge that racialization is what is significant and not the socially constructed notion of race. In any case, no one disputes the significance of the concept in justifying or legitimating ways of treating people. The concept of "race" has historically been used to justify inequitable treatment—sometimes economic and social disadvantage, sometimes death—in all cases, not contributing anything satisfactory to our understanding of human behaviour. As summarized by Fleras and Elliott (1999:36), "Race matters because people perceive others to be different and rely on these perceptions to justify unequal treatment and condone indifference."

The Meaning of Majority and Minority Groups

When sociologists use the terms *majority group* and *minority group*, they are referring to power differentials among groups, not to the numerical sense in which the words *majority* and *minority* are generally used. A **majority (or dominant) group is one that is advantaged and has superior access to resources and rights in a society** (Feagin and Feagin 2011). Majority groups often are determined on the basis of racialized factors or ethnicity, but they can also be determined on the basis of gender, sexual orientation, class, age, or physical ability. A **minority (or subordinate) group is one whose members, because of supposed physical or cultural characteristics, are disadvantaged and subjected to negative discriminatory treatment by the majority group and regard themselves as objects of collective discrimination** (Wirth 1945). In Canada, people "of colour," all women, people with disabilities, gay men, lesbians, and trans people tend to be considered minority group members, regardless of their proportion in the overall population. The term "minority" is formally applied to non-White people in Canada, as in the official government category "visible minority."

White Privilege and Internalized Dominance

In Canada, the racialized and ethnic majority group is associated with *White privilege*—privilege that accrues to the people who have "white" skin, trace their ancestry to Northern and Western Europe, and think of themselves as European Canadians or WASPs (White Anglo-Saxon Protestants).

In a paper called "Deconstructing Whiteness," Gabriel Bedard (2000:45) makes the point that "in Canada, Whiteness holds political, economic and moral power." In addition, Whiteness is a condition that White people every day can count on to ease their lives *because* they are White. In general, having "white" skin in Canada confers two overarching benefits: the invisibility and normalization of privilege and the choice of whether or not to support the struggle against racialized oppression (Wildman and Davis 2002). The normalization of privilege means that characteristics and attributes associated with Whiteness or White people's cultures are viewed as the standard, as the "normal" way of doing things. Normalization of privilege is manifested when all members of a society are judged against the characteristics or attributes of those who are privileged, and typically this is seen as a neutral process—the standard is typically invisible to those who do the judging. Objectivity is the dominant group's subjectivity. In this system, when people—usually those who are most like the privileged norm—succeed, it is seen as the result of individual effort or merit, not due to any invisible or unearned privilege (Wildman and Davis 2002:93). Janet Sawyer (1989) called this *"internalized dominance"*—**all the ways that White people learn they are normal, feel included, and do not think of themselves as "other" or "different."** White people carry this privilege around with them at all times, everywhere they go, and they are generally unaware of it.

The second benefit conferred on people with "white" skin is having the choice about whether to work against oppression. If White people choose, they do not have to engage in working against racist oppression. This privilege is commonly exercised as silence when witnessing racist behaviour or hearing racist comments. As legal scholars Stephanie Wildman and Adrienne D. Davis (2002:94) conclude, "Privilege is not visible to its holder; it is merely there, a part of the world, a way of life, simply the way things are. Others have a *lack*, an absence, a deficiency." Most White Canadians are unaware of the benefits that they derive from White privilege (see Rothenberg 2008).

What is also true is that many White people in Canada suffer from a clear lack of privilege, associated with class, gender, ability, age, and/or sexual orientation or preference. What White privilege does for people who experience oppression on other measures is reflect one place where they are not discriminated against in a White-dominant society. Non-White people may experience gendered oppression or be impoverished and *also* have to contend with racism, the kind of multiple jeopardy or intersectionality discussed elsewhere in this chapter and text. Nevertheless, the advantage/disadvantage and power/exploitation relationships of majority and minority groups in this country are deeply rooted in patterns of prejudice and discrimination. One group, however, appears to be much more disadvantaged than other groups: our Indigenous peoples.

The Special Case of Indigenous Peoples

Any textbook discussion of racism and ethnic inequality in Canada should include a section about our Indigenous peoples, called Aboriginals by Statistics Canada and others. Indigenous peoples migrated to and all over the Americas over 12 000 years ago. In Canada today, they comprise three main groups: First Nations, Métis, and Inuit. The First Nations and Inuit groups include scores of nations, each with their own language, culture, and resources (e.g., oil, forests, fisheries, and minerals). Table 3.1 shows how numerous these groups were in 2011. They constitute about 4 percent of the Canadian population, with First Nations being the largest group at over 800 000 people.

TABLE 3.1 Indigenous Identity Population, Canada, 2011

Indigenous identity	Number	Percent
Total Indigenous identity population	1 400 685	100.0
Métis single identity	451 795	32.3
Inuit single identity	59 445	4.2
Indigenous identities not included elsewhere	26 475	1.9

Source: *Statistics Canada, 2011*, "National Household Survey." Retrieved August 31, 2014 (*http://www12.statcan.gc.ca/nhs-enm/2011/as-sa/99-011-x/2011001/tbl/tbl01-eng.cfm*).

Métis are the second largest group with over 400 000 people, and Inuit are third with almost 60 000 people.

Indigenous peoples are our most disadvantaged groups in many ways. When the Europeans first came to this country, they needed the help of Indigenous people for survival, as guides and as allies (e.g., against surviving the harsh conditions). When Europeans came later in great numbers, the Indigenous peoples were exploited, driven off their land, or killed (see The Conflict Perspective later in this chapter). A very large number of land claims with Indigenous groups have still not been settled, especially in the West. In the late 1800s and early 1900s, in an attempt to assimilate the Indigenous peoples, the federal government took over 100 000 children from their families and placed them in residential schools. In these schools, students were actively discouraged from speaking their language or learning about their culture, and many were physically and sexually abused. Residential schools also indirectly prevented the children from having the experience of seeing their parents as role models for how to raise children. (The problem of residential schools will be discussed in Chapter 12.)

Indigenous peoples are disadvantaged in four central ways: life expectancy, education, income, and incarceration. In terms of life expectancy, figures suggest there is a gap of six years between the life expectancies of the Indigenous and non-Indigenous population (see Chapter 10). In 2011, 89 percent of the non-Indigenous population aged 18–44 years had a high school diploma or equivalent, while in 2012, according to the Aboriginal Survey only 72 percent of First Nations, 77 percent of Métis, and 42 percent of Inuit had this level of education (Statistics Canada 2014a). Without a high school diploma or equivalent, post-secondary education is not possible. Given the importance of post-secondary education to an individual's future prosperity (see the economic benefit of degrees in Chapter 12), this difference in high school graduation rates is a major disadvantage.

In terms of employment, Statistics Canada has stated that it does not survey Indigenous peoples on distant reserves. The employment rates are likely lower and the unemployment rates are likely higher for Indigenous peoples than for the rest of the population. Finally, Figure 3.1 shows that Indigenous peoples' incomes in 2005 were substantially lower than that of the non-Indigenous population. In 2005, the non-Indigenous population aged 25–54 years earned about $33 000/year, while the First Nations people earned about $19 000/year, the Métis earned almost $28 000/year, and the Inuit earned almost $25 000/year (Statistics Canada 2014b). Overall, Indigenous peoples earned about two-thirds of the income that non-Indigenous people earned.

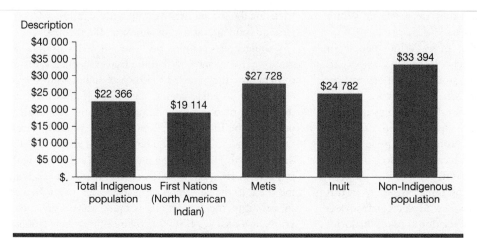

Description

Figure 3.1   Median Total Income for Indigenous Groups Ages 25–54 Years, 2005.

Source: Statistics Canada, 2014a, "Aboriginal Statistics at a Glance." Retrieved September 22, 2014 (http://www.statcan.gc.ca/pub/89-645-x/2010001/c-g/c-g011-eng.htm).

Finally, in terms of incarceration, Figure 3.2 shows that while Indigenous peoples constituted about 4 percent of the population in 2011–2012, they constituted 20 percent of adults in federal custody (see the right vertical bars labelled CSC (Correctional Service Canada)). The figure also shows that in some provinces (e.g., the Atlantic provinces, Quebec, and Ontario), they represent a small percentage of the population and do not constitute a very high percentage of those in custody, but Indigenous peoples are still overrepresented in custody. In Manitoba, Saskatchewan, and the territories, Indigenous peoples represent a much larger percent of the population and constitute over 70 percent of those in custody (Statistics Canada 2013b).

In addition to the reasons discussed above, Indigenous peoples are at a disadvantage compared to non-Indigenous populations, as a result of the disappearance of over 1100 Indigenous women. After the death of Tina Fontaine in 2014, there has been widespread demand for a national inquiry.

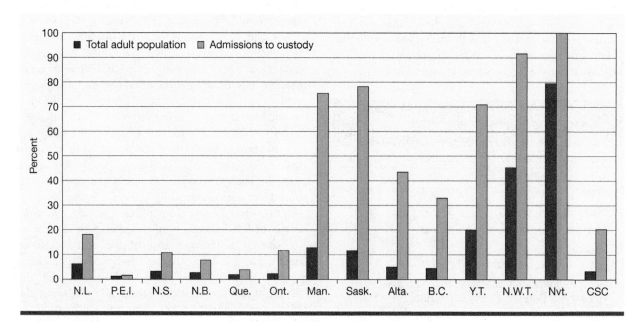

Figure 3.2   Percent of Indigenous Population in Custody by Province/Territory, 2011–2012.

Source: Statistics Canada, 2013b, "Canadian Centre for Justice Statistics Adult Correctional Services Survey 2011/2012 and National Household Survey 2011." Retrieved September 20, 2014 (http://www.statcan.gc.ca/pub/85-002-x/2014001/article/11918-eng.htm).

Should there be an Inquiry into the Murders and Disappearance of Indigenous Women?

The body of Tina Fontaine was found in August 2014 in the Red River in Manitoba. She was one of the more than 1100 Indigenous women who have gone missing or were killed since 1980. After the discovery of her body, the Indigenous community demanded a national inquiry about the problem. Since so many women had disappeared, many believed that an examination of some common factors, like particular kinds of discrimination, violence, and lack of opportunities, could provide suggestions to help end the disappearances. A national inquiry might help shine a spotlight on those factors. The prime minister suggested that this killing was a crime, not a "sociological phenomenon," and the crime should be handled by the police and no inquiry was necessary. (We will skip over the obvious fact that crimes are sociological phenomena.) He also reported in a year-end interview that a national inquiry wasn't high on the government's radar (Strueck 2014:A6). In contrast, the two major opposition parties (NDP and Liberal) have called for an inquiry.

It is true that national inquiries are not necessarily useful. First, they cost millions of dollars. Wally Oppal, a former attorney-general of British Columbia, conducted an inquiry into missing women in that province, including victims of Robert Picton, who was convicted of being a serial killer. Oppal said that the inquiry cost $10 million and suggested that depending on the scope, a national inquiry would cost about $100 million. He stated it would be much more worthwhile to tackle issues like poverty, alcohol and drug abuse, and homelessness of Indigenous women (Stueck 2014: A6). Second, inquiries often do not provide easy policies to implement. The B.C. Inquiry concluded that police did not show proper respect for poor, drug-addicted women, some of whom were sex workers (Strueck 2014:A6)—and little seems to have changed. Finally, the reports from inquiries can collect dust on shelves for decades, as has the Le Dain Commission of Inquiry into the Non-Medical Use of Drugs from the 1970s.

The disappearances of Indigenous women are also more than a federal government problem; they are also a provincial problem. Some premiers, like Kathleen Wynne of Ontario, have urged the prime minister to conduct an inquiry into this matter. In the fall of 2014, the Stop Racism and Hate Collective devised a poll that would allow anyone to vote about whether or not to conduct an inquiry (available at www.stopracism.ca). As of early 2015, they have not yet reported results.

The leadership of the Assembly of First Nations has called for an inquiry. Since Tina Fontaine's death, a number of other Indigenous women have been attacked and survived, and they too have called for an inquiry. Finally, the UN has called for an inquiry. Law professor James Anaya, the UN's special rapporteur on Indigenous rights, has called on the Canadian government to conduct an inquiry (Campion-Smith 2014). After a fact-finding mission, he reported that Indigenous women are proportionately much more likely to be attacked than are non-Indigenous women. He went on to cite the well-known (and above mentioned) disparities in education, health, life expectancy, etc., and advocated for a nation-wide inquiry.

In early 2015, it seems that an inquiry will not take place. However, that could change with more pressure or a change in government.

Questions for Consideration:

1. Do you think a national inquiry should be held? If an inquiry was held, what would you hope to come from it?
2. If 1000 professional men and women disappeared, how quickly do you think an inquiry would be called?
3. In the 2014–15 federal budget, Canada offered those families with one worker and one non-worker and with at least one child under 18 years of age (not the most vulnerable Canadians) the opportunity to share incomes for tax reduction purposes. Indigenous women are a much more vulnerable group. What should Canada be doing for our most vulnerable people?

RACISM, PREJUDICE, AND DISCRIMINATION

Racism **is a set of attitudes, beliefs, and practices used to justify the superior treatment of one racialized or ethnic group and the inferior treatment of another racialized or ethnic group.** In sociology, racism is sometimes referred to as White racism. *White racism* refers to socially organized attitudes, ideas, and practices that deny Indigenous people and people "of colour" the dignity, opportunities, freedoms, and rewards that are typically available to White Canadians (Feagin and Vera 1995:7). From this perspective, Indigenous people and people "of colour" pay a direct, heavy, and immediately painful price for racism, while White discriminators pay an indirect and seldom-recognized price.

Prejudice **is a negative attitude about people based on such characteristics as racialization, gender, age, religion, or sexual orientation.** If we think of prejudice as a set of negative attitudes toward members of another group simply because they belong to that group, we quickly realize that all people have prejudices, whether or not they acknowledge them. Prejudice is rooted in *ethnocentrism*—**the assumption that one's own group and way of life are superior to all others.** For example, most school children are taught that their own school and country are the best. Singing the national anthem is a form of *positive ethnocentrism*. However, *negative ethnocentrism* can result if individuals come to believe, because of constant emphasis on the superiority or "normalcy" of their own group or nation, that other groups or nations are inferior and should be treated accordingly (Feagin and Feagin 2011). Negative ethnocentrism is manifested in stereotypes that adversely affect many people.

Stereotypes **are fixed and distorted generalizations about the appearance, behaviour, or other characteristics of all members of a particular group.** Stereotypes are rigid perceptions that are believed to be true for all members of a group, even in the face of contradictory evidence. They ignore individual differences and specific situations (Speier 1991). Stereotypes should be distinguished from generalizations. *Generalizations* **are ideas held about a group of people that are open to revision or change and that can be rejected entirely at any time.** Everyone generalizes—it is an efficient way to organize our experiences and a useful method of applying information from situation to situation without having to relearn it every time. Stereotyping often leads to discrimination, while generalizing usually does not.

Discrimination may be carried out by individuals acting on their own or by individuals operating within the context of large-scale organizations or institutions, such as schools, corporations, and government agencies. *Individual discrimination* **consists of one-on-one acts by members of the dominant group that harm members of the subordinate group or their property** (Carmichael and Hamilton 1967). Individual discrimination results from the prejudices and discriminatory actions of bigoted people who target one or more subordinate group members. The taxi driver who refuses to pick up passengers who are members of Indigenous groups in Canada is practising individual discrimination. The neo-Nazi member of an organized racist group who paints a swastika on a synagogue is practising individual discrimination. Another common example in Canada involves the treatment of non-White-looking Canadians who, regardless of how many generations their families have been in Canada, and who may even be of mixed ethnic origins, are assumed to be from somewhere other than Canada, in ways White-looking Canadians are not assumed to be.

Additionally, people who embody mixed racialized or ethnic backgrounds and who look visibly non-White are often asked by strangers, "Where are you from?" The desired response that is being sought is one that differs from "from Canada" or "from Winnipeg." The desired response is one that emphasizes the person's "exoticness" (e.g., she or he should be from a culturally "different" and non-White nation) and, in the bargain, revokes her or his claims to Canadianness (Taylor 2008). Canadian educator Leanne Taylor (2008:86) notes that "the more that mixed-race identities challenge the norms of what is understood as 'Canadian,' the more mixed-race people will be positioned as doubly different, doubly strange, and doubly foreign." Many visible minority citizens can be members of many generations born in Canada.

In contrast to individual discrimination, *institutional discrimination* **consists of the day-to-day practices of organizations and institutions that have a harmful impact on members of subordinate groups.** For example, many mortgage companies are more likely to make loans to White people than to people "of colour" or to members of Indigenous groups (see Squires 1994). Institutional discrimination is carried out by the individuals who implement policies and procedures that result in negative and differential treatment of subordinate group members. Jewish immigrants in the late 1800s experienced institutional discrimination in accommodations and employment. Signs in hotel windows often read "No Jews Allowed," and many "help wanted" advertisements stated "Christians Only" (Levine 1992:55). Such practices are referred to as *anti-Semitism*—**prejudice and discriminatory behaviour directed at Jews.** Anti-Semitism is not the same as racism, although both have to do with prejudice and discrimination against a group of people presumed to have certain characteristics.

Anti-Semitism is one of the longest-standing forms of discrimination recorded in history (Fleras and Elliott 1999). A little-known fact about Canada is that in 1939, authorities refused to admit to Canada, as refugees, 900 German Jews who were fleeing the Holocaust. They were forced to return to Nazi Germany, where many were imprisoned and killed in concentration camps. In Toronto, Jews (and dogs) were disallowed public beach access at Lake Ontario. Public signage warning Jews (and Catholics) not to apply for police work was posted by the Toronto Police Force, and many other types of employment and education in Canada were closed to Jews (see Abella 1989; Abella and Troper 1991).

Anti-Semitism is one of the longest-standing recorded forms of discrimination in history. Today, in Canada and throughout the world, discrimination against Jews is often carried out in the destruction and defacing of property, as this photo illustrates, and in the distribution of hate propaganda.

Nick Corrigall/CP Images

Today, discrimination against Jews is often carried out through the destruction and defacing of property and the distribution of hate propaganda, increasingly over the Internet. Based on the pernicious history of intolerance and overt discrimination against Jews in Canada, there is a long-standing debate about whether or not anti-Semitism should be taken up under the anti-racism banner. In defence of keeping the issues separate, but cooperating as allies with common interests, activist Joshua Goldberg (1998), a White Jew, wrote in correspondence to a friend, "Solidarity is not built on pretending we all experience the same struggles. As a white Jew, I get all the race-based privileges afforded Gentile white people." While this is no doubt true, Jewish people today still experience being on the receiving end of negative stereotyping, prejudice, and discrimination. In fact, with the upsurge of organized racist activity around the world, Jews are active targets of virulent hatred. In addition, they are often disbelieved when they try to raise issues of anti-Semitism. Short (1991:37), for example, states that even "anti-racists appear to have eschewed any interest in anti-Semitism." Reasons for the neglect of anti-Semitism in anti-racist work may be remnants of anti-Semitism among those who are active anti-racists or a belief in the

stereotype of Jews as powerful people in society who are therefore not subject to economic and educational disadvantage in the same ways that people "of colour" (Jewish or not) or Indigenous people are. Racism and anti-Semitism come from different histories of oppression: colonization and slavery on the one hand, and expulsion and persecution on the other.

In all anti-oppression work, it is important to acknowledge people's distinct histories and distinct struggles and not become complicit in furthering people's oppression through competition. This point speaks also to the issue of analogizing as a way of unintentionally furthering the oppression of people as we try to understand their situations. Legal scholars Tina Grillo and Stephanie Wildman (1996:86) talk about the contradictory use of analogies as both "the key to greater comprehension and the danger of false understanding." Trying to understand another's experience by comparing it with an experience one has had is common. This can ease the process of comprehension and pave the way for greater understanding. It can also, however, perpetuate existing relations of domination, and thus cause more pain by centring on and shifting the focus back to the analogizer's issues or by taking over or denying the existence of pain through the analogizer's belief that she or he understands the pain the other is experiencing.

A final type of institutional discrimination that deserves mention occurs in what American anti-racism trainer and diversity consultant Byron Kunisawa (1996) refers to as an "institutional design of omission." Kunisawa points out that the design of the whole range of systems, from education to health care and not-for-profit organizations, government, and judicial systems, reflects the needs, values, practices, and priorities of those who created them. Members of every group in society were not consulted, and their needs and priorities were not considered. It may have nothing to do with intentional exclusion, but rather may reflect the (racist) protocols and values consistent with the era in which the systems were developed. Kunisawa contributes to understanding and overcoming racism by pointing out that we have never actually dealt with the exclusionary nature of the system design. Rather, we attempt to remedy situations by "adding on" another piece. For example, in phase 1 of Kunisawa's model Institutional Designs of Omission a system or an organization gets designed by people who represent 70 percent of the population but who *think* they represent 100 percent. In phase two, those left out of the original design want inclusion. The way of balancing people's demands for inclusion is to create separate systems, or add-ons, with the belief that these add-ons will sufficiently meet the needs of those previously excluded.

The add-ons do not meet their needs, however, because people are still not included in the original or "mainstream" systems. People are still set apart and, given how pervasive racism is, not treated equally. What we need to do, according to Kunisawa, is work toward changing the fundamental design criteria of the organizations and systems we take part in by including historically marginalized people in their redesign. This process will take time, but will yield an inclusive and truly multicultural society; however, we still have a long way to go when we consider how little progress has been made historically.

Historical Roots of Racism

As Europeans participated in campaigns to expand their empires, they increasingly came into contact with "exotic others." Their responses to these others ranged from benign curiosity to outright hostility. As a way of making sense of the diversity they encountered, they employed the pseudo scientific "race" theories that were gaining a foothold in society. It was the time known as the Enlightenment, and people searched for rational and scientific ways to classify and explain their worlds. Using the legitimacy of the scientific enterprise (but arbitrary criteria), these theories explained that some people were superior to others.

The most common doctrine of "racial" supremacy, widely accepted in the first part of the 19th century, was what later became known as social Darwinism (Fleras and Elliott 1999). Notions of "survival of the fittest," the "struggle for survival," and unilinear evolution legitimized colonial expansion with the rationale that those who were better adapted would thrive, while those less adapted would become extinct. As with all who have the power to define, the Europeans defined themselves at the top of the evolutionary hierarchy, with all others ranked according to how closely they emulated European civilization and Christianity. Therefore, colonialism was viewed as a "natural" and inevitable process, just like capitalism and imperialism. Colonialists saw themselves as assisting those whom they were exploiting in their evolutionary progression from savagery through barbarism to civilization. Civilization meant European and Christian civilization, of course. This doctrine added legitimacy to many practices, such as slavery and forced labour, the appropriation of land and resources, and the destruction of whole cultures and ways of life.

The Many Forms of Racism in Canadian Society

Racism is not a uniform process. It has many permutations and varieties, demonstrating its complexity and multidimensionality. Several authors have created a typology of the forms of racism in Canada as a way of pointing to the necessity for a range of diverse solutions to the problem (Fleras 2001; Fleras and Elliott 1999; Henry et al. 2000). Fleras and Elliott (1999) outline three broad categories of racism, each with specific subcategories: interpersonal, which includes redneck racism and polite racism; institutional, which includes systematic racism and systemic racism; and societal, which includes everyday racism and cultural racism.

Interpersonal Racism

Interpersonal racism occurs between individuals and is directed at an individual because of who or what he or she stands for. The typical depiction of a racist is the redneck racist whose racism is explicit and who generally is not intimidated by the label "racist." This is the "Bubba" stereotype of our collective view. "Bubba" participates in highly personalized attacks on others, such as name calling or racial slurs, based on the notion that his or her culture is superior. An example of redneck racism is the type of racism exhibited by members of White supremacist groups in Canada, such as the Heritage Front or the White nationalist Aryan Guard, which parades in Calgary each year on March 21 to protest the International Day for the Elimination of Racism (see Box 3.2 for more discussion).

The use of the "Bubba" stereotype in our cultural view can be dangerous for two reasons. First, it is a stereotype, and as such can be misleading and inaccurate and can be applied to people erroneously. Second, and more subtle, is the fact that if we define racism as only the type of behaviour exhibited by "Bubba," we miss the majority of racism that goes on in Canada. In other words, the stereotype provides a cover for other harmful attitudes and practices. Human rights legislation and the *Charter of Rights and Freedoms* have done a great deal to erode redneck racism in public discourse. In its place, due to increasing risks of legal and social consequences, polite racism has evolved. *Polite racism* refers to the ways that people may couch criticisms of racialized others in bland tones or use language that appears non-prejudicial on the surface. Polite racists are often good at phrasing a sentence so it delivers a racist message to anyone looking for it, but makes it obscure enough to enable the deliverer to deny that there was any racist intent. Unsurprisingly perhaps, polite racists tend to be those with higher education. Polite racism can be difficult to prove and therefore difficult to combat. An example is when a member of a dominant group makes a comment to another member of a dominant group about a subordinate group that he or she would not make, knowingly, to a member of the subordinate group in question.

Social Problems in Global Perspective

Box 3.2

Canada's Acceptance of Diversity and Organized Racism—Canada's Links to a World of Hatred

Canada has a reputation as a country that welcomes immigrants, especially visible minorities. This is supported by Canada's ranking among other high-income countries in terms of reporting how accepting respondents' neighbourhoods have been of different racial, ethnic, and cultural groups prior to 2013. Figure 3.3 shows that Canada placed first, with over 80 percent of respondents accepting diversity. Many other countries were very close, including the United States, but a couple of countries, namely Italy and Japan, had scores lower than 60 percent.

But just because we generally welcome people of different visible minorities does not mean there have not been hate crimes, varying support for immigrants—including visible minorities—and organized racism in our country. For example, Figure 3.4 shows the most frequent types of hate crimes reported in Canada in 2012. The data indicate that most hate crimes had to do with race and ethnicity. Little change has occurred in these data over the last few years (see Chapter 9).

In addition, an Ekos poll released in March 2015 showed that a higher percentage of Canadians felt that there were too many immigrants and visible minorities coming to Canada now than they did a decade ago. In 2005, less than 25 percent of Canadians polled said that too many immigrants and visible minorities were coming to Canada. In constrast, in 2015, 46 percent said too many immigrants were coming to Canada, while 41 percent of those polled said the same of too many visible minorities. As might be expected, a higher percentage of older than younger, high school than university educated, and

Conservative than Liberal or NDP supporters indicated that there were too many immigrants and visible minorities. Interestingly, the percentage of respondents saying too many immigrants were coming to Canada in 1995 was almost identical to the percentage saying it in 2015 (Graves 2015). The pollsters indicated that a change in polling method might have contributed to the recent difference over time. In 2005, people were surveyed by a person, while the latest survey responses were submitted anonymously to a machine, perhaps allowing respondents to be more candid.

Another indicator of the presence of racism in Canada is evident in the increasing membership in organized anti-immigrant and sometimes racist groups around the Western world since the decline of communism in Europe and the former U.S.S.R., and the economic recession beginning in 2008. Racist groups worldwide have fairly easily traceable links to a number of networks and groups in Canada. While it may be surprising to many Canadians, the history of organized hate groups in Canada is, unfortunately, a long one. The Ku Klux Klan (KKK), which began as a U.S. group, became a thriving organization in Canada in the 1920s and 1930s and has recently resurfaced here.

Organized racism is often referred to as neo-fascism, neo-Nazism, White supremacism, or organized hate. It differs from other forms of Canadian racism in both its virulence and its intent. Organized racists differ from regular racists in that their hatred of non-White people, and of Jews in particular, coupled with their active membership in a hate group, give them a predisposition to *act* on their

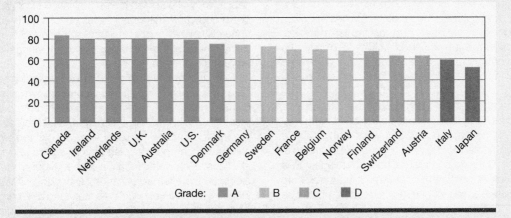

Figure 3.3   Acceptance of Diversity, by Nation, 2011.

Source: Conference Board of Canada, 2014, "Society." Retrieved September 2, 2014 (http://www.conferenceboard.ca/hcp/details/society/acceptance-of-diversity.aspx).

Social Problems in Global Perspective

Box 3.2 continued

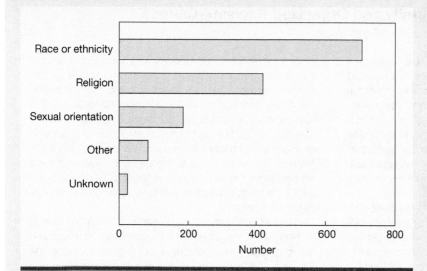

Figure 3.4   Type of Police-reported Hate Crimes in Canada.

Source: Statistics Canada, 2013, "Police-reported Hate Crimes, 2012." Retrieved Sepember 21, 2014 (http://www.statcan.gc.ca/daily-quotidien/140626/dq140626b-eng.htm).

racism by committing violence, publishing messages of hate, recruiting others to their cause, and participating in a host of other activities.

The intent of the many hate groups ranges, but they have one basic activity in common—to rid the province/state/nation/world of "undesirables" and to fight against what they view as the "racial takeover" of "their" geographic space. As anthropologists Frances Henry and Carol Tator, lawyer Winston Mattis, and race relations and diversity specialist Tim Rees (2000:99) state, "All these groups share an ideology that supports the view that the Aryan, or White, 'race' is superior to all others, morally, intellectually, and culturally, and that it is Whites' manifest destiny to dominate society." Also, as the term implies, organized racism is an organized activity. Typically, the group has a designated leadership and a well-established hierarchy of followers. Most Canadians are completely unaware of this kind of organized activity. Those who are aware of the existence of such groups tend to dismiss their adherents as "nutters" or people on the fringe. While many of us do not wish to believe it when a 65-year-old Sikh janitor is beaten to death at a Surrey, B.C., temple, or an elderly Calgary journalist is beaten savagely in a surprise attack at his home, or Jewish synagogues are defaced across Canada, or burning crosses are placed on the lawns of people believed to be non-White or Jewish, it is difficult to discount White supremacists as harmless.

Augie Fleras and J.L. Elliott reported (1999) that in Canada there was a proliferation of groups, including known racist organizations such as the KKK, the Western Guard, the Aryan Nations, the White Aryan Resistance, the Heritage Front, the Nationalist Party, the Posse Comitatus, and the Church of the Creator, and alleged groups such as the Canadian Free Speech League, the Council on Public Affairs, and the Coalition for Humanistic British Canada. Information about organized hate groups in Canada is now easy to access through the Internet and telephone call-in lines, such as Canadian Liberty Net, although organized hate groups still carry out physical recruitment drives as well.

The question is, What do these people want? Different groups have different aims. Some of the more radical right-wing groups desire the downfall of the Canadian state (viewed as traitorous because it has allowed non-White and Jewish immigration) and political control over a bounded territory (a sovereign "Aryan Nation") completely free of non-White and Jewish people and of "race traitors" (those who associate with non-Whites or Jews). For many, violence is an acceptable means for achieving these ends, and in preparation for the coming "race war," paramilitary training is carried out in several areas of Canada (e.g., northern British Columbia, Alberta, and Ontario) and at some "Whites only" compounds in the United States (e.g., Hayden Lake, Idaho, and other areas in the southern States).

Many of these groups believe that it will take an extreme incident, like the near-extinction of Whites, before White people will wake up and realize they need to join supremacist groups and "take back" their nation. While some are content to wait for the majority of Whites to "wake up," many others take matters into their own hands by actively recruiting members.

Recruitment into hate groups takes many forms. It may be a simple pamphlet left in a mall washroom or on a city bus seat. It may be a racist comic book given out to elementary school children. It can be a book table at a public lecture. It can be a personal visit to a person's home. It can be through political platforms in legitimate democratic elections. Recruitment can also be through music. For example, the alternative hate rock band RaHoWa (which stands for Racial Holy War) was managed by George Burdi, who was also the band's lyricist and vocalist. Burdi was a self-proclaimed leader of the violent Church of the Creator and a Heritage Front member. Bands like RaHoWa and others, such as Odin's Law from Surrey, B.C., market and

Social Problems in Global Perspective

Box 3.2 continued

George Burdi

distribute their hate-filled lyrics worldwide. George Burdi, whose real name is George Eric Hawthorne, recently left the White Power movement after a stint in prison for assault. He is now married to a non-White woman, is a Buddhist, and is involved in a multiethnic music group called Novacosm.

While membership in organized hate groups tends to increase during economic recessions, it is by no means restricted to the working class. On the contrary, although much of the membership may be from economically disenfranchised classes, leadership and financial support are often from middle- and upper-middle classes (CTV 1995). As Barrett (1991:87) concludes, "It is improbable that such organizations could exist unless there was some degree of compatibility with the institutional fabric of the larger society." This comment may explain how it is that organized hate groups are able to access tolerance from many liberal thinkers who otherwise claim to be non-racist. The racists play on people's deep emotions about personal freedoms and democracy. Making a heartfelt case for an issue such as freedom of speech, organized racists say that even if most Canadians do not like exactly what they are saying, as Canadians they should have the right not to be censored. Fleras and Elliott (1999:80) point out that because of a deeply rooted history of racism and the

ability of organized racists to hide behind this liberal facade, extremists may always have the ability to undermine societal values and practices. Leo Adler, the director of national affairs for a Toronto Jewish human rights organization, notes that there are approximately 6000 Internet sites operating that promote hatred. Fleras argued recently that even though "there is no way of gauging the number of hardcore supremacists in Canada . . . even a small number of racist ideologues have the potential to destabilize a society where prejudice is pervasive and the economy is sputtering" (2010:74).

Questions for Consideration

1. Do you think people in Canada should have the freedom to publicly express views and messages of hatred against groups?

2. Can you imagine any situation where there would be less friendly treatment of visible minorities in Canada? Can you think of anything that might be done to anticipate it? The Ekos poll also shows that the wearing of the niqab erodes support for immigrants. Can you think of ways of ensuring the niqab has greater acceptance in Canada?

3. In October 2014, three students staged an anti-Muslim "social experiment" at a bus stop in Hamilton, Ontario (after the killings in Ottawa and Quebec). During the "experiment," a person appeared to persecute a Muslim. Two bystanders at different times challenged this persecution, coming to the defence of the apparently innocent Muslim. The video went viral on YouTube. Do you think Canadians would be more likely to challenge this persecution?

The comment is often carefully benign on the surface, to allow room for the denial of racism, but the receptor of the comment *knows* what the thrust of the comment is.

Institutional Racism

Institutional racism refers to various organizational practices, policies, and procedures that discriminate, either purposely or inadvertently. If there is the intent to deny privilege or to exclude, it is referred to as institutional. If not, it is referred to as systemic. *Systemic racism* is embedded in the design of the organization, is formalized, and is legally sanctioned by the state. Discriminatory practices reflect the values of the dominant culture and act to deliberately prevent certain groups from participating in the culture. Examples are the exclusion of Indigenous people and Black Canadians from movie theatres and

restaurants until the 1950s, the restricting of the enrolment of Jewish Canadians in Canadian universities in the 1940s, and the disallowing of Japanese Canadians from voting in British Columbia until 1949 (Fleras and Elliott 1999). Indigenous people were only allowed the vote provincially beginning in 1949 and through to 1969, and were disenfranchised federally until 1960.

Systemic racism is also embedded in the organization, procedures, and norms of an organization. It tends to be impersonal and unconscious in that discrimination is unintended but has the effect of discriminating anyway. It occurs because seemingly neutral rules are applied evenly to all, even when this may be inappropriate. The impact is the favouring of certain groups whose members most closely resemble the rule makers while disadvantaging those who are different. An example is the height and weight requirements once used for police recruits in Canada, which inadvertently disallowed most Asians, Indigenous people, and women from participation. A well-publicized example was the headgear policy for the RCMP that stated that members had to wear RCMP-issue headgear. This policy, which was fought and defeated, effectively disenfranchised Sikhs who, for religious reasons, wear a turban.

Societal Racism

Societal racism refers to the generalized, and typically unconscious, patterns of interaction between people that perpetuate a racialized social order. It is part of the general functioning of society and is said to precede other forms of racism (Henry et al. 2000). *Everyday racism* refers to general, and seemingly benign, ideas about the relative superiority and inferiority of certain groups. These ideas are widely accepted as normal by dominant group members. The main way that ideas are perpetuated is through language that is held to be neutral. Language, of course, is far from neutral, as we socially construct our reality through it. Words convey images and associations, both positive and negative, that we draw upon to order and imagine our worlds. As Fleras and Elliott (1999:84) point out, "[Language] provides a cultural frame of reference for defining what is desirable and important."

Some examples of everyday racism can be found in the use of colour symbolism (e.g., associating white with good, black with evil), or the use of emotionally loaded terms like "Indian massacres" in the past or now "Islamic terrorist." Everyday racism can be further distinguished into active and passive racism (Henry et al. 2000:55). *Active racism*, according to social psychologist Philomena Essed (1990), includes any act (including the use of language) that is motivated by the intention of excluding or making a person or group feel inferior *because* of his/her/their minority group status. *Passive racism* includes being complicit in another's racism, for example laughing at a racist joke or "not hearing" racist comments. *Cultural racism* refers to cultural values that reinforce the interest of the dominant group while undermining the interests of subordinate groups. Cultural racism is manifested in the notion that minority groups are acceptable in Canada, as long as they know and understand their place in society and act in ways the dominant majority wants them to. Cultural values support equality, but measures toward ensuring that it happens are resisted. An example can be cultural support for the notion of equal opportunity in employment in all sectors, but hostility toward employment equity programs or the *Canadian Employment Equity Act*. This can also be seen in stereotyped commercials where visible minorities are underrepresented (see Chapter 14).

PERSPECTIVES ON RACIALIZED AND ETHNIC INEQUALITY

Over the course of more than 100 years, sociologists have developed different perspectives to explain why racialized and ethnic inequality occurs and why it persists. Some perspectives focus on sociological factors such as migration, assimilation, conflict, and exploitation, while others focus on more social-psychological factors.

The Symbolic Interactionist Perspective

One interactionist approach emphasizes how racialized socialization contributes to feelings of solidarity with one's own racialized or ethnic group and hostility toward all others. *Racialized socialization* is a process of social interaction that contains specific messages and practices concerning the nature of one's racialized or ethnic status as it relates to (1) personal and group identity; (2) intergroup and inter-individual relationships; and (3) one's position in the social stratification system. Although racialized socialization may occur through direct statements about "race" made by parents, peers, teachers, and others, it may also include indirect modelling behaviours, which occur when children imitate the words and actions of parents and other caregivers (Thornton et al. 1990). Racialized socialization affects how people view themselves, other people, and the world.

Though all groups practise racialized socialization, White racialized socialization emphasizes White "racial" bonding. According to multicultural education scholar Christine E. Sleeter (1996), White racial bonding occurs when White people act in ways that reaffirm the common stance on ethnic or cultural issues and draw "us–them" boundaries, thus perpetuating racism and discrimination. Such people choose to live near other Whites, to socialize with other Whites, and to vote for other Whites, thus maintaining racialized solidarity. Although many Whites do not support racist beliefs, actions, or policies, they fear breaking bonds with other Whites and may simply remain silent in the face of prejudice and discrimination (Sleeter 1996).

The Functionalist Perspective

To functionalists, social order and stability are extremely important for the smooth functioning of society. Consequently, "racial" and ethnic discord, urban unrest, and riots are dysfunctional and must be eliminated or contained. One functionalist perspective focuses on **assimilation,** the

process by which members of subordinate racialized and ethnic groups become absorbed into the
dominant culture. Functionalists view assimilation as a
stabilizing force that minimizes differences that otherwise
might result in hostility and violence (Gordon 1964). In its
most complete form, assimilation becomes *amalgamation,*
**a process in which the cultural attributes of diverse
racialized or ethnic groups are blended together to
form a new society incorporating the unique contributions of each group.** Amalgamation occurs when
members of dominant and subordinate racialized or ethnic groups intermarry and procreate to produce "mixed-
ethnicity" children.

Early assimilation in Canada focused primarily on
the Anglo-conformity model, rather than amalgamation. The *Anglo-conformity model* **refers to a pattern
of assimilation in which members of subordinate
racialized/ethnic groups are expected to conform
to the culture of the dominant (White) Anglo-
Saxon population.** Assimilation does not always lead
to full social acceptance. For example, many successful members of designated minority groups have been
excluded from membership in elite private clubs and
parties in the homes of co-workers.

Another functionalist perspective emphasizes *ethnic
pluralism*—**the coexistence of diverse racialized/
ethnic groups with separate identities and cultures
within a society.** In a pluralistic society, political and
economic systems link diverse groups, but members of
some racialized/ethnic groups maintain enough separation from the dominant group to guarantee that their
group and ethnic cultural traditions continue (Gordon
1964). Ethnic pluralism is the formal model of ethnic relations in Canadian society; however, Anglo-conformity
is such a strong force that pluralism may be more of a
myth than a reality for ethnic groups. In Canada, pluralism can take the form of *segregation* because subordinate
racialized/ethnic groups have less power and privilege
than do members of the dominant group (Marger 1994).
Segregation **is the spatial and social separation of
categories of people by racialization, ethnicity,
class, gender, religion, or other social characteristics.** Some recent sociological studies have found that
when high levels of segregation based on racialization
are followed by inter-ethnic contact, competition may
ensue, which creates the potential for conflict between
groups (Olzak et al. 1996).

The Conflict Perspective

Conflict theorists explain racialized and ethnic inequality
in terms of economic stratification and access to power.
As discussed in Chapter 1, there is more than one conflict

perspective. This chapter focuses on the critical-conflict
approach, which explains racialized and ethnic inequality in terms of economic stratification and unequal access
to power. We will briefly examine class perspectives,
split-labour market theory, internal colonialism, and the
theory of "racial" formation.

Class perspectives on racialized and ethnic inequality highlight the role of the capitalist class in racialized
exploitation. For example, according to sociologist
Oliver C. Cox (1948), the primary cause of slavery was
the capitalist desire for profit, not racialized prejudice.
People were enslaved because, through force, they could
be made to do heavy labour and other duties for basically
the costs of feeding and housing them. A contemporary
class perspective suggests that members of the capitalist class benefit from a split-labour market that promotes
racialized divisions among workers and suppresses wages.
According to the *split-labour market theory,* the economy
is divided into two employment sectors: a primary sector
composed of higher-paid workers in more secure jobs
and a secondary sector composed of lower-paid workers
in jobs that often involve hazardous working conditions
and little job security (Bonacich 1972, 1976). Dominant
group members are usually employed in primary sector
positions, while subordinate group members are concentrated in the secondary sector. Workers in the two job
sectors tend to have divergent interests and goals because
of their different relations to the labour market, therefore
worker solidarity can be difficult to achieve (Bonacich
1972, 1976). Members of the capitalist class benefit from
these divisions because workers are less likely to band
together and demand pay increases or other beneficial
changes in the workplace. Historically, White workers
in the primary sector who accepted racist arguments
attempted to exclude subordinate group members from
higher-paying jobs by barring them from labour unions,
lobbying against employment equity, and opposing
immigration. Some of these tactics still occur today.

A second critical-conflict perspective examines *internal colonialism*—**a process that occurs when members of a racialized/ethnic group are conquered or
colonized and forcibly placed under the economic
and political control of the dominant group.**
According to sociologist Robert Blauner (1972), people
in groups that have been subjected to internal colonialism remain in subordinate positions in society much longer than do people in groups that voluntarily migrated
to this country. For example, Indigenous peoples were
forced into subordination when they were colonized
by Europeans. Hundreds of culturally and linguistically
diverse Indigenous groups lost property, political rights,
components of their culture, and often their lives; some

Indigenous groups were virtually extinguished as victims of *genocide*—**the deliberate, systematic killing of an entire people or nation. Meanwhile, the capitalist class acquired cheap labour and land, frequently through government-sanctioned racialized exploitation (Blauner 1972).** The legacy of internal colonialism remains visible today in the number of Indigenous people who live in poverty, particularly those who live on federal reserves, often lacking essential services such as water, electricity, and sewage disposal.

Psychologists Michael Chandler and Christopher Lalonde have been studying Indigenous youth suicide on reserves in Canada, primarily in British Columbia, for over a decade. Studying the wide discrepancy in youth suicide rates—some Indigenous communities have zero youth suicides, while others have rates as high as 800 times the national average—they convincingly demonstrate that the more protective factors a band has in place, the fewer suicides their community experiences. The community factors that affect the suicide rate include self-government, getting title for land claims, education, health, cultural facilities, police and fire services, women in government, and child protection. Chandler and Lalonde note that in British Columbia, more than 90 percent of the suicides by youth occur in only 10 percent of the communities (2004). The protective factors they identify have to do with overcoming the legacy of internal colonialism described above. The most striking finding by Chandler and Lalonde is that where self-government is present in a community, the suicide rate is about 7.5 per 100,000 people, compared to a rate of 40 in communities without self-government.

The last critical-conflict perspective we will look at is the *theory of racial formation*, **which states that the government substantially defines racialized and ethnic relations.** From this perspective, racialized bias and discrimination tend to be rooted in government actions, ranging from the passage of "race"-related legislation to imprisonment of members of groups that are believed to be a threat to society. According to sociologists Michael Omi and Howard Winant (1994), governments are responsible for shaping the politics of racialized inequality through actions and policies that have resulted in the unequal treatment of Indigenous people and visible minorities. Immigration legislation, for example, reveals specific racialized biases. Fleras (2010:250), for example, notes that "initial practices regarding whom to let in and whom to keep out could be described as essentially racist in orientation, assimilationist in objective, nativist in content, and exclusionary in outcome." As an example, until the 1960s, Western Europeans were the preferred immigrants, and

when immigration was extended to Eastern Europeans, Jewish and Mediterranean people required special permits. Further, Asians of Chinese and Indian origin were only reluctantly admitted during times of capitalist expansion, when the state required large pools of cheap labour, and even then, only males were permitted to immigrate. Family members were not allowed. Overtly racially selective immigration policies, closely following Canada's nation-building requirements, were in force until the first major revision in 1962.

Feminist and Anti-Racist Perspectives

One feminist perspective is based on a critical-conflict perspective and links racialized inequality and gender oppression. ***Gendered racism* may be defined as the interactive effect of racism and sexism in exploiting Indigenous women and women "of colour."** According to Essed (1991), not all workers are exploited equally by capitalists. For many years, the majority of jobs in the primary sector of the labour market were held by White men, while most people of colour and many White women were employed in secondary sector jobs. Below the secondary sector, in the underground sector of the economy, many Indigenous women and women "of colour" worked as domestic servants and nannies, in sweat shops, or in the sex trade to survive. Work in this underground sector is unregulated, and people who earn their income in it are vulnerable to exploitation by many, including unscrupulous employers, greedy pimps, and corrupt police officers (Amott and Matthaei 1991).

In Canada, anti-racist feminist theorizing—deconstructing the interconnectedness of racism and sexism, colonialism and imperialism—has been engaged in since the 19th century (Dua 1999). Anti-racist feminist theorizing differs from mainstream feminist theorizing: it challenges the notion of a common experience that all women share under capitalism; and it focuses on the specific ways that class, gender, *and* ethnicity play out as interconnections. Anti-racist feminist scholar and critical theorist Himani Bannerji (1995:77) points out that "the erasure of the factors 'race,' racism, and continual immigration prevents an adequate understanding of the Canadian economy." Building on this, women's studies scholar Enakshi Dua (1999:21) concludes that "the discourse of race is as 'foundational' to the creation and maintenance of the Canadian political economy as are capitalist relations and patriarchy." Dua (1999:16) outlines three priorities within much of Canadian anti-racist feminist thought: (1) to interrogate feminist theory and practice to assess its complicity in perpetuating racism; (2) to raise questions about ways of theorizing about the connections between gender and racialization; and (3) to continue to document the ways that racialized differences are created and maintained among women.

Many proponents of anti-racist feminism also investigate the impacts of racism on women of colour, examining the ways that gender, racialization, and class intersect, for example, when well-to-do White women employ racialized and poor women from non-industrialized nations to do domestic labour for them on temporary work visas. Other impacts that have been examined are the wages of women of colour and Indigenous women compared to White women's wages, and the ways that equity measures for women disproportionately privilege White women relative to non-White women. Some anti-racist feminist theorists have suggested a *standpoint analysis*, that is, beginning theorizing and analysis from the situated standpoint of the person and her experiences—employing a kind of "outsider-within" perspective (Dua 1999:19). However, women's experiences with racialization vary along class lines according to sexual orientation and personal history. Therefore, it is important to account for the whole of a person's identity or locations.

Taking anti-racist feminism a step further, sociologist Daiva Stasiulis (1999) makes a convincing case for feminist intersectional theorizing. Feminist intersectional theorizing, or intersectionality, is a trend away from what Stasiulis (1999:350–351) calls the "race-gender-class trinity" or the "iron triangle of race-gender-class" and a move toward an understanding of the myriad ways that oppressions are linked and the impacts on individuals and groups of those intersections. In addition to a focus on the triad of issues mentioned, nationality, language, religion, sexuality, citizenship, ability, and so on are interrogated, with the emphasis on seeing the ways the "simultaneity of racism, sexism and class exploitation" plays out (Satzewich and Liodakis 2007:24).

With the increase in economic globalization, interest in this mode of analysis has been heightened and developed. However, in developing an analysis of intersectionality, the challenge is to steer clear of the trap of essentializing all women this way and all people "of colour" that way, and so on, as well as to avoid using terms euphemistically, such that "gender" means "women" and "racialized" means "brown," and so on.

HOW CAN RACIALIZED AND ETHNIC INEQUALITIES BE REDUCED?

According to symbolic interactionists, prejudice and discrimination are learned, and what is learned can be unlearned. Only individuals and groups at the grassroots level, not government and political leaders or academic elites, can bring about greater ethnic equality. Many authors point to anti-racist education as an important means of promoting change and building alliances (Bakanic 2009; Bishop 2002; Fleras 2001; Fleras and Elliott 1999; Henry et al. 2000; Kivel 1996, 2002; Robertson 1999).

How do functionalists suggest reducing racialized/ethnic inequality? Because they believe a stable society requires smoothly functioning social institutions and people who have common cultural values and attitudes, functionalists suggest restructuring social institutions to reduce discrimination and diffuse racialized/ethnic conflict. According to sociologist Arnold Rose (1951), discrimination robs society of the talents and leadership abilities of many individuals especially people of colour. Rose suggests that societies invest time and money fostering racialized/ethnic inclusion and eliminating institutionalized discrimination in education, housing, employment, and the criminal justice system. Employing a global perspective, functionalists argue that Canadian racialized discrimination should be reduced because it negatively affects diplomatic and economic relations with other nations made up of diverse racialized/ethnic groups.

From a conflict perspective, racialized and ethnic inequality can be reduced only through struggle and political action. Conflict theorists believe that inequality is based on the exploitation of subordinate groups by the dominant group, and that political intervention is necessary to bring about economic and social change. They agree that people should mobilize to put pressure on public officials. According to social activist Paul Kivel (1996, 2002), racialized inequality will not be reduced until this country has significant national public support and leadership for addressing social problems directly and forcefully.

Feminists and anti-racist feminists advocate critical analysis that begins from the myriad standpoints and situated experiences of people. In addition to building on insights developed from various standpoints, they advocate rendering the connections between locations or standpoints visible so that silences can be heard, hypocrisies can be exposed, and myths can be evaporated. When White people become more clearly aware of their complicity in perpetuating racism and systems of domination, the foundation for solid alliances can be built. We must work toward those ends tirelessly if we intend to create a better place for all.

Whether or not the people of Canada will work for greater equality for all racialized/ethnic groups, one thing is certain: the Canadian population is rapidly becoming increasingly diverse. Table 3.2 provides the latest figures for the size of visible minority groups in Canada's major cities.

TABLE 3.2 Visible minority population and top three visible minority groups, selected census metropolitan areas, Canada, 2011

	Total population number	Visible minority number	Population percentage	Top 3 Visible Minority Groups
Canada	32 852 325	6 264 755	19.1	South Asian, Chinese, Black
Toronto	5 521 235	2 596 420	47.0	South Asian, Chinese, Black
Montréal	3 752 475	762 325	20.3	Black, Arab, Latin American
Vancouver	2 280 695	1 030 335	45.2	Chinese, South Asian, Filipino
Ottawa - Gatineau	1 215 735	234 015	19.2	Black, Arab, Chinese
Calgary	1 199 125	337 420	28.1	South Asian, Chinese, Filipino
Edmonton	1 139 585	254 990	22.4	South Asian, Chinese, Filipino
Winnipeg	714 635	140 770	19.7	Filipino, South Asian, Black
Hamilton	708 175	101 600	14.3	South Asian, Black, Chinese

Source: (Statistics Canada, 2013r, "Immigration and Ethnocultural Diversity in Canada." Retrieved September 2, 2014 [http://www12.statcan.gc.ca/nhs-enm/2011/as-sa/99-010-x/2011001/tbl/tbl2-eng.cfm]).

In 2011, 19.1 percent of Canadians in these major cities were visible minorities. A much higher percentage reported being visible minorities in Toronto and Vancouver. Projections suggest that these visible minority percentages will be much higher in the future. Thus, a vision of the future in Canada must be inclusive and be based on a collective endeavour to bring about the thorough eradication of racism at all levels of society—the individual, the institutional, and the societal. The time to begin is immediately. Given that we are the most accepting of high-income countries (see Figure 3.4 above), there is some reason for optimism, but that support can rise and fall (e.g., with economic slowdowns) (Graves 2015). As a result, continuous vigilance is necessary.

WHAT CAN YOU DO?

- Join (or start) a local anti-racism group and develop or take part in a "social action" mandate.
- Learn how to address racist comments and jokes when you hear them. This can sometimes be accomplished by asking people for clarification about their comments and providing information counter to their stereotypes. This can also sometimes mean just clearly telling the perpetrator that you find these remarks upsetting or unsettling and do not wish to hear them.
- Join and/or monitor anti-racist discussion groups online such as http://icare.to.
- Make an effort to get to know people from cultural groups different from your own. Take stock of your friendship circle right now. Do you regularly hang out with people who are different from you? If not, why do you think that is?
- Report suspected or known hate crimes or White supremacist activity to http://www.stopracism.ca.
- Attend cultural activities that are open to the public to get to know people different from you and find out about cultures different from your own. What things do you have in common? What things are different? What differences can you celebrate?
- Do not assume that eating sushi or falafel or listening to "world music" gives you enough cross-cultural experience! It's often a beginning. Challenge yourself and others to broaden that knowledge.
- To begin to learn how to unlearn racism, enroll in an anti-racism or diversity course or workshop.
- Get educated about contemporary Indigenous issues such as land claims, treaty rights, and self-determination. Recognize that what you may read or hear in the media is usually only one perspective and that careful attention to information from legitimate sources on both (or more) sides of an issue may be something you need to research to find out.
- Attend public forums on issues concerning immigration, refugees, and Indigenous people. Check into Canada's immigration and refugee policies and investigate recent immigration and refugee statistics to get a better understanding of what is fact and what is fiction.
- Look at the cultural makeup of the boards, staff, and volunteers at organizations you belong to or at places you frequent. Where there is diversity, what positions do people

fill in your organization? Are there any non-White people in positions of authority or working on the front lines (e.g., visible to the public as soon as they walk in?).

- Carefully read the policies of organizations you are part of. Are they inclusive? Are they welcoming of diversity? If you are unsure, contact a local anti-racism organization and have them come in to do a policy workshop, or consult with them using your policies as examples.

- Address stereotypical comments that may be made by your family and friends. Do not let any such remarks go by. Ask them for more information about a stereotype they hold, or why they believe the stereotype to be true; or, if they really believe the stereotype to be true, ask them what evidence they have that it is. Ask yourself what investment they may have, if any, in continuing to hold a certain view.

- March in solidarity with people of all backgrounds when the opportunity to publicly declare your stance against racism arises. If you are a White person, demonstrate your position as an ally.

- Write letters or editorials for your local or post-secondary newspaper debunking stereotypes. Interview people of diverse groups.

- If you are White, do not make your unlearning of racism the work of people of colour or Indigenous people. Make this your own project. Read. Talk to other White people who are grappling with these issues. Be reflective about the biases and stereotypes you hold and analyze them critically. Do not wallow in guilt. This serves no one. Become a force for positive change. "No one is free, until all are free."

- Think about your social locations and determine which of your statuses confer privilege on you and which ones confer disadvantage. Think carefully about what you are willing to give up or to do to ensure equality for all people in Canada. This is a hard one!

SUMMARY

How Do Racialized and Ethnic Groups Differ?
According to sociologists, racialized groups are defined on the basis of arbitrarily selected characteristics, and ethnic groups are defined on the basis of cultural or nationality characteristics. "Race" does not exist biologically but does exist as a socio-cultural phenomenon.

What Are Majority and Minority Groups?
When sociologists use the terms *majority group* and *minority group*, they are referring to power differentials. A majority (or dominant) group is one that is advantaged and has superior resources and rights in a society. A minority (or subordinate) group is one whose members are disadvantaged and subjected to unequal treatment by the dominant group and regard themselves as objects of collective discrimination.

How Are Prejudice and Discrimination Related?
Prejudice is a negative attitude that may or may not lead to discrimination, which is an action or practice of dominant group members that has a harmful impact on subordinate group members.

How Do Individual Discrimination and Institutional Discrimination Differ?
Although individual discrimination and institutional discrimination are carried out by individuals, individual discrimination consists of one-on-one acts by members of the dominant group; institutional discrimination refers to actions and practices that are built into the day-to-day operations of large-scale organizations and social institutions.

How Do the Interactionist and Functionalist Perspectives View Racialized and Ethnic Relations?
Interactionists focus on microlevel issues, such as how people develop a racialized/ethnic identity and how individuals from diverse racialized/ethnic groups interact with each other. Functionalists focus on macrolevel issues, such as how entire groups of people assimilate or do not assimilate into the mainstream of society.

What Are the Major Conflict Explanations for Racialized/Ethnic Inequality?
Conflict perspectives include class perspectives, split-labour market theory, internal colonialism, and racial formation theory.

How Do Feminist and Anti-Racist Feminist Theories Explain Racialized/Ethnic Inequality?
Feminists and anti-racist feminists advocate using critical analysis, beginning from the lived experiences of people. Additionally, they advocate an analysis that examines the intersections of locations, such as gender, ethnicity, sexual orientation, and class.

What Types of Discrimination Have Been Experienced by Minority Group Members in Canada?
Minority group members have experienced every type of discrimination in Canada, from exclusion and expulsion to cultural genocide, slavery, and internment; from discrimination in hiring and retention and in housing to physical violence on a personal level. The legacy of racism for Indigenous people is particularly acute.

What Commonalities Can Be Seen in the Experiences of All Subordinate Racialized/Ethnic Groups?
Members of most subordinate racialized/ethnic groups have these commonalities in their experiences in Canada: (1) each has been the object of negative stereotypes and discrimination; (2) each has resisted oppression and continued to strive for a better life for their members and their

children; and (3) each has been the object of some government policy that has shaped its place (or lack thereof) in Canadian ethnic relations over the past four centuries. Since the surveys of Statistics Canada show a high percentage of visible minorities in Canada, almost 50 percent visible minorities in Toronto and Vancouver and greater percentages in the future, Canada must be inclusive in the future to survive.

KEY TERMS

amalgamation, p. 57
Anglo-conformity model, p. 57
anti-Semitism, p. 50
assimilation, p. 56
ethnic group, p. 44
ethnic pluralism, p. 57
ethnocentrism, p. 50
gendered racism, p. 58

generalization, p. 50
genocide, p. 58
individual discrimination, p. 50
institutional discrimination, p. 50
internal colonialism, p. 57
internalized dominance, p. 46
majority (or dominant) group, p. 46
minority (or subordinate) group, p. 46

prejudice, p. 50
racialized group, p. 45
racism, p. 49
segregation, p. 57
social construct, p. 45
stereotypes, p. 50
theory of racial formation, p. 58

QUESTIONS FOR CRITICAL THINKING

1. Do you consider yourself part of the dominant racialized/ethnic group or part of a subordinate racialized/ethnic group in Canada? Consider what specific ways your life might be different if you were in another group.

2. Sociologists suggest that we acquire beliefs about our self and others through socialization. What specific messages have you received about your racialized/ethnic identity? What specific messages have you received about dealing with people from other racialized/ethnic groups? What hidden, subtle, or covert messages do you think you have received about your cultural group and about others?

3. Have all White Canadians, regardless of class, gender, or other characteristics, benefited from racialized prejudice and discrimination in Canada? Why or why not? In what ways have White people benefited from racism against non-Whites? In what ways have they been harmed by racism against non-Whites?

4. Compare recent depictions of Indigenous people, Black Canadians, Asian Canadians, and other racialized/ethnic groups in Canada in films, television shows, and advertisements. To what extent have we moved beyond the traditional stereotypes of those groups? To what extent have the stereotypes remained strong?

GetStock.com

VIOLENCE AGAINST WOMEN

The killing of 14 women in Montreal, Quebec, on December 6, 1989, shocked the nation. Most news reports in the days and weeks following cited the act as that of a madman—an isolated, bizarre event carried out by a deranged individual. While there can be no doubt that the act was extreme, feminists and other analysts continue to question this individualistic analysis, pointing instead to the pervasiveness of sexism in a patriarchal society, a pervasiveness they say creates a climate for actions such as this, and other forms of violence against women, to play out. *Sexism is the subordination of one sex, female, based on the assumed superiority of the other sex, male; patriarchy refers to a hierarchical system of social organization in which cultural, political, and economic structures are controlled by men.* According to some social analysts, problems of sexism are overblown: sexism was a problem in the past when women were underrepresented in organizations and in the paid labour force generally; now, however, women have made significant inroads in education and employment. In August 2014, 60.8 percent of women and 72.1 of men 25 years and over participated in the labour force (Statistics Canada 2014b). Many more women than men today have gained post-secondary degrees (see Figure 12.2 in Chapter 12) and are employed in an increasing variety of professional fields. With obvious changes such as these, some people believe that women should just be happy and stop complaining about the "past." Many feel that, while the events of December 6, 1989, were tragic, conditions that may have caused such an event to occur (assuming a social *versus* an individualized analysis) are over now—they are historical conditions that we have overcome in the years since. These people believe that today women and men in Canada are equal.

The 1993 National Violence Against Women Survey (VAWS) conducted by Statistics Canada represents the most comprehensive report on women's experience of violence. Statistics Canada added questions to the quinquennial (occurring every five years) General Social Survey (GSS) about family violence and gendered violence that allow some ongoing statistical comparisons. A Violence Against Women Survey was also administered in 2011, but it is not as comprehensive as the 1993 survey. The 1993 VAW Survey, which asked a sample of 12 300 women to report their lifetime experiences of assault, sexual assault, and sexual harassment, found that most assaults go unreported to police. Only 14 percent of all assaults had been reported; wife assaults were reported at a rate of 26 percent. Fifty-one percent of Canadian women had experienced at least one incident of physical or sexual assault since the age of 16. Forty-five percent of these women were assaulted by men known to them, and an additional 23 percent were assaulted by a stranger.

The 2011 Violence against Women Survey showed that over 173 000 women over the age of 15 were victims of violent crime in Canada in 2011 according to police reports. As you will see in Chapter 9 (Table 9.2), a very high percent of violent crime goes unreported to the police. But it is possible to show some magnitude and trends of the problem. The rate of violent crime against women is slightly higher than that against men, as Figure 4.1 shows, and young people are more subject to violent crime than are older people. The rate of violent crime against women ages 15–24 was about double that of women ages 35–44. Men and women tended to be victims of similar offences except for criminal harassment (women's were three times men's reports) and sexual offences (women's were 11 times men's reports) (Statistics Canada 2013b).

In terms of injuries, 41 percent of female victims were injured while 46 percent of male victims were injured, and generally injuries were minor. Most victims, both male and female, experienced assault 1, not assault 2 or 3, which are more injurious (see Table 11.4 in Chapter 11). Female victims were more likely to sustain physical injury when a spouse or a date was involved. Reporting to police was more likely when women had sustained an injury, when they feared for their lives, or when the abuse had gone on for some time. This report is not meant to downplay the homicides and homicide attempts among intimate partners (again, see Table 11.4), but fortunately homicides/attempts among intimate partners (146 women) is a small number relative to the total number of women who were

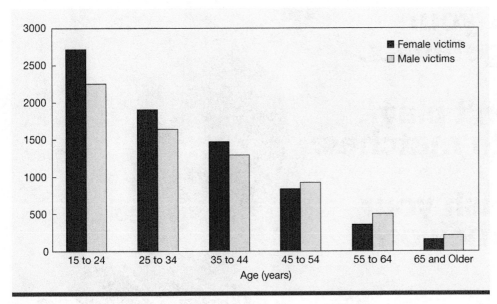

Figure 4.1   Police-Reported Victims of Violent Crime in Canada, 2011.

Source: *Statistics Canada, 2013b*, Violence Against Women, 2011. *Retrieved September 15, 2014* (*http://www.statcan.gc.ca/daily-quotidien/130225/dq130225a-eng.htm*).

victims of violence. Although rates of police-reported physical assaults against women, including common assaults, serious physical assaults, and attempted murder, have trended down from 2009 to 2011, the rate of sexual assaults against women remained stable in 2011 after increasing between 2009 and 2010.

Just as women have not historically been viewed as equal to men, not all women are viewed as equal to one another. For example, the murders of the 14 women in Montreal sparked annual December 6th memorials, to raise awareness of the violence against women, that continues today. The White Ribbon Campaign, begun in 1991 and carried out by Canadian men to raise awareness and educate men and boys about violence against women, continues to gain support each year. In fact, this campaign is the largest worldwide effort by men to end violence against women and is currently operating in over 80 countries. In contrast, the disappearances and deaths of many women in Vancouver and other Western cities have received only a small amount of attention compared to the women in Montreal. Analysts highlight the class, ethnic, and lifestyle differences between the groups; for instance, the Montreal Massacre, as it quickly came to be called, involved 14 young, White, middle-class women, most of whom were enrolled as students in engineering at

the "Poly." The disappearances in Vancouver and elsewhere have mainly involved women believed to be drug users and/or sex-trade workers, many of whom are also Indigenous. However, since mid-August 2014, a great deal of attention has been given to the 1100+ Canadian Indigenous women who have been murdered or missing, according to the RCMP, and there is a fierce debate about whether the federal government should hold a national inquiry into the problem (see Chapter 3).

Violence against women will be discussed in several chapters of this book. To study the basic facts and survey results, visit the Canadian Women's Foundation's Web page entitled The Facts about Violence against Women. While the facts are drawn from various years, they are all referenced, usually from data provided by Statistics Canada or other governmental agencies.

Violence against women in its many forms is one particularly devastating result of sexism and gender inequality. Other manifestations of sexism discussed in the following sections include inequalities in the paid labour force and in domestic labour. The ways that gender socialization perpetuates these inequalities are highlighted, as are various theories for analyzing gender inequality.

Eat your vegetables.

Don't play with matches.

Finish your homework.

Respect women.

AWAITING INSTRUCTIONS.

Violence against women is a tragic reality. We must teach our sons early and often what it means to be a real man – that women deserve honor and respect, and that violence never equals strength. A safer world is in their hands. Help them grasp it.

Family Violence Prevention Fund
www.endabuse.org

It is important that children are brought up to respect women.
Family Violence Prevention Fund, www.endabuse.org

GENDER INEQUALITY AS A SOCIAL PROBLEM

Similar to the ways that racialized ethnic group members experience discrimination based on supposed innate characteristics, women experience discrimination based on their sex. Since 51 percent of the people in Canada are female, women constitute a numerical majority. However, they are often referred to as the country's largest minority group because as a group, they do not possess as much wealth, power, or prestige as men. As a telling example involving income alone, for all full-time workers in Canada in 1967—the first year the data were gathered on male to female earnings—women earned 58.4 percent of what men earned, a 42 percent gap (Nelson 2010:236). In 1980, the gap declined to 35 percent, and by 2010, the gap had declined to a still substantial 19 percent (see Figure 4.2).

Defining Sex and Gender

What is the difference between sex and gender? Although many people use these terms interchangeably, sociologists believe there are significant differences in their meanings. **Sex refers to the biological, physiological, hormonal, and chromosomal attributes of females, males, and intersex people.** Our sex is the first label we receive in life and is an ascribed status. Before birth or at the time of birth, we are typically identified as either male or female on the basis of our sex organs and genes. Despite the fact that many children do not exhibit the genitalia or chromosomes consistent with either a male or female designation, most people act as though there are only two dichotomous and "opposite" sexes. For example, when a child is born *intersexed*—**that is, with either unrecognizably male or female genitalia or with both male and female genitalia**—we surgically alter the child to fit our current two-sex model of reality. Within the two-sex model, males are seen as the central or standard sex against which females,

the "opposite" sex, are measured. This **practice of putting males at the centre is known as** *androcentricity*. As an illustration of the fluidity of our notions, even in something as seemingly fixed or static as biology, in the past, Westerners had a one-sex model of humanity, with the one sex being male. Females and their bodies were viewed as imperfect or flawed versions of the male. Historian Thomas Laqueur (1992:4), in a book called *Making Sex*, states that several early "scientists," such as Galen and Herophilus, claimed that women were less perfect men and compared women's genitalia to men's. Scholars and lay people alike were "caught up in the female-as-male model" until approximately 1800, when many began to insist that there "were fundamental differences between the male and female sexes" (Laqueur 1992:5).

Following, then, from a two-sex model, *gender* **refers to the culturally and socially constructed sets of attitudes that dictate what behaviours, thoughts, and emotions are appropriate for each sex—these are culturally specific, change over time, and are associated with notions of femininity and masculinity.** For many people, being *masculine* means being aggressive, independent, and unemotional, while being *feminine* means the opposite—being passive, dependent, and emotional. Understanding the difference between sex and gender is important, according to sociologists, because what many people think of as *sex differences*—for example, being aggressive or independent—are actually socially constructed *gender differences* based on widely held assumptions about men and women. In other words, males are supposed to be aggressive and independent not because they have male sex organs, but because that is how people in this society think males should act. Psychologist S.L. Bem (1974) talked about masculinity and femininity being represented on two continuums. Where individuals are located on each continuum gives an indication as to their personal combination of masculine and feminine

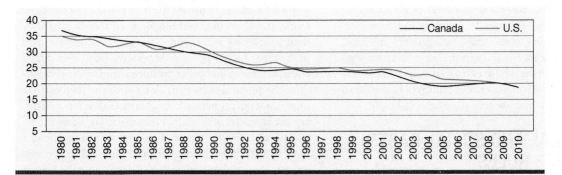

Figure 4.2   Gender Income Gap, 1980–2010 (percent).

Source: *Conference Board of Canada, 2013*, Society. Retrieved September 15, 2014. (*http://www.conferenceboard.ca/hcp/details/society/gender-income-gap.aspx*).

This young F to M couple is celebrating graduation from university. They have to contend not only with transphobia in their daily lives, but also with homophobia.
Vicki L. Nygaard

traits. Again, though, masculinity and femininity are presented as the central elements in a dichotomy instead of as simply two out of a multiplicity of possibilities for genders.

Because gender is socially constructed, people can choose a gender identity that is in keeping with the way they view themselves. Some people choose a more feminine gender identity, while others choose a more masculine identity. Most people choose a gender identity that is consistent with their biological sex. However, some may choose an identity that others feel is inappropriate. It is important to remember that currently, most people in Canada believe there are two sexes and hence two genders. The category of "trans" focuses our attention on the fluidity of gender. According to a 2001 publication created by Transcend Transgender Support and Education Society, the terms "trans" and "transgender" are used, often interchangeably, to refer to anyone who is not simply a male or female, whose behaviour contravenes societal norms, and who experiences a transphobia, similar to homophobia, for contravening the norms (2001:9).

BIOLOGICAL AND SOCIAL BASES OF GENDER ROLES

To study gender inequality, sociologists begin with an examination of the biological and social bases for gender roles, which are the rights, responsibilities, expectations,

and relationships of women and men in a society. Gender roles have both a biological and a social basis. The biological basis for gender roles is rooted in the chromosomal and hormonal differences between men and women. When a child is conceived, the mother contributes an X chromosome and the father contributes either an X chromosome (which produces a female embryo) or a Y chromosome (which produces a male embryo). As the embryo's male or female sex glands develop, they secrete the appropriate hormones (androgens for males, estrogens for females) that circulate through the bloodstream, producing sexual differentiation in the external genitalia, the internal reproductive tract, and possibly some areas of the brain. At birth, medical personnel and family members distinguish male from female infants by their *primary sex characteristics:* the genitalia that are used in the reproductive process. At puberty, hormonal differences in females and males produce *secondary sex characteristics,* the physical traits that, along with the reproductive organs, identify a person's sex. Females develop secondary sex characteristics such as menstruation, more prominent breasts, wider hips and narrower shoulders, and a layer of fatty tissue throughout the body. Male secondary sex characteristics include the development of larger genitals, a more muscular build, a deeper voice, more body and facial hair, and greater height. Although both males and females have androgens and estrogens, it is the relative proportion of each hormone that triggers masculine or feminine physical traits.

Is there something in the biological and genetic makeup of boys or girls that makes them physically aggressive or passive? As sociologist Judith Lorber (1994:39) notes, "When little boys run around noisily, we say 'Boys will be boys,' meaning that physical assertiveness has to be in the Y chromosome because it is manifest so early and so commonly in boys." Similarly, when we say "She throws like a girl," according to Lorber, people mean that "she throws like a female child, a carrier of XX chromosomes." However, Lorber questions these widely held assumptions: "But are boys universally, the world over, in every social group, a vociferous, active presence? Or just where they are encouraged to use their bodies freely, to cover space, take risks, and play outdoors at all kinds of games and sports?"

According to Lorber, boys and girls who are given tennis racquets at the age of 3 and encouraged to become champions tend to use their bodies similarly. Even though boys gradually gain more shoulder and arm strength and are able to sustain more concentrated bursts of energy, after puberty girls acquire more stamina, flexibility, and lower-body strength than before. Coupled with training and physical exercise, these traits enhance, compensate for, or override different physical capabilities (Lorber 1994). Thus, the girl who throws "like a girl" is

probably a product of her culture and time: she has had more limited experience than many boys at throwing the ball and engaging in competitive games at an early age. The implication that social roles "are an unproblematic reflection of biology (sex)" is analytically flawed (Marshall 2000:24).

The social basis for gender roles is known as the gender belief system or *gender ideology—ideas of masculinity and femininity that are held to be valid in a given society at a specific historical time* (Lorber 1994). Gender ideology is reflected in what sociologists refer to as the *gendered division of labour—the process whereby productive tasks are separated on the basis of gender.* How do people determine what constitutes "women's work" or "men's work"? Evidence from cross-cultural studies shows that social factors, more than biological factors, influence the gendered division of labour in societies. In agricultural societies, for example, women work in the fields and tend to their families' daily needs; men typically produce and market cash crops but spend no time on household work. In industrialized nations, an increasing proportion of women are in paid employment but still have heavy household and family responsibilities. Figure 4.3 shows that although newer cohorts of men are doing housework, most of this work is still done by women. Across cultures, women's domain is viewed as the private and domestic, and men's domain

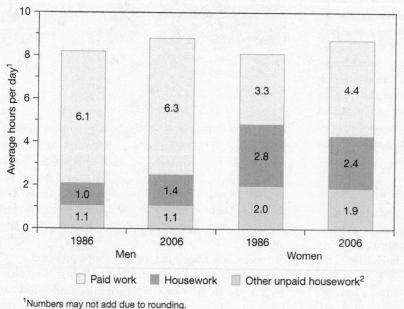

Figure 4.3 *Hours per Day Spent on Paid and Unpaid Work: Males and Females, 1986 and 2006.*

Source: Reprinted with permission from the House of Commons, Parliament of Canada.

[1]Numbers may not add due to rounding.
[2]Primary child care and shopping for goods and services.

is viewed as the public, economic, and political. This difference in how labour is divided, how workers are rewarded, and what cultural value is accorded to paid versus unpaid labour affects access to scarce resources such as wealth, power, and prestige. Given their domain, men have greater access to these resources, a situation that leads to gender inequality in other areas.

To explain gender inequality, some sociologists use a *gender-role approach*, focusing on how the socialization process contributes to male domination and female subordination. Other sociologists use a *structural approach*, focusing on how large-scale social structures determine the boundaries of individual behaviour. Let's look first at how socialization can perpetuate gender stereotyping and inequality.

GENDER INEQUALITY AND SOCIALIZATION

Numerous sociological studies have found that gender-role stereotyping is one of the enduring consequences of childhood gender socialization. Socialization into appropriate "feminine" behaviour makes women less likely than men to pursue male-dominated activities, and socialization into appropriate "masculine" behaviour makes men more likely than women to pursue leadership roles in education, religion, business, politics, and other spheres of public life (Peterson and Runyan 1993). We learn our earliest and often most long-lasting beliefs about gender roles from a variety of *agents of socialization*—those people, groups, or institutions that teach us what we need to know to participate in society.

Among the most significant agents of socialization are parents, peers, the education system, and the media. Although all four agents of socialization are important, this chapter will focus on peer and media gender socialization, since parental gender socialization is well known, and education and gender socialization is dealt with in the education chapter.

Peers and Gender Socialization

Peer groups are powerful socializing agents that can reinforce existing gender stereotypes and pressure individuals to engage in gender-appropriate behaviour. Peer groups are social groups whose members are linked by common interests and, usually, by similar age. Even in kindergarten and the early grades, peers influence how we do in school and our perceptions of ourselves and others. Children are more widely accepted by their peer group

This young man challenges gender conformity through his choice of clothes.

Vicki L. Nygaard

when they conform to the group's notion of gender-appropriate behaviour. Male peer groups place more pressure on boys to do "masculine" things than female peer groups place on girls to do "feminine" things. For example, most girls today wear jeans and many play soccer and softball, but boys who wear dresses or play hopscotch with girls are banished from most male peer groups.

Peers are important in both women's and men's development of gender identity and their aspirations for the future. Among college and university students, for example, peers play an important part in career choices and the establishment of long-term, intimate relationships. They have also played an important role in the misogynistic attacks by groups of men against women, such as the Facebook attack on women by dentistry students at Dalhousie University, the attacks by sports team members on women like those of the University of Ottawa Gee-Gees and Steubenville in the United States, and the attacks against women by fraternity brothers in many fraternity houses, especially in the United States.

The Media and Gender Socialization

Females' acceptance or praise for being "good" and/or "compliant" is consistently reinforced throughout all types of media. From television to the Internet, from magazines to billboards, we are inundated by media on a daily basis. Because media are socially constructed, they reflect the realities and/or fantasies of their creators. Communications scholar Julia T. Wood (2001) identifies three themes in contemporary media that reflect gender. The first theme is the underrepresentation of women and other minority groups. The overrepresentation of able-bodied, youngish, White men in media conveys the message that they make up the majority of the population (which they do not) and, as such, that they are the cultural standard. When women and other minority groups are depicted in media, they are typically shown in ways that reinforce and perpetuate, subtly or overtly, negative stereotypes about the group. The second theme is the stereotypical fashion in which males and females are presented. Males continue to be presented as competent, powerful, serious, confident, and independent, while females continue to be presented as incompetent, unintelligent, young, thin, beautiful, dependent, and passive sex objects (Wood 2001:283–284). To redress past voids, contemporary media have made attempts to show women involved in activities outside the domestic sphere; however, they have not made a corresponding attempt to show men involved in the domestic sphere. Where men are shown involved in domestic labour or child care, they are typically portrayed as helpless ("hopeless"?) buffoons (Wood 2001:284), reinforcing men's lack of "suitability" for child care and domestic activities. Family sociologists historically have referred to this phenomenon as "learned incompetence." The third theme is the portrayal of male–female relations along traditional lines and in ways that perpetuate and normalize violence against women (Wood 2001:281). Wood (2001:287–294) suggests there are four themes that reflect and promote gender-stereotypical, and perhaps even dangerous, relations between the sexes: (1) women's dependence and

men's independence; (2) women's incompetence and men's authority; (3) women as primary caregivers and men as primary breadwinners; and (4) women as victims and sex objects and men as aggressors.

While some critics argue that the media simply reflect existing gender roles in society, others point out that the media also have a unique ability to shape ideas. Sociologist Linda Lindsey (2005:69) notes that "heavy television viewing is strongly associated with traditional and stereotyped gender views, a pattern that is demonstrated for all [ethnic groups] and age groups." From children's cartoons to adult shows, television programs offer many more male than female characters. Furthermore, the male characters often act in a manner strikingly different than the female ones. Male characters in both children's adult programs are typically aggressive, constructive, and direct, while female characters defer to or manipulate them by acting helpless, seductive, or deceitful. Nurturing males, along with females generally, are most often found in comedies with females who inhabit highly stereotypical roles, suggesting that they need not be taken seriously (Nelson 2010). Furthermore, in cartoons, where male characters outnumber female characters five to one, females are typically cast in minor supportive roles (e.g., the wife or the younger sister) and display only a small repertoire of stereotypical behaviours and emotions such as fear, support, romance, or good manners (Nelson 2010:198). Males, particularly in the many police and detective dramas available today, tend to be stereotyped as hyper-masculinized: they are either aggressive, criminal, thrill-seeking, and callous toward women ("bad guys"), or aggressive, thrill-seeking, and tough ("good guys") (Nelson 2010:200). Some have argued that even educational programs such as *Sesame Street* perpetuate gender stereotyping and male dominance because most of the characters have male names and masculine voices and participate in "boys' activities" (Wood 2001).

Studies of televised music videos have found that they often show stereotyped gender roles and condone harassment of and discrimination against women. In the words of Linda Lindsey, "The misogyny in most rock videos is blatant." (2005:358). A 1992 study found most female characters were dressed in revealing clothing, made sexual advances toward men, and usually were presented as sex objects. Further studies from 1999 and 2002 demonstrate that women do not appear at all or appear only in the background in over half of music videos, but where they do appear, sexual images are increasingly combined with violence. Male characters routinely pursue fantasy adventures or engage in aggression and violence (Seidman 1992). Further, women are shown either satisfying male sexual fantasies or being ostracized or punished for not engaging in this way. Sociologist Sut Jhally, in his *Dreamworlds* documentaries, links music videos and sexual assault, describing the fantasy world of music videos as the male videographer's and consumer's dreamworld. This "dreamworld" objectifies and dehumanizes women and denies them subjectivity, all of which puts women at risk for violence by reinforcing a *rape culture*—**the pervasive system of cultural values, attitudes, and practices that support and perpetuate sexualized violence against women.** It includes rigid gender scripts for males and females and equally rigid notions of gender-appropriate behaviours. Many music videos overtly depict male violence against women, and increasingly, over the years, rape scenes have been enacted in music videos (Lindsey 2005). Jhally, in the latest edition of *Dreamworlds* (2007) makes the case that many music video producers and directors today are also producers and directors of pornography, and that the line between music video and pornography is now indistinct. Psychologists Harmony Sullivan and Maureen McHugh (2009:746) note that Jhally's film "elucidates how the dominant cultural narrative expressed in music videos and other media confers to men a sense of entitlement to comment on and even touch women's bodies in public" and that through indoctrination by various media, such as music videos, "women may be seen, by men but also by women [themselves], as decorative, dehumanized and perhaps deserving of abuse."

While changes have occurred in the roles men and women play in movies, most still embrace stereotypes. Even though there are many movie stars who are female, with a few exceptions, there are few notable roles for women, and even fewer films that examine women's lives and issues from their perspectives. Movies featuring boys and men focus on saving the nation, the world, or the universe, while films featuring girls and women focus on saving money on shoes by finding *the most fabulous discount ever!* Females are usually depicted as "bimbos," as shopaholics, and as sexually available. Things may be changing somewhat: in some recent films, women are not portrayed as helpless, even if they are conventionally attractive, and even the token "smart females" are sometimes portrayed as also attractive. However, even when females are portrayed positively as smart *and* attractive, as characters in the *Harry Potter* and *Star Wars* series are, they are still only supporting characters to the males who save the day. There has been a spate of movies featuring "kick-ass" females (*Underworld, Mr. and Mrs. Smith, The Matrix*); however, these women are depicted as cold-blooded

killers, very masculine in their approach to the world and dressed in highly sexualized attire. According to social psychologist Hilary Lips (1993:19), "We are surrounded with the message that masculine males can be powerful, but feminine females cannot, or that women's only effective source of feminine influence is beauty and sex appeal." Moreover, the dominant message conveyed still remains that females must use their influence, however paltry, in an attempt to garner that pinnacle of feminine achievement and self-definition—an intimate relationship with a man.

Why is awareness of gender socialization important for understanding gender discrimination and gender inequality? Social analysts who use a gender-role approach say that because parents, peers, teachers, and the media influence our perceptions of who we are and what our aspirations should be, gender-role socialization contributes to a gendered division of labour, creates a *wage gap* between women and men workers, limits occupational and other choices for women and men, and perpetuates gendered violence and shapes our (lack of) responses to it. It is important, therefore, to keep in mind that gender is a social construction and, in the words of sociologist Judith Lorber (1986:576), "what is socially constructed can be reconstructed, and social relations can be rearranged." In this way, social change is always possible.

However, some social analysts say that the decisions that people make (such as the degrees they choose to achieve and the occupations they choose to pursue) are linked not only to how they were socialized, but also to how society is structured. We now examine structural features that contribute to gender inequality.

CONTEMPORARY GENDER INEQUALITY

How do tasks in a society get defined as either "men's work" or "women's work," and why are they differentially rewarded? Many sociologists believe that through various social institutions and structures, people assign different roles and responsibilities to women and men based on notions of gender appropriateness and, in the process, restrict women's opportunities. According to feminist scholars, gender inequality is maintained and reinforced through individual and institutionalized sexism. The term *individual sexism* refers to individuals' beliefs and actions that are rooted in anti-female prejudice and stereotypical beliefs. The term *institutionalized sexism* refers to the power that men have to engage in sex discrimination at the organizational and institutional levels of society. This pattern of male domination and female subordination is known as *patriarchy*, defined earlier as a hierarchical system of social organization in which cultural, political, and economic structures are controlled by men. According to some analysts, the location of women in the workforce and on the economic pyramid is evidence of patriarchy (Epstein 1988). In this section, we focus on five structural forms that contribute to contemporary gender inequality: the gendered division of labour, the wage gap, sexual harassment, the glass ceiling and the glass escalator, and the double shift.

The Gendered Division of Paid Work

Whether by choice or economic necessity, women have entered the paid labour force in unprecedented numbers in recent years. In 1946, fewer than 20 percent of women over the age of 25 were employed in the Canadian paid labour force. This number had risen to 30 percent as of 1961. Today as discussed earlier, women have a participation rate of 60.8 percent. Until the 1950s, employed women were typically single, young, and childless. Today, however, many women with preschool children are in the paid labour force. As of 2003, 80 percent of all married Canadian women were in the paid labour force (the Statistics Canada 2014 survey does not mention marital status), with the largest increases in participation coming from those aged 25 to 44 years—those most likely to have dependent children at home (Mitchell 2009; Nelson 2010).

There are several reasons for these dramatic increases in participation. First, economic growth after World War II saw an increase in available jobs, particularly jobs that were deemed suitable for women such as "supportive" clerical jobs, nursing, and teaching (Mitchell 2009:96). Additionally, structural pressures such as inflation necessitated higher incomes generally, and the shift from a goods-producing or manufacturing economy to a service economy—with the attendant lower wages—and cost-of-living increases in the 1960s drove the increase in dual-earner families. As well, service jobs are ones in which we disproportionately find women. Along with this, cultural values about women's roles, paid employment, marriage, and parenting shifted to the point where today, women working for pay, regardless of their marital or parental status, are no longer so negatively stigmatized as they once were (Mitchell 2009; Nelson 2010). Even as women's labour force participation has been increasing, male participation has been gradually declining due to young men staying in school longer, layoffs in the industrial sector, downsizing of business and government, and the long-term trend toward early retirement,

either voluntary or involuntary, by men in their 50s and older (i.e., "buyouts"; Nelson 2010).

While many people who know these statistics are optimistic about the gains Canadian women have made in paid employment, this should be a cautious optimism given that women's position in the labour force is still lower than men's in terms of status, opportunities, and salaries. Today, most women and men remain concentrated in occupations that are segregated by gender (see Table 4.1). The term *gender-segregated work* refers to the extent to which men and women are concentrated in different occupations and places of work (Reskin and Padavic 1994). For example, women are predominant in nursing and child-care centres, whereas men are predominant in the construction trades and engineering.

Women continue to be concentrated in jobs where they receive lower wages, less prestige, and fewer benefits, on average, than men receive. However, this **inequity is further compounded by racialization, older age, and (dis)ability, a situation known as** *multiple jeopardy or intersectionality*. For those who experience multiple barriers to employment, it is nearly impossible to determine which particular barrier was most salient in a given instance of discrimination.

The Wage Gap

The *wage gap—***the disparity between women's and men's earnings—**is the best-documented consequence of gender-segregated work (Reskin and Padavic 1994). No matter what group men belong to in terms of age, racialization, or ability, they earn more than women of that same group. It is well known that a wage gap persists in Canada across full- and part-time employment and in both annual income and hourly wages. The fact that women have historically been a cheaper source of labour has been one of the factors in their attractiveness to employers. In the past 30 years, while women's participation in the labour force has increased, inequality still occurs between men's and women's wages. Figure 4.2 (above) shows that the gap in wages has declined from 35 percent in 1980 to 19 percent in 2010.

This gap places Canada 11th of 17 in the ranking of wage inequality among the high-income countries. Among the reasons for the decline are that women are achieving higher levels of education and are marrying later, giving them a chance to establish themselves in their careers. Women have increased their proportion of those graduating with all degrees by more than 10 percent for those 25–34 years of age compared to those 55–64 years of age (see Chapter 12 for details). In addition, younger women have earnings closer to younger

TABLE 4.1 Women as a Percentage of Total Employed in Occupation, 1987, 1994, 2003, 2006					
	1987	1994	1999	2003	2006
Managerial					
Senior management	16.9	19.8	26.8	24.2	26.3
Other management	30.6	36.9	35.7	36.1	36.9
Total management	28.9	35.1	35.1	35.4	36.3
Professional					
Business and finance	40.7	44.6	49.4	48.4	51.6
Natural sciences/engineering/mathematics	16.7	17.0	19.6	22.0	22.0
Social sciences/religion	47.8	56.5	58.2	63.8	71.3
Teaching	57.3	59.4	62.1	62.9	63.9
Doctors/dentists/other health-related	44.1	48.7	47.1	52.1	55.3
Nursing/therapy/other health-related	87.3	87.1	86.5	87.7	87.4
Artistic/literary/recreational	50.4	53.6	54.6	53.4	54.1
Total professional	49.8	52.2	51.8	53.4	55.9
Clerical and administration	74.4	74.9	75.3	75.1	75.0
Sales and service	55.7	56.4	58.7	58.7	56.8
Primary	20.0	21.3	21.6	19.7	20.5
Trades, transport, and construction	5.3	5.4	6.2	6.6	6.5
Processing, manufacturing, and utilities	30.2	29.2	29.8	28.9	31.1
Total*	43.0	45.3	45.9	46.6	47.1

* Includes occupations that are not classified.

Source: *Adapted from Statistics Canada, Women in Canada: Work Chapter Updates, 2003, Cat. No. 89F0133X (March 25, 2004). Adapted in Gender in Canada, Fourth Edition by Adie Nelson, 2010, p. 227, Pearson Canada. Reprinted with permission of Pearson Canada Inc.*

men's earnings. Table 4.2 shows the median incomes of men and women in various occupations who are university educated and are 25–29 years of age and 30–34 years of age for 2006. (Unfortunately, these data were not collected in the 2011 census.) For these women, the inequality wage gap is much lower than the 19 percent seen above, and in a few cases (e.g., health, recreation, and fitness and physical and life sciences and technologies), women's wages are higher than men's.

Statistics Canada (1999a) notes that one-half the differential of the gap can be explained by not only education and age, but also occupation. Table 4.3 shows that while the gap is still present, the gap has declined more for women in business and professions than women in primary industry (e.g., resources and agriculture). Another reason given for the reduction of the wage gap has been the stagnation and long-term decline of men's

wages generally, particularly in primary (resources) and secondary (manufacturing) industries (Nelson 2010; Roos and Reskin 1992; Wilson 2001).

Sexual Harassment

Millions of men never harass women in the workplace or elsewhere, but so many men do, that, sadly, it is almost impossible for women to avoid the experience (Langelan 1993). **Sexual harassment is a form of intentional, institutionalized gender discrimination that includes all unwelcome sexual attention affecting an employee's job conditions or creating a hostile work environment.** Sociologists Walter S. DeKeseredy and Ronald Hinch (1991:103) define it as "unsolicited, unreciprocated male behaviour that values a woman's sex role over her function as a worker." Sexual harassment includes, but is not limited to, verbal abuse or threats,

TABLE 4.2 Median Earnings of University Graduate Employees by Field of Study and Age Group in Canada, 2006

Field of study	25 to 29					30 to 34				
	Distribution		Median income			Distribution		Median income		
	Women	Men	Women	Men	ratio	Women	Men	Women	Men	ratio
	percentage		dollars			percentage		dollars		
Education	9.5	2.3	41 154	43 174	0.95	10.7	3.4	47 561	52 916	0.90
Visual and performing arts, and communications technologies	4.6	4.1	30 530	33 496	0.90	3.6	3.7	39 041	40 482	0.96
Humanities	5.4	3.3	34 407	36 304	0.95	5.7	3.8	41 392	47 200	0.88
Social and behavioural sciences and law	15.9	6.9	38 402	41 448	0.93	16.8	8.3	47 303	56 000	0.84
Business, management, and public administration	27.9	17.2	41 728	46 539	0.90	27.9	17.3	50 250	64 833	0.78
Physical and life sciences, and technologies	4.2	3.5	37 677	36 827	1.02	4.0	3.8	46 647	55 182	0.85
Mathematics, computer, and information sciences	3.7	11.0	44 745	47 987	0.93	4.1	8.9	53 090	62 227	0.85
Architecture, engineering, and related services	4.3	37.0	47 977	52 175	0.92	4.3	36.1	55 027	65 281	0.84
Agriculture, natural resources, and conservation	1.9	3.3	41 162	45 355	0.91	1.7	3.3	47 506	56 278	0.84
Health, parks, recreation, and fitness	16.9	4.4	49 969	46 872	1.07	16.6	5.2	55 650	58 666	0.95
Personal, protective, and transportation services	5.8	7.0	38 200	45 135	0.85	4.8	6.4	55 000	66 612	0.83

Note: Full-year employees: self-employed workers are excluded from this table. University graduates include persons with a Bachelor's degree or higher.

Source: *Statistics Canada, 2010*, Women and Education. *Retrieved September 15, 2014 (http://www.statcan.gc.ca/pub/89-503-x/2010001/article/11542/tbl/tbl012-eng.htm).*

touching, staring or leering, making jokes, demanding sexual interactions, making repeated propositions, offering comments or questions about a person's sex life, displaying sexually offensive materials, and sexual assault on the job (Benokraitis and Feagin 1995; Nelson 2010). The Violence against Women 2011 study shows that harassment is still widespread.

People who are accused of sexual harassment frequently claim that their actions were merely harmless expressions of (supposedly) mutual sexual attraction. Sociologist Adie Nelson reports that "research has indicated that behaviour that women defined as unacceptable or offensive, especially in the workplace, was viewed by men as normal and appropriate" (2006:179). Sexual harassment is not about attraction; it is about abuse of power. Sexual harassment constitutes a form of intimidation and aggression: the recipient has no choice in the encounter or has reason to fear repercussions if she or he declines. Prominent media figure in Canada have been charged with harassment (see Box 4.1).

The Glass Ceiling and the Glass Escalator

More recently, feminist researchers have used the advancement (or lack of advancement) of women into

TABLE 4.3 Relative Earnings of Women and Men by Occupation, Canada (ratio of female to male earnings)

	1986	2010
Natural and applied sciences	0.63	0.94
Art, culture, recreation, and sport	0.54	0.88
Management	0.59	0.71
Social science, education, government service, and religion	0.57	0.70
Processing, manufacturing, and utilities	0.52	0.65
Business, finance, and administrative	0.58	0.60
Trades, transport and equipment	0.50	0.59
Sales and service	0.48	0.57
Primary industry	0.46	0.49
Health	0.48	0.47

Source: *Conference Board of Canada. 2013. Society. Retrieved September 15, 2014 (http://www.conferenceboard.ca/hcp/details/society/gender-income-gap.aspx)*

top-tier management jobs as a litmus test for how well women are faring in the labour force as a whole. They have found that women hold only a handful of top positions. Although they are inching their way up the corporate ladder, women almost always encounter barriers when they try to enter the lucrative and prestigious top positions of their occupations. This is because of what is known as the *glass ceiling*—the invisible institutional barrier constructed by male management that prevents women from reaching top positions in major corporations and other large-scale organizations. Among the reasons cited for this barrier are male executives who believe that male workers will not work for female supervisors, that female workers are supposed to be in support roles only, that the prestige of the profession will decrease if females are admitted, and/or that "the ideal worker is normatively masculine" (Benokraitis and Feagin 1995; Martin 1992:220; Nelson 2010).

The glass ceiling is particularly evident in the nation's largest companies. Leading Boards, a website that tracks the gender balance of 80 large corporations (more than $1 billion in revenue), found that though the representation of women on boards in Canada rose from 15 percent in 2008 to 20 percent in 2013 (Leading Boards 2014), this is still far below women's proportion (almost half) of the labour force. In 2013, Canada had a slightly higher score than the United Kingdom or the United States. The *Corporate Knights* survey released in 2015 used the percentage of women on boards of directors as one factor to identify the 100 most sustainable corporations in the world. Twelve Canadian corporations made the list. Canadian corporations where more than 33 percent of the board members were women include the Toronto-Dominion Bank, the Bank of Montreal, Intact Financial, and Encana (Runnalls 2015:38). Overall, women are most likely to reach top positions in the service sector (for example, banking and diversified finance, publishing, retailing, food services, and entertainment), a sector in which they have traditionally been employed in great numbers. Their percentages are lower in mining and energy companies, where traditionally few women are employed, except for Encana.

Even with nearly equivalent numbers of women and men in a workplace, a chilly climate may exist. The *chilly climate* is a concept used to draw attention to the fact that equality of access does not necessarily guarantee equality of treatment within any given institution. The chilly climate can be manifested as an inhospitable workplace for a person of "the wrong sex" through exclusionary, isolating, dismissive, or generally "cool" behaviours, based on cultural notions of gender-appropriate labour (The Chilly Collective 1995; Nelson 2010:240).

Unlike women who enter male-dominated occupations, men who enter female-dominated occupations are apt to find little difficulty rising to the top. In research on men working as registered nurses, elementary teachers, librarians, and social workers, sociologist Christine L. Williams (1995) found that they tended to

I SAID...
"YOU'VE COME
A LONG WAY
BABY!"...

EARNING POWER

Women   Men

Brian Gabel Globe

rise in disproportionate numbers to administrative positions at the top of these occupations. Further, they very often gain quick access to promotion and higher salaries (Nelson 2010:230). Williams (1995:12) calls the upward movement of men in "women's professions" the *glass escalator effect*.

The Double Shift

Although there have been dramatic changes in the participation of women in the labour force, the household

division of labour by sex has changed little in many families. While more married women now share responsibility for earning part—or all—of the family income, many married men still do not participate in routine domestic chores. Consequently, many employed women must deal with a double workload. In the words of sociologist Arlie Hochschild (1989), women with dual responsibilities as wage earners and unpaid household workers work "the second shift." Interestingly, there have been some changes recently in the daily participation rate of what has been identified as "core housework"—tasks such as meal preparation, cleaning, and laundry. Men's participation went from 40 percent in 1986 to 59 percent in 2005, while women's participation actually decreased from 88 percent to 85 percent (Marshall 2006). There has also been an increase in women's hours per day at paid labour, from 4.5 hours to 5.4, and a corresponding decrease in hours spent doing housework (see Figure 4.3). Basically, a higher percentage of people are doing some daily housework than in the past, but they are spending less time at it (Marshall 2006:9). Figure 11.4, in the chapter concerned with family, shows more recent cohorts of males are slightly more likely to do more housework.

While things are becoming slightly more equitable, albeit slowly, on the domestic labour front, the kinds of chores men and women do vary significantly. Women do most of the *daily* chores, such as making beds, cooking, cleaning up after meals, chauffeuring, and taking care of children ("core" household work). As sociologist Adie Nelson states, "women's tasks tend to be routine, repetitive, monotonous and invisible (i.e., not noticed unless undone)" (2006:253). Men are more likely to do chores that do not have to be done every day ("non-core" work) and hence allow considerable scheduling autonomy. For example, men typically mow the lawn, repair cars or other equipment, clean out the eavestroughs, and do home improvements (Marshall 2006; Nelson 2006; Shelton 1992).

From 1996 to 2006, the census included questions on unpaid labour. Data from the 2006 census demonstrated that the current value of unpaid work in Canada, at least two-thirds of which is performed by women, was approximately 41 percent of Canada's GDP (Mitchell 2009:98). As sociologist Augie Fleras points out, this result concedes "the collapse of Canada's market economy" without the invisible labour of women's unpaid work (Fleras 2005:114). Globally, unpaid work is worth US$11 billion annually (Mitchell 2009:98).

Now that figures on particular problems in Canada have been presented, how does Canada rank among other (not just high-income) countries? Box 4.2 attempts to provide an answer.

Box 4.1

Can Media Help Solve the Major Social Problem of Harassment?

In this text, media are often found to be part of a problem as a result of the way they frame topics or their lack of inclusion of groups like visible minorities (Chapter 14) and the elderly (Chapter 5). But can media contribute to bringing about a solution to major social problems, such as harassment of and non-consensual violence toward women? In the last week of October 2014, several media stories appeared that led to much discussion about these topics.

According to reports in all the Toronto newspapers and news programs, Jian Ghomeshi, the host of CBC's radio program *Q with Jian Ghomeshi*, was accused by nine women of non-consensual abuse (e.g., slapping, punching, and choking). As a result, the CBC fired him, the Giller Prize dropped him as host, and even a public relations firm hired to support him dropped him as a client. Some of these incidents happened many years ago, but women have had a history of not reporting sexual assault because of related problems of feelings of shame, indignities in collecting evidence, not being believed by police, and the very long criminal proceedings that can result. In the Statistics Canada General Social Survey, *Criminal Victimization 2004*, the sample survey reported that about half a million people were victims of sexual assault (see Chapter 9 for definitions of 1, 2, and 3), but about 450 000 (88 percent) did not report it (Statistics Canada 2005).

Some people in the media are trying to help. For example, another CBC show, George Stromboulopoulos's *The Strombo Show*, has provided information about crisis line telephone numbers and encouraged people who have experienced sexual violence to contact them. There have been suggestions that with all the publicity this news story is getting, this could be a turning point about violence against women. But there have been other highly publicized examples of violence against women like the Steubenville and the Rehtaeh Parsons assaults (see Chapter 9) and the missing 1100 Indigenous women (see Chapter 3). Perhaps this story can at least start a discussion about consent.

A second media story from October 2014 was the Twitter hashtag #BeenRapedNeverReported, started by a retired CBC and *Toronto Star* reporter, Antonia Zerbisias,

and *Montreal Gazette* reporter, Sue Montgomery. They wanted to let the world know how widespread the non-reporting of rape was in Canada in earlier years. According to the *Toronto Star*, the site received 41 519 tweets between October 29 and November 3, 2014 (Teotonio 2014). Many more have come in since that time and the story has been featured on the BBC and Al-Jazeera. Many of those who responded echoed the above concerns of feeling shame and not being believed by the police. It has taken some women years before they felt confident enough to report being raped, and doing so on this site and getting mostly supportive comments has helped them heal and feel empowered.

By coincidence, a video of a woman walking in New York and receiving cat calls was released on YouTube in this same time period. Although the video was taken over a 10-hour period and reduced to two minutes, it shows that a woman walking on the street can be harassed many times in a day. Many hope that these media incidents will start a widespread conversation about harassment and violence toward women.

Questions for Consideration

1. What steps should media hosts and writers take to keep these discussions going?

2. What other things should media do to highlight this problem?

3. You are reading this after the incidents occurred. To what extent has a conversation started and continued about harassment and violence?

4. Men are often afraid to speak up and support women, but the White Ribbon Campaign, the organization mentioned at the opening of this chapter, is trying to redefine what it means to be masculine. Representatives of this organization are talking in Canada about Jian Ghomeshi's behaviour to groups across the country. Has this organization had any impact in your area? To what extent do this organization and like-minded groups contradict the claims about the pervasiveness of rape culture?

Women in Canada's Position in the Gender Inequality Index

How do women fare in our country relative to those in other countries? Table 4.4 shows Canada's ranking relative to other countries on a number of aspects of human development.

While the Gender Inequality Index (GII) does not provide comparisons about harassment, glass ceilings, etc., it does measure gender inequalities in three important aspects of human development:

- reproductive health, measured by maternal mortality ratio and adolescent birth rates;
- empowerment, measured by proportion of parliamentary seats occupied by females and proportion of adult females and males aged 25 years and older with at least some secondary education; and
- economic status, expressed as labour market participation and measured by labour force participation rate of female and male populations aged 15 years and older.

Although Canada ranks in the top 10 of the Human Development Index (HDI) measured by life expectancy, education levels, and per capita income, it ranks 23rd of over 180 countries in the world in the GII. (The United States ranks far lower with a rank of 47.) In large part, Canada's position is due to the low participation of women in politics, and a higher maternal mortality and adolescent birth rate than most countries in the top 10. The GII values vary tremendously across countries, ranging from 0.021 (Slovenia ranking 1st) to 0.709 (Niger ranking 187th).

Questions for Consideration

1. Canada scores poorly for political participation. What kind of intervention might increase political participation by women in Canada?
2. Adolescent birth rates are on the decline in Canada (see Chapter 11). Is there anything that could be done to reduce it further?
3. Are there any more variables that you would like to see in the GII?

TABLE 4.4 Canada's Position in the Gender Inequality Index, 2013

HDI rank	Country	Gender Inequality Index Value, 2013	Gender Inequality Index Rank, 2013	Maternal mortality ratio, 2010	Adolescent birth rate, 2010/2015	Share of seats in parliament, 2013	Population with at least some secondary education, 25+, female, 2005–2012	Population with at least some secondary education 25+, male, 2005–2012	Participation rate, 15+, female, 2012	Participation rate, 15+, male, 2012
Very high human development										
1	Norway	0.068	9	7	7.8	39.6	97.4	96.7	61.5	69.5
2	Australia	0.113	19	7	12.1	29.2	94.3	94.6c	58.8	71.5
3	Switzerland	0.030	2	8	1.9	27.2	95.0	96.6	61.2	75.3
4	Netherlands	0.057	7	6	6.2	37.8	87.7	90.5	79.9	87.3
5	United States	0.262	47	21	31.0	18.2	95.1	94.8	56.8	69.3
6	Germany	0.046	3	7	3.8	32.4	96.3	97.0	53.5	66.4
7	New Zealand	0.185	34	15	25.3	32.2	95.0	95.3	62.1	73.9
8	Canada	0.136	23	12	14.5	28.0	100.0	100.0	61.6	71.2
9	Singapore	0.090	15	3	6.0	24.2	74.1	81.0	59.0	77.5
10	Denmark	0.056	5	12	5.1	39.1	95.5	96.6	59.1	67.5

Source: Selection from Table 4: Gender Inequality Index, United Nations Development Programme Human Development Reports. Retrieved June 1, 2015 (http://hdr.undp.org/en/content/table-4-gender-inequality-index).

PERSPECTIVES ON GENDER INEQUALITY

Unlike functionalist and conflict perspectives, which focus on macro level sources of gender inequality, feminist perspectives focus on both macro structural levels and micro interactional levels. Interactionist perspectives typically focus on social constructs such as language. It is language, interactionists say, that structures our thinking and discourses about domination and subordination.

The Interactionist Perspective

Symbolic interactionists focus on the differential socialization processes that create masculinity and femininity in people. When a child is assigned a gender at birth, typically corresponding to sex, culturally appropriate gender socialization begins wholeheartedly. Children learn which attitudes, skills, behaviours, likes and dislikes, and so on are appropriate for each gender. Many people believe that socialization today has changed, with fewer restrictions on the ways children are taught to act, think, and feel. It is important to recognize that some differences may exist that are class-based, with people from working classes typically enforcing greater conformity to stereotypical roles, as this may mirror the expectations many of them face in their work lives. People from the middle classes often allow children more autonomy, in keeping with their occupations. In all cases, however, despite our ideas that things have changed, gender roles based on stereotypes are so entrenched and pervasive in the dominant culture that pressure to conform is enormous for most children.

Interactionists, who view society as the sum of people's interactions, consider language extremely significant in defining social realities because it provides people with shared meanings and social realities. Historically, what men have thought, written, and concluded have been the givens of our discourse (Peterson and Runyan 1993). Today, however, English and other languages are being criticized for *linguistic sexism*—that is, for words and patterns of communication that ignore, devalue, or sexually objectify women.

Linguistic sexism, some analysts believe, perpetuates traditional gender-role stereotypes and reinforces male dominance. These analysts note that the idea that women are secondary to men in importance is embedded in the English language: the masculine form (*he*) has traditionally been used to refer to human beings generally, and words such as *chairman* and *mankind* are now mostly replaced with *chair* and *humanity*. When a woman enters a profession such as medicine or law, she was frequently referred to as a "female doctor" or "woman lawyer"; these terms are now mostly replaced by doctor and lawyer.

Language can also be used to devalue women by referring to them in terms that reinforce the notion that they are sex objects. Terms such as *fox, bitch, babe, kitten,* or *doll* further devalue women by ascribing petlike, childlike, or toylike attributes to them (Adams and Ware 1995). According to one analyst, at least 220 terms exist for women considered sexually promiscuous, but only 22 terms exist for men considered sexually promiscuous (Stanley 1972). Further, the terms for women are more likely to be derogatory, while those reserved for men are complimentary.

Research by scholars in a variety of disciplines has demonstrated not only the importance of language in patterning our thoughts but also how gender—and the hierarchy it constructs—is built into the English language (Peterson and Runyan 1993). According to sociologists Claire M. Renzetti and Daniel J. Curran (1995:151), "Given that women are denigrated, unequally defined, and often ignored by the English language, it serves not only to reflect their secondary status relative to men in our society, but also to reinforce it."

Linguist Deborah Tannen (1990) has examined how power differentials between women and men at home and in the workplace are reflected in their communication styles. According to Tannen (1990), men and women speak different *genderlects:* women are socialized to speak and hear a language of intimacy and connection, while men are socialized to speak and hear a language of status and independence. For example, women's conversations tend to focus more on relationships with others and include "rapport talk." Men's conversations are more likely to convey messages about their position in the workplace or social hierarchies and include "report talk." In explanation, Tannen (1990:77) states that for most women conversation is about rapport, and for most men talk is about preserving independence and one's position in the social hierarchy.

Men's and women's communication styles also differ. Men are taught to have a more direct style of communication and are more likely to dominate conversations than women are. Men are taught to seek immediate solutions for problems, while women are taught to consider a variety of alternatives before reaching a decision. From this perspective, communication not only reflects women's and men's relative power in society, but also perpetuates gender inequalities.

At the micro level of interactions, we can see some of the ways that male dominance is perpetuated through non-verbal forms of communication, such as bodily movement, posture, eye contact, use of personal space, and touching. Men typically control more space than women do, whether they are sitting or standing. Men tend to invade women's personal space by standing close to them, touching them, or staring at them. Such actions are not necessarily sexual in connotation; however, when a man pats and fondles a flight attendant or a co-worker in the office, these actions do have sexual overtones that cannot be dismissed. Recent sexual harassment cases show that women do not appreciate such acts and feel threatened by them, especially when the toucher is the employer.

Although the interactionist perspective has been criticized for ignoring the larger, structural factors that perpetuate gender inequality, it is important to note that language and communication patterns are embedded in the structure of society and pass from generation to generation through the socialization process.

The Functionalist Perspective

In focusing on macro level issues affecting gender inequality, functionalists frequently examine employment opportunities and the wage gap between men and women.

According to such early functionalists as Talcott Parsons (1955), gender inequality is inevitable because of the biological division of labour: men generally are physically stronger than women and have certain abilities and interests, whereas women, as the only sex able to bear and nurse children, have their own abilities and interests. Given these biological attributes, Parsons said, men find themselves more suited to *instrumental* (goal-oriented) *tasks* and women to *expressive* (emotionally oriented) *tasks*. In the home, therefore, husbands perform such instrumental tasks as providing economic support and making the most important decisions for the family, while wives perform such expressive tasks as nurturing children and providing emotional support for all family members. The division of labour by gender ensures that important societal tasks—such as procreation and the socialization of children—are fulfilled and that the family is socially and economically stable.

According to Parsons, this division of labour continues in the workplace, where women again do expressive work and men again do instrumental work. Thus, women cluster in occupations that require expressive work, such as elementary school teaching, nursing, and secretarial work, because of their interests and abilities. Women also are concentrated in specific specialties within professions such as law and medicine because of their aptitude for expressive work and their desire to spend more time with their families than men, who are in the more lucrative specialties. For example, many women in law specialize in family law, and many women in medicine specialize in pediatrics (infants and children), obstetrics and gynecology (women), or family practice. In corporations, women are thought to be more adept at public

relations and human resources; men are viewed as more adept at financial management.

Other functionalist explanations of gender inequality focus on the human capital that men and women bring to the workplace. According to human capital explanations, what individuals earn is based on choices they have made, including choices about the kinds of training and experience they accumulate. For example, human capital analysts argue that women diminish their human capital when they leave the labour force to engage in child-bearing and child-care activities, which, of course, are not valued and therefore do not increase human capital. While women are out of the labour force, their human capital deteriorates from non-use. When they return to paid employment, they earn lower wages than men do because they have fewer years of work experience and "atrophied human capital" because their education and training may have become obsolete.

Critics of the human capital model note that it is based on the false assumption that all people, regardless of gender, racialization, or other attributes, are evaluated and paid fairly on the basis of their education, training, and other job-enhancing characteristics. It fails to acknowledge that White women, Indigenous people, people of colour, and people with disabilities tend to be paid less when they are employed in occupations dominated by White males, even when they take no time off for family duties.

Conflict Perspectives

Conflict perspectives on gender inequality are based on the assumption that social life is a continuous struggle in which members of powerful groups (males, in this case) seek to maintain control of scarce resources such as social, economic, and political superiority. By dominating individual women and commanding social institutions, men maintain positions of privilege and power. However, as conflict theorists note, not all men are equally privileged: men in the upper classes have greater economic power because they control elite positions in corporations, universities, the mass media, and government.

Conflict theorists using a Marxist approach believe that gender inequality primarily results from capitalism and private ownership of the means of production. The gendered division of labour is seen to be inherent in capitalism and, therefore, will disappear with its demise. With the development of private property and inheritance based upon primogeniture, women were transformed from equal, productive members of society in hunting-and-gathering and feudal economies into subordinate wives (and also into property or "chattel"). Further, with the institution of bourgeois marriage, women found it necessary to exchange their sexual and reproductive services for economic support. As industrialization progressed and production moved further from the home, women's skills and education became increasingly separate from those required in the paid labour force. Therefore, according to conflict theorists, the subordinate position of women is the result not of biology, as functionalists believe, but of structural and historical relations.

Conflict theories have been criticized for their view that gender inequality is an inherent and inevitable feature of capitalist relations and for the simplistic and androcentric view that the liberation of women is dependent solely on the liberation of the working class.

Feminist Perspectives

Feminist perspectives in general challenge the status quo with regard to the unequal position of females in society. Feminism, however, is far from being a unified voice. Instead, it is multifaceted, critical, and activist, seeing both the scope of the problem of gender inequality and its solutions differently. Basing their work on a Marxist approach, *socialist feminists* state that under capitalism, men gain control over property and over women. Thus, *capitalism* exploits women in the workplace, and *patriarchy* exploits women at home. According to this perspective, capitalists benefit from the gendered division of labour in the workplace because they can pay women lower wages and derive higher profits. Cultural ideas about the appropriateness of women in the home ensure that women return to the home after any stints in the paid labour force (for example, as a worker in the reserve army of labour required by a capitalist economy— see Chapter 2). At the same time, individual men benefit from the unpaid work women do at home by simply not having to do it and by having more leisure time to recuperate from labouring in the capitalist marketplace. The capitalist economic system is maintained because women literally reproduce the next generation of workers while also providing current employees (often including also themselves) with food, clean clothes, and other goods and services that are necessary for those who must show up at the workplace each day. In addition, men who labour under capitalism can feel a sense of power by having a superior social position to women and may be less apt to agitate. Marxist feminist perspectives have been criticized for their emphasis on male dominance without a corresponding analysis of how men may also be oppressed by capitalism and/or patriarchy.

Unlike socialist feminists, *radical feminists* focus exclusively on *patriarchy* as the primary source of gender inequality. From this perspective, men's oppression of women is deliberate, with ideological justification provided by other institutions such as the media and religion. The subordination of women is naturalized through gendered assumptions inherent in patriarchy. Radical feminism challenges patriarchy and male hegemony, seeing many traditional institutions—the nuclear family in particular—as sites of female enslavement and "domestic servitude" (Fleras 2001:133). Radical feminists are criticized for their focus on patriarchy to the exclusion of other structures of domination (such as class oppression and racism).

Liberal feminists believe that gender inequality is rooted in *gender-role socialization*, which perpetuates women's lack of equal rights and educational opportunities. This type of feminism arises out of classical liberal notions of individual freedoms or liberty. Women are seen to be unequal because they are not given access to the opportunities to make comparable wages and so on. The aim of this type of feminism, therefore, is to ensure that women are equally distributed in education and the paid labour force, alongside men. The system is seen as inherently sound and would be transformed with the removal of discriminatory barriers. Liberal feminism is criticized for its lack of focus on the structural roots of inequalities.

Black feminists, Indigenous feminists, and other feminists "of colour" believe that Indigenous women and women of colour face heightened inequalities based on the multiplicative effect of racialization, class, and gender as simultaneous forces of oppression. Oppressions are seen as intersecting patterns of subordination that cannot be viewed or treated as separate issues, but rather must be seen as a complex whole (see Chapter 3). Solutions to gender inequality, therefore, are inextricably linked with solutions to oppression generally. Lesbians and women with disabilities also experience the effects of this matrix of domination in our hierarchically organized society. Feminists from the so-called margins, those who experience multilayered oppressions, have led the much-needed critique of other feminist perspectives, advancing the incisiveness of feminist perspectives overall and strengthening activism across difference.

HOW CAN GENDER INEQUALITY BE REDUCED?

Although the rights and working conditions of women have improved during the past 50 years, much remains to be done before gender inequality is eradicated or even significantly reduced. As for how, specifically, to go about reducing gender inequality, a point that was made in previous chapters bears repeating: how people view social problems directly affects how they think the problem should be solved. Interactionists, for example, think that one way gender inequality can be reduced is to redefine social realities such as linguistic sexism. In their view, language should be modified so that it no longer conveys notions of male superiority and female inferiority, which are then transmitted through the socialization process.

Some functionalists believe that traditional gender roles should be redefined for the well-being of individuals and society, but other functionalists suggest that women should become more aware of how their human capital is diminished by decisions they make. From this perspective, to be competitive in the workplace, women must have the same educational background and qualifications for positions that men have. As part of the plan to educate women, International Women's Day (IWD) was founded and now takes place every March 8. The theme of the 2015 IWD was *Make It Happen*, designed to encourage effective action for advancing and recognizing women. There have been close to annual international women's days since 1911. In some places, like China, Russia, and Bulgaria, it is a national holiday. The IWD has a global hub home page, which outlines the major themes, identifies the participating countries and their programs (in 2015 Canada had 156 programs), provides resources, and so on. The website states that 1000+ programs from around the world are uploaded to their site. It is also possible to follow IWD on Facebook, Twitter, Pinterest, LinkedIn, and other social media. Functionalists suggest that overt sex discrimination can be reduced by enforcing existing legislation such as the *Canadian Charter of Human Rights and Freedoms* or various provincial human rights codes, which forbid discrimination on the basis of sex or gender. However, this approach would not affect covert or institutionalized discrimination, which has a negative and differential impact on White, non-White, and Indigenous women.

While some conflict theorists view elimination of sex discrimination as the primary solution for gender inequality, those using a Marxist approach believe that gender equality will occur simultaneously when capitalism is abolished. Socialist feminists agree that it should be discarded and a new economy that eliminates the gendered division of labour and the wage gap between women and men should be developed. Liberal feminists say that we could reduce gender inequality by dramatically changing gender socialization and what children learn from their families, teachers, and the media about appropriate masculine and feminine attitudes and behaviour. Radical feminists suggest that gender inequality can be reduced only when patriarchy is abolished. To achieve this goal, they say that the legal system must continue to provide relief for sex discrimination, especially sexual

harassment in schools and the workplace, and that alternative institutions must be developed to replace existing gendered social institutions. For example, women's health care centres should replace male-dominated medical practices, and child-care and elder-care centres should assume some of women's caregiving burdens. Finally, Black feminists and other feminists "from the margins" believe that equality will occur only when all women—regardless of racialization, class, gender, age, religion, sexual orientation, and ability or disability—are treated equitably (Andersen and Collins 1997).

Clearly, many gender issues remain unresolved. As a result of technological changes and the proliferation of service jobs, such as information clerk, nurses' aide, and fast-food restaurant worker, which often are equated with "women's work," gender-segregated jobs may increase rather than decrease. Moreover, if the number and quality of "men's jobs" shrink, some men at all class levels may become more resistant to women entering traditionally male-dominated occupations and professions. Many analysts suggest that for a significant reduction in gender inequality to occur, women have to become more involved in the political arena and take action themselves (see Chapter 13). Box 4.2 showed that Canada has a low number of women in parliament. Again, however, this view implies that the system itself is essentially sound and that reform is possible using the tools that have been traditionally available. What do you think?

WHAT CAN YOU DO?

Gender inequality is a complex social problem that is rooted in structural sexism and manifests itself every day in actions in interpersonal interactions. In terms of proactive things that you can do, then, much depends on the situations you most often find yourself in, as well as what your interests are. Below are a few suggestions for social action that is either preventative or interventionist. What others can you think of?

- Get involved in political actions in your province or territory by joining in protests and teach-ins and by writing letters to MPs/MLAs and the newspapers (e.g., about pay equity).
- Create a program for International Women's Day and upload it to their website for next March 8.
- Lobby government to restore and increase core funding for women-serving organizations such as women's shelters, women's centres, and sexual assault centres. Write letters to government officials linking your thoughts with your vote.
- Fundraise alone (smaller-scale effort) or with others (larger-scale effort) to support women-serving organizations in your municipality.

- Create coalitions, along with other justice-seeking groups, to raise awareness of the gender inequality issue of interest to you.

- Start or join a group aimed at effecting change on an issue of interest to you. For example, many small groups of men at university and college campuses across Canada have started groups and campaigns to end violence against women. After the shooting in Montreal, men organized a White Ribbon Campaign to talk to their peers about the relationship of men to sexualized violence against women.

- Sign on to Internet listservs and websites of groups and organizations whose interests you share as a means of keeping up to date on the issues and informing others.

- Break the cultural taboo about wage secrecy and share information about wages as widely as possible with co-workers. Many businesses explicitly instruct employees not to discuss their wages. It is very possible that these places are paying people inequitably. You may be surprised to find where you are on the wage scale, despite what company representatives imply. If there are inequities, expose them and lobby the company to redress the situations of underpaid workers.

- When you are being told a sexist joke (or a joke that is typically inherently sexist, like a "blonde joke"), explain to the person that the joke perpetuates harmful and derogatory stereotypes about women and that you do not find it amusing to demean others.

- Be alert and open to hearing about (other) women's experiences with sexism or violence. Ask women you know what their experiences have been. Educate yourself about people's differing experiences—talk to males and females, White women and non-White women, lesbians, trans people, and so on. Try to hear the experience without judgment.

- Report violence whenever you see or hear it by calling 911. Do not get involved in a situation that is unsafe physically: call law enforcement.

- Go to court and watch the trials of men charged with sexual assault, assaulting a woman, or femicide. Critically analyze the approach of the justice system to the case. How did police handle it? How did lawyers handle it? How did the judge handle it? Write a letter to the local newspaper and/or your college/university newspaper with your analysis.

- Think about all the words you use that are gender exclusive and/or sexist. Think of words you can use to replace them and begin practising. (Don't worry about not being perfect! It takes a long time to unlearn this.)

- Educate yourself and others about trans issues. You may even know a trans person and be unaware of it. Try not to assume. Support trans people when and wherever they are.

- Support people's inalienable right to feel comfortable in their own skin.

- Include trans issues whenever you talk or write about gender. In the words of renowned feminist scholar Adrienne Rich (1984:13), "When someone with the authority of a teacher describes the world and you are not in it, there is a moment of psychic disequilibrium, as if you looked into a mirror and saw nothing."

- Next time you, a friend, or a relative has a child, look for gender-neutral clothing, accessories, and toys and books that promote gender equality.

- Think of any gender-stereotypical assumptions you have and challenge them.

- Consumerism is power. Begin a boycott campaign against companies that use women in narrow, stereotypical, and objectified ways in advertising. Write to the company and tell it what you are doing and why and in what ways you are planning to get your boycott message out (examples can be found on the Canadian White Ribbon Campaign site.

- Write a letter to the newspaper or advertise in some other way about companies that have gender-equitable policies, wages, and so on. This demonstrates to all companies that the public is watching and does care.

- Report offences and breeches to the appropriate person or office (e.g., police, ombuds offices, or anti-harassment offices on campuses). Be persistent. Get support. Be an advocate for people whose voices are marginalized in these systems. Help them to report and follow up, if appropriate.

- Volunteer for crisis lines, sexual assault centres, and women's shelters (men can volunteer in many of these places by going out and doing community education and/or fundraising, for example). It is important to demonstrate to the community that violence against women is not a women's issue—it is a community issue.

- If you witness sexual harassment in a public place, lend support to the person suffering and/or make it uncomfortable for the perpetrator to harass (again, do not take risks to your own safety, but intervene where and when possible).

- Think about ways in which your actions and words maintain current beauty standards. Think of ways to celebrate and support all women.

- Read books by pro-feminist men that analyze and help unravel male privilege and that suggest alternatives to "going with the flow" and perpetuating sexism. Some great examples are *The Macho Paradox* by Jackson Katz, *Unraveling the Gender Knot* by Allan Johnson, *New Black Man* by Mark Anthony Neal, and *Guyland* by Michael Kimmel.

- Begin discussions with your family and friends about an issue of sexism that interests you. Inform people about some of the facts you have learned and explain why you feel the situation is unjust.

- Make music, make art, make word collages, make zines—whatever—that promote the message that gender inequality is unjust and has got to go. Get your message out there!

SUMMARY

How Does Sex Differ from Gender?

Sex refers to the biological and physiological aspects of being male or female or intersex; gender is the socially constructed sets of attitudes that dictate what is deemed appropriate, in term of masculinity and/or femininity, for the sexes. In short, sex is what we (generally) are born with; gender is what we acquire through socialization. We currently operate under a two-sex, two-gender system that views male–female and masculine–feminine as not only different, but also binary opposites.

What Are the Primary Socializing Agents?

The key socializing agents are parents, peers, teachers and schools, and the media, all of which may reinforce gender stereotypes and gender-based inequalities as they attempt to teach culturally based gender-appropriate behaviour.

How Are Sexism and Patriarchy Related?

Individual and institutional sexism are maintained and reinforced by patriarchy, a hierarchical system in which cultural, political, and economic structures are dominated by males.

What Are Some of the Primary Causes of Gender Inequality?

Gender inequality results from economic, political, and educational discrimination against women as evidenced in gender-segregated work, which in turn results in a disparity—or wage gap—between women's and men's earnings. Even when women are employed in the same job as men, on average they do not receive the same (or even comparable) pay.

What Is the Second Shift? Why Is It a Problem for Women?

The second shift is the unpaid household work and child care performed by employed women. Many women have a second shift because of their dual responsibilities in the workplace and at home. The typical woman in Canada who combines paid work in the labour force with parenting and housework does not have enough hours in the average day to fulfill all her responsibilities, and many men have been unwilling or unable to pick up some of the slack at home. Women, thus, employ a variety of creative strategies for coping with this problem such as sacrificing leisure time and sleep.

How Does Symbolic Interactionism Explain Gender Inequality?

Symbolic interactionists view gender inequality as the result of faulty gender-role socialization, in which language use, including body language, plays a significant role. Inequality between the sexes is seen to exist and be perpetuated through the use of gender-exclusive and/or sexist language and through non-verbal actions, such as male invasion of female space or males touching females in mixed-gender interactions.

How Do Functionalist and Conflict Analysts Explain the Gendered Division of Labour?

According to functionalist analysts, women's caregiver roles in contemporary industrialized societies are crucial in ensuring that key societal tasks are fulfilled. While the husband performs the instrumental tasks of economic support and decision making, the wife assumes the expressive tasks of providing affection and emotional support for the family. According to conflict analysts, the gendered division of labour within families and the workplace results from male control and dominance over women and resources.

What Are the Major Feminist Perspectives? How Do They Explain Gender Inequality?

In liberal feminism, gender equality is connected to equality of opportunity. In radical feminism, male dominance is seen as the cause of oppression. According to socialist feminists, women's oppression results from capitalism and patriarchy and women's dual roles as paid and unpaid workers. Antiracist feminism and other feminisms focus on matrices of oppression, linking gender inequality with other forms of oppression, such as class oppression, racialization, sexual orientation or preference, ability, and age.

KEY TERMS

androcentricity, p. 67
gender, p. 67
gendered division of labour, p. 69
gender ideology, p. 69
glass ceiling, p. 76

intersectionality, p. 73
intersexed, p. 67
patriarchy, p. 64
rape culture, p. 72
sex, p. 67

sexism, p. 64
sexual harassment, p. 74
wage gap, p. 73

QUESTIONS FOR CRITICAL THINKING

1. Examine the various administrative offices and academic departments at your college or university. What is the gender breakdown of administrators, faculty, and staff in selected departments? Can you identify a gender-related pattern associated with women's and men's work at your school? What conclusions can you draw about the relationship between gender and employment, based on your observations? Are there any policies in place to counteract gendered inequities in that workplace? Do they work? Why or why not?

2. Will the increasing numbers of women in higher education, the workplace, and the military, particularly in non-traditional positions or majors, tip the balance of power between men and women and result in greater gender equality in the future? Explain why or why not.

3. What is the role of violence against women in our culture? In what ways do music videos perpetuate a "rape culture" and violence against women in Canada? What could be done to change this?

4. In what ways does traditional gender socialization support capitalism?

ANN ELIZABETH CARSON—poet, writer, sculptor, feminist—was selected as one of Toronto's Mille Femmes at the 2008 Luminato Festival, which paid tribute to women who have made a contribution to the arts. Ann has published *Shadows Light* (a collection of poetry and sculptures), *My Grandmother's Hair* (a tale about how our family stories make our memories and shape our lives), *The Risks of Remembrance* (a collection of new poems), and *We All Become Stories* (12 conversations about the experiences of old age and memory). Her latest book, *Laundry Lines*, includes reflections in prose and poetry. Ann is a former counsellor, a supervisor and instructor at York University, and a recently retired psychotherapist focusing on expressive therapies. At age 84, she continues to write, sculpt, and read from her work in solo and collaborative events, and to lead workshops in the arts. She enjoys music, theatre, gardening, gallery hopping, bookstore browsing, and the company of her family and friends.

Author's personal communication, April, 2013

It has been frequently noted that our society is aging. Figure 5.1 shows the growth of the proportion of seniors in our population from a small segment of the population pyramid in 1956 to the largest segment in 2056, if conditions remain as projected. But this aging might not be as negative as some suggest when so many seniors like Ann Carson are contributing to our society.

Ann Carson's example indicates that it is still possible to make a substantial contribution to society years after the traditional retirement age. Two terms can help us distinguish between people's actual age and their performance. Although Ann's *chronological age*—age based on date of birth—is quite high, her *functional age*—individual attributes such as physical appearance, mobility, strength, coordination, and mental capacity that are used to assign people to age categories (McPherson and Wister 2008:17)—is considerably lower. Although we may appear to be younger or older than our chronological age, there are some things that we do in life, such as driving a car or voting, that are determined by our chronological age rather than our functional age. For the younger person, then, changes in

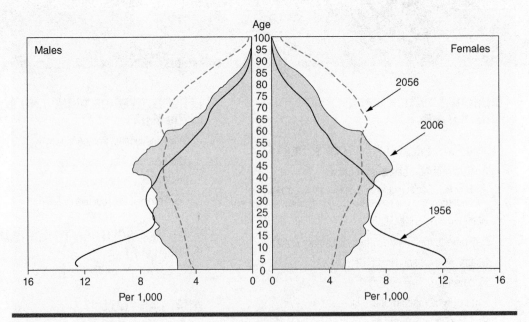

Figure 5.1 Changes in Age Structure of the Canadian Population.

Source: *Statistics Canada, 2007, "Canadian Demographics at a Glance," Catalogue number 91-003-XWE. Retrieved April 6, 2012 (http://www.statcan.gc.ca/pub/91-003-x/2007001/figures/4129870-eng.htm).*

chronological and functional age are positive. However, as some people age, they begin to lose some of their functional abilities, such as vision or hearing, that are necessary for driving. Thus, the older person may view changes in chronological and functional age negatively. The field of *gerontology* examines the biological, physical, and social aspects of the aging process. In this chapter, we focus primarily on *social gerontology*—**the study of the social (nonphysical) aspects of aging**—as we examine age classifications in Canada and such problems as ageism, workplace discrimination, retirement, income security, leisure, health, illness and health care, victimization, family relationships, housing and long-term care, and death and dying. To provide a comparative portrait of the situation and experiences of seniors, we also make several comparisons to younger people.

Finally, the sociological perspectives are used to help explain aging problems. The chapter concludes with a discussion of ways to reduce inequality based on age and what you can do about it.

CHARACTERISTICS OF LATER MATURITY AND OLD AGE

Later maturity is usually considered to begin in the 60s. The major changes associated with this stage are social. Although many people in their 60s retain sufficient physical strength to be able to carry on an active social life, their peer groups can shrink noticeably as friends and relatives die. Many people in later maturity find themselves caring for people of their own age and older.

Old age is usually considered to begin in the late 60s or in the 70s. Although some people continue to work past age 70, most have left paid employment by their 70th birthday. The chances of heart attacks, strokes, and cancer increase, along with the likelihood of some diseases that primarily affect the elderly. Alzheimer's disease, a degenerative disease that attacks the brain and severely impairs memory, thinking, and behaviour, may be the best-known example. People with this disease have an impaired ability to function in everyday social roles; over time, they cease to be able to recognize people they have always known, and they lose all sense of their own identity. Finally, they may revert to a speechless childishness, at which point others must feed them, dress them, sit them on the toilet, and lead them around by the hand. According to the Alzheimer's Society, today in Canada there are likely over 747 000 people suffering from dementia. The organization projects that in 2031, 1.4 million Canadians will be suffering from one of several kinds of dementia (Alzheimer's Society 2013).

Gerontologists have come to realize that there are significant differences among people who are now called the "young-old" (ages 65 to 74), the "middle-old" (ages 75 to 84), and the "old-old" (ages 85 and older). Although more than half of all people aged 65 and older are in the young-old category, the old-old category has grown more rapidly over the past two decades than has any other age group in Canada. In 2011, the number of seniors aged 65 or older was estimated at 5,186,800. They represented 14.9 percent of the total population, up from 11.6 percent in 1992. The proportion of seniors will grow rapidly in the coming years as baby boomers reach the age of 65 (see Figure 5.1). Another indication of the growth of seniors is the growth of centenarians (those 100+ years old). Statistics Canada projects that the number of centenarians will increase from 5825 in 2011 to 63 700 in 2056 (Statistics Canada 2013c). As with other age categories, it is difficult to make generalizations about older people. But it is not true that all old people feel lonely and lost in retirement, live in institutions, and are uniform in their health, activities, and financial situation. In addition, many seniors provide a great deal of time and financial support for their families and/or charitable organizations. (Novak and Campbell 2010:296).

PROBLEMS LINKED TO BEING ELDERLY

Ageism and Age-Based Stereotypes

Ageism—**prejudice and discrimination against people on the basis of age**—is a social problem that particularly stigmatizes and marginalizes older people. Gerontologist Robert Butler (1969) introduced the term *ageism* to describe how myths and misconceptions about older people produce age-based discrimination. According to Butler, just as racism and sexism perpetuate stereotyping and discrimination against people of colour and all women, ageism perpetuates stereotyping of older people and age-based discrimination. Most research has therefore focused on the negative and differential impact ageism has on older people. There are more stereotypes about the physical and mental abilities of older people than there are about the abilities of people in any other age category (see Box 5.1).

In 2012, Revera, a leading provider of seniors' accommodation, care, and services, conducted a study on ageism that probed Canadians (N = 1501) aged 18–32 (Gen Y), 33–45 (Gen X), 46–65 (Boomers), 66–74 (Seniors), and 75+ (Older Seniors) to find out their attitudes about aging and to gauge their level of awareness and experience with ageism. The report was written with The International Federation on Ageing

(IFA), an international, non-governmental organization and point of global connection for experts and expertise in the field of aging (Revera 2012:16).

The findings included the following:

- Six in ten (63 percent) seniors 66 years of age and older say they have been treated unfairly or differently because of their age.
- One third (35 percent) of Canadians admit they have treated someone differently because of their age; this statistic goes as high as 43 percent for Gen X and 42 percent for Gen Y respondents.
- Half (51 percent) of Canadians say ageism is the most tolerated social prejudice when compared to gender- or race-based discrimination.

- Over three quarters (79 percent) of Canadians agree that seniors 75 years and older are seen as less important and are more often ignored than younger generations in society.
- Seven in ten (71 percent) of respondents agree that Canadian society values younger generations more than older generations.
- One in five (21 percent) respondents says older Canadians are a burden on society (Revera 2012:5).

The study recommended that individuals should shine a spotlight on ageism; organizations should increase awareness of ageism and make contributions to ensure that it does not occur in the workplace and other institutions; and policy makers such as government and non-governmental

Social Problems in the Media

Media Ageism: Preferring Younger and Stereotyping Older Age Groups

Although media coverage of teenagers can be negative, as soon as teenagers turn 18 years of age, the media want to attract them. Advertisers focus on 18- to 34-year-olds because the advertisers believe that if this segment is attracted to products, they will maintain "brand loyalty." Older segments of the population, according to the advertisers, have already made up their minds.

One of the other consequences of advertisers' beliefs is that television and radio networks change or drop programs well established with the 50+ age group to appeal to younger viewers and listeners. Whereas many programs with older actors, such as Angela Lansbury (*Murder She Wrote*), Andy Griffith (*Matlock*), and Betty White and the rest (*The Golden Girls*), were on prime time until the mid-1990s, and *The West Wing* until mid-2006, few shows have older actors.

But this might be changing. Perhaps surprisingly, a continuing demand exists for *The Golden Girls*. In June 2009, Betty White said, "When the DVD came out, I thought who's going to watch it? We're on four times a day. They know the lines better than we ever did. But sure enough, the DVD keeps selling all over the world. I hear from Finland, Bangladesh, Sri Lanka" (Ehrbar 2009:49). More people want to watch older women than advertisers think. Betty White went on to have another successful series, *Hot in Cleveland*. Several other senior females are in great demand. Helen Mirren still has a successful television career starring in many British TV series, some of which have been shown in North America (such as *Prime Suspect* and *Elizabeth I*), and a movie career (starring recently in *Hitchcock* and *Red*). Judi Dench continues to enjoy several movie roles (e.g., *Shakespeare in Love* and playing Queen Victoria in *Mrs. Brown*) and M in

James Bond movies. Meryl Streep is well known for many Academy Awards nominations, winning three. Actors Jessica Lange and Charlotte Rampling, both over 65 years of age, are also seen in cosmetics advertisements.

Some older men are in demand as well. Christopher Plummer has received an Academy Award, a Golden Globe Award, an Emmy, and Tony Awards. Donald Sutherland is still making TV shows and has won two Golden Globe Awards. It was true that a couple of decades ago seniors were treated in an ageist fashion, but this seems to be over. As the population ages, more opportunities are occurring for older actors, who will not tolerate being the butt of jokes.

However, magazine and TV ads still promote products that attempt to make people look younger. Advertisements for vacations or for community living show people who look young (i.e., in their late 50s and early 60s), while older people are not actually moving into residences until they are in their mid-80s.

Questions for Consideration

1. What should media do about the nature of their coverage of elderly people?
2. Do the media treat men and women differently?
3. To what extent should the media, particularly public media like the CBC, organize their programming to appeal to different age groups?

Independent Research

Review magazines ads to determine those which treat men and women across age categories as worthy. Do these ads emphasize physical appearance? What other attributes do they highlight?

organizations should develop policies to reduce its impact (Revera 2012:14).

Clearly, our place in the social structure changes during our life course, and if we live long enough, any of us may become the target of stereotyping and discrimination directed at older people.

Workplace Discrimination

Despite the *Canadian Charter of Rights and Freedoms,* which protects all Canadians against discrimination based on many characteristics including age, many subtle forms of age discrimination in the workplace remain. This does not include mandatory retirement, which has now been eliminated in all the provinces and territories. Still, some employers prefer younger workers to older workers, whom they believe have health problems, poor motivation, and low ability. Employers may hire younger workers because they believe that they can pay them less than older workers and make more demands on their time and energy. Older employees sometimes find that their employers have downgraded their job descriptions, failed to promote them or grant them raises, or are trying to push them out of their jobs so that cheaper workers can be hired. In a study of Statistics Canada's employment numbers from 2000 to 2004, Chhinzer and Ababneh reported that younger workers aged 25 to 34 were a third less likely to experience a layoff than an older worker (Grant 2008:B10).

Despite the negative stereotypes, some employers have found it profitable to keep or hire older employees, and some older employees, especially professionals, continue working long past 65 years. Since the numbers of people 55+ is increasing (see Figure 5.1), a higher percentage of workers 55+ is working now than in the past. As shown in Figure 5.2, the percentage of total workers both male and female 55+ years has increased since 1976 from 12 percent to almost 18 percent.

The end of mandatory retirement makes it possible for older people to continue working. However, new problems will likely emerge, perhaps around removing people who are thought to be unable to do the job.

Retirement: Income Security and Leisure Activities

The *retirement principle* is the "idea that at a fixed age, regardless of mental or physical ability, a person leaves work" (Novak and Campbell 2010:211). In the past, people in many occupations and professions (including tenured faculty members at universities, police officers, and fire fighters) faced mandatory retirement at age 65, regardless of their health or desire to continue working. It was simply assumed that everyone experienced a decline in physical and mental ability at a specific age.

The severe decline in the value of pensions and investments that occurred because of the market crash in the fall of 2008 may have resulted in many more people continuing to work after age 65. An October 2008 study by Desjardins Financial found that 42 percent of Canadians over the age of 40 plan to delay retirement because of the global recession (Grant 2008:B10). The Toronto and New York stock markets have now mostly recovered (as of spring 2015), so much of seniors' assets have also recovered. Do you think this will change retirement patterns?

Another advantage of continuing to work is a reduction in the chances of early dementia. The Associated Press reported findings from the French government's research agency which studied the charts of 429 000 people, mostly small shopkeepers and craftsmen and women, whose average age was 74. The results indicated that those who retired at age 65 had a 15 percent lower risk of contracting dementia than had earlier retirees (Associated

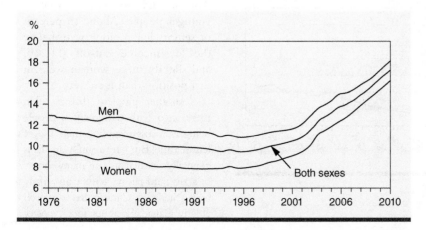

Figure 5.2 Percentage of Workers over 55 in Canadian Labour Force, 1976–2010.

Source: *Statistics Canada, 2011. "Delayed retirement: A new trend?" Retrieved August 19, 2013 (http://www.statcan.gc.ca/pub/75-001-x/2011004/charts-graphiques/11578/cg00d-eng.htm).*

Press 2013). This reduction in risk is probably present for anyone who keeps their mind active.

The next problem to deal with is the orientation of the retiree. Many are well prepared with good health, friends, and financial resources. Others are not so well prepared. A small percentage of people exist who are enjoying life less after retirement, and these are the people whose health is fair or poor, who do not have much financial support, and who did not plan for retirement.

While some retirees are enjoying life less than others, fewer Canadians are suffering now from income insecurity in their retirement than in the past, and most retirees are far from being dependent. Some even provide financial support to children and grandchildren. The results of a global study conducted by Oxford University's Institute of Ageing showed that "16 percent of those in their 60s and nearly one-third of those in their 70s provide financial support to grandchildren" (Galt 2007:B5). Using data collected from 1983 to 2004 by Statistics Canada, on average, Canadian workers had family disposable incomes at age 75, when most are retired, that were 80 percent of their incomes at age 55, when they were working. Naturally, the extent to which Canadians maintained their income in retirement varied with their level of income and availability of pensions. However, those with the lowest incomes did not experience a worse financial situation, whereas wealthier Canadian workers experienced a substantial financial decline after they retired. The richest workers, those in the top 20 percent of the income distribution at age 55, received on average about 70 percent of their working income during their 70s. The people in the lowest 20 percent of income earners saw no decline in their income because they received various transfer payments, such as Old Age Security

(OAS) and Guaranteed Income Supplement (GIS), an income supplement for those with a low income or no income other than OAS, and, if they were working, the Canada or Quebec Pension Plan (CPP/QPP). Over this period, as illustrated in Figure 5.3, the percentage of senior low-income earners declined substantially. The percentage of low-income Canadians aged 65 and older declined from more than 33 percent in 1976 to just over 10 percent in 2010. Canada had the third lowest poverty rate of seniors of all the OECD countries (Conference Board 2013).

A new retirement financial concern has recently been raised: the percentage of a RRIF (registered retirement income fund, which the RRSP must be converted to), that must be withdrawn and taxed each year might eliminate the fund too quickly. In fact, 7.38 percent of the income must be withdrawn at age 71, and that percentage increases until age 90 when 20 percent of the fund must be withdrawn. Given how long people are living, very little of this fund could be left in one's final years.

Most seniors in Canada are doing well. The Global Age Index of 2013, an index that ranks the well-being of older people (60+ years), places Canada fifth among 91 nations of the world regarding a combination of health status, income security, employment and education, and enabling environment, just two points behind first place Sweden (Global Age Watch 2013). But a recent rise in poverty over the last few years (see Figure 5.3) and subgroups of seniors experiencing problems are reasons for concern. The cause of the former concern is that the rate of the government's increases in payouts has not been as high since the mid-1990s as it was before that time. Regarding the latter concern, a major subgroup not doing so well is those seniors living alone. Figure 11.5 in Chapter 11 shows that in 2010, seniors living alone, especially women, did not fare as well as younger people. About 15 percent of seniors living alone were below the low-income cut-off (LICO), and slightly more women were in that position than men were.

Another problem that is often mentioned with retirement is people being at a loss regarding their use of leisure time. But here again, Canadians generally participate in many hours of active and passive leisure on a daily basis. Statistics Canada has surveyed elderly Canadians about four types of

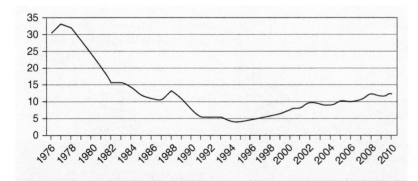

Figure 5.3   Canada's Elderly Poverty Rate (percent).

Source: *Conference Board of Canada, 2013, "Elderly Poverty." Retrieved June 21, 2013 (http://www.conferenceboard.ca/hcp/details/society/elderly-poverty.aspx).*

leisure activity: passive leisure, cognitive leisure, social leisure, and physical leisure:

- Passive leisure consists of such activities as watching television, listening to the radio, and taking pleasure drives.
- Cognitive leisure is made up of reading books or newspapers, taking part in educational activities, attending entertainment events, participating in hobbies, playing cards, and using the computer or the Internet.
- Social leisure includes socializing with friends and relatives and talking on the phone.
- Physical leisure includes all physical recreation.

Cognitive leisure, social leisure, and physical leisure can be combined to form active leisure in comparison to the passive leisure activities.

Passive and active leisure both increase after 65 years for men and women. Men participate in about four hours of active and passive active leisure, and women participate in four hours of active leisure and slightly more than three hours of passive leisure per day (Turcotte and Schellenberg 2007).

Health, Illness, and Health Care

Many seniors lead active lives. Studies show that many older people are not developing the disabling diseases that were common in the past, and the vast majority function quite well. Improvement in the health status of older people has been attributed, at least in part, to better education (knowing what to do and not to do to stay healthy),

nutrition, and public health care. Figure 5.4 shows that a high percentage of people 65 years of age and older with university education report having excellent or very good health. Since the number of people with university education is increasing, it is likely that in the future a higher percentage of people will report excellent or very good health.

However, this positive outlook is not true for Indigenous people in Canada. Figure 10.2, shows that for both Indigenous males and females, the percentage of seniors who report excellent or very good health is much below that of the total Canadian population. The percentage of Indigenous seniors who report a high level of health is slightly lower than those with less than high-school education in the total population (see Figure 5.4). This finding might also be predicted from the fact that 79 percent of Indigenous seniors have less than high-school education.

Despite feeling healthy, people aged 65 and older account for about one third of all dollars spent on health care, and this figure is expected to rise dramatically with the aging of the Canadian population. Many believe the cost problems associated with health care will be further intensified by the feminization of aging—the formerly increasing proportion of older people who are female—because women, on average, have a greater likelihood of being poor and having no spouse to care for them (Weitz 1996). Some researchers state that dire predictions of skyrocketing costs are greatly overstated. The National Health Expenditure Trends 1975–2012 report

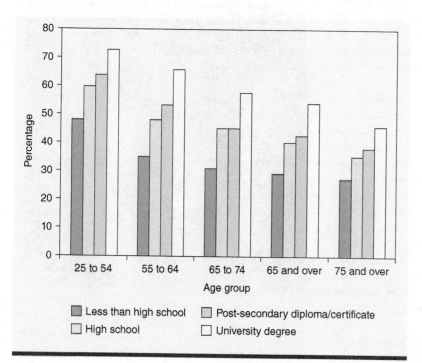

Figure 5.4 Percentage of Canadians Reporting Excellent or Very Good Health, by Age Group and Level of Education, 2003.

Source: *Martin Turcotte and Grant Schellenberg, 2007,* A Portrait of Seniors in Canada, *Ottawa: Statistics Canada, Social and Aboriginal Statistics Division.*

states that population aging has been a relatively modest contributor to costs. A study by Ramlo and Berlin of British Columbia's growth in health care costs found that only 14 percent of the change in health care costs from 1976 to 2009 was due to the aging of the population. Increased consumption of services and industry specific inflation was the greatest driver of expenditure (59 percent), followed by CPI inflation (19 percent) and population growth (7 percent) (2010:8). However, the impact of the aging of the population on health care spending varied considerably by province. It was more significant in the Atlantic provinces and Quebec, for example, than in Ontario and the west (Canadian Institute for Health Information 2013:16).

Victimization

Although older people are in fact less likely than younger people to be victims of violent crime (see Figure 4.1), they fear this type of crime more than people in other age categories do. According to police-reported statistics, in 2011 (see Figure 4.1), there were more than 2850 senior victims of family-related violence, representing 61 senior victims per 100 000 population. Data from a subset of police-reported crimes show that violence against seniors has remained stable over the past three years. In addition, seniors were more likely to be victimized by someone they knew than by a stranger. Senior victims of violence were more likely to be victimized by an adult child or a current or former spouse. Among both men and women, the rate of family violence against seniors was considerably lower compared to victims of other ages. For example, the rate of family violence among senior women was close to 10 times lower than the rate for women aged 25 to 34 (Brennan 2013).

Older victims of violence may be more vulnerable to complications resulting from physical violence than younger victims are, since physical injuries may worsen pre-existing health problems or inhibit an older person's ability to function independently. Many analysts believe that family violence is under-reported because people who know of the abuse are unwilling to report it, and older people who are the victims are either too ashamed or afraid to notify authorities. Although some analysts initially believed that younger people were likely to exploit older people who were psychologically and economically dependent on them, just the opposite has often proven true: younger people are more likely to exploit elders on whom they themselves are dependent (Novak and Campbell 2010:322).

Safe havens have now been created for abused seniors. The first one was created in Calgary. Edmonton has one that has expanded to seven apartment units. There are now apartments in Surrey, B.C., Winnipeg, and Toronto, the last one called Pat's Place (addresses are not given to protect the seniors). Pat's Place is not a traditional shelter, but rather an apartment where a person can receive counselling and will be helped to create a long-term plan.

Other kinds of abuse besides violence exist, including emotional, financial, sexual, and neglect. A study of abuse was conducted in 2009 by the Canadian Association of Retired People (CARP) of its own members (N = about 2500) who received *ActionOnline* an E-Newsletter, who are likely to be more educated, more active, and more wealthy than senior Canadians generally. The authors reported that 10 percent of their members reported some kind of abuse: 15 percent emotional, 5 percent financial, 2 percent sexual, 1 percent physical, and 1 percent neglect. Those with part- or full-time caregivers were twice as likely to report abuse than were those living on their own (CARP 2009). Thus a much larger percent of seniors are subjected to other types of abuse than those seniors who are cited as victims of violence.

However, older people are often the targets of other types of crime. Con artists frequently contact them by mail, telephone, or Internet to perpetrate scams that often promise prizes, involve a "stockbroker" selling a "hot" stock or other commodity, or promise a large

Retirement is a time for leisure and reflection if it comes by choice and the individual is healthy and financially prepared. But for others, adapting to less income, increased dependency, and the loss of roles can be difficult.
Jeffery Allan Salter/Corbis

sum of money if money can be provided upfront. Seniors have also been scammed by foreign bride organizations promising a beautiful, young woman to the victim in return for money and/or marriage in the West, after which the woman leaves or even brings assault charges against a man. In some cases, the beautiful woman is a front for illegal activity. A high-profile example of such a case was reported in the *New York Times Magazine*. In November 2011, Paul Frampton, age 68, a theoretical particle physicist and recent widower, met Denise Milani, supposedly a Czech bikini model, on the online dating site Mate1.com. Many things went wrong in his attempt to meet her: an airline e-ticket was invalid; a supposed associate of hers asked him to take a suitcase to Argentina; the suitcase was discovered to have drugs in it; he was arrested in Buenos Aires; and he is now awaiting trial in prison for smuggling drugs (Swann 2013).

CARP, an advocacy group for those 45-plus years of age and/or retired, created a National Forum on Scams and Frauds, which produced recommendations such as providing more information to seniors, instituting cooling-off periods for contracts, and freezing assets of scam artists.

Family Problems and Social Isolation

Older people can easily become socially isolated from their families. Younger family members who once asked for advice stop asking, perhaps because they think that their older relatives are out of touch or perhaps because of some miscommunication. Sometimes younger family members feel unduly burdened by the concerns of their elders, which don't seem truly important to them. For one reason or another, older people can come to believe (rightly or wrongly) that they are isolated from the rest of the family.

Of the nearly 5 million seniors aged 65 and over in 2011, most (92.1 percent) lived in private households, including 56.4 percent who were part of couples, 24.6 percent who lived alone, and 11.0 percent who had other arrangements such as living with relatives. The remaining 7.9 percent lived in collectives such as nursing homes or residences for senior citizens. A decade earlier, in 2001, fewer seniors were living as part of a couple (54.1 percent), while more were living alone (26.7 percent) (Statistics Canada 2012a).

But, living alone is not always the equivalent of social isolation. Many older people have networks of family and friends with whom they engage in activities. Contrary to the myth that older people are abandoned by their families, Canadian research has shown that most seniors live in a situation called "intimacy at

a distance"—families usually provide much support for their older members (C. Rosenthal 1987). For those without children, many form other ties (McMullin and Marshall 1996). Many seniors also engage in a variety of work, as shown by Ann Elizabeth Carson in the vignette at the beginning of this chapter. To a large degree, the extent to which older people associate with others has to do with social class: people with more money are able to pursue a wider array of activities and take more trips than are those with more limited resources.

Perhaps one of the saddest developments in contemporary society is the growing number of older people who are homeless. While some older homeless people have lived on the streets for many years, others have become homeless because they have been displaced from low-income housing, such as single-room occupancy (SRO) hotels. In recent years, many SROs in cities such as Vancouver and Toronto have been replaced by high-rise office buildings, retail space, and luxury condominiums. Older people who are homeless typically lack nutritious food, appropriate clothing, adequate medical care, and a social support network. They tend to die prematurely of disease, crime victimization, accidents, and weather-related crises, such as winter blizzards, when an individual without shelter can freeze to death on a park bench. Fortunately, the picture is not this bleak for many older people who remain in residences they have occupied for many years.

Housing Patterns and Long-Term Care Facilities

Many people mistakenly assume that most older people live in long-term care facilities such as nursing homes. As Figure 5.5 shows, even for those 85 years and over, only about a quarter of the men and a third of the women live in institutions.

More than people of any other age category, older people are likely to reside in the housing in which they have lived for a number of years and own free and clear of debt. Because of the high cost of utilities, insurance, taxes, and repairs and maintenance, older women, who are more likely to live alone than are older men, are at a distinct disadvantage if they attempt to maintain their own homes. And, as shown in Figure 11.5, a high percentage of women living alone have a low income.

Before identifying levels of housing, it is important to note that an increasing number of older people are homeless. A survey of Toronto homeless people (see Chapter 15) shows that the percentage of older people

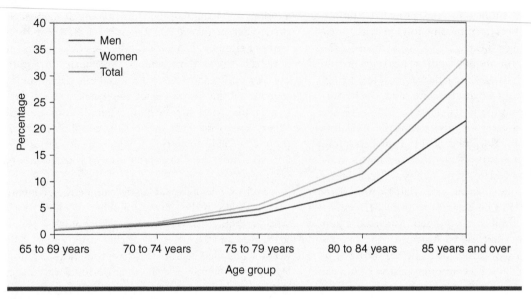

Figure 5.5   Percentage of Seniors Living in Institutions, by Age Group and Sex, 2011.

Source: *Statistics Canada, 2013, "Living arrangements of seniors." Retrieved June 3, 2015. (http://www12.statcan.ca/census-recensement/2011/as-sa/98-312-x/98-312-x2011003_4-eng.cfm)*

who are homeless has doubled from 2009 to 2013 (from 4.7 to 10.0 percent for people 61 years+) (City of Toronto 2013).

Some low-income older people live in planned housing projects that are funded by federal and local government agencies or private organizations, such as religious groups. Older people with middle and upper incomes are more likely to live in retirement communities or in seniors' residences that provide amenities such as housekeeping, dining facilities, and transportation services. In recent years, religious organizations and for-profit corporations have developed *multilevel* facilities, which provide services ranging from independent living to skilled nursing care all at the same site.

When we refer to housing the elderly, it is important to distinguish between residences for the elderly and long-term care facilities. Long-term care is defined as many services for people needing help with activities of daily living (ADL), such as eating, dressing, and bathing. This help is often combined with pain management, medication, rehabilitation, and finally palliative care.

Long-term care is expensive. How much does Canada spend for this essential service? The Organisation for Economic Co-operation and Development (OECD), an organization of the major Western industrialized nations and Japan, has provided some data about provision of long-term care among most of its members. Canada spends 1.23 percent of its GDP on long-term

care (.99 percent is public, .24 percent is private funding, 1.06 percent is for institutions, and .17 percent is for home care). The OECD average for 19 countries is 1.25 percent of GDP in total, with a similar public/private distribution, slightly higher support for home care, and slightly lower support for institutions. Thus, Canada is an average contributor to long-term care among industrialized nations. As might be

Although only about 7 percent of older people live in nursing homes or other long-term care facilities in Canada, living in an institutional setting remains the only option for some older individuals. What alternative living arrangements can you suggest for older people in the future?

Boris Spremo/CP Images

predicted, Sweden, with a higher percentage of elderly and a collective orientation, contributes a higher percentage of GDP to long-term care, and the United States, with a lower percentage of elderly and an individualist orientation, contributes a lower percentage of GDP to long-term care (Huber 2005:26).

While some seniors' residences may be excellent, other long-term care facilities have undergone extensive media scrutiny and public criticism for violations of regulations and harmful practices such as elder abuse. These facilities are also very expensive. In Ontario, for example, the cost of a private residence is $3066/month for a bachelor private room (Infographic 2013). As a result, many people select home care, adult day care, or assisted living for older relatives rather than institutional settings. Home care is being seen now as a way to reduce costs in the health care system. The price of home care in Ontario is about $2791/month for four hours of daily in-home care (Infographic 2013). Although home care has received increased resources in the past decade, problems with getting needed home care still exist.

Death and Dying

In previous generations, death was a common occurrence in all stages in the life course, but today most deaths occur among older people. Table 5.1 shows the leading causes of death for Canadians in 2000 and 2009.

About 50 percent of deaths among Canadians are due to heart disease and cancer, with cancer now being the leading cause of death (Statistics Canada 2012b). Stroke, chronic lower respiratory diseases, diabetes, influenza and pneumonia, Alzheimer's disease, and kidney disease follow these causes of death for older people. A comparison of rates in 2000 and 2009 shows that the death rates declined for most of these diseases, but it is still true that most deaths occur among older people. Euphemisms such as "pass away" or "sleep" are often used to refer to death by those who are trying to avoid its reality. Researchers have found, however, that many people do not actually fear death itself as much as they fear the possibility of pain and suffering, loss of control, and the consequences of their death for survivors (Marshall

TABLE 5.1 Mortality Rates for the 10 leading causes of death in Canada, 2000 and 2009

Cause of death	2000		2009	
	Rank	Standardized rate[1]	Rank	Standardized rate[1]
All causes of death	...	615.5	...	515.0
Males	...	778.3	...	629.9
Females	...	493.2	...	423.5
Malignant neoplasms (cancer)	1	180.4	1	160.3
Diseases of heart (heart disease)	2	152.0	2	101.4
Cerebrovascular diseases (stroke)	3	42.2	3	28.4
Chronic lower respiratory diseases	4	27.2	4	22.9
Accidents (unitentional injuries)	5	25.8	5	24.5
Diabetes mellitus (diabetes)	6	18.9	6	14.9
Alzheimer's disease	7	13.2	7	11.8
Influenza and pneumonia	8	13.2	8	11.7
Intentional self-harm (suicide)	9	11.4	9	10.7
Nephritis, nephrotic syndrome, and nephrosis (kidney disease)	10	8.6	10	7.2

1. Age-standardized mortality rate per 100 000 standard population.

Note: The order of the causes of death in this table is based on the ranking of the 10 leading causes of death in 2009.

Source: *Statistics Canada, 2012, "Leading Causes of Death in Canada." Retrieved August 28, 2014* (http://www.statcan.gc.ca/pub/84-215-x/2012001/table-tableau/tbl007-eng.htm).

and Levy 1990). Given a chance to choose, most people would choose a painless death over prolonged physical and mental deterioration and the prospect of being a burden on their families. Quoting Ann Elizabeth Carson again:

> At age 86 (now), death will come sooner rather than later. Like so many others I've talked to, it's not death I fear, but the process of dying. As the result of an adverse drug reaction 13 years ago, most of the commonly used drugs are toxic for me or cause an allergic reaction. In dealing with chronic pain over the years, I have researched alternative methods of pain control like acupuncture, coditron (a little gizmo that delivers electrical stimulation to the meridian points identified by Chinese acupuncture), and meditation, and am now looking into these and other ways to alleviate pain during palliative care. However, it is very difficult to find allopathic (traditional) medical practitioners willing to discuss the toxic or allergic consequences of anaesthetics and painkillers. I can only hope that there will soon be significant advances in this respect, or that I will not need surgery in my last years. (personal communication, April 2013)

There are four widely known frameworks for explaining how people cope with the process of dying: the stage-based approach, the trajectories of grief, the dying trajectory, and the task-based approach. The *stage-based approach* was popularized by Elisabeth Kübler-Ross (1969), who proposed five stages in the dying process: (1) denial ("Not me"); (2) anger ("Why me?"); (3) bargaining and asking for divine intervention to postpone death ("Yes me, but . . . "); (4) depression and sense of loss; and (5) acceptance. According to some social scientists (Kalish 1985; Marshall 1980), Kübler-Ross's study is limited because she focused primarily on the attitudes of younger people who had terminal illnesses. These scientists argue that the same stages may not apply to older people who believe that they have already lived a full life.

The second approach, the trajectories of grief approach, was introduced by George Bonanno (2009, 2010), who claims that bereavement studies have disproved the stages of grief approach and helped researchers identify four common trajectories of grief:

1. **Resilience**—the ability of people to maintain a relatively stable, healthy level of psychological and physical functioning while dealing with a death of a relative or a life-threatening situation.

2. **Recovery**—a gradual return to previous levels of normal functioning after a period of stress, e.g., post-traumatic stress disorder.
3. **Chronic dysfunction**—inability to function after experiencing grief.
4. **Delayed grief**—appearing to have a normal adjustment followed by an increase in distress.

Bonanno coined the term *coping ugly* to describe inappropriate behaviour like telling jokes that may help the person move on from a loss.

The third approach, referred to as the *dying trajectory*, focuses on the perceived course of dying and the expected time of death. From this perspective, not all people move toward death at the same speed and in the same way. A dying trajectory may be sudden (e.g., a heart attack) or slow (e.g., lung cancer), and is usually shaped by the condition causing death. A dying trajectory involves three phases: the *acute* phase, in which maximum anxiety or fear is expressed; the *chronic* phase, in which anxiety declines as the person confronts reality; and the *terminal* phase, in which the dying person withdraws from others (Glaser and Strauss 1968).

The *task-based approach* suggests that daily activities can still be enjoyed during the dying process and that fulfilling certain tasks makes the process of death easier, not just on the dying person, but on everyone involved. *Physical tasks* are performed to satisfy bodily needs and to minimize physical distress. *Psychological tasks* help to maximize psychological security, autonomy, and richness of experience. *Social tasks* sustain and enhance interpersonal attachments and address the social implications of dying. *Spiritual tasks* are performed to identify, develop, or reaffirm sources of spiritual energy and to foster hope (Corr et al. 1994). Most important in any approach are the rights of the dying person and the way in which care is provided.

Technological advances in medicine have helped to focus attention on the physical process of dying and, in recent years, the needs of dying patients and their families. Many people are choosing to sign a *living will*—a document stating a person's wishes about the medical circumstances under which his or her life should be allowed to end. Rejecting the idea of being kept alive by elaborate life-support systems and other forms of high-tech medicine, some people choose to die at home rather than in a hospital or nursing home. The hospice movement has provided additional options for caring for the terminally ill. **Hospices are organizations that provide a homelike facility or home-based care (or both) for persons who are terminally ill.** Some hospices have facilities where care is provided, but hospice

Social Problems and Social Policy

Box 5.2

Euthanasia

At the age of 72, Susan Griffiths of Winnipeg went to Switzerland to get physician-assisted suicide to prevent being overwhelmed by multiple system atrophy, a disease similar to Parkinson's disease. Griffiths reported that while it was wonderful to have some family present, she wished that more of her family and friends could be with her at the end (Lambert 2013).

According to Greek etymology, *euthanasia* means, literally, a "good death," and it comes in several types. *Passive euthanasia* means withholding or ceasing treatment of someone not likely to recover from a disease or injury. *Active euthanasia* means intervening to hasten someone's terminal illness, with, for example, a lethal dose of sedatives. *Assisted suicide* means helping someone end his or her life with, for example, drugs. Since advances in medical technology have made it possible to keep people alive longer than in the past, questions are arising about the best time and method of dying.

In the past, a number of high-profile cases, such as those of Sue Rodriguez, Robert Latimer, and Gloria Taylor, have spotlighted the problems in this area. Sue Rodriguez was a 42-year-old woman suffering from ALS (Lou Gehrig's disease) who appealed all the way to the Supreme Court of Canada to have the legal right to have someone help her commit suicide when she wanted to die. In 1993, the Supreme Court decided against her, supporting the law prohibiting assisted suicide. Sue Rodriguez actually did die with the assistance of an unidentified doctor. Robert Latimer is a Saskatchewan farmer who administered a lethal dose of carbon monoxide gas to his daughter, Tracy, who suffered from severe cerebral palsy. He was accused of second-degree homicide. After his first trial, at which he was found guilty, the judge imposed a two-year sentence. This sentence was appealed to the Saskatchewan Court of Appeal, which sentenced Latimer to the mandatory penalty for second-degree homicide,

life imprisonment with no chance of parole for 10 years. Later, in 2001, the Supreme Court of Canada refused to review that sentence. More recently in June 2011, Gloria Taylor, an ALS sufferer, filed a case with the BC Supreme Court saying that not being able to get physician-assisted suicide violated her rights under the Charter of Rights and Freedoms. The BC Supreme Court agreed to allow her to have physician-assisted suicide, but she died in July 2012 of a severe infection. In February 2015, the Supreme Court decided unanimously that people should have the right to assisted suicide and gave the government a year to put forward legislation.

In 2012, an Angus Reid poll inquired about Canadians' attitude toward euthanasia. It found that 80 percent of Canadians are quite supportive of legalizing euthanasia for competent, fully informed, terminally ill patients. In addition, 38 percent of Canadians believe it is acceptable for a parent to commit a mercy killing if his/her child is suffering from a severe disease like cerebral palsy (Angus Reid 2013). The Netherlands permits mercy killing of severely deformed children, and Belgium is considering it also. But it will take some time for the government and medical profession to agree with the Canadian people.

Questions for consideration

1. Do you agree with the 2015 Supreme Court decision that Canada should legalize euthanasia?

2. The Netherlands, Switzerland, and some U.S. states (e.g., Oregon, Montana, and Vermont) have made euthanasia legal. What problems have they encountered?

3. Do you think that young people might want to euthanize older relatives to make their own lives easier? If we do legalize euthanasia, what safeguards do you think should be imposed?

4. What do you think of mercy killing one's own child?

---

is primarily a philosophy that affirms life, not death, and offers holistic and continuing care to the patient and family through a team of visiting nurses, on-call physicians, and counsellors. Home care enables many people to remain in familiar surroundings and maintain dignity and control over the dying process (Corr et al. 1994).

Because many people want a dignified death, the topic of euthanasia will likely become very prominent in the future (see Box 5.2).

PERSPECTIVES ON AGING AND SOCIAL INEQUALITY

Although each of the major sociological perspectives focuses on different aspects of aging and social inequality, they all provide insights into how people view the aging process and how ageism toward the young and the old contributes to social inequality in society.

The Functionalist Perspective

According to functionalists, dramatic changes in such social institutions as the family and the economy have influenced how people look at the process of growing old. Because of these influences, both the complexity and the stability of society require that people spend much time preparing for occupational roles and then leaving them at an arbitrary time, such as age 65, when it is likely that they are no longer able to keep up with the role demands and jobs must be made available to younger people. Encouraging older people to leave is referred to as *disengagement theory*; this theory suggests that older people want to be released from societal expectations of productivity and competitiveness. At the same time, disengagement facilitates a gradual and orderly transfer of statuses and roles from one generation to the next instead of an abrupt change, which might result in chaos. Retirement policies, then, are a means of ensuring that younger people with more up-to-date training (for example, newer computer skills) move into occupational roles while ensuring that older workers are recognized for years of service (Williamson et al. 1992).

Critics of this perspective object to the assumption that disengagement is functional for society and say that it is dysfunctional. Older people may not want to disengage when they are still productive and gaining satisfaction from their work. Some have suggested that CPP/QPP and other pension systems will be strained by the proportionately fewer workers who are paying into the plans, which must support an increasing number of retired workers (see *elderly dependency ratio* on page 101). As mentioned above, mandatory retirement has been eliminated in Canada, so pension plans may be less strained if people continue to work after age 65.

The Interactionist Perspective

Interactionist perspectives on aging focus on the relationship between life satisfaction and levels of activity. The *interactionist activity theory* is based on the assumption that people who are active are happier and better adjusted than are less-active persons. According to this theory, older people shift gears in late middle age and find meaningful substitutes for previous statuses, roles, and activities (Havighurst et al. 1968). Those who remain active have a higher level of life satisfaction than do those who are inactive or in ill health (Havighurst et al. 1968). In contrast to disengagement theory, activity theory suggests that older people must deny the existence of old age by maintaining middle-age lifestyles for as long as possible. But some older people are themselves critiquing this idea. According to an interview study conducted by Stephen Katz, some older people object to the idea that those preferring their inner world to being active are thought to be problem people. Katz (2000) suggests that this emphasis on activity could be transformed into a means of controlling older people.

The Conflict Perspective

In analyzing the problems of older people in contemporary capitalistic societies, conflict theorists focus on the political economy of aging. From this perspective, class constitutes a structural barrier to older people's access to valued resources, and dominant groups attempt to maintain their own interests by perpetuating class inequalities. According to conflict theorists, aging itself is not a social problem. The problem is rooted in societal conditions that older people often face without adequate resources, such as income and housing. People who were poor and disadvantaged in their younger years become even more so in old age. Today, in Canada, a much smaller percentage of seniors live in low-income situations now than as recently as two decades ago (see Figure 5.3). Figure 5.3 shows that whereas in 1976, 30 percent of seniors lived in poverty (the low-income cut-off [LICO] is discussed in Chapter 2), in 2010 that percentage was just over 10 percent. However, health care costs could be a greater problem in the future, as very expensive drugs are not included in support plans and other costs could emerge.

In the capitalist system, many older people are set apart as a group that depends on special policies and programs. Fortunately, in Canada, seniors do not have to depend on special government programs; Canada's health program is universal. But it is under siege by those who would like to see greater privatization of services and who claim among other things that seniors will bankrupt the system.

Conflict analysts draw attention to the ways that class, gender, and racialization divide older people, just as they do everyone else. The conflict perspective adds to our understanding of aging by focusing on how capitalism devalues older people, especially women. Critics assert, however, that this approach ignores the fact that industrialization and capitalism have been positive forces in society, greatly enhancing the longevity and quality of life for many older people.

The Feminist Perspective

Feminist theorists emphasize inequalities between men and women. It is well known that although women live longer than men, they are subject to higher rates of disability (see Chapter 10) and their incomes are lower.

In 2010, whereas 11.5 percent of unattached men had low incomes, 15.6 percent of females had low incomes (see Figure 11.5).

In addition, feminists argue that more attention should be paid to the health problems of women, as in the study done by the Ontario Women's Health Council to determine whether this difference in disability is alterable.

IS THERE A SOLUTION TO AGE-BASED INEQUALITY?

The inequality experienced by older people needs to be addressed. People who have had no opportunity to engage in leisure activities earlier in their life are unlikely to suddenly become leisure-oriented. Employment, family responsibilities, and leisure must become less compartmentalized, and changes in technology and employment may make this possible. At present, however, it is difficult for most people to have *free time* and *money* at the same time.

For older people many dimensions must be addressed. As we have seen, technological innovations and advances in medicine have contributed to the steady increase in life expectancy in Canada. Advances in the diagnosis, prevention, and treatment of diseases associated with old age, such as Alzheimer's, may revolutionize people's feelings about growing older. Technology may bring about greater equality and freedom for older people (Novak and Campbell 2006:90–94). Home-based computer services, such as online banking and shopping, make it possible for older people to conduct their daily lives without having to leave home to obtain services. Computerized controls on appliances, lighting, and air conditioning make it possible for people with limited mobility to control their environment. Soon, sensing devices may be developed that could monitor a person's daily behaviour, such as the use of a kettle or accidents like a fall, and report any deviation over the Internet to a concerned relative or central office.

Technology also brings recreation and education into the home. For example, Senior Net is a computer network that encourages discussion of diverse topics and provides hands-on classes in computer use. Robotics and computer systems may eventually be used by frail older people who otherwise would have to rely on either family or paid caregivers to meet their needs or move to a nursing home. In mid-2013 a cute, pint-sized (34 cm tall and weighing 1 kg) talking robot was sent into space to be a future companion of a Japanese astronaut at the space station. The robot was called Kirobo. It has the ability to remember conversations with the astronaut and can relay commands from mission control. This robot could act as a mediator between a man and a machine or the Internet or between people (BBC News 2013). It is also hoped that this robot could provide aid to seniors living alone, performing tasks or monitoring their state of health. However, income is again a factor: while much of home care is covered by the health care system in Canada, many home accessibility features, including robots, are and would be paid for by users or their families.

Economic concerns loom large in the future as baby boomers (those born between 1946 and 1964) will be retiring soon if they have not already done so, bringing about a dramatic shift in the ***elderly dependency ratio*— the number of workers necessary to support those over age 64** (see Figure 5.6). Obviously, as the percentage of seniors in the population rises, there would be a smaller percentage of workers to support them, and ultimately, according to some speculation, seniors would bankrupt the system. Box 5.3 asks you to consider what would be an appropriate response to the changing elder dependency ratio.

Advocates of *productive aging* suggest that instead of pitting young and old against each other, we should change our national policies and attitudes. We should encourage older people to continue to create their own roles in society, not to disengage from it. To some extent, as mentioned, this will happen with the end of mandatory retirement. In addition, real value should be placed on unpaid volunteer and caregiving activism, and settings should be provided in which older people can use their talents more productively (Hooyman and Kiyak 2008).

Functionalists suggest that changes must occur in families and other social institutions if we are to resolve problems brought about by family diversification and increased workplace demands. Some adult children have to provide economic and emotional support for aging parents and grandparents at the same time as they are caring for their own children. These people are called the *sandwich generation*. According to the 2012 GSS, almost 3 in 10 people aged 35 to 44 years with unmarried children under 25 in the home were also caring for a senior (Statistics Canada 2013d). This is over 2.2 million people, mostly women, in Canada. Various sacrifices made by these people include changing hours, losing income, missing promotional opportunities, and incurring medical expenses. Women tend to devote more hours than men do caring for seniors, and they tend to provide more personal care while men provide economic and transportation care. Although some tax incentives are available for those taking care of seniors, given that the

Critical Thinking and You

Box 5.3

To what extent is the future elderly dependency ratio a problem?

Ever since it was realized that there would be a great decline in workers and a great increase in seniors, people (mostly conservatives) have made strong claims that the age "tsunami" would overwhelm our Social Security and Medicare systems. Figure 5.6 shows that indeed the ratio of workers to seniors is falling quickly, and that in another two dozen years it will be half of what it is now.

These claims have become more strident and were combined with concerns about government deficits and debt during the current recession. In an effort to keep people employed by supporting automobile companies and infrastructure projects, like roads and bridges, governments have been taking on increased debt. This has caused people who believe in austerity to use expressions like, "we are bankrupting the next generation" since the next generation will be repaying the debt. This is not entirely true, since seniors are still paying taxes and they are still transferring money to their children during their lifetimes or through their bequests.

A variety of transfers occur between and among generations. Sometimes they are private transfers from the elderly to help the young get started. Sometimes they are private transfers from children to their parents so they can live comfortably in their later years. Generally people are happy to make private transfers when they are given to members of their own family. Sometimes the transfers are public transfers from taxpayers to the young, like public education. Sometimes they are public transfers from young and previously working people (now receiving payments) through taxes to the elderly for OAS and Medicare. To this point, Canadians have supported public transfers to both the young and the elderly. But will they be as eager to do so when the price goes up substantially to pay for both transfers and debt and fewer workers are paying taxes for this?

The federal government has been taking this into account in part for some time. The federal government has for years clawed back OAS money from those with high incomes (in 2012, clawing back begins with incomes of $69 562 and becomes complete for those earning $100 000+). It changed the pension systems in Canada to bring about a decline in the number of low-income seniors without creating many high-income seniors (Myles 2000:312–313). In 2013, the federal government created new regulations. Since people have longer life expectancies and are fitter for longer, the federal government increased the usual retirement age from 65 to 67 years for those now in their mid-50s and younger. As a result, the standard OAS transfer and CPP will begin later.

In addition, provincial governments can make their own regulations. For example, the Ontario government has said it will claw back money from high-income elderly for their to-date almost free drugs program for seniors. Supporting these measures and putting forth more comprehensive recommendations is the Ontario government's commission on the Reform of Ontario's Public Services Report,

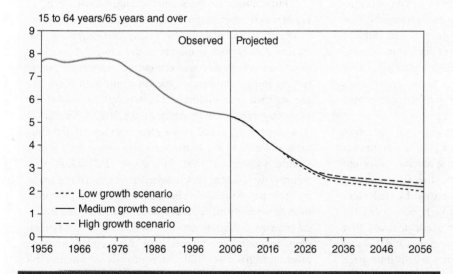

Figure 5.6   Ratio of Workers to Seniors.

Source: *Statistics Canada, 2007, "Canadian Demographics at a Glance," Catalogue number 91-003-XWE. Retrieved April 6, 2012 (http://www.statcan.gc.ca/pub/91-003-x/2007001/figures/4129872-eng.htm).*

the so-called Drummond Report, named after the chief author, Don Drummond, a noted economist. Basically, the report said that the past decade's annual increases in health care (7 percent), education (4.5 percent), and post-secondary education (8.2 percent) expenditures cannot be maintained because our growth will be less than 2 percent annually. The report said that future annual increases must be drastically reduced (e.g., 2.5 percent for health and 1.5 percent for post-secondary) so we do not accumulate a huge debt like some European countries have (Drummond 2012).

Some deficit "hawks," admittedly more in the United States than in Canada, have suggested drastic cuts in government spending, including transfer payments to eliminate the debt so young people will not be bankrupted repaying it. On the other hand, if infrastructure projects (e.g., roads, bridges, etc.) are not repaired now, and reduced transfers to education, health, and social service do not bring about a healthy, educated populace, then the young will have to pay for these problems in the future.

Questions for Consideration

1. Some have suggested that we will have a new form of inequality where seniors are better off than younger cohorts. Do you think that a new kind of inequality (a birth cohort inequality) will emerge with the current and near future seniors (the baby boomers) forcing too high a financial burden on those who are younger (e.g., Gen X and Y)?

2. If so, what sociological insights might be used to reduce the burden?

3. If not, what percent of their income should people pay in taxes to gain all the services they use? How progressive should taxes levied be?

4. If you accept this as a new kind of inequality, how important do you think it is relative to other kinds of inequalities (e.g., gender, class, ethnicity, and sexual orientation)?

Independent Research

Research the federal and provincial tax rates in your province. Talk to your friends about how much they feel they should be taxed for government services and transfer payments to different groups like the elderly and parents of small children (e.g., Child Care Benefit). Interview people from seniors' advocacy groups like CARP to discover what they think should be transferred from the young to help the elderly (keeping in mind that many seniors are paying quite substantial taxes themselves).

sandwich generation reports generally feeling stressed, more support would certainly be welcomed by them.

Other social analysts suggest that people need to rely more on themselves for their retirement and old age. Younger workers should be encouraged to save money for retirement in RRSPs. As conflict theorists have pointed out, however, many young people have education loans to repay or do not have jobs or adequate income to meet their current economic needs, much less their future needs.

From the conflict perspective, age-based inequality is rooted in power differentials, and short of dramatic changes in the structure of political and economic power in society, the only way for older people to hold on to previous gains is through continued activism. Advocacy groups like CARP make presentations to government and hold forums (e.g., on scams and frauds) about policies that would benefit many older people. According to interactionists, however, individuals like Ann Elizabeth Carson, who maintain strong relationships with others and remain actively involved throughout their lifetime, have reason to be optimistic about life when they reach old age.

WHAT CAN YOU DO?

- Study the amount of caregiving that your elderly relatives and those of your friends require.

- Volunteer for an agency that helps seniors in your neighbourhood. Helping a senior person may be as simple as listening to one on a regular basis.

- Set up a system of habits, such as exercise, recreational reading, and saving for retirement in an RRSP, to establish an activity pattern that will prepare you for later years.

- Help some seniors lobby for some improvements, such as educational and fitness programs in communities.

- Challenge some of the ageist stereotypes held by some young people. When one of the authors was showing a news clip about people over 80 years of age and their romantic interests, he heard sounds of disgust from the back of the classroom. You might start a discussion of ageism with questions about romantic expectations after age 80. The vast majority of your age group will be there someday.

- Study the differences in problems currently faced by senior men and women. To what extent will these problems change as more women become more self-supporting?

SUMMARY

What Do We Experience in Later Maturity and Old Age?

The life course is generally divided into infancy and childhood, adolescence and young adulthood, middle age, later maturity, and old age. In later maturity, we increasingly find ourselves involved in caring for people of our own age and older people. Problems of older adults vary widely because of the diverse needs of the "young-old" (ages 65 to 74), the "middle-old" (ages 75 to 84), and the "old-old" (ages 85 and older).

Problems Linked to Being Elderly

Ageism is prejudice and discrimination against people on the basis of age. Ageism is a social problem because it perpetuates negative stereotypes and age-based discrimination, particularly against older people. Despite laws to the contrary, older workers may experience overt or covert discrimination in the workplace. Retirement brings about changing roles and a loss of status for those older people whose identity has been based primarily on their occupation, but most Canadians have until now maintained income security and been active in leisure activities. For some older people, low incomes, disease, and lack of health care or home care are problems. Older people may become the victims of scams by con artists and elder abuse by family members or nursing-home personnel, but they experience the lowest rates of violent crime for any age group. For some older people, moving into a nursing home represents a loss of autonomy.

How Do People Cope with the Process of Dying?

Four explanations have been given for how people cope with dying. Kübler-Ross identified five stages that people go through: (1) denial; (2) anger; (3) bargaining; (4) depression; and (5) acceptance. Second, there is a trajectories of grief approach, suggesting that people have more than one way of dealing with grief. Third, the dying trajectory suggests that individuals do not move toward death at the same speed and in the same way. Fourth, the task-based approach suggests that daily activities can still be enjoyed during the dying process and that fulfilling certain tasks makes the process of death easier not just on the dying person, but on everyone involved.

How Do Functionalist and Interactionist Explanations of Age-Based Inequality Differ?

According to functionalists, disengagement of older people from their jobs and other social positions may be functional for society because it allows the smooth transfer of roles from one generation to the next. However, interactionists suggest that activity is important for older people because it provides new sources of identity and satisfaction later in life.

How Do Conflict and Feminist Theorists Explain Inequality Based on Age?

According to conflict theorists, aging itself is not a social problem. The problem is rooted in societal conditions that older people often face when they have inadequate resources in a capitalist society. In the capitalist system, older people are set apart as a group that depends on special policies and programs. Feminists argue that older men tend to be in a more advantageous social and economic position than older women. Since this disadvantage for women begins much earlier, institutions such as schools and businesses should work to eliminate the inequality they generate.

KEY TERMS

ageism, p. 89
elderly dependency ratio, p. 101

hospice, p. 98
social gerontology, p. 89

QUESTIONS FOR CRITICAL THINKING

1. Some people believe they can live to 150 years of age. In June 2013, a Japanese man who was believed to be 116 years of age, died. If we live much longer than our current life expectancy, what will be some consequences for society?

2. Since we have eliminated laws regarding retirement for older people, are there limits we should consider?

3. Does disengagement theory or activity theory more closely reflect how you plan to spend your later years? What other approaches to aging can you suggest?

4. Think of synonyms, both formal and informal, for *senior*, and look up the word *senior* in a thesaurus. How ageist are these synonyms? Make up new synonyms that are not ageist.

Natasha Kramskaya/Shutterstock

6

Inequality Based on Sexual Orientation

A number of diverse issues needs to be considered when looking at sexual orientation and discrimination. This chapter will examine many issues surrounding sexual orientation, beginning with a look at definitions of various orientations and the extent of homosexuality, bisexuality, homophobia, and biphobia in Canada.

We will try to understand how and why prejudice and discrimination against people based on sexual orientation still happens in Canadian society, a society that prides itself on its high levels of "tolerance" and even "acceptance." We will review some of the laws that deal with sexual orientation and look specifically at hate crimes and ways they are being dealt with. Finally, we will review several theories that pertain to sexual orientation and discrimination and consider ways we can advocate for social change.

Simplistically, *sexual orientation* **refers to a preference for emotional–sexual relationships with individuals of the "same" sex (homosexuality), the "opposite" sex (heterosexuality), or both (bisexuality)** (Lips 1993). This type of definition, however, encourages us to think of sexual orientation as an "either–or" proposition—you are *either* heterosexual *or* you are homosexual *or* you are bisexual—when, in fact, not only do many people exhibit a shifting sexual orientation over their lifetimes, they may identify differently depending upon whether we are talking about behaviour, attraction, fantasy, desire, or self-identity. This will be discussed further shortly. **Pansexuality is a relatively new term used to refer to people who are attracted to male, female, trans, androgynous, gender fluid, and non-gendered people.**

The terms *homosexual* and *gay* are most often used in association with males who prefer "same"-sex relationships; the term *lesbian* is used in association with females who prefer "same"-sex relationships. Heterosexual individuals, or those who prefer "opposite"-sex relationships, are sometimes referred to as *straight* (e.g., "Is everyone else in your family straight?"). It is important to note, however, that heterosexual people are almost never labelled by their sexual orientation, unlike people who are gay, lesbian, bisexual, or pansexual, because heterosexuality is presumed normal and is taken for granted. We will discuss this presumption of normalcy later in the chapter when we examine heterosexual privilege and heteronormativity. It is also important to note that while in lay terms we talk about the "opposite" sex, there are biologically, physiologically, cognitively, and emotionally very few differences between males and females. In effect, there is no such thing as an "opposite" sex. The myth of the opposite sex is one of the most persistent and foundational binaries we adhere to in our culture.

What criteria do social scientists use to classify individuals as gay, lesbian, or bisexual? In a groundbreaking study of sexual orientations published in the mid-1990s, researchers at the University of Chicago established three criteria for identifying people as homosexual or bisexual: (1) *sexual attraction* to persons of one's own sex, (2) *sexual involvement* with one or more persons of one's own sex, and (3) *self-identification* as gay, lesbian, or bisexual (Michael et al. 1994). According to these criteria, then, engaging in a homosexual act does not necessarily qualify a person as homosexual. Many participants in the Chicago study indicated that although they had had *at least* one homosexual encounter when they were younger, they were no longer involved in homosexual conduct and never identified themselves as lesbians, bisexuals, or gay. Self-definition plays a critical role in confounding attempts to classify people definitively. For example, many people who engage in same-sex behaviours on an occasional or even regular basis perceive themselves as and identify as heterosexual. In fact, among many (mostly young) people, bisexual behaviour at parties or raves has achieved a sort of cachet, sometimes called "bisexual chic" in academic literature. Further, in important longitudinal research by psychology and gender studies professor Lisa Diamond, sexual orientation among the 79 women in her research tended to be fluid; two-thirds of the women changed their identity labels once in ten years (e.g. from lesbian to bisexual) and one-third changed their labels two or more times (Diamond 2008).

NATURE AND EXTENT OF INEQUALITY BASED ON SEXUAL ORIENTATION

How many homosexuals and bisexuals are there in Canada? That question is likely impossible to answer definitively for the reasons already discussed. The 2001 Canadian Census was the first to ask questions specifically about same-sex couples, a full four years before same-sex marriage was legalized.

In that year, 34 200 Canadian couples, or one-half of 1 percent of all couples, claimed same-sex common-law status (Statistics Canada 2002a). In 2006, the number reporting same-sex couple status (common law and married) increased 11 percent to 37 885 couples (0.6 percent of all couples in Canada) (Statistics Canada 2008f). By 2011, 64 575 couples reported same-sex partnerships, compared with 7 797 280 heterosexual couples. Of these, 29 380 were female couples and 35 195 were male couples (Statistics Canada 2013e). Independent and Statistics Canada researchers caution, however, that the reported numbers of same-sex couples may still be quite low in relation to the actual number of same-sex couples in Canada, as reporting same-sex couple status to the government is quite new and many people are understandably wary. Indeed, in their report of recent research of Canadian lesbians, researchers for Status of Women Canada Irene Demczuk, Michele Caron, Ruth Rose, and Lyne Bouchard (2002:viii) state that "to this day, most lesbian couples still hide their sexual orientation and their conjugal situation, especially in the workplace, in order to protect themselves against the negative reactions of those around them." Jerome Ryckborst, a Vancouver writer, described the conflict that many gay and lesbian Canadians had to grapple with when faced with reporting, in essence, their sexual orientation to the Canadian government: "It does feel risky . . . but the need for our community to grow up, stand up and be counted outweighs the personal concerns" (Anderssen 2002:A9). While a higher number of males than females reported being in a same-sex partnership in 2006 and 2011, in keeping with gender socialization norms and typical post-divorce custody arrangements in Canada, a considerably higher number of female couples had children (Statistics Canada 2007; #1 New Statistics Canada 2013e – 02–27).

While we now have a count, however inaccurate, of same-sex common-law and married couples in Canada, the general population census has yet to count people according to their sexual orientation. Most estimates of the homosexual population have historically placed percentages between 1 and 10 percent. While there are many reasons, discussed later in this chapter, why people in Canada may wish to keep information about their sexual orientation from being scrutinized by government agencies, legalization of same-sex marriage has opened the door for the collection of official statistics. For example, the 2003 Canadian Community Health Survey (CCHS) was the first Statistics Canada survey to include a question on sexual orientation (Statistics Canada 2008a). The CCHS asks questions of Canadians aged 12 and up regarding health-related matters, such as health status and health care usage. The CCHS found that of Canadians aged 18 to 59 years, 1.0 percent identified themselves as gay or lesbian and a further 0.7 percent identified themselves as bisexual. The CCHS in 2005 reported higher numbers as people became more comfortable disclosing sexual orientation. In a Statistics Canada study of health care use, 1.9 percent of Canadian adults (aged 18–59 years) identified as gay, lesbian, or bisexual (see Table 6.1 for the breakdown of people with different sexual orientations by age, marital status, education, etc.).

Further, in the 2004 GSS (released February 2008), a survey of criminal victimization conducted every five years, found that 1.5 percent of Canadians identified as homosexual, 94 percent identified as heterosexual, and 5 percent did not identify their sexual orientation (Statistics Canada 2008a). Regardless of the numbers of people who identify as other than heterosexual, the central issue is the need to eliminate prejudice and discrimination against people based on their sexual orientation.

Homosexuality has existed in most, if not all, societies throughout human history. Acceptance (and tolerance) of homosexuality and bisexuality exist along a continuum. Most tribal societies regard some homosexual acts as socially acceptable at least some of the time. For example, the Siwans, the Azande, the Dahomy, and the !Kung of Africa, and the Sambians of New Guinea regard same-sex relations as a "normal" part of maturing (Blackwood 1986). In contrast, for most of the past 2000 years, there have been groups—sometimes entire societies—that considered homosexuality "a crime against nature," "an abomination," or "a sin" (Doyle 1995:224). In any case, most societies have norms pertaining to *sexuality*—**attitudes, beliefs, and practices related to sexual attraction and intimate relationships with others.** Cultural sexuality norms are based on the assumption that some forms of attraction and relationships are *normal* and *appropriate* while others are *abnormal* and *inappropriate*. Up until very recently, in many societies, including modern North American and European societies, homosexuality had been classified as a form of deviance. This classification made people the targets of prejudice and discrimination so severe that some have even been killed for being or presumed gay. Prejudice toward gay men and lesbians is known as *homophobia*—**the irrational and excessive fear or intolerance of homosexuals and homosexuality.** Additionally, *biphobia* **refers to fear and intolerance of bisexuality.** According to sociologists, homophobia and biphobia are actually *socially determined prejudices,* not medically recognized *phobias* (Lehne 1995; Wilton 2000). In recognition of this, a quote attributed to actor Morgan Freeman started appearing on social media in

TABLE 6.1 Distribution of Household Population Aged 18 to 59, by Gender, Sexual Identity, and Selected Socio-Demographic and Economic Characteristics

	Men			Women		
	Hetero-sexual	Gay	Bisexual	Hetero-sexual	Lesbian	Bisexual
	%	%	%	%	%	%
Age group						
18 to 24	16.3	9.7*	23.9*	15.4	10.5*E	35.9*
25 to 34	21.8	22.5	18.1	22.3	22.1	26.8*
35 to 44	27.6	36.3*	22.2*	26.9	36.4*	21.2*
45 to 59	34.3	31.5	35.7	35.3	30.9	16.1*
Marital status						
Married or common-law	64.4	31.8*	39.9*	65.6	38.5*	40.9*
Previously married	6.0	4.0*	7.3E	10.1	9.3	10.5
Single (never married)	29.6	64.2*	52.9*	24.3	52.2*	48.6*
Children younger than 12 in household	29.5	2.6*E	18.5*E	31.1	8.4*	26.1*
Education (aged 25 to 59)						
Less than secondary	12.1	4.4*E	16.2	10.6	6.1*E	10.7
Secondary	16.7	10.2*	15.8E	18.1	13.4*	19.1
Some postsecondary	6.7	9.3	14.4E	6.8	6.1E	9.4E
Postsecondary	64.5	76.1*	53.6*	64.4	74.4*	60.7
Income quintiles						
Lowest	17.0	15.5	34.9*	22.0	19.0	42.7*
Second-lowest	19.5	14.6*	29.1*	21.2	15.3*	22.0
Middle	20.1	17.9	12.4*	20.3	22.1	14.5
Second-highest	21.2	22.0	11.6*	19.2	20.0	12.0*
Highest	22.1	29.9*	12.0*E	17.3	23.4*	8.8*E
Racial or cultural group						
White	82.4	88.1*	76.0	82.7	89.1*	81.9
Non-white	17.6	11.9*	24.0	17.3	10.9*E	18.1
Place of residence						
Montreal, Toronto, or Vancouver	34.9	55.9*	47.0*	35.1	41.0*	34.9
CMA 100 000 to 2 million	31.9	28.3*	24.9*	32.1	35.1	31.3
Non-CMA (less than 100 000)	33.1	15.8*	28.1	32.8	23.9*	33.8

* Significantly different from estimate for heterosexual population of same gender (p < 0.05)

E Use with caution (coefficient of variation 16.6% to 33.3%)

Note: Missing values are excluded

Source: Statistics Canada, 2008, Health Reports, Vol. 19, No. 1, March, page 57, *http://www.statcan.gc.ca/pub/82-003-x/2008001/article/10532-eng.pdf.*

2012: "I hate the word homophobia. It's not a phobia. You are not scared. You are an asshole." Morgan Freeman never said this; it is believed to have originated in August 2010 from an anonymous Twitter account that used a picture of Morgan Freeman.

Elisabeth Young-Bruehl, a psychotherapist and professor at Columbia University in the United States, classifies what she calls "primary prejudices," such as racism, sexism, homophobia, and anti-Semitism, into three categories: obsessive, hysterical, and narcissistic (1996, in Baird 2007). People who embody *obsessive* prejudices feel the objects of their prejudice are "omnipresent conspirators or enemies set on one's destruction" and as such, they "must be eliminated" (Baird 2007:80). Anti-Semitism is an example of obsessive prejudice. People who embody *hysterical* prejudices are those who view the objects of their prejudice as "'other,' as inferior, and as sexually threatening" (Baird 2007:80). Racism is an example of hysterical prejudice. Finally, people who embody *narcissistic* prejudices "cannot tolerate the idea that there exist people who are not like them" (Young-Bruehl 1996, quoted in Baird 2007:80). Young-Bruehl notes that homophobia alone represents all three categories, a factor that may help to explain its pervasiveness (1996, in Baird 2007:80).

Homophobia and biphobia are intensified by the ideology of **compulsory heterosexism**, or **heteronormativity**, **a belief system that offers no acceptable options other than heterosexual behaviour and feelings and denies, denigrates, and stigmatizes gay, lesbian, or bisexual behaviour, identity, relationships, and community.** Through this ideology, heterosexuality is naturalized and viewed as universal. Somewhat like institutional racism and sexism, compulsory heterosexism and heteronormativity are embedded in a society's social structures and maintained by ideologies that are rooted in religion and law (Herek 1995). **Heterosexism is the belief that heterosexuality is the only normal, natural, and moral mode of relating, and hence is superior to homosexuality, bisexuality, or pansexuality** (Wilton 2000). It often leads to homophobia and biphobia.

IDEOLOGICAL BASES OF INEQUALITY BASED ON SEXUAL ORIENTATION

Support for Elisabeth Young-Bruehl's idea that homophobia constitutes a special case of prejudice is echoed in the work of cultural critics such as Bruce Bawer (1994:81). Bawer also believes that homophobia differs significantly from other forms of bigotry:

In a world of prejudice, there is no other prejudice quite like [homophobia]. Mainstream writers, politicians, and cultural leaders who hate Jews or Blacks or Asians but who have long since accepted the unwritten rules that forbid public expression of those prejudices still denounce gays with impunity. For such people, gays are the Other in a way that Jews or Blacks or Asians are not. After all, they can look at Jewish or Black or Asian family life and see something that, in its chief components—husband, wife, children, workplace, school, house of worship—is essentially a variation of their own lives; yet when they look at gays—or, rather, at the image of gays that has been fostered both by the mainstream culture and by the gay subculture—they see creatures whose lives seem to be different from theirs in every possible way. Bawer (1994:81)

According to Bawer, heterosexuals cannot identify with the daily lives of lesbians and gay men, who—unlike them—exist as identifiable categories primarily because there is such strong anti-gay prejudice in Canada. In fact, the stereotypical beliefs that dominant (heterosexual) group members hold about gay men and lesbians are a major impediment to reducing inequalities based on sexual orientation (Nava and Dawidoff 1994).

Stereotypical beliefs about lesbians and gay men often equate people's sexual *orientation* with sexual *practice*. For example, gay men and lesbians—regardless of the nature and extent of their sexual activity—are often still stereotyped as "sex obsessed, sexually compulsive, and sexually predatory" (Nava and Dawidoff 1994:32). Despite increases in the profile of homosexuals in mainstream media, media depictions still tend to reinforce stereotypes of gay men as sexual predators or effeminate sissies while lesbians are still depicted as butch, man-hating "dykes" (Nava and Dawidoff 1994; Wilton 2000). More recently, movies such as *The Kids are Alright, The Family Stone, Imagine Me and You,* and *A Touch of Pink* have attempted to demonstrate the normalcy of same-sex partnerships, while others, including *Brokeback Mountain* and *Milk,* have attempted to demonstrate some of the harms to bisexual and other non-heterosexual people caused by living in a homophobic culture. Television shows such as *Game of Thrones, Modern Family,* and *Glee* have sought to bring gay and lesbian issues into prime-time programming, while hit series such as *Revenge, Dexter,* and *Grey's Anatomy* profile bisexual characters. Although some shows perpetuate negative stereotypes about lesbians and gay men, others have attempted, with varying levels of success, to change public perceptions about issues related to sexual orientation (see Box 6.1).

Social Media and Questioning Youth: Boon or Bane?

In a heteronormative environment such as ours, heterosexual practices and values are considered the norm and deviations from them are seen as a threat to the dominant value system. However, the Internet, and social media in particular, now offers the opportunity for minority groups to create virtual spaces in which their values and practices can be normative.

In 2013, the Pew Research Center, which styles itself as a "nonprofit, nonpartisan and non-advocacy fact tank" in the United States, conducted a large study (nearly 1200 people) regarding Internet use among LGBT people. Their findings indicated that gays, lesbians, and bisexuals use social media proportionately more than heterosexuals, although the age of the research participants may be a factor in the differences to some degree. A total of 80 percent of participants stated that they use social networking sites such as Facebook and Twitter, as compared with 58 percent of the general population (Duggan and Smith 2013). The researchers also found that 55 percent of LGBT Internet users said they had met a new friend online, and over one-half of the participants said they had come out on a social networking site.

Recently, hundreds of LGBT-focused social media websites have emerged, both locally and internationally. Some examples include Hornet, Jake, Connexion, DList, BigJock, OutEverywhere, and Planetout. Many of these websites are highly specialized in their focus. Some are used for searching out dating relationships, while others serve as support networks for members of the LGBT community. The research by Pew Research Center found that gay men are more likely to have met someone online compared with lesbians and bisexual people (Duggan and Smith 2013). Only 16 percent of study participants said they used the Internet to discuss issues surrounding LGBT.

Niche social networks are a viable business because they allow specialized functionality and create a subjective community-feel as opposed to general interest sites, like Facebook, which cater to the general population. Many LGBT people want to participate in social networks, but often prefer networks specifically set up for people they can relate to and who may share similar experiences, such as coming out at work or the process of adopting a child as a gay parent. Specialized social networks have allowed many minority communities to come together in a context in which they are, often for the first time, the majority.

However, even mainstream social networks have taken certain steps to support the LGBT community. For example, Facebook has recently added two new options to its list of relationship status possibilities, "in a civil union" and "in a domestic partnership." These new features have been received with open arms by many LGBT advocacy groups, who view it as a sign of support for gay rights. The relationship status changes were made in consultation with Facebook's *Network of Support*, a group that includes LGBT organizations such as the Gay and Lesbian Alliance Against Defamation, the Gay, Lesbian, and Straight Education Network, and the Human Rights Campaign.

Potential Benefits of Social Media to Members of the LGBT Community

Facebook and other social media can act as a lifeline for young people struggling with their sexuality. Isolated teens and transgender teens, in particular, are able to get support with what they are experiencing and find a sense of community online. Speaking to and learning from other people who are, or who have been, in a similar position allows many questioning teens to find security and comfort with their situation.

Teens who are struggling with coming out to their families and friends now have a way to reach out to others and get support, advice, and encouragement. Online gay communities such as R U Coming Out and the It Gets Better project were created to show young people that the struggles they are going through are temporary and to demonstrate that they are not alone.

Facebook, as the dominant social networking website, has become a major part of coming out for many people. Making one's sexual orientation public on Facebook (making it "Facebook official") can be beneficial in the sense that asserting one's whole, authentic self can be an effective way to end any rumours and assumptions that others may have made while enabling one to claim an identity to feel proud of.

Potential Detriments of Social Media to Members of the LGBT Community

Because teens are not fully prepared for the rapidity and replicability of online information, social media can also create potential risks. Before social media, if someone was rumoured to be gay, the rumour had to be passed from one person to another. Now, rumours or truths can be posted for thousands to read, and possibly also see, if there is some kind of photographic element. In addition, 55.2 percent of LGBT students in the United States reported being cyber-bullied, via texts and social media sites, because of their sexual orientation (GLSEN 2011). The effects of this widespread rumour mongering, forced "outing," and general harassment can be disastrous for a young person struggling with sexual orientation or gender identity issues.

Another source of stress for LGBT youth is that Facebook asks people to identify their relationship status, and whether they are interested in men, women, or both, leaving very little room for ambiguity, no "questioning" choice, and no way to account for pansexual preferences. Young people also feel pressure to be completely open online, whereas adults who remember the old norms have less trouble simply leaving certain fields blank or hidden.

Do you think that social media are mostly beneficial for LGBT people? Have you experienced or seen social media used for the benefit of, or to the detriment of, someone questioning sexual orientation, gender identity, and so on? What ways can social networking sites continue to change to accommodate non-heterosexual users?

Religion and Sexual Orientation

The major difference between homophobia and biphobia and other forms of discrimination, such as sexism or racism, is that many people believe that homosexuality or bisexuality is morally wrong. These beliefs are often, although not always, linked to religious affiliation. For example, health researcher Tamsin Wilton (2000:9) cites a strong association found by many researchers between homophobic and biphobic attitudes and strong religious beliefs. Some people use their religious affiliation as a way of reinforcing their existing prejudices against gays and lesbians, while others interpret their religious doctrines as genuinely forbidding same-sex relations (Wilton 2000:9). In Canada, while civil marriages are now legalized between same-sex couples, the law has stated that no religion or faith is compelled to endorse or marry same-sex couples in faith-based ceremonies.

Most of the major religions of the world—Judaism, Christianity, Islam, and Hinduism, as well as Confucianism—have historically regarded homosexuality as a sin. Indeed, the only major world religion that does not condemn homosexuality is Buddhism (Dynes 1990), although historically acceptance of sexual diversity has varied across Buddhist cultures (Baird 2007). This is not to suggest that all, or even most, practising religious people are homophobic, only that most of the major religions provide justifications for homophobia, should people want them. Fundamentalists of all religions particularly denounce homosexual conduct as a sign of great moral decay and societal chaos.

Some Canadian churches, such as the United Church of Canada, have declared that all people, regardless of sexual orientation, are entitled to become full members of the church, including the right to become ordained ministers. In this spirit, the Unitarian Universalist Church also welcomes LGBT individuals and families to join their congregations through their website:

Unitarian Universalist congregations extend a warm welcome to Bisexual, Gay, Lesbian, and Transgender (BGLT) people and their families. We encourage you to seek your own spiritual path and visit our congregations, places where people gather to nurture their spirits and put their faith into action by helping to make our communities—and the world—a better place. (Unitarian Universalist Association of Congregations 2009)

Still, increasing numbers of lesbians and gay men are carving out their own niches in religious organizations. Some gay men and lesbians have sought to bring about changes in established religious denominations; others have formed religious bodies, such as the Metropolitan Community Church, that specifically focus on the spiritual needs of LGBT communities. Like anyone, gay men and lesbians believe that they should not have to choose between full participation in their church and a committed relationship (Dunlap 1996).

Law and Sexual Orientation

However divided Canadians are in their opinions about the rights gays and lesbians should be afforded in society, both tolerance and acceptance of homosexuality and bisexuality have increased in Canada in past decades. Canadian citizens are much more tolerant of homosexual and bisexual relations than are U.S. citizens, although the vast majority of people in both countries believe that, with regard to employment, there should be no discrimination on the basis of sexual orientation. In a 1996 Gallup poll, 60 percent of Canadians said they believed that homosexuality was acceptable, compared with 44 percent of people in the United States. Similarly, 64 percent of Canadians believed that consensual homosexual acts between adults should be legal, while 48 percent of people in the United States agreed. The most recent poll covering same-sex relationships, conducted by Angus Reid in January 2013, offered a random sample of adults in Canada, the United States, and Britain a list of 21 issues with which to state their opinion as to their morality (see Table 6.2). On the question of "sexual relations between two people of the same sex" being morally acceptable, 64 percent of Canadians, 58 percent of Britons, and only 40 percent of Americans agreed. Increasingly, Canadians are becoming more accepting, or at least more "tolerant," of same-sex relationships.

Over the past four decades, Canadians have witnessed first the decriminalization of sexual practices associated with same-sex relations; second, the inclusion of sexual orientation as a prohibited ground in human rights legislation; and third, the enactment of federal and provincial legislation aimed at recognizing rights of same-sex couples (Demczuk et al. 2002:viii). Therefore, in Canada, discrimination on the basis of sexual orientation is prohibited everywhere. In Alberta, the provincial legislation deliberately omitted sexual

orientation as a prohibited ground for discrimination; however, the Supreme Court of Canada stated in a groundbreaking April 1998 case (*Vriend v. Alberta*) that Alberta's human rights legislation would be *interpreted* as including sexual orientation as a prohibited ground for discrimination, whether the legislation specifically stated this or not, in order to bring Alberta's legislation in line with that of the rest of the provinces and territories.

These advances have been diligently pushed for and won by gay, lesbian, bisexual, and queer advocates, mainly through successful legal challenges and not, as Demczuk and colleagues (2002:viii) point out, through "the expression of any political will on the part of the federal [territorial] and provincial governments to systematically eliminate discrimination."

TABLE 6.2 Personal Morality of Canadians, Americans, and Britons, 2013

Regardless of whether or not you think each of the following issues should be legal, please indicate whether you personally believe they are morally acceptable or morally wrong. *Only responses indicating "morally acceptable" are listed in this table.*	Morally acceptable responses		
	Canada	United States	Britain
Contraception	91%	79%	91%
Sexual relations between an unmarried man and woman	83%	59%	82%
Divorce	80%	65%	79%
Having a baby outside of marriage	78%	53%	74%
Gambling	70%	63%	60%
Medical research using stem cells obtained from human embryos	65%	52%	56%
Doctor-assisted suicide	65%	35%	61%
Sexual relations between two people of the same sex	64%	40%	58%
Abortion	60%	36%	54%
The death penalty	53%	58%	50%
Buying and wearing clothing made of animal fur	50%	42%	21%
Pornography	42%	32%	40%
Prostitution	41%	23%	34%
Medical testing on animals	38%	31%	29%
Cloning animals	26%	23%	20%
Using illegal drugs	24%	17%	16%
Suicide	22%	13%	29%
Married men and/or women having an affair	14%	7%	13%
Polygamy, when one husband has more than one wife at the same time	14%	13%	10%
Cloning humans	10%	12%	9%
Paedophilia	1%	2%	1%

Source: *Angus Reid Public Opinion Poll, January 31, 2013, "Americans More Morally Conservative Than Canadians or Britons" (http://www.angusreidglobal.com/wp-content/uploads/2013/01/2013.01.31_Morality.pdf).*

In the late 1960s, the Canadian government debated many much-needed reforms to the *Criminal Code* in order to make it more reflective of current and changing Canadian values and practices. In a 1969 omnibus bill, sexual acts that were committed between consenting adults fell within the parameters of individual freedoms, and thus many sexual practices, some believed to be associated with homosexuality—for example, anal sex or "sodomy"—were decriminalized. It still took until 1977 for the federal government to do away with the immigration regulation prohibiting homosexuals from immigrating to Canada.

> The 1969 Act . . . did not represent "a legalization of homosexuality," but rather a partial decriminalization of certain sexual practices that were not limited to homosexuals but were often associated with them. Beyond these changes to the Criminal Code, violence, discrimination in employment, police harassment and distinctions in terms of conjugality continued to exist with impunity. (Demczuk et al. 2002:6)

In the 1960s, the United Nations adopted the *Universal Declaration of Human Rights*. As a liberal democracy and member nation, Canada was obligated to both respect this and similar declarations and to make illegal any government acts that infringe on people's individual rights. Along with the federal government, most provinces also enacted their own human rights legislation in the late 1960s and early 1970s. When Canada repatriated its Constitution in 1982, the *Canadian Charter of Rights and Freedoms* gained ascendancy, and its section 15 provided a vehicle for disenfranchised groups to seek remedy through court challenges. Section 15(1) of the *Charter* reads,

> Every individual is equal before and under the law and has the right to the equal protection and equal benefit of the law without discrimination and, in particular, without discrimination based on race, national or ethnic origin, colour, religion, sex, age, or mental or physical disability.

In 1977, Quebec became the first province to include sexual orientation as a prohibited grounds of discrimination in its provincial human rights legislation. Ontario followed nine years later, but it still took 21 years and the *Vriend* decision for sexual orientation to be extended as a prohibited ground in all Canadian provinces and territories.

Throughout the 1980s and 1990s, through legal challenges about pensions, bereavement leaves, alimony, and various other family-law issues, individuals pushed, with varying levels of success, for recognition of same-sex

couples as legally no different from heterosexual couples. Governments continued to make case-by-case decisions, in several cases insisting that the decisions be non–precedent setting and that they be given more time to integrate the rights of minority groups into existing law. Finally, in the *Vriend v. Alberta* case, the Supreme Court of Canada stated:

> The need for government incrementalism was an inappropriate justification for *Charter* violations. . . . In my opinion, groups that have historically been the target of discrimination cannot be expected to wait patiently for the protection of their human dignity and equal rights while governments move toward reform one step at a time. If the infringement of the rights and freedoms of these groups is permitted to persist while governments fail to pursue equality diligently, then the guarantees of the *Charter* will be reduced to little more than empty words. (*Vriend v. Alberta* 1998. S.C.R. 493, paragraph 122, cited in Demczuk et al. 2002:17)

One year later, following a Supreme Court ruling that made distinctions between heterosexual couples and homosexual couples unconstitutional, several provincial governments amended their *Family Law* acts to include provision for same-sex couples by changing the definition of "spouse." The first to make these changes were British Columbia, Quebec, and Ontario in 1999 and Nova Scotia in 2000 (see Figure 6.1). Besides allowing same-sex partners the same benefits and responsibilities as heterosexual partners (e.g. inheritance, pensions), same-sex couples today are usually able to adopt an unrelated child with both potential parents formally applying and being listed as parent applicants. This follows the 1999 Supreme Court of Canada ruling in *M v. H* that opposite-sex definitions being read into the word "spouse" were "unconstitutional." This ruling came into effect as of March 1, 2000, and had implications for adoption acts that stated "spouses" could adopt children. Each province and territory in Canada oversees its own adoptions, and many same-sex couples have successfully adopted children in Canada.

Same-sex couples in British Columbia, Ontario, and Quebec challenged Canada's marriage laws in 2000. Many advocates believed that until same-sex couples were granted the right to legally marry across Canada, they would not be viewed by society as legitimate and would continue to be disenfranchised from some of the financial and many of the social benefits—such as holding hands in public, bringing one's spouse to the company picnic, having one's partnership recognized by one's parents as more than a "phase"—enjoyed by heterosexual spouses. In July 2002, two men who married in a church ceremony but were denied a marriage licence

Figure 6.1 Provinces and Territories Permitting Same-Sex Marriage Before Nationwide Legalization in 2005.
Source: *Map Courtesy of Ink Blot Visual Communications.*

by the Ontario provincial government took their case to court. Three Ontario Superior Court judges ruled that the law prohibiting same-sex marriages was unconstitutional. The Government of Canada was appealing the ruling, but on June 17, 2003, on the recommendation of federal Justice Minister Martin Cauchon, Prime Minister Chrétien announced that the federal government would no longer engage in the legal battle and would support marriage for gays and lesbians across Canada.

As Canadians debated the issue of same-sex marriage, the courts were doing their work. On December 9, 2004, the Supreme Court of Canada ruled that Ottawa *did* have the exclusive right to determine who had the right to marry in Canada. The government's same-sex marriage bill, Bill C-38, came up for the vote in Cabinet on June 28, 2005. It passed by a 158–133 margin, with the support coming from most Liberals, the NDP, and the Bloc

Québécois. Bill C-38 became law on July 20, 2005, after being passed by the Senate and receiving Royal Assent.

Canada became the fourth country, after the Netherlands, Belgium, and Spain, to legalize same-sex marriage. Since legalization in Canada in 2005, 11 other countries have legalized same-sex marriage, along with several American and Mexican states, and many additional countries offer some type of legal recognition of same-sex unions (Angus Reid 2009; Desilver 2013). The most recent (and 21st) nation to allow same-sex marriage at the time of publication is the United States, occurring June 26, 2015. See Figure 6.2 for a snapshot of countries that allow same-sex marriage. As of 2011, Statistics Canada counted 64 575 same-sex couples in Canada in the 2011 Census (Statistics Canada 2013f). Of the same-sex couples reported in 2011, 29 380 are female and 35 195 are male (Statistics Canada 2013f).

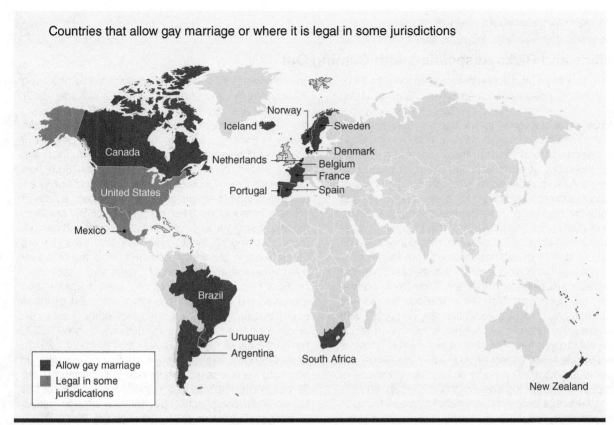

Figure 6.2 Gay Marriage Around the World.

Source: *Drew Desilver, 2013, "A global snapshot of same-sex marriage,"* Pew Research Center. *Retrieved from http://www.pewresearch.org/fact-tank/2013/06/04/global-snapshot-sex-marriage/.*

In a June 2006 Angus Reid poll, 62 percent of Canadians stated clearly that the matter of giving same-sex couples the same right to civil marriage as opposite-sex couples was "settled," and only 27 percent felt the government should reopen the issue (Angus Reid 2006b). The issue has not been raised in Canadian polls since.

Further to these positions, some Canadians suggest that the inclusion of homosexual couples in definitions of "family" and "marriage" and the like will act to destabilize those definitions and categories, perhaps fundamentally and radically altering them for the betterment of all persons (Blasius 2001b; Currah 2001; Gamson 1996; Goldie 2001). This debate mirrors the debate waged between those who use the term "queer" politically—as an essentialist category, to describe themselves, to be recognized and valued for who they are, and to be included as equals with the rest of society—and those who use the term "queer" more theoretically—as a destabilizing entity, a descriptor only in that it implies non-mainstream but refuses to define, in any essential way, what "queer" is or is not. This debate will be discussed in more detail later in the chapter.

DISCRIMINATION BASED ON SEXUAL ORIENTATION

As the campaigns for equal rights and an end to anti-gay discrimination have progressed, more people have come forward to declare that they are gay, lesbian, or bisexual and to indicate their support for LGBT organizations. Lesbian, gay, and bisexual people continue to seek all the same rights and privileges that heterosexual people enjoy. Many people, however, continue to find themselves the victims of discrimination and hate (see Box 6.2).

Victimization and Hate Crimes

On November 17, 2001, Aaron Webster, a 41-year-old Vancouver photographer, was viciously beaten to death near Second Beach in Stanley Park by a group of three or four men. While gay bashing in Vancouver, Toronto, and other large Canadian cities is well documented (see EGALE 2013; Janoff 2005; Lindell and Mickleburgh 2010), Webster's death marked the first time a person

Politics and Risks Associated with Coming Out

In line with most social psychological models of identity formation, psychologist Jean Baker (2001:45) states that coming out is a "complex discovery process that children or adolescents go through as they gradually recognize their homosexual identity and acknowledge it to themselves and then to others." Unlike homosexuals or bisexuals, heterosexuals have no such process to undergo. As a member of the group that is the norm, or cultural standard, they learn from a very early age what social work researcher Janet Sawyer (1989) calls "internalized dominance." Internalized dominance refers to all the messages, overt and otherwise, that signify to White people or straight people or people with no disabilities or men that they are normal; they are the standard; they are acceptable just being who they are. They are in no way "other," as people of colour or Indigenous people are; as women are; as sexual minorities are; as people with disabilities are. One of the privileges of being part of the dominant group is the privilege of never having to consider how a fundamental aspect of your self—your sexual orientation, for example—impacts on your life. Contrast this with people who belong to a marginalized group, and it is easy to see that people in marginalized groups must, at least potentially, deal with or consider their status every day. They must consider how being openly gay or lesbian will impact their job search or apartment search or family holiday or grade in a class. Will it get them verbally or physically harassed or assaulted today?

Baker (2001:46) notes that "coming to terms with one's homosexual identity is a developmental task required of the gay, [lesbian, bisexual, or pansexual individual] but one for which he or she receives little guidance and for which successful role models are seldom available." This situation is changing for the better today with access to the Internet, and particularly to social media (see Box 6.1). Taking a slightly different approach from Baker, political theorist and LGBT activist Mark Blasius (2001a:155), in a discussion of an "ethos" of gay and lesbian existence, states that coming out is a multifaceted and lifelong process. Blasius believes that coming out, the goal of which is to live one's life as a lesbian or gay man, is not just about disclosure of one's gay or lesbian identity to one's self and others: "Rather than being an end-state in which one exists as an 'out' person, coming out is a process of becoming, a lifelong learning of how to become and of inventing the meaning of being a lesbian or a gay man in this historical moment." Coming out thus refers both to "an ontological recognition of the self by the self" and a "fundamental political act" (Blasius 2001a:155).

Defining oneself as gay or lesbian or bisexual or pansexual can have serious, and often negative, consequences for youth due to the prevalence of homophobia and biphobia in society. According to Parents and Friends of Lesbians and Gays (PFLAG) Canada, LGBT youth hear anti-gay slurs an average of 26 times every day (2009). Further, a recent national school climate survey in the United States found that 71.3 percent of youth heard homophobic remarks such as "faggot" and "dyke" frequently or often at their schools, 56.9 percent heard these kinds of remarks from teachers, overall making 63.5 percent of LGBT youth feel unsafe at school. In addition, 81.9 percent of LGBT students reported being verbally harassed at school, 38.8 percent reported being physically harassed, and 18.3 percent reported being physically assaulted within the past year due to their sexual orientation. Unsurprisingly, the majority (60.4 percent) of students who were harassed and assaulted did not report the incidences and of those who did, 36.7 percent reported that nothing was said or done by the school (for the full report, see GLSEN National School Climate Survey 2011; PFLAG 2013). Unsurprisingly, one-quarter of youth who identify as non-heterosexual leave school due to harassment, and 40 percent report that their performance at school has been negatively affected by conflicts around sexual orientation (Dobinson 2004; Mooney et al. 2003).

In a Canadian study conducted by sociologist Cheryl Dobinson (2004:55), homophobia in schools is overt and includes "violence, threats of violence, intimidation, verbal abuse, and homophobic slurs." As one young woman states, "I wanted to just forget about the teasing. I thought, it'll just go away, but it didn't. It definitely affected my actions. I started ditching school" ("Amy," quoted in Dobinson 2004:66). Further, queer-friendly counselling and support services are often nonexistent in schools, as are positive role models and library and other resource materials (Dobinson 2004). Often, LGBT youth feel they cannot come out at home or at school, leading to violence against oneself and suicide attempts, the ultimate example of internalized oppression. One survey of gay youth found that 30 percent of those identifying themselves as homosexual had attempted suicide in the past year, compared with 7 percent of those identifying themselves as heterosexual (PFLAG 2009; Platt 2001, in Mooney et al. 2003). Recent statistics from PFLAG NYC state that LGBT youth are 8.4 times more likely to have attempted suicide and 5.9 times more likely to experience high levels of depression (PFLAG 2013). A Calgary study found that gay and bisexual males were nearly 14 times more likely to have seriously attempted suicide than heterosexual males were (Mooney et al. 2003). This study also demonstrated that non-heterosexual youth of colour (lesbians, gay males, and bisexuals) were "dramatically overrepresented in the attempted-suicide statistics" ("Pierre Tremblay" in

Social Problems and Social Policy

Box 6.2 continued

Fisher 1999, in Mooney et al. 2004:299). As this young man relays, "I realize that I made some choices, but when I first started cutting [classes] I felt I was making the only choice. It was for simple survival. I wasn't choosing to fuck up, I was choosing to not kill myself . . . I decided I didn't feel pride in graduating from a school that had treated me in this way" ("Brent," in Dobinson 2004:66).

When LGBT youth feel they have no choice but to quit school because the bullying is unbearable, not only are their lives impacted in that moment, but that "choice" affects their future, socially and with regard to employment and further education. Twenty-six percent of LGBT youth are told to leave home when their parents find out they are gay or lesbian, and LGBT youth are much more likely to become homeless at an early age (PFLAG 2009). There

is also evidence that gay, lesbian, and bisexual youth are coming out at earlier ages today than in the past (Baker 2001; Dobinson 2004). This speaks to the need for more and earlier supports, particularly in schools, such as LGBT-straight Alliances and specific policies about LGBT bullying. Internet chat rooms and dedicated LGBT phone lines are two supports that youth can access from almost anywhere in Canada. Dobinson, who volunteered at an LGBT youth phone line, notes that "I have no doubt that being able to reach out over the phone and talk to another gay, lesbian or bisexual young person contributes directly to saving lives" (2004:69).

What do you think should be done to decrease the numbers of suicides and attempted suicides among non-heterosexual youth?

---

could have been charged with a hate crime in British Columbia regarding sexual orientation. It would not, unfortunately, be the last.

In Canada, under the *Criminal Code,* there is no "hate crime legislation" per se. Rather, under "Purposes and Principles for Sentencing," section 718.2 states that:

a court that imposes a sentence shall also take into consideration the following principles:

(a) a sentence should be increased or reduced to account for any relevant aggravating or mitigating circumstances relating to the offence or the offender, and, without limiting the generality of the foregoing . . .

(i) evidence that the offence was motivated by bias, prejudice or hate based on race, national or ethnic origin, language, colour, religion, sex, age, mental or physical disability, sexual orientation, or any other similar factor. . . . (Department of Justice Canada 2006b)

Before the early 1990s, few acts of violence against gays and lesbians were ever reported in the media. Indeed, hate crimes against gay men and lesbians were not even acknowledged as such. Although research is finally being done, the scope and extent of hate crimes based on sexual orientation is not yet known (MacMillan and Claridge 1998). However, hate crimes appear to be most prevalent where homophobic attitudes and behaviours are tolerated or at least overlooked. The 2001 murder of Adam Webster was not an isolated hate crime—many other incidents are reported across the country every week, and hate crimes based on sexual orientation continue to increase

whereas hate crimes based on other social characteristics (e.g. ethnicity, religion) have decreased. Alarmingly, the 2009 General Social Survey (GSS) found that only one-third of those who believed they had been victimized by a hate crime had actually reported it to the police (GSS 2009; Dauvergne and Brennan 2011). Further, the B.C. Hate Crimes Team estimates that only between 5 and 10 percent of all hate crimes are actually reported to police (MacMillan and Claridge 1998:2) and that "based on the number of hate/bias crimes 'reported' to the police in the late 1990s, gay males were the most victimized group in Vancouver" (MacMillan and Claridge 1998:5). In fact, due to the increases in attacks against non-heterosexual people and the disproportionate amount of violence of these attacks, Vancouver has been dubbed "the gay bashing capital of Canada" (Lindell and Mickleburgh 2010).

In July 2011, Statistics Canada released a study of hate-motivated crime (see Figure 6.3). While 52 percent of hate crimes are motivated by racism, 18 percent are motivated by homophobia. What is of particular note, corroborating the findings of the B.C. Hate Crimes Team over a decade earlier, is that 65 percent of hate crimes based on sexual orientation are violent crimes, generally assault, and are the most likely to result in physical injuries. This is in striking contrast to crimes motivated by racism (41 percent are violent crimes) or religious intolerance (16 percent are violent).

Statistics Canada's recent police-reported hate crime study also found that 92 percent of those accused of a hate crime based on sexual orientation were male and 71 percent were under the age of 25. Victims of hate crimes motivated by sexual orientation tended also to

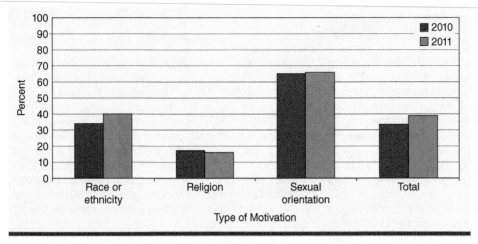

Figure 6.3   Percentage of hate crimes involving violent offences, by motivation, Canada 2010 and 2011.

Source: "Police-reported hate crime in Canada, 2011". Mary Allen and Jillian Boyce. Canadian Centre for Justice Statistics. *Juristat.* Catalogue no. 85-002-x. ISSN: 1209-6393).

be young (50 percent under age 25 years) and male (85 percent) (Allen and Boyce, 2013).

Further, data from Ontario show that most hate crimes (95 percent) are committed by individuals who are not connected to an organized hate group, despite most people's beliefs that organized hate groups such as racist groups are most often responsible for hate crimes (MacMillan and Claridge 1998:6). Clearly, stronger and more pervasive measures must be taken to eliminate homophobia, biphobia, and associated hate crimes.

Sexual orientation inequality can be understood from various perspectives. Sociological explanations focus primarily on how various aspects of sexual identity and homophobia are associated with social learning and/or social structural factors in society. We'll look at each perspective separately.

PERSPECTIVES ON SEXUAL ORIENTATION AND SOCIAL INEQUALITY

Interactionist Perspectives

Similar to some social psychological perspectives, interactionist perspectives view all sexual conduct—heterosexual and homosexual—as learned behaviour; therefore, they tend to focus on the process by which individuals come to identify themselves as gay, lesbian, bisexual, pansexual, or straight. According to interactionists, most people acquire the status of *heterosexual* without being consciously aware of it. Because heterosexuality is the established norm in Canadian society, heterosexuals do not have to struggle over

their identity. They have the privilege of not ever thinking about sexual orientation. But the same is not true of people who come to identify themselves as *homosexual, bisexual* or *pansexual*. In fact, some sociologists suggest that sexual orientation is likely to be a master status for many non-heterosexuals (Schur 1965). A **master status is the most significant status a person possesses, the one that most determines how the individual views him- or herself and how he or she is viewed and treated by others.** Master status based on sexual orientation is particularly significant when it is linked to other subordinate racialized/ethnic group statuses in a matrix of interlocking oppressions (see Chapter 1 for more discussion). For example, working-class gay Latinos may be more hesitant than White, middle-class gay men to come out to their families because of cultural norms pertaining to *machismo* (masculinity) and the fear that relatives will withdraw the support that is essential for surviving at the subordinate end of racialized and class hierarchies (see Almaguer 1995).

Interactionists have identified several common themes that people may experience in the process of accepting a lesbian, gay, bisexual, or pansexual identity (Weinberg et al. 1994). First, people may experience identity confusion—a situation in which they feel different from other people they know and struggle with admitting that they are attracted to individuals of the same sex. For example, "Brandon," a 17-year-old in Bass and Kaufman's 1996 study, stated,

> If my "naturalness" wasn't going to come by itself, then I was ready to force it on myself. . . . I did some really drastic things—all of which I hoped would make me do a complete turnaround and become a heterosexual. (quoted in Dobinson 2004:63)

Another youth in the same study, "Matt," explains his attempts to come to terms with the possibility that he might be gay, saying,

> I'll do anything for this not to be me. I decided I just won't have sex with men. I'll just have sex with women and get married and live a normal life. That was my attitude for a long time. I didn't know anyone gay, not anyone. So, I tried all this different stuff to make myself be straight, like going to dances with girls. (quoted in Dobinson 2004:63)

In the past, many gay and lesbian people had nowhere to turn in their quest for answers and support from others; today, many use the Internet and other forms of global communication to connect with others who share their concerns (see Box 6.1) (Gabriel 1995). It is important to keep in mind, however, that in a more accepting and less homophobic society, young people would not need to feel their lives were "over" when experiencing feelings of attraction for those of the same sex.

A second part of the process of establishing a non-heterosexual identity can be seeking out others who are openly lesbian or gay and perhaps engaging in sexual experimentation or making other forays into a homosexual subculture. A typical third theme that many people report as part of their coming-out process is an attempt to integrate their self-concept and acceptance of a label such as "homosexual," "gay," or "lesbian" by pursuing a way of life that conforms to their definition of what those labels mean (Cass 1984; Coleman 1981/2; Ponse 1978). This may take a variety of forms. As with most of the "stage" theories that deal with identity construction, it is important to note that not all people experience the same things in coming to terms with their sexual orientation, whatever it is. It is worth noting that many young people today do not experience coming out as especially traumatic; more often today than before, youth may have supportive parents, school counsellors, peers, and other family members.

Studies on how people come to accept their sexual identity as gay, bisexual, or lesbian show the significance of labelling in identity construction. Labelling, while potentially helpful in some instances, can also create barriers to full participation in Canadian society. However, studies on labelling to date have been typically based on a relatively narrow selection of people, which makes it difficult to generalize the findings to larger populations. That is, research participants who openly identify themselves as gay or bisexual may not be characteristic of the larger homosexual or bisexual population (Weinberg et al. 1994).

Longitudinal research on women who self-identified as bisexual, lesbian, or unlabelled suggests that sexual orientation can be fluid, among women at least (Diamond 2008). In Lisa Diamond's ongoing research with 79 women in the United States, she has been exploring questions around bisexual identity formation. She was interested in evidence that supported one of three theories about bisexuality. One theory posits that bisexuality is a transitory stage of denial and experimentation after which individuals choose one or the other orientation (heterosexual or homosexual). A second theory suggests that bisexuality is a third category of sexual orientation in which people remain attracted to people of both sexes. A third theory argues that bisexuality is really an intensified form of human beings' capacity for sexual fluidity, its particular manifestation influenced by openness to other forms of sexual expression (e.g., not just heterosexual) and opportunities for openness to be translated in action. What Diamond has found so far, over a 10-year period, is that two-thirds of women changed their identity once and one-third changed it twice or more, suggesting that "identity change is more common than identity stability" (Diamond 2008:13). Diamond concludes that there is strong evidence to support the second and third theories put forth.

Functionalist and Conflict Perspectives

Unlike the interactionist approach, which focuses primarily on how individuals come to identify themselves as homosexual, bisexual, or heterosexual, functionalist perspectives focus on the relationship between social structure and sexual orientation. To functionalists, social norms and laws are established to preserve social institutions and maintain stability in society. From this perspective, then, many societies punish homosexual conduct because it violates the social norms established by those societies and thus undermines their stability. Sociologist David P. Aday, Jr., provides an overview of this perspective:

> Marriage and family are structural arrangements that contribute to the continuity of our contemporary society. . . . [Homosexuality undermines] arrangements that currently operate to replace societal members in an orderly way—that is, the arrangement has survival value. . . . If homosexual conduct were allowed to exist unchallenged and unpunished, then it might in time undermine norms and laws that underpin monogamous marital sex, at least some of which results in the production of offspring to repopulate the society. . . . The punishment of

homosexual conduct, from ridicule and discrimination to imprisonment, reinforces expectations about heterosexual and marital sex and defines the boundaries of society. (Aday 1990:25)

The functionalist perspective supports the ideas of those people who do not believe homosexual conduct or marriages between lesbian or gay couples should be protected legally. It also explains why some religious and political leaders call for a renewal of heterosexual "family values" in North America. But, as pointed out by political scientist and gay rights activist Andrew Sullivan (1997:147), non-heterosexual people are part of heterosexual families too:

> [They] are sons and daughters, brothers and sisters, even mothers and fathers, of heterosexuals. The distinction between "families" and "homosexuals" is, to begin with, empirically false; and the stability of existing families is closely linked to how homosexuals are treated within them.

Importantly, as a popular slogan states, "Hate is *NOT* a family value."

Critics suggest that the functionalist approach supports the status quo and ignores a need for more current definitions of marriage and family. If marriage is understood to be the decision of two people to live together in a partnership—to be a family—then the intention or the capacity to have children should not be a condition. Furthermore, when heterosexual couples do not have children, they can still be defined as a family, so reproductive capacity should not play a role. Critics of the theory say that nothing but custom mandates that marital partners must be of different genders and sexes (Nava and Dawidoff 1994).

Whereas the functionalist approach focuses on how existing social arrangements create a balance in society, the conflict approach focuses on *tensions* in society and *differences* in interests and power among opposing groups. From this perspective, people who hold the greatest power are able to have their own attitudes, beliefs, and values—about sexual orientation, in this case—represented and enforced, while others are not (Aday 1990). Therefore, norms pertaining to *compulsory heterosexuality* reflect the beliefs of dominant group members who hold high-level positions in the federal, territorial, and provincial governments and other social institutions. However, critics assert that the conflict approach fails to recognize that some people who have wealth and power are gay or lesbian yet take no action to reduce discrimination based on sexual orientation. People inhabit multiple social locations in their lives, and sexual orientation is often only one of many—and it is often not a master status for many non-heterosexuals.

Many individuals go through similar processes of accepting their identities as lesbian, gay, bisexual, or pansexual over time. Being accepted for who they are by family and friends, and finding others who are open about their sexual orientation, can help the journey to self-acceptance.

Anton Gvozdikov/Shutterstock

According to Karl Marx, conflicts over values are an essential element of social life, and less-powerful people often challenge the laws imposed on them by those in positions of power. For example, adverse decisions by provincial courts and the Supreme Court of Canada have often resulted in increased political activism by gay and lesbian rights groups. In recent years, more openly lesbian and gay people can be found in public office, as elected or appointed officials; in the medical and legal professions; as educators and business leaders; and in all walks of life. However, regardless of their location in the power structure, most non-heterosexuals remain acutely aware that many social barriers have not been lifted and that major shifts in people's attitudes toward homosexuality and bisexuality are still not realized.

With rapid Internet communications and social media, non-heterosexuals around the world keep informed about political decisions that may affect them. Many coalitions have been formed to organize gay pride marches and protests around the world. For example, the International Lesbian, Gay, Bisexual, Trans and Intersex Association (ILGA) reports that more than 750 lesbian and gay groups exist, on every continent and in more than 110 nations (Hendriks et al. 1993; ILGA 2009; ILGA 2013).

Feminist and Postmodern Perspectives

Feminist perspectives on sexual orientation have shifted considerably over the past few decades. In the late 1960s and through the 1970s, sexual orientation was mainly discussed by radical feminists who, by embracing binary and essentialist notions of males and females, claimed that women everywhere were bonded together in a sisterhood founded on their common oppression by men everywhere. As feminist writer Robin Morgan wrote in 1969, "Women have been subjugated longer than any other people on earth" (1993:42). Feminist scholars Robyn Rowland and Renate Klein echoed this in 1996: "The first and fundamental theme is that women as a social group are oppressed by men as a social group and that this is the primary oppression for women" (1996:11). Along with the radical feminist theories of patriarchy came, necessarily, the analyses of compulsory heterosexuality as the cornerstone of male privilege and sexism. Feminist writer Adrienne Rich (1984), in her now famous essay "Compulsory Heterosexuality and Lesbian Existence," pointed out that heterosexuality, far from being a "natural" inclination, was, in fact, systematically imposed upon women through various means, including violence, as well as through hegemonic notions that heterosexuality was natural, inevitable, and universal. The radical feminist response to compulsory heterosexuality was varying degrees of separatism, at least for the short term. As theorist Chris Weedon (1999:36) points out,

> a heterosexual lifestyle was often regarded as incompatible with feminism. To relate sexually to men was to consort with the enemy. This radical version of separatism implied having nothing to do with men, the first step in the process of freeing oneself from patriarchal power structures. This process involved a decolonization of patriarchally defined female consciousness, body image and ways of living. The result, it was thought, would be the discovery of a truly woman-defined womanhood.

This is not to suggest that men, and gay men in particular, are not oppressed by heterosexism or compulsory heterosexuality, but sociologist Mariana Valverde (1987/2000:257) points out, "it weighs particularly heavily on women [as] men do not need female validation for their identity."

The weight of this radical feminist perspective resulted in feelings of guilt and confusion for many heterosexual feminists, estranging some from feminism altogether and reducing many to silence on the question of sexuality (Overall 2000; Valverde 1987/2000; Weedon 1999). However, many feminists became discontented with past analyses and took up the issue of sexuality, focusing on what it means to be both heterosexual and feminist. So, by the late 1980s, Valverde (1987/2000:260) argued that,

> feminism asserts the right of all women to make their erotic choices, and this includes choosing men exclusively. Feminism also rejects the hierarchy of

sexual practices, and so does not seek to substitute a lesbian priority for heterosexism. The goal of feminism in the area of sexuality is to establish true sexual pluralism, where no one choice is presented as "the norm."

Following on the notion of sexual pluralism, some feminist analyses focused on the possibility of being heterosexual and feminist but "conscious" of both the privileges and constraints of one's choice of heterosexuality (Overall 2000). What this question brings up is the thorny issue of privilege. Women as a group may be disenfranchised. Gay men, lesbians, and bisexuals may be disenfranchised. Men have privilege. Heterosexuals have privilege. Therefore, as sociologist Zoe Newman (2001:134) points out, "We need to map our complicity in structures of domination in order to 'move out of the subject position we claim on the margins and into the shifting and multiple subject positions of oppressed and oppressor.'" In effect, theorizing and identifying oneself as both heterosexual and feminist carries with it the discomfort of "disrupt[ing] identity posited on marginality, and reveal[ing] the coexistence of innocence and complicity" (Newman 2001:131). Despite some heterosexual feminists' claims that their relationships with men are completely egalitarian and non-oppressive,

> it nonetheless remains *possible* for the man to take advantage of his potential power. All that stands in the way of his using that power is his own good will, while he is not similarly dependent on the woman's good will. And he still benefits, however indirectly, from male hegemony, and "even the advantages that he is in a position to refuse are waiting for him if he changes his mind." (Overall 2000:267)

Newman draws upon the work of theorist Michel Foucault (2001:134), stating that "even the act of shedding power is born of power; power circulates throughout our relations, it enables and it restricts." Contemporary feminists, then, with regard to the question of sexual orientation, have been focusing on the politics of difference. This is to say that because of the "hierarchization of difference in heterosexist societies," homosexuality and bisexuality continue to be hotly debated political issues within feminism, as much as they are personal ones (Weedon 1999:46). Contemporary feminist scholars also increasingly focus on intersectionality, examining how age, gender, sexual orientation, class, and so on come together in personal identity formation, and on the power of interlocking oppressions, such as ableism, racism, and heterosexism, for example, to create specific time- and context-contingent experiences (Hulko 2008).

Common ground between gay men and lesbians is discussed much more in contemporary liberal feminist perspectives, due, as Weedon (1999) points out, to the achievements of the lesbigay rights movements. For example, feminist psychologist Celia Kitzinger (1987:44) states that "the lesbian and gay man are no longer a species apart, but human beings of equal worth and dignity to heterosexuals, contributing to the rich diversity of humankind." The shift from feminist critiques of patriarchy and male power to a more inclusive politics of difference perspective accompanied the rise of postmodern thought, in particular in the form of *Queer theory*.

The quintessential feature of Queer theory is its staunch theoretical repudiation of any defining features, of any "normality" or "fixedness." Accepting the basic tenets of postmodern thought generally, those who subscribe to Queer theory, or to notions of "queer" in general, allow that nothing is "normal," nothing is "natural"; everything is socially constructed and hence arbitrary. Queer theorists view gender and sexuality as performance (see Judith Butler's 1990 groundbreaking work on "gender as performativity" in *Gender Trouble*) and refuse to hierarchize any sex above another, any gender above another, any mode of sexual expression above another (Weedon 1999:73). Feminist psychologists Sue Wilkinson and Celia Kitzinger (1996:377) summarize one of the main thrusts of Queer theory, which is,

> most popularly . . . [the] "genderfuck" . . . or "fucking with gender." The genderfuck is supposed to "deprive the naturalizing narratives of compulsory heterosexuality of their central protagonists: 'man' and 'woman'" . . . and to illustrate the social constructedness of "sex" in all its multiple meanings.

While Queer theory seeks to subvert notions of "natural" and "normal," making any and every form of sexuality acceptable, many feminists and others find it problematic from a political or social change perspective, for a number of reasons. Queer theorists often view feminism as a "grand narrative," the assumptions and foundational propositions of which must be open to question and critique. Therefore, sexualized violence, pornography, and other heterosexually eroticized models of sexuality that are based in profoundly oppressive patriarchal relations may, within a Queer theory perspective, all be endorsed as "unimportant," "transitory," and "provisional" (Wilkinson and Kitzinger 1996:381): "Power relations within and between heterosexuality and homosexuality become invisible, allowing for a liberalism which hides oppression" (Weedon 1999:76).

Another potential problem is the widespread practice of gays and lesbians reclaiming the term "queer" as a means of self-identification, shifting the term from the pejorative to the celebratory. In doing this, they subvert the radical potential of the term "queer" by using it as an almost essentialist, but certainly bounded or fixed, category that has political value on the one hand but subverts the "mind fuck" potential on the other. From this perspective, then, a more radical use of the term may be for "straights" to begin to identify as "queer," thereby highlighting the multiplicity and arbitrariness of "queer." Indeed, many heterosexual people whose sexuality does not fit the norm for a variety of reasons do identify as queer. In this case, the value of queer as a destabilizing element is highlighted, rather than the term being used as simply a new category; as Newman (2001:129) describes it, defining one's "identity as always founded on a sense of marginality." She further points out that, used in this way, "the potential of queer seems to be that we do not come together around an assumption of sameness, but around a critique of 'the normal'" (Newman 2001:132). Sociologist Joshua Gamson (1996:396) cites queer activists Allan Bérubé and Jeffrey Escoffier in saying that queer is often employed "to affirm sameness by defining a common identity on the fringes." Other critics of Queer theory note that while it may appear radical to reinterpret oneself as "queer," in terms of political activism, it can be problematic. Anthropologist Max H. Kirsch (2000:97) cautions: "It is misguided as political action: it cannot generate the collective energy and organization necessary to challenge existing structures of power."

Defining oneself as queer—as "other" from a norm of heterosexuality—has concrete consequences. Some of these consequences include internalized and external oppression played out in depression, apathy, and violence. Kirsch (2000:97) notes, "We cannot simply refuse to acknowledge these facts of social life in our present society and hope that our circumstances will change." Queer theory therefore contains both the ability to be radical and destabilizing in challenging all things deemed natural or normal and, conversely, the potential to render one completely apolitical and paralyzed by apathy in the abyss of "anything goes." This is neatly summarized by political scientist Paisley Currah (2001:193–194), who also quotes feminist legal scholar Kimberlé Crenshaw (1991):

> "At this point in history, a strong case can be made that the most critical resistance strategy for disempowered groups is to occupy and defend a politics of social location rather than to vacate and destroy it." The appropriation of queer theory's useful theoretical insights by advocates of gay rights and the rights of sexual minorities requires maintaining a delicate balance between the politics of location and the politics of deconstruction.

HOW CAN INEQUALITIES BASED ON SEXUAL ORIENTATION BE REDUCED?

As we have emphasized in previous chapters, how people view a social problem is related to how they believe the problem should be reduced or solved. Inequality based on sexual orientation is no exception. From an interactionist perspective, homosexual conduct is learned behaviour, and people go through a process in establishing a non-heterosexual identity. Society should, therefore, be more accepting of people as they come to understand and accept their sexual identity, even if that identity shifts over time or due to circumstance (Diamond 2008). Legal and social barriers that prevent non-heterosexuals from fully participating in society should be removed, thereby making the often complex psychological and social process of coming out to friends, family, and co-workers easier for those who choose to do so.

According to the functionalist perspective, social norms and laws exist to protect the family and maintain stability in society. Given this, sexual orientation becomes a social issue: activists' demands for equal rights, including legal recognition of same-sex marriages, become major threats to the stability of society. With the legalization of marriage for gays and lesbians in Canada, some groups said that there would be no stopping others who wish to strike down what remains of "foundational truths once thought to be self-evident" (Thomas 1996:A15).

Some advocates of this position believe that lesbians and gay men can change their sexual orientation:

> Homosexuals can and do change. My files bulge with stories of those who once engaged in sex with people of the same gender, but no longer do. They testify to the possibility of change for those who want to. The struggle to maintain what remains of the social fabric will ultimately determine whether we will continue to follow ancient Rome on the road to destruction, or come to our senses, turn around and re-enter a harbour of safety ordained by God for our own protection. (Thomas 1996:A15)

Whether gay, lesbian, bisexual, and pansexual individuals can or should change their sexual orientation is the subject of some disagreement. However, most functionalists agree that homosexuality may be dysfunctional for society if it does not contribute to society's need for new members or if it undermines social norms and laws that preserve the family unit and maintain stability in society.

Conflict theorists believe that prejudice and discrimination against non-heterosexuals are embedded in the social structure of society and are reinforced by those who hold the greatest power and thus are able to perpetuate their own attitudes, beliefs, and values about what constitutes "normal" sexual conduct. From this perspective, homophobia is similar to (but not the same as) racism, sexism, ableism, and ageism, and the overt and covert discrimination that gay men and lesbians experience is similar to (but not the same as) the discrimination experienced by people of colour, Indigenous peoples, all women, people with disabilities, elderly people, and children and youth. According to the conflict approach, the best way to reduce inequality based on sexual orientation is to continue to pass laws that ban all forms of discrimination against non-heterosexuals and to remove barriers to their equality with heterosexuals. However, to gain equal rights, activism is necessary: people must continue to demand social change.

In the past, feminist theorists, using a radical critique of patriarchy, advocated separation of men and women. Lesbianism was promoted as the only rational and non-oppressive mode of relationship. This perspective led to deep divisiveness in the movement as heterosexual feminists had difficulties reconciling their sexual orientation with the political demands of the radical feminist separatists. More recently, feminists have approached questions of sexual orientation from the perspective of sexual pluralism, with the idea that all people, regardless of sexual orientation or gender, need to support one another to combat interlocking matrices of oppression. Therefore, according to contemporary feminists, to reduce inequality based on sexual orientation, people need to understand their commonalities in the face of oppression and also need to be clear about their varying positions of privilege in order to form alliances across social locations. In this way, everyone can fight against inequality based on sexual orientation as well as other inequalities.

Queer theorists believe that gender is a social construction, and therefore sexual orientation is also socially constructed and fluid. People use a queer perspective in one of two ways. Either they use the term "queer" as a descriptive category, or they use it as a stand-in for the terms "gay," "lesbian," or "bisexual." This use is political in that it represents a reclaiming of a term that, in most uses, has been regarded as disparaging. However, the radical potential of "queerness" as something fluid is thus subverted. From this perspective, the category or term is a means of overcoming people's homophobia by being "out," "loud," and "proud"—by demonstrating the normalcy of being outside the "norm" and raising challenging questions such as, "Who defines what or who is normal?" Using "queer" as a political category gives people something to rally around; it helps make collective action possible. Additionally, many people identify themselves as "queer" for a variety of reasons, and so it is an identity marker to use to provide common ground for all those who see themselves in opposition to heteronormativity. Others use a queer perspective to refuse to define self or others, in this way enabling people to grapple with identity, subjectivity, and location.

People may define themselves as queer but refuse to explain what makes them so, forcing people to engage with postmodernist-inspired questions about the importance of categorizing at all. From this perspective, by transgressing gender or sexuality norms (e.g. through cross-dressing or remaining attracted to, and with, a partner who has changed her/his sex or gender), people can flout the norms and demonstrate their arbitrariness and fluidity and thereby have an impact on changing or broadening norms and definitions. This is typically done on an individual basis, making collective actions difficult to organize. However, as pointed out by political scientist James Scott, "most of the political life of subordinate groups is to be found neither in overt collective defiance of powerholders nor in complete hegemonic compliance, but in the vast territory between these two polar opposites" (1990:136).

In the 21st century, gay advocacy is perhaps the most effective means of reducing homophobia and bringing about greater equality for non-heterosexual people. In fact, it took a small riot at the Stonewall Inn in 1969 in New York to make the general public really aware of inequality based on sexual orientation and the need for social change (Weinberg and Williams 1975). As recently as the 1970s in Canada, the RCMP conducted raids on bars known for or suspected of patronage by gays and lesbians. Hundreds of organizations seek equal rights and protections for non-heterosexuals or queer folk; these groups represent a wide cross-section of the Canadian population.

Despite some changes in the attitudes and laws pertaining to homosexuality, discrimination and anti-LGBT prejudice remain strong:

> Gay rights advocates argue that gay men, lesbians, and bisexuals should not be the only ones responsible for reducing or eliminating inequality based on sexual orientation: It all comes down to this: Are people equal in this society by virtue of their citizenship, or not? If the answer is no, then we will be saying that equality does not exist . . . anymore but has been replaced by tiers of citizenship, and that what tier you occupy depends on whether people like you or not. And if we accept this, then we will have repudiated the constitutional principles of liberty and equality. . . . We believe that you will join in this cause because it is your cause, too, the cause of individual liberty and human equality. (Nava and Dawidoff 1994:167)

Some analysts suggest that people in the future will ask, "What was all the fuss over gay men and lesbians (or sexual orientation) about?" Valverde (1998) took the position in 1998 that 20 years in the future, it would have become as socially unacceptable to discriminate against people based on sexual orientation as it has become to discriminate against people based on skin colour. We have arrived at the date she suggested. What do you think? Was Valverde correct, or must we wait yet another 20 years for her prediction to materialize?

WHAT CAN YOU DO?

- Reflect on the assumptions you hold about homosexuals, heterosexuals, bisexuals, and pansexuals, and about sexual orientation in general.
- Attend a Pride Day or parade in your community, regardless of your sexual orientation.
- Consider voting in favour of same-sex marriages and other equality issues that support queer folk, in newspapers, on the Internet, and in opinion polls.
- Do not claim heterosexual privilege. Refer to your girlfriend or boyfriend or husband or wife as your "partner" or your "spouse." Don't let people assume heterosexual privilege. Keep people guessing.
- Incorporate sexual orientation issues into your relevant research papers.
- Do not refer to gay, lesbian, or bisexual friends or colleagues as "my gay friend Kim" unless you typically refer to your straight friends as "my straight friend Lee."
- Do not assume you know someone's sexual orientation. Instead, allow people to define their gender or sexuality for you if they wish.
- Do not treat bisexuality as an "identity of confusion" . but accept it as a real and valid (and queer) identity of its own.
- Get educated about hate crime so you know what to do if you are targeted by one or if you witness or hear about one.
- Object to harassment, discrimination, and prejudice whenever you see or hear it. Don't ignore, condone, or accept this in others.
- Intervene when you hear homophobic or biphobic jokes or slurs. Your silence can be all the encouragement a person needs to continue this hurtful behaviour.
- Encourage diversity, inclusion, and respect in your school, your classrooms, your workplace, and your friendship circles.
- Work on being nonjudgmental about others' preferences, life choices, and orientations.
- Use gender-inclusive and non-heterosexist language.
- Don't "out" anyone to others if you know she or he is non-heterosexual. Respect people's rights to disclose

their sexual orientation if and when they choose. This is especially important as many people may be "out" only in certain spaces or with certain people they deem safe. Outing someone could put her or him at risk for many serious consequences such as losing friends, family members, employment, or housing.

- Don't assume that being LGBT is a negative thing or that LGBT people are always suffering. There is much to celebrate and much humour found and shared.

- Recognize people's complexity. Sexual orientation is just one part of identity that people carry around with them. This means that sexual orientation is only part of the picture, and it intersects with multiple other parts of our identities to both enfranchise and disenfranchise us, sometimes simultaneously.

- Never force anyone to "come out" or remain "out."

- Accept public displays of affection (PDAs) between people of the same sex as natural and normal.

Participate in them, to show solidarity with same-sex couples, to whatever degree you are comfortable (e.g., linking arms with a same-sex friend while walking down the street; hugging a same-sex friend when you meet him or her).

- If you are heterosexual and involved in an intimate partnership with a person of the other sex, try to keep this relationship "in the closet" for one week. This could involve (a) having no physical contact with the person if anyone else (friends, family, general public) is around; (b) being careful where or even if you are seen together; (c) not mentioning this person or the relationship to anyone; and (d) not being seen or heard talking on the phone to this person.

- Don't assume that people's orientations are fixed forever. Accept people's self-definitions and identities as who they are at the moment.

SUMMARY

What Criteria Do Sociologists Use to Study Sexual Orientation?

Sociologists define sexual orientation as a preference for emotional–sexual relationships with persons of the "same" sex (homosexuality), the "opposite" sex (heterosexuality), or both (bisexuality). Recent studies have used three criteria for classifying people as homosexual or bisexual: (1) sexual attraction to persons of one's own gender; (2) sexual involvement with one or more persons of one's own gender; and (3) self-identification as a gay man, lesbian, or bisexual. Further, recent longitudinal research indicates that people's (and especially women's) sexual orientations may be much more fluid than previously thought.

How Do Religion and Law Influence People's Beliefs About Homosexuality?

Most major religions, with the exception of Buddhism, regard homosexuality as a sin. Contemporary religious fundamentalists denounce homosexual conduct as a sign of great moral decay and societal chaos. Throughout Canadian history, moral and religious teachings have been intertwined with laws that criminalize homosexual conduct. While many religions do not condone homosexuality, many adherents to them do. With acts believed to be associated with homosexuality decriminalized, with the inclusion of sexual orientation in the Charter as a prohibited ground for discrimination, and with the legalization of same-sex marriage in Canada, Canadians continue to move toward increased acceptance of non-heterosexual relations.

What Types of Discrimination Do Gay and Lesbian People Experience?

Although lesbians and gay men experience discrimination in many aspects of daily life such as housing, medical care,

and employment, a major concern, because of the seriousness of its consequences, is hate crime. Hate crimes based on sexual orientation continue to increase while others decrease, and they are more often violent in nature than hate crimes based on other characteristics.

How Have Changes in the Definition of Hate Crimes Affected Non-heterosexuals?

Despite sexual orientation being a "protected ground" in the Charter and in most provincial and territorial human rights legislation, Canada's *Criminal Code* still does not include specific hate crime legislation, except under section 718.2 on sentencing. Provincial hate crimes units, however, such as British Columbia's, are going a long way to collect those data, perhaps influencing further and broader legislative changes in the future. Hate crimes against gays, lesbians, and bisexuals appear to be most prevalent where homophobic attitudes are tolerated or overlooked.

How Do Interactionists Explain Issues Associated With Sexual Orientation?

According to interactionists, most people acquire the status of heterosexual without being consciously aware of it. For lesbians, gay men, and bisexuals, sexual orientation may be a master status because it largely determines how individuals view themselves and how they are treated by others. Interactionists identify a process of accepting the identity of lesbian, gay, bisexual, or pansexual that some people may experience: (1) experiencing identity confusion; (2) seeking out others who are openly lesbian or gay and sometimes engaging in sexual experimentation; and (3) attempting to integrate self-concept and acceptance of a label such as "homosexual," "gay," or "lesbian." Recent research suggests that identity formation regarding specific sexual orientations (e.g., bisexual) is not static and fixed. Rather, people often change their sexual identities one or more times over a period of time.

How Do Functionalists Explain Issues Associated With Sexual Orientation?

Functionalists focus on how social norms and laws are established to preserve social institutions such as the family and to maintain stability in society. They also analyze reasons why societies find it necessary to punish sexual conduct that violates social norms prohibiting non-marital sex and same-sex sexual relations. According to functionalists, homosexual conduct is punished because it undermines social institutions and jeopardizes the society.

How Do Conflict Theorists Explain Issues Associated With Sexual Orientation?

Conflict theorists believe that the group in power imposes its own attitudes, beliefs, and values about sexual orientation on everyone else. Thus, norms enforcing compulsory heterosexuality reflect the beliefs of dominant group members in the federal and provincial governments, the military, and other social institutions. According to conflict theorists, social change can occur only if people demand that laws be changed to bring about greater equality for non-heterosexuals.

How Do Feminist Theorists Explain Issues Associated With Sexual Orientation?

Like conflict theorists, feminist theorists believe that the group in power can impose its own agenda. The group in power in this case is seen to be males, however, and notions of compulsory heterosexuality work to serve the interests of men in an unequal and gendered social system. Feminist theorists from a radical perspective first suggested that lesbianism was a rational, political choice, based on a critique of patriarchy. Today, many feminists reject the separatist stance of earlier writers on these issues and instead opt for a model that values all diversity and encourages acceptance of all people, regardless of gender, sexual orientation, and so on. Increasingly, feminist theorists are focusing on the intersectionality of identity and interlocking matrices of oppression that serve to shape and define people's experiences in much more nuanced ways. Feminist theorists then argue that theorizing and activism must take into account the multiple locations of both privilege and oppression that people may inhabit simultaneously. Non-heterosexuals need to be made equal within all institutions and facets of society.

How Do Postmodern Queer Theorists Explain Issues Associated With Sexual Orientation?

Many Queer theorists believe that problems associated with sexual orientation are the result of a homophobic and biphobic culture. They advocate playing with the categories, labels, definitions, and understandings of the various genders, sexes, and sexual orientations as a way of subverting consciousness. Queer theorists believe that when people's taken-for-granted realities are disrupted, people will be enabled to see sex, gender, and sexual orientation as the social constructions they are, and thus, ease off of rigid and harmful stereotyping and actions.

How Have Gay Rights Advocates Sought to Reduce Inequality Based on Sexual Orientation?

Beginning with the Gay Liberation movement in the 1960s, advocates have argued that lesbians and gay men are citizens and entitled to the same rights and protections that all other citizens enjoy, including the right to equal employment and housing, legally sanctioned marriage, adoption of children, and protection from harassment and hate crimes. Some analysts suggest that future social change depends on the continued vigilance of gay, lesbian, and bisexual advocacy organizations.

KEY TERMS

biphobia, p. 107
compulsory heterosexism, p. 109
heteronormativity, p. 109

heterosexism, p. 109
homophobia, p. 107
master status, p. 118

pansexuality, p. 106
sexuality, p. 107
sexual orientation, p. 106

QUESTIONS FOR CRITICAL THINKING

1. Think of any assumptions you hold about homosexuals, bisexuals, and heterosexuals. What actions flow from your assumptions? What impact might your actions have on people whose sexual orientation or preference differs from your own?

2. Following a Queer theory approach, critically analyze the discomfort generated by allowing or asking people to define their gender, sex, and sexual orientation for you. What assumptions are disrupted when you do this?

3. What things can heterosexual individuals and couples take for granted that homosexual individuals or couples cannot?

4. The B.C. Hate Crimes Team, created by the provincial government and including members of the RCMP, reports that gays, lesbians, and bisexuals are often reluctant to report violence that is perpetrated against them. Explain why this might be so.

5. How has the social institution of heterosexuality constrained and limited all Canadians—heterosexual and non-heterosexual alike?

6. How does pansexuality differ from homosexuality and bisexuality? What are some of the implications of pansexuality for advocacy of gay, lesbian, and bisexual rights?

Igor Shootov/Shutterstock

There are a multitude of reasons why people enter the sex trade. Some men and women involved in the sex trade view what they do as oppressive and see the causes of their involvement in it as exploitive, as these two Canadian women who entered the sex trade as youths share:

I just fell for it . . . I was in a vulnerable state, I lost my virginity to rape, and I was consistently abused by my mother. I was ashamed of myself, who I was, what I looked like and, when I met this man, he was the world to me. He said, "Oh you're so pretty" and I fell for it [and became a prostitute for him]. (Kingsley and Mark 2000:54)

A lot of our issues are the same, all the way across the country, whether we want to see it or not, and it all comes back to the same thing, that abuse in our families and our communities. (Kingsley and Mark 2000:23)

At the other end of the spectrum are sex workers who view their work as a career choice—with willing buyers and sellers, a purely economic exchange—that is no more or less degrading than any other profession (Aalbers 2005; Alexander 1987; Chapkis 1997; Doezema 1998; Kempadoo 1998, 2005; McWilliams 1996). The words of a woman from British Columbia reflect this perspective: "It's just a job, that's it. I don't come home and break down. There have been times when I'm not too happy with what I do, but if I stay in that head space I get depressed. It's not about having sex, it's about the money, it's about providing a good living for myself" (Hallgrimsdottir, Phillips, and Benoit 2006:276). A male sex worker from New Brunswick shares what he sees are the benefits of sex work for himself: "I won't even work for anything under $10 an hour, I won't. 'Cause what's the sense of busting my balls for that? and listen to somebody yelling at you, telling you what to do. 'Cause I can't take authority from nobody, I can't let nobody tell me what to do. This job [sex work], that's how it turned me. I'm kinda my own boss, and I get so much money off it. No, it [a 'straight' job] just won't work" (Jeffrey and MacDonald 2006:322). Certainly, in this country, it is a thriving multimillion-dollar industry that includes prostitution, the film and video trade, printed pornography, escort services, massage parlours, and strip and table- and lap-dancing clubs. However, prostitution and other types of sex work have always been controversial; not all social analysts even agree on whether or not the sex industry is a social problem. To better understand the controversy over prostitution, pornography, and other sex work, we will look at each of these issues and examine varying views on what the work means to those involved. Looking at the way elements of the sex trade are currently organized, as well as looking into the future, nationally and globally, may help you to decide if any of the explanations provided by various sociological and feminist perspectives clarify *your* opinions.

PROSTITUTION IN HISTORICAL AND GLOBAL PERSPECTIVE

Narrowly defined, *prostitution* **is the sale of sexual services (of oneself or another) for money or goods and without emotional attachment.** More broadly defined, systems of prostitution refer to any industry in which women's, men's, and children's bodies are bought, sold, or traded for sexual use (Giobbe 1994). According to this broader definition, systems of prostitution may include pornography, live sex shows, peep shows, international sexual slavery, and prostitution as more narrowly defined above. The vast majority of sex-trade workers around the globe are women and female children (80 to 90 percent), although men and male children also work in the sex trade. In all cases, regardless of the age or sex of the sex-trade worker, the clients or buyers are nearly always adult males (see Browne and Minichiello 1995; Lauer et al. 2006; Leuchtag 2003; McNamara 1994; Snell 1995; Wolff and Geissel 2000). What factors in our global society may help explain this gendered phenomenon?

The World's Oldest Profession?

Prostitution has been referred to as the "world's oldest profession" because references to it can be found throughout recorded history. Still, over the past 4000 years, prostitution has been neither totally accepted nor completely condemned. For example, while female prostitution was widely accepted in ancient Greece, where upper-class prostitutes were admired and frequently became the companions of powerful Greek men, the prostitutes themselves were refused the status of wife—the ultimate affirmation of legitimacy for women in Greek society—and were negatively compared with so-called virtuous women in a "bad woman–good woman" ("Madonna–Whore") dichotomy (see Bullough and Bullough 1987; Jolin 1994; Roberts, 1992).

In other eras, attitudes and beliefs about prostitution have ranged from generally tolerant to strongly averse. Such early Christian leaders as St. Augustine and St. Thomas Aquinas argued that prostitution was evil, but encouraged tolerance toward it. According to Aquinas, prostitution served a basic need that, if unmet, would result in greater harm than prostitution itself. Later Christian leaders such as Martin Luther in 16th-century Europe believed that prostitution should be completely eliminated on moral grounds (Jolin 1994; Otis 1985).

In the 19th-century feminist movement, women for the first time voiced their opinions about prostitution. Some believed that prostitution led to promiscuity and moral degeneracy in men and should therefore be eradicated. Others believed that prostitution should be legitimized as a valid expression of female sexuality outside of marriage. Over the past two decades, an increasing number of advocates have suggested that prostitution should be viewed as a legitimate career choice (prostitute as independent sex worker), but others have argued that prostitution is rooted in global gender inequality (prostitute as victim of oppression as most prostitutes are women). This argument will be discussed further when we examine feminist perspectives on the issue as feminists can be found at both ends of this continuum.

In terms of prostitution being Canada's oldest profession, it is not. Sociologist Dan Allman (1999) notes that though there were some interpretations that describe "prostitution-like" relations among Indigenous people, sex work was not actually introduced in Canada until Europeans began to settle here. Early writings about the Canadian sex trade (late 1800s to early 1900s) are limited to females who were in the public eye.

The Global Sex Industry

The past three decades have seen the industrialization, normalization, and globalization of prostitution. Although *industrialization* typically refers to the mass production of manufactured goods and services for exchange in the market, sociologist Kathleen Barry (1995:122) suggests that this term should also apply to commercialized sex manufactured within the human self. Prostitution becomes *normalized* when sex work is treated as merely a form of entertainment and there are no legal impediments to promoting it as a commodity. Certainly the plethora of television advertisements encouraging viewers to call or text "hot singles" in their area help speed the process of normalization. The *globalization* of prostitution refers to the process by which the sex industry has become increasingly global in scope (e.g., international conglomerates of hotel chains, airlines, bars, sex clubs, massage parlours, brothels, and credit card companies that have an economic interest in the global sex industry), which has occurred as people's political, economic, and cultural lives have become increasingly linked globally (Barry 1995; Davidson 1996; Maticka-Tyndale, Lewis, and Street 2005). Political scientists and International Relations specialist Cynthia Enloe critically comments that,

> Sex tourism requires Third World (sic) women to be economically desperate enough to enter prostitution; having done so, it is made difficult to leave. The other side of the equation requires men from affluent societies to imagine certain women, usually women of colour, to be more available and submissive than the women in their own countries. Finally, the industry depends on an alliance between local governments in search of foreign currency and local and foreign businessmen willing to invest in sexualized travel (1990:36–37).

For evidence of exactly this sort of globalization, one has only to look at the increase in Canada of migrant—often trafficked—sex workers from the former Soviet Union and Eastern and Central Europe, often referred to as "Natashas." While the women trafficked into Canada rarely benefit economically or otherwise and are often assaulted, abused, and confined (McDonald et al. 2000), the allure of trafficking women for sex work for the traffickers is unmistakably worth the risk, as this sex trafficker states: "You can buy a woman for $10 000 and you can make your money back in a week if she is pretty and she is young. Then everything else is profit" (Malarek 2003:45).

The globalization of the industry can also be seen through the plethora of Internet sites, such as World Sex Archives and World Sex Guide. These sites (and many others) post listings for hundreds of cities all over the world. Would-be travellers can simply log on, click on their destination city, and find out about specific women and agencies in the area, including rates, services offered (e.g., if she allows "oral" on herself, if she will perform "oral" on you, how "good" the experience is, etc.), photos, laws of the particular jurisdiction, and so on. Many Canadian cities are listed, along with detailed advice and reports from businessmen, tourists, long-haul truckers, and others who travel domestically. One has only to spend two minutes looking through the photo galleries of any of these sites to see the evidence of globalization.

In June 2010, the Canadian Centre for Justice Statistics published a report on the need for and feasibility of a national framework to assess the extent of trafficking in Canada (Ogrodnik 2010). The most recent United Nations Office on Drugs and Crime report (December 2012) states that women and girls account for 75 percent of those trafficked annually, and that the majority of trafficking is for the purposes of sexual exploitation (UNODC 2012a). It is difficult to gain reliable statistics for any aspect of trafficking, however, because of the illicitness of the acts and because definitions and perceptions of "trafficking" vary. This dilemma has led many people worldwide to adopt the United Nations definition of trafficking proposed in 2000 in their *Protocol to Prevent, Suppress, and Punish Trafficking in Persons*. The UN definition is as follows:

"Trafficking in persons" shall mean the recruitment, transportation, transfer, harbouring or receipt of persons, by means of the threat or use of force or other forms of coercion, of abduction, of fraud, of deception, of the abuse of power or of a position of vulnerability or of the giving or receiving

of payments or benefits to achieve the consent of a person having control over another person, for the purpose of exploitation. Exploitation shall include, at a minimum, the exploitation of the prostitution of others or other forms of sexual exploitation, forced labour or services, slavery or practices similar to slavery, servitude or the removal of organs. (UN 2000)

The first estimate of global trafficking was published by the International Labour Organization in 2005, which estimated that 2.45 million people were trafficked, resulting in $31.6 USD billion in profit. By 2012, they estimated 20.9 million victims. World Bank consultant Saltanat Sulaimanova states that trafficking is one of the fastest growing organized crime activities precisely because risks are relatively low while profits are extremely high (2006:61). While trafficking is a crime perpetrated mainly by men, it is also the crime in which the highest proportion of females are found—approximately one-third of people convicted of trafficking offences are women, most of whom are used to lure young girls (UNODC 2012a). In Canada between 2007 and 2010, the RCMP convicted seven males and one female and detected 11 children and 43 adult victims, 76 percent of whom were trafficked for sexual exploitation (UNODC 2012b). More recently, Statistics Canada reported 60 incidents of trafficking in persons in 2011 and 54 in 2012 (Statistics Canada 2013t) (see Table 7.1).

Traditionally, the demand for prostitution was greatest when large numbers of men were congregated for extended periods of time in the military or on business far from home. Natural disasters or wars saw many displaced or marginalized women taken to or drawn to these areas to make a livelihood. As noted by anthropologists Ward and Edelstein, "[s]erving men sexually is one of the leading forms of employment and survival for women on the planet" (2014:197). Further, a connection between wartime rape and increased prostitution

TABLE 7.1 Canadian Crime Statistics: Trafficking in Persons and Child Pornography Offences

Year	2011	2012
Trafficking in persons—actual incidents	60	54
Total persons charged	36	46
Total incidents cleared	50	42
Child pornography—actual incidents	1958	1919
Total persons charged	523	500
Total incidents cleared	790	788

has been documented for the Vietnam War, for the wars in El Salvador, Kosovo, and Bosnia, and more recently in conflicts in Democratic Republic of Congo, Colombia, and Sudan, according to Amnesty International (Smith-Spark 2004/2014; Amnesty International 2014a, 2014b). Large populations of refugees and victims of rape and sexual violence tend to be exploited by networks of pimps and organized crime gangs in such places (Amnesty International 2014; Leuchtag 2003; Seager 1997; Women's International Network 1995). For example, Amnesty International heard reports of increased incidents of rape of women and girls in Darfur during the 2013 clashes. As one mother reported:

> First they beat me with sticks on my back . . . I fell, and they hit me again on my neck with the back of their rifles. They took my daughter . . . she is six-years-old . . . and tied her to a tree, beat her, and raped her. Now, she can't walk on her own, she needs [walking] sticks. (Amnesty International 2014b:21)

Besides ongoing physical problems for victims, there are also issues of PTSD and shame and stigma. Jyoti Sangera (1997) refers to serving men sexually as the first or traditional tier of sex work. Linked to the first tier, but different from it, exists a second tier. This second tier is tied intricately to global tourism and business, key strategies for modernization and development globally, and "women and sex are prominent enticements of tourist destinations" (Ward and Edelstein 2014:198). In many countries, sex tourism began with the establishment of brothels that served foreign military bases (Seager 1997). The second tier has grown up around major tourist destinations and business centres. The size of the first tier has remained relatively stable, while the size of the second tier is ever expanding, providing "R and R for the corporate world workforce" (Sangera 1997:11), particularly as women get in on the action as sex tourists. There is evidence that increasing numbers of Western women are engaging in sex tourism, and several studies have examined the extent and consequences of it in places like Bali, Kenya, Jamaica, Barbados, and the Dominican Republic (see, for example, Taylor 2001; Taylor 2006; Phillips 2005; Bindel 2013). Women's involvement in international sex tourism as customers has been largely ignored in the past as ideas of exploitation and victimization are implicitly gendered as feminine, therefore the fact of wealthy (in relation) White women potentially exploiting poor, Black men has been viewed as a contradiction in terms. This patriarchal view of gendered power has all but made invisible the fact that sexual relations between White female tourists and local Black men are not simply relationships between two equals, but are rather complex dynamics that involve inequities in gender, racialization, age, social class, colonialism, and education. It is particularly important for female sex tourists to cling to the notion of colour-blindness and male dominance, as that enables them to view themselves, at worst, as "romance tourists," and simultaneously as desirable and worthwhile, sexual, and feminine, without acknowledging the importance of their White privilege and class power over the men they "romance" while on holiday (Bindel 2013; Phillips 2005).

In a case study of Windsor, Ontario, as a destination for male sex tourism, Maticka-Tyndale, Lewis, and Street (2005) discuss the notion of *liminal space* as it relates to sex tourism. They suggest that people who travel to other locations are able to engage in exotic or forbidden practices because they "move into liminal space . . . [and are] 'betwixt and between,' in a socially condoned marginality, where they are bound neither by the mores of home, nor by those of the host community" (Maticka-Tyndale et al. 2005:46). This notion of liminality is reflected in a quote shared by "Barbara," a divorced, White administrator in her late 50s, about her first "holiday romance" with a local man in Jamaica, "It was like total freedom. Chris was all over me and I couldn't get enough of that beautiful body. He showered me with compliments . . . [Before this, I felt] worthless and like no man would ever look at me again. Chris made me feel gorgeous and special straightaway" (Bindel 2013:35). Many women do not view themselves as sex tourists or these men as prostitutes as they believe they are in love and downplay the economic exchanges that are inevitably part of the deal, "I fell head over heels with him when we first met and he couldn't get enough of me, but I'm not daft . . . I knew he was as keen on my money as he was on me but they have nothing here and live like paupers" (in Bindel 2013:37). UK journalist Julie Bindel's decade-long research uncovered that many women engage in interracial holiday romances with "boyfriends" whom they never would dare to date at home, and that they often view their activities while abroad as overt expressions of being both liberal and anti-racist (2013). However, using a feminist and post-colonialist framework, she concludes that:

> Our hesitation in describing women such as Barbara as "sex tourists" and the acceptance of the illusion that it's about romance and love, further allow us to justify a racist and colonialist view of Black male sexuality. For the women it perpetuates a view of themselves as worthless, because most of these faux romances have no longevity or honesty. For the men

it confirms that the legacy of slavery, under which the Black body was commodified and dehumanized, is not far behind them. (Bindel 2013:37)

For residents of these tourist destinations, however, this is their home. Residents inhabit a space "where visitors come for the explicit purpose of violating the dominant norms and mores of Western sexuality" (Maticka-Tyndale et al. 2005:47). As one White woman ("Dawn") states in Bindel's research as a justification for the expenses she incurs maintaining her Black boyfriend when she visits Jamaica, "What do I get out of it? A lot of fun, and a beautiful body and massive cock to have my wicked way with whenever I want" (2013:37). Both local males and local females who trade sex and romance for money and/ or goods may feel used when they come to understand that they are dehumanized and used by tourists for the stereotypes they represent (Taylor 2006; Phillips 2005).

Although research has indicated that the global sex industry, especially prostitution, contributes to the transmission of HIV, the virus that causes AIDS (Gil et al.

Human trafficking is a serious crime.

NinaMalyna/iStock/Getty Images

1996; Purvis 1996), many agencies and governments have not come to grips with the problem. Moreover, the threat of HIV/AIDS may be fuelling the increased demand for children and younger, inexperienced sex workers as a "safe sex" strategy in the booming sex tourism business (Seager 1997). This strategy, along with myths in many cultures that sex with virgins cures HIV, has led to increasing sexual exploitation of children. Globally, the traffic in children has increased between 2007 and 2012, with two-thirds of the children being female (UNODC 2012a).

The picture of the global sex industry reflects the economic disparity between the poorest regions of the world—where women and children (mainly) may be bought, sold, or traded like any other commodity—and the richest regions, such as Europe and North America, where many of the global sex industry's consumers reside (see Bauerlein 1995; Davidson 1996; Seager 2003). Canada consistently places near the top of the list of countries that sex tourists live in and leave from (Seager 2003, 1997; Ward and Edelstein 2014). Additionally, as discussed earlier, rich nations increasingly import the sexual services of people from poorer nations. As geographer and women's studies scholar Joni Seager (2003:56) notes, "As poverty deepens in Eastern Europe, it becomes a major source region for prostitutes; as wealth expands in China and Malaysia, men in those countries fuel an increased demand for the traffic in women and girls."

PROSTITUTION IN CANADA

Prostitution, among consenting adults, has never been illegal in Canada. However, sections 210–214 of the Canadian *Criminal Code* do prohibit many transactions that are quite necessary to prostitution, particularly to the safer sale of sexual services. The activities that are illegal in Canada relating to the sex trade are communicating in a public place for the purposes of buying or selling sexual services (section 213); procuring or soliciting a person to exchange sexual services for money and living off the avails (section 212); being involved in a common bawdy house (section 210); providing direction to or transporting someone to a bawdy house (section 211); and purchasing sexual services from someone under the age of 18 years (section 214[4]; Maticka-Tyndale et al. 2005:47; Millar 2002:38; Wolff and Geissel 2000:254). These activities are considered a threat either to public decency or to public order. However, many sex workers and advocates argue that what these laws really do is create a situation where sex workers must work in potentially dangerous conditions while not impacting the sale of sexual services. Recent court challenges in British

Columbia and Ontario have raised the issue of safety, citing constitutional concerns such as freedom of association and freedom of expression among others (Barnett and Nichol 2011, 2012:8). Those convicted of prostitution-related offences are often fined, although jail terms are possible. For example, communicating for the purposes of prostitution carries the maximum penalty of a $2000 fine or six months in jail or both. Given the economic situation of many street prostitutes, hefty fines may ensure continued sex-trade work and do not in any way act as a deterrent. As one female Saskatoon youth explains:

> [When I was arrested for prostitution] all my friends were there and it hurt so much, it made me feel much lower . . . they [the judicial system] treat you like such a bad person or that you're a slut, tramp, or whore. You're forced to go there [the streets], you were forced into that spot and if you said no, you were beat up or something worse, you could be killed. And they make it out like you're nothing, they don't try to help you, they just charge you and send you on your merry way . . . they know where you're going off to, you have to pay off your fine. (Kingsley and Mark 2000:27)

Federal laws on prostitution-related activities ensure that it is almost impossible to engage in the trade without breaking the law. Criminologist John Lowman (2000) argues that this fact adds to the already existing moral–political marginalization that sex-trade workers endure, increasing the risks of the work. Lowman (2000:1006) says our "system of quasi-criminalization":

1. contributes to legal structures that tend to make the prostitute responsible for her [or his] own victimization, and thus reinforces the line of argument that says that, if people choose to prostitute themselves, they deserve what they get—they are "offenders" not "victims";
2. makes prostitution part of an illicit market. As such, it is left to primitive market forces and creates an environment in which brutal forms of manager-exploitation can take root;
3. encourages the convergence of prostitution with other illicit markets, particularly the drug trade. Once the price of a habit-forming, mind-altering substance is driven up by criminal prohibition, a drug like heroin can be as demanding a "pimp" as any man; and
4. alienates persons who engage in prostitution from the protective-service potential of the police. Why would prostitutes turn to police for help when police are responsible for enforcing the laws against prostitutes? . . . Criminal law sanctions institutionalize an adversarial relationship between prostitutes and police.

This may be why, instead of going to the police when they are beaten, raped, or robbed, sex-trade workers report "bad tricks" or "bad dates" to various organizations that keep, post, and monitor Bad Date Sheets. One of the first organizations in Canada to publish a Bad Date Sheet was the Alliance for Safety of Prostitutes (ASP) in 1983. Bad Date Sheets typically report the type of offence, where the offender picked the worker up, the date and time of the offence, description of and characteristics of the offender (age, racialization/ethnicity, gender, other identifying features such as tattoos, etc.) and vehicle, the type of person victimized (e.g., woman, man, transsexual, youth), and whether the person is known to be a repeat offender or not. The sheets are then circulated monthly by street and other social service workers and posted in various agencies and places prostitutes are known to go to for services (Lowman and Fraser 1995). John Lowman and Laura Fraser's study (1995) *Bad Trick Reports in Vancouver, B.C. 1985–1994* shows that most "bad tricks" are Caucasian males, perceived to be in their 20s and 30s, and most victims are adult females. The most common types of bad dates were physical and sexual assaults, followed by robbery and, in a quarter of the cases, a weapon was used. Lowman and Fraser (1995) encourage us to see this violence as part of a continuum of male violence against women, not as an acceptable risk associated with the job. One study of 80 men who purchased sex in Vancouver, BC reported that only 6.5 percent of the men surveyed (n=5) had ever committed a violent act against a commercial or non-commercial sexual partner:

> . . . our findings are consistent with many contemporary accounts suggesting that the problem of violence against sex workers is perpetrated by a relatively small proportion of very violent men who prey on the marginalized social and situational position of street sex workers (Lowman and Atchison, 2006:293).

Many Canadians are involved in the sex trade as sex workers, as "managers," or as customers, both overseas and at home. Sex work has always been a feature of modern Western societies and, although some characteristics of it are changing with increasing technology, globalization, and economic disparity between more and less industrialized nations, it certainly appears to be here to stay. As "Megan," an ex-sex-trade worker in British Columbia, reports:

> A sex worker friend of mine and I sat down one night and figured out how many tricks we'd had in our illustrious careers as street sex trade workers. We came up with about 10,000 each, so anyone who says

there aren't very many men out there buying sex are just wrong (Megan in Rabinovich and Lewis 2001:7).

How we approach the myriad issues raised by the sex trade (e.g., some of the associated dangers, like violence, particularly against street sex-trade workers) will depend upon how we view it. (For a discussion on some implications of Facebook on the sex trade, for example, see Box 7.1).

Some Characteristics of Prostitution in Canada

Clearly, not all sex-trade workers are alike: life experiences, family backgrounds, years of formal education, locales of operation, types of customers, and methods of doing business vary widely. Even with these differences, however, sociologists have identified five tiers of prostitution, ranging from escorts to those exchanging sex for drugs in crack houses.

Top-tier prostitutes are typically referred to as *escorts*. They are considered the upper echelon in prostitution because they tend to earn considerably higher fees and typically have more years of formal education than other sex workers do and many of them do not think of themselves as prostitutes. They usually dress nicely—often conservatively—so that they do not call undue attention to themselves at the luxury hotels, clubs, and apartment buildings they may be called to work in. Maybe most importantly, escort sex workers have more selectivity in their working conditions and customers than do other prostitutes (Chapkis 1997; Macy 1996; Maticka-Tyndale et al. 2005). An escort named Terry clearly differentiates between herself and other, less fortunate sex workers:

> One of the reasons I think I can enjoy my work, is because I carefully screen my clients. I have no tolerance for any assholes. I'm providing a service to these men, and as far as I'm concerned, they're privileged to have it. So they have to show me the proper respect. I deserve that respect. If they don't think so then they should keep their cock in their pants and their money in their pocket. It means that I may make less money than I might otherwise, but my safety is worth it. People in more desperate circumstances have to put up with a lot more. (Chapkis 1997:100)

Escorts work "on call," going out to see customers who are referred to them by their escort service, pimp, or other procurers such as hotel concierges and taxi drivers who may receive a percentage of the sex worker's fees. Other escorts may "freelance," brokering their own calls and deals, advertising online and in local newspapers, and so on. One home-based male escort in Victoria, B.C.,

"Peter," speaks to his experience of the relative autonomy offered by freelancing, stating, "[w]hen it comes right down to it, I have full control over what I'm doing. I know that I can make my own decisions, my own rates, and I can make my own hours" (Hallgrimsdottir, Phillips and Benoit 2006:277).

Although their work is not as visible as that of many other sex workers, escorts can face some of the same hazards, including abusive customers and sexually transmitted diseases. An exploratory study of off-street sex workers' experiences of violence in Vancouver, BC by SFU criminologist Tamara O'Doherty, reported that two-thirds have never experienced violent behaviour while working (Meadahl, 2007). O'Doherty's findings support earlier research in Vancouver, BC (see Lowman and Fraser, 1995) that suggests that potentially violent men may specifically target street workers, which comes as ". . . no surprise . . . street sex workers, forced to work in isolation with little or no protection from police [and] are ideal prey for violent men" (O'Doherty quoted in Meadahl, 2007). A global review of research on the sex trade by sociologist Ronald Weitzer (2005) supports that "street workers are significantly more at risk for violence and more serious violence than indoor workers" (Lever and Dolnick quoted in Weitzer 2005:216) because indoor workers "are in a better position to screen out dangerous customers and also have a greater proportion of low-risk, regular clients" (Weitzer, 2005:216).

The municipal council in Windsor, Ontario created a task force in 1995 on the use of city bylaws to regulate sex work. The goal was to create a bylaw that would not violate the *Criminal Code* statutes on prostitution, nor be seen as licensing sex work, but at the same time provide sex workers with safety and autonomy and the police with the ability to monitor the industry. As one police representative stated at the time, "Escort work is particularly difficult to police. You can't find it. . . . When it's licensed we know who they are and where they are. We can keep tabs on it. . . . We can prevent the worst elements from moving in (Maticka-Tyndale et al., 2005:49). Three factors were seen as important in the creation of a bylaw:

> (a) escorts should remain integrated in their local communities and not be isolated in a red-light district; (b) escorts should be able to determine their own working conditions within the limits set by law; and (c) escorts should be provided with information that could help them conduct their work safely and contribute to their over-all well-being (Maticka-Tyndale et al. 2005:49).

Windsor escorts and agency receptionists are able to work from their own homes or through an agency.

Escorts are licensed after meeting certain criteria such as a minimum age of 18 years and a clean police record. Work must be out-calls only, and workers are required to carry and produce their licences when asked by police. Agency personnel are required to keep records of who went where and when and to turn these records over to police if requested. Recently, there have been several groups advocating complete decriminalization of sex work with the goal of improving the working conditions, remuneration, and health and safety of sex workers. These advocates, including the Canadian Union of Public Employees (CUPE), Canada's largest union, tend to approach sex work from a "harm reduction/labour rights framework" (Shaver, Lewis, and Maticka-Tyndale 2011:61). The issues, however, are complex, with some people working within the sex trade disagreeing about which work in the sex trade is legitimate and which is not. Many escorts like to maintain that their work does "not necessarily involve sexual services" (Maticka-Tyndale et al. 2005:50), and many see themselves as very different from other sex-trade workers, particularly from street prostitutes:

> I'm not like them. They're disgusting, all dirty and smelly. Several of them look like they got AIDS. I'm not anything like them, no way, I'd never be a whore. (quoted in Maticka-Tyndale et al. 2005:50)

The second tier of prostitutes is comprised of hustlers, strippers, and table dancers who engage in sex work on the side. People in this tier work primarily out of nightclubs, bars, and strip clubs. The hustlers are supposed to pressure (hustle) customers to buy drinks. Most hustlers are not paid by the bar but earn their livelihood by negotiating sexual favours with bar customers, who often are lonely and want someone to talk to as well as to have sex with (Devereaux 1987).

The third tier is made up of *house girls* who work in brothels (houses of prostitution) run by a madam or a pimp, who collects approximately half of the fees earned by the women. Customers choose a "date" from women lined up in a parlour or receiving room. Most house prostitutes are not allowed to turn down a customer (Devereaux 1987). Operating a bawdy house or living off the avails of prostitution is illegal in Canada, and thus houses of prostitution typically operate as body-painting studios, massage parlours, or other legal businesses. A controversial proposition to open a cooperative brothel near Vancouver, BC in time for the 2010 Olympics raised many issues from health and safety to complete decriminalization. Some of the arguments that may support the "pro opening" side include that hundreds of brothels already exist in the city but are

merely quasi-hidden behind massage parlour and other "fronts"; that nearly all Canadian research has demonstrated that sex-trade worker's safety is nowhere near as at-risk in indoor work; that the brothel would provide other legitimate work opportunities and help workers who want to exit the trade; that worker's health could be better monitored; that it would help reduce the stigma against sex workers; and that it would get the sex trade off the streets, out of the public view. Based on their eight years of research on legalized brothels in Nevada, sociologists Barbara G. Brents and Kathryn Hausbeck argued "that legal brothels generally offer a safer working environment than their illegal counterparts" (2005:293). Those who are against the opening of a legal brothel in Canada, even as "an experiment," state that a cooperatively owned and operated brothel still won't solve any problems for those engaged in the sex trade for survival (e.g., those who are drug addicted, the abused, etc.); that it is still akin to slavery; that if prostitution is legitimized, it means legitimizing pimps and sex traffickers; and that prostitution in any form is violence against women (Lee 2004; Joyce 2008).

Near the bottom tier of prostitution are *streetwalkers,* who publicly solicit customers and charge by the "trick." This type of prostitution is believed to account for between 10 and 20 percent of the sex trade in most large urban centres in Canada (Lowman and Atchison 2006:285). Most street workers work a specific location and many are managed by a pimp. Some streetwalkers derive status and some degree of protection from violent "johns" from their pimps, although in most cases, pimps are not out on the streets monitoring the workers enough to provide protection (Weitzer 2006). Further, researchers have also documented the exploitative and too-often violent nature of the pimp–prostitute relationship (BC Ministry of Attorney General 1996; Kingsley and Mark 2000; Lauer et al. 2006; Sexually Exploited Youth Committee of the Capital Regional District [SEYCCRD] 1997). There is little available research on pimps—most information comes from the women who work for them. One British study found pimps "exercised almost total control over their workers" (May et al. 2000 in Weitzer 2006:227). Whether at risk for violence from pimps or johns, street prostitution is significantly more dangerous than sex work in indoor (and often screened and controlled) environments.

The very bottom tier of prostitution is occupied by people who are addicted to crack cocaine, heroin, or other drugs and who engage in drugs-for-sex exchanges (Fullilove et al. 1992; Kingsley and Mark 2000). Researchers have found that many crack-addicted women perform unprotected oral sex on men or have sexual intercourse with them in crack houses in exchange for hits of crack, a practice known as "freaking" (Erickson, Butters, McGillicuddy, and Hallgren 2000). As explained in one study:

> Some men will enter a crack house, purchase enough rocks for two people for several hours, and then make it clear to every woman in the house what he has in mind. . . . [There] seems to be an expectation [in the crack house] that if a man wants to have sex with a woman, she will not oppose the offer. The expectations are implicit. Everyone involved—the house owner, the male user/customer, and the female user/prostitute—are all aware of what is expected. (Inciardi et al. 1993:74–75)

In the words of one young Winnipeg woman, "I met a bunch of guys I knew, they were always giving me rock [crack] for free, I never had to do anything, except for this one guy. Then we met these guys, [and] you had to go around the whole room to get a piece [of crack from each guy]" (Kingsley and Mark 2000:21).

Although less research has been done on prostitution tiers with males, the tiers appear to be similar to those of females except that, with males, most customers are of the same sex as the sex worker. In the words of journalist Marianna Macy (1996:249), "Men normally go see men." Most of Canada's larger cities, for example Vancouver, Toronto, and Montreal, have some form of "Boystown," where male sex workers line the "stroll," on display for the primarily male customers. Some male prostitutes work as hustlers in bars and nightclubs, where they typically wear blue jeans, leather jackets, and boots, seeking to project a strong heterosexual image. Julian Marlowe, a graduate student who was putting himself through university by working as an escort, reports that "the sugar daddy of a former acquaintance of [his] once admitted he used to get a rush from picking up hustlers on his lunch break due to the sheer element of danger: the person he picked up could conceivably beat him to a pulp" (1997:141).

Despite the fact that most customers of male sex workers are male, many male sex workers do not define themselves as gay and limit the types of sexual acts they are willing to perform. Others view sex strictly as an economic exchange and define work-related sex as "not real sex" (Browne and Minichiello 1995). Other research suggests that for hustlers who are part of gay culture, "knowing that one is attractive enough to command payment raises, rather than lowers, one's self-esteem. Why would a man have low self-esteem if he's being sought out and given money for his body?" (Marlowe 1997:143). Most research shows that although many males are involved in the sex trade as sex workers, there

are not anywhere near as many boys and men as there are girls and women.

Much research in Canada has focused on identifying the factors that bring people into the sex trade, particularly into the relatively dangerous street prostitution tier. A few studies have also looked into the influence of Facebook in involving people in the sex trade (see Box 7.1). Studies of youth in the sex trade in British Columbia, as well as nationally, reveal that several factors are nearly always implicated in engaging youth in the sex trade. The use of the term "youth" is not accidental here, as research shows that most people (96 percent) became prostitutes before age 18 (Hallgrimsdottir, Phillips, and Benoit 2006; Rabinovich and Lewis 2001; Wolff and Geissel 2000). There is evidence across Canada that males remain in the trade for much shorter durations than females do, with the average length of time being just over five years for men. Allman suggests that by the time males in the trade reach the age of 20 to 22, the youthful looks that attracted the customers are beginning to fade, so they have to move on to other things.

Most adults involved in the sex trade, females and males alike, report that the money is an enticement (Allman 1999; Hallgrimsdottir, Phillips, and Benoit 2006; Jeffery and MacDonald 2006). Although dated, a 1993 Montreal study found that prostitutes were earning anywhere from $600 to $2000 per week, with females earning considerably more than males per week (maybe due to demand) (Allman 1999). In her Vancouver, BC study of off-street workers, criminologist Tamara O'Doherty (2011) found that women typically worked four days per week and earned $60 000 per year. A 2008 article focusing on escorts in British Columbia cited earnings of $4000 to $10 000 per month for independent female escorts (Severinson 2008). Key factors leading youth into the sex trade are generally reported to be homelessness and/or a lack of basic necessities for survival of self or of their own children (e.g., shelter, food, clothing, etc.); emotional abuse, sexual abuse/assault, and/or other physical assaults at home; the development of an alcohol and/or drug addiction; a lack of satisfactory assistance with a health/mental health issue (e.g., depression, eating disorder, bipolar disorder); a lack of life skills and employment; dropping out of school; and low self-esteem (BC Ministry of Attorney General 1996; Kingsley and Mark 2000; Lauer et al. 2006; SEYCCRD 1997; Wolff and Geissel 2000). As stated by a female former street worker from Thunder Bay, Ontario, "[I wouldn't have worked in the trade if] I could have had better self-esteem, I didn't have any boundaries, and I didn't care. I didn't know my worth at that time" (Kingsley and Mark 2000:31). One Ottawa-area study of

Facebook and the Sex Trade: Some Issues to Consider

Facebook and other social media have an undisputed impact on many aspects of social life, and the sex trade is not exempt. Prostitution in North America is in a transitional stage due primarily to the influence of Facebook. However, what remains to be seen is whether or not these transitions are beneficial. There are issues to consider on both sides of the debate about the role Facebook plays in the sex trade.

Some Negative Effects of Using Facebook for the Sex Trade

Facebook has become a primary way in which pimps lure young, often underage, women into the sex trade. Pimps will often troll through Facebook profiles looking for girls who appear to be isolated and vulnerable (e.g., young women and girls who are maybe dressed provocatively and/or who look like they have few friends). They will then message these women and girls, complimenting their looks and asking if they would like to hang out or make some easy money. To attract the vulnerable, the pimps' profile pictures will often show them surrounded by money, drugs, alcohol, and other glamorous items such as expensive cars and jewellery.

Targeted young women and girls will often accept friend requests from these strangers, and by doing so, provide all kinds of personal information (photos, cell phone number, address, friends). Pimps will then start looking for cracks in the targeted females' lives that they can potentially fill, whether that is as a father figure, a boyfriend, or a new, older, glamorous friend, and will attempt to arrange a meeting.

After successfully arranging a face-to-face meeting, pimps will use a variety of strategies such as free drugs and alcohol, gifts, and expensive dinners, and other forms of mental and physical coercion, to persuade their targets to begin sex work at hotels as escorts or to work on the streets. The teenage daughter of one of this text's authors was targeted by a local pimp in the interior of BC. This man, calling himself "Paul," friended the young woman on Facebook, complimented her looks, commiserated with her about her troubles at home and school, and asked if she would like to make a lot of money easily and quickly. This same man was reported to be handing out business cards to young women working late night shifts at local fast food establishments' drive through windows, telling them if they were interested in making $200 in 15 minutes to give him a call.

Why would young females fall for the lines of these predators? Commonly, it is because pimps tend to target young women who exhibit low self-esteem and who have troubled lives at school, or home, or both. By initially showering these girls with compliments and affection and exploiting their insecurities, pimps can often gain their trust and use that to initiate a meeting. Other times it is the promise of money, drugs, and luxuries that coaxes young women into engaging with these strangers.

Some Positive Effects of Using Facebook for the Sex Trade

While Facebook has been used by pimps to recruit young women to work for them in the sex trade, it is also being used by sex workers themselves to free themselves from the grasp of pimps and other exploitive relationships, including drug addiction.

Recent research at Columbia University found that 83 percent of sex workers have a Facebook page that they actively use to find customers. Using Facebook, sex workers are able to control their images, set their prices, and sidestep some of the exploitation that accompanies pimps, madams, and other intermediaries who once took a large share, or all, of the revenue.

In 2008, 25 percent of sex workers received their clients from Facebook, while 31 percent received them from escort agencies. In the years since, Facebook has overtaken escort agencies as the more popular method of receiving customers, and it seems as if this avenue for soliciting clients will only become more popular over time. Sex workers who primarily use Facebook are also able to avoid physically walking on the streets and all the potential dangers that they encounter there (e.g., law enforcement, violent men, addictions).

Conversely, male customers seeking companionship may do so much more discreetly than in the past. No longer must they lean out of their car windows and call out to women at traffic lights. Instead, they can arrange meetings from the safety of their computers and smartphones, out of the public's scrutinizing eye.

On a broad scale, the increased ability for sex workers to run their own independent businesses via Facebook (without the hazards of pimps, streets, drugs, etc.) can potentially be a step forward in fostering the safety and legalization of prostitution everywhere.

youth sex-trade workers found that the "sex for survival" motif was more common for females than for males. Many homeless males were able to "couch surf," while females were expected to trade sex for food, shelter, or money (reported in Allman 1999).

The presence of several or even all of these factors obviously does not guarantee entry into the sex trade, of course. It does, however, heighten the risk of a young person having fewer choices. As stated in one Canadian report on youth sex-trade workers, "They do not move directly from a 'normal' teenage life of home, school and extra-curricular activities to being a prostitute. Long before that, most have a long history of school problems or family problems or emotional problems or all three" (SEYCCRD 1997:4). Criminologist John Lowman reports that most female street sex workers are from lower socio-economic backgrounds and are extremely dissatisfied with their home lives (1995). As clearly stated by Wolff and Geissel (2000:257), "Adolescent prostitution can be viewed as a survival behaviour." However, as BC sociologists Hallgrimsdottir, Phillips, and Benoit (2006:275) caution:

> . . . a more accurate interpretation [for why people enter the sex trade] of the empirical data is that persons involved in the sex industry represent populations that face barriers to mainstream employment, are more likely to belong to discriminated identities, and come from current and historical backgrounds of economic and social hardship. Such an interpretation positions sex industry workers as structurally disadvantaged, not morally corrupt or helpless victims.

The Extent of Prostitution in Canada

There are few reliable estimates of the extent of prostitution in Canada, for several reasons. First, the activity is quasi-legal, and hence most of the activity is clandestine or otherwise hidden behind massage parlours and escort services. Second, criminal charges, which are basically our only official source for quantitative data on prostitution, deal almost entirely with street prostitution. Although this is only one component of the sex trade, accounting for 10 to 15 percent of prostitution overall in Canada, it is the most visible, with 95 percent of all charges in recent years being for "communicating." Throw into all this confusion is the fact that people don't always agree on how to define certain types of sex work (i.e., is it "prostitution" or not?) and the fact that people move around, change their names and addresses, and so on. Many people drift into and out of sex work, considering it as temporary work between full-time jobs or as part-time work while attending post-secondary (Allman 1999; Lowman 2000; Reynolds 1986; Potterat et al. 1990).

Prostitution and Age, Class, Education, Racialization, and Ethnicity

The vast majority of Canadian sex workers are between the ages of 17 and 24 years. However, one cross-provincial community consultation on prostitution in British Columbia found that the average age of entry to prostitution is 14 years, with some beginning as early as age 8 or 9 (BC Ministry of Attorney General 1996). Another study, conducted in Victoria, BC, found the average age of entry to be 15.5 years, although some started as early as 11 (SEYCCRD 1997). Allman (1999) reported that approximately 10 to 12 percent of sex-trade workers were under 18 years of age, and most males in the trade admit to starting by age 16. The peak earning age appears to be about 22, although this may apply mainly to street workers. For example, O'Doherty's study of off-street sex workers in Vancouver, BC found that the women involved were aged 22 to 45 years, and a Victoria, BC study found the mean age of 201 sex workers they interviewed was 32, with ages ranging from 18 to 63 (Clinard and Meier 1989; DePasquale 1999; Hallgrimsdottir, Phillips, and Benoit 2006; Meadahl, 2007). Male customers are often considerably older than the sex workers they hire and are usually White and married, although some teenage and university-age males also hire prostitutes (Lowman and Atchison 2006; National Victims Resource Center 1991; Weitzer 2005). Often, the age difference between young prostitutes and older customers is striking, as a woman forced into prostitution at age 13 by a pimp explains:

> The men who bought me—the tricks—knew I was an adolescent. Most of them were in their 50s and 60s. They had daughters and granddaughters my age. They knew a child's face when they looked into it. . . . It was even clearer that I was sexually inexperienced. So they showed me pornography to teach me and ignored my tears as they positioned my body like the women in the pictures, and used me. (Giobbe 1993:38)

Although a small percentage of teenagers enter prostitution through coercion, most are runaways who have left home because of sexual abuse or other family problems. Some teen sex workers are "throwaways"—thrown out of their homes by parents or other family members (Snell 1995; Vissing 1996). Regardless of their prior history, many teens become prostitutes because prostitution is the best—or only—job they can get. As "Dawn" explains:

> I have often heard men say that I had a choice, and I did, work as a prostitute or starve to death because it is illegal in Canada to work at 12, not to mention

that no one will hire you if you have no address and are only 13 or 14 (quoted in Parrot and Cummings 2008:4).

Social class is directly linked to prostitution: lower-income and poverty-level women and men are far more likely to become sex workers than are more affluent people (Hallgrimsdottir, Phillips, and Benoit 2006; Lowman 1995; Miller 1986). Some people with little formal education and few job skills view prostitution as an economic necessity. As one woman stated, "I make good money [as a prostitute]. That's why I do it; if I worked at McDonald's for minimum wage, then I'd feel degraded" (quoted in McWilliams 1996:340). However, women working for exclusive escort services are more likely to have attended college or university and come from the middle or upper-middle class. O'Doherty's research supports this, as 90 percent of her sample of off-street sex workers had some post-secondary education and more than one-third had a university degree (Meadahl 2007).

Racialization is also an important factor in prostitution. Sociologist Patricia Hill Collins (1991) suggests that African-American women are affected by the widespread image of Black women as sexually promiscuous. Collins traces the roots of this stereotype to the era of slavery, when Black women—and Black men and children—were at the mercy of White male slave-owners and their sexual desires. Indigenous women are affected by similar stereotyping. Historically, First Nations women have been viewed as "exotic sexual commodities" (Farley and Lynne 2004:111) and sexually freer than White women (Allen 1986), a view that has, over the years, translated into the stereotype of sexual promiscuity. This stereotype has had the effect of devaluing and even dehumanizing Indigenous women, and has been used as a justification for sexualized violence against them. As psychologist Melissa Farley and social worker Jacqueline Lynne note, "[h]ierarchies within prostitution locate Indigenous women at the bottom of a brutal 'race' and class hierarchy" (2004:111). For example, sociologists Augie Fleras and Jean Leonard Elliott (1996:148) report on the prairie practice of "squaw hopping," the "acknowledged practice for White men to harass and sexually assault native women." Collins (1991:175) supports Farley and Lynne, stating that prostitution exists within a "complex web of political and economic relationships whereby sexuality is conceptualized along intersecting axes of 'race' and gender." Sexually-exploited-youth advocates Cherry Kingsley and Melanie Mark (2000:28–29), in a national consultation of sexually exploited Indigenous youth, found Indigenous women and girls overrepresented in the visible sex trade, with Indigenous youth accounting

for as much as 90 percent of the visible trade in some communities. These findings are echoed in a Victoria, B.C. study as well, where Indigenous people accounted for 15 percent of the workers, but only 2.8 percent of the census area population (Hallgrimsdottir et al. 2006). Farley and Lynne's research in Vancouver, BC's downtown East side found 52 percent of their sample identifying as "Native," and a further 5 percent identifying as "African Canadian" (2004:115). High rates of Indigenous participation in visible sex work can be attributed, in part, to poverty and to many young people's experiences in foster care. For example, researchers Kingsley and Mark found that, "consultations with [Indigenous] youth identified their [foster] care experiences as paving the way for their commercial sexual exploitation" (2000:26). Today, prostitution remains linked to the ongoing economic, political, and social exploitation of people of colour and Indigenous people, particularly women. As Sociologist Ronald Weitzer notes from his research on prostitution, "street prostitution is stratified by 'race', gender, age, appearance, income and locale—all of which shape worker's daily experiences" (2005:215).

A Closer Look at "Johns"

Until very recently, there have been few comprehensive studies conducted in Canada about the sex-trade customer or "john." This may be a reflection of the relative power of the john's social location in relation to the sex-trade worker's. Since both are, theoretically, equally liable for prosecution under Canada's communicating laws, we should have access to similar information about both groups. This power differential is well understood by one youthful sex-trade worker in Saskatoon:

> They are always looking down on us and blaming us, but it's not only us. It's their husbands that are picking us up. Everybody is in denial: everybody pinpoints us, and blames us because we're the ones out on the street. But they're the ones that are picking us up and giving us money. They're always calling us little sluts and whores, but they never say anything about the johns . . . like they're picture perfect guys. (Kingsley and Mark 2000:25)

Available information indicates that typically johns are men in their mid-20s to mid-40s (although older is common also), White, married, and gainfully employed (Brannigan et al. 1989; Lowman and Atchison, 2006; Lowman, Atchison, and Fraser 1997; National Victims Resource Center 1991). A report by the Canadian Advisory Council on the Status of Women (1984:49) notes that most observers of prostitution report that johns are "ordinary men who go to prostitutes for simple

This self-inking money stamp was made available by the Sex Workers Alliance of Vancouver, in 1999, to sex workers in the community. Its aim is to raise public awareness that money generated by the sex trade is an important part of the Canadian economy.

Pearson.

reasons," such as experiencing sexual acts they cannot have in their other relationships, experiencing sexual relationships without lasting obligations or long-term complications, engaging in "therapy" for problems like impotence, or having a good time (see also Weitzer 2005).

A British Columbia consultation with johns that was arranged through Sexual Addicts Anonymous provided some insights into some johns' behaviour that offer a contrast to the picture of johns as ordinary, well-adjusted men. Given the nature of the group consulted, however, these men cannot be seen to be representative of all johns (BC Ministry of Attorney General 1996). This consultation found that many johns reported childhood sexual abuse and believed themselves to be "addicted" to sex. The use of prostitutes resulted in the men feeling a great deal of shame, which related to their childhood experiences and caused them to act in ways that perpetuated those feelings (engaging the services of a prostitute, for example). These johns also reported that part of the attraction to cruising for prostitutes and the use of their services was the risk of getting caught, therefore indicating that "shame the johns" campaigns may in fact work counter to the stated purpose of the campaigns. The view of the men interviewed was that stopping prostitution could only be achieved by ensuring there was a treatment component inherent in the sentencing, and that punishments alone would not be successful.

Other strategies aimed at customers are being tried, such as charging a john but offering the removal of the charge from the man's record if he agrees to pay a fine and attend "John School." The one-day workshop typically provides a legal overview, shows slides of various venereal diseases, and showcases ex-sex workers who talk about how much they despised their clients. The program seems to have been moderately successful in reducing people's return to buying sex, but only a small proportion of johns limit their sex buying to one time (Lauer et al. 2006). Most johns are repeat customers; for example, only 5 percent of the participants in Lowman and Atchison's Vancouver BC study had purchased sex only once—the highest proportion, one-third of the study participants, had purchased sex between 11 and 50 times, with 10 percent reporting 51 to 100 times (2006:288). Lowman and colleagues further report that in a survey of 120 johns in the United States, a quarter of the people said they had seen a sex worker 51 or more times, and 16 percent reported seeing a sex worker more than 100 times. Another study of 101 johns found they use the services of sex workers over several years, with two-thirds of the men reporting weekly contact with a sex worker (reported in Lauer et al. 2006:36).

In an attempt to obtain a broader picture of people who buy sexual services, the BC Ministry of Attorney General funded an Internet survey in 1996–1997, conducted by John Lowman, Chris Atchison, and Laura Fraser (1997). The attitudes and behaviours of 130 men worldwide who buy sex are represented in this report. As in the Canadian studies (Brannigan et al. 1989; Lowman and Atchison 2006; Van Brunschot 2003), the mean age of johns was 37, with a range from 18 to 67. Most men were married or common-law; had children; were heterosexual, White, high school graduates; and were employed full-time. Most of the men who responded online reported that their first sexual experience was with a friend or acquaintance, not with a relative or a stranger. Twenty percent reported childhood sexual abuse; however, we do not have comparable figures for childhood sexual abuse for men generally.

When asked about attitudes, the men who participated in this survey believed that loneliness, sexual problems at home, the desire for specific sexual acts that partners would not perform, the desire for uncomplicated sex, and a strong male sex drive were important reasons for seeking out a sex worker. Just over one-half of the participants believed that travel to a city other than one's normal residence is important for the sex-trade transaction to occur. Most men believed female sex-trade workers are "normal," hard-working women who are "just doing another job" and "provid[ing] a valuable service"; most of the participants disagreed that prostitutes are the "victims of a sexist society" (Lowman et al. 1997). When asked whether prostitution should be criminalized, unsurprisingly most of these men believed it should not be. The exception here was that most of these men believed that sex with children under age 13 is morally reprehensible and should be prohibited. In terms of deterrents to buying sex, nearly all the men who

responded stated they would buy sex even if it was completely illegal. However, when asked which strategies would be useful in preventing men from buying sex on the street, having viable off-street options was listed, as well as the fact of their spouses finding out, public exposure or public recognition by someone they know, and fear of HIV/AIDS (Lowman et al. 1997). An American study of research on prostitution depicted some interesting attitudes toward prostitution held by 140 male customers who had been arrested (Weitzer 2005:225), as shown in Table 7.2.

The way that prostitution is dealt with under the *Criminal Code of Canada* makes the prostitution-related offence, "communicating" (s. 213) a "nuisance" offence. It is the most frequently prosecuted prostitution offence, but sentencing is minimal. Generally, when sentencing occurs, it is female sex-trade workers who receive sentences of a few days in jail and the male customers who receive "discharges or negligible fines" (Barnett and Nichol 2011, 2012; Department of Justice Canada 1998). "Procuring" (s. 212), an indictable offence, is viewed as much more serious, particularly when youth are involved, and currently carries a maximum sentence of 5, 10, and 14 years' imprisonment, depending on the sub-section of the code. Keeping a bawdy house (s. 210)

TABLE 7.2 Customers' Attitudes toward Prostitution

	Agree (%)	Disagree (%)
Currently in a sexual relationship	59	41
Usually enjoys sex with prostitutes	36	64
Tried to stop using prostitutes	50	50
Patronizing prostitutes has caused problems for me	40	60
Prostitutes are victims of pimps	61	39
Prostitutes make a lot of money	44	56
Women are prostitutes because they want to be	42	58
Prostitutes enjoy their work	27	73
Prostitutes genuinely like men	43	57
There is nothing wrong with prostitution	46	54
Prostitution should be legalized	61	39
I would marry a prostitute	24	76
It would be okay if my son went to prostitutes	24	76
It would be okay if my daughter became a prostitute	8	92

N=140 men arrested for soliciting a prostitute in a midwestern city and west coast city in the United States.

Source: *Weitzer, Ronald. Crime, Law & Social Change (2005) 43:211–235, DOI: 10.1007/s10611-005-1735-6 C.*

is also an indictable offence and can result in a sentence of up to two years' imprisonment, while transporting (s. 211), not an indictable offence, can result in a summary conviction, as in s. 213. The Vancouver brothel pursued by The West Coast Co-operative of Sex Industry Professionals (WCCSIP), discussed earlier, would see an experimental exemption to Criminal Code sections 210, 211, and 213 similar to the kind of exemption awarded the Vancouver safe injection site during its pilot phase.

PERSPECTIVES ON PROSTITUTION

Sociologists use a variety of perspectives to examine the sex trade as a social problem. Functionalists focus on the notion of deviance and on how deviance—sex work as deviant behaviour—serves important functions in society. Interactionists investigate microlevel concerns, such as how and why people become sex workers or how people come to buy sexual services or how negative stigmatization affects sex worker's self-concepts and experiences. Conflict perspectives seek to explain how the powerful enact their moral beliefs into law and how prostitution is related to capitalism and/or patriarchy, and feminist theorists focus on sex-trade work as gendered (and generally inequitable) labour.

The Functionalist Perspective

Functionalists believe that the presence of a certain amount of deviance in society contributes to its overall stability. According to early sociologist Emile Durkheim, deviance clarifies social norms and helps societies to maintain *social control*—**the systematic practices developed by social groups to encourage conformity and discourage deviance**—over people's behaviour. By punishing those who engage in deviant behaviour such as prostitution, the society reaffirms its commitment to its sexual norms and creates loyalty to the society, particularly as people come together to oppose the behaviour.

Prostitution "is one of the few areas of consensual sexual activity that is still subject to legal control and punitive measures" in Canada (Sutdhibhasilp 2002:173). According to sociologist Kingsley Davis (1937), in societies such as Canada that have certain restrictive norms governing sexual conduct, prostitution will always exist because it serves important functions. First, it provides impersonal sexual gratification that does not require emotional attachment or a continuing relationship with another person (Freund et al. 1991). Second, prostitution provides a sexual outlet for those who do have difficulty finding a partner in a conventional relationship (Weitzer 2005). Third, prostitution provides people with the opportunity to engage in a variety of sexual practices and experiences—multiple sex partners, same sex partners, "interracial" partners, fellatio (oral stimulation of the male genitalia), cunnilingus (oral stimulation of the female genitalia), anal intercourse, or any of a range of behaviours associated with BDSM (bondage, discipline, sadism, and/or masochism), including the use of devices such as restraints, gags, riding crops, and dildos. Fourth, prostitution protects the family as a social institution by making a distinction between "bad girls" or "bad boys"—with whom one engages in "promiscuous" sexual behaviour—and "good girls" and "good boys"—with whom one establishes a family. Finally, prostitution can benefit the economy by providing jobs for people who have limited formal education and job skills.

The Interactionist Perspective

Why do people enter the sex trade? Why do they stay? Why do some enjoy their work while others loathe it? What makes some people choose to pay for sex? How do sex-trade workers experience their work? Interactionists investigate questions such as these by examining people's lived experiences and first-hand accounts. An excerpt from an interview with "Dolores" is instructive:

> I set my own schedule. I set my own limits and made my own rules, and I didn't have to answer to anyone. I learned a lot about myself: what I would and would not do for money, and what I was willing to do for the right amount of money. . . . I didn't have to see anyone I didn't want to see. If a man was too boring or too rough or too crude or took too much time, I didn't have to see him again. I loved it. (French 1988:180)

"Dolores's" remarks suggest that some people become sex workers because it provides them with greater autonomy and more career options than they otherwise would have. These reasons fit with sociologist Howard Becker's (1963) suggestion that entering a stigmatized or deviant career is similar in many ways to entering any other occupation. The primary difference is the labelling that goes along with a deviant career. Public labelling of people as deviant and their acceptance or rejection of that label can be crucial factors in determining whether or not a person stays in a deviant career or at the very least, can determine their experience of it and of themselves. Some people are more willing than others to accept the label "deviant" or may believe they have no other option. Others successfully redefine their work and their roles within it:

> See and the worst thing too, in the paper they try to fabricate. . . "prostitute, prostitute." The way

they talk about it: how dare you! I am more than a prostitute. I'm somebody's mother. I'm somebody's friend. I'm somebody's sister. I'm not just a prostitute, you know, I have, I have a story. I have lived, you know? I'm not just that. Get off it. . . . And what people are like nowadays, it's just the stigma of the whole thing. But it's. . . hey, walk in my shoes for a week, see if you survive ("Alyssa" Saint John, NB quoted in Jeffrey and MacDonald 2006b:172).

There are now many qualitative Canadian studies that seek to understand the experiences of those involved in the sex trade at all levels. People's experiences vary widely in the sex trade, with conclusions showing that sex workers in Canada "overwhelmingly view sex work as a job" (Jeffrey and MacDonald 2006a). It has to be remembered that the vast majority of sex work is not street work. Many of those who work on the streets may define their experiences somewhat more negatively, and certainly do if they have been trafficked or otherwise victimized. As Weitzer states, "in general, the type of prostitution is the best predictor of worker experiences" (2005:219).

Why do some men prefer to pay for sex? Research by interactionists suggests that some young men seek out prostitutes to fulfill what they believe is a rite of passage from boyhood to manhood. Further, social analysts suggest that the desire of men of all ages to validate their sexual prowess or reaffirm their masculinity can be a factor in their seeking out prostitutes (Raphael 1988). Other research demonstrates that men who feel shy or awkward around women generally may enjoy the straightforward transactions with a prostitute (Weitzer 2005). Additionally, some clients may define the risk of "illicit or risky conduct thrilling" (Weitzer 2005:223). Interactionist perspectives such as these highlight the different ways that people define social realities—such as the importance of sexual prowess or the thrill of illicit behaviour—in light of competing and often contradictory values they have learned through socialization.

Conflict and Feminist Perspectives

Conflict perspectives on prostitution highlight the relationship between power in society and sex work: the laws that make certain activities associated with prostitution illegal are created by powerful dominant group members who seek to maintain cultural dominance by criminalizing sexual conduct that they consider immoral or in bad taste (Barry 1995).

Some conflict analysts using a liberal feminist framework believe that prostitution should be *decriminalized*—meaning that laws making activities around prostitution

a crime should be eliminated. These analysts argue that prostitution is a *victimless crime*—**a crime that many people believe has no real victim because it involves willing participants in an economic exchange.** Therefore, neither sex workers nor johns should be harassed by police and the courts. According to Margo St. James, a former prostitute and founder of an activist group called COYOTE (Call Off Your Old Tired Ethics), "The profession itself is not abusive; it's the illegality; it's the humiliation and degradation that is dealt to them at the hands of the police" (quoted in McWilliams 1996:340). In other words, prostitution is sex work in the sex industry and should be treated and regulated as any other labour issue. In a September 2004 St. John's, Newfoundland, radio broadcast, Wayne Lucas, then provincial president of Canada's largest union, the Canadian Union of Public Employees, agreed, stating that sex workers clearly should be unionized:

> Work is work. The people who work in that trade, they certainly deserve some of the benefits that other workers have traditionally received in their work fields. [They] should have access to benefits such as health care and pensions. They're people, just like your next-door neighbour. They could be a sister of ours, a mother, a cousin. They're out and they're in a dangerous field. ("Unionize Prostitutes" 2004)

Some conflict perspectives that use Marxist feminist and radical feminist frameworks suggest that women become prostitutes because of structural factors such as economic inequality and patriarchy (Jolin 1994). Capitalism and patriarchy foster economic inequality between women and men and force women, especially, to view their bodies as commodities: "When a man has bought a woman's body for his use as if it were like any other commodity . . . the sex act itself provides acknowledgment of patriarchal right. When women's bodies are on sale as commodities in the capitalist market . . . men gain public acknowledgment as women's sexual masters" (Pateman 1994:132). Taylor Lee, a young woman who entered the sex trade as a dancer first, acknowledges the roles of economics and power in a capitalist market: "Many believe that women profit from prostitution, when in fact the largest portion goes to pimps, club owners, and other businessmen. . . . The managers, owners, and investors are the ones in power. . ." (2004:57). Summarizing a historical feminist position, the Canadian Advisory Council on the Status of Women (1984:3), in its report on prostitution in Canada, pointed out that:

> Prostitution is not an exchange among equals. Men, who as a group, still hold most of the powerful positions of social, economic and political power

in our society, buy services from the less powerful: women (often poor, young and under-educated women) and male and female adolescents and children. The sellers have little or no defense against the risks of physical or sexual abuse of economic exploitation . . . The buyer . . . has the money: as a group, buyers do not depend on sellers for their income, while sellers generally do depend on buyers. This economic dependence reinforces the social vulnerability that prostitutes experience.

Feminists who hold this view believe that the exploitation involved in prostitution is an extension of the kind of exploitation women experience generally, not only with regard to economic disadvantages but also with regard to cultural standards of female attractiveness, which are bound up in youthfulness, slimness, and so on. Male customers, on the other hand, like men in general in society, are not constricted by these cultural standards, as they make up the rules and have the economic means to reinforce their desires. Many feminists believe that women who are prostitutes do not understand their exploitation and need to be saved from the "false consciousness" that traps them in these degrading occupations. Taylor Lee explains:

> The first time I had sex, I was raped by someone close enough to my family to call my mother "mom." Now I was sure what I was for. I knew that my greatest asset was my sexuality and knew how badly it was desired. I also realized that I had little control over my sexuality, that it could be taken at will. It was easy to give it for profit; at least then I was in control (2004:58).

The prostitute-as-victim stance continues to be challenged by many people who are advocates for and/or engaged in the sex trade, including many sex workers who identify as feminists. As Jeffrey and MacDonald state, "attempts to portray the sex worker as 'victim' infantilizes her [and] denies her agency . . ." (2006a:314). Hallgrimsdottir and colleagues further note that in "victim" narratives, "sex workers appear to be legally and morally incapacitated, incapable of making safe and reasonable choices for themselves" (2006:272). These sociologists all have a view of prostitution as a service for which workers charge a fee, much like any other service in society. The difference, about which the workers are fully conscious, is that they are hiring out their bodies in ways most people would find too distasteful to engage in. They do not necessarily view themselves as exploited, and often encourage those who view them as "victims" to instead respect them as self-directed, independent, hard-working women who have made the conscious

choice to be involved in the sex trade; to do what they wish with their own bodies. This debate, between feminists, on prostitution, like the debate on pornography to follow, has been going on for decades and likely will continue. As Carol Queen, a well-known sociologist, film-maker, and sex-trade worker, states:

> Unfortunately, the exciting politics that promised me sexual freedom twenty-five years ago have veered toward dogma . . . Please . . . don't assume that you know what someone else's experience has been just because you can't imagine liking to do it yourself. Please don't require that all people be one certain "politically correct" way. Please don't assume I can't make my own decisions, that my exhibitionism somehow makes me a victim . . . Don't tell me I don't have a soul. (Queen 1997:138–141)

According to some Marxist feminists, the only way to eliminate prostitution is to reduce disparities in income levels between women and men and eliminate poverty. However, most radical feminists believe that prostitution will not be eliminated until patriarchy is ended.

Conflict theorists and feminists, who in examining social problems focus on the interrelationship of racialization, class, and gender, suggest that the criminalization of prostitution uniquely affects poor women, especially poor women of colour and Indigenous women, who are overrepresented among street prostitutes and the most vulnerable to violence, arrest, fines, and so on. According to these theorists, White male supremacy—which traditionally preserves the best-paying jobs for men—makes women of colour and Indigenous women particularly vulnerable to recruitment or coercion into sex work. Kingsley and Mark (2000:14) found, in a national consultation of commercially sexually exploited Indigenous children and youth in Canada, that "for the Aboriginal youth who participated in these consultations, economic need dictated their actions . . . [their] engagement in the sex trade."

Analysts using this framework also note that discrimination in law enforcement uniquely affects women of colour and Indigenous women, as these groups are overrepresented among prostitutes in Canada. For example, law-enforcement officials typically target street prostitutes and other sex workers, particularly when political elites decide to crack down on "deviant" behaviour such as prostitution and pornography (Barry 1995). Lowman notes that there is a lack of political will to create safer conditions for prostitutes to ply their trade, as this would be seen as condoning prostitution, a stance Lowman (1995) calls "odd" as well as "hypocritical" given that prostitution in Canada is legal and hence already condoned.

Instead, Lowman (1995) notes that crackdowns, which disproportionately affect street prostitution, occur when property-holders get up in arms about their neighbourhoods, demonstrating that "public propriety and property values heavily outweigh all other considerations." Most recently in many Canadian communities, police "sting" operations have targeted johns, arresting them for "communicating offences" and then publicizing their names, levying fines, and demanding community service hours and other conditions of probation.

In opposition to those analysts who view all sex work as violence against women, many Third World or transnational feminist analyses view sex work as a practice that emerges from the intersections of racism, patriarchy, imperialism, and capitalism. Women in this perspective are seen not simply as victims of patriarchal oppression, but equally as,

> . . . agentic, self-determining, differentially positioned subjects who are capable of negotiation, complying with, as well as consciously opposing and transforming relations of power, whether these are embedded in institutions of slavery, prostitution, marriage, the household, or the labour market. (Kempadoo 2005:37)

Kempadoo concludes, therefore, that sex work or the sex trade itself is not necessarily problematic: much depends upon the will of the person involved in the sex trade (2005). She notes that many prostitutes' rights and anti-trafficking organizations, including feminist ones, now make a distinction between "free and forced prostitution," with "traffic in persons and forced prostitution [as] 'manifestations of violence against women'" being viewed entirely differently from that of "respect for the self-determination of adult persons who are voluntarily engaged in prostitution" (2005:37). As noted in Anthropologist Denise Brennan's ethnographic account of sex worker's lives in the Dominican Republic, "[s]ex work is never just about money and sex; it is about hopes, possibilities, and the realities of transnational capitalism and the local structures of class" (2004:ix–x). Brennan's research "unscrambles the transnational economies of desire and intimacy and shows how sex workers, with few opportunities and fewer resources, strategize to make a way for themselves in a global economy of enduring inequalities" (Brennan 2004:x).

PORNOGRAPHY

Nina Hartley (1994:176–177), founder of the Pink Ladies club, a group of women in the pornography industry, wrote of herself:

"A feminist porno star? Right, tell me another one," I can hear some feminists saying . . . why porno? Simple—I'm an exhibitionist with a cause: to make sexually graphic (hard core) erotica, and today's porno is the only game in town. . . . As I examine my life, I uncover the myriad influences that led me to conclude that it was perfectly natural for me to choose a career in adult films. . . . I stripped once a week while getting my bachelor's degree in nursing. . . . I went into full time [adult] movie work immediately following graduation.

While Hartley identifies herself as a feminist porn star, many social analysts, as Hartley herself notes, believe that this is a contradiction in terms. Many academics, such as journalism professor Robert Jensen (2007) and sociology professor Gail Dines (2010), believe pornography is a pressing contemporary social problem. But what kind of social problem is it? Many researchers have framed the issue historically as a problem of patriarchy—male oppression of women—by analyzing power differentials between the actors (Dines 2010; Jensen 2007; Leong 1991). The specific nature of pornography as a social problem is not clear-cut. Canadian sociologist Mariana Valverde (1985:124) discusses some of the difficulties with even defining what pornography is, saying that pornography "is a collection of images and texts, representations which have something in common." But what is that "something"? In noting there are no concrete ways to measure what is or is not pornography, Valverde (1985:125) explains,

> Pornography is not a natural object that can be classified, like a particular species of butterfly, but rather is a complex cultural *process*. . . . Pornography does not drop from heaven onto our local corner store shelves. It is first *produced* by certain people who relate to one another via the pornography industry; it is then *consumed* by customers who buy porn in the expectation of being aroused; and finally porn derives most of its meaning and significance from the *social context* in which it exists. (italics in original)

The social context in which pornography exists is all-important (Diamond 1988; Valverde 1985). This can be demonstrated using Valverde's classic example of the *Playboy* centrefold. While the distribution and consumption of pornography has come a long way from the magazine centrefolds of Valverde's analysis, the analysis is no less accurate today. She argues that the picture, typically of a nude, young, attractive, White woman whose genitals are featured prominently, does not have much meaning in and of itself. When viewed in a North American context of sexism, racism, ableism, ageism, and so on, however, the picture is imbued with layers of meaning. She is beautiful and helpless-looking and posed in such a way as to engender a specific response (arousal) in North American men: "He will not merely glance at the photo as he would at a landscape or a family photograph; he will gaze intently, stare at, and *possess* that woman with his eyes" (Valverde 1985:125–126). Further, the point of the picture is not to celebrate femaleness or the female body, but rather, in the context of capitalism, the purpose is to use the female body for profit making. Finally, besides the feelings the picture may arouse in many men, it also heightens feelings for many women; feelings of embarrassment for the model, whose seeming naivety is a ploy used to enhance the male viewer's pleasure in dominance. Many women may feel angry, at risk, and vulnerable. As Valverde (1985:126) concludes, "It is not the picture itself which creates these feelings. If men never raped women in real life, the same picture would not have the same power to make us feel violated." As sociologist Sara Diamond (1988:400) points out, pornography will always exist, underground or in the mainstream, until sexism is eliminated. How differently might pornography look in the absence of sexism? Would it even exist? Would it still be called pornography? What about gay and lesbian pornography? Certainly it is not separable from or immune to sexist stereotyping and attitudes in mainstream culture, but is all pornography sexist? Must it be? Professor, feminist, and erotica author Susie Bright addresses this issue head-on, stating,

> We saw the sexism of the porn business. . . but we also saw some intriguing possibilities and amazing maverick spirit. We said, "What if we made something that reflected our politics and values, but was just as sexually bold?" (2006, quoted in Nathan 2007:61)

Determining or interpreting what is pornographic will always be a difficult task.

Over time, public attitudes change regarding what should be tolerated and what should be banned because of *obscenity*—**the legal term for pornographic materials that are offensive by generally accepted standards of decency.** But, who decides what is obscene? According to what criteria? Typically, governments decide. A publication is deemed to be obscene according to the Canadian *Criminal Code*, section 163, if its dominant characteristic is the "undue exploitation of sex" or is of "sex and any one or more of the following subjects, namely, crime, horror, cruelty, and violence." Most mainstream pornography today, and certainly

gonzo pornography—**openly misogynist pornography with no pretensions of a plot**—seems to clearly meet the qualifications for obscenity, and yet it is easily and widely available to anyone. The fact that some pornography has been criminalized, at least as it pertains to children, has helped in its construction as a social problem.

The Social Construction of Pornography as a Social Problem

The social construction of pornography as a social problem involves both a cognitive framework and a moral framework. The cognitive framework refers to the factualness of the situation that constitutes the "problem." In regard to pornographic materials, one cognitive framework might be based on the assumption that pornography *actually affects* people's actions or attitudes; an opposing cognitive framework might be based on the assumption that pornography is a fantasy mechanism that enables people to express the forbidden without actually engaging in forbidden behaviour (Kipnis 1996; Loftus 2002). The moral framework refers to arguments of whether something is immoral or unjust. In the case of pornography, moral condemnation arises from beliefs that graphic representations of sexuality are degrading, violent, and/or sinful. From this perspective, pornography is less about sex than about violating certain norms or taboos in society. The moral framework often distinguishes between pornography and *erotica*—**materials that depict consensual sexual activities that are sought by and pleasurable to all parties involved.** According to sociologist Diana E. H. Russell (1993), materials can be considered erotic—rather than obscene—only if they show respect for all human beings and are free of sexism, racism, and homophobia. Contemporary erotica might include romance novels that describe two consenting adults participating in sexual behaviour (see Snitow 1994). On the other hand, materials depicting violent assaults, rapes, or the sexual exploitation of children would be considered pornographic or obscene. However, the distinction appears to be highly subjective, as feminist scholar Ellen Willis (1981:222) notes: "Attempts to sort out good erotica from bad porn inevitably come down to 'What turns me on is erotic: what turns you on is pornographic.'" These are issues that the Canadian justice system is continually called upon to debate; but, in the words of the report of the Special Committee on Pornography and Prostitution (the Fraser Committee 1985:7), "Activities which threaten the physical well-being of others can find no real place in civilized society."

The Nature and Extent of Pornography

As part of the multibillion-dollar sex industry, pornography is profitable to many people, including investors, filmmakers, and owners of stores that distribute such materials. *Hard-core* pornography is material that explicitly depicts sexual acts and/or genitals. In contrast, *soft-core* pornography is "suggestive" but does not depict actual intercourse or genitals. Gonzo pornography has taken hard-core pornography to new levels, generally featuring overt violence and pain—including extreme sadism—against whatever women happen to be in the scenes.

Technological innovations such as digital media and widespread broadband Internet access have greatly increased the amount and variety of pornographic materials available, as well as methods of distribution. The major factor here is the fact that people can easily consume pornography, in private, any time. According to a 2003 Canadian study, "Canadians lead the world in terms of the amount of time they spend downloading porn from the Internet" (Kimmel and Holler 2011:265). Although some people still visit live peep shows and adult boutiques, hard-core, sexually explicit materials are easily and widely available on one's computer or smartphone, and through mail-order services, movies on cable television channels, Internet chatrooms, and sexually explicit websites. Today, the porn industry is estimated to gross approximately $100 billion globally, and approximately $15 billion USD per year in the United States alone (Kimmel and Holler 2011:265; Dines 2010:47). Some adult production and distribution companies are listed today on the American stock exchange. On the Internet, the number of pornographic webpages increased 1800 percent between 1998 and 2003—from 14 million pages to 260 million pages (Kimmel and Holler 2011:265). Pornography has become increasingly corporatized and makes a great deal more money than what Hollywood takes in for mainstream movies per year (Kinnick 2007; Nathan 2007). A lot of the financial disparity is due to the sheer volume of pornography movies made. For example, by the early 2000s, over 13 000 porn movies—from amateur to pro—were being produced annually around the world, compared to Hollywood's 400. As examples, Vivid, one of the largest porn producing companies in the world today, turns out a minimum of 80 movies per year; Private Media, Europe's largest producer, turns out approximately 100 films per year (Nathan 2007). It is not known how much revenue is made in Canada from the pornography industry, but due to digital media technology, porn is relatively easy, cheap, and quick to produce (Kinnick 2007). Most porn in Canada is made in Quebec, which is also home to other thriving porn-related businesses, such as recruiting agencies for new male and female "talent" to export to Los Angeles (where most U.S. porn is made). While pornography can command excellent returns on investment for owners and producers, wages and salaries for actors in the business vary widely.

According to some social analysts, pornography is a prime example of the principle of supply and demand. As long as demand remains high, which it likely will, pornographers will continue to market their goods and services and find new ways to use technology. According to Walter Kendrick, a scholar whose research focuses on pornography,

> Pornographers have been the most inventive and resourceful users of whatever medium comes along because they and their audience have always wanted innovations. Pornographers [have been] excluded from the mainstream channels, so they look around for something new, and the audience has a desire to try any innovation that gives them greater realism or immediacy. (quoted in Tierney 1994:H18)

Each new development in technology changes the meaning of pornography and brings new demands for regulation or censorship. Today, pornography is employing various types of interactive media, including virtual reality and Digital Video Disk, which operates much like a video game where the buyer can choose which of several characters to enact, change the view, and so on as they do in the popular mainstream game "the Sims." One of the first popular pornographic games, called *Chasing Stacy* (produced by VCA Labs), allows the player to interact with Stacy the porn star, asking her out on a date, having the date, and then choosing the location of the inevitable sexual tryst (Hughes 2004:42) As stated by one producer,

> If a viewer wants something different, we give it to him. The viewer can go inside the head of the person having sex with [name deleted], male or female. He can choose which character to follow. He can re-edit the movie. It's a great technology. (Rich 2001 quoted in Hughes 2004:41)

These technological innovations, along with other sexually explicit pornography on the Internet, are widely believed to have a far more powerful influence on people than the printed word has.

Research on Pornography

In June 1983, the Department of Justice convened a seven-member committee to investigate and report on

Canada's Role in Cracking Down on Internet Child Pornography

Anonymity on the Internet makes it difficult to detect child pornography and to apprehend those who distribute or consume such materials (Simon 1999). Most "seasoned" people who distribute and trade child pornography have sophisticated methods for avoiding detection. Material flows globally through various servers, as Nathan notes, "the person posting the picture, the server, the picture site where other users could locate the image [and download it if deemed "worthwhile"] and the site with the access password—could each be in a different country (2007:116). Additionally, many sites with the most serious material are what historian Philip Jenkins calls "ephemeral sites," and may only last a matter of hours before they are closed down, making it difficult to track both distributors and consumers (Jenkins 2001:22). Historically, sexually abusive images of infants and children were traded privately, in person or through the mail, between people who knew one another and through clubs.

Since its inception in 1989, the Internet has become the source of vast amounts of beneficial information. However, this new form of information technology has also facilitated the dissemination of child pornography. According to one legal analyst, the Internet has changed the manner in which pornography can be created, distributed, and accessed:

> Prior to the invention of the Internet, consumers and distributors of child pornography had to know each other or have connections to exchange materials. Underground networks facilitated the trade of photographs or videos through the mail or in person. Currently, however, subscribers . . . can simply download graphic images through their modems to be able to view and print images.
>
> The anonymity available on the Internet hinders the detection of child pornography. A user can create any identity and transmit a message from [Calgary] through New Zealand, and then on to Halifax, making it impossible to determine the origin. Furthermore, "anonymous remailers" enable a user to re-route outgoing messages by removing the source address, assigning an anonymous identification code number with the remailer's address, and forwarding it to the final destination. (Simon 1999:7)

Just as the distribution of child pornography has been facilitated by the Internet, sexually explicit visual depictions of children (and adults) have become much easier to create and mass produce. Scanners, video cameras, and graphics software packages are an integral part of the production of child pornography today (Simon 1999),

and much child pornography production is easily accomplished within the relative safety (legally speaking) of people's homes (Jewkes and Andrews 2007).

What social policy issues are raised by the increasing availability of pornographic materials? One major consideration is the use of children under the age of 18 in pornographic depictions. Another is the question of whether or not child pornography contributes to pedophilia (defined as an abnormal condition in which an adult has a sexual desire for children). Further complicating this issue is the fact that some child pornographers claim that the actors they use are over the age of 18 and simply appear to be younger, or that the children shown are not actual children but rather computer-generated images—"virtual" actors.

This argument, however, is rendered irrelevant under section 163.1 of the Canadian *Criminal Code,* which states that child pornography is "(a) a photographic, film, video or other visual representation, whether or not it was made by electronic or mechanical means, (i) that shows a person who is or *is depicted as being* under the age of eighteen years and is engaged in or is depicted as engaged in explicit sexual activity, or (ii) the dominant characteristic of which is the depiction, for a sexual purpose, of a sexual organ or the anal region of a person under the age of eighteen years; or (b) any written material or visual representation that advocates or counsels sexual activity with a person under the age of eighteen years that would be an offence under this Act."

In Canada, anything illegal off-line is illegal online. In May 2004, the National Child Exploitation Coordination Centre (NCECC) was expanded to focus on sexual exploitation of children on the Internet. Many officers within Canada's police forces have been gaining valuable Internet training focused specifically on Internet-based exploitation. This training includes investigative techniques for the search and seizure of illegal computer data (RCMP 2006a). Police, however, as always, are bound by the *Charter* and Canadian laws pertaining to protection of privacy issues.

Mystery hackers like "Citizen Tipster" are not so bound, or at least choose not to be. On June 29, 2002, the *Vancouver Sun* reported on the activities of a 21-year-old Langley, B.C., computer hacker who used a computer program he wrote to monitor the private emails of suspected child-porn producers and child molesters worldwide. He had read hundreds of communications each day for three years, and his tips to police resulted in the arrests of several child predators in Canada, the United States, and Russia. His online evidence led to the arrest in 2001 of an Orange County Superior Court Judge for possession of more than 100 images of child pornography and involvement in a plot to sexually exploit young boys at a private health club. The hacker forwarded his evidence to an online organization, Predator-Hunter.com, focused on ending the exploitation of children; it, in turn, forwarded the files to the California Department of Justice. Citizen Tipster's online evidence also led to the arrest and conviction of an Alberta man who was using the Internet to sell his eight-year-old daughter for sex in 1999. Police threatened Omni-Potent (the tipster's online handle) with arrest for violations of citizens' privacy, but it took them a long time to actually find him. When they finally tracked him down, via a website, they demanded his hard-drive and all his files. In the words of 21-year-old Omni-Potent, though, "Sure, a violation of privacy you must cry, but, if you have nothing hurting kids, the future of the world, then there's no reason to worry as that is all Omni-Potent protects . . . [those] who can't protect themselves" (Dimmock 2002:A14).

The vulnerability of children to online predators led to the introduction into the House of Commons, on March 14, 2001, of a bill to fortify existing legislation protecting children from sexual exploitation, particularly through the Internet. On June 10, 2002, the Justice Minister and Attorney General of Canada announced that "Bill C-15A, containing tough new legislation protecting children from sexual exploitation, Internet luring and child pornography" had received Royal Assent. Specific to child pornography, amendments to the *Criminal Code* include:

- **Internet luring and child pornography:** It is now illegal to communicate with a child over the Internet for the purpose of committing a sexual offence against that child as well as to transmit, make available, export, and access child pornography;
- **Child sex tourism:** Amendments to the Child Sex Tourism Law (enacted in 1997) will simplify the process used to prosecute Canadians who sexually exploit children in other countries; and
- **Enhanced judicial powers:** Judges can now order both the deletion of child pornography posted on computer systems in Canada and the forfeiture of any materials and equipment used in the commission of a child pornography offence. They can keep known sex offenders away from children by using prohibition orders, long-term offender designations, and one-year peace bonds for offences relating to child pornography and the Internet (Department of Justice Canada 2002).

Following the October 2004 Speech from the Throne committing to a "crackdown on child pornography," Bill C-2, an *Act to Amend the Criminal Code* (protection of children and other vulnerable persons) *and the Canada Evidence Act* was passed into law in the summer of 2005.

The bill includes new and tighter provisions around child pornography, new sexual exploitation offences, procedures that facilitate testimony, new voyeurism offences, and reforms to existing federal measures protecting children. The new child pornography laws were put to the test immediately. In 2005, Gordon Chin of Alberta was sentenced to 18 months' probation, 100 community service hours, no computer or Internet access for the duration of his probation, and his name added to a sex-offender registry for five years. His crime? Possessing anime comic books that included images of naked, tied-up children and babies being raped with pistols. Chin's investigation stemmed from customs officials seizing a package with the comic books destined for Chin's home. His sentence was viewed as "lucky" by the Crown in the case because it was handed down days before the amendment came into full effect on November 1, 2005, requiring a minimum sentence of 90 days in jail for importing or distributing child pornography ("Man Guilty of Child Porn Cartoons" 2005). Today, anyone convicted of possessing child pornography is required to register with the sex-offender registry even if they are not "contact" offenders (Jewkes and Andrews 2007).

Acknowledging the global scope of the issue, the Canadian government and the RCMP are also joined by experts from 30 other nations through the Virtual Global Taskforce, and 24-hour law-enforcement points of contact have been established to facilitate cooperation and share information between countries of the G-8 (RCMP 2006b). Canada also launched a National Strategy to Protect Children from Exploitation on the Internet in May 2004, with $42 million in funding over five years. Part of that funding was for the launch of "*cybertip.ca,* a 24/7 public national tip line" (Department of Justice Canada 2005). As of January 2008, reports to the tip line had resulted in 43 arrests and the removal of 2850 websites from the Internet (cybertip.ca). Not only is the issue global, but its scope is also immense because it involves the Internet. Chidley noted in 1995 that a conservative estimate of information passed on the Internet equated to approximately 300 paperback pages per second. Most current estimates suggest that there are millions or hundreds of millions of websites currently supplying billions of pages of information and materials and billions of images. In this context, attempts to eliminate or censor internet child pornography may well be futile.

Certainly many people are not happy about any movement toward censorship of the Internet. Jeffrey Shallit, a computer scientist at the University of Waterloo in Ontario, was also involved with an organization called Electronic Frontier Canada, which is focused on maintaining free speech in cyberspace. Shallit (cited in Chidley 1995:58)

Social Problems in the Media

Box 7.2 continued

and many others believe that the issue of Internet pornography has been blown way out of proportion—that it represents a minimal amount of online material. While few condone child pornography, members of online communities are nervous about where crackdowns and censorship may lead generally. How much freedom and privacy should be exchanged for problems that everyone is opposed to like child pornography? Is censorship causing more problems than it solves and could other methods be effective?

Others, such as the Coalition for Lesbian and Gay Rights in Ontario (CLGRO 1998), raise concerns about what censorship of the Internet may do to advances for people with non-heterosexual sexualities, noting that with the passage of laws, "there is no reason to believe the police and courts will suddenly become less homophobic or that serious attempts will be made to educate and empower children and youth in the area of sex or encourage the autonomy of lesbian, gay and bi-sexual teens." The CLGRO also points out the inconsistency in defining people 12 and under as children in the *Young Offenders Act*, and then defining people 18 and under as children with regard to sex-related offences (CLGRO 1998).

Historian Philip Jenkins, author of *Beyond Tolerance: Child Pornography on the Internet*, was one such sceptic about the pervasiveness of child pornography on the Internet. In order to demonstrate that the "social menace" of child pornography on the Internet was "vastly overblown," Jenkins set out to academically research the issue (Jenkins 2001:9). He quickly discovered that he was wrong: "It is a substantial presence, and much of the material out there is much worse than most of us can imagine, in terms of the types of activity depicted and the ages of the children portrayed. This is not just a case of softcore pictures of precociously seductive fifteen year olds" (Jenkins 2001:9). However, while Jenkins wishes to rid the world of child pornography, like the others cited here, he does not support censorship of the Internet: "We have to find means of killing or crippling the subculture without destroying the Internet, with which so much good can be accomplished" (2001:224).

So, how pervasive is this problem? Many sceptics have suggest that child porn is the purview of a "few grubby, inadequate loners," however the seizure of *one* Texas-based subscription website that served as a portal for porn sites with sexually abusive images of infants and young children offered up the names and credit card details of 390 000 subscribers in 60 nations—35 000 of those subscribers were U.S. citizens, 2300 were Canadian, and 7200 were from the U.K. (Jewkes and Andrews 2007:62). A recent estimate suggests that there are currently at least 250 000 Britons who use child pornography, so the

390 000 caught in the one seizure likely represent only a fraction of the self-described "Loli Lovers" or "Lolita Lovers" (Jewkes and Andrews 2007). Further, between 2002 and 2004, one study found that the number of dedicated child porn and pedophilia websites grew to 19 246, half of which were hosted in the United States (Yar 2006). The same study found that people in the United States were the most frequent visitors to such sites, representing an estimated 32 percent of global users, and that half of these sites were commercial (Yar 2006). It is believed that the online trade in child porn is worth $3 billion USD per year (Yar 2006).

Using research spanning a 15-year period on the victims of child pornography, Jewkes and Andrews (2007) report five clear trends: (1) the age of victims is decreasing, possibly because younger children are less able or likely to disclose abuse; (2) there is an increase in "in-home" production; (3) more than half the images are of girls, but images of boys are increasingly prevalent; (4) there is an ethnic and racialized dimension in that Asian children are more likely to be found in posed erotic or posed sexually explicit images, while most images of children, especially those that demonstrate explicit sexual activity, assault, gross assault, and/or sadism or bestiality are of White children, and Black children are rarely represented in child porn; and (5) there has been an increase in images of children from eastern Europe (Jewkes and Andrews 2007:63–64; Yar 2006:113). Another U.S. study of pornography found in offenders' possession found that most (58 percent) of the images found were of very young children (younger than five years old) and most images were of girls (Jewkes and Andrews 2007:65). An international study found that most child pornography seized in Japan depicted girls, whereas 50 percent of the child pornography seized in the United States and 75 percent seized in Canada depicted boys (Yar 2006:113).

The overwhelming majority of people who download child pornography are White men over age 30, although there is a "small but significant number" of women, teens, and children who trade in abusive images of children (Jewkes and Andrews 2007; Yar 2006). As Jewkes and Andrews summarize, "The only conclusion about Internet child pornography offenders that can be drawn from international research, then, is that, while almost exclusively male and usually reported to be White professionals, in all other ways offenders are a diverse and heterogeneous group" (2007:69).

What social policy issues are raised by the legislation on child pornography and the Internet, especially given that production, consumption, and distribution span the globe? Some critics argue that freedom of expression involving youthful-looking adults is limited by our laws, and therefore, our laws are unconstitutional (e.g., in Canada it is illegal to possess pornography that depicts people who look like children). Other critics raise the issue of privacy, asserting that people should be able to read and view whatever they want. Suppose, they say, someone else used your computer, downloaded child pornography, and then you were accused of possessing that pornography? On the other hand, supporters of the new legislation argue that these concerns are outweighed by the necessity of protecting children from being victimized by child pornographers. What do you think?

---

the situation of pornography and prostitution in Canada. This resulted in the 1985 Fraser Committee report. The report concluded, with regard to pornography, that "there is agreement that the current situation is problematic [e.g., that current laws on availability and control are unsatisfactory], [but] . . . that is where consensus ends" (Special Committee on Pornography and Prostitution 1985:5). The Committee also stated that legal reform was only part of the solution, and that social policies and actions were necessary elements of any long-term strategy. Regarding its stance on pornography generally, and informing the recommendations the Committee made, were these two points:

> In essence we see two forms of harm flowing from pornography. The first is the offence which it does to members of the public who are involuntarily subjected to it. The second is the broader social harm which it causes by undermining the right to equality which is set out in section 15 of the *Charter of Rights and Freedoms.* (Special Committee on Pornography and Prostitution 1985:10)

Sociologists do not agree on the extent to which pornography that depicts excessive sex, violence, and the domination of one person by another affects behaviour. The majority of films in the adult market include scenes where women are dominated by men. The violence and aggression against women in porn today makes many earlier pornographic movies appear the equivalent of the tame after-school specials targeted at teens in the 1970s. Recent publications on pornography suggest that as people become increasingly desensitized to violence, more and more extreme acts are necessary to keep viewers' interest (Dines 2010; Jensen 2007):

> The awkward truth, according to one study, is that 90 percent of 8-to-16-year-olds have viewed pornography online. Considering the standard climax to even the most vanilla hard-core scene today, that

means there's an entire generation of young people who think sex ends with a money shot to the face. (Details, quoted in Dines 2010:59).

Sociologist Gail Dines (2010) critiques the socialization into ultra-violent forms of masculinity that are readily available to young men today through television, the Internet, and video games. Dines argues,

> In this emotional economy, porn is appealing; it offers men a no-strings-attached, intense, disconnected sexual experience, where men always get to have as much sex as they want, in ways that shore up their masculinity. The sex acts are always successful, ending in supposed orgasm for both, and he is protected from rejection or ridicule since in porn, women never say no to men's sexual demands, nor do they question their penis size or technique. In this world, men dispense with romantic dinners, vanilla sex, and post-coital affection and get down to the business of fucking. In porn, sex is the vehicle by which men are rendered all powerful and women are rendered all powerless. . . . (Dines 2010:63)

Based on his analysis of pornography since 1988, journalism professor Robert Jensen discusses three themes that are central to mass-marketed heterosexual porn, whether mainstream or gonzo. These themes are (1) "all women at all times want sex from all men"; (2) "women like all the sexual acts that men perform or demand"; and (3) "any woman who does not at first realize this can be easily turned with a little force. Such force is rarely necessary, however, for most of the women in pornography are the 'nymphomaniacs' that men fantasize about" (Jensen 2007:56–57). As sociologists Michael Kimmel and Jacqueline Holler note, in the world of mainstream porn, "both women and men want what men want, or what pornography thinks men want" (2011:267). Jensen critiques the messages in pornography as being a reflection of mainstream culture where the normalization of cruelty toward, and degradation and dehumanization of women are increasingly commonplace: "[m]irrors can be dangerous and pornography is a mirror" (2007:14).

An increasing number of websites (and the films available through them) are dedicated specifically to violent sex and rape and the complete dehumanization of women. For example, one website registered in Russia is advertised as "the best and most violent rape site on earth" (in Hughes 2004:46). Subscribers are offered 30 000 hard-core porn images, 500 online video channels, and 100 lengthy videos depicting "violent rapes, ass rapes, mouth rapes, gang rapes, nigger (sic) rapes, torn vaginas, and tortured clits" along with a free film showing a "hooded perpetrator raping a woman in an office" (Hughes 2004:46). Typical of the Gonzo porn genre (and increasingly of mainstream porn), women are never presented as human beings or even referred to as women. Any quick Internet search will yield thousands of images of "sluts, whores, cunts, nasty bitches" (Jensen 2007:57) and "cumdumpsters," and "horny bitches" (Dines 2010:66) who love being mistreated sexually and "beg" for more and worse treatment. Jensen suggests that porn today "[sexualizes] the degradation of women" (2008:np). The most violent and humiliating forms of porn available today are likely anything conceived of by Max Hardcore, a particularly sadistic actor who has been jailed for obscenity based on his multiple movies and the ATM (ass-to-mouth) where the woman in the scene is forced to put a penis in her mouth that has been in her own or another woman's anus. The viewer's sexual pleasure derived from these scenes and others where it is clear that the women are not enjoying the acts, even openly demonstrating real pain and agony, is based on desensitization and a complete lack of empathy for women (Dines 2010). Most male porn viewers, however, insist that the women in the porn industry love what they do, especially the acts that debase them the most, making them a particular type of women, quite different from the women in their real lives. However, increasingly porn seems to be leaking into people's real lives and real relationships.

Some studies have demonstrated a link between violent porn and increased aggressive attitudes toward women by men, but research has not demonstrated that attitudinal changes cause rapes or assaults on women that would otherwise have not taken place (Valverde 1985:121). For example Diamond (1988:396) remarks that "[t]he suggestion that consumers of pornographic material or other media products respond in zombie-like, imitative fashion to all-powerful images is both false and frightening." However, as Gail Dines (2010) points out, that kind of argument is far too simplistic, and that we should really be looking at and asking ourselves how porn affects our culture and relationships generally and how it shapes the ideas, attitudes, and practices of the men and women who consume it. Dines argues that, "taken together, pornographic images create a world that is at best inhospitable to women, and at worst dangerous to their physical and emotional well-being" (2010:85). Kimmel and Holler echo Dines's perspective, stating that "[w]e need a conversation about pornography that looks at why porn's version of sex works for so many men (and an increasing number of women)" (2011:268). In any case, in recent years, most people do not support outright efforts to censor adults' access to pornographic material, unless the material involves children (see Box 7.2).

Pornography and Age, Gender, Class, Racialization, and Ethnicity

Because viewing pornography used to be considered obscene by most Canadians, it was a secretive activity, making data on the consumers of various forms limited, historically. Today, as pornography increasingly becomes part of the mainstream (fashions, video games, language, soft core on prime time television) "fully recognizable fixtures of popular culture," people are more open about their consumption habits (Williams 2004:1). Studies in the past found that the typical customer of an "adult bookstore" was a White, relatively well-educated, married, middle-class man between the ages of 25 and 66. Other studies have found that younger and more-educated adults express more accepting attitudes toward pornography than do older, less educated adults (Lottes 1993). In a "porn census" put together by journalist Debbie Nathan, it appears that the picture has shifted again somewhat to more female viewers and younger viewers. For example, in early 2007, 48 percent of U.S. visitors to adult websites were women, while 35 percent of Grade 8 boys and 8 percent of Grade 8 girls say they have viewed Internet porn "too many times to count" (Nathan 2007:41).

Overall, men watch more sexually-explicit material and hold more favourable attitudes toward it than women do. The June 2006 Angus Reid Poll on Canadians' views about immoral behaviour supports this, with 58 percent of Canadians overall stating they felt pornographic films are immoral, representing 46 percent of men polled and 68 percent of women polled (Angus Reid 2006).

Some analysts attribute this difference to gender-role socialization. In a society in which men are socialized to be sexual initiators but often fear rejection, pornography may be satisfying because it typically shows a willing female partner—in the words of legal scholar Margaret Baldwin, "[i]n pornography . . . women live to be fucked, men inevitably fuck" (1984:631). In contrast, women have been socialized to respond negatively to material showing nude bodies and male pleasure that may occur at the expense of a woman's sense of safety and dignity. However, in recent years, more women have become consumers of magazines such as *Playgirl*, erotic novels, and videos that are made specifically for women, such as those produced, directed, and distributed by Nina Hartley, Veronica Hart, Susie Bright, and Candida Royalle, all women in their 60s and former porn actors (Nathan 2007). Certainly there has been a substantial increase in female consumers of porn (Kimmel and Holler 2011:265). There is evidence that many more women are becoming involved in the pornography industry, not only as actors, but as directors, producers, camera operators, and, of course, as consumers. As writer Paula Gilovich discusses,

> Women are discovering in pornography an incredible new tool: If porn has been one of the major engines of objectification in the hands of men, it holds the potential to become an engine of subjectification in the hands of women. What better field to transmute the woman in the camera's gaze from an object to—at long, long last—the subject? Female filmmakers have begun using pornography—and female pornographers have begun using film—to challenge the relationship of sex and power. There is a transfer of ownership underway: More and more, porn now belongs to the women who make it.

> What makes this transfer of ownership so powerful is that pornography is one of the primary cultural engines of objectification. Women are most harmed through porn because they are objectified almost beyond all recognition. In porn, the female has always been the object of the male viewer's attention; she is strictly an extension of his fantasy, a tool to get him off. And this is why the feminine subversion of porn is especially feministic. We are just beginning an era when power in the porn industry is being defined by the new recognition of an old truth: there is no porn without women. (Gilovich 2002)

Further, younger women are now getting in on the action too. Canadian director Angela Phong, working out of Toronto's women-run and feminist company Dirty Pillows, produces lesbian porn for lesbian audiences (Nathan 2007). Young women are also producing porn with a violent or aggressive edge, showing scenes of women being dragged by the hair and so on—porn that

many women feel degrades women. Director Mason disagrees, stating that the ideas come from her own sexual fantasies and that the work is "woman-oriented" (Nathan 2007:69). Other young female porn producers see themselves as feminists and as activists, using their websites and film roles to engage in intelligent and critical commentary about the images and about other elements of popular culture. Examples include BurningAngel.com and Suicidegirls.com (Nathan 2007). Explicitly looking at porn as a vehicle for activism, producers like Tristan Taormino believe the porn they produce is a political act:

> I consciously work to create images that contradict (and hopefully challenge) other porn that represents women only as objects and vehicles for male pleasure. The lack of female pleasure in porn just sucks. . . . I think making porn can be a political act, just as valid and valuable as other forms of activism within the women's movement. (2006, quoted in Nathan 2007:69)

For all the inroads women and feminists have made as directors, producers, and distributors, porn continues to be a male-dominated industry that makes porn for mainly male viewers—both gay and straight.

Historically, women have been more vocal than men in opposing pornography. According to sociologist Michael Kimmel, men have been relatively silent for several reasons: embarrassment or guilt for having enjoyed pornography; anger at women's interference in male privilege; lack of interest in what they perceive to be a non-issue; fear that speaking out will lead to questions about their masculinity; reluctance to talk openly about their sexual feelings; and confusion about "what it means to be a 'real man' in contemporary society" (Kimmel 1987:121).

According to film scholar Laura Kipnis (1996), much of the sentiment against pornography is rooted in class-based elitism: opposition to pornography is a form of snobbery related to maintaining class distinctions in society. From this perspective, rejecting pornography amounts to rejecting all that is vulgar, trashy, and lower class. Although Kipnis does not suggest that all consumers of pornography are lower class, she believes that members of the upper classes typically view pornography consumers as lower-class people who may imitate the images they see. Similarly, women who appear in pornography or consume it are seen as brainwashed or unenlightened people who lack "class." It is worth noting that more recent research shows that pornography consumption, as well as participation in it, appears to cut across class lines. A 2005 paper prepared by the legal branch of the adult entertainment industry in the United

States reports that 50 percent of hotel guests order pay-per-view porn (Nathan 2007), creating annual hotel revenue from porn worth about $500 million USD (Dines 2010:52). The editor of Adult Video News stated, "Porn doesn't have a demographic—it goes across all demographics. . . . [The market is] as diverse as America" (quoted in Williams 2004:2). Further, another study of actors at big production houses conducted by sociologist Sharon Abbott found that many of the actors were well-educated, with approximately one-third having graduated from post-secondary before going into the porn industry (Nathan 2007). Most of the 50 actors Abbott interviewed in her study called their work "stupid" and "ridiculous"—apparently none took it to be "serious art" (Nathan 2007:81).

In another class analysis of pornography, philosopher Alan Soble (1986) linked men's use of pornography to the feelings of boredom and powerlessness that result from the alienating work that most people do in a capitalist marketplace. For these men, pornography becomes a diversion—a means of escaping from the dull, predictable world of work. Soble suggests that consumers of pornography use the material to construct fantasies and gain a sense of control; it gives men the opportunity—otherwise rarely available—to organize the world and conduct its events according to their own wishes and tastes. In Soble's eyes, pornography consumption is not an expression of men's power as much as it is an expression of their lack of power (Soble 1986). How would this analysis account for women's greatly increased consumption of pornography? Certainly if we look at the incredible increase in women's labour force participation in recent years, an increase in consumption to rival men's could make sense. However, in most porn, women do not control any of the action, and instead are acted upon and controlled by one or more men, as well as controlled by the typically male directors and producers.

In other research, sociologists Alice Mayall and Diana E. H. Russell (1993) have detailed how different racialized/ethnic groups are portrayed in pornography. Examining materials in a heterosexual-oriented pornography store, the researchers found that skin colour is a highly salient issue: White women were featured in 92 percent of the pornography, perhaps because they fulfill traditional stereotypes equating female beauty with white skin and Caucasian features (Mayall and Russell 1993). Non-White performers are believed to be "less sexually desirable in the sexual marketplace," according to the mostly White producers, distributers, and directors (Nathan 2007:85).Also in Mayall and Russell's research, people of colour were more likely to be found in materials featuring rape, bondage, and sadomasochism, anal sex, sex with children, and sex between women. Among women of colour, Black women were most frequently featured, followed by Asian women and Latinas. People who consume pornography have a choice of buying magazines portraying only Whites, White men with Black women, or Black men with White women. The researchers were unable to determine whether these options were based on the preferences of consumers or those of the makers of pornography (Mayall and Russell 1993). Collins (1991) suggests that racism in pornography can be traced to the oppression of Black women in slavery: African women were depicted as animals and used as sex objects for the pleasure of White men. Others have noted that, at the same time that the White man was exploiting the Black woman, he was obsessive about protecting the White woman from the Black man (Gardner 1994). Interestingly, White men from the southern U.S. have been shown to be avid consumers of porn depicting Black men with White women, engaging in acts that would have resulted in both partners being killed not many decades ago (Nathan 2007). The breaking of taboos through viewing pornography, without engaging in taboo acts oneself, may be part of what makes some pornography compelling for so many people.

A final consideration of the characteristics of those involved in the porn industry must be income level. Just like those involved in prostitution, men, and particularly women, who are poor may face the most pressure to work in the industry. Using a global example, approximately one-quarter of European pornography is produced in Hungary, a country known for its cheap labour, and most European porn stars are Hungarian. As Nathan notes, "Porn producers complain that in prosperous countries such as France, it is hard to find women who want to make porn. In Hungary, would-be actresses are turned away" (2007:84).

THE FUTURE OF PORNOGRAPHY AND THE SEX INDUSTRY

Public opinion polls have consistently shown that people in Canada are mainly ambivalent about pornography and other aspects of the sex industry. While they acknowledge that the sex industry may produce goods and services that serve as a "safety valve" for some, many others believe that these goods and services can also be a "trigger" for some. There does seem to be a consensus regarding children and pornography Children should be shielded from some materials. At this point, however, the consensus breaks down. Who should do the shielding (the state or families?), what materials should be banned, and what is the appropriate definition of "child" with regard to sexually explicit materials? Certainly with most Canadian children having access to the Internet, and a great many youths admitting to viewing pornography online, the questions may not even be relevant.

The controversy over sexually explicit materials is particularly strong in schools, and some school boards have banned books and audiovisual materials they consider obscene, while others believe the materials to be educational and constructive to children's psycho-sexual development. For example, materials discussing or depicting homosexuality in a positive (or at least not negative) way have been banned in some schools. Many adults would also like to see children shielded from sexually explicit movies, television shows, and rock music videos—to say nothing of the sophisticated adult entertainment on many gaming platforms (Dines 2010; Stefanac 1993). The censorship wars—both online and in public life—continue to pose serious social policy questions.

All of the issues pertaining to pornography and censorship discussed bring us back to a point we have made in previous chapters: how people view social problems affects how they believe such problems should be solved. People seem to view pornography in one of four ways: liberal, religious conservative, antipornography feminist, or anticensorship feminist (Berger et al. 1991; Dines 2010; Jensen 2007; Kinsman 1996; Loftus 2002; Nathan 2007; Nelson 2010; Segal 1990; Williams 2004; Valverde 1985). Each point of view espouses a different solution to the problem of pornography.

According to the *liberal* point of view, pornography may offend some people but brings harmless pleasure to others. It may even serve as a safety valve for those who have no other sexual outlet. Moreover, no evidence links pornography to actual sexual violence or degradation of women (except in the pornography itself, of course). Therefore, the social problem is not really pornography but censorship—people attempting to impose their morals on others and thereby violating the *Canadian Charter of Rights and Freedoms* (Cottle et al. 1989).

In contrast, from a *religious conservative* point of view, pornography is a threat to the moral values of society, especially to "family values." Pornography encourages people to have sexual intercourse outside marriage and to engage in deviant sexual behaviour. Therefore, sexually explicit and violent materials should be censored to protect families and societal values.

Some feminist analysts are generally critical of pornography because it is mainly sexist in its portrayal of women, reinforces gender scripts that emphasize male dominance and female submission, and encourages the valuing of women according to their ability to please men. However, not all feminists agree on what—if

anything—should be done about pornography. *Antipornography feminists* believe that pornography is a primary source of male oppression of, and violence against women. Viewing pornography as a form of sexual discrimination that dehumanizes women and diminishes women's opportunities in all areas of life, including employment, education, and freedom of movement, they believe it should be eliminated (see Dworkin 1988; Dines 2010; Jensen 2007; MacKinnon 1987). In this view, pornography becomes a human rights issue, and anti-pornography feminists argue that communities should pass anti-pornography laws that would enable people who have been victimized by pornography to have legal recourse.

In contrast, *anti-censorship feminists* do not believe that any single factor, such as pornography, causes women's subordination. Focusing on pornography as the primary source of sexual oppression, they say, "downplays the sexism and misogyny at work within all of our most respectable social institutions and practices, whether judicial, legal, familial, occupational, religious, scientific, or cultural" (Segal 1990:32). Therefore, pornography should not be censored because open discussions about sexuality and sexual practices promote women's sexual freedom and their right to express themselves (Kaminer 1990; Willis 1983). Instead, it is argued, we should have even more breadth in the portrayal of women in sexually explicit materials. This is perhaps likely to happen as more and more women enter the ring as pornography producers, directors, and distributors in their own right.

In a world linked by the Internet and other rapid sources of communication, the controversy over censorship may be obsolete. In such a world, whose community standards should be applied in determining whether online materials are obscene? Should we use the standards of St. John's, Newfoundland, or those of Tokyo, Japan? Should we use the standards of the community where the image is posted, or the community where it is viewed, or both? Censorship is a very complicated proposition in an increasingly global village. To restrict local access to a picture, story, or idea on the Internet, access must be blocked to computer users all over the world. What are Internet service providers such as CompuServe and America Online to do? As a historical example that brought these issues into public view, in 1996, German authorities asked one U.S.-based corporation to not let German subscribers access 200 discussion groups and picture databases that allegedly violated German pornography laws. To meet this request, CompuServe had to block worldwide access to those sites. Although the ban was only temporary, it sent shock waves throughout the community of Internet users, who became concerned that material deemed pornographic or obscene by people anywhere in the world could become unavailable everywhere. Among the materials Germany sought to ban were sexuality support groups for people with disabilities and a bulletin board for gay men and lesbians that provided a support network for gay youths ("A Journey of 10,000 Miles Begins with the Shoes" 1996).

In this chapter, we have focused on prostitution and materials that are defined as pornographic, obscene, and erotic. However, it is important to note that mainstream media—including magazines, movies, DVDs, television programming, and online media—also can contribute to negative images of women and men and the exploitation of children. Furthermore, the mainstream media can desensitize people to sexual assault, rape, violence, and murder through repeated exposure to depictions of women as victims and sex objects and men as aggressors, rapists, and killers. What do you think? Is the sex trade more likely than the media in general to encourage violence aimed at women and children?

WHAT CAN YOU DO?

- Educate yourself further about the anti-pornography and anti-censorship debates and decide which view makes the most sense for you.
- Find out what is happening regarding youth prostitution in your area and sit on an existing committee. For example, there may be a committee to establish a "safe house" for youth desiring to leave the trade.
- If your community has a safe house, volunteer at it or help educate others about the issues faced by people attempting to leave the sex trade.
- As many youth in prostitution come from abusive homes, get involved in child-abuse prevention programs in your area.
- Put together an education/information package, with others if you wish, to send to schools so that they may include the issue of sexual exploitation in career and personal planning curricula.
- Lobby the local school district to have such information available in public schools.
- Get involved in local organizations that support making the working conditions for people in the sex industry safer (e.g., Prostitutes Empowerment and Education Resource Society–PEERS).

- Get involved in international organizations to work toward ending sexual exploitation of women and children (e.g., Global Alliance Against Trafficking in Women–GAATW).
- Volunteer to teach English or French with immigrant and refugee settlement organizations. Because cuts to funding for these programs often mean men have the first priority for language training (within certain racialized/ethnic communities and families), offer to teach women and/or youth.
- Lobby federal MPs and provincial MPPs/MLAs to have health inspectors tour entire establishments (not only kitchens) as part of their job descriptions to ensure safer working conditions for people employed in clubs.
- Work with health care organizations to ensure that information on physical, mental, and emotional health-related issues is accurately translated into many languages and distributed in places where sex-trade workers convene.
- Write a letter to the newspaper discussing some of the issues for people in the sex trade from your point of view (e.g., Do you think prostitution or pornography should be decriminalized? Why or why not?).
- Lobby federal MPs and provincial MPPs/MLAs to shift the focus in prosecution from the most vulnerable sex-trade workers onto pimps, traffickers, child-porn film-makers, and so on—whomever you think should be prosecuted, if anyone.
- Work on a media awareness campaign with the goal of "deglamourizing" work in the sex trade.
- Get involved with or create, with others, a public-education campaign about why young people get involved in prostitution and pornography.
- Lobby in your community for higher minimum wages so that there may be less incentive to enter the sex trade rather than pursue other occupations.
- Work in your community to get better addiction services and housing for those who need it.
- Talk with friends and family members about how pornography makes them (and you) view men and women; about whether they (and you) feel it impacts people's actions and attitudes.
- If you have been (or are) involved in the sex trade, use your knowledge to mentor others who are involved about health and safety and options.

SUMMARY

What is prostitution? how has it changed in recent years?

Prostitution is the sale of sexual services (one's own or another's) for money or goods and without emotional attachment. According to some social analysts, prostitution has recently become industrialized, normalized, and globalized. The industrialization of prostitution refers to commercialized sex as a product manufactured within the human self. Normalization is the process whereby sex work comes to be treated as a form of entertainment with no legal impediments to promoting it as a commodity. The globalization of prostitution refers to the process by which the sex industry has increasingly become global in scope, travelling across borders with relative ease.

What levels, or tiers, of prostitution have sociologists identified?

Sociologists have identified several categories: Escort prostitutes earn higher fees and can be more selective in their working conditions and customers than other prostitutes. Hustlers work out of nightclubs, bars, and strip joints, where they solicit their customers. House prostitutes work in brothels, and a substantial portion of their earnings goes to the house manager or pimp. Street prostitutes publicly solicit customers and charge by the "trick." The last tier includes those who exchange sex for drugs.

How do functionalists view prostitution?

Functionalists point out that prostitution—like other forms of deviance—is functional for society. Prostitution continues because it provides people with (1) quick, impersonal sexual gratification without emotional attachment; (2) a sexual outlet for those who have no ongoing sexual relationships; (3) the opportunity to engage in non-traditional sexual practices; (4) protection for the family as a social institution; and (5) jobs for people with few traditional job skills.

How do interactionists view prostitution?

Interactionists believe that prostitution—like other forms of deviance—is socially constructed. Entering a career such as prostitution is like entering any other occupation, but public labelling of the occupation as deviant—and the individual's acceptance or rejection of that label—determines whether a person stays in that career.

How do conflict theorists and feminists view prostitution?

There are several conflict perspectives on prostitution. Liberal feminists consider prostitution a victimless crime—involving a willing buyer and a willing seller—that should be decriminalized. Marxist feminists see prostitution as linked to the capitalist economy. Radical feminists trace the roots of prostitution to patriarchy in society. Feminist theorists who focus on the intersection of racialization/ethnicity, class, and gender believe that the criminalization of prostitution is a form of discrimination against poor women, particularly poor women of colour and Indigenous women. Third World or transnational feminists view sex work and trafficking as one possibility emerging from the intersections of many relations of dominance that conditions women's lives.

Does pornography differ from obscenity and erotica?

It is difficult to distinguish among these categories as everyone interprets what they see differently, but pornography usually refers to the graphic depiction of sexual behaviour through pictures and/or words—including delivery by electronic or other data retrieval systems—in a manner that is intended to be sexually arousing. Obscenity is the legal term for pornographic materials that are offensive by generally accepted standards of decency. Erotica refers to material depicting consensual sexual activities that are sought by and pleasurable to all parties involved.

How has pornography changed in recent years?

Technological innovations have greatly increased the variety of pornographic materials available, as well as their methods of distribution. According to some analysts, as long as the desire for such materials is high, the multibillion-dollar pornography industry will continue to produce and market goods and services, adapting to new technologies as they become available.

Does research indicate that pornography contributes to sexual violence?

No conclusive answer has been found to this question. Some studies have found that hard-core pornography is associated with aggression in males and sexual violence in society, but other studies have found no conclusive evidence that pornography actually contributes to sexual violence. Many commentators today insist we need to ask more sophisticated questions about the impacts of pornography, not just focus on the issue of rape. Additionally, some feminist scholars insist that pornography exploits all women and sometimes men and children, while other feminist scholars disagree as adamantly.

How do people react to the censorship of pornography?

Reactions to the censorship of pornography are varied. People with a liberal view of pornography believe that it is a safety valve for society and that censorship—not pornography—is the social problem. Religious conservatives consider pornography a threat to moral values and encourage censorship of most materials. Anti-pornography feminists view pornography as a primary source of male oppression and violence against women and argue for its elimination. Anti-censorship feminists believe that some pornography may be oppressive to women, but that censorship is worse; they argue that more variety in porn is what is needed.

KEY TERMS

erotica, p. 146

gonzo pornography, p. 146

obscenity, p. 146

prostitution, p. 128

social control, p. 142

victimless crime, p. 143

QUESTIONS FOR CRITICAL THINKING

1. There have been ongoing suggestions by citizens to create "red-light" districts or legal brothels in major urban centres in Canada. What arguments would you present in favour of this suggestion? What arguments would you present against it?

2. In what ways are prostitution and pornography linked to sexism, racism, homophobia, and class-based inequality?

3. In what ways does our Canadian culture generally sustain and perpetuate an environment where commercial sexual exploitation of children and youth, in prostitution and in pornography, flourishes?

4. Libertarian author Peter McWilliams suggests that the problem with censorship can be summed up in two words: Who decides? Who do you think should decide what materials—if any—should be censored as pornographic or obscene? Besides deciding what's acceptable and what isn't, who should decide on the punishments for violating these standards?

5. What challenges exist in tackling the problem of online child pornography?

Addictions

Rob Wilson/Shutterstock

T he health and well-being of a wide variety of people are affected by alcohol, tobacco, drugs, and gambling, and the financial costs are very high. While the health and well-being effects of drugs and gambling are well known, the costs are not. Since total costs are not calculated every year, costs of drug use and misuse from the most recent survey (2002) will be reported here for Canada. First, the number of deaths was substantial. Over 43 000 deaths were attributed to substance use and abuse:

- 4258 deaths to alcohol;
- 37 209 to tobacco; and
- 1695 to illegal drugs.

The total costs of use and abuse were about $40 billion in 2002, over $1200/person. Breaking this figure down, the costs were $463/person for alcohol; $262/person for illegal drugs; and $541/person for tobacco. Tobacco and alcohol accounted for 43 percent and 37 percent of the costs respectively.

In terms of indirect costs from drugs and gambling, 61 percent were due to productivity losses, 22 percent were due to health care costs, and 14 percent were due to law enforcement costs. In addition, about 3.8 million hospital days were attributable to substance use and abuse, mainly to tobacco (Rehm et al. 2007).

This is a substantial rise in costs since 1992, even taking inflation into account, when researchers found that the overall costs were $18.4 billion (Single et al. 1996). While similar comprehensive analyses have not been done for those affected by gambling, Tepperman (2009:8) estimated from the survey of Wiebe et al. (2006) that in a population of 32 million of whom 75 percent are over age 25, "roughly 1.2 million Canadians have a gambling problem or are at serious risk of a gambling problem."

In this chapter, we will examine legal drug use and abuse (e.g., alcohol, tobacco, and prescription drugs); illegal drug use and abuse (e.g., marijuana, narcotics, and stimulants); and gambling and severe problem gambling. To reduce unnecessary complexity of expressions, we will label all psychological and physiological need for these problems as addictions, and we will examine explanations of addictions, addiction prevention and treatment programs, and what you can do about addictions.

DRUG USE AND ABUSE

What is a drug? There are many answers to this question, so the definition is not always consistent or clear. For our purposes, a **drug is any substance—other than food or water—that, when taken into the body, alters its functioning in some way**. Drugs are used for either therapeutic or recreational purposes. *Therapeutic* use occurs when a person takes a drug for a specific purpose, such as reducing a fever or controlling an epileptic seizure. Sometimes, individuals who take prescription drugs for therapeutic purposes cross the line to drug abuse. *Recreational* drug use occurs when a person takes a drug for no other purpose than achieving some pleasurable feeling or psychological state. Alcohol and tobacco (nicotine) are *licit* (legal) drugs that are used for recreational purposes; heroin and cocaine are *illicit* (illegal) recreational drugs (Levinthal 2011). Licit drugs, which include such substances as vitamins, aspirin, alcohol, tobacco, and prescription drugs, are legal to manufacture, sell, possess, and use. Illicit drugs, such as marijuana, cocaine, heroin, and LSD (lysergic acid diethylamide), are socially defined as deviant, and using them is criminal behaviour and hence a social problem.

Defining Drug Abuse

What is drug abuse? *Drug abuse* is the excessive or inappropriate use of a drug that results in some form of physical, mental, or social impairment. A more difficult question to answer is, "What constitutes drug abuse?" When looked at from this perspective, drug abuse has both objective and subjective components. The *objective component* is physical, psychological, or social evidence that harm has been done to individuals, families, communities, or the entire society by the use of a drug. The *subjective component* refers to people's perceptions about the consequences of using a drug and the social action they believe should be taken to remedy the problem.

Sometimes, when people talk about drug abuse, the subjective component—the perception of consequences—overrides the objective component. Consider, for example, the subjective and objective components underlying our society's view of the use of marijuana. The subjective component of marijuana use is the general belief that marijuana is harmful and therefore should not be legal, even though there is little evidence that marijuana use is detrimental to health (see Box 8.3 for a discussion of the legalization debate). The subjective component of alcohol use is the general belief that it is harmless and acceptable, even though there is considerable evidence that it impairs more people and produces greater costs to individuals and society than marijuana use.

Drug Addiction

The term *drug addiction* (or *drug dependency*) **refers to a psychological and/or physiological need for a drug to maintain a sense of well-being and avoid withdrawal symptoms.** Drug dependency has two essential characteristics: tolerance and withdrawal. *Tolerance* **occurs when larger doses of a drug are required over time to produce the same physical or psychological effect that was originally achieved by a smaller dose.** Tolerance is a matter of degree: some drugs produce immediate and profound levels of tolerance, whereas others produce only mild tolerance. For example, when a person first drinks a five-ounce cup of coffee, containing about 100 milligrams of caffeine, the stimulant effect is usually quite pronounced. After that person drinks the same amount of coffee over a period of several days or weeks, the effect is greatly diminished, and a second or third cup of coffee (for a total of 200 to 300 milligrams of caffeine) becomes necessary to duplicate the earlier feeling (Levinthal 2011). *Withdrawal* **refers to a variety of physical and/or psychological symptoms that habitual drug users experience when they discontinue drug use.** For example, people who suddenly terminate their alcohol intake after long-term, heavy drinking experience various physical symptoms ranging from insomnia to DTs (*delirium tremens,* or mental confusion often accompanied by sweating and tremor) and psychological symptoms such as a reduced sense of self-worth.

ALCOHOL USE AND ABUSE

Much of the data in this section come from the 2011 Canadian Alcohol and Drug Use Monitoring Survey (CADUMS), the most recent national study of Canadians' use of alcohol and other drugs. In addition, results of a couple of the waves of the National Population Health Study (NPHS) are also reported. This study was conducted by Health Canada and Statistics Canada and consisted of in-depth interviewing of over 17 000 Canadians. It is an ongoing study designed to measure changes in the health status of Canadians.

The use of alcohol—ranging from communion wine in religious ceremonies to beer, wine, and liquor at business and social gatherings—is considered an accepted part of the dominant culture in Canada. *Alcohol* and *alcoholic beverages* are terms that refer to the three major forms in which ethyl alcohol (ethanol) is consumed: *wine,* which is made from fermentation of fruits and contains between 12 and 14 percent ethyl alcohol; *beer,* which is brewed from grains and hops and usually contains 3 to 6 percent alcohol; and *liquor,* which includes whiskey, gin, vodka, and other distilled spirits and usually contains 40 percent (80 proof) to 50 percent (100 proof) alcohol.

According to sales data from 2012, Canadians (aged 15 years and older) purchased 7.5 litres of spirits, 16.9 litres of wine, and 80.3 litres of beer per capita, for a total of 104.7 litres. Interestingly this number is identical to the

104 litres purchased in 2002 (Statistics Canada 2013u). Some people do not drink at all, and others drink heavily. If Canada follows the American pattern, this rate means that 10 percent of the population could account for roughly half the total alcohol consumption (Levinthal 2011).

Many people do not think of alcohol as a drug because it can be purchased legally—and without a prescription—by adults. It is, however, a psychoactive drug that is classified as a *depressant* because it lowers the activity level of the central nervous system. The impairment of judgment and thinking associated with being drunk is the result of alcohol depressing brain functions. Alcohol also affects mood and behaviour. One to two drinks often bring a release from tensions and inhibitions. Three to four drinks affect self-control—including reaction time and coordination of hands, arms, and legs—and judgment, muddling the person's reasoning ability. Five to six drinks (binge or heavy drinking) affect sensory perception, and the person may show signs of intoxication, such as staggering, belligerence, or depression. At seven to eight drinks, the drinker is obviously intoxicated and may go into a stupor. Nine or more drinks affect vital centres, and the drinker may become comatose or even die. Of course, factors such as sex (women are more affected than men by the same amount of alcohol because they have a lower percentage of water in their bodies), body weight, physical build, and recent food and fluid consumption must be taken into account in estimating the rate of alcohol absorption in the body.

Although negative short-term effects of drinking are usually overcome, chronic heavy drinking or alcoholism can cause permanent damage to the brain or other parts of the body. Social scientists divide long-term drinking patterns into four general categories. *Social drinkers* consume alcoholic beverages primarily on social occasions; they drink occasionally or even relatively frequently. *Heavy drinkers* are more frequent drinkers who typically consume greater quantities of alcohol when they drink and are more likely to become intoxicated. *Acute alcoholics* have trouble controlling their use of alcohol and plan their schedule around drinking. *Chronic alcoholics* have lost control over their drinking and tend to engage in compulsive behaviour such as hiding liquor bottles and sneaking drinks when they are not being observed.

High Alcohol Consumption and Gender and Age

The CADUMS study found that about 90 percent of Canadians have drunk alcohol. But where does problem drinking begin? In the past, frequent binge drinking, five plus drinks at one sitting, was the standard for problem drinking. This standard has been changed to low-risk drinking guidelines. There are two low-risk drinking guidelines, chronic and acute:

- Low-risk drinking Guideline 1: Chronic – People who drink within this guideline must drink no more than 10 drinks a week for women, with no more than 2 drinks a day most days and 15 drinks a week for men, with no more than 3 drinks a day most days. They must also plan non-drinking days every week to avoid developing a habit.
- Low-risk drinking Guideline 2: Acute – Those who drink within this guideline must drink no more than three drinks (for women) and four drinks (for men) on any single occasion. They must plan to drink in a safe environment and stay within the weekly limits outlined in Guideline 1. (Health Canada 2012)

These new guidelines are not an arbitrary limit, like five drinks, but standards related to liver disease and some cancers (chronic), injuries, and overdoses (acute).

Table 8.1 shows the extent to which people exceed these low-risk drinking guidelines (LRDG).

Table 8.1 shows that 14.4 percent of Canadians exceed the LRDG chronic standard and 10.1 percent exceed the acute standard. In each case, a higher percentage of men exceed the standard than women. Little difference was seen between young and older Canadians in either acute or chronic standards. The percentages "among drinkers" are not much different since such a high percentage of Canadians drink.

Alcohol-Related Social and Health Problems

Alcohol consumption is linked to many kinds of harm, both to oneself and to others. Harms to oneself refer to harm to physical health, family and work functioning, friendships, legal problems, and so on. Harms to others refer to being insulted or humiliated, receiving verbal abuse, being in serious quarrels, family or marriage problems, or being assaulted.

Although not all heavy drinkers and chronic alcohol abusers exhibit the major health problems that are typically associated with alcoholism, their risk of these problems is greatly increased. For alcoholics, the long-term health effects include *nutritional deficiencies* as a result of poor eating habits. Chronic heavy drinking contributes to high caloric consumption but low nutritional intake. Alcoholism is also associated with fluctuations in blood sugar levels that can cause adult-onset diabetes. Structural loss of brain tissue may produce *alcoholic dementia,* which is characterized by difficulties in problem solving, remembering information, and

TABLE 8.1 Exceeding Low-risk Drinking Guidelines by Sex and Age					
	Overall	Males	Females	15–24	25+yrs
Exceeding low-risk drinking guidelines[1]					
Exceeds LRDG chronic	14.4 [13.1–15.8]	18.1 [15.9–20.3]	11.1 [9.5–12.6]	14.9 [10.6–19.2]	14.4 [13.0–15.7]
Exceeds LRDG acute	10.1 [8.9–11.2]	13.5 [11.5–15.4]	7.0 [5.6–8.3]	12.8 [8.7–16.9]	9.5 [8.4–10.7]
Exceeds LRDG chronic - among drinkers	18.7 [17.0–20.4]	22.3 [19.7–25.0]	15.0 [13.0–17.1]	21.1 [15.2–26.9]	18.3 [16.6–20.0]
Exceeds LRDG acute - among drinkers	13.1 [11.6–14.5]	16.6 [14.3–19.0]	9.5 [7.7–11.2]	18.1 [12.5–23.7]	12.2 [10.7–13.6]

[95% Confidence Interval]

1 Based on alcohol consumption in the previous 7 days

Source: *Health Canada 2012 CADMUS. Retrieved June 23, 2013 (http://www.hc-sc.gc.ca/hc-ps/drugs-drogues/ stat/_2011/tables-tableaux-eng.php#t1).*

organizing facts about one's identity and surroundings (Levinthal 2011).

Chronic alcohol abuse is also linked to *cardiovascular problems* such as inflammation and enlargement of the heart muscle, poor blood circulation, reduced heart contractions, fatty accumulations in the heart and arteries, high blood pressure, and cerebrovascular disorders such as stroke (Levinthal 2011). However, studies show that moderate alcohol consumption—such as a glass of wine a day—may improve body circulation, lower cholesterol levels, and reduce the risk of certain forms of heart disease.

Over time, chronic alcohol abuse also contributes to irreversible changes in the liver that are associated with *alcoholic cirrhosis*—a progressive development of scar tissue in the liver that chokes off blood vessels and destroys liver cells by interfering with their use of oxygen. Given all the possible health problems, perhaps it is not surprising that alcoholics typically have a shorter life expectancy— often by as much as 10 to 12 years—than non-drinkers or occasional drinkers who consume moderate amounts of alcohol.

Unlike an earlier study, the Canadian Addiction Study (2004), CADUMS did not survey harms done by one's own or others' drinking. The researchers surveyed harms only for drug-taking behaviour. However, it is likely safe to assume that much harm was committed as a result of problem drinking.

Abuse of alcohol and other drugs by a pregnant woman can damage the fetus. **Fetal alcohol spectrum** **disorder (FASD) is an umbrella term used to describe the range of disabilities and diagnoses that result from drinking alcohol during pregnancy.** But *fetal alcohol syndrome* and *fetal alcohol effects* are still noted separately. Specific birth defects and the degree of the disability can depend on how much alcohol was drunk, and how often and when during the pregnancy; they can also depend on the state of health of the pregnant woman. No amount or type of alcohol during pregnancy is considered safe.

In Canada, the incidence of FAS is greater than the incidence of either Down's Syndrome or Spina Bifida. The incidence of FAE is 5 to 10 times higher than the incidence of FAS. This means that each year in Canada, between 123 and 740 babies are born with FAS, and around 1000 babies are born with FAE (based on 370 000 births per year) (Health Canada 2013).

Driving and Drinking

Drivers who have been drinking often do not realize how much alcohol they have consumed or what effect it has on their driving ability. As a result, many people drive dangerously even when they are not legally drunk—that is, driving with a blood alcohol level over 0.08 percent, which is referred to as impaired driving. Alcohol-related driving accidents occur, for example, when drivers lose control of their vehicles; fail to see a red traffic light, a car, or a pedestrian in the street; or miss a sharp curve in the road (Gross 1983). In 2001, the latest information available from Health Canada,

Social Problems in Global Perspective

Box 8.1

Drinking Around the World

In 2011, the World Health Organization (WHO) published *The Global Status Report on Alcohol and Health*. This comprehensive report on the global, regional, and national consumption of alcohol included patterns of drinking, health consequences, and policy responses in member states. Figure 8.1 shows the per capita consumption of pure alcohol in the member states. Eastern and most of Western Europe have the highest consumption levels. The Americas are at the mid-point, and the middle-Eastern countries consume the least since Islam forbids drinking. In Canada, the per capita consumption of pure alcohol per year for adults (15+ years of age) is 9.8 litres, vs. 6.1 litres for the world as a whole. Additional information on Canada's drinking patterns is available on the Web. See References for specific URLs.

Alcohol has always been known to be a serious health problem, but it has never had the prominence of HIV/AIDS, though it kills and injures many more people. Almost 4 percent of all deaths worldwide are attributed to alcohol, greater than deaths caused by HIV/AIDS, violence, or tuberculosis. Alcohol consumption is

- the world's third largest risk factor for disease and disability (in middle-income countries, it is the greatest risk);
- a causal factor in 60 types of diseases and injuries and a component cause in 200 others; and
- associated with many serious social issues, including violence, child neglect and abuse, and absenteeism in the workplace (WHO, 2011).

Questions for Consideration

1. What age restrictions would you suggest for the purchase of alcohol?
2. Taxing of cigarettes has reduced smoking. Should we have a similar heavy tax on alcohol?
3. What advertising restrictions would you place on alcohol?

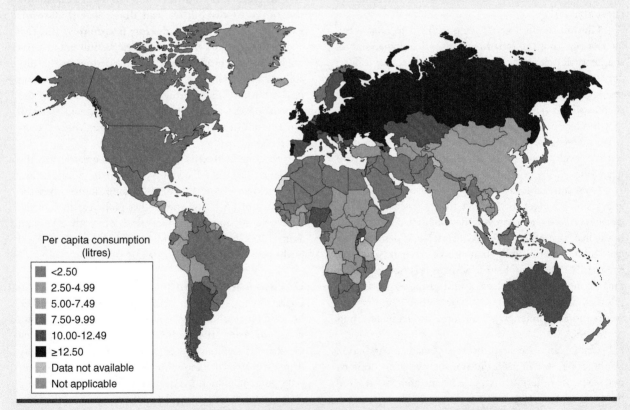

Per capita consumption (litres)
- <2.50
- 2.50-4.99
- 5.00-7.49
- 7.50-9.99
- 10.00-12.49
- ≥12.50
- Data not available
- Not applicable

Figure 8.1   Total adult (15+) per capita consumption, in litres of pure alcohol, 2005.

Source: *WHO, 2011*, Global Status Report on Alcohol and Health. *Retrieved July 6, 2013 (http://www.who.int/substance_abuse/publications/global_alcohol_report/msbgsru-profiles.pdf).*

approximately 40 percent of the estimated 3000 deaths each year from motor vehicle crashes were attributable to alcohol (Health Canada 2014).

Family Problems

Chronic alcohol abuse or alcoholism makes it difficult for a person to maintain social relationships and have a stable family life. According to social scientist Charles F. Levinthal (2011), for every person who has a problem with alcohol, about four other people are directly affected on a daily basis. Domestic abuse and violence in families are frequently associated with heavy drinking and alcohol abuse by one or more family members. Women whose partners consume five or more drinks at one time, compared to those whose partners never drink, are at six times the risk of violence, and abused women frequently use drugs to deal with the pain (Health Canada 1993). Growing up in a family that is affected by alcohol can have a profound impact on children. The extent to which alcohol abuse affects other family members depends on the degree of alcoholism and the type of alcoholic. Some alcoholic parents are violent and abusive; others are quiet and sullen or withdrawn. To outsiders, the family of an alcoholic may appear to be normal, but family members may feel as though they have a serious problem to contend with.

Family members of alcoholics frequently become *enablers*—people who adjust their behaviour to accommodate an alcoholic. Enabling often takes the form of lying to cover up the alcoholic's drinking, absenteeism from work, and/or discourteous treatment of others, and even financially supporting the drinking. Enabling leads many families to develop a pattern of *codependency*—a **reciprocal relationship between the alcoholic and one or more non-alcoholics who unwittingly aid and abet the alcoholic's excessive drinking and resulting behaviour** (Jung 1994). When codependency occurs, the spouse or another family member takes on many of the alcoholic's responsibilities and keeps the alcoholic person from experiencing the full impact of his or her actions. Children who grow up in alcoholic families tend to have higher than normal rates of hyperactivity, antisocial behaviour, low academic achievement, and cognitive impairment (Levinthal 2011). However, although the risk of becoming an alcoholic increases if one's parent was an alcoholic, most children of alcoholics (as many as 59 percent) do not become alcoholics themselves (Sher 1991).

How does Canada's consumption of alcohol compare with others around the world? The World Health Organization has released its first report on drinking in its member states. Some results are found in Box 8.1.

TOBACCO (NICOTINE) USE AS A SOCIAL PROBLEM

The nicotine in tobacco is a toxic, dependency-producing psychoactive drug that is more addictive than heroin. It is categorized as a *stimulant* because it stimulates central nervous system receptors, activating the release of adrenaline, which raises blood pressure, speeds up the heartbeat, and gives the user a sense of alertness. Some people claim that nicotine reduces their appetite, helps them to lose weight, and produces a sense of calmness and relaxation. Perhaps these physical and psychological effects of nicotine dependency help to explain why even though smoking rates have declined substantially (see Figure 8.2), just less than one in five Canadian adults over the age of 15 (23 percent of men and 17 percent of women) still smoked in 2011 (Statistics Canada 2012e).

Although the overall proportion of smokers in the general population has declined substantially since the pioneering 1964 U.S. Surgeon General's warning that smoking is linked to cancer and other serious diseases, tobacco is still responsible for more than 37 000 deaths per year in Canada, or five times the number of deaths from car accidents, murder, suicides, and alcohol abuse combined, according to Health Canada (2009d). People who smoke cigarettes, cigars, or pipes have a greater likelihood of developing lung cancer and cancer of the larynx, mouth, and esophagus than non-smokers do because nicotine is ingested into the bloodstream through the lungs and soft tissues of the mouth. Furthermore, many cases of bronchitis, emphysema, ulcers, and heart and circulatory disorders can be traced to nicotine consumption. When tobacco burns, it forms carbon monoxide, which disrupts the transport of oxygen from the lungs to the rest of the body and hence contributes to cardiovascular disease (Levinthal 2011).

Smoking typically shortens life expectancy. It is estimated that about half a pack (10 cigarettes) a day on average reduces a person's life expectancy by four years, and smoking more than two packs a day (40 cigarettes) reduces life expectancy by eight years. Even people who never light up a cigarette are harmed by *environmental tobacco smoke*—**the smoke in the air as a result of other people's tobacco smoking** (Levinthal 2011). When someone smokes a cigarette, about 75 percent of the nicotine ends up in the air. Researchers have found that non-smokers who carpool or work with heavy smokers are more affected by environmental smoke than are non-smokers who are only occasionally exposed to it. Therefore, smoking has been banned in many public and private facilities throughout the country.

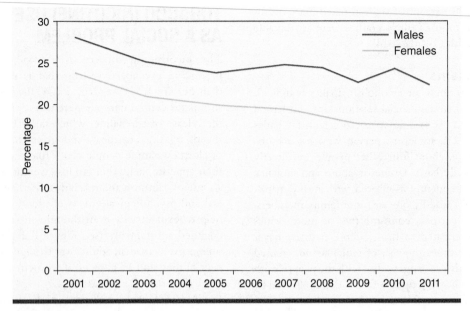

Figure 8.2 Percentage of Smokers by Sex, Aged 12 or Older, in Canada, 2001–2011.
Source: *Statistics Canada, 2012, "Smoking, 2011". Retrieved June 21, 2013 (http://www.statcan.gc.ca/pub/82-625-x/2012001/article/11668-eng.htm)*.

Not surprisingly, cigarette smoking adversely affects infants and children. Infants born to women who smoke typically have lower-than-average birth weights and sometimes slower rates of physical and mental growth. When a pregnant woman smokes, blood vessels constrict, which reduces the amount of oxygen reaching the fetus. Carbon monoxide transmitted from the mother's blood to the fetus interferes with the distribution of oxygen that does reach the fetus. Children who grow up in households where one or both parents smoke are more apt to suffer from frequent ear infections, upper respiratory infections such as bronchitis and sinusitis, allergies, asthma, and other health problems than are children whose parents do not smoke.

Why do so many people use nicotine if it is so dangerous? Several reasons have been suggested. First, nicotine creates a high level of dependency, so once a person has begun to use tobacco regularly, the withdrawal symptoms may be strong enough to make the person light up another cigarette. Some researchers have found that the majority of people who smoke recognize that smoking is bad for them and would like to quit, but cannot. Second, in the past, sophisticated marketing campaigns associated smoking with desirable cultural attributes, such as achieving maturity, gaining wealth and happiness, gaining liberation and personal experiences, or being thin and sexy (see Box 8.2).

In Canada, the *Tobacco Act* of 1997 (amended in 1998 and 2000) prohibits cigarette manufacturers from advertising their products on radio or television or in magazines or newspapers; they are also prohibited from sponsoring sports and arts events. In addition, the manufacturers must print large health warnings and graphic anti-smoking pictures on cigarette packages and report marketing campaigns to the federal government. Finally, smoking has been used by youth as a form of rebellion and a method of showing solidarity with peers. Thus, many forces combine to promote the continuation of Canada's number one public health problem.

A new tobacco problem has recently emerged: the electronic cigarette or e-cigarette. It has become very popular in the United States, but so far it is not prominent in Canada or regulated by Health Canada. The e-cigarette looks like a cigarette, but contains a liquid that includes nicotine that is heated by a battery that turns the liquid into vapour which is then inhaled. The advantage is that the vapour does not contain the dozens of carcinogens in the regular cigarette smoke. But, while this product could be used as a harm-reduction method, flavours in the liquid like lemon/lime and watermelon could be used to attract children, which could lead to nicotine addiction or at least acceptance of smoking again. In addition, the long-term inhaling of the propylene glycol, the liquid in the e-cigarette, is unknown. Health Canada should test these cigarettes and determine if they should be regulated like regular cigarettes.

Advertising to Encourage Women to Smoke

Cigarette companies target women through a complex combination of psychosocial need, time period, and age group, according to a study by Anderson, Glantz, and Ping (2005). Reviewing market research by cigarette companies and conducting a content analysis of advertisements, they were able to show how needs satisfaction can be communicated often without referring to smoking. For example, they suggest that

- Lorillard's "Spoil Yourself with Satin" ad was attractive to the mature, feminine women, aged 35–59 years in the early to mid-1980s;
- Brown and Williamson's "She's Gone to Capri" ad was attractive to those seeking fantasy escape to older women, aged 35–59 years in the mid-1990s to 2000; and
- Philip Morris's "You've Come a Long Way Baby" in the late 1970s and "It's a Woman thing" ads were attractive to newly liberated women in their 20s, in the late 1970s and late 1990s.

The authors suggest that partial bans on advertising smoking, by eliminating smoking from the ad, are ineffective for reducing smoking and only comprehensive bans on all tobacco products can be effective. Now that we have comprehensive bans and smoking among women is declining, the authors' suggestions appear to be supported.

Questions for Consideration

1. Since a small percentage of women continue to smoke, what kind of advertising should be undertaken now to further reduce consumption? Do you think offering prizes to stop smoking would be effective?
2. Do you think that an ad showing how smoking just adds to other problems would be effective?
3. Can advertising on needs satisfaction bring about a reduction in other public health problems like obesity?

PRESCRIPTION DRUGS, OVER-THE-COUNTER DRUGS, AND CAFFEINE

When most people think of drug abuse, they picture unscrupulous drug dealers in dark alleys selling illegal drugs. But legal drugs may also be abused. Legal drugs fall into two categories: *prescription drugs,* which are dispensed only by a registered pharmacist on the authority of a licensed physician or dentist, and *over-the-counter (OTC) drugs,* which are available off the shelf and are restricted only by the customer's ability to pay.

Prescription Drugs

Table 8.2 from the CADUMS study shows the amount of consumption of prescription drugs by Canadians in 2011, and also shows the great variety of drugs consumed. CADUMS includes questions relating to the abuse of three classes of psychoactive pharmaceutical drugs:

- opioid pain relievers (such as Percodan, Demerol, and OxyContin);
- stimulants (such as Ritalin, Concerta, Adderall, and Dexedrine); and
- tranquillizers and sedatives (such as Valium, Ativan, and Xanax).

While these drugs are prescribed for therapeutic purposes, they have the potential to be abused due to their psychoactive properties.

Pain medication is probably the prescription drug that is most frequently abused. According to Table 8.2, 16.7 percent of Canadians used this type of medication in 2011. The numbers in this table are small so interpret with caution. Women's use is slightly higher than men's, and older people's use is higher than younger people's. Stimulants are seldom used, but among users, a quarter of users use them to get high. In summary, just over a fifth of Canadians use pharmaceuticals, and among users, less than 5 percent abuse them. Though millions of people benefit from *narcotics*—natural or synthetic opoids—that relieve pain, suppress coughing, control chronic diarrhea, and reduce heroin withdrawal symptoms, there are risks of short-term abuse and long-term psychological and physical dependence. Over time, users develop tolerance for the drug they are taking and must continue to increase dosages to obtain the same effect that was derived from the lower dose. Drug dependency that results from physician-supervised treatment for a recognized medical disorder is called *iatrogenic addiction.* Iatrogenic addiction is most likely to occur with long-term use and/or high dosages of a prescription drug; it most often affects people from the middle or upper class who have no previous history of drug abuse or addiction (Levinthal 2011).

TABLE 8.2 Prescription Drug Use by Sex and Age, 2011

	Overall	Males	Females	15–24 yrs	25+ yrs
Pain Relievers	16.7 [15.4–18.0]	15.8 [14.0–17.7]	17.4 [15.7–19.2]	14.3 [10.3–18.4]	17.1 [15.8–18.4]
Pain Relievers to get high	S	S	S	S	S
Pain Relievers to get high— among users	S	S	S	S	S
Abuse of pain relievers (includes to get high)	S	S	S	S	0.2Q [0.1–0.4]
Abuse of pain relievers (includes to get high)—among users	S	S	S	S	S
Stimulants	0.9Q [0.6–1.2]	1.2Q [0.7–1.8]	0.5Q [0.3–0.8]	2.4Q [0.9–3.8]	0.6Q [0.4–0.8]
Stimulants to get high	S	S	S	S	S
Stimulants to get high—among users	S	S	S	S	S
Abuse of stimulants (includes to get high)	S	S	S	S	S
Abuse of stimulants (includes to get high)—among users	27.4Q [10.5–44.3]	S	S	S	S
Sedatives	9.1 [8.1–10.0]	5.9 [4.8–7.1]	12.0 [10.6–13.5]	4.0Q [1.5–6.4]	10.1 [9.0–11.1]
Sedative to get high	S	S	S	S	S
Sedatives to get high—among users	S	S	S	S	S
Any pharmaceutical	22.9 [21.5–24.4]	20.2 [18.1–22.3]	25.5 [23.5–27.6]	17.6 [13.3–21.9]	23.9 [22.4–25.5]
Any pharmaceutical to get high	0.3Q [0.1–0.5]	S	S	S	0.2Q [0.1–0.3]
Any pharmaceutical to get high—among user	1.5Q [0.6–2.4]	S	S	S	0.9Q [0.3–1.4]
Abuse of any pharmaceutical (includes to get high)	0.7Q [0.4–1.1]	0.6Q [0.2–1.0]	S	S	0.5Q [0.3–0.7]
Abuse of any pharmaceutical (includes to get high)—among	3.2Q [1.6–4.8]	3.1Q [1.3–4.9]	S	S	1.9Q [1.1–2.8]

Source: *Health Canada, 2012, CADUMS. Retrieved June 22, 2013 (http://www.hc-sc.gc.ca/hc-ps/drugs-drogues/ stat/_2011/tables-tableaux-eng.php#t1).*

Two widely prescribed drugs that have been the subject of controversy regarding their use and abuse are methylphenidate (Ritalin) and fluoxetine (Prozac). Ritalin is a stimulant that is prescribed for children who are diagnosed with *attention-deficit hyperactivity disorder* (ADHD). According to the American Psychiatric Association, ADHD is characterized by emotionality, behavioural hyperactivity, short attention span, distractibility, impulsiveness, and perceptual and learning disabilities. Although some children are probably correctly diagnosed with this disorder, some commentators worry that Ritalin is overprescribed in Canada. According to the continuing survey of drug use among Ontario students conducted by drug-use researchers Angela Paglia-Boak and colleagues (2011), 1.0 percent of students used drugs for ADHD in 2011 (see Table 8.3 below). Boys are slightly more likely than girls to be diagnosed with ADHD and to be prescribed drugs to treat it. Advocates believe that children with normal to above-average intelligence who are performing poorly in school can benefit from Ritalin, which has proven to be safe for more than 40 years. But critics argue that many parents, doctors, and teachers see Ritalin as a quick fix for dealing with troublesome children.

One of the most abused prescription drugs for adults is Prozac, an antidepressant. Introduced in 1987 as a breakthrough medication for clinical depression, Prozac has become a cure-all for the blues, a far milder form of depression. Advocates believe that Prozac enhances the quality of life for many people, freeing them from depression and suicidal thoughts. But the long-term side effects of the drug are unknown, and there is some evidence that Prozac is associated with intense, violent suicidal thoughts in some patients. Both Prozac and Ritalin are approved by Health Canada and are considered safe and effective if taken as directed.

Over-the-Counter Drugs

A fine line exists between prescription and over-the-counter (OTC) drugs. Today, both types of drugs are advertised in electronic and print media directly to the consumer, with suggestions to "ask your doctor or pharmacist about [our product] on your next visit." Some drugs are available both by prescription and over the counter, depending on their strength and dosage. For example, medication for stomach ulcers (e.g., Zantac and Tagamet) is sold over the counter in lower doses and by prescription in higher doses. Some drugs that are now sold over the counter were previously available only by prescription.

Widely used OTC drugs include analgesics, sleep aids, and cough and cold remedies. Since the CADUMS survey did not study OTC drugs, data from an earlier study are used. According to the NPHS, 65 percent of Canadians 12 years old and older took pain relievers, 20 percent took cold and cough remedies, and 11 percent took stomach remedies. In each case, a higher percentage of women than men took the drugs (Statistics Canada 2001b:36). Abuse of aspirin and other analgesics can cause gastric bleeding, problems with blood clotting, complications during surgery and during labour and delivery, and Reye's syndrome (a potentially life-threatening condition that can arise when children with flu, chicken pox, or other viral infections are given aspirin). Overdoses of analgesics such as acetaminophen (e.g., Tylenol and Anacin-3), aspirin, and ibuprofen (e.g., Motrin, Advil, and Midol) have been linked to cases of attempted suicide, especially by White females between the ages of 6 and 17 years. Few of these suicide attempts have resulted in death, except when the analgesics were combined with alcohol or other drugs (Levinthal 2011). Like analgesics, sleep aids are dangerous when combined with alcohol or some cough and cold remedies because they are depressants that slow down the central nervous system. Even cough and cold medications alone have side effects, such as drowsiness, that can be hazardous—if, for example, users attempt to drive a car or operate heavy machinery. To counteract drowsiness, some drug companies add caffeine to their products.

Caffeine

Although it is a relatively safe drug, caffeine is a dependency-producing psychoactive stimulant (Gilbert 1986). Caffeine is an ingredient in coffee, tea, chocolate, soft drinks, and stimulants such as NoDoz and Vivarin. According to the 2010 Canadian Coffee Drinking Study, two-thirds of Canadians drink 2.8 cups of coffee per day (Coffee Association of Canada 2013). Most people ingest caffeine because they like the feeling of mental alertness and reduced fatigue that it produces.

The extent to which caffeine actually improves human performance, however, is widely debated. Caffeine may improve concentration when a person is performing boring or repetitive tasks, but it has little effect on the performance of complex tasks such as critical thinking and decision making (Curatolo and Robertson 1983; Dews 1984). The short-term effects of caffeine include dilated peripheral blood vessels, constricted blood vessels in the head, and a slightly elevated heart rate (Levinthal 2011). Long-term effects of heavy caffeine use (more than three cups of coffee or five cups of tea per day) include increased risk of heart attack and osteoporosis—the loss of bone density and increased brittleness associated with fractures and broken bones (Kiel et al. 1990).

Overall, however, the social problems associated with the abuse of caffeine and prescription and OTC drugs are relatively minor when compared with the social problems associated with illegal drugs.

ILLEGAL DRUG USE AND ABUSE

Are some drugs inherently bad and hence classified as illegal? What constitutes an illegal drug is a matter of social and legal definitions that are subject to change over time. During the 19th and early 20th centuries, people in Canada had fairly easy access to drugs that are currently illegal for general use. In the early 1800s, neither doctors nor pharmacists had to be licensed. *Patent medicines,* which sometimes contained such ingredients as opium, morphine, heroin, cocaine, and alcohol, could be purchased in stores, through mail-order advertisements, and from medicine wagons run by people who called themselves doctors and provided free entertainment to attract crowds (Young 1961). Over time, because of the rapidly growing number of narcotics addicts, prescriptions became required for some drugs. Some forms of drug use were criminalized because of their association with specific minority groups. For example, in Canada, opium could be consumed legally in cough syrup, but smoking the same amount of opium was banned by the *Opium Act* of 1908 after an investigation by Mackenzie King on the use of opium. The reason for the ban was that opium smoking was a favourite pastime of the Chinese workers building railroads in Western Canada (Small 1978). In Canada, the Division of Narcotic Control was part of the Department of Health. Its head was Col. C.H.L. Sharman, who undertook the moral entrepreneurial role against drugs by criminalizing them in Canada that Harry Anslinger played in the United States.

The most recent legislation dealing with drugs in Canada is the *Controlled Drugs and Substances Act,* which came into effect in 1996, last amended in 2012. This legislation, according to *Canada's Drug Strategy* (Health Canada 1998), has enforcement measures "for the interdiction and suppression of unlawful import, export, production, distribution, and possession of controlled

TABLE 8.3 Illicit Drug Use in the Past Year by Sex and Age, 2011

	Overall	Males	Females	15–24 yrs	25+ yrs
Illicit drug use past year					
Cocaine/Crack	0.9Q [0.5–1.3]	1.4Q [0.7–2.2]	S	S	0.7Q [0.3–1.0]
Speed	0.5Q [0.2–0.7]	S	S	S	S
Methamphetamine/Crystal meth	S	S	S	S	S
Hallucinogens	0.6Q [0.3–0.9]	0.9Q [0.4–1.4]	S	2.0Q [0.8–3.1]	S
Hallucinogens (including salvia)	0.9Q [0.5–1.2]	1.3Q [0.6–1.9]	S	3.4Q [1.5–5.2]	S
Ecstasy	0.7Q [0.4–1.0]	0.9Q [0.4–1.3]	S	2.6Q [1.1–4.1]	S
Salvia	S	S	S	S	S
Heroin	S	S	S	S	S
Any 6 drugs (hallucinogens excl. salvia)[a]	9.4 [8.3–10.5]	12.4 [10.6–14.3]	6.5 [5.2–7.7]	21.9 [17.2–26.6]	6.9 [6.0–7.9]
Any 5 drugs (hallucinogens excl. salvia)[b]	1.7 [1.2–2.2]	2.4Q [1.5–3.3]	1.0Q [0.5–1.5]	4.8Q [2.5–7.2]	1.1Q [0.7–1.5]
Any 6 drugs (hallucinogens incl. salvia)[a]	9.4 [8.3–10.5]	12.5 [10.6–14.3]	6.5 [5.2–7.7]	21.9 [17.2–26.6]	6.9 [6.0–7.9]
Any 5 drugs (hallucinogens incl. salvia)[a]	1.9 [1.3–2.4]	2.7Q [1.7–3.7]	1.1Q [0.6–1.6]	5.8Q [3.2–8.5]	1.1Q [0.7–1.5]
Any drug[c]	9.9 [8.7–11.0]	13.0 [11.1–14.9]	6.9 [5.6–8.2]	23.1 [18.2–28.0]	7.3 [6.4–8.3]

[a] Cannabis, cocaine/crack, speed, ecstasy, hallucinogens, heroin
[b] Cocaine/crack, speed, ecstasy, hallucinogens, heroin
[c] Cannabis, cocaine/crack, meth/crystal meth, ecstasy, hallucinogens, salvia, inhalants, heroin; abuse of pain relievers, stimulants; sedatives to get high

Source: *Health Canada, 2012, CADUMS. Retrieved June 22, 2013 (http://www.hc-sc.gc.ca/hc-ps/drugs-drogues/ stat/_2011/tables-tableaux-eng.php#t1).*

substances and for the forfeiture of any property used or intended to be used in the commission of such offences and profits derived from such offences." Nevertheless, drugs are still widely available. Table 8.3 provides an aggregate portrait of illicit drug use in Canada.

Table 8.3 shows the past year use by Canadians of any of the following drugs: cannabis, cocaine, speed, methamphetamines, hallucinogens, ecstasy, salvia, and heroin. Of Canadians aged 15 and over, 9.4 percent reported past year use of any of these six illicit drugs. A higher percentage of males than females reported using them (12.4 vs. 6.5 percent, respectively). In addition, a higher percentage of younger than older people reported using them (21.9 vs. 6.9 percent). The numbers in this table are small so interpret with caution.

To explore the use of these drugs by teenagers, we turn to the continuing (since 1977) study by Angela Paglia-Boak and colleagues (2011) of drug use among Ontario students. This study includes students from Grades 7 to 12 inclusive (aged approximately 12 to 17 years). Table 8.4 shows drug use during 2011 reported by male and female students. Alcohol and energy drinks are by far the drugs that are used most, and little difference exists between the sexes in their use. Only a tiny percentage of students use a wide variety of illicit and prescription drugs. But these percentages indicate that a high number of actual users exist.

Marijuana

Marijuana is ingested by mixing it with food or smoking it, either in a hand-rolled cigarette known as a *reefer* or *joint,* or through a pipe or other smoking implement. Potent marijuana—marijuana with high levels of the plant's primary psychoactive chemical, delta-9 tetrahydrocannabinol (THC)—has existed for many years, but potency has increased in recent years because of indoor gardens. Marijuana is both a central nervous system depressant and a stimulant. In low to moderate doses, the drug produces mild sedation; in high doses, it produces a sense of well-being, euphoria, and sometimes hallucinations. Marijuana slightly increases blood pressure and heart rate and greatly lowers blood glucose levels, causing extreme hunger. The human body manufactures a chemical that closely resembles THC, and specific receptors in the brain are designed to receive it. Marijuana use disrupts these receptors, impairing motor activity, concentration, and short-term memory (Cowley 1997). As a result, complex motor tasks such as driving a car or operating heavy machinery are dangerous for a person who is under the influence of marijuana. Some studies show that heavy marijuana use can impair concentration and recall in high-school and college and university students

(Wren 1996). Users become apathetic and lose their motivation to perform competently or achieve long-range goals, such as completing their education. Overall, the short-term effects of marijuana are typically milder than the short-term effects of drugs such as cocaine.

High doses of marijuana smoked during pregnancy can disrupt the development of a fetus and result in lower-than-average birth weight, congenital abnormalities, premature delivery, and neurological disturbances (Levinthal 2011). Furthermore, some studies have found an increased risk of cancer and other lung problems associated with inhaling, because marijuana smokers are believed to inhale more deeply than tobacco users.

Though not included in Table 8.3, CADUMS found that overall, 9.1 percent of Canadians had used marijuana in the past year (12.2 vs. 6.2 percent respectively for males and females, and 21.6 vs. 6.7 percent respectively for 15 to 24 year olds and 25+ year olds respectively). The same research also indicates a slight decline in the use of drugs from 2004 to 2011.

According to the 2011 Ontario Student Drug Use Survey report, 22.3 percent of students used marijuana, with little difference between the sexes. Students often laugh to hear that marijuana use is still considered deviant behaviour. While the federal government has considered the decriminalization of marijuana possession during Liberal administrations, the current (2015) Conservative government has no plans to decriminalize it.

Many teenage users report that marijuana is as easy to acquire as alcohol, and easier than cigarettes. According to one teenager, "It is so popular, so well known, it is around everywhere. Nobody is afraid of the consequences of selling it or buying it. . . . It is really easy to get" (quoted in Friend 1996:2a). In addition, many young people buy the drug from friends who grow their own plants.

Box 8.3 reviews the controversy about legalizing marijuana.

Stimulants

Cocaine and amphetamines are among the major stimulants that are abused in Canada. Cocaine is an extremely potent and dependency-producing drug derived from the small leaves of the coca plant, which grows in several Latin American countries. In the 19th century, cocaine was introduced as a local anesthetic in medical practice and a mood-enhancer in patent medicines. It was an ingredient in Coca-Cola from the 1880s to the early 1900s. Today, cocaine is the third most widely used psychoactive drug after alcohol and marijuana. Users typically sniff, or "snort," the drug into their nostrils, inject it intravenously, or smoke it in the form of crack—a potent form of cocaine that is specially processed for smoking.

TABLE 8.4　Percentage of Ontario Secondary Students Reporting Past-Year Drug Use, 2011			
	Total	**Males**	**Females**
Alcohol	54.9	54.6	55.1
High-Caffeine Energy Drinks	49.5	52.2	46.5
Binge Drinking	22.3	22.7	21.8
Cannabis	22.0	23.0	21.0
Opioid Pain Relievers (NM)	14.0	12.9	15.2
Cigarettes	8.7	9.3	8.2
OTC Cough/Cold Medication	6.9	8.0	5.7
Inhalants (Glue or Solvents)	5.6	5.3	5.9
Smokeless Tobacco	4.6	7.5	1.6
Stimulants (NM)	4.1	3.0	5.3
Mushrooms (P silocybin) or Mescaline	3.8	5.0	2.6
Salvia Divinorum	3.7	5.1	2.1
Ecstasy (MDMA)	3.3	3.5	3.2
Cocaine	2.1	2.5	1.6
Tranquillizers/Sedatives (NM)	1.9	1.8	2.1
Jimson Weed	1.7	2.2	1.2
OxyContin (NM)	1.2	1.5	1.0
LSD	1.2	1.8	0.6
Methamphetamine (incl. Crystal Meth.)	1.0	1.2	0.8
ADHD Drugs (NM)	1.0	1.2	0.7
Ketamine	0.9	1.4	s
Crack	0.7	0.9	s
Any NM Use of a Prescription Drug	16.7	15.1	18.5
Any illicit Drug Use, ind. NM Prescr. Drug	37.4	37.7	37.0

Source: Paglia-Boak, A., Adlaf, E.M., & Mann, R.E. (2011). Drug use among Ontario students, 1977-2011: Detailed OSDUHS findings (CAMH Research Document Series No. 32). Toronto, ON: Centre for Addiction and Mental Health.

Cocaine and Crack

According to CADUMS, in 2011, past-year use of the most commonly reported illicit drugs after cannabis was estimated to be less than one percent for each (hallucinogens including salvia: 0.6 percent; ecstasy: 0.7 percent; cocaine or crack: 0.9 percent; and speed: 0.5 percent). The only statistically significant change noted among these substances over time was a decrease in use of cocaine or crack to 0.9 percent in 2011 from

1.9 percent in 2004. Table 8.4 shows that 2.1 percent of students reported using cocaine in 2011, and more males than females (2.5 versus 1.6 percent) used it. That too is slightly lower than what earlier studies showed. For some central-city residents living in poverty, with no hope of gainful employment, dealing cocaine is a major source of revenue and an entry point for other drug-related crime.

The effects of cocaine on the human body depend on how pure the dose is and what effect the user

The Battle over Marijuana: Medicalization, Availability, Decriminalization, and Legalization

The controversy over marijuana is long-standing and will certainly continue for a long time. In the mid-1970s in Canada, the Le Dain Commission suggested that government should consider legalizing it. It was not legalized, but since then a number of concessions have been made. First marijuana was medicalized. As of July 30, 2001, Canada allowed people with medical need to use marijuana. Restrictions applied to certain types of need, such as having a terminal illness with a prognosis for a remaining life span of less than 12 months; having particular diseases such as multiple sclerosis, spinal cord injury, some cancers, and HIV/AIDS; and having other serious medical conditions where conventional treatments are not relieving symptoms (Health Canada 2001). In addition, a doctor had to declare that conventional procedures had been tried and were unsuccessful.

Not all doctors agree with the decision to medicalize marijuana. Both the Canadian Medical Association and the Canadian Medical Protective Association have urged physicians not to sign patients' forms, to protect the physicians against being accused of recommending an unproven treatment. In addition, Physicians for a Smoke-Free Canada say that marijuana contains many cancer-causing ingredients and more tar than tobacco, and thus should not be smoked for health reasons. Its effectiveness has not yet been shown in controlled experiments.

In April 2005, Canada was the first country to approve the sale of a cannabis-based prescription painkiller. It is being prescribed for people suffering from multiple sclerosis who have severe nerve pain and those with nerve pain from other diseases, ranging from cancer to shingles. The dose can be regulated more easily than smoking pot (Picard 2005). For over a dozen years (from July 30, 2001), Canada has allowed people with medical need to use marijuana. Since 2001, the numbers taking marijuana for medical reasons have grown to over 30 000 people known to the authorities in 2013, and more are thought to be taking it. New regulations state that as of April 2014, marijuana can no longer be grown in homes. Quality-controlled growing will take place under secure and safe conditions, and medical practitioners will be able to prescribe it without submitting medical information to Health Canada (Health Canada 2013).

Given the difficulties of making marijuana available to people with a medical need, the difficulties of decriminalizing or legalizing it seem substantial. But, in 2012, 66 percent of Canadians polled by Ipsos-Reid supported decriminalization, and 57 percent polled by Angus-Reid supported full legalization (Ibbitson 2013). Advocates of decriminalization or legalization suggest that small amounts of marijuana for personal use should no longer be subject to legal control. In the Netherlands, it has been possible for some time to use a variety of drugs without fear of prosecution; some U.S. states have already adopted some form of decriminalization for the possession of small amounts—usually less than one ounce or so—of marijuana; and in the 2012 U.S. elections, two states, Colorado and Washington, voted to legalize marijuana. Early reports suggest that they are earning millions through taxes and not having the great predicted social and health problems. But the U.S. Congress is not expected to legalize it. Similarly in Canada, despite the pioneering work in medical marijuana, the Harper government is not expected to legalize or even decriminalize it.

Obviously a number of benefits could flow from the legalization of marijuana in Canada:

- Fewer resources needed to fight and punish drug crime;
- Possibly fewer deaths due to drunk driving;
- Fewer deaths and injuries with the expected decline of criminal activity; and
- Reduction of government debt as a result of taxes on marijuana and income taxes on the related workers (like those on alcohol and tobacco).

But a number of problems would also likely occur:

- How would we deal with unintended health side effects, since very little scientific research has been devoted to marijuana's effects? This lack of research has led some doctors to refuse to prescribe it.
- How would we limit advertising and provide inspection for safety?
- How would we price it to discourage heavy use and not create another black market?
- How would we deal with marijuana use and drugged driving?
- Would big business (like Big Tobacco) take over production, with its focus on increasing consumption and profits?
- If Canada legalized it before the United States did, how would that affect relations between the two countries, especially regarding border security? However, because a couple of states voted to legalize marijuana in November 2012, security may be less of a problem.

In the summer of 2013, Justin Trudeau, leader of the Liberal Party of Canada, admitted not only to using marijuana, but also advocated legalizing it, so this issue may figure prominently in the 2015 federal election.

Can you think of any more pros and cons to decriminalizing/legalizing marijuana?

Questions for Consideration

1. Since Canadians are now interested in treating marijuana more leniently, should Canada decriminalize/ legalize marijuana to respond to the will of the people?

2. Do you think it likely that the federal government would decriminalize/legalize cannabis soon?

3. What would you expect will be the policy about legalization in another 20 years?

---

expects. Most cocaine users experience a powerful high, or "rush," in which blood pressure rises and heart rate and respiration increase dramatically. Reactions vary in length and intensity, depending on whether the drug is injected, smoked, or snorted. When the drug wears off, users become increasingly agitated and depressed. Some users become extremely depressed and suicidal; others develop such a powerful craving that they easily become addicted to the drug. Occasionally, cocaine use results in sudden death by triggering an irregular heart rhythm.

People who use cocaine over extended periods of time have higher rates of infection, heart disturbance, internal bleeding, hypertension, cardiac arrest, stroke, hemorrhaging, and other neurological and cardiovascular disorders than non-users. Although these problems may develop gradually as cocaine use continues, some users experience the problems after a single dose. Intravenous cocaine users who share contaminated needles and syringes are also at risk for HIV/AIDS. The risk of contracting HIV is especially high in crack houses, where women addicts often engage in prostitution (see Chapter 7) to acquire drugs.

Cocaine use is extremely hazardous during pregnancy. Children born to crack-addicted mothers usually suffer painful withdrawal symptoms at birth and later show deficits in cognitive skills, judgment, and behaviour controls. "Crack babies" must often be cared for at public expense in hospitals and other facilities because their mothers cannot meet their basic needs or provide nurturance. But social scientist Philippe Bourgeois suggests that blame for the problem cannot be placed on the women alone. Instead, Bourgeois blames patriarchal definitions of "family" and the dysfunctional public sector that relegates the responsibility for nurturing and supporting children almost exclusively to women. For change to occur, fathers and the larger society must share women's burden (Bourgeois 1995).

Like cocaine, amphetamines ("uppers") and a subclass, methamphetamines, stimulate the central nervous system. Amphetamines in the form of diet pills and pep formulas are legal substances when they are prescribed by a physician, but many people, believing that they cannot lose weight or have enough energy without the pills, become physically and/or psychologically dependent on them. Speed freaks—heavy users who inject massive doses of methamphetamine several times a day—often do "runs," staying awake for extended periods of time, eating very little, and engaging in bizarre behaviour such as counting cornflakes in a cereal box or pasting postage stamps on the wall before "crashing" and sleeping for several days. Recent concern about amphetamine abuse has focused on methamphetamine, a drug with a much stronger effect on the body. Table 8.4 shows that 1 percent of students used this drug in 2011. Chronic methamphetamine abuse can change how the brain functions, which may lead to reduced motor skills, impaired verbal learning, and changes in brain areas associated with memory and emotion.

Depressants

Many people who abuse stimulants also abuse depressants—drugs, including alcohol, that depress the central nervous system and may have some pain-killing properties. The most commonly used depressants are barbiturates (e.g., Nembutal and Seconal) and anti-anxiety drugs or tranquilizers (e.g., Librium, Valium, and Miltown). Table 8.4 shows that 1.9 percent of Ontario students (females slightly more than males) used tranquilizers in 2011. Relatively low oral doses of depressants produce a relaxing and mildly disinhibiting effect; higher doses result in sedation. Users may develop both physical addiction to and psychological dependence on these depressants. Users sometimes use depressants for *potentiation*—the interaction that takes place when two drugs are mixed together to produce a far greater effect than the effect of either drug administered separately. Heroin users, for example, will sometimes combine heroin and barbiturates in hopes of prolonging their high and extending their heroin supply (Levinthal 2011).

Rohypnol has been a topic of concern on university and college campuses. Rohypnol is used as an anesthetic and sleep aid in other countries, but it is not approved for use in Canada. For some people, Rohypnol works like a powerful sleeping pill.

For other users, however, the consequences are more dire. Rohypnol, a benzodiazepine, known colloquially as "roofies," is known as the "date rape drug" because a number of women have reported that they were raped after an acquaintance secretly slipped the drug into their drink. Victims, including men, become drowsy and pass out, not remembering what happened. The combination of alcohol and Rohypnol has also been linked to automobile accidents and deaths from overdoses, which occur because it is difficult to judge how much intoxication will result when depressants are mixed with alcohol

Narcotics

Narcotics, or opioids, are available in several forms: natural substances (e.g., opium, morphine, and codeine); opioid derivatives, which are created by making slight changes in the chemical composition of morphine (e.g., heroin and Percodan); and synthetic drugs, which produce opioid-like effects but are not chemically related to morphine (e.g., Darvon and Demerol). Because heroin is the most widely abused narcotic, we will focus primarily on its effects.

Who uses heroin? The percentage of Canadians using it is very small. The CADUMS results in Table 8.3 show than less than 1 percent of Canadians were using any one of these drugs, but this increased to 9.4 percent for using any one of six drugs. Table 8.4 shows that 1 percent of Ontario students used methamphetamine and none used heroin in 2011. Some people who try the drug have adverse side effects, such as nausea and vomiting, and never use it again; others become addicted.

What effect does heroin have on the body? Most heroin users inject the drug intravenously—a practice known as *mainlining* or *shooting*—which produces a tingling sensation and feeling of euphoria that is typically followed by a state of drowsiness or lethargy. Heroin users quickly develop a tolerance for the drug and must increase the dosage continually to achieve the same effect. Heroin and other opioids are highly addictive; users experience intense cravings and have physical symptoms such as diarrhea and dehydration if the drug is withdrawn.

What are the long-term effects of heroin? Although some users experience no long-term physical problems, there are serious risks involved in use. In high doses, heroin produces extreme respiratory depression, coma, and even death. Because the potency of street heroin is unknown, overdosing is always a possibility. Street heroin also tends to be diluted with other ingredients that produce adverse reactions in some users. Shooting up with contaminated needles can lead to hepatitis or HIV/AIDS. As well, heroin use has been linked more directly to crime than have some other types of drug use. Because hard-core users have difficulty holding a job and yet need a continual supply of the drug, they often turn to robbery, burglary, shoplifting, pimping, prostitution, or working for the underground drug industry (B. Johnson et al. 1985).

Hallucinogens

Hallucinogens, or psychedelics, are drugs that produce illusions and hallucinations. Mescaline (peyote), lysergic acid diethylamide (LSD), phencyclidine (PCP), and MDMA (ecstasy) produce mild to profound psychological effects, depending on the dosage. Mescaline or peyote—the earliest hallucinogen used in North America—was consumed during ancient Native American religious celebrations.

In the 1960s, LSD became a well-known hallucinogen because of Timothy Leary's widely publicized advice, "Turn on, tune in, drop out." LSD is one of the most powerful of the psychoactive drugs; a tiny dose (10 micrograms) of the odourless, tasteless, and colourless drug can produce dramatic, highly unpredictable psychological effects for up to 12 hours. These effects are often referred to as a *psychedelic trip*, and users report experiences ranging from the beautiful (a good trip) to the frightening and extremely depressing (a bad trip). Consequently, some LSD users take the drug only with the companionship of others who are familiar with the drug's effects. However, some studies have found that there is a possibility of *flashbacks* in which the user re-experiences the effects of the drug as much as a year after it was taken. Most long-term psychiatric problems associated with the drug involve people who were unaware that they had been given LSD, who showed unstable personality characteristics before taking the drug, or who experienced it under hostile or threatening circumstances (Levinthal 2011).

Among the most recent hallucinogens are PCP ("angel dust") and MDMA (ecstasy). PCP can be taken orally, intravenously, or by inhalation, but it is most often smoked. Initially, PCP was used as an anesthetic in surgical procedures, but it was removed from production when

TABLE 8.5 Percentage Reporting One or More Harms from Drug Use in the Past Year, by Sex and Age

	Overall	Males	Females	15–24 yrs	25+ yrs
Drug-related harms in past year[3]					
Any drug harm to self of total population	1.8 [1.3–2.3]	2.3Q [1.5–3.2]	1.3Q [0.8–1.9]	5.8Q [3.4–8.1]	1.1Q [0.7–1.5]
Any drug harm to self among users any 5 drugs	41.6Q [26.9–56.3]	38.21 Q [20.7–55.7]	49.7Q [25.6–73.7]	45.0Q [22.3–67.7]	38.1Q [19.1–57.1]
Any drug harm to self among users any drug	17.6 [13.0–22.1]	16.6Q [10.8–22.4]	19.3Q [11.7–26.9]	23.1Q [14.0–32.2]	14.2Q [9.3–19.2]

Source: *Health Canada, 2012, CADUMS. Retrieved June 22, 2013 (http://www.hc-sc.gc.ca/hc-ps/drugs-drogues/stat/_2011/tables-tableaux-eng.php#t1).*

patients who received it showed signs of agitation, intense anxiety, hallucinations, and disorientation. Production then went underground, and PCP became a relatively inexpensive street drug that some dealers pass off as a more expensive drug, such as LSD, to unknowing customers.

In the mid-1980s, MDMA (ecstasy) hit the street market. Manufactured in clandestine labs by inexperienced chemists, ecstasy, or "E," is a "designer drug" that is derived from amphetamines and has hallucinogenic effects. Users claim that it produces a state of relaxation, insight, euphoria, and heightened awareness without the side effects of LSD. Ecstasy has a high abuse potential and no recognized medical use. Table 8.4 shows that 1.2 and 3.3 percent of students reported using LSD and ecstasy, respectively, in 2011.

Inhalants

Inhalants are products that people inhale to get high. Commonly available products that are used as inhalants include gasoline, glue, paints, cleaning fluids, and toiletries. Inhalants are often called solvents because so many of them are used as inhalants. Abuse is common because inhalants are inexpensive, easy to obtain, and fast acting. They contain poisonous chemicals that can make abusers sick, damage their nerve and brain cells, and even kill them. As with many kinds of substance abuse, precise figures about use are either unavailable or questionable. However, Table 8.4 shows that 5.6 percent of students used solvents in 2011.

Overall Harm from Drug Use

Table 8.5 shows the percentage of Canadians reporting harm to themselves because of illicit drug use,

according to CADUMS. Overall, 17.6 percent of drug users reported harm to self in the past year from their drug use. This figure has been consistent since 2004. Little difference was found between men and women users of drugs for the past year, but a higher percentage of women who used any of five drugs reported harm to themselves. A higher percentage of younger than older Canadians reported harm.

One might think that reducing harm due to drug use would be considered a good thing, but a new controversy has emerged about the topic of safe injection sites. Should governments pay for safe injection sites (see The Future of Addictions below)?

GAMBLING AND PROBLEM GAMBLING

Although Canadians, like people everywhere, have always gambled, only recently has gambling become a billion-dollar business in Canada, and we have begun to learn about the characteristics of gamblers and the consequences of problem gambling. Since the early 1990s, great growth has occurred in the gambling industry. Net revenue from government-run lotteries, video lottery terminals (VLTs), casinos, and slot machines not in casinos rose from $2.7 billion in 1992 to $13.6 billion in 2007, and employment in the gambling industry rose from 11 000 in 1992 to 46 000 in 2007 (Statistics Canada 2008h). Since then the revenue and work force have plateaued.

Types of Gamblers

A study conducted in Ontario in 2005 by psychologist Jamie Wiebe and colleagues provides a comprehensive and detailed picture of the types of gambling and consequences for participants. The researchers employed the Canadian Problem Gambling Index (CPGI), included in one cycle of the Canadian Community Health Survey, and within it the Problem Gambling Severity Index (PGSI). This study found that about 36 percent of the population were non-gamblers, 54 percent were non-problem gamblers, about 6 percent were at risk, 2.6 percent had moderate gambling problems (level 3–7), and 0.8 percent had severe gambling problems (level 8+) (compare this with drinkers who exceed risk levels above) (Wiebe et al. 2006:41). The PGSI is a nine-dimension instrument that assesses several domains of gambling problems and is divided into four categories (0, 1–2, 3–7, and 8+) to indicate increasing levels of problems. The 3–7 level denotes a significant risk. It is associated with heavy gambling and related gambling problems, such as making increased wagers, returning to win back losses, and borrowing money or selling something to gamble. In addition, this level may or may not yet be accompanied by adverse consequences from gambling, including feeling guilty about gambling, experiencing financial problems, and developing health problems such as stress and anxiety. The 8+ level represents severe problem gamblers— those who have experienced adverse consequences from gambling and might have lost control of their behaviour. The severe problem gamblers participated more in every kind of gambling (tickets, electronic, games with friends, casinos, horse racing, bingo, sports betting, and speculative investments) than other gamblers (Wiebe et al. 2006:30). Individuals with severe gambling problems spent about 20 times as much money as an average gambler in any month. Whereas an average gambler spent 2.2 percent of his or her income on gambling, those with severe gambling problems spent about 21 percent of their income (Wiebe et al. 2006:34).

Gambling and Gender, Age, Income, and Marital Status

National gambling data show no difference in the percentage of men and women who gamble. While there is little difference in gambling by age, men's participation increases with age, and women 65 and over are least likely to gamble. People at all income levels participate, and participation and expenditure rates increase with household income. For example, 54 percent of households with incomes of less than $20 000 gambled in 2006 and spent an average of $469 per year, while equivalent figures for those with incomes of $80 000 or more were 82 percent and $566, respectively. People living alone are likely to gamble more. One in seven women and men living alone reported spending money on casinos, slot machines, or VLTs; however, men spent more than three times as much as women ($1396 versus $434.3) (Statistics Canada 2008h).

Problem Gambling and Province, Gender, Age, Marital Status, Education, and Income

To determine the prevalence of problem gambling in Canada, psychologist Brian Cox and colleagues (2005) also used the CPGI and within it, the PGSI. These researchers found that while the vast majority of Canadians had not experienced gambling problems, about 2 percent of Canadians were problem gamblers (levels 3–7 and 8+) and that some variation occurred among the provinces, ranging from 1.5 percent of people in New Brunswick to 2.9 percent of people in Manitoba (Cox et al. 2005).

Since the Ontario study by Wiebe and colleagues contains more detailed data of severe problem gamblers, it will be used to create a more complete portrait of this type of person. A higher percentage of men than women were severe problem gamblers (1.2 versus 0.5 percent). A higher percentage of young people (18 to 24 years) were severe problem gamblers compared with older people (1.4 versus 0.4 to 0.8 percent). A higher percentage of severe problem gamblers were found among those who were single and never married than those married or living with a partner (1.2 versus 0.7 percent). Those who had completed post-secondary education were less likely to be severe problem gamblers. A higher percentage of those who had the highest level of income ($100 000+) were likely to be severe problem gamblers (2.4 versus 0 to 1.7 percent), but otherwise employment status was unrelated to severe problem gambling. Region of residence in Ontario was also unrelated to severe problem gambling (Wiebe et al. 2006:41–42). Paglia-Boak and colleagues also inquired into the gambling behaviour of students and questioned them about problem gambling using a shortened version of the South Oaks Gambling Screen for Adolescents. They found the percentage of problem gamblers in Ontario in Grades 7 to 12 was similar to the previous findings. Two percent of students are likely to have a problem, and males are more likely than females. No differences were found among grades and regions of Ontario (Paglia-Boak et al. 2012:19).

Gambling-Related Social Problems

Wiebe and colleagues also identified difficulties experienced by gamblers. While few gamblers overall reported difficulties, almost half of severe problem gamblers reported one or more problems, including:

- difficulty making a paycheque last (64.5 percent of severe problem gamblers);
- gambling with money budgeted for something else (51.6 percent);
- negatively affected personal relationships (45.2 percent);
- negatively affected work (13.3 percent); and
- thoughts of suicide (9.7 percent) (Wiebe et al. 2006:37).

The following three quotations from sociologist Lorne Tepperman's interview study *Betting Their Lives: The Close Relations of Problem Gamblers* (2009) illustrate particular difficulties gamblers or their relations experience:

- A person who had properties now has nothing. Now he hopes to repay his debts and rebuild his family.
- A child is concerned that her father is very consumed with money making and does not care about other people's well-being.
- A mother could not buy formula for a baby, because her husband would return it for cash for gambling (2009:145–147).

EXPLANATIONS OF ADDICTIONS

As mentioned at the outset of this chapter, we will use the term *addictions* to describe dependence on alcohol, drugs, and tobacco, along with severe problem gambling. Since less research is available for severe problem gambling than for the other addictions, the research reported here will refer to specific kinds of addictions. Why do people become addicted? Various explanations have been given. Some focus on biological factors; others emphasize environmental influences. Sociologists stress environmental factors. We will focus on these factors, but it is important to remember that other factors contribute. For example, studies have found convincing evidence that drugs such as alcohol, heroin, and cocaine act directly on the brain mechanisms responsible for reward and punishment. As the drugs stimulate the areas of the brain that create the sensation of pleasure and suppress the perception of pain, the user receives reinforcement to engage in further drug-taking behaviour.

Drugs that provide an immediate rush or intense euphoria (e.g., cocaine and heroin) are more likely to be abused than drugs that do not. Similarly, drugs that produce pleasant but rapidly dissipating effects (e.g., alcohol) tend to encourage users to take additional doses to maintain the pleasurable effects. Prescription drugs, like dopamine agonists for Parkinson's disease, can also produce feelings of bliss after a gambling win. Patients can be so overcome that they continue in a compulsive fashion and can lose everything gambling (Lehrer 2009).

The Interactionist Perspective

Like social psychologists, sociologists who use an interactionist framework believe that an addiction is learned behaviour that is strongly influenced by families, peers, and other people. In other words, individuals are more likely to use or abuse drugs if they have frequent, intense, and long-lasting interactions with people who use or abuse drugs. For example, some children learn to be addicts by watching their parents' addictive behaviour. Tepperman and colleagues have applied this theory to gambling. They found that parent modelling behaviour was a good predictor of problem gambling, in addition to other factors like stressful events (Tepperman et al. 2013:106). Other young people learn from their peer group. In his classic study of marijuana users, sociologist Howard S. Becker (1963) concluded that drug users learn not only how to "do" drugs from other users, but also what pleasurable reactions they should expect to have.

People are also more prone to accept attitudes and behaviours favourable to drug use if they spend time with members of a *drug subculture*—**a group of people whose attitudes, beliefs, and behaviours pertaining to drug use differ significantly from those of most people in the larger society.** Over time, people in addictive subcultures tend to become closer to others within their subculture and more distant from people outside the subculture. Given this, participants in hard-core subcultures quit them only when something brings about a dramatic change in their attitudes, beliefs, and values regarding drugs. Although it is widely believed that most addicts could change their behaviour if they chose to do so, *labelling theory* suggests that it is particularly difficult for individuals to discontinue once they have been labelled "alcoholics" or "drug addicts." Because of the prevailing ideology that alcoholism and drug addiction are personal problems rather than social problems, individuals tend to be held solely responsible for their behaviour.

The Functionalist Perspective

Why does the level of addiction remain high in Canada? Functionalists point out that there is virtually no society in which people do not use drugs of some kind or do not gamble. Drugs contribute to many rituals, including weddings and other celebrations, and some drugs, such as alcohol, are often a part of daily mealtimes. Other functionalists would suggest that social institutions such as the family, education, and religion, which previously kept deviant behaviour such as addictions in check, have become fragmented and somewhat disorganized. Because they have, it is now necessary to use formal mechanisms of social control to prohibit people from taking illegal drugs or driving under the influence of alcohol or other drugs. External controls in the form of law enforcement are also required to discourage people from growing, manufacturing, or importing illegal substances. But these controls are not available for problem gambling. Gambling is legal and provides employment and a substantial portion of government budgets (see the above figures on gambling).

Governments also earn a large amount of money from alcohol, as Figure 8.3 shows.

In 2011, revenue for all governments was more than $5 billion, though after controlling for inflation it was slightly more than the same revenue from 1988, $3 billion.

Functionalists believe that activities in society continue because they serve important societal functions. Alcohol can facilitate social interaction and reduce stress. Prescription and over-the-counter drugs, for example, are functional for patients because they ease pain, cure illness, and sometimes enhance or extend life. They are functional for doctors because they provide a means for treating illness and help to justify the doctor's fee. They are functional for pharmacists because they provide a source of employment; without pills to dispense, there would be no need for pharmacists. Gambling is also very profitable.

The growth in the gambling industry in Canada has been noted. But dysfunctions also occur with addictions: patients may experience adverse side effects or develop a psychological dependence on the drug; doctors, pharmacists, and drug companies may be sued because they manufactured, prescribed, or sold a drug that is alleged to cause bodily harm to users. The dysfunctions of severe addictions are losses of wealth, health, and relationships. In addition, there are costs to society of disability and death, etc. (see costs at the beginning of the chapter). Illicit drugs also have functions and dysfunctions. On the one hand, the illicit drug trade creates and perpetuates jobs at all levels of the criminal justice system, in the federal government, in social service agencies that deal with problems of alcoholism and drug addiction, and in criminology departments. What, for example, would employees in various police services do if Canada did not have an array of illicit drugs that are defined as the "drug problem"? On the other hand, the dysfunctions of illicit drug use extend throughout society. At the individual level, addictive drugs such as heroin, cocaine, and barbiturates create severe physical and mental health problems as well as economic crises for addicts, their families, and acquaintances. At the societal level, drug

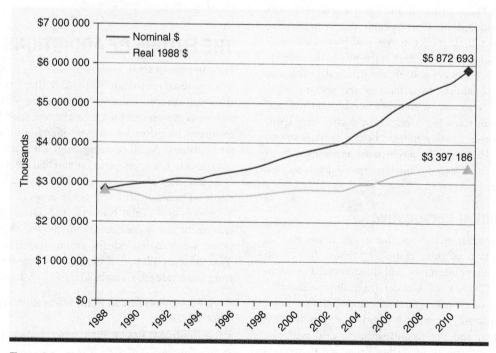

Figure 8.3 Net income of provincial/territorial liquor authorities from the control and sale of alcoholic beverages, Canada, 1988–2011.

Source: *Thomas, Gerald. 2012:4*

abuse contributes to loss of productivity, human potential and life expectancy, and money. Hundreds of millions of dollars in taxpayers' money that might be used for education or preventive health care are spent making and enforcing drug laws and dealing with drug-related crime and the spread of HIV/AIDS by addicts who shoot up with contaminated needles. Addiction to illegal drugs, the abuse of legal drugs, the abuse of alcohol and tobacco, and severe problem gambling exacerbate the loss of human potential and undermine the stability of society. Should such drugs like marijuana be legalized or at least decriminalized (see Box 8.3)?

The Conflict Perspective

According to conflict theorists, people in positions of economic and political power make the sale, use, and possession of drugs abused by the poor and the powerless illegal. We mentioned earlier that opium smoking was outlawed because it was associated with the Chinese. Restricting the drugs that members of a subordinate racialized/ethnic group use is one method of suppressing the group and limiting its ability to threaten dominant group members or gain upward mobility in society. Those who control the nation's political and legal apparatus decide whether a drug is legal or illegal.

Conflict theorists also point out that powerful corporate—and, in the case of alcohol, smoking, drug use, and gambling, corporate and government—interests perpetuate addictions. Corporations that manufacture, market, and sell alcohol, tobacco, and pharmaceuticals and the gaming industries reap huge profits from products that exact a heavy toll on the personal health and well-being of addicts, their families and communities, and the larger society. Using their wealth and political clout, elites in Canadian tobacco companies have spent years vigorously fighting measures to discourage smoking. Since sales of tobacco products are approximately $4 billion per year, tobacco companies are not likely to give up the fight.

The Feminist Perspective

Feminist theorists point out that a significant part of the explanation of drug abuse by women has to do with women's vulnerability and disadvantaged position in society. Chapter 4, "Gender Inequality," discussed many forms of inequality, such as vulnerability to sexual and spousal abuse, the wage gap and fewer promotional opportunities, and the second shift. To deal with the feelings these forms of inequality bring about, women sometimes turn to drug abuse: "Women use drugs to cope, to deal with stress, to nurture themselves, to escape from the pain of past events or of their current status, or to continue their social roles" (Harrison 1997:230).

A feminist approach to the problem emphasizes the different types of drug abuse by males and females. Data presented earlier in the chapter showed that males are much more likely to use alcohol and illicit drugs than females are, and females are more likely to use licit, psychotherapeutic drugs than males are. Several hypotheses have been suggested to account for gender differences in health behaviour. Two hypotheses that help to explain the differences in drug taking are the risk-taking behaviour of men and the willingness of women to adopt the "sick role" (see Chapter 10 for a discussion of the sick role). Men are socialized to take risks, and women are socialized to be more cautious and take care of their health (Waldron 1997). Thus, men would engage in risky behaviour such as drinking or illicit drug use to solve problems and women would seek out medical help and use prescription drugs for problems rather than engage in risky behaviour. On the other hand, the social acceptability hypothesis suggests that women are more willing than men to admit being sick, adopt a sick role, and accept medical help such as using drugs to deal with their problems (Gee and Kimball 1987).

Main focus for feminists is the fact that many women and children suffer from the consequences of men's severe gambling problems.

THE FUTURE OF ADDICTIONS

How to prevent abuse of alcohol and other drugs and how to treat drug-related problems after they arise are controversial issues in contemporary society. What kinds of addiction prevention programs are available? Will future treatment programs for addicts differ from the ones that are available today? Regarding drugs, the Canadian federal government has developed a comprehensive strategy—the National Anti-Drug Strategy. This national, concerted effort addresses alcohol and other drugs in Canada. The long-term goal of the National Anti-Drug Strategy is to reduce the harm associated with the use of alcohol and other drugs to individuals, families, and communities. This is accomplished through pursuing the following three plans (Health Canada 2013):

- The **Prevention Action Plan**, which aims to prevent illicit drug use;
- The **Treatment Action Plan**, which aims to treat those with drug dependencies; and
- The **Enforcement Action Plan**, which aims to combat the production and distribution of illicit drugs.

Prevention Programs

Addiction prevention programs can be divided into three major categories: primary, secondary, and tertiary. *Primary prevention* **refers to programs that seek to prevent drug problems before they begin.** Most primary prevention programs focus on people who have had little or no previous experience with drugs. In contrast, *secondary prevention* programs seek to limit the extent of drug abuse, prevent the spread of drug abuse to substances beyond those already experienced, and teach strategies for the responsible use of licit drugs such as alcohol (Levinthal 2011). For example, a program directed at university or college students who already consume alcohol might focus on how to drink responsibly by emphasizing the dangers of drinking and driving. Finally, *tertiary prevention* programs seek to limit relapses by individuals recovering from alcoholism or drug addiction. The purpose of tertiary prevention is to ensure that people who have entered treatment for some form of drug abuse become free of drugs and remain that way.

Primary prevention, according to Canada's Drug Strategy, is best done through a combination of public awareness campaigns, educational resources, training of service providers, and community action. Some of these programs have been organized by MADD (Mothers against Drunk Driving) and SADD (for Students). The programs should be part of every year's school curriculum, should involve students in planning and conducting presentations, and should present honest, factual material about why people use drugs and give alternatives to their use.

Scare tactics and negative-education programs do not work; they turn students off and do not achieve their desired goal. Effective prevention programs are family-, school-, and community-based. They offer alternative activities and outlets to drug use. These programs— like other drug abuse prevention efforts—take into account issues that affect people differently depending on their racialization/ethnicity, religion, or other factors. Reaching across lines of racialization, class, and gender, successful drug abuse prevention programs will use television and the Internet to make people aware of the effects of drugs on the human body and how to get help in dealing with alcoholism and drug addiction.

A controversial example of *secondary prevention* is the InSite program. InSite is a safe injection (of drugs) site that opened in 2003 in Vancouver's downtown East Side. InSite is called a "harm reduction site" because drug users are given clean needles (not drugs) and a safe place to shoot up to prevent needle sharing and the subsequent spread of disease; provided nursing help to prevent fatalities due to overdoses; and offered routes to rehabilitation.

The World Health Organization has endorsed the site, and it is one of over four dozen safe injection sites, primarily in Europe and Australia. The Canadian Conservative government has opposed this site, questioning whether it is appropriate for health care professionals to allow the giving/using of drugs that cannot be prescribed legally (Editorial, *Globe and Mail,* August 20, 2008:A16).

However, though the site is costly, it's been projected that InSite will save the health care system at least $14 million and prevent more than 1000 HIV infections and 54 cases of hepatitis C over a 10-year period (Weeks 2008:L1). The current director, Russ Maynard, has said, "Since InSite has been operating in 2003, we've seen 30 percent decrease in overdoses" and "in addition, 450 people a year go straight from InSite into pyjamas and slippers in a treatment and detox centre" (Ellison 2013:A4).

InSite also gained judicial support from the BC Court's 2008 decision that allowed the site to remain because to deny access to its health care services would violate drug users' *Charter* rights. The federal government appealed this decision to the Supreme Court of Canada, and the Supreme Court not only upheld the BC judicial ruling on September 30, 2011, but also said that other sites should have the opportunity to create similar programs where there is little or no impact on public safety.

In 2013, in Toronto, Dr. David McKeown, Toronto's medical officer of health, looked for support for a pilot site in Toronto, but the Toronto Police Service and the premier of Ontario, Kathleen Wynne, did not show enthusiasm for it.

Treatment Programs

Tertiary prevention programs are programs that aim to ensure that people who have sought help for some form of drug abuse remain drug-free. It follows from the biological and social learning explanations for substance abuse and alcohol addiction that treatment must deal with the body's physiological and psychological responses. Therefore, *alcohol and drug treatment* involves the use of activities designed to eliminate physical and psychological addiction and to prevent relapse—returning to abuse and/or addiction. Most treatment programs are based on a medical model or therapeutic community.

The Medical Treatment Model

The *medical treatment model* considers drug abuse and alcoholism to be medical problems that must be resolved through medical treatment by medical officials. Treatment may take the form of *aversion therapy* or *behavioural conditioning.* For example, drugs such as Cyclazocine and Nalozone are given to heroin and opioid addicts to prevent the euphoric feeling that they associate with taking the drugs. Supposedly, when the pleasure is gone, the person will no longer abuse the drug. Some heroin addicts also receive methadone detoxification to alleviate withdrawal symptoms associated with stopping heroin use. Over a one- to three-week period, the patient receives decreasing doses of methadone, a synthetic opium derivative that blocks the desire for heroin but does not have its negative side effects.

Antabuse is used in the treatment of alcoholism. After the person has been detoxified and no alcohol remains in the bloodstream, Antabuse is administered along with small quantities of alcohol for several consecutive days. Because this combination produces negative effects such as nausea and vomiting, the individual eventually develops an aversion to drinking, which becomes associated with uncomfortable physical symptoms. Although the medical treatment model works for some people, it is criticized for focusing on the physiological effects of alcohol and drug dependency and not dealing with the psychological and sociological aspects of dependency.

The Therapeutic Community

According to a booklet entitled *Alcohol and Drug Treatment in Ontario: A Guide for Helping Professionals* published by the Centre for Addiction and Mental Health, many short- and long-term services (both live at-home and live-in) are available (at no charge, except for some specialized services) for people seeking help with addictions. (The authors acknowledge that some services may not be locally available.) Short-term services include withdrawal management (detox) services, which give people a place to stay while their bodies get rid of alcohol or drugs and adapt to a drug-free state, and services that provide a place to stay for a month and insight into leading a healthy life.

When substance abusers are perceived to have an underlying psychological problem, treatment generally involves long-term services like counselling, rehabilitation, and/or the therapeutic community. Counselling often employs rehabilitated alcoholics or addicts who encourage participants to take more responsibility for their lives so that they can function better in the community. Some counselling and rehabilitation programs take place on an outpatient basis or as day treatment; others involve residential treatment. *Outpatient programs* allow drug abusers to remain at home and continue working while attending regular group and individual meetings. *Day treatment* takes place in a hospital setting where the abuser participates in day-long treatment groups and individual counselling sessions and returns home in the evening. The *therapeutic community approach* is based on the idea that drug abuse is best treated by intensive individual and group counselling in a residential setting. Residential treatment takes place in a special house or dormitory where alcoholics or drug addicts remain for periods of time, ranging from several months to more than a year, while they learn to rebuild their lives without alcohol or drugs.

Perhaps the best-known non-residential therapeutic communities are Alcoholics Anonymous (AA), founded in 1935, and its offshoots, Narcotics Anonymous (NA) and Gambling Anonymous (GA). AA, NA, and GA provide members with support in their efforts to overcome drug dependence and addiction. AA was established in 1935 in the United States by two alcoholics who were seeking a way of returning to sober life. Members use only their first names to ensure anonymity, and recovering addicts serve as sponsors and counsellors for others. AA, NA, and GA are based on a 12-step program that requires members to acknowledge that they are addicts who must have the help of a higher power and other people to remain sober or drug-free.

All the approaches for reducing alcohol and drug abuse that we have discussed can help certain individuals, but none addresses what to do about social structural factors that contribute to the drug problems. Because drug- and alcohol-related problems and their solutions are part of deeper social issues and struggles, they cannot be dealt with in isolation. If Canada sets out to reduce inequalities, perhaps the drug problem would be substantially reduced. What do you think it would take to make this happen?

WHAT CAN YOU DO?

- Volunteer at an agency such as Mothers Against Drunk Driving (MADD) or, if a local chapter exists, Students Against Drunk Driving (SADD). If a local chapter does not exist, contact MADD via their website (included in the References).

- Participate in or organize a committee for challenging the various kinds of drug companies and their influence on universities. Since the influence of pharmaceutical companies on research practices is likely to be a continuing problem, much scope exists for future educational programs.

- Develop an educational program to help students stop binge drinking. Generally, peer-initiated programs have better results. Several years ago, students at colleges in Ontario undertook a promotional campaign based on the slogan, "If you drink, don't bowl," based on the double meaning of *bowl* as a game and a place to vomit (toilet bowl). Try to devise a new catchy and effective slogan for your program. You might include some first-aid suggestions for dealing with consequences of binge drinking.

- Study the way students use prescription medicines, not only antidepressants, but also diet pills and stimulants, and study the relationship between alcohol consumption and acquaintance or date rape.

- Design a program to alert students, particularly women, to the problems of excessive body-consciousness (see also Chapter 10), as well as the need to use drugs with particular care when on dates.

SUMMARY

What Are the Major Patterns of Problem Drinking?
Health Canada is using a new approach for determining whether a person meets or exceeds the Low-Risk Drinking Guidelines, standards found to be related to diseases like cancers and cirrhosis of the liver. About 14 percent and 10 percent of Canadians (15 years+) are exceeding the chronic and acute guidelines respectively, with higher percentages for men than women, but no differences between young and old.

What Are the Major Hazards Associated with Tobacco Use?
Nicotine is a toxic, dependency-producing drug that is responsible for about 37 000 deaths per year in Canada. People who smoke have a greater likelihood of developing cardiovascular disease, lung cancer, and/or cancer of the larynx, mouth, and esophagus. Even those who do not smoke may be subjected to the hazard of environmental tobacco smoke—the smoke in the air as a result of other people's tobacco smoking. Infants born to women who smoke typically have lower-than-average birth weights and sometimes have slower rates of physical and mental growth. Fortunately, smoking has declined among all groups in Canada, especially youths.

What Problems Are Associated with Use of Prescription and Over-the-Counter Drugs?
Some prescription drugs have the potential for short-term abuse and long-term psychological and physical dependence. This form of dependency is known as *iatrogenic addiction*—drug dependency that results from physician-supervised treatment for a recognized medical disorder. Over-the-counter drugs, which are widely advertised and readily available, may be dangerous when combined with alcohol or other drugs.

In Canada, What Are the Major Stimulant Drugs?
Cocaine and methamphetamines are the major stimulant drugs abused in Canada. Cocaine is an extremely potent and dependency-producing stimulant drug. Methamphetamines can be obtained legally in the form of diet pills and pep formulas when they are prescribed by a physician.

What Are Depressants and What Health-Related Risk Do They Pose?
As the name indicates, depressants depress the central nervous system; they also may have some pain-killing properties. The most common depressants are barbiturates and anti-anxiety drugs or tranquilizers. Users may develop both physical addiction and psychological dependency on these drugs. There is also the risk of *potentiation*—the drug interaction that takes place when two drugs are mixed together and the combination produces a far greater effect than that of either drug administered separately.

What Is Severe Problem Gambling, and What Difficulties Do Such Gamblers Experience?
Severe problem gambling is associated with heavy gambling and related gambling problems such as increased wagers, returning to win back losses, and borrowing money or selling something to gamble. It may or may not yet be accompanied by adverse consequences from gambling, including feeling guilty about gambling, having financial problems, and experiencing health problems such as stress and thoughts of suicide.

How Do Sociological Perspectives View Alcohol, Drug, and Gambling Addictions?
Interactionists believe that these are learned behaviours that are strongly influenced by families, peers, and others who serve as role models. People are more prone to accept attitudes and behaviours that are favourable to drug use or gambling if they spend time with members of a subculture or see models (e.g., at home). Functionalists believe that drug and gambling-related problems have increased as social institutions such as the family, schools, and religious institutions have become fragmented and somewhat disorganized. However, use of alcohol and other drugs serves an important function, even though some aspects of drug use are dysfunctional for society. All of these addictions provide jobs for people, and most provide income for governments. According to conflict theorists, people in positions of economic and political power are responsible for making the sale, use, and possession of some drugs illegal. Conflict theorists also point out that powerful corporate interests perpetuate the use and abuse of alcohol, tobacco, other legal drugs, and gambling. Feminist theorists emphasize the vulnerability and disadvantaged position of women who abuse drugs.

What Is the Purpose of Prevention and Treatment Programs?
Primary prevention programs seek to prevent problems before they begin. Secondary prevention programs seek to limit the extent of abuse, prevent the spread of abuse to

other substances beyond the problems already experienced, and teach strategies for responsible use. The InSite program is a good example. Tertiary prevention programs seek to limit relapses by individuals recovering from addiction. They may be based either on a medical model or the therapeutic community. The best-known therapeutic community is Alcoholics Anonymous (AA) and other Anonymous programs.

What Other Factors Must be Taken into Account in Efforts to Reduce Drug and Gambling Problems?
Addictions are intertwined with other social problems, such as dramatic changes in the economic and technological bases of society, the growing gap between the rich and poor, and inequalities based on ethnicity and gender.

KEY TERMS

codependency, p. 165
drug, p. 160
drug addiction (drug dependency), p. 161

drug subculture, p. 178
environmental tobacco smoke, p. 165
fetal alcohol spectrum disorder (FASD) p. 163

primary prevention, p. 181
tolerance, p. 161
withdrawal, p. 161

QUESTIONS FOR CRITICAL THINKING

1. Does public tolerance of alcohol and intolerance of tobacco lead to increased and decreased use of these drugs respectively? Why do many people view the use of alcohol and tobacco differently from the use of illicit drugs?

2. If stimulants, depressants, hallucinogens, and inhalants have such potentially hazardous side effects, why do so many people use these drugs? If drug enforcement policies were more stringently enforced, would there be less drug abuse in this country?

3. As a sociologist, how would you propose to deal with the problem of addictions in Canada? If you were called upon to revamp existing drug laws and policies, what, if any, changes would you make in them?

4. How have changes in technology affected the problem of alcohol, drug, and gambling addictions over the past century? How have changes in the global economy affected drug-related problems in this country and others? (See Box 9.1 on page 194 about international organized crime.)

Crime and Criminal Justice

Jacob Henefin/AP Photo/CP Images

When people think about crime they usually think of violent crimes like robbery and murder. However, white-collar crime, or crime occurring during a (high social status) person's normal occupational activities (like kickbacks for contracts, insider trading (trading stocks before news about the company is public), and corruption by public officials, can cost far more and affect more people than violent crime does.

In this chapter you will learn about the problem of defining crime and measuring crime with official statistics or victimization surveys; the rates of various kinds of crime (e.g., violent, property, and youth crime); and how the rates of some of these crimes in Canada compare to those in the United States. You will also learn about the nature of occupational and organized crime; why people commit crimes (the sociological explanations of crime); and the nature of the criminal justice system. The chapter concludes with some suggestions for ways you might help deal with the problem of crime.

CRIME AS A SOCIAL PROBLEM

Many people in Canada fear crime and may even be somewhat obsessed with it even though they have no direct daily exposure to criminal behaviour. Their information about crime comes from the media and sometimes from watching real-crime dramas such as *America's Most Wanted* (sightings by Canadians have led to the arrest of a few of the suspects). They are also influenced by fictionalized crime stories on television, such as *Flashpoint, Murdoch Mysteries,* and *CSI.* Media coverage of crime is extensive, but it is not because crime is increasing.

Crime rates have fallen now for the last two decades, as seen in Figure 9.1. That is not to say that crime isn't a problem. Crime statistics tell only part of the story. Crime *is* a significant social problem because it endangers people's lives, property, and sense of well-being. In 2011, over 1.9 million crimes (down from 2.3 million reported in 2006) were reported to police (see Table 9.1).

Given that many victims do not report crimes to the police (see Table 9.2), a substantial portion of Canadians have been victimized. Since much money is spent on the police, courts, and prison system, even individuals who are not directly victimized by crime are affected because they have to pay taxes to fight it, high insurance rates for theft, high interest rates for credit card fraud, and so on.

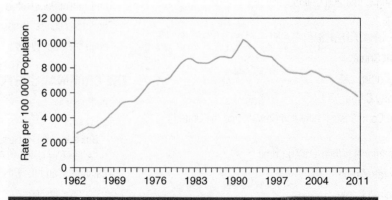

Figure 9.1 Crime Rates in Canada, 1962–2011.
Source: *Statistics Canada 2012. Crime, 2011 Retrieved June 28, 2013*
(http://www.statcan.gc.ca/pub/85-005-x/2012001/article/11745-eng.htm)

TABLE 9.1 Police-Reported Crime Statistics

	2001	2006	2011
	actual incidents		
Criminal Code violations (excluding traffic)	**2 353 330**	**2 359 804**	**1 984 916**
Violent *Criminal Code* violations	457 043	451 652	424 410
Property crimes	1 589 425	1 566 315	1 213 885
Other *Criminal Code* violations	306 862	341 837	346 621
Selected violations			
Homicide	553	606	598
Sexual assault (levels 1 to 3)	24 044	22 245	21 821
Assault (levels 1 to 3)	236 957	240 629	226 440
Prostitution	5087	5679	2459
Break and enter	279 461	251 361	181 217
Motor vehicle theft	168 595	158 638	82 411
Drugs	89 395	96 175	113 164
Impaired driving	82 718	76 127	90 277

Source: *Statistics Canada 2013. "Canada at a Glance." Retrieved June 18, 2013 (http://www.statcan.gc.ca/pub/12-581-x/2013000/cri-eng.htm#t11).*

Problems with Official Statistics

Over the past two decades, sophisticated computer-based information systems have not only improved rates of detection, apprehension, and conviction of offenders, but also have provided immediate access to millions of bits of information about crime, suspects, and offenders. The leading source of information on crimes reported in Canada is the *Uniform Crime Report* (UCR). The UCR was developed by Statistics Canada with the cooperation and assistance of the Canadian Association of Chiefs of Police. The survey became operational in 1962, and collects crime and traffic statistics reported by all police agencies in Canada. UCR data are based on reported crime substantiated by police investigation (Logan 2001:13) and are made available by the Canadian Centre for Justice Statistics (CCJS) in its online periodical, *Juristat*, for use in presentations and documentation. Since 1988, the UCR has been using an incident-based reporting system (collecting data on each criminal event, offender, and victim) instead of an aggregate system. It thus provides a more complex portrait of crime in Canada than previously available. The crime rate reported in Table 9.1 includes offences such as homicide, assault, sexual assault, break and enter, robbery, theft,

motor vehicle theft, and fraud. It does not include other violations, such as traffic offences.

How accurate are these crime statistics? Any answer to this question must take into account the fact that the statistics reflect only crimes that are reported to law enforcement agencies or that police officers see occur.

The downward trend in crime from the early 1990s probably reflects several factors, including increasing job opportunities (at least until the 2008 recession) and an age shift upward in the population; older people commit fewer crimes than younger people (see Chapter 5). The percentage of the Canadian population under age 26—the age group most likely to commit crimes—began to decline in 1992.

Because the number of crimes *reported* is not necessarily the number of crimes *committed,* Statistics Canada conducts victimization surveys. The most recent example is the General Social Survey (GSS) of 2009, which surveyed 24 000 randomly selected households to identify victims of personal crimes (e.g., theft of personal property, break and enter, assault, sexual assault, robbery, motor vehicle theft, and hate), and to determine whether the crime was reported or not. These surveys indicate

	TABLE 9.2 Self-reported Victims of Personal Crime, 1999, 2004, and 2009					
	Total violent victimization[1]		**Total household victimization**[2]		**Theft of personal property**	
Year	number (thousands)	rate[3]	number (thousands)	rate[4]	number (thousands)	rate[3]
1999	2691	111	2656	218*	1831	75*
2004	2751	106	3206	248	2408	93*
2009[†]	3267	118	3184	237	2981	108

† reference category

* significantly different from reference category (p < 0.05)

1. Total violent victimization includes: sexual assault, robbery and physical assault.
2. Total household victimization includes: break and enter, motor vehicle theft/parts, theft of household property and vandalism.
3. Rates are calculated per 1000 population age 15 years and older.
4. Rates are calculated per 1000 households.

Note: Excludes data from the Northwest Territories, Yukon, and Nunavut, which will be published at a later date.

Source: *Statistics Canada, 2013. "Criminal Victimization in Canada," Juristat. Retrieved June 28, 2013 (http://www.statcan.gc.ca/pub/85-002-x/2010002/article/11340/tbl/tbl1-eng.htm).*

that the number of crimes committed is substantially higher than the number reported (compare Tables 9.1 and 9.2), and note that the figures in Table 9.2 (Statistics Canada 2013z) are not rising or falling in a consistent way. The main reason given for not reporting crimes to police was that the incident was not considered significant enough. Victims of sexual assault reported seeking help from social services and support centres.

However, the GSS also has limitations:

1. Responses are based on recall, and some people don't remember specifically when a crime occurred. (They are supposed to report on the previous 12 months.)
2. For various reasons, respondents may not be truthful.
3. The surveys focus on theft and assault and do not measure workplace crimes, such as embezzlement or bribery, and organized crime.

Defining Crime and Delinquency

Crime is behaviour that violates the criminal law and is punishable by fine, jail term, or other negative sanctions. There are two components to every crime: the act itself, and *criminal intent*—expressed in the concept of *mens rea*, meaning "guilty mind." An individual's intent in committing a crime may range from wilful conduct (hiring someone to kill one's spouse) to an unintentional act of negligence that is defined as a crime (leaving a small child unattended in a locked automobile in extremely hot weather, resulting in the child's death).

Criminal law is divided into two major categories: summary and indictable offences. **Summary conviction offences are relatively minor crimes that are punishable by a fine or less than a year in jail.** Examples include public unlawful assembly, theft ($5000 and under), and traffic violations. **Indictable offences are more serious crimes, such as murder or aggravated assault, that are punishable by more than a year's imprisonment.** Adolescents (12 to 17 years of age) who commit illegal or antisocial acts usually are adjudicated as *delinquent* or *youth crime* by a youth court judge.

TYPES OF CRIMES

To make the study of crime—a large and complex subject—manageable, sociologists and criminologists categorize types of crime. In this section, we will look at seven categories of crime: violent crime, hate crime, property crime, occupational crime, corporate crime, organized crime, and youth crime. Table 9.1 shows the rate of particular crimes in 2001, 2006, and 2011. Interestingly, violent crimes are down, but homicide varies; motor vehicle thefts and prostitution offences are down, but drug offences are up.

Violent Crime

While it is well known to occur frequently in the United States, violent crime occurs much less frequently in Canada. **Violent crime consists of actions involving force or the threat of force against others and** includes homicide, attempted homicide, the three levels of assault and sexual assault, robbery, and other violent offences like criminal negligence causing death. Violent crimes are committed against people; non-violent crimes are usually committed against property. People tend to fear violent crime more than other kinds of crime because victims are often physically injured or even killed and because violent crime receives the most sustained attention from law enforcement officials and media.

Homicide

The UCR defines *homicide* as the unlawful, intentional killing of one person by another. (Killing by accident, in self-defence, or as an act against an enemy during wartime is not homicide.) By this definition, murder involves not only an unlawful act, but also *malice aforethought*—the *intention* of doing a wrongful act. A person who buys a gun, makes a plan to kill someone, and carries out the plan has probably committed homicide. In contrast, *manslaughter* is the unlawful, *unintentional* killing of one person by another. An intoxicated person who shoots a gun into the air probably holds no malice toward the bystander who is killed by a stray bullet. Sometimes a person's intentions are clear, but many times they are not, and the lines between intentional, unintentional, and accidental homicides are blurred. Homicides are rare in Canada and in other high-income countries (see Chapter 1), except in the United States. The Conference Board of Canada Report Card on Society shows that Canada and 14 other countries have a homicide rate of less than two per 100 000 inhabitants (Conference Board of Canada 2014).

Mass murder is the killing of four or more people at one time and in one place by the same person. Fortunately, the examples of mass murder in Canada are few. Marc Lepine's killing of 14 women in 1989 at the École Polytechnique in Montreal is an extreme example of mass murder (see Chapter 4). Although mass murders are extremely rare in Canada, it occurred in 2014 with the killing of five young people in Calgary by another young person in May. The killing of three members of the RCMP in Moncton in June 2014 by Justin Bourque, however dreadful, does not count as a mass murder because three people were killed.

According to criminologists, mass murderers tend to kill in the areas where they live. They are likely to be male, problem drinkers, and collectors of firearms and other weapons, which they often hide (Dietz 1986). Some mass murderers have been disgruntled employees or former employees who seek out supervisors and

co-workers in the workplace. An example of this kind of mass murder was the 1992 killing of four faculty members by Valery Fabrikant, a professor of engineering, at Concordia University in Montreal. A number of major mass murders have occurred recently in the United States, including a second Fort Hood shooting which killed four people in 2014.

Serial murder is the killing of three or more people over more than a month by the same person. Serial murders account for few homicides, but receive extensive media coverage. In Canada, Clifford Olson, who killed 11 boys and girls and was sentenced to life imprisonment in 1982, and Michael Wayne McGray, who pleaded guilty to six murders in 1998, are examples of serial killers. The murders committed by Robert Picton on his pig farm in Port Coquitlam, a suburb of Vancouver, is another example of serial murder. The remains of 27 victims were discovered on the farm, and in 2007, he was convicted of killing six people. The Crown decided not to pursue convictions for additional murders. It is difficult to characterize serial killers, outside of the fact that the best-known ones are White males. Some travel extensively to locate their victims; others kill near where they live. One study identified four basic types of serial killers: (1) *visionaries,* who kill because they hear a voice or have a vision that commands them to commit the murderous acts; (2) *missionaries,* who take it on themselves to rid the community or the world of what they believe is an undesirable type of person; (3) *hedonists,* who obtain personal or sexual gratification from violence; and (4) *power/control seekers,* who achieve gratification from the complete possession of the victim (Holmes 1988).

Characteristics of Victims and Accused

Statistics on homicide are among the most accurate official crime statistics available. Homicides rarely go unreported, and suspects are usually apprehended and charged. Although annual rates vary slightly (see Table 9.1), homicide follows certain patterns in terms of gender, age, racialization, and region of the country, as analyses from earlier years show. Men make up the vast majority of murder victims and offenders. In 2011, just less than three-quarters of homicide victims were male and 90 percent of the accused were male. In Canada, unlike the United States, homicide is not an urban phenomenon, and it is more likely to occur in western than eastern provinces (Statistics Canada 2013v).

In 2011, in 80 percent of solved homicides the victim knew their killer (Statistics Canada 2013v). In 2011, there were 89 intimate partner homicides (76 female victims and 13 male victims), almost identical to the rate recorded in each of the previous four years (Statistics Canada 2013v). In 2011, a knife or other cutting instrument was the weapon most often used to commit a homicide, accounting for more than one-third (35 percent) of all homicides in Canada. The next most common methods used to commit homicide in 2011 were firearms (27 percent), strangulation (7 percent), and beatings (2 percent). Contrary to people's general expectations, only 158 homicides were committed with a firearm in 2011, 13 fewer than the previous year (Statistics Canada 2013v).

Sexual Assault

Many people think of *sexual assault* (the term "rape" is no longer used in Canadian criminal law) as a sexually motivated crime, but it is actually **an act of violence in which sex is used as a weapon against a powerless victim.** Both men and women can be victimized by sexual assault. For example, men can be assaulted in prison. In Canada, sexual assault is classified into three levels:

- Level 1 includes touching, grabbing, kissing—the category of least physical harm to the victim.
- Level 2 includes assault with a weapon, threats to use a weapon, or causing bodily harm.
- Level 3, or aggravated assault, includes wounding, maiming, or endangering the life of the victim.

Date rape is forcible sexual activity that meets the legal definition of sexual assault and involves people who first meet in a social setting (Sanday 1996). This definition is preferred by some scholars because it encompasses dates and casual acquaintances but excludes spouses (marital rape) and relatives (incest). The phrase was coined to distinguish forced, non-consensual sex between people who know one another from forced, non-consensual sex between strangers—but both are against the law. Date rape is often associated with alcohol or other drug consumption (see "roofies" on page 175 in Chapter 8), especially among college and university students. We probably know much less about the actual number of date rapes than we do about the number of stranger assaults, because victims are less likely to report sexual attacks by people they know.

On university or college campuses, date or acquaintance rape sometimes takes the form of gang or party rape. The Steubenville case in 2012 is a notorious example. In this case a girl was raped by small-town high school football stars, and teens spread evidence of the assault on social media. Then a conflict erupted between the football fans and the victim's supporters. Similar attacks by university students have also occurred in Canada. For example, two former University of Ottawa hockey players have been charged with an alleged sex assault against a woman in Thunder Bay in February 2014 (see also Chapter 4). Unlike individual acquaintance rape, gang rape is used as a reinforcing mechanism for membership in a group of men (Warshaw 1994). In fact, men who rape in groups might never commit individual rape. As they participate in gang rape, they experience a special bonding with each other and use rape to prove their sexual ability to other group members and thereby enhance their status among members.

Characteristics of Victims and Accused

Statistics on sexual assault are misleading at best because the crime is often not reported. According to the 2013 Violence Against Women Survey, the five most common violent offences committed against women in 2011 were common assault (49 percent), uttering threats (13 percent), serious assault (10 percent), sexual assault level I (7 percent), and criminal harassment (7 percent) (Statistics Canada 2013w). According to UCR data for 2011 (see Table 9.1), sexual assaults constituted less than 5 percent of violent crime and have declined by about an eighth since 2001. Some women may not report that they have been assaulted because they believe that nothing will be done about it or that the attacker may try to get even.

Like homicide, sexual assault follows certain patterns in terms of gender, age, racialization, and education. With the proviso that inmates of correctional institutions may not fully represent the population that commits these crimes, we can gain much information from the last major inmate survey by consultant David Robinson and his colleagues (1999:275). According to the census of inmates conducted on October 5, 1996, incarcerated sexual offenders were male (99 percent), older than other violent offenders (35 versus 31 years of age), slightly more likely to be of Indigenous status than other violent offenders (23 versus 19 percent), and less educated (Grade 9 education or less) than the rest of the prison population (41 versus 19 percent).

Gang Violence

Gang violence includes homicide, sexual assault, robbery, and aggravated assault. But actually defining a "gang" is difficult. Police define gangs so broadly—"two or more persons engaged in antisocial behaviour who form an allegiance for a common criminal purpose and who individually or collectively are creating an atmosphere of fear and intimidation within a community" (quoted in Abbate 1998:A10)—that to identify violence as gang violence using this definition is too inclusive. Criminologist Robert M. Gordon (2000:48) has identified six types of gangs in Vancouver:

1. *Youth movements*—like skinheads and punks who perpetrate hate crimes;

2. *Youth groups*—youth who hang out together in public places, like malls;

3. *Criminal groups*—small groups who band together for a short time for illegal financial gain;

4. *"Wanna-be" groups*—loosely structured groups, frequently substitute families, that indulge in impulsive criminal behaviour;

5. *Street gangs*—young adults who plan criminal behaviour; and

6. *Criminal business organizations*—older, well-established groups, sometimes with ethnic membership, like the Lotus, Flying Dragons, Hells Angels, and Bandidos.

Typically, gangs are composed primarily of young males of the same ethnicity. Some gangs are basically peer groups that hang out together, seeking a sense of belonging, like a family, but others are well organized and violent. Violence often erupts in disputes over control of drug territory and enforcement of drug debts. Drug trafficking includes marijuana, cocaine, heroin, Ecstasy, and methamphetamine. In Canada, the rate of gang-related homicides steadily increased from the early 1990s until 2008, before declining in both 2009 and 2010. In 2013, there were 85 gang-related homicides, the first decline after the rate remained unchanged from 2010. At a rate of 0.24 per 100 000 population, gang-related homicides are the lowest they have been since 2004 (Statistics Canada 2013v).

In recent years, gang activity and gang-related violence have increased significantly not only in large metropolitan areas, but also in smaller cities and suburbs.

The rate of gang-related homicide was highest in British Columbia and Manitoba, the only two regions where the number of gang-related homicides increased compared with 2012. Kelowna and Regina recorded the highest rates of gang-related homicide. (See Chapter 1 for a note about gang violence in other parts of the world.)

Intervention by law enforcement officials and the criminal justice system has had only limited success. Monetary rewards for criminal behaviour far outweigh what individuals could have earned in legitimate jobs. But sometimes legal intervention works. In spring 2002, "Mom" Boucher, the closest thing to a godfather in the Hells Angels in Quebec, was convicted on several counts of homicide; and police arrested 36 members of the Bandidos, the second largest biker gang.

Hate Crime

Hate crimes are crimes that are motivated by the offender's hatred of certain characteristics of the victim (e.g., national or ethnic origin, language, colour, religion, gender, age, mental or physical disability, or other similar factors). In 2010, 1401 crimes were classified as hate crimes, down from 1482 in 2009, but up from 892 in 2006. Of these, half were motivated by race/ethnicity; 30 percent were motivated by religion; 15 percent were motivated by sexual orientation; and 5 percent were motivated by other characteristics (Statistics Canada 2012f). Since most hate crimes were motivated by ethnicity, we have chosen to highlight this kind of hate crime in Table 9.3.

TABLE 9.3   Police-reported Hate Crimes Motivated by Ethnicity in Canada, 2009 and 2010

Type of race or ethnicity	2009	2010
	percentage of racially motivated hate crimes	
Black	38.0	39.3
Arab or West Asian	10.4	10.9
South Asian	12.7	9.7
East and Southeast Asian	9.8	6.0
Caucasian	4.7	5.2
Aboriginal	3.6	2.5
Multiple races or ethnicities[1]	13.3	15.5
Other[2]	7.6	10.9

1. Includes hate crimes that target more than one race or ethnic group.
2. Includes motivations based upon race or ethnicity not otherwise stated (e.g., Latin American, South American).
Note: Information reflects data reported by police services covering 87% of the population of Canada in 2009 and 99% in 2010. Percentages have been calculated excluding unknown motivations.
Source: *Statistics Canada, 2012*, Police Reported Hate Crime 2010. *Retrieved June 29, 2013* (http://www.statcan.gc.ca/pub/85-002-x/2012001/article/11635-eng.htm).

The highest percentage of hate crimes were against Blacks (39.3 percent) and the lowest (2.5 percent) against Indigenous people. Hate crimes can have more severe psychological consequences for the victim and community and require longer recovery times than other crimes.

Property Crime

Property crime is the taking of money or property from another without force, the threat of force, or the destruction of property. Breaking and entering, possession of stolen goods, theft, motor vehicle theft, and fraud are examples of property crimes. Over 1.2 million property crimes were reported in 2011 (see Table 9.1), although property crime has fallen by a fifth since 2001. According to victimization surveys, the most frequent property crime is *breaking and entering*—the unlawful or forcible entry or attempted entry of a residence or business with the intent to commit a serious crime. Breaking and entering usually involves theft—the burglar illegally enters by, for example, breaking a window or slashing a screen (forcible entry) or through an open window or unlocked door (unlawful entry). Although breaking and entering is normally a crime against property, it is more serious than most non-violent crimes because it carries the possibility of violent confrontation and the psychological sense of intrusion that is associated with violent crime.

According to victimization surveys, the young have a higher risk of being subject to property crime than older people do. Risk of victimization is also much higher for families with incomes under $15 000 living in rental properties or in inner-city areas. In contrast, people who live in well-maintained residences with security systems on well-lit streets or cul-de-sacs are less likely to be victimized (Logan 2001:1). The UCR likely does not accurately represent the number of burglaries committed because people tend to report them only when very valuable, insured goods are taken.

The most frequently reported crime is called *theft $5000 and under*—unlawfully taking or attempting to take property from another person. This kind of theft includes purse snatching and pickpocketing. Statistics on auto theft are more accurate than those for many other crimes because insurance companies require claimants to report the theft to police. Analysts have identified four basic motives for auto theft:

1. Joyriding—the vehicle is stolen for the fun of riding around in it and perhaps showing off to friends.

2. Transportation—the vehicle is stolen for personal use.
3. Crime—the vehicle is used as an aid in the commission of another crime.
4. Profit—the vehicle is sold or taken to a "chop shop," where it is dismantled for parts.

Shoplifting accounts for billions of dollars in losses to retail businesses each year. For some stores, the annual loss can be as high as 2 to 5 percent of the total value of inventory. Criminologists generally put shoplifters into three categories: the *snitch*—someone with no criminal record who systematically pilfers goods for personal use or to sell; the *booster* or *heel*—the professional criminal who steals goods to sell to *fences* (people who receive and dispose of stolen property) or pawnshops; and the *kleptomaniac*—someone who steals for reasons other than monetary gain (e.g., for sexual arousal).

The last types of non-violent property crime are *identity theft* and *identity fraud*. Identity theft refers to the acquiring and collecting of someone else's personal information for criminal purposes. "Identity fraud is the actual deceptive use of the identity information of another person (living or dead) in connection with various frauds (including, for example, personating another person and the misuse of debit card or credit card data)" (RCMP 2013). The RCMP reports that the Internet facilitates identity theft and in 2009, the Canadian Anti-Fraud Centre received identity fraud reports from 11 095 Canadians, totalling a loss of more than $10 million (RCMP 2013).

Crime Comparisons between Canada and the United States

Canadians absorb much of their crime information from the U.S. media. It is therefore worthwhile to show the differences in Canadian and U.S. crime rates so that we do not automatically assume that their crime problem is our crime problem. Over the past 20 years, Canada has had a much lower violent crime rate than the United States. In 2011, the U.S. homicide rate was about three times our rate, almost 5/100 000 versus 1.73/100 000 population (Statistics Canada 2012g). Although Canada had a higher burglary rate in the early 2000s, since 2006 it has had a lower rate than the United States (600 vs. 700/100 000) (Conference Board 2013).

Occupational (White-Collar) Crime

Occupational (white-collar) crime refers to illegal activities committed by people in the course of their employment or normal business activity.

When sociologist Edwin H. Sutherland (1949) first introduced the term *white-collar crime,* referring to people who work in service industries as opposed to the blue-collar workers who work in factories, he was referring to such acts as employee theft, fraud (obtaining money or property under false pretenses), embezzlement (theft from an employer), and soliciting bribes or kickbacks. Today, the concept of white-collar crime may sound outdated because it referred to an era when men in high-paying jobs wore white-collared shirts and neckties. However, in the 21st century, occupational or white-collar criminals wear all kinds of clothing and engage in a wide variety of illegal practices ranging from fraud, to bribery, to money laundering, to embezzlement, to insider trading. Some observers are now calling it occupational fraud.

The amount of white-collar crime is difficult to determine because some of it is unreported. But according to a recently released report by PricewaterhouseCoopers LLP about white-collar crime worldwide, while Canada's rate of economic crime is lower than that of the rest of the world, still a third of those surveyed in 2011 said they were victims of white-collar crime. This figure was lower than a comparable one in the mid-2000s when 50 percent said they were victims. The four most common types of crime are theft of assets, fraud in the procurement process, accounting fraud, and cybercrime (e.g., viruses and stolen data). The cost can be substantial; 10 percent of those surveyed said they lost more than $5 million (McKenna 2014).

Corporate Crime

Some white-collar offenders engage in *corporate crime*—**illegal acts committed by corporate employees on behalf of the corporation and with its support.** Examples include acts injurious to the public or employees; pollution; manufacturing of defective products; antitrust violations (seeking an illegal advantage over competitors); deceptive advertising; infringements on patents, copyrights, and trademarks; unlawful labour practices involving the exploitation or surveillance of employees; price fixing; and financial fraud like tax evasion and insider trading. These crimes arise from deliberate decisions by corporate personnel to profit at the expense of competitors, consumers, employees, and the general public. A striking Canadian example of the economic effects of corporate crime was the case of the gold-mining company Bre-X Minerals Ltd. A company geologist, Michael de Guzman, added gold to survey samples, making the results look like those of a great gold mine. When the deception was discovered in 1997, the company and its stock became worthless, wiping out millions of dollars from various portfolios, including pension funds, and de Guzman apparently committed suicide. Other examples are found in the crimes of multinational companies such as Arthur Andersen—convicted in the spring of 2002 of obstructing justice—that have consequences for the companies' branches and accounting practices in Canada.

Other examples include mortgage fraud such as misstating information like interest rates and consequences of interest rate hikes; insurance fraud, like staged accidents and taking disaster relief money; mass marketing fraud, where potential victims are told of winning something but must put up money in advance, which then is taken; and money laundering, where crime proceeds are converted into business expenses or accepted by banks.

Corporate crime has huge direct and indirect injurious as well as economic effects. Direct injury and death from corporate crime are immense in comparison to crime rates of murder and manslaughter. Sociologist John L. McMullan reports that before the mid-1980s in Canada, the corporate death rate was more than six times greater than the street crime rate of murder and manslaughter (1992:24). A notable example of lethal corporate crime is Nova Scotia's Westray mine, whose failure to follow good safety procedures resulted in the death of 26 workers in 1992. The top executives were not prosecuted for this disaster. More recently, the train explosion in Lac-Mégantic that killed 47 people in 2013 also appears to be a corporate crime. It is very difficult to determine what constitutes corporate crime. The banking recession that began in 2008 had an enormous impact on the financial fortunes of many people and institutions. Because Canadian banks were not as cavalier about mortgages as American banks were, they did not need financial support, and no fines have been levied against Canadian banks. In the United States as of August 2014, three banks have agreed to pay fines for mortgage-related misconduct: Citigroup Inc. agreed to pay $7 billion; J.P. Morgan Chase & Co. agreed to pay $13 billion; and Bank of America Corp. agreed to pay $17 billion to the government.

Organized Crime

Organized crime **is a business operation that supplies illegal goods and services for profit.** These illegal enterprises include drug trafficking, prostitution, gambling, loan sharking, money laundering,

Social Problems in Global Perspective

Box 9.1

Organized Crime: The Global Empire

According to Havocscope (2015a), a website and information centre that focuses on black market activities around the world, the monetary value of global black market products was US$1.81 trillion in 2015, or about the size of the Canadian economy (see Chapter 13). Havocscope is recognized by agencies like the World Economic Forum and publications like *Bloomberg News*, *National Geographic*, and *The Atlantic Monthly*. This sum came from the production and sale of marijuana, cocaine, opium/heroin, counterfeit technological products, counterfeit pharmaceutical drugs, cigarettes, and counterfeit software; Web video piracy; and human trafficking. Canada ranked seventh, after the United States, China, Spain, Italy, Japan, and Mexico, in a long list of countries involved with the black market, gaining an estimated US$77.83 billion, primarily from the growth, smuggling, and sale of marijuana in British Columbia. According to Misha Glenny, a former BBC reporter who has toured the world investigating global crime and coined the term "McMafia" to describe the global organization of crime and the franchising nature of many criminal organizations, British Columbia's criminal marijuana enterprise generated over $4 billion in 2012 (Diplock et al. 2013:6), about 5 percent of the BC GDP. The industry employs around 100 000 full- and part-time workers in the growing, distributing, smuggling (to the United States), and sale of marijuana—thousands more than the 55 000 working in forestry, mining, oil, and gas combined (Glenny 2008:214).

According to Glenny, much of the increase in global crime is due to failed states and the large numbers of unemployed youth and security workers, and the general chaos that results. In addition, globalization and deregulation of trade have made it easier to move (or launder) money in off-shore banking systems. The collapse of the Soviet Union is "the single most important event promoting the exponential growth of organized crime around the world in the last two decades" (Glenny 2008:52). Glenny found that chaos in other areas led to organized crime, such as the Balkans and in India, where the collapse of the textile industry rendered 1.5 million textile workers jobless, causing great hardship to families (Glenny 2008:129). Canada had a similar experience when, contrary to the NAFTA Agreement, the United States imposed a tariff on the export of softwood lumber sales. The Canadian government estimated that 7000 jobs were lost directly in the softwood industry, and another 7000 were lost indirectly in the community. This event produced a ready labour force to produce and sell marijuana. "Most of those who once worked in the traditional industries have moved into marijuana" (Glenny 2008:215).

This is not the only organized crime in Canada. When researching a novel, John McFetridge found that over 900 gangs are located in Canada. These gangs conduct a wide variety of criminal activities, including high-tech crime (software piracy), meth labs, manufacturing and importing of counterfeit goods, and human trafficking (McFetridge 2008:71). While one might expect Canadians to be involved in high-tech crime and meth labs, one might not think that people would resort to human trafficking in Canada. However, human trafficking does not occur only in Europe, the Middle East, and the Far East. "An estimated 600 to 800 people a year are brought into Canada illegally with the promise of better life, and then pushed into prostitution, domestic servitude and forced labour" (*Metro* 2006:1). Many speakers at a sex crimes conference in 2006 reported that Canada is being presented to victims as a land of opportunity. While some people are able to escape from their enslavers, it is known that fear and distrust of police make prosecuting these cases difficult, and it is often difficult to distinguish between victims and illegal migrants. To help eliminate human trafficking, Canada has a policy of allowing victims of human trafficking to "stay in Canada up to 120 days to help them decide if they wish to assist in the investigation or return home" (*Metro* 2006:1) (see also Chapter 7).

Globally, according to Havocscope, thousands of gangs with hundreds of thousands of people are involved with organized crime (2015b). For example, 3600 gangs operate across Europe, 100 gangs operate in Latin America, 300 000 people are involved in Russian gangs worldwide, and 80 000 people are involved in the Japanese Yakuza.

Questions for Consideration

1. What can Canada do about global organized crime?
2. Can any one nation or organization—such as the United Nations—reduce international human and drug trafficking?
3. Drug trafficking accounts for a large proportion of the work of organized crime. Should we make the use of some drugs, like marijuana, legal to reduce the level of crime, and will crime be reduced if we do?

controlling labour markets, controlling building con-tracts, and large-scale theft such as truck hijacking. No single entity controls the entire range of corrupt and illegal enterprises. Instead, there are many groups—syndicated crime networks, including biker gangs—that can thrive because there is great demand for illegal goods and services. Syndicated crime networks operate at all levels of society, and even globally (see Box 9.1). Criminologist Margaret Beare (1996) suggests that groups vary according to their dependence on orga-nized crime. Whereas some groups are organized to carry out organized-crime activities (e.g., Russian and Nigerian groups and Colombian cartels), other groups have different goals and use organized-crime activities to support them (e.g., terrorist groups and motorcycle gangs). Sometimes these groups form alliances with businesspeople, law enforcement officials, and politi-cians. The RCMP website explains some ways of how organized crime affects Canadians:

- It can be an extra tax burden to pay for treatment of addicts and victims of trafficking;
- It can add to property tax by requiring extra policing, etc.;
- It can add to insurance bills for auto theft and break-and-enter crimes; and
- It can add to banking and credit card fees to compensate for fraud.

It is estimated that organized crime costs Canadians $5 billion/year or $600/year for a family of four (RCMP 2014).

Youth Crime

Youth crime **involves a violation of law or the com-mission of a status offence by a young person 12 to 17 years of age.** Many behaviours identified as youth crime or juvenile delinquency are not criminal acts per se but *status offences*—acts that are illegal because of the age of the offender—such as cutting school, buy-ing and consuming alcoholic beverages, or running away from home. But measuring youth crime is diffi-cult because youth who come into contact with the law can be charged or cleared by a variety of other means, such as a warning or an extrajudicial sanctions program, or the complainant's decision not to lay a charge. The *Youth Criminal Justice Act* (YCJA) of 2003 recognizes that effective responses to youth crime may be outside the courts. Figure 9.2 shows that overall, youth crime and severe youth crime have been in decline over the past decade, with declines in property crime and increases in "other" (e.g., drug offences) and violent crime (Statistics Canada 2013x). Figure 9.3 shows an increase in the clearance rate since the introduction of the Act, resulting in a steady decline in charging youth. The YCJA appears to be effective in diverting youth from courts.

Generally, police-reported rates of offending tend to be higher among youth and young adults. Rates tend to increase incrementally among those aged 12 to 17 years, peak among those aged 18, and then decrease with increasing age. Youth crime, like adult crime, has decreased greatly since the early 1990s.

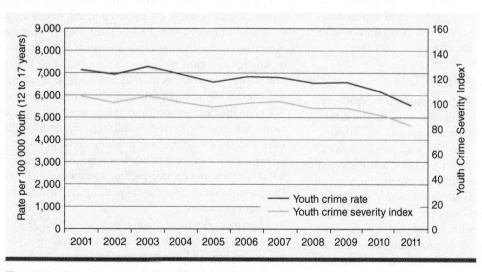

Figure 9.2   Rates of Youth Crime in Canada, 2001–2011.

Source: *Statistics Canada, 2013,* Youth Crime 2011. *Retrieved June 18, 2013 (http://www.statcan.gc.ca/pub/85-005-x/2012001/ article/11749-eng.htm).*

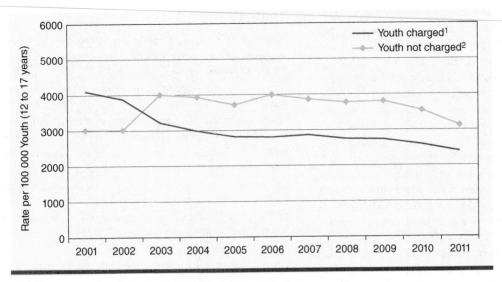

Figure 9.3　Youths Charged by Clearance Status in Canada, 2001–2011.

1. Refers to youths (12 to 17 years) who were formally charged by police (or recommended for charging).

2. Refers to youths (12 to 17 years) who were cleared by other means (e.g. alternative measures).

Source: *Statistics Canada, 2013*, Youth Crime, 2011. *Retrieved June18, 2013 (http://www.statcan.gc.ca/pub/85-005-x/2012001/ article/11749-eng.htm).*

SOCIOLOGICAL EXPLANATIONS OF CRIME

As with other social problems, crime and delinquency have been explained in biological, psychological, and sociological terms. Most biological and psychological explanations assume that criminal behaviour is an inherent trait, with genetic, biological, or psychological roots. Unlike biological and psychological explanations that focus on individual behaviour, sociological explanations focus on those aspects of society that may contribute to delinquent or criminal behaviour.

The Functionalist Perspective

Although there are numerous functionalist perspectives on crime and delinquency, we will focus on two: strain theory and control theory, as illustrated in social bond theory.

Functionalist explanations for why people commit crimes can be traced to Émile Durkheim, who believed that the macrolevel structure of a society produces social pressures that result in high rates of deviance and crime. Durkheim introduced the concept of *anomie* to describe a social condition that engenders feelings of futility in people because of weak, absent, or conflicting social norms. According to Durkheim (1895/1964), deviance and crime are most likely to occur when anomie is present in a society. On the basis of Durkheim's theory, sociologist Robert Merton (1938; 1968) developed strain theory to explain why some people conform to group norms while others do not. **Strain theory states that people feel strain when they are exposed to cultural goals that they cannot reach because they do not have access to a culturally approved means of achieving those goals.** When some people are denied legitimate access to cultural goals such as success, money, or other material possessions, they seek to acquire these things through deviant—and sometimes criminal—means. This lack of legitimate access is typical of many of Canada's inmates. According to Robinson and colleagues (1999:57), the one-day snapshot of inmates shows that criminals are much more likely to be unemployed than the general population are (52 percent versus 7 percent). A more recent study of crime patterns over a 40-year period (from 1962 to 2003) found that economic factors were associated with some kinds of crime. For example, periods of inflation, like in the 1970s, were associated with robbery, breaking and entering, and motor vehicle theft, and unemployment is associated with homicide (Statistics Canada 2005g). The recession of 2008 will also provide an opportunity to examine the influence of economic factors.

Merton identified five ways in which people respond to cultural goals: conformity, innovation, ritualism, retreatism, and rebellion (see Table 9.4).

- *Conformity* occurs when people accept the culturally approved goals and pursue them through the approved means. People who choose conformity work hard and

TABLE 9.4　Merton's Strain Theory

Mode of Adaptation	Method of Adaptation	Agrees with Cultural Goal	Follows Institutional Means
Conformity	Accepts culturally approved goals; pursues them through culturally approved means	Yes	Yes
Innovation	Accepts culturally approved goals; adopts disapproved means of achieving them	Yes	No
Ritualism	Abandons society's goals but continues to conform to approved means	No	Yes
Retreatism	Abandons both approved goals and the approved means to achieve them	No	No
Rebellion	Challenges both the approved goals and the approved means to achieve them	No—seeks to replace	No—seeks to replace

Source: *Adapted from Robert King Merton, 1968*, Social Theory and Social Structure, *New York: Free Press.*

save their money to achieve success. Someone who is blocked from achieving a high level of education or a lucrative career typically conforms by taking a lower-paying job and attending school part-time, joining the military, or trying alternative (but legal) avenues, such as playing the lottery.

- *Innovation* occurs when people accept society's goals but use illegitimate means to achieve them. Innovations for acquiring material possessions include shoplifting, theft, burglary, cheating on income taxes, embezzling money, and other kinds of occupational crime.

- *Ritualism* occurs when people give up on societal goals but still adhere to socially approved means for achieving them. People who cannot obtain expensive material possessions or wealth seek to maintain the respect of others by being "hard workers" or "good citizens" to an extreme degree.

- *Retreatism* occurs when people abandon both the approved goals and the approved means of achieving them. Retreatists include hard-core drug addicts and some middle- or upper-income people who reject conventional trappings of success and the means to acquire them, choosing to "drop out" instead.

- *Rebellion* occurs when people reject both the approved goals and the approved means for achieving them and advocate an alternative set of goals and means. Rebels may use violence (such as vandalism or rioting) or non-violent tactics (such as civil disobedience) to change society and its cultural beliefs. Or they may withdraw from mainstream society, like the Amish, to live their own lives.

Another functionalist perspective—*control theory*—seeks to answer the question, "Why do people *not* engage in deviant behaviour?" According to control theory, people are constantly pulled and pushed toward deviant behaviour. Environmental factors (pulls), such as adverse living conditions, poverty, and lack of educational opportunity, draw people toward criminal behaviour, while at the same time, internal pressures (pushes), such as feelings of hostility or aggressiveness, make people not want to act according to dominant values and norms (Reckless 1967). If this is true, why doesn't everyone who is poor or has a limited education commit crimes? According to control theorists, people who do not turn to crime or delinquent behaviour have *outer containments*—supportive family and friends, reasonable social expectations, and supervision by others—or *inner containments*—self-control, a sense of responsibility, and resistance to diversions. This lack of outer and inner containments is found among Canada's inmates. According to Robinson and his colleagues, inmates are much more likely to be unmarried than the general adult population is (31 percent versus 63 percent; 1999:57) and have high levels of crime-causing needs, such as personal and emotional problems, substance abuse, and problems functioning in the community (1999:66).

The best-known control theory is **social bond theory—the proposition that criminal behaviour is most**

likely to occur when a person's ties to society are weakened or broken. According to criminologist Travis Hirschi (1969), who proposed this theory, social bonding consists of (1) *attachment* to other people, (2) *commitment* to conformity, (3) *involvement* in conventional activities, and (4) *belief* in the legitimacy of conventional values and norms. When a person's social bonds are weak and when peers promote antisocial values and violent behaviour, the probability of delinquency and crime increases (Massey and Krohn 1986).

When analyzing violent crime, some functionalists believe that a sense of anomie is the root cause. Others believe that violence increases when social institutions such as the family, schools, and religious organizations weaken and the primary mechanisms of social control in people's everyday lives become external—law enforcement and the criminal justice system. Others accept the *subculture of violence hypothesis*, that **violence is part of the normative expectations governing everyday behaviour among young males in the lower classes** (Wolfgang and Ferracuti 1967). These violent subcultures are most likely to develop when young people, particularly males, have few legitimate opportunities available in their segment of society and when subcultural values accept and encourage violent behaviour.

Another functionalist perspective on violence, discussed in Chapter 1, is the *lifestyle–routine activity approach*, which holds that the patterns and timing of people's daily movements and activities as they go about obtaining the necessities of life—such as food, shelter, companionship, and entertainment—are the keys to understanding violent personal crimes and other types of crime in our society (Cohen and Felson 1979). In other words, changes in social institutions, such as more families in which both parents (or the sole parent) work outside the home or the extension of shopping hours into the night, put some people at greater risk than others of being victims of violent crime (Parker 1995).

Functionalist explanations contribute to our understanding of crime by emphasizing that individuals who engage in such behaviour are not biologically or psychologically impaired but are responding to social and economic conditions in society. However, functionalists are not without their critics. Strain theory may point out that people from low-income and poverty-level backgrounds are prevented from achieving success goals through legitimate channels, but it is still criticized for focusing almost exclusively on crimes committed by the lower classes and ignoring crimes committed by people in the middle and upper classes. Critics of social bond theory say that it is limited in its ability to explain more serious forms of delinquency and crime (Krohn 1995).

The Conflict Perspective

Conflict theorists explain criminal behaviour in terms of power differentials and/or economic inequality in society. One approach focuses on how authority and power relations can contribute to some people—but not others—becoming criminals. According to sociologist Austin Turk (1966, 1971), crime is not a *behaviour* but a *status* that is acquired when people with the authority to create and enforce legal rules apply those rules to others.

A second conflict approach focuses on the relationship between economic inequality and crime. Having roots in the work of Karl Marx, the *radical critical-conflict approach* argues that social institutions (such as law, politics, and education) create a superstructure that legitimizes the class structure and maintains capitalists' superior position. In fact, say these theorists, the crimes people commit are based on their class position. Thus, crimes committed by low-income people typically involve taking things by force or physical stealth, while white-collar crime usually involves non-physical means, such as paper transactions or computer fraud. Some critical theorists believe that affluent people commit crimes because they are greedy and continually want more than they have, whereas poor people commit street crimes such as robbery and theft to survive (Bonger 1916/1969).

In sum, the conflict approach is useful for pointing out how inequalities of power, class, and racialization can contribute to criminal or delinquent behaviour. Nevertheless, critics say that conflict theorists have not shown that powerful political and economic elites manipulate law making and enforcement for their own benefit. Rather, say these critics, people of all classes share a consensus that acts such as homicide, sexual assault, and armed robbery are bad (Klockars 1979).

The Interactionist Perspective

Interactionists emphasize that criminal behaviour is learned through everyday interaction with others. We will examine two major interactionist theories: differential association theory and labelling theory. *Differential association theory* states that **individuals have a greater tendency to deviate from societal norms when they frequently associate with people who tend toward deviance rather than conformity.** According to sociologist Edwin Sutherland (1939), who formulated this theory, people learn not only the techniques of deviant behaviour from people with whom they associate but also the motives, drives, rationalizations, and attitudes. Former gang member

Nathan McCall (1994:93–94) describes such a learning process in his own life:

> Sometimes I picked up hustling ideas at the 7-Eleven, which was like a criminal union hall: Crapshooters, shoplifters, stickup men, burglars, everybody stopped off at the store from time to time. While hanging up there one day, I ran into Holt. . . . He had a pocketful of cash, even though he had quit school and was unemployed. I asked him, "Yo, man, what you been into?" "Me and my partner kick in cribs and make a killin'. You oughta come go with us sometimes. . . ." I hooked school one day, went with them, and pulled my first B&E [breaking and entering]. . . . After I learned the ropes, Shell Shock [another gang member] and I branched out, doing B and Es on our own. We learned to get in and out of houses in no time flat.

As McCall's description indicates, criminal activity often occurs within the context of frequent, intense, and long-lasting interactions with people who violate the law. When more factors favour violating the law than not, a person is likely to become a criminal. Although differential association theory contributes to our knowledge of how deviant behaviour reflects the individual's learned techniques, values, attitudes, motives, and rationalizations, critics note that many individuals who are regularly exposed to people who break the law still conform most of the time. Many critics think that the theory does not adequately take into account possible connections between social inequality and criminal behaviour.

Labelling theory, which was mentioned briefly in Chapter 1, takes quite a different approach from differential association theory. According to **labelling theory, delinquents and criminals are people who have been successfully labelled as such by others.** No behaviour is inherently delinquent or criminal; it is defined as such by a social audience (Erikson 1962). According to sociologist Howard Becker (1963), labelling is often done by *moral entrepreneurs*—people who use their own views of right and wrong to establish rules and label others "deviant." Furthermore, the process of labelling is directly related to the power and status of the people who do the labelling and those who are being labelled. In support of this theory, one study of juvenile offenders has found that youths from lower-income families were more likely to be arrested and indicted than were middle-class juveniles who did the same things (Sampson 1986). Sociologists have also noted that the criminal justice system generally considers such factors as the offender's family life, educational achievement (or lack thereof), and social class in determining how to deal with juvenile offenders. According to one study,

the individuals who are most likely to be apprehended, labelled delinquent, and prosecuted are people of colour who are young, male, unemployed, and undereducated and who live in urban high-crime areas (Vito and Holmes 1994).

Sociologist Edwin Lemert (1951) expanded labelling theory by distinguishing between primary and secondary deviance. **Primary deviance is the initial act of rule-breaking in which the individual does not internalize the delinquent or criminal self-concept.** **Secondary deviance occurs when a person who has been labelled a deviant accepts that new identity and continues the deviant behaviour.** The concept of secondary deviance is important to labelling theory because it suggests that when people accept a negative label or stigma that has been applied to them, the label may actually contribute to the behaviour it was meant to control. In other words, secondary deviance occurs if a person is labelled a juvenile delinquent, accepts that label, and then continues to engage in delinquent behaviour. Labelling theory is useful for making us aware of how social control and personal identity are intertwined. Critics, however, do not think that labelling theory explains what causes the original acts that constitute primary deviance, nor do they think that it adequately explains why some people accept deviant labels and others do not (Cavender 1995).

In 1843, Daniel M'Naughton was acquitted by reason of insanity of attempting to kill the British prime minister and shooting an official. This was the beginning of the plea of not guilty by reason of insanity, but it did not provide any clear definition or measure of irrational behaviour. Since that time, a wide variety of defences involving a loss of self-control by the accused due to medical problems have been advocated by defence attorneys. The process has been called the **medicalization of crime, the converting of criminal behaviour to a medical condition or disease.** It is parallel to the medicalization of deviance—the converting of deviance, such as alcoholism, to a medical condition. Given the current and likely future development of our understanding about the influence of biological factors on serious violent crime, questions about the definition of personal responsibility versus medical conditions for irrational behaviour will be central to many future criminal proceedings.

Feminist Perspectives

Feminist scholarship focuses on why women commit crimes or engage in delinquent behaviour. We have already noted the differences in victimization rates for men and women. Criminologist Elizabeth Cormack (1999) reminds us that studies of offenders in prison often find that the women have experienced physical and/or sexual abuse. Scholars who use a *liberal feminist* framework believe that women's delinquency or crime is a rational response to gender discrimination in society. They attribute crimes such as prostitution and shoplifting to women's lack of educational and job opportunities and to stereotypical expectations about roles women should have in society (Daly and Chesney-Lind 1988). Scholars who espouse *radical feminism* believe that patriarchy contributes to crimes such as prostitution because, according to society's sexual double standard, it is acceptable for a man to pay for sex but unacceptable for a woman to accept money for such services. A third school of feminist thought, *socialist feminism,* believes that women are exploited by capitalism and patriarchy. Because most females have relatively low-wage jobs and few economic resources, crimes such as prostitution and shoplifting become a means of earning money and acquiring consumer products. Feminist scholars of colour, and other feminist scholars who wish to broaden the perspective of criminology beyond the patriarchy, suggest that consideration be given to "the complex and diverse ways in which patriarchal (along with class and racialization) privilege and power invade people's subjectivities and experiences" (Cormack 1999:166).

THE CRIMINAL JUSTICE SYSTEM

The *criminal justice system* **is the network of organizations, including the police, courts, criminal prosecutions, and corrections, involved in law enforcement and the administration of justice** (CCJS 1999:4). Originally, the criminal justice system was created to help solve the problem of social disorder and crime. Today, however, some social analysts wonder whether the criminal justice system is part of the problem. Most cite two reasons for concern: (1) the criminal justice system fails in its mission to prevent, control, or rehabilitate offenders; and (2) unequal justice occurs because officials discriminate against people on the basis of racialization, class, gender, age, sexual orientation, or other devalued characteristics.

The Police

The police are the most visible link in the criminal justice system because they determine how to apply the law to control crime and maintain order. Four factors seem to influence the occurrence of an arrest:

1. the nature of the alleged offence or problem;
2. the quality of available evidence;
3. the age, racialization, and gender of the alleged offender; and
4. the level of deference shown to police officers (Mastrofski 1995).

Given these factors, law enforcement officials have fairly wide *discretion*—use of personal judgment regarding whether and how to proceed in a given situation—in deciding who will be stopped and searched and which homes and businesses will be entered and for what purposes (Donziger 1996). Sociologist Jerome Skolnick (1975) argues that because police officers must often make these decisions in a dangerous environment, they develop a sense of suspicion, social isolation, and solidarity.

Some police departments have begun *community policing* as a way of reducing crime. Community policing involves integrating officers into the communities they serve—getting them out of their patrol cars and into a proactive role, recognizing problems and working with neighbourhood citizens to find solutions. It is difficult to inquire into the effectiveness of community policing because there are so many variations in how it is practised and crime rates have been going done overall. In Toronto, outgoing (in 2015) Police Chief Bill Blair increased the amount of community policing. The crime rates in Toronto are lower, but it is difficult to show community policing's influence when overall crime rates are lower. More community policing has also brought about more carding of people by the police, and that is considered discriminatory (see Box 9.2). In one study in a U.S. suburb, officers were interviewed and crime data were collected over eight years for the test area of community policing and two comparable police beats. The researchers found a significant reduction in violent and property crimes in the test area, but not in the other areas in the county (Connell et al. 2008).

The Courts

Criminal courts are responsible for determining the guilt or innocence of people who have been accused of committing a crime. In theory, justice is determined in an adversarial process: a prosecutor (a Crown attorney who represents the state) argues that the accused is guilty, and a defence attorney argues that the accused is innocent. In reality, judges have a great deal of discretion. Working with prosecutors, they decide who will be released, who will be held for further hearings, and—in many instances—what sentences will be imposed on people who are convicted.

Because courts have the capacity to try only a small fraction of criminal cases, an attrition process occurs.

Social Problems and Social Policy

Box 9.2

Racial Profiling and What to Do About It

In the past, Toronto police could stop someone and "card" them when they were investigating a crime, saw suspicious acts, etc. (The police service has a website about what to expect when stopped. The process, called carding, consists of obtaining a name, address, height and weight, and skin colour (white, black, brown, and other), along with other information. Toronto police also carded associates with the person. The police believe that this information could be helpful when a crime victim is already carded, and associates might help with the investigation. A very large number of cards (350 000+/year) are collected, but they have never been analyzed to determine the influence of demographic factors. It was considered discriminatory to do so. Jim Rankin, a *Star* reporter, analyzed the cards in 2012 and discovered that Blacks were over three times more likely to be carded than White people were, and Browns were one and a half times more likely to be carded than White people were.

While Blacks constituted about 8 percent of the population, they constituted 25 percent of the people carded. The number of Black and Brown males aged 15 to 24 years who have been documented since 2008 outnumbered the actual Black and Brown men who live in the city, since some have been carded more than once. Civil rights advocates like Toronto Police Accountability Coalition and Black is Not a Crime have spoken out against this practice at police board meetings. Some wonder if it is a Human Rights Code violation.

The police board passed several resolutions in April 2013, including:

- that police must give a copy of the document card—with the reason for the stop—to the individual;
- Police Chief Bill Blair must report carding statistics to the board every three months; and
- the Chief must monitor and address discriminatory practices.

According to a report in the *Toronto Star*, Chief of Police Bill Blair said there is never a justification for racial profiling. "The chief also said he didn't dispute the *Star's* analysis of the police carding data" (Winsa 2013).

In November 2013, the chair of Toronto's police board, Alok Mukherjee, released a report with 18 recommendations. Some of these included removing those cards not collected for a legitimate reason, collecting only details that are relevant to the stopping, and stopping using card counts for advancement in the service (Star 2013:A1 and 22). In April 2014, the board approved new policies that police should inform those stopped that they are free to leave if not arrested or detained, and the practice of carding can no longer be used to meet performance quotas or raise an awareness of the police presence in the community.

Interestingly, carding is supported by some members of the Black community as a crime fighting tool in high-crime areas, and the belief that carding could expose systemic biases in particular police officers' treatment of minorities.

A follow-up survey reported by the *Star* in the fall of 2014 indicated that the recommended practices are not being followed in the Jane-Finch area. This area is in the north-west of Toronto and is known for higher crime rates than neighbouring areas. Over 50 percent of those who were carded since June 2014 were not told a reason for their being stopped, and 86 percent did not get a receipt with the officer's name and badge number. Carding fell by 75 percent because the police greatly reduced their carding (Winsa 2014:A1 and A11). On January 1, 2015, Chief Blair suspended carding (but not stopping and interrogating) young people. In 2015, Chief Blair's contract was not renewed. His successor, Mark Saunders, who happens to be Black, supports carding. In early June, a panel consisting of two former mayors and a former Ontario chief justice joined others in calling for an end to carding. Mayor John Tory, who had previously supported carding, also called to end it. In mid-June, the Ontario government said that it will bring in regulations to govern carding in Ontario in the fall of 2015. These regulations will be open to challenges under the Charter of Rights. Since carding takes place in other jurisdictions across the country, these regulations could have a widespread influence. So we must wait until later in 2015 to see what kind of accountability will take place. If challenges take place, then the issue will not be resolved for some time afterward.

A video about this topic, including interviews with members of the Black community and Police Chief Bill Blair, is available.

Questions for Consideration

1. What kind of data do you think that police should be able to obtain from people they stop?
2. What kinds of accountability measures should be in place to protect the privacy of people stopped?
3. Are giving copies of cards to those stopped and regular reporting enough to prevent profiling from occurring?

This process begins with the police, who clear about a third of all offences reported to them. The police clear a fifth of all reports with a charge. About 15 percent of the total reports result in conviction, and 4 percent of reports result in a sentence to custody (CCJS 1999:xiii). This attrition process has been called a "crime funnel" (Silverman et al. 1996, cited in Sacco and Kennedy 1998:205). Many cases are resolved by *plea bargaining*— **a process whereby the Crown attorney negotiates with a defence attorney for a guilty plea for a less serious crime.** In other words, defendants (especially those who are poor and cannot afford to pay for an attorney) plead guilty to a lesser crime in return for not being tried for the more serious crime for which they were arrested. As cases are sifted and sorted through the legal machinery, steady attrition occurs. At each stage, various officials determine what alternatives will be available for the cases that remain in the system (Hills 1971).

Sometimes plea bargaining occurs to get a conviction in a high-profile case when no other avenue seems available. A notorious example was the case of the sentencing of Karla Homolka to 12 years in prison in return for her testimony and evidence (tapes, missed in the search by police, recording the homicides of two girls) to convict Paul Bernardo of the girls' homicides.

In 2010–2011, following three consecutive annual increases, the number of adult criminal court cases remained relatively stable. Canadian adult criminal courts completed almost 403 000 cases in 2010–2011 involving nearly 1.2 million *Criminal Code* and other federal statute offences, such as drug-related offences. In 2010–2011, a guilty finding was reached in about two-thirds (64 percent) of cases, a proportion that has remained relatively consistent over the past decade. Another 32 percent of cases were stayed, withdrawn, dismissed, or discharged at preliminary inquiry, and 3 percent were acquitted (Dauvergne 2013).

Punishment and the Prisons

Punishment **is any action designed to deprive a person of things of value (including liberty) because of an offence the person is thought to have committed** (Barlow 1996). Punishment is seen as serving four functions:

1. *Retribution* imposes a penalty on the offender. Retribution is based on the premise that the punishment should fit the crime.
2. *Social protection* results from restricting offenders so that they cannot continue to commit crimes.
3. *Rehabilitation* seeks to return offenders to the community as law-abiding citizens. Often, the job skills (such as agricultural work) that are taught in prison do not transfer to the outside world, and offenders are not given help in finding work that fits the skills they might have obtained once they are released.
4. *Deterrence* seeks to reduce criminal activity by instilling a fear of punishment. Criminologists debate, though, whether imprisonment has a deterrent effect, given that 30 to 50 percent of those who are released from prison commit further crimes.

Table 9.5 shows the 2010–2011 counts of adults under correctional supervision. Although some believe the Canadian justice system is punitive, less than one-third of the adults are in custody.

Despite the few people sentenced to custody, certain problems remain. For example, there is an overrepresentation of Indigenous people in prison. Whereas Indigenous people constitute 3 percent of the adult population, they make up 18.73 percent of the federal prison population, according to a report from Statistics Canada (2009f). Incarcerating Indigenous people for crimes such as drunkenness and vagrancy, crimes for which Whites are less likely to be incarcerated, has been a longstanding feature of our justice system.

Restorative Justice

In Canada, Europe, Australia, and New Zealand, the concept of restorative justice comprises diverse practices, including conferencing, sentencing circles, and victim–offender mediation. *Restorative justice* **focusses on repairing the harm caused by crime by holding moderated meetings of crime victims, offenders, and others affected by crime, which can be used at different sites in the justice system, for example, as a diversion from court, a pre-sentencing option, and after the release from prison.**

Current applications of the idea began to emerge in the 1970s in North America, beginning with a victim–offender reconciliation program in Ontario in 1974. Another example is the response of the parents of Reena Virk, killed in 1997, and one convicted killer, Warren Glowatski. In fall 2005 in a church in Mission, BC, and in the summer of 2006, they hugged each other during an Indigenous healing circle that was part of Glowatski's parole hearing (Mason 2006:A3). The Virks hugged him, they said, to release some of the anger that had built up inside them and to help him to not "carry a heavy heart around with him for the rest of his life" (Mason 2006:A3).

But the recommendations of sentencing circles are not always followed. Another example began in January, 2007, when Christopher Pauchay, an Indigenous person, drank heavily after arguing with his wife. Later, he began to worry about one of his daughters. Pauchay took his two girls out in the cold winter air to get help, dressed

TABLE 9.5   Average Counts of Adults under Correctional Supervision, Canada

	2010/2011 number	rate[1]	Percent change in rate 2009/2010 to 2010/2011
Total correctional supervision[2,3]	**163 229**	**615.9**	**−0.9**
Custody			
Federal custody	13 758	50.6	2.6
Provincial and territorial custody	24 461	89.9	−0.1
Sentenced custody	10 916	40.1	7.1
Remand	13 086	48.1	−6.2
Other	458	1.7	31.9
Total custody	**38 219**	**140.5**	**0.9**
Community supervision			
Probation[2,3]	103 955	393.2	−0.9
Conditional sentences[2,3]	13 211	50.0	−4.2
Full parole	3652	13.4	−3.3
Statutory release	2389	8.8	−4.9
Day parole	1143	4.2	−1.1
Provincial parole[4]	659	3.9	−8.1
Total community supervision[2,3]	**125 010**	**472.9**	**−1.5**

1. Rates are calculated per 100 000 adult population (18 years and over).
2. Data for 2010/2011 excludes community supervision counts in Nova Scotia.
3. The percent change in rates from 2009/2010 to 2010/2011 exclude Newfoundland and Labrador and Nova Scotia.
4. The 2010/2011 figures as well as the percent change in rate reflect data from Quebec and Ontario, the only provinces that currently operate provincial parole boards.

Source: *Statistics Canada, 2012h,* Adult Correctional Services, *The Daily. Retrieved July 1, 2013* (http://www.statcan.gc.ca/daily-quotidien/121011/t121011c001-eng.htm).

only in their T-shirts. Both girls were found dead in the following days. Pauchay pleaded guilty to criminal negligence causing death and requested that a sentencing circle be convened. The sentencing circle said that he should not be jailed, but be entrusted to the guidance of the community where he committed his crimes. The community recommended that he be sentenced to service in the community. Though the judge was not obliged to follow the community's recommendation, he took it into account (Libin 2009). The judge did not agree with the recommendation and sentenced Pauchay to prison for three years because of the seriousness of the crime.

A recent prominent case of restorative justice concerned the dozen male dentistry students from Dalhousie University and the six female students they profiled in a sexist way in Facebook in 2015. Although many people criticized this process, these students and others from the DDS2015 class went ahead with it and produced a very thoughtful report. First, the men who wrote the misogynistic notes accepted full responsibility and expressed great remorse. They offered apologies, which were accepted. They felt the process helped them to appreciate what they did and hoped that they could become better professionals. Second, the women named in the Facebook notes chose to enter this process despite great criticism from others. They believed that they could engage with safety and respect. They also believed that it allowed them to address systemic factors influencing the climate and culture of the school. They hoped that this would contribute to effecting important change in the climate and culture. Third, all those who participated thought restorative justice was worthwhile and wanted privacy from the publicity that sometimes became harmful even to families and friends. They hoped that this process would contribute to the ongoing discussion about sexism, misogyny, inclusion, and professionalism.

Is the solution to our "crime problem" to build more prisons? Only about 20 percent of all crimes result in a charge, only half of these lead to a conviction, and fewer than 4 percent of convictions result in a jail term. The "lock 'em up and throw away the key" approach has little chance of succeeding. As for individuals who commit occupational and corporate crime, the percentage that enters the criminal justice system is so minimal that prison is relatively useless as a deterrent to others. Furthermore, the high rate of recidivism strongly suggests that the rehabilitative efforts of our existing correctional facilities are sadly lacking. One thing is clear: the existing criminal justice system cannot solve the crime problem.

Is equal justice under the law possible? As long as social problems exist in our society, equal justice under the law may not be possible for all people; however, that does not keep it from being a goal that citizens and the criminal justice system should strive to reach.

WHAT CAN YOU DO?

- Seek out a community/police liaison committee in your neighbourhood and learn about local problems and what people are trying to do about them.

- Seek out an advocacy group and participate in one of its activities. For example, in Ontario, an organization called Justice for Children and Youth challenged the Ontario law banning squeegee kids' solicitations and various kinds of begging (e.g., while intoxicated). This organization seeks participation on its Youth Advisory Committee to help it deal with the problems of young people. It is located in Toronto.

- Organize seminars to discuss or debate ideas like the publication of racialized/ethnicity data for crime or the value of restorative justice.

- Work with campus groups to alert female students to the problem of date rape.

SUMMARY

■ **Why Is It Difficult to Study Crime and Youth Crime?**
Studying crime, criminals, and youth crime is difficult because it involves complex human behaviour, and many criminals and victims hide their involvement. There also are problems inherent in using official sources of data, such as the *Uniform Crime Report,* because they reflect crimes that are reported rather than crimes that are committed, and they do not provide detailed information about offenders.

■ **How Does Violent Crime Differ from Property Crime?**
Violent crime consists of actions involving force or the threat of force against others and includes homicide, sexual assault, robbery, and aggravated assault. Property crime consists of taking money or property from another without force, the threat of force, or the destruction of property.

■ **Why Is Sexual Assault as a Violent Crime Not Well Understood? How Is This Lack of Understanding Reflected in Our Social Response to Sexual Assault?**
First, many people think that sexual assault is a sexually motivated crime, but it is actually an act of violence in which sex is used as a weapon against a powerless victim. Moreover, statistics on sexual assault are misleading at best because sexual assault is often not reported. Many reasons keep victims from coming forward. Some victims may be so traumatized that they just want to forget about it. Others fear the attacker will try to get even. Many also fear how they may be treated by the police and, in the event of a trial, by Crown attorneys.

■ **What Is Occupational Crime?**
Occupational (white-collar) crime refers to illegal activities committed by people in the course of their employment or normal business activity. Occupational crime includes crimes such as employee theft, fraud (obtaining money or property under false pretenses), embezzlement (theft from an employer), soliciting bribes or kickbacks, and insider trading of securities.

■ **How Does Occupational Crime Differ from Corporate Crime?**
Occupational crimes are illegal activities committed by people in the course of their employment or normal business activity. Corporate crimes are illegal acts committed by corporate employees on behalf of the corporation and with its support.

■ **What Is Organized Crime and Why Does It Flourish in Canada?**
Organized crime is a business operation that supplies illegal goods and services for profit. These illegal enterprises include drug trafficking, prostitution, gambling, loan sharking, money laundering, and large-scale theft. Organized crime thrives because there is great demand for illegal goods and services.

■ **How Does Youth Crime Differ from Adult Crime?**
Youth crime refers to a violation of law or the commission of a status offence by people who are younger than a specific age. Many behaviours that are identified as juvenile delinquency are not criminal acts per se but status offences—acts that are illegal because of the age of the offender—such as cutting school or purchasing and consuming alcoholic beverages. Juvenile hearings take place in juvenile courts or before juvenile court judges, whereas adult offenders are tried in criminal courts.

Who Is Most Likely to be Arrested for a Crime in Canada?

Men are more likely to be arrested than women. Teenagers and young adults are most likely to be arrested for serious crimes such as homicide, sexual assault, and robbery. Although individuals from all social classes commit crimes, people from lower socioeconomic backgrounds are more likely to be arrested for violent and property crimes, whereas people from the upper classes generally commit white-collar or corporate crimes. Indigenous people and Blacks are overrepresented in arrest data.

How Do Functionalists Explain Crime?

Functionalists use several theories to explain crime. According to strain theory, people are socialized to desire cultural goals, but many people do not have institutionalized means to achieve the goals and therefore engage in criminal activity. Control perspectives, such as social bond theory, suggest that delinquency and crime are most likely to occur when a person's ties to society are weakened or broken.

How Do Conflict Theorists Explain Crime?

Conflict theorists explain criminal behaviour in terms of power differentials and/or economic inequality in society. One approach focuses on the relationship between authority and power and crime; another focuses on the relationship between economic inequality and crime.

How Do Interactionists Explain Crime?

Interactionists emphasize that criminal behaviour is learned through everyday interaction with others. According to differential association theory, individuals have a greater tendency to deviate from societal norms when they frequently associate with people who are more likely to deviate than conform. Labelling theory says that delinquents and criminals are those people who have been successfully labelled by others as such.

How Do Feminist Theorists Explain Crime?

Feminist approaches offer several explanations of why women commit crimes: gender discrimination, patriarchy, a combination of capitalism and patriarchy, and a combination of family structure and socialization.

What Are the Components of the Criminal Justice System?

The criminal justice system is a network of organizations involved in law enforcement, including the police, the courts, and the prisons. The police are the most visible link in the criminal justice system because they are responsible for initially arresting and jailing people. Criminal courts are responsible for determining the guilt or innocence of people who have been accused of committing a crime. Imprisonment, conditional sentences, probation, parole, and restorative justice are mechanisms of punishment based on retribution, social protection, rehabilitation, and deterrence.

KEY TERMS

corporate crime, p. 193
crime, p. 188
criminal justice system, p. 200
date rape, p. 190
differential association
theory, p. 198
homicide, p. 189
indictable offence, p. 188
labelling theory, p. 199
mass murder, p. 189

medicalization of crime, p. 199
occupational (white-collar)
crime, p. 192
organized crime, p. 193
plea bargaining, p. 202
primary deviance, p. 199
property crime, p. 192
punishment, p. 202
restorative justice, p. 202
secondary deviance, p. 199

serial murder, p. 189
sexual assault, p. 190
social bond theory, p. 197
strain theory, p. 196
subculture of violence
hypothesis, p. 198
summary conviction
offences, p. 188
violent crime, p. 188
youth crime, p. 195

QUESTIONS FOR CRITICAL THINKING

1. Do you think that putting surveillance cameras in public places to monitor people and their possible deviant behaviour is a good idea? Why or why not?

2. How would sociologists argue with the claim that crime is committed by disturbed people?

3. Does the functionalist, conflict, or interactionist perspective best explain why people commit corporate crimes? Organized crimes? Explain your answer.

4. How would you reorganize the criminal justice system so that it would deal more equitably with all people in this country and prevent problems like profiling?

CHAPTER 10

Health, Illness, and Health Care as Social Problems

The Terry Fox Run

Rene Johnston/Toronto Star/CP Images

his chapter examines health, illness—including both physical and mental illness—health care problems, and current issues in providing health services in this country. The chapter also draws attention to inequalities regarding disease and disability for people of different sex, gender, class, and racialization or ethnicity; problems such as HIV/AIDS and obesity; mental illness as a social problem; and the crisis faced by the Canadian health care system and recommendations to improve it. The sociological perspectives are used to explain health problems, and the chapter concludes with suggestions for what you can do to improve your health and the health of others.

HEALTH AND ILLNESS AS SOCIAL PROBLEMS

According to the World Health Organization (WHO 1946:3), *health* is a state of complete physical, mental, and social well-being. In other words, health is not only a biological issue, but also a social issue. After all, physical and mental health are intertwined: physical illness can cause emotional problems, and mental illness can produce physical symptoms. Many people think there is a positive relationship between the amount of money a society spends on health care and the overall physical, mental, and social well-being of its people—that spending a great deal of money on health care should result in physical, mental, and social well-being. But if this were true, people in the United States would be the healthiest and most fit in the world, and they are not.

While physical, mental, and social well-being are difficult to measure, *life expectancy*, **an estimate of the average lifetime of people born in a specific year, is relatively easy to measure.** Table 10.1 shows the life expectancies for females and males in Canada. Canadian females born in 2007–09 can expect to live 83.3 years and males can expect to live 78.8 years (Statistics Canada 2012). The Conference Board of Canada in their Report Card on Health indicates that Canadians score highly on this measure, ranking sixth of 17 high-income countries (Conference Board of Canada 2013). If we use this widely accepted measure of the effectiveness of the health care system, we find that the relationship between health expenditure and health of the population is not strong. In 2010, the United States spent the equivalent of $8233 U.S. per person and Canada spent $4445 U.S. per person on health care (see Figure 10.6 later in this chapter) (Canadian Institute for Health Information 2013). Although the health service industry accounts for more than 15 percent of GDP in the United States and 11.6 percent in Canada in 2012, Canadians live on average three years longer than Americans (78 years vs. 81 years respectively).

Besides life expectancy, another widely used measure of the effectiveness of the health care system is the *infant mortality rate*, **the number of deaths of infants under one year of age per 1000 live births in a given year.** During the past century, Canada's infant mortality rate has decreased greatly. Table 10.1

TABLE 10.1   Canadian Health Data

Check-up on Canada's health

Total fertility rate (average number of children per woman) (2011)	**1.61**
Current smokers (2012)	**20.3%**
Infant mortality rate (per 1000 live births) (2009)	**4.9**
Has a doctor (2012)	**85.1%**
Heavy drinkers (2012)	**17.4%**
High blood pressure (2012)	**17.4%**
Life expectancy at birth - males (2007–2009)	**78.8 years**
Life expectancy at birth - females (2007–2009)	**83.3 years**
Overweight or obese adults (2012)	**52.5%**
Overweight or obese youth (12–17) (2012)	**21.8%**
Physically active (leisure time) (2012)	**53.9%**

Source: *Statistics Canada, 2013*, Health in Canada. *Retrieved July 10, 2013* (*http://www.statcan.gc.ca/health-sante/index-eng.htm*).

TABLE 10.2   Health Indicators, 2011

	Both sexes	Males	Females
		% of population	
Arthritis	17.0	12.7	21.2
Diabetes	6.1	6.7	5.6
Asthma	8.6	7.4	9.8
High blood pressure	17.6	17.4	17.7
Current smoker, daily or occasional	19.9	22.3	17.5
BMI (18 and older), overweight	33.8	40.2	27.3
BMI (18 and older), obese	18.3	19.8	16.8
Influenza immunization, in past year	30.2	26.9	33.4
Perceived mental health, very good or excellent	72.6	73.5	71.7
Perceived mental health, fair or poor	5.6	5.2	6.1
Life satisfaction, satisfied or very satisfied	92.3	92.4	92.1
Pain or discomfort that prevents activities	14.5	12.3	16.7
Has a regular medical doctor	84.7	80.6	88.8

Notes: Population aged 12 and older.

BMI = body mass index.

Source: *Statistics Canada, 2013, "Health at a Glance 2013."* Retrieved June 17, 2013 (http://www.statcan.gc.ca/pub/12-581-x/2013000/h-s-eng.htm).

shows that the infant mortality rate (per 1000 live births) for Canada was 4.9 in 2009. The infant mortality rate is an important indication of a society's level of preventive (prenatal) medical care, maternal nutrition, childbirth procedures, and care for infants. While this rate is much lower than before, it is still high relative to other high-income countries (see Canada's rank in Table 10.6).

Table 10.1 provides basic health data about Canadians and Table 10.2 provides a set of health indicators, many of which will be referred to below. Some overlap and slight discrepancies between tables occur because they were created at different times.

Acute and Chronic Diseases

Life expectancy in Canada and other developed nations has increased largely because vaccinations and improved nutrition, sanitation, and personal hygiene have virtually eliminated many acute diseases, including measles, polio, cholera, tetanus, typhoid, and malaria. *Acute diseases* **are illnesses that strike suddenly and cause dramatic incapacitation and sometimes death** (Weitz 2010). Acute diseases that are still common in Canada include chicken pox and some strains of influenza.

With the overall decline in death from acute illnesses in high-income nations, however, has come a corresponding increase in *chronic diseases*—**illnesses that are long term or lifelong and that develop gradually or are present from birth** (Weitz 2010). In Chapter 8, we discussed two of the most common sources of chronic disease and premature death: tobacco use, which increases mortality among both smokers and people who breathe the tobacco smoke of others, and alcohol abuse. According to some social analysts, we can attribute many chronic diseases in our society to the *manufacturers of illness,* groups that promote illness-causing behaviour and social conditions, such as smoking (McKinlay 1994). The effect of chronic diseases on life expectancy varies because some chronic diseases are progressive (e.g., emphysema worsens over time), whereas others are constant (e.g., paralysis after a stroke); also, some are fatal (lung cancer), but others are not (arthritis and asthma). And many of these diseases are becoming more prevalent all over the world, as reported in Box 10.1. Because of the combination of longer life expectancies and the disabling consequences of some diseases, new terms have been coined—for example, "active" life or health expectancy and "disability-free" life expectancy.

Global Burden of Disease 2010

The GBD (Global Burden of Disease) 2010 study was a tremendous effort by at least 486 scientists from 302 institutions in 50 countries to contribute to our understanding of present and future health priorities for countries and the global community. The study was supported by the Bill and Melinda Gates Foundation. GBD 2010 is the first systematic and comprehensive assessment of data on disease, injuries, and risk since 1990. In 1990, 107 diseases and injuries, together with 10 risk factors, were assessed. For 2010, 235 causes of death and 67 risk factors were included. The results, which appeared in the *Lancet,* show that although 52.8 million deaths occurred in 2010 versus 46.5 million deaths in 1990, great progress is being made in population health. For example:

- Life expectancies for men and women are increasing.
- Deaths from HIV and malaria are falling.
- Far fewer children younger than five years are dying because infectious diseases are increasingly being controlled.
- In high-income parts of the world, there has been substantial progress in preventing premature deaths from heart disease and cancer.

On the other hand, disease is still a major problem in the world. For example:

- Tuberculosis and malaria are estimated to have killed around 1.2 million people each in 2010.
- Cancer killed 8 million people in 2010, over a third more deaths than 20 years ago.
- Heart disease or stroke killed one in four in 2010.
- Diabetes killed 1.3 million in 2010.
- Road traffic injuries deaths increased by almost half.
- Blood pressure is the biggest global risk factor for disease, followed by tobacco, alcohol, and poor diet.
- Maternal, newborn, and child mortality, along with a broad array of vaccine-preventable and other communicable diseases, are substantial (Horton et al. 2012).

Questions for consideration

1. How would it be possible to reduce chronic diseases in the world?
2. Do Western corporations contribute to worldwide chronic disease?
3. How do medical people prevent the emergence of new diseases like Ebola?

Sex and Gender, Class, and Indigenous Status

Life expectancy and chronic diseases vary substantially by major demographic variables. Females have longer life expectancies than males, as Table 10.1 shows. But according to Table 10.2 (Statistics Canada 2013y), larger percentages of females than males reported having arthritis (21.2 percent vs. 12.7 percent) and pain preventing activities (16.7 percent vs. 12.3 percent). On the other hand, larger percentages of males than females reported being overweight (40.2 percent vs. 27.3 percent). On most other indicators, the differences are minimal. The reasons for these differences could be a combination of factors that contribute to females' longer lives, and having longer lives can lead to the development of more chronic disease. Class or income is also related to longevity, as Figure 10.1 shows.

Figure 10.1 shows that in 2005–07, people in the lowest neighbourhood income quintiles (Q1) (a measure of class by Statistics Canada) had a shorter life expectancy measured in years than those in the highest neighbourhood income quintile (Q5). Specifically, Q1 life expectancy for males and females was 75.6 and 81.7 respectively, while Q5 life expectancy for males and females was 80.3 and 84.0 respectively. A more complex study of income and cause-specific mortality showed the same inverse relation between age-specific mortality rates and income. Between 1991 and 2007, 2.7 million Canadians 25+ years were followed. During that period, about half a million died, and their death rates were related to income, measured by income quintile. As mentioned in Chapter 8, deaths from alcohol and smoking diseases were definitely related to income. Although some diseases, like prostate cancer and pancreatic cancer, were not related to income, just about all other disease deaths were related to income, especially HIV/AIDS, diabetes mellitus, and suicide. Overall death rates showed a 12 percent higher death rate in the second richest quintile than in the richest, 21 percent higher for third richest, 35 percent higher for the fourth richest, and 67 percent higher for the poorest quintile (Tjepkema 2013).

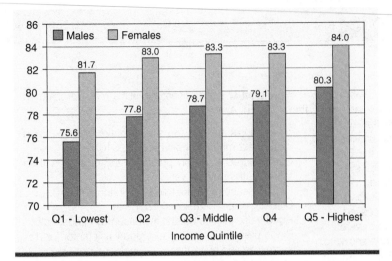

Figure 10.1 Life Expectancy by Sex, Neighbourhood Income Quintiles, 2005–2007
Source: *Statistics Canada, 2011, "Vital Statistics." Retrieved June 18, 2013 (http://www.statcan.gc.ca/pub/82-624-x/2011001/article/chart/11427-06-chart5-eng.htm).*

The reasons for these differences are likely a combination of people with lower levels of income:

• being unable to afford nutritious food;
• engaging in risky health behaviour such as smoking, drinking, and drug use (see Chapter 8);
• working in dangerous industries; and
• living in some areas, including the North, far from medical care.

Indigenous status is a very important predictor of life expectancy and illness, both acute and chronic. A gap of two to three years exists between the life expectancy of Indigenous people at age 25 years and that of the general population (Tjepkema and Wilkins 2011). In addition, a substantial difference in both perceived physical and mental health of about 10 to 12 percent exists between First Nations (off the reserve), Metis, and Inuit compared to non-Indigenous Canadians, as Figure 10.2 shows.

The reasons for these differences are similar to those for class-related differences in health, including:

• high levels of poverty, with the accompanying poor housing, nutrition, and sanitary conditions;
• higher rates of risky health behaviour; and
• being distant from medical care in Nunavut, Yukon, and the Northwest Territories.

Disability

Some chronic diseases and injuries produce disabilities that significantly increase personal suffering and health care costs for individuals and for society. *Disability* can be defined in several ways. Medical professionals tend to define it in terms of organically based impairments—that is, the problem is entirely within the body. However, disability rights advocates believe that disability is a physical or health condition that stigmatizes or causes discrimination. Perhaps the best way to define disability

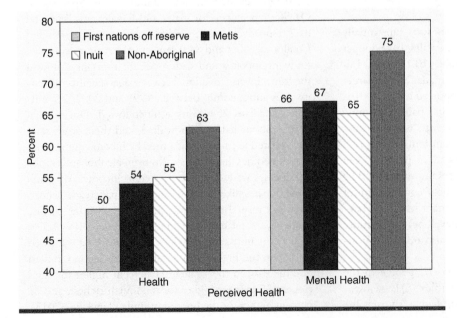

Figure 10.2 Very Good or Excellent Perceived Health of Indigenous and non-Indigenous Populations in Canada
Source: *Gionet and Roshanasfar, 2013, "Health at a Glance." Retrieved June 19, 2013 (http://www.statcan.gc.ca/pub/82-624-x/2013001/article/chart/11763-01-chart1-eng.htm).*

TABLE 10.3	Prevalence of Disability by type in Canada, 2012
Disability type	**%**
Pain	9.7
Flexibility	7.6
Mobility	7.2
Mental/psychological	3.9
Dexterity	3.5
Hearing	3.2
Seeing	2.7
Memory	2.3
Learning	2.3
Developmental	0.6
Unknown	0.3

Source: *Statistics Canada, 2013p,* Canadian Survey on Disability, 2012. *Retrieved December 3, 2013 (http://www.statcan.gc.ca/pub/89-654-x/89-654-x2013002-eng.htm).*

is, as medical sociologist Rose Weitz (2010) has said, in terms of both physical and social factors: *disability* **is a restricted or total lack of ability to perform certain activities as a result of physical or mental limitations or the interplay of these limitations, social responses, and the social environment.** In Canada, the 2012 Canadian Survey on Disability reported that about 3.8 million people (13.7 percent of Canadians) aged 15 years and over reported being limited in a daily activity because of a disability. Predictably, older people have more disabilities than younger; women have a higher prevalence of disabilities than men do in most age groups; and many kinds of disabilities exist. The survey identified 10 types of limitation. Table 10.3 shows the prevalence of these limitations.

Disabilities are an important social problem because, among other problems, people with disabilities have higher unemployment rates and lower incomes than those without disabilities. While some of these differences are likely due to those living with disabilities being unable to work, others point instead to discrimination against those with disabilities. This is called ableism, following the examples of racism and sexism. *Ableism* **is prejudice and discrimination against people because of a physical or mental disability.** In the past, among those 25 to 64 years of age in 2001, 10.7 percent of the disabled were unemployed versus

5.9 percent of the non-disabled. By 2012, about half the disabled were employed and half reported that their employer was unaware of the disability. The median income of those aged 15 to 64 years with disabilities was reported to be $20 000 in comparison with $30 000 for those without disabilities. Pensions, lump-sum payments, or investment income was the source of income for just over a third of persons with disabilities (Statistics Canada 2015).

The number of disabled people continues to increase for several reasons. First, with advances in medical technology, many people who in the past would have died from an accident or illness now survive with impairment. Second, as people live longer, they are more likely to experience chronic diseases (such as arthritis) that may have disabling consequences. Third, people born with serious disabilities are more likely to survive infancy because of medical technology. (However, only a small percentage of people with a disability today were born with it; accidents, disease, and violence account for most disabilities in this country.) Many people with a chronic illness or disability will not live out the full life expectancy for people in their age category.

HIV/AIDS

AIDS—acquired immune deficiency syndrome—was a devastating health problem until the mid-1990s. Since that time, inexpensive and highly active anti-retroviral therapy (HAART) has made it more manageable. AIDS is caused by infection with a virus called human immunodeficiency virus (HIV), which is passed from one person to another through sexual contact and/or blood-to-blood (sharing needles with an infected person, or earlier in the 1980s from blood transfusions).

However, many cases of HIV, and smaller numbers of cases of AIDS, are still found annually. In 2012, the Public Health Agency of Canada (PHAC) estimated that there were approximately 71 300 people living with HIV/AIDS in Canada, 25 percent of whom were unaware of their infection due to a lack of testing and/or diagnosis. The estimated number of new HIV infections in 2011 was 3175. This number was down from 2010, but since 1996 the number of new cases appears like a roller coaster track. Less than a quarter of new cases were females. The primary causes for males were men having unprotected sex (61.4 percent), heterosexual contact (20.5 percent), and injection drug use (13.6 percent); the primary causes for females were heterosexual contact (64.5 percent) and injection drug use (29.9 percent). Ontario had the highest proportion of cases, but not the highest rate, which was in Saskatchewan (PHAC 2012).

Since AIDS reporting began in 1979, there has been a cumulative total of 22 322 AIDS cases reported to PHAC through the end of 2011. The annual number of reported AIDS cases in Canada has been decreasing steadily over the past 18 years. In 2011, 151 AIDS cases were reported to PHAC, representing an 82.6 percent decrease since 1993, when 1827 AIDS cases were reported—the highest number ever in Canada (PHAC 2012).

Though HIV/AIDS appears under control in high-income countries, it is still a major problem in low- and middle-income countries. It is estimated that 34 million people, mostly in sub-Saharan Africa, are living with HIV/AIDS (WHO 2013). Estimates have improved in recent years. For example, in 2008, the number of people estimated to be living with HIV/AIDS in the world was 42 million.

Besides being a serious health issue, HIV/AIDS can be a criminal and human rights issue. In Canada, any person who has HIV and does not disclose it to a partner and does not take some sort of protective measure (such as condom use) is guilty of aggravated sexual assault. One person was convicted of first degree murder when two of his partners died from the disease. Human rights organizations have suggested that these convictions will discourage people from testing themselves. What do you think should be the consequences of non-disclosure of HIV?

Obesity

A relatively new health risk—being overweight—is now affecting about half the Canadian population. Obesity is more prevalent in the United States and as of June 2013, obesity is now called a disease by the American Medical Association. It was thought that naming obesity a disease would increase research funding and encourage medical schools to pay more attention to it. Excess weight is linked to heart disease, Type II diabetes, back problems, certain forms of cancer, and stroke. A healthy weight range is indicated by the body mass index (BMI), which is calculated by dividing weight in kilograms (kg) by height in metres squared (m^2). A person with a BMI of less than 18.5 is considered underweight; a BMI of 18.6 to 24.9 is considered of normal weight; a BMI of 25.0 to 29.9 is considered overweight; and a BMI of over 30.0 is considered obese.

According to Table 10.2, in 2011 one third of Canadians were overweight and 18.9 percent were obese. Men were much more likely to be overweight than women were, but little difference was found in the percentage of men and women who were obese.

According to a Canadian Community Health Survey, 23 percent of adult Canadians are obese. What kinds of problems does this increasing trend present for the health care system in the future?

Guy Erwood/Shutterstock

A curvilinear pattern was found for age, with middle-aged people being the most likely to be obese. Region of the country is also important. People in Newfoundland and Labrador and New Brunswick were found to have higher rates of obesity than people in the rest of the country have. But the growth of the obesity problem may be over. A comparison of figures from the Canadian Community Health Survey in 2007 and current figures shows that dramatic increases in obesity seem to have ended. In 2007, the percentage of people over the age of 18 years who are overweight (32 percent) or obese (16 percent) (Statistics Canada, 2008c) are almost identical to the current ones.

Obesity is not just a problem for Canadians; it is a problem worldwide. Although data are difficult to confirm, as of 2008, the WHO estimated that more than 1.4 billion adults were overweight and more than half a billion were obese (WHO 2013).

How can we reduce the overweight/obesity problem? Besides the usual suggestions for self-help groups, increased physical activity, and better diets, suggestions now include putting caloric counts on menus; putting health warnings, like those found on cigarette packages, on packages of junk food; adding a tax to junk food; and banning very large drinks to discourage consumption (see Box 10.2).

On the other hand, people of size take exception to the prejudicial attitudes and discrimination they experience from society. They would call this the equivalent of ableism. Several organizations are working to change society's attitudes and behaviour toward people who

Taxing Food, Banning Very Large Drinks, and Restricting Added Salt

In an effort to help reduce obesity, some American communities, including California, New York, Seattle, and Maine, have made it mandatory for fast-food restaurants to prominently post caloric counts of their menus. In February 2014, Ontario Health Minister Deb Matthews introduced a bill to make menu calorie labelling mandatory in large chain restaurants after consultations with the food industry and health care sector. As of January 1, 2017, restaurants with 20 or more locations will be required to display the number of calories on menus or on menu boards.

Few would object to caloric information and educational campaigns to promote weight control and physical activity. But would you go along with increased taxation on or an outright ban of very large sugared drinks? We know that the intake of sugared beverages is associated with increased body weight and poor nutrition, and consumption increases risk for obesity and diabetes (Brownell and Frieden 2009). We also know that sugared beverages are marketed extensively to children and adolescents, and in the mid-1990s in the United States, children's intake of sugared beverages surpassed that of milk (Brownell and Frieden 2009).

The advocates, or nudgers (those who nudge people in a particular direction) as they are called, then argued for a tax on sugared beverages to reduce their consumption and to pay for some of the costs of obesity. Brownell and Frieden reported that some have estimated the annual costs of consumption of sugared beverages at US$79 billion (2009). To support the effectiveness of a tax, Brownell and Frieden use the analogy that taxing smoking was effective in reducing consumption of tobacco and the huge costs of its health effects. In the same way, taxing sugared drinks can help reduce consumption and obesity and offset the costs of its effects. In 2012, Mayor Bloomberg of New York City went a step further and proposed banning very large soft drinks (larger than 16 ounces or about 473 ml) at restaurants and other food-service outlets.

Objections to the tax include that it is regressive in taxing the poor the most; that it singles out one kind of food for a tax (e.g., why tax soft drinks and not packaged desserts and candy?); and that taxing will not eliminate obesity, as it has not eliminated smoking. However, the poor are at greatest risk from obesity; no

other food provides as many extra calories; and taxing smoking did have an influence on reducing, if not eliminating, consumption of cigarettes (see Chapter 8). Although hefty taxes are recommended by Brownell and Frieden to reduce consumption, too high a tax can have the unintended consequence of encouraging smuggling, as Ontario discovered in 1993–1994 when high tobacco taxes resulted in an increase in cigarette smuggling.

The arguments for restrictions on food additives are similar. Although we know that reducing salt is related to reducing high blood pressure, considerable controversy exists about whether overall low levels of salt are beneficial in the long run. For example, reducing salt can cause problems with blood flow to the kidneys and insulin resistance, which can increase the risk of strokes and heart attacks. Scientists also have discovered that salt, like chocolate and cocaine, can enhance the mood of rats, and rats deprived of salt experience lack of enjoyment of everyday activities. Thus, salt may prevent feelings of depression (Tierney 2009). While no figures are available on the support for salt restrictions, Brownell and Frieden report that a small majority of polled New Yorkers support a "soda tax," and that figure rises to 72 percent when the revenue is used to prevent obesity.

Objections to the outright ban on large soft drinks include claims that public health problems cannot be changed by such a narrow ban and that it involves too much government control. In March 2013, a judge of the New York Supreme Court ruled that such a ban overstepped the powers of the Board of Health of New York. Although Mayor Bloomberg is appealed the judgment, in 2014 the state's highest court refused to reinstate the ban.

Questions for Consideration

1. Would you buy fewer soft drinks if they were taxed an extra 10 percent?

2. Do you think that restricting food additives by large amounts like 50 percent is a good thing?

3. Do you think that government should ban certain types and sizes of soft drinks? What would you tell your local board of health?

are fat, including the International Size Acceptance Association and the National Association to Advance Fat Acceptance (see references for links to these sites) with up-to-date media releases, education, community, and other links.

MENTAL ILLNESS AS A SOCIAL PROBLEM

Mental illness is a social problem because of the number of people it affects, the difficulty of defining and identifying mental disorders, and the ways in which mental illness is treated. Although most social scientists use the terms *mental illness* and *mental disorder* interchangeably, many medical professionals distinguish between a *mental disorder*—a condition that makes it difficult or impossible for a person to cope with everyday life—and *mental illness*—a condition that requires extensive treatment with medication, psychotherapy, and sometimes hospitalization.

The most widely accepted classification of mental disorders is the American Psychiatric Association's (2013) *Diagnostic and Statistical Manual of Mental Disorders 5 (DSM-5)* The *DSM* is now in its fifth edition, and with each revision, its list of disorders has changed and grown. Listings change partly because of new scientific findings, which permit more precise descriptions that are more useful than broad terms covering a wide range of behaviours, and partly because of changes in how we view mental disorders culturally (at one time, for example, homosexuality was considered a mental disorder and now prolonged grief is considered a disorder). This edition is supposed to have much more empirical support for its claims, but critics argue that the DSM-5 so lowers the thresholds for mental illnesses (e.g., grief) that life could be considered a treatable disease.

How many people are affected by mental illness? According to the Canadian Community Health Survey (2012), as shown in Table 10.4, one third of Canadians experiences some form of mental or substance use disorders over their lifetimes, and 1 in 10 have experienced this in the past year. Most of these disorders are well known. The substance disorders were discussed in Chapter 8; however, generalized anxiety may need an elaboration. It is a condition characterized by a pattern of frequent, persistent worry and excessive anxiety about several events or activities.

Rates of mental illness are affected by gender, age, class, and Indigenous status. It is often thought that

TABLE 10.4   Rates of Mental or Substance Use Disorders in Canada, 2012

	Lifetime %	12-month %
Mental or substance use disorders[1]	**33.1**	**10.1**
Substance use disorder[2]	21.6	4.4
Alcohol abuse or dependence	18.1	3.2
Cannabis abuse or dependence	6.8	1.3
Other drug abuse or dependence (excluding cannabis)	4.0	0.7
Mood disorder[3]	12.6	5.4
Major depressive episode	11.3	4.7
Bipolar disorder	2.6	1.5
Generalized anxiety disorder	8.7	2.6

1. **Mental or substance use disorders** is comprised of: substance use disorders, mood disorders and general anxiety disorder. However, these three disorders cannot be added to create this rate because these three categories are not mutually exclusive, meaning that people may have a profile consistert with one or more of these disorders.
2. **Substance use disorder** includes alcohol abuse or dependence, cannabis abuse or dependence, and other drug abuse or dependence.
3. **Mood disorder** includes depression (major depressive episode) and bipolar disorder.
Source: *Statistics Canada, 2012,* Canadian Community Health Survey – Mental Health, 2012. *Retrieved September 18, 2013 (http://www.statcan.gc.ca/pub/82-624-x/2013001/article/tbl/tbl1-eng.htm).*

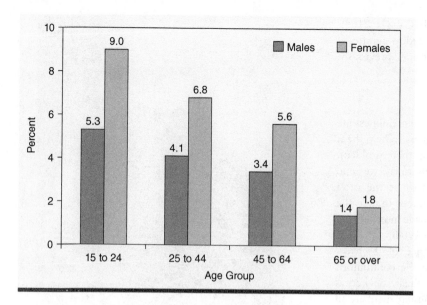

Figure 10.3   Rates of Depression by Age and Sex in Canada, 2012

Source: *Statistics Canada, 2012,* Canadian Community Health Survey – Mental Health, 2012. *Retrieved September 18, 2013 (http://www.statcan.gc.ca/pub/82-624-x/2013001/article/c-g/11855-c-g-01-eng.htm).*

females have higher rates of mental illness. Figure 10.3 shows this is true for depression in the past 12 months. Figure 10.3 also shows that young people are more likely than older people to experience these problems, which also applies to Chapter 5 on aging (i.e., aging does not bring about a decline in every kind of health).

Figure 10.4 shows that men have higher rates of substance abuse drug dependence. When these two types of problems (mental disorders and substance use) are combined, it appears that mental health problems are not related to gender.

People in lower social classes have higher rates of mental disorders than people in upper classes do. But according to sociologist Harley Dickinson (2002), this relationship could be explained by the "downward drift hypothesis"—that people with mental illnesses are unable to function properly, neither getting an education nor keeping a job. Thus, they slip into the lower classes (Dickinson 2002:376). Health Canada reports that the suicide rate of First Nations youth is about five or six times as great as for non-Indigenous youth. Suicide rates for Inuit youth are among the highest in the world, at

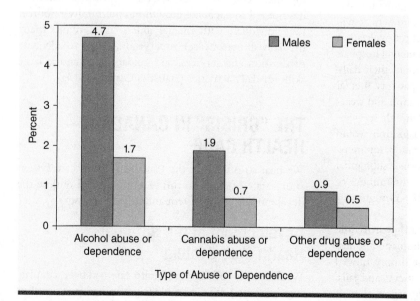

Figure 10.4   Rates of Substance Use Disorders by Sex in Canada, 2012

Source: *Statistics Canada, 2012,* Canadian Community Health Survey – Mental Health, 2012. *Retrieved September 18, 2013 (http://www.statcan.gc.ca/pub/82-624-x/2013001/article/c-g/11855-c-g-02-eng.htm).*

11 times the national average (Health Canada 2103). Reasons for these differences are attributed to significant differences in living conditions, as mentioned previously, and lack of opportunities.

Treatment of Mental Illness

People who seek professional help for mental illness are treated with medication and psychotherapy to help them understand the underlying reasons for their problem. Because medication is used so routinely today, we tend to forget that institutionalization used to be the most common treatment for severe mental illness. In fact, the development of psychoactive drugs made possible the deinstitutionalization movement of the 1960s.

Deinstitutionalization is the practice of discharging patients from mental hospitals into the community. Although deinstitutionalization was originally devised as a solution for the problem of warehousing mentally ill patients in large, prison-like mental hospitals in the first half of the 20th century, many social scientists now view deinstitutionalization as a problem. To understand how this solution evolved into a problem, one must understand the state of mental health care in Canada during the 1950s and 1960s. The practice of *involuntary commitment* (i.e., without a patient's consent) allowed many patients to be warehoused in mental hospitals for extended periods of time, with only minimal and sometimes abusive custodial care. According to sociologist Erving Goffman (1961), a mental hospital is a classic example of a **total institution**—**a place where people are isolated from the rest of society for a period of time and come under the complete control of the officials who run the institution.** Patients are stripped of their individual identities—or depersonalized—by being required to wear institutional clothing and follow a strict regimen of activities, meals, and sleeping hours. The deinstitutionalization movement sought to release patients from mental hospitals so that they could live at home and go about their daily activities. Professionals believed that the patients' mental disorders could be controlled with medication and treatment through community-based mental health services. Other advocates hoped that deinstitutionalization would remove the stigma attached to hospitalization for mental illness. Deinstitutionalization occurred in a substantial way in Canada. Between 1960 and 1976, the number of beds in mental hospitals declined from 47 633 to 15 011 (Cochrane et al. 1997:1).

Although deinstitutionalization had worthwhile goals—protection of civil rights, more humane and less costly treatment—in too many cases, it simply moved people out of mental hospitals into the streets and jails. Today, critics of deinstitutionalization argue that it

Although there are many causes of homelessness, ranging from lack of affordable housing to drug dependency, some analysts believe that the deinstitutionalization of patients from mental hospitals has significantly increased the number of people living on the streets in Canada. What other alternatives can you suggest for dealing with mental illness?

wrangler/Shutterstock

exacerbated long-term problems associated with treating mental illness. They say that deinstitutionalization has not led to adequate growth in community resources for individuals with mental illness. As a result, many mentally ill persons lack supervision, access to adequate medication and services, and guidance to acquire basic skills for daily activities (Statistics Canada 2013g).

THE "CRISIS" IN CANADIAN HEALTH CARE

We hear so often that the Canadian health care system is in a state of crisis. In this section, we will outline the development of the system and its current issues.

Development of the National Health Care System

While the idea of universal health care had been circulating for some time, and Saskatchewan had pioneered its major elements, the features of the national health care system emerged with the following pieces of federal legislation and more recent changes in funding:

- The *Hospital Insurance and Diagnostic Service Act* 1957 provided insurance for hospital and diagnostic services.

- The *Medical Care Act* 1966 provided insurance for medical services, to which all the provinces agreed by 1972, emphasizing five principles: universality—all Canadians should be covered; accessibility—reasonable access must be unimpeded by financial or other barriers; comprehensiveness—all medically necessary services should be guaranteed; portability—Canadians should be able to have their benefits transferable to other provinces or other countries; and public administration—the system would be operated by a public body on a non-profit basis.

- The *Canada Health Act* 1984 confirmed the five principles and prohibited private charges or extra billing by doctors or hospitals.

- The federal government substantially reduced its contributions to the provinces in the mid-1990s to 26 percent or less of the total cost.

- The federal government increased its contributions to the provinces in 1999, but not to the 50 percent level established at the beginning.

- A federal–provincial agreement in February 2003 saw the Liberal federal government state that it would inject almost $35 billion into the health care system over the next five years to deal with wait times for operations like hip and knee replacements, catastrophic drug costs, electronic health records (EHRs), and so on. This was increased to $41 billion in the 2005 budget. In addition, a Health Council of Canada was formed to monitor progress toward these goals.

In 2012, the Conservative government said that it would continue to give money to the health care system at a reduced rate given reduced revenues. However, it would give the money directly to the provinces to allocate as they saw fit. According to some observers, this was the end of the national health care system. Since the federal government decided not to try to set a national policy for health care, they also eliminated the Health Council of Canada.

Current Issues in the Health Care System

Accessibility and Wait Times

These two topics are often thought to be the same, but accessibility also refers to having or finding a doctor. The vast majority (85.1 percent) of Canadians have a family doctor (see Table 10.1); the ones who do not

have a doctor tend to be young, and in most cases they do not need one. Besides having a doctor, another concern is how quickly the doctor can be seen in case of a problem. In the 2012 Commonwealth Fund International Health Policy Survey of Primary Care Physicians, which asked Canadian family physicians to rate the health system, fewer than half of the doctors (47 percent) said that patients can get same-day or next-day appointments when requested. In contrast, over 95 percent of doctors in France said this is possible for their patients. Other accessibility issues for patients identified by doctors include:

- Seeing a physician after the practice is closed—46 percent of the doctors said yes;

- Experiencing difficulty often in getting diagnostic tests—38 percent said yes; and

- Experiencing difficulty paying for drugs, etc.—26 percent said yes (Health Council of Canada 2012).

Turning to wait times for selected elective procedures (not life-threatening ones, which are dealt with immediately), a number of benchmarks were set in 2005. While wait times were reduced substantially from 2004 to 2008, many seem to have levelled off (Health Council of Canada 2013). Table 10.5 shows the wait times in Canada as of 2012 and progress since 2005. Recent efforts to improve wait times seem to have stalled, perhaps because a greater volume of these operations are taking place.

The Ontario Government has developed a website to help people determine wait times for various procedures (see references for link). At this site, a patient can seek out wait times for emergency rooms, various kinds of adult and pediatric surgeries, and diagnostic procedures at hospitals all over the province.

A terrible example of the problem of wait times occurred in Manitoba in 2010. Brian Sinclair, a 45-year-old double amputee, Indigenous, homeless person, died of a preventable bladder infection during a 34-hour wait at Winnipeg's Health Sciences Centre. Mr. Sinclair's family brought a law suit against the Winnipeg Regional Health Authority in 2012. Even if average wait times improve, health care personnel have to be extra vigilant to ensure that this kind of death does not happen again.

Electronic Health Records (EHRs)

While substantial progress has been made in encouraging doctors to convert paper records to electronic health records (EHRs) (in 2006, 28 percent of doctors in Canada used EHRs, while in 2012, 57 percent of doctors did), Canadian doctors are very far behind doctors of other

TABLE 10.5 Progress on 2005 Benchmarks	
2005 Benchmarks	**Progress in 2012**
radiation therapy for cancer within four weeks of patients being ready for treatment	All provinces met the radiation therapy benchmark for at least 90% of patients (except Nova Scotia at 89%).
hip/knee replacement within 26 weeks	15% more hip and knee replacement surgeries were performed in Canada than two years earlier. But the proportion of these surgeries performed within the pan-Canadian benchmark decreased by 4%. Among all priority areas, patients seeking knee replacements have the longest waits.
hip fracture repair within 48 hours	Wait times for hip fracture repair have remained fairly stable since 2010. From 2010 to 2012, wait times for hip fracture repair improved in only two provinces—Ontario and Saskatchewan.
cataract surgery within 16 weeks for those at high risk	Wait times for cataract surgeries have remained fairly stable since 2010. Alberta is the only province in which the percentage of cataract surgeries performed within the benchmark increased.
coronary artery bypass graft (CABG) surgery within 2 weeks for level 1 urgency, 6 weeks for level 2 urgency, and 26 weeks for level 3 urgency	Due to the lack of comparable data for CABG, CIHI no longer includes CABG wait times in its annual report. However, CIHI's website indicates that on average, 90% of Canadian patients receive CABG surgery within 46 days, although waits range from 19 days in Saskatchewan to 84 days in Alberta.

Source: *Health Council of Canada, 2013*, Progress Report 2013: Health Care Renewal in Canada.

high-income countries (e.g., Norway, the Netherlands, the United Kingdom, and New Zealand have close to 100 percent of doctors using EHRs). In addition, for six major topics (registries, diagnostic imaging, drug information systems, lab test results, clinical reports, and immunizations), only 52 percent of Canadians have EHRs. While EHRs could improve coordination of care, thus reducing costs, they might also help with innovative projects like identifying unused hours of doctors' time and making use of them by connecting them with isolated patients, reducing visits to distant emergency wards or providing continuing care (Health Council of Canada 2013).

Costs of Care

The overall costs of the health care system and the way they are paid is increasingly an issue. Figure 10.5 shows the comparative costs per capita of health care (measured in U.S. dollars) in 2010 in OECD countries.

As mentioned at the beginning of the chapter, Figure 10.6 shows that Canada spent US$4445 per capita, around the average for OECD high-income countries. In comparison, the United States was far in front, spending $8233 before the Affordable Care Act (commonly known as Obamacare) came into effect. The expectation is that this Act will encourage more competition in the

health care field, and will thus reduce costs over time. Figure 10.6 shows how health care dollars are distributed among the segments of the health care system. In 2010, hospitals got the most, over a quarter of the expenditures at 29.1 percent. Drugs are next, at 15.9 percent, followed by doctors at 14.2 percent.

Although Canada has a single-payer, public method of financing health care, a private segment exists in our system—for cosmetic surgery, dental practice, eyeglasses, drugs outside hospitals, and other out-patient aids and services. This segment amounts to 30 percent of the total health care expenditures (CIHI 2013). While this private-care figure is high relative to that of some European countries, it is well below the United States's comparable figure of 55 percent.

In some countries with universal health care, people have an opportunity to pay for their own operations and thereby jump the public queue. The two-tier system of health care, with both public and private funding and delivery of health care, results in differential access—poorer access for those who cannot afford to pay. Pressure groups in the private sector are advocating that private clinics and services be made available in Canada for people who can afford to pay for them. But many others fear that allowing two tiers in the health system will reduce overall support for the public system.

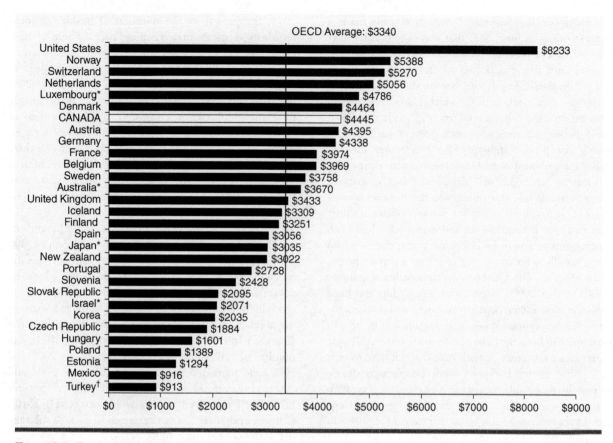

Figure 10.5   Total Health Expenditures per Capital for Selected Countries, 2010

Source: *Canadian Institute of Health Information, 2013*, National Health Expenditure Trends 1975–2012.

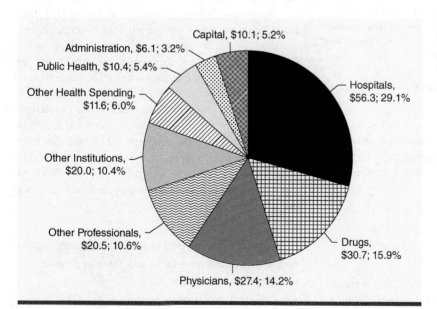

Figure 10.6   Total Health Expenditures by Use of Funds in Canada, 2010

Source: *Health Council of Canada, 2012*, National Health Expenditure Trends 1975–2012

However, the Supreme Court of Canada made a historic ruling in June 2005 that may significantly alter our health care system. In a battle that originated in Quebec and that pitted two institutions against each other (the public health care system and the *Charter of Rights and Freedoms*), both of which Canadians hold in high esteem, the Supreme Court of Canada ruled that the Quebec government cannot prevent people from paying for private insurance for procedures covered under the public system. Unreasonable wait times pose a threat to our rights to "life, liberty, and security of the person." While this ruling was for the province of Quebec, it has implications for the rest of the country. The case was brought by an individual who had been waiting almost a year for hip surgery, and also involved Dr. Chaoulli, who was trying to set up a private hospital in Quebec. The Quebec government has stated that as of October 2009, 56 procedures (e.g., hip and knee replacements, cataracts, mastectomies, and hysterectomies) can be contracted out, and doctors will be able to participate in both the public and private systems. People with private insurance or with cash will not have to wait in a public queue. However, while people may decide to pay for reasonably inexpensive elective surgery, such as hip replacement and cataract surgery, to get it quickly, they likely will not be able to pay for cancer care that can cost hundreds of thousands of dollars.

Since 2009, very little was heard about this precedent. However, on June 25, 2013, the Alberta Court of Queen's Bench began to hear two cases (Allen and Cross) that challenge the Government of Alberta's health care monopoly. It will be the first time that a court outside Quebec hears an application to extend *Chaoulli* outside Quebec (Justice Centre Constitutional Freedoms 2013).

What is the recent news about two-tier health care in your province? How do you expect it to change in the future?

Supply and Demand of Health Care Professionals

While it is difficult to know how many doctors, nurses, and other health professionals are needed now or in the future, the Health Council of Canada, in their Progress Report of 2012, identified the increase in the supply of some professionals from 2006–2010:

- The number of physicians grew by 12 percent to 69 699.
- The number of nurses grew by 6 percent to 268 512.
- The number of pharmacists grew by 16 percent to 31 195 (Health Council of Canada 2012).

Since these increases are larger than the increase in the Canadian population of 5 percent from 2006 to 2011, the growth of the numbers of health care professionals is more than keeping pace. There is now some talk of unemployed or underemployed doctors. According to the 2013 report of the Royal College of Physicians and Surgeons of Canada, one in six (208) new specialists and subspecialists reported being unable to secure employment, compared to 7.1 percent of all Canadians. Of these, over one half stated they were or would be pursuing further training, and over one third reported that they were unemployed and without a training post (Fréchette et al. 2013). Doctors may now be subject to the same pressures experienced by teachers and lawyers.

A relatively new group of nurses, nurse practitioners (NPs)—nurses with extra training to diagnose disease, prescribe pharmaceuticals, and perform specific procedures—are able to do work previously done by doctors, especially in rural and remote areas, and are thought to be a means of reducing costs and increasing accessibility. According to a media release from the Canadian Institute for Health Information (CIHI), the number of NPs more than doubled between 2005 and 2009, and increased by 22 percent between 2008 and 2009. However, 2486 NPs represent only 0.7 percent of the total registered nursing workforce (CIHI 2010). Consequently they are not expected to make a substantial difference for some time.

Quality of Care

Quality of care can be measured in many ways: people's feelings of satisfaction with services provided by the system, the quality of the institutions (hospitals) that provide care, and international comparisons of effectiveness.

Regarding feelings of satisfaction, Figure 10.7 shows that Canadians rate their system at a lower than average level for major high-income countries. Over half of those surveyed say that the system has some good features, but fundamental changes need to be made to make it work better (Health Council of Canada 2010:9).

The CBC program "The Fifth Estate" undertook a study of hospitals across the country to determine their quality. The journalists rated 239 hospitals across the country in a couple of ways. First, they obtained data from the CIHI that showed the hospitals' ranking in terms of dealing with major surgery and medical procedures, including:

- mortality after surgery;
- nursing-sensitive adverse events, surgical patients;
- nursing-sensitive adverse events, medical patients;
- readmission after surgery; and
- readmission after medical treatment.

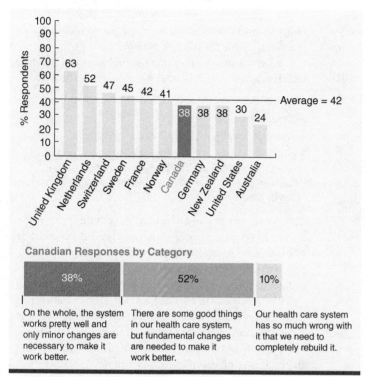

Figure 10.7 Level of Agreement with the Statement: On the whole, the system works pretty well and only minor changes are necessary to make it work better.

Source: *Health Council of Canada, 2010*, How Do Canadians Rate the Health Care System? Results from the 2010 Commonwealth Fund International Health Policy Survey. *Canadian Health Care Matters, Bulletin 4*. Toronto: Health Council of Canada (www.healthcouncilcanada.ca).

TABLE 10.6	Canada's Health Report Card	
Health		
1	Japan	A
2	Switzerland	A
3	Italy	A
4	Norway	B
5	Finland	B
6	Sweden	B
7	France	B
8	Australia	B
9	Germany	B
10	Canada	B
11	Netherlands	C
12	Belgium	C
13	Austria	C
14	U.K.	C
15	Ireland	D
16	Denmark	D
17	U.S.	D

Source: *Conference Board of Canada of Canada, 2013*, Health. *Retrieved May 26, 2013* (http://www.conferenceboard.ca/hcp/details/health.aspx).

Then, the journalists surveyed the hospitals about the actions they are taking to improve care regarding safety, being patient friendly, and quality of care. Lastly, the journalists obtained judgments of people regarding respect shown, communication provided, timeliness, cleanliness, and whether they would recommend the hospital. Hospitals with complete data were given a grade ranging from A+ to D. To discover how hospitals in your area were graded, see the link in the references.

Regarding international health care comparisons, the Conference Board of Canada continues to chart the effectiveness of the Canadian health system relative to 17 high-income nations. As Table 10.6 shows, Canada ranks 10th of the 17 countries, receiving an overall B grade, the same as noted in 2008. Countries were ranked on 11 measures.

- Canada received an A or B, an above average ranking, in life expectancy, self-reported health status, premature mortality, mortality due to respiratory diseases, mortality due to circulatory diseases, mortality due to mental disorders, and mortality due to medical misadventures.
- Canada received a C, a below average ranking, in mortality due to cancer, mortality due to diabetes, mortality due to muscular skeletal diseases, and infant mortality.

Canada has had a high B ranking since the 1960s, but the relative ranking has declined since other countries have improved their records more than Canada has (Conference Board of Canada 2013).

PERSPECTIVES ON ILLNESS AND HEALTH CARE PROBLEMS

What are the primary causes of health care problems in Canada? How can health care be improved? The answers that social scientists give to these questions depend on their theoretical framework. Analysts approaching these questions from a functionalist perspective focus on how illness affects the smooth operation of society and how medicine serves as a social institution. Sociologists using a conflict perspective focus on how a capitalist economy affects health and health care delivery. Those who use an interactionist framework look at the social and cultural factors affecting communication between doctors and patients. Finally, feminist theorists look at inequalities of racialization, class, and sex and gender.

The Functionalist Perspective

The functionalist perspective views illness as a threat to a smoothly functioning society, which depends on all people fulfilling their appropriate social roles. According to this view, when people become ill, they cannot fulfill their everyday responsibilities to family, their employer, or the larger society and instead adopt the *sick role*—patterns of behaviour expected from individuals who are ill. Sociologist Talcott Parsons (1951) identified four role expectations of the sick role:

1. Sick people are not responsible for their incapacity.
2. They are exempted from their usual role and task obligations.
3. They must want to leave the sick role and get well.
4. They are obligated to seek and comply with the advice of a medical professional.

In other words, illness is a form of deviance that must be controlled. According to Parsons, physicians are the logical agents of social control. By certifying that a person is physically or mentally ill and by specifying how the ill person should behave, doctors use their professional authority to monitor people with illnesses, thereby granting them only a temporary reprieve from their usual social roles and responsibilities. Today, however, the dramatic increase in chronic illness and disorganization in the delivery system for medical services mean that many people have less access to doctors, and doctors have less control over those aspects of patients' lives that can increase their chances of becoming ill. Acknowledging these major changes, sociologist Alexander Segall has modified the original conception of the sick role by identifying six expectations. The rights of sick people comprise:

- making decisions about health-related matters;
- being exempt from performing usual well roles; and
- making use of social support and depending on others outside the medical profession.

The duties of sick people comprise:

- maintaining health and managing illness;
- engaging in routine self-health management; and
- making use of available health care resources (Segall and Chappell 2000:2).

These changes take into account both the increase in chronic conditions and the need for a more active rather than passive role for the sick person.

Functionalists believe that the problems in Canadian health care are due to macrolevel changes, such as:

- the development of high-tech medicine and drugs;
- overspecialization of doctors;
- over-diagnosing of patients; and
- increased demand for health care by consumers (see Ramlo and Berlin in Chapter 5 for a critique of the notion that seniors' health problems will overwhelm the health care system).

As a result of these changes, the equilibrium of the system has been greatly affected, and procedures must be implemented to restore the equilibrium. Some observers, writing in a functionalist manner, state that incremental changes will solve the problems. The section "Crisis" in Canadian Health Care identifies a number of such changes, like improving wait times, using electronic health records, funding senior's drug plans, dehospitalizing the system, ensuring the supply of professionals (including using more nurse practitioners), and specifying quality of care that would solve some of the problems. The progress identified by the Health Council of Canada shows that some improvements are occurring.

The Conflict Perspective

The conflict approach is based on the assumption that health care is a common good that should be provided and regulated by the government, just like highways, schools, and national defence. This is the case in most high-income countries, except the United States—but the United States is changing. Whereas in the past a large percentage of people did not have health insurance, the Affordable Care Act is making it possible for all those who want insurance to have it, even those with pre-existing conditions. The Act will take time to be implemented, so problems will remain for the uninsured. For example, the Affordable Care Act's website could not accommodate all who wanted to sign up in the fall of 2013. Figure 10.8 shows the extent to which health care is a common good in Canada disproportionally supported by high-income earners who pay more taxes than they receive in services, and subsidizing use by low-income earners who receive more services than they pay in taxes.

Over a lifetime, tax payments made to finance health care are progressive in that the most affluent pay relatively more of their income, Whereas Q5 earners contribute $8700 dollars to the system annually and use $3400 of services, Q1 earners contribute $1000 annually

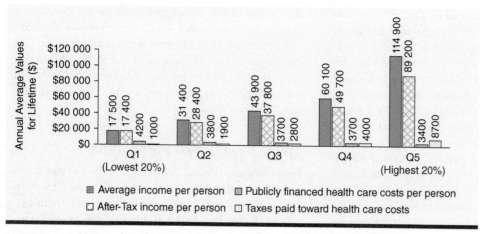

Figure 10.8   Lifetime Health Care Costs and Tax Payments in Relation to Income, by Income Group

Source: *Canadian Institute for Health Information, 2013,* Publicly financed health care in Canada: Who pays and who benefits over a lifetime? *Retrieved August 21, 2013 (https://secure.cihi.ca/estore/productFamily.htm?locale=en&pf=PFC2192).*

and use $4200 of services. People in Q1 could have faced hardship when attempting to pay for their health care costs without access to publicly funded health care. In fact, some Americans in this situation faced bankruptcy before the Affordable Care Act was available. Among the unintended benefits of this approach is that this pattern contributes to a decrease in the income gap between the highest and lowest quintile (CIHI 2013).

The ***medical–industrial complex* (the industry that produces and sells health goods and services)** encompasses both local physicians and hospitals, as well as global health-related industries such as the pharmaceutical and medical supply companies that deliver health care. Although this expression was coined to typify the U.S. health care system, it applies in part to the Canadian system also. For example, pharmaceutical companies have been well known to put profits first, as outlined by physician Joel Lexchin (2002). Lexchin (2002:402) argues that when profit and health considerations come into conflict, profit is likely to be the primary consideration. He gives the examples of Lilly's anti-arthritis drug, benoxaprofen, where the company did not mention to the Canadian Health Protection Branch reviewing the drug that eight deaths had occurred in Britain, and Bristol-Myers Squibb's statin drug, Pravachol (pravastatin), where the Canadian Coordinating Office for Health Technology Assessment reported that all statins were equivalent (Bristol-Myers Squibb sued them).

Another problem exists with pharmaceutical companies. For example, Goldacre showed in *Bad Pharma: How Drug Companies Mislead Doctors and Harm Patients* how drug trials with positive outcomes are more likely

to get published than are trials with negative results (Goldacre 2013). Since doctors depend on published data, they may have skewed information about a drug's effectiveness.

Some conflict theorists believe that only when inequalities—e.g., gender, income, and racialization—are reduced and a more comprehensive approach to health care is implemented that not only includes health care, but also lifestyle and the environment, will inequalities in health outcomes be eliminated. Four decades ago, a comprehensive approach by then federal Minister of Health Marc Lalonde (1974) (thereafter called the Lalonde Report) included applying the four determinants of health—human biology, lifestyle, environment, and health care—to provision of services. As a result, provision of services should: emphasize health maintenance and promotion; improve occupational and income opportunities; and improve the physical and social environment. As long as variable societal conditions—environmental pollution, lack of affordable housing, high levels of stress associated with working conditions or unemployment, inadequate nutrition, lack of early diagnosis for diseases such as breast cancer and heart disease, and type of available health model—affect people, health outcomes will be unequal.

Some conflict theorists also call attention to the unintended negative effects of doctors and suggest that the doctor–patient relationship should be demystified. An early theorist of the negative effects of doctors and the system was Ivan Illich, who coined the term ***iatrogenesis* to describe problems caused by doctors and the health care system.** These problems are of three types. *Clinical iatrogenesis* occurs when pain, sickness, and death result from medical care. The term used in Canada is "medical misadventures" or "adverse effects" (see one of the indicators in the Conference Board of Canada's Report Card in the Quality of Care section, which shows Canada places 7th among 15 high-income countries). A study of hospital records in Canada in 2000–2001 found that adverse effects, such as the wrong medication or dose, infection, adverse transfusion reactions, and in-hospital hip fractures, occurred in 7.5 percent of hospital admissions, and of these, 36.9 percent were preventable and 20.8 percent resulted in death (Baker et al. 2004). This study is still used to measure adverse effects. Projected to Canada's 2.5 million annual admissions, this study suggests that 185 000 adverse effects occur annually, and 70 000 of these are preventable. *Social iatrogenesis* occurs when the health care system creates dependency and ill health, for example, by discouraging home births. *Cultural iatrogenesis* occurs when the system undermines the ability of people to care for themselves (Illich 1975:165). Conflict theorists argue that if patients were given the information and resources they need for prevention, self-treatment, and home care, the need and demand for expensive medical care would be greatly reduced (Stewart 1995). And some of these theorists are doctors themselves.

The Medical Reform Group is a Toronto-based voluntary association of physicians and medical students who believe that the medical profession must look to the social, economic, and political forces shaping health and health care in Canada. They believe that health care is a right and that today's health care is too hierarchical, giving too much power to doctors and not enough to patients. Some lay people have also formed an organization called Patients Canada to bring patients into the discussion. But they are not just an advocacy group. They also acknowledge outstanding work by health care professionals in partnership with the Ontario Medical Association. They invite patients and caregivers to nominate candidates who have performed exceptionally well. The stories are reviewed by a panel, and in 2014 five awards were presented to family physicians and hospital-based specialists in Ontario communities.

Another group that challenges accepted thinking in the area of health is disability rights' organizations. They are especially concerned with the public's support of euthanasia, or "mercy killing," of people with disabilities who cannot speak for themselves. An example of this is the Tracy Latimer story (see Box 5.2 on page 99 in Chapter 5). Tracy Latimer was a 12-year-old girl with severe cerebral palsy. Her father asphyxiated her, was tried and convicted of her killing, and was sentenced to prison. Disability rights advocates argue that it would not be a problem to have a disability if persons with disabilities were not discriminated against and oppressed. In the United States, a rights group that campaigns against euthanasia is called Not Dead Yet (from the film *Monty Python and the Holy Grail*, in which someone about to be put on a cart of plague victims says, "I'm not dead yet").

The Interactionist Perspective

Interactionists believe that many problems pertaining to health and illness in our society are linked to social factors that influence how people define our health care system. According to interactionists, we socially construct notions of crisis according to our desire to promote political objectives.

Interactionists are also interested in using telecommunications to promote health. People can call for advice, such as learning when they should see a doctor or go to an emergency room. A now well-used method is Telehealth, a toll-free, 24/7, confidential telecare service. In 2010, 5710 Telehealth sites were being used in at least 1175 communities across the country, accounting for close to 260 000 Telehealth interventions/meetings held between providers and patients, including an estimated 94 000 in rural or remote areas (Health Council of Canada 2012).

For example, Telehealth Ontario provides information on symptoms, illness, medications, nutrition and health, help for teens, and so on, but does not provide prescriptions or specific doctor referrals, and it is not a substitute for emergency (911) calls.

In the past, most patients relied on doctors for health-related information. Today, many people obtain medical information from the media and the Internet. Many thousands of websites are devoted to health and medical information, ranging from potentially life-saving research in top medical journals to alternative therapies such as herbal preparations and colon irrigation. Computer bulletin boards, chat groups, and Facebook groups have emerged to support people with conditions such as HIV/AIDS, multiple sclerosis, and others. Some sites (e.g., CarePages) allow people with a particular disease or condition to write a daily report on their condition so that friends can keep up with how they are progressing. Google can also be used as a source of information about the spread of diseases (when people in particular areas inquire about symptoms) and can thus alert health authorities to the possibility of epidemics more quickly than physicians' reports can. Because of the proliferation of medical information on the Internet, Health Canada is working to provide guidance to the consumer. Whether or not this proliferation of information helps to demystify doctor–patient relationships remains to be seen.

Interactionists also examine how individuals can construct their own health, to be producers rather than consumers of health. Writing in the interactionist manner, K. Green (1985) introduced the concept of self-health management, which recommends that people engage in practices to promote their own health—from following good health behaviour guidelines to seeking alternative care or seeking comfort from a friend. ***Self-health management* includes self-care practices, mutual aid, and membership in self-help groups** (Segall and Chappell 2000:131).

While the last two items are self-explanatory, the notion of self-care requires some expansion. This concept originated with Ivan Barofsky (1978) and has been developed by Alexander Segall (Segall and Chappell 2000:135–138). Self-care comprises four components:

- *Regulatory* self-care consists of daily habits that affect health, like eating a balanced diet, getting rest, and exercising.
- *Preventive* self-care consists of deliberate actions taken to reduce the risk of illness, such as brushing and flossing teeth.
- *Reactive* self-care consists of determining what to do when one feels ill and may involve seeking over-the-counter remedies and/or advice from friends or experts.
- *Restorative* self-care consists of compliance with treatments and medications prescribed by professionals, or part compliance, according to self-determination.

Self-care emphasizes lay control over health decision making and health maintenance.

The Feminist Perspective

Feminist theorists examine the extent to which women are treated in a disadvantageous manner in health or health care through processes like medicalization. ***Medicalization* is the treating of a person's condition as an illness.** This topic is of particular concern to women because many of women's natural conditions have been treated as physical or psychological illnesses. Deborah Findlay and Leslie Miller have written on the medicalization of women's bodies and women's lives. They begin by describing the rise of the medical profession, showing how healing became "men's work" and women's bodies "offered a lucrative new territory for profit-making" (Findlay and Miller 2002:188). First, mothering, child rearing, and childbirth were defined as medical problems; then, disorders suffered mostly by women—anorexia nervosa, for example—were defined as diseases.

Second, feminists have been critical of the traditional pattern of treating women according to findings from studies of men. In 2013, a major study of women was published at Women's College Hospital (Toronto), called Project for an Ontario Women's Health Evidence-Based Report (P.O.W.E.R.), which has produced information to support campaigns of women's organizations everywhere. The report provides data about women's health status, access to health care, and the quality of services across the continuum of care. In addition it provides data about the social determinants of health, differences between men and women, and differences among women associated with age, income, education, ethnicity, and neighbourhood.

A third concern of feminists has been the presence and treatment of women in the medical profession itself. It is well known that until a few decades ago, it was not easy for women to enroll in medical faculties, and thus not easy to become a doctor. With the increase of women in medical schools came the corresponding increase in women in medicine. In 2011, according to the CIHI (2013), women constituted 36 percent of physicians. Since the percentage of women doctors under 30 years of age is over 60 percent (see also Figure 12.1), the percentage of women doctors will certainly grow to over 50 percent over time.

Finally, some feminists have a special concern with disability. They have created the Disabled Women's Network. Their website provides a variety of useful links and recent updates.

WHAT CAN YOU DO?

- Volunteer at a downtown health agency (e.g., Street Health, a non-profit community agency in Toronto) that deals with people who are on welfare, are homeless, are recovering addicts, or are recently released from prison. Among the sociological insights you will get is an appreciation of how health is affected by social status. You may also make a difference in the life of a participant.
- Some students on your campus may not be able to afford nutritious meals, especially at the end of term when meal cards and money run out. Students at the University of Calgary organized a food bank for students. The bank gets funds from grants and student fees, uses student volunteers, and gives food to students who can no longer afford it (go to their website for more information). Other post-secondary schools have done the same. If your college or university does not have a food bank, you might help to create one.

- Develop a self-care management program. Consider how you could make use of mutual aid and the self-help groups that are available on university and college campuses, and how you could follow the four types of self-care to maintain your health.
- Study the way women, and men too, are exploited for profit in the cosmetic surgery and other health-related ways. Develop a seminar on body conscious-ness. You might start with the work of Tovée and associates (1997), who compare the BMIs of post-secondary female students, glamour and fashion models, and anorexic females. Fashion models (BMI = 17.6) are halfway between the female students (a normal BMI = 21.6) and anorexic females (BMI = 14.7).

- If you plan to do research in this area in the future, apply for a grant from the Canadian Institute of Health Research. One of its four goals is to improve the health status of vulnerable populations and create institutes for specific populations, such as Indigenous peoples, and children and youth. Included in this list is the Institute of Gender and Health, which supports research about how sex and gender interact with other health factors, leading to different risk factors and interventions for women and for men. Of particular interest is research on gender inequalities.

SUMMARY

Why Are Illness and Health Care Social Problems?

Health care is a social issue because, according to the World Health Organization, health is a state of complete physical, mental, and social well-being. Although people in Canada pay less for health services than people in the United States do, our measures of health show better outcomes than theirs. Thus, high expenditures do not translate into improved life expectancy for everyone.

How Have Health Care Problems Changed Over the Past Century?

Life expectancies increased greatly during the 20th century. Since acute illnesses (e.g., measles, polio) are largely under control with vaccinations and improved public health practices, most health problems today are chronic diseases (e.g., arthritis, diabetes, heart disease) or disabilities (e.g., back injuries, hearing or vision problems, brain injuries), which require long-term treatment. Medical advances mean that many people born with serious disabilities survive, as do many who would have died from acute illnesses or accidents in earlier times. As more people survive and live longer, more are likely to experience chronic illnesses and disabilities. But all these improvements are influenced by demographic variables like gender, class, and Indigenous ancestry.

Why Is Obesity a Social Problem?

Over half of Canadians over 18 years of age are overweight, and a fifth of Canadians are obese. Being overweight is related to a number of diseases, such as heart disease and Type II diabetes. People in rural Canada are more likely to be overweight than are people in urban Canada. The problem exists worldwide, even in developing countries. Suggestions to reduce this problem are similar to those suggested to reduce smoking, such as warnings on packages and taxes on junk food.

Why Is Mental Illness a Social Problem?

Mental illness is a social problem because of the number of people it affects, the difficulty in defining and identifying mental disorders, and the ways in which it is treated. Deinstitutionalization—discharging mental patients from hospitals into the community—was considered a solution to the problem of warehousing patients, but it has created new problems.

How Do Sex and Gender, Class, and Indigenous Ancestry Affect Physical and Mental Health?

Men, the poor, and Indigenous people have lower life expectancies than women, the rich, and non-Indigenous people. Women report more chronic conditions and disabilities than men do, while the poor and elementary-educated report more disability and poorer health than the rich and highly educated do. Although more women than men report mental illness, when addictive behaviour is included, men have higher rates of mental illness. Indigenous people have lower rates of very good and excellent perceived health than non-Indigenous people do. Indigenous youth are five to six times more likely to commit suicide than non-Indigenous youth are.

What Are the Five Characteristics of the Canadian Health Care System?

Our system is universal—covering all Canadians; accessible—unimpeded by financial and other barriers; and comprehensive—providing service on the basis of need. It is portable across provinces and territories. Lastly, it is publicly managed and funded.

Why Is the Health Care System Considered a Problem?

People find a number of issues with the health care system. The coverage of care including home care, drugs, and dental care needs to be expanded. Wait times, though decreasing, could decrease further. Will the supply of health care professionals be adequate with an aging population? How can technology help with health care (e.g., EHRs)? How are the costs of care distributed? Can the portion going to hospitals be reduced?

What Are the Sociological Explanations for Health Care Problems?

Functionalists consider the sick role a form of deviance that medicine as an institution controlled until recently. Some functionalists believe that the whole health system must be reorganized; others believe that incremental change is the best answer. Some conflict theorists believe that our health problems are rooted in capitalism and the medical–industrial complex. Some, like Ivan Illich, criticize the control of the system and would like to see people take more responsibility for their own health. Others, including some doctors, believe that only when inequalities based on sex and gender, class, and Indigenous status are reduced will inequalities in health care be reduced. Interactionists believe that communication problems among politicians, advocates, health care professionals, and the public create much of our concern about the health care system, but that these problems can be resolved through negotiation. They promote Telehealth. They believe that people must become more involved in self-health management and health care reform. Feminists believe that women have been treated in a disadvantageous manner regarding their bodies and health, the distribution of money to diseases that affect them, and their participation in medical careers. Women's organizations and studies like P.O.W.E.R. have improved knowledge of women's health issues, and higher graduation rates of women than men from medical schools have helped to reduce the dominance of male doctors.

KEY TERMS

ableism, p. 211
acute diseases, p. 208
chronic diseases, p. 208
disability, p. 211

iatrogenesis, p. 223
infant mortality rate, p. 207
life expectancy, p. 207
medical–industrial complex, p. 223

medicalization, p. 225
self-health management, p. 225
total institution, p. 216

QUESTIONS FOR CRITICAL THINKING

1. Because Canadians take pride in their high level of life expectancy, they are usually surprised to learn that the infant mortality rate of Indigenous people is double the rate of Canadians generally. Why is this rate so high, and what do you think individuals can do at the community level to save these young lives?

2. In what ways are sex and gender, class, and Indigenous status intertwined with physical and mental illness? Consider causes and treatments.

3. Do you know people with mental illness? What do you think would help them function better in our society?

4. Our health care system is growing in cost and could grow substantially higher. How much of our gross domestic product would you allocate with your tax dollars to health care in light of our education, research (e.g., on alternate sources of energy), social service, and security needs, and our future debt levels because of our current stimulus spending?

11

The Changing Family

Christian Adams/Photographer's Choice/Getty Images

M any people today experience the following family-related problems: women wanting equality, worries about long-term commitment, economic hardship after divorce, and sexual abuse. Although most sociologists believe that the family as a social institution will endure in one form or another, they also acknowledge that family-related problems are a challenge not only to individuals, but also to our entire society.

THE NATURE OF FAMILIES

What is a family? That question generates heated debate: some say that any definition of the family must emphasize tradition and stability; others argue that any useful definition must take into account diversity and social change. Traditionally, *family* has been defined as a group of people who are related to one another by blood, marriage, or adoption and who live together, form an economic unit, and bear and raise children. Today, however, the traditional definition of family is often modified to incorporate diverse living arrangements and relationships such as single-parent households, cohabiting unmarried couples, partners living apart together, blended or stepfamilies, marriages of lesbian or gay couples, and several generations of family members (grandparent, parent, and child) living under the same roof. To encompass all these arrangements, we will use the following definition as we look at family-related social problems: a **family is an institution found in all societies that unites people in cooperative groups to care for one another, including children** (Macionis and Gerber 2008:465).

Changing Family Structure and Patterns

The basis of the traditional family structure is **kinship, a social network of people based on common ancestry, marriage, or adoption.** Kinship is very important in pre-industrial societies because it serves as an efficient means of producing and distributing food and goods (clothing, materials for building shelter) and transferring property and power from one generation to the next. In many pre-industrial societies the primary kinship unit is the **extended family, a family unit composed of relatives in addition to parents and children, all of whom live in the same household.** Extended families typically include grandparents, uncles, aunts, or other relatives in addition to parents and children. When the growing and harvesting of crops is the basis of economic production, extended families mean that large numbers of people participate in food production, which can be essential to survival. Living together also enables family members to share other resources, such as shelter and transportation. Though extended families are not common in Canada, except in some immigrant communities, they are prevalent in some countries in Latin America, Africa, Asia, and parts of eastern and southern Europe.

    With industrialization, other social institutions begin to fulfill kinship-system functions. The production and distribution of goods and services, for example, largely shifts to the economic sector.

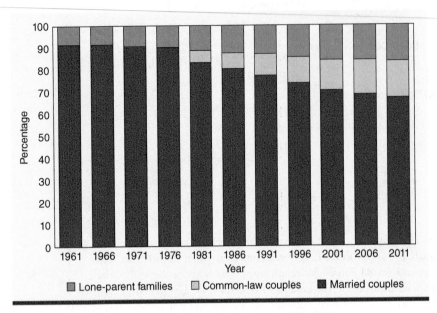

Figure 11.1   Distribution of Families by Family Structure in Canada, 1961–2011.

Source: *Statistics Canada, 2011, Census. Retrieved May 2013 (http://www12.statcan.gc.ca/census-recensement/2011/as-sa/98-312-x/2011003/fig/fig3_1-1-eng.cfm).*

The form of kinship that is most typical in industrialized nations is the *nuclear family*, **a family unit composed of one or two parents and her/his/their dependent children who live apart from other relatives.** The nuclear family in an industrialized society functions primarily to regulate sexual activity, socialize children, and provide family members with affection and companionship.

In the past, many people would have said that an ideal family consisted of a married couple and children. But lone-parent families have existed in the past, often because of a death of one of the parents, and common-law couples have existed in substantial and growing numbers for the last half century. Figure 11.1 shows the distribution of families by family structure from 1961 to 2011. Although substantial change occurred in the structure of families until the turn of the century, the distribution has remained quite stable from 2001 to 2011.

Table 11.1 shows more clearly the stability in the different types of families from 2001 to 2011. The only slight changes were increases in the number of common-law couples and male parent lone-parent families.

Are Canadian Families in Decline?

Will the family as a social institution disappear in the future? Social analysts answer this question differently,

	2001		2006		2011		Percentage change 2006 to 2011
TABLE 11.1 Changes in Family Structure in Canada, 2001–2011							
Census family	**number**	**percentage**	**number**	**percentage**	**number**	**percentage**	
Total census families	8 371 020	100.0	8 896 840	100.0	9 389 700	100.0	5.5
Couple families	7 059 830	84.3	7 482 775	84.1	7 861 860	83.7	5.1
Married	5 901 420	70.5	6 105 910	68.6	6 293 950	67.0	3.1
Common-law	1 158 410	13.8	1 376 865	15.5	1 567 910	16.7	13.9
Lone-parent families	1 311 190	15.7	1 414 060	15.9	1 527 840	16.3	8.0
Female parents	1 065 360	12.7	1 132 290	12.7	1 200 295	12.8	6.0
Male parents	245 825	2.9	281 775	3.2	327 545	3.5	16.2

Source: *Statistics Canada, 2011*, Censuses of Population, 2001 to 2011. *Retrieved May 10, 2013 (http://www12.statcan.gc.ca/census-recensement/2011/as-sa/98-312-x/2011001/tbl/tbl1-eng.cfm).*

depending on whether they adopt a traditional definition of the family or a modified definition. But new patterns have emerged over the past 50 years:

- New types of families include common-law, living apart together, blended or stepfamilies, and same-sex.
- While the types of families appear to be stabilizing, the percentage of people in traditional families has declined. Figure 11.2 shows that the percentage of single-person households has increased dramatically from less than 10 percent in 1961 to almost 30 percent in 2011, and the percentage of families with many members has also substantially declined.
- Chapter 4 showed that large numbers of married women have left the role of full-time mother and housewife to go into the labour market, and not all the functions of the former role are being fulfilled.
- The focus of many families has shifted away from childbearing to the needs of the adult members. Increasingly, even when parents have young children to raise, they break up if their psychological and self-development needs are unmet in the marriage relationship. Some sociologists have suggested that if marriage and the family weaken enough and no satisfactory substitute for marriage emerges, industrial societies will not survive.

Some analysts say the family isn't declining, it's simply changing. From this social change perspective, families are becoming more complex and diverse; they are not in a state of irreversible decline (Cherlin 1992; Skolnick 1991). In fact, according to sociologist Andrew

Cherlin (1992), the family will last as a social institution precisely because it can adapt to social change and modify its form. However, Cherlin goes on to say that the best way to minimize the costs of change in the family unit is to modify the other social institutions of daily life—such as the economy and workplace.

Changing Views on Marriage and Families

The term *marriage* refers to a legally recognized and/or socially approved arrangement between two individuals that carries certain rights and obligations and usually involves sexual activity. In Canada, the only legal form of marriage is **monogamy, a marriage between two people, either heterosexual or homosexual.** Some advocates have suggested that since marriage does not depend on opposite sexes any more, why limit the number of people in a marriage? Polygamy is widely practised outside high-income countries, why not in Canada? Actually it is practised in Canada. In Bountiful, B.C., polygamy has been practised with no prosecutions being considered until relatively recently (see Box 11.1).

Marriage was once a cultural imperative. There was "something wrong" with a person who didn't marry. But since the 1970s, people's attitudes toward marriage and the family have changed as other aspects of society have changed. Cultural guidelines on marriage and childbearing have grown weaker as our society has experienced

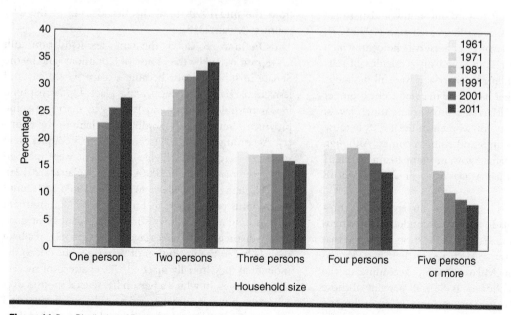

Figure 11.2 Distribution of Private Households by Household Size in Canada, 1961–2011.

Source: *Statistics Canada, 2011,* Censuses of Population, 2001 to 2011. *Retrieved May 19, 2013 (http://www12.statcan.gc.ca/census-recensement/2011/as-sa/98-312-x/2011003/fig/fig3_1-4-eng.cfm).*

Social Problems and Social Policy

Box 11.1

Polygamy

In early 2009, the attorney general of British Columbia announced criminal prosecutions against Winston Blackmore and Jim Oler, two leaders of the Fundamentalist Church of Jesus Christ of Latter Day Saints (FLDS) in Bountiful, B.C., on the charge of polygamy. This was an important case because it pitted the criminal ban on polygamy against freedom of religion in the *Charter of Rights and Freedoms* according to the FLDS. This freedom, however, is not supposed to extend to behaviour that harms others, particularly the most vulnerable, such as underage girls. Since this original charge, laws against polygamy were upheld in the B.C. Supreme Court in November 2011.

The FLDS is the Canadian branch of a group now residing in Texas that broke away from the Mormons. The Mormons have rejected the FLDS, whose prophet, Warren Jeffs, is now serving a prison term for being an accomplice to child sexual assault. The Canadian group is divided after a split between Blackmore, who was again charged with marrying 24 women on August 13, 2014, and Oler, who is charged with marrying four women.

Besides possible Charter protection, some say that polygamy is just another marriage form, like same-sex marriage. Some observers suggest that the best approach to deal with this problem is prosecution for trafficking and impregnation of underage girls. These alleged crimes might be the easiest to prove.

Since leaders are now charged with polygamy, we will see how the case is resolved.

Questions for Consideration

1. If marriage can be between any two people (no longer just a man and a woman), why not any three or more people?
2. Should religious rights trump other rights? If so, which ones?
3. How might young women in these communities come to reject this system?

Sources: Canadian Press, 2014, Polygamy charges against B.C. men raise Charter questions, *CBC NEWS. Retrieved June 19, 2015* (http://www.cbc.ca/news/canada/british-columbia/polygamy-charges-against-b-c-men-raise-charter-questions-1.2739179); *Geordon Omand, 2015,* Bountiful leader Winston Blackmore didn't get' fair notice' polygamy is illegal, argues lawyer, *CBC NEWS. Retrieved June 19, 2015* (http://www.cbc.ca/news/canada/british-columbia/bountiful-leader-winston-blackmore-didn-t-get-fair-notice-polygamy-is-illegal-argues-lawyer-1.3104352).

---

a broader cultural shift toward autonomy and personal growth. In the 1970s, according to Cherlin (1992:127), "family life became a matter of personal choice in which individuals made decisions based on a calculus of self-interest and self-fulfillment. Marriage was still desirable, but no one any longer had to be married to be a proper member of society." Marriage also became much less of an economic necessity for women in the 1970s because of new job opportunities and rising incomes. Although women's wages remained low in comparison to men's during this time, their wages rose in absolute terms (Cherlin 1992).

Still, marriage is a persistent preference for most people today. In a national survey conducted by Angus Reid, two-thirds of Canadian adults strongly agreed that their families were the greatest joy in their lives (Angus Reid 1994, cited in Milan 2000:5). According to the 1995 General Social Survey (GSS), 98 percent of those in marriages and 96 percent of those in common-law unions feel that a long-term relationship is important for their happiness (quoted in Milan 2000:5). Figure 11.3 shows the quite stable state of marriages and divorces

from the mid-1990s until the first decade of the 21st century (Milan 2013).

On June 28, 2005, the same-sex legislation, Bill C-38, was passed by the House of Commons (and by the Senate in July). Canada became a place where gay and lesbian marriage could legally take place. Up to that time it was possible for gays and lesbians to marry in some provinces, but it is now possible anywhere in the country. According to the 2011 census, 64 575 couples were same-sex couples, of which 32.5 percent were married (twice the percentage in 2006) (Statistics Canada 2012a).

Though many believe marriage should last "until death do us part," others feel marriage is a commitment "for as long as love allows." Through a pattern of marriage, divorce, and remarriage, many people reaffirm their belief in the institution of marriage, but not to the individual they initially married. This pattern of successive marriages, in which a person has several spouses over a lifetime but is legally married to only one partner at a time, is referred to as *serial monogamy*. Some social analysts consider serial monogamy a natural adaptation to other social changes in society; others think it is detrimental to

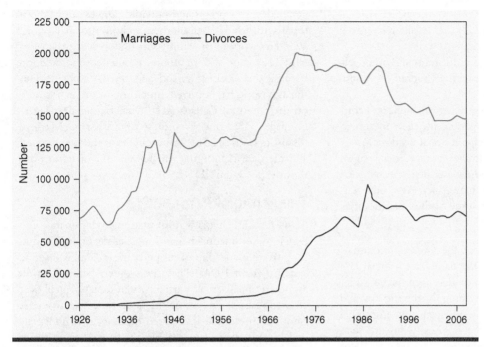

Figure 11.3 Number of Marriages and Divorces in Canada, 1926–2008.

Source: *Statistics Canada, 2011,* Canadian Vital Statistics. *Retrieved September 25, 2013* (*http://www.statcan.gc.ca/pub/91-209-x/2013001/article/11788/fig/fig7-eng.htm*).

individuals and to society and serves as further evidence of the decline of the family (see Popenoe 1996). Who is right? As with other social problems we have examined, the view of causes, effects, and possible solutions for family-related problems depends on the theoretical framework the analyst uses.

PERSPECTIVES ON FAMILY-RELATED PROBLEMS

What purposes do families serve in contemporary societies? Do families create problems for society or solve them? The latter, say functionalists, who believe that the family fulfills important functions for individuals at the microlevel and for the entire society at the macrolevel. Conflict and feminist theorists, on the other hand, consider families a primary source of inequality—and sometimes abuse and violence—in society. Taking a microlevel approach, interactionists analyze family-related social problems in terms of socialization and social interactions among family members.

The Functionalist Perspective

Functionalists emphasize the importance of the family in maintaining the stability of society and the well-being of

individuals. According to Emile Durkheim, marriage is a microcosmic replica of the larger society; both marriage and society involve a mental and moral fusion of physically distinct individuals (Lehmann 1994). Durkheim also believed that a division of labour contributed to greater efficiency in marriage and families (and in all areas of life). In his study of family life in the United States, sociologist Talcott Parsons (1955) also viewed a division of labour as important. He saw the husband in an ideal nuclear family as fulfilling an *instrumental role*—meeting the family's economic needs, making important decisions, and providing leadership—and the wife as fulfilling an *expressive role*—running the household, caring for children, and meeting family members' emotional needs.

Using Durkheim's and Parsons's work as a basis for their model of the family, contemporary functionalists believe that a division of labour makes it possible for families to fulfill a number of functions that no other social institution in high-income nations can perform as efficiently and effectively:

1. Regulate sexual behaviour and reproduction: Families are expected to regulate the sexual activity of their members and thus control reproduction so that it occurs within specific boundaries. Sexual regulation of family members by the family is supposed to

protect the *principle of legitimacy*—the belief that all children should have a socially and legally recognized father (Malinowski 1964).

2. Socialize and educate children: Parents and other relatives are responsible for teaching children the values and norms of their culture.

3. Provide economic and psychological support: Families are responsible for providing for their members' physical (food, shelter) and emotional needs.

4. Provide social status: Families confer social status on their members, including ascribed statuses such as racialization, ethnicity, nationality, class, and religious affiliation, although some of these statuses may change later in life.

Considering their view of the family, functionalists believe that problems in the family are a social crisis. The functional family provides both social order and economic stability by providing for the survival and development of children; the physical and emotional health of adults; and the care of those who are sick, injured, elderly, or have disabilities. The family is also the front line for reinforcing society's norms and values. Functionalists consider the family to be part of the solution to many problems faced by people in contemporary societies. In this view, dysfunctions in families are problems that threaten the well-being of individuals, groups, and nations.

Functionalists believe that changes in other social institutions, such as the economy, religion, education, law, medicine, and the government, contribute to family-related problems. For example, some functionalists think that changing the law to recognize no-fault divorce contributed to higher rates of divorce and dramatically increased lone-parent households, which do not provide children with the nurture and guidance they get in a two-parent home (Popenoe 1996).

The Conflict Perspective

Most conflict analysts believe that functionalist views on family problems are idealized and inadequate. Rather than operating harmoniously and for the benefit of all members, families, these analysts say, are sources of social inequality and conflict over values, goals, and access to resources and power.

Conflict theorists who focus on class relations in capitalist economies compare family members to workers in a factory, emphasizing the inequality in each institution. Women are dominated by men in the home, just as workers are dominated by managers and capitalists in factories (Engels 1972). As wives and mothers, women contribute to capitalism by producing the next generation of workers and providing the existing labour force with food, clean clothes, and emotional support. Women's work in the family not only benefits the capitalist class, but also reinforces women's subordination because the work is unpaid and often devalued. This unpaid work has received much attention in research on the family in Canada (see "Dual-Earner Marriages" on page 237). But, according to Katherine Marshall (Statistics Canada 2011), in recent years younger women and men are converging on the amount of housework they do (see Figure 11.4).

The Feminist Perspective

Many feminist theorists think that male dominance and female subordination began long before capitalism and the private ownership of property arose as an economic system (Mann 1994). They see women's subordination as rooted in patriarchy, particularly in men's control over women's labour power. At the same time that women's labour in the home is directed by men, it is undervalued, which allows men to benefit from their status as the family breadwinners (Firestone 1970; Goode 1982). Sociologist Jane Riblett Wilkie (1993) found that most men are reluctant to relinquish their status as family breadwinner. Although only 15 percent of the families in Canada are supported solely by a male breadwinner, many men continue to construct their ideal of masculinity based on this role. It is acceptable for wives to enter the paid workforce if their role is simply to earn money; they should not, however, challenge the ideal roles of male breadwinner and female homemaker.

Like conflict theorists, feminist theorists argue that family problems derive from inequality—not just within the family, but in the political, social, and economic arenas of the larger society as well (Aulette 1994). In fact, pervasive societal inequality leads to one of the most tragic family problems: intimate partner (including dating) violence. According to feminist theorists, intimate partner and other forms of domestic violence may even be conscious strategies that men use to control women and perpetuate gender inequality (Kurz 1989). Fortunately, the rates seem to be declining with the general crime rates. However, during the past 30 years, the rate of women's homicide (or attempts) has been about three times greater than the rate of men's homicide (or attempts). According to the 2010 edition of the report *Family Violence in Canada: A Statistical Profile* (Statistics Canada 2012c:39), from 1991 to 2010, the rate of female victims of spousal homicide dropped from 11 per million women in spousal relationships to 3, and the rate of male victims was stable around 2. (The rates of overall intimate partner violence are illustrated in Table 11.4.)

According to feminist theorists, family-related problems, including domestic violence and wife abuse, can be solved only if all social institutions work to eliminate the subordination of women in society. Increased educational and occupational opportunities for women over the past quarter-century may be contributing to a reduction in intimate partner violence. Related to increased opportunities for women, the increase in the age of first marriage (see "Postponing Marriage" on page 236) may be another contributing factor to the decline in violence.

The Interactionist Perspective

Some interactionists view the family communication process as integral to understanding the diverse roles that family members play; therefore, these analysts examine how husbands, wives, and children act out their roles and react to the parts played by others. Although societies differ widely on the rules and norms that should shape family and kin relationships, people are socialized to accept their society's form of the family as the acceptable norm. According to sociologists Peter Berger and Hansfried Kellner (1964), marital partners develop a shared reality through their interactions with each other. Although newlyweds bring separate identities to a marriage, over time they construct a shared reality as a couple. In the process, the partners redefine their past identities to be consistent with their new realities. Interactionists say that the process of developing a shared reality is continuous and occurs not only in the family, but also in any group in which the couple participates together. In cases of separation and divorce, the process is reversed: couples may start with a shared reality but once again become individuals with separate realities in the process of uncoupling their relationship.

How do interactionists explain problems in a family? Some look at the subjective meanings and interpretations people give to their everyday lives. According to sociologists Charles Jones, Lorna Marsden, and Lorne Tepperman (1990), over the past few decades, women have gained more choice and opportunities in life. Women have become more "individualized." One of the consequences of this dramatic change is that women have few role models to follow; as a result, new expectations about work and child rearing could cause problems for the family. Obviously, men would also be uncertain about how to behave with these changed expectations. According to sociologist Jessie Bernard (1982), women and men experience marriage differently. While the husband may see his marriage very positively, the wife may feel less positive. The reverse may also be true. Evidence for the different realities of marriage comes from research that shows that husbands and wives often give very different accounts of the same event (Safilios-Rothschild 1969).

Still other interactionists view family problems in terms of partners' unrealistic expectations about love and marriage, which can lead to marital dissatisfaction and, sometimes, divorce. These analysts note that our culture emphasizes romantic love—a deep and vital emotion based on significant need satisfaction, caring for and acceptance of another person, and the development of an intimate relationship (Lamanna and Riedmann 1994). Indeed, most couples in Canada get married because they are in love, but being a "nation of lovers" doesn't mean that men and women have the same ideas about what constitutes romantic love. According to sociologist Francesca Cancian (1990), women tend to express their feelings verbally, whereas men tend to express their love through such non-verbal actions as preparing dinner or doing household repairs. Women may not always interpret these actions as signs of love. One man complained (Rubin 1976:146), "What does she want? Proof? She's got it, hasn't she? Would I be knocking myself out to get things for her—like to keep up this house—if I didn't love her? Why does a man do things like that if not because he loves his wife and kids? I swear, I can't figure what she wants." His wife replied, "It's not enough that he supports us and takes care of us. I appreciate that, but I want him to share things with me. I need for him to tell me his feelings."

Whatever their different viewpoints on marriage and family, most social theorists agree on one fact: three decades ago, the nuclear family was the most common family form, and today it is only one of many patterns.

DIVERSITY IN INTIMATE RELATIONSHIPS AND FAMILIES

Greater diversity, and thus, potential problems in intimate relationships and families in Canada has come about because of dramatic increases in (1) singlehood, (2) postponed marriage, (3) living together without marriage (called common-law or cohabitation), (4) living apart together, (5) dual-earner marriages, and (6) one-parent families.

Singlehood

Although most young singles will eventually marry, 10 percent of the population will remain single for their lives. When this figure is combined with those who have been widowed, separated, or divorced, the proportion of Canadian single-person households is almost 30 percent (see Figure 11.2). Some people choose singlehood over marriage because it means greater freedom from commitments to another person. Others choose it because of increased career opportunities (especially for women), the availability of sexual partners without marriage, the belief that the single lifestyle is full of excitement, or the desire for self-sufficiency and freedom to change and experiment. As an indication of this, online dating sites have a huge following (e.g., one site, Match.com had 1.2 million members in early 2013) and are some of the most profitable companies on the Web.

Some people are single not by choice but by necessity. Because of structural changes in the economy, many young working-class people cannot afford to marry and set up their own households. Indeed, some college and university graduates have found that they cannot earn enough money (Boyd and Norris 1999) or since the great recession, recover from student debt, to set up households separate from those of their parents.

Postponing Marriage

Young people today are less eager to get married than they were four decades ago; many are remaining single into their late 20s. In 2008, the average age at which men first married was 31.0 years, and the average age for women was 29.6 years; the pattern has changed from the 1960s and 1970s, when the average age for men was 25 and for women, 23 years (Milan 2013).

Why are more people postponing first marriages? Although some reasons are the same as those for staying single, sociologist Robin Wolf (1996) suggests four key factors: (1) economic uncertainty due to the changing job structure in Western societies; (2) women's increasing participation in the labour force; (3) the sexual revolution of the 1970s that made sexual relationships outside marriage more socially acceptable; and (4) the rising divorce rate—young people watching their parents divorce may be less anxious to jump into marriage themselves. Other analysts suggest that a significant increase in cohabitation and domestic partnerships also contributes to the percentage of people who are counted as single or postponing marriage.

Common-Law or Cohabitation

The popularity of cohabitation has increased in the past two decades. **Common-law,** or *cohabitation,* **is two adults living together in a sexual relationship without being legally married.** According to the 2011 census (see Table 11.1), 1.4 million couples—18 percent of all couples—were living common-law, up from 5.6 percent in 1981. Now almost 40 percent of men and women aged 30 to 39 are expected to choose common-law as their first union (Statistics Canada 2002:3). The proportion of cohabiting couples still varies significantly by language spoken. In Quebec, 31.5 percent of all couples were living common-law in 2011, about the same as 2001 (Statistics Canada 2013h). This seems counter-intuitive in a predominantly Roman Catholic province. What do you think?

For some couples, cohabitation is a form of trial marriage and constitutes an intermediate stage between dating and marriage. According to anthropologist Margaret Mead (1966), dating patterns do not adequately prepare people for marriage and parenting responsibilities. Mead proposed a two-stage marriage process, each with its own ceremony and responsibilities. In the first stage, the individual marriage, two people would make a serious commitment to each other but agree not to have children during this stage. In the second stage, the parental marriage, the couple would decide to have children and to share responsibility for their upbringing. Many people today seem to be following this pattern, though without intention, and with different partners. Divorce in the first couple of years of marriage is quite common, and the break-up of a common-law relationship is even more likely. *American Demographics* editor Pamela Paul, having been through an early divorce herself, interviewed 60 other young, divorced couples and wrote a book about what she called a "starter marriage." She claimed that most of her sample had not given marriage much thought before getting married; they had developed "matrimania" due to a marriage-oriented culture (Paul 2002).

For other couples, cohabitation is not necessarily a first step toward marriage. In one study, researchers found that slightly more than 50 percent of cohabitation relationships eventually culminated in marriage, whereas 37 percent broke up and 10 percent were still ongoing at the time of the study (London 1991).

Does cohabitation contribute to marital success? The evidence is mixed. Some studies show that cohabitation has little or no effect on marital adjustment, emotional closeness, satisfaction, or intimacy. Other studies indicate that couples who cohabit first are more likely to divorce than those who do not. Apparently, partners in this study who had cohabited were less satisfied with their marriage and less committed to the institution of marriage than were those who had not lived together before marrying. The researchers theorized that cohabitation may contribute to people's individualistic attitudes and values, while making them more aware that alternatives to marriage exist (Axinn and Thornton 1992; Thomson and Colella 1992).

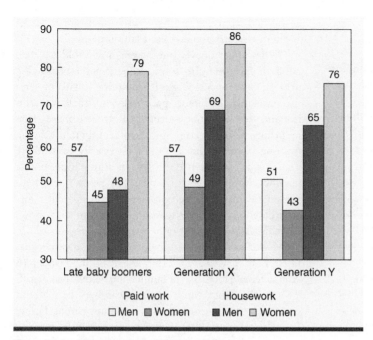

Figure 11.4   Convergence of Participation in Housework.

Source: *Marshall, Katherine. 2011. Generational change in paid and unpaid work. Canadian Social Trends. No. 92 Catalogue No. 11-008:13-26.*

Living Apart Together (LAT)

As was suggested at the beginning of the chapter by the general definition of families, families may not even choose to live together. A form of relationship that has been recently surveyed involves couples who are living apart together, meaning they are married, single, widowed, divorced, or separated but are in an intimate relationship with someone living in another dwelling/location. In 2011, 7 percent of couples or 1.9 million Canadians, mostly young LATs, were not living in the same residence, whether for job or other opportunities. Of the young, 80 percent wanted to live together; but of the older couples, only 30 percent wanted to live together, perhaps to maximize benefits or minimize care-giving burdens. Since older couples are more likely always to live apart, with the aging of the population we may see a higher percentage of these couples (Statistics Canada 2013i).

Dual-Earner Marriages

More than two-thirds of all marriages in Canada are *dual-earner marriages*, **marriages in which both spouses are in the labour force.** Over half of all employed women hold full-time, year-round jobs, and in a change from the past, there are more married women with young children in the paid labour force today than ever before.

Many married women who are employed outside the household face hours of domestic work and child care when they get home. Sociologist Arlie Hochschild (1989) refers to the latter half of women's dual workdays as the *second shift*—**the domestic work that many employed women perform at home after completing their workday on the job.** According to Hochschild, the unpaid housework that women do on the *second shift* (see Chapter 4) amounts to an extra month of work each year. In households with small children or many children, the amount of housework increases (Hartmann 1981). Across racialization and class lines, numerous studies confirm that domestic work remains primarily women's work (Gerstel and Gross 1995).

In recent years, more husbands or partners have been sharing some of the household and child-care responsibilities, especially when both individuals' earnings are essential to family finances (Perry-Jenkins and Crouter 1990). But even when husbands or partners assume some of the household responsibilities, they typically spend much less time in these activities than do their wives. A Canadian time-budgeting study of young people aged 20 to 29 years in three generations (Baby boomers born mid-1940s to mid-1960s, Gen Xers born mid-1960s to late 1970s, and Gen Yers born early 1980s to late 1990s) shows that later generations of men are doing more housework. Figure 11.4 shows that whereas 48 percent of baby boomers are doing housework, 69 percent of Gen X men are doing housework and 65 percent of Gen Y men are doing housework (Marshall 2011:18).

In the age of dual-earner marriages, it has become increasingly important for fathers to assume child-care and household duties. How does this photo show the competing demands faced by many employed parents?
Ariel Skelley/Taxi/Getty Images

Comparing Two-Parent and One-Parent Households

When the mother and father in a two-parent household truly share parenting, children have the benefit of two primary caregivers. Some researchers have found that when fathers take an active part in raising their children, the effect is beneficial for all family members. Fathers find that increased contact with their children provides more opportunities for personal and emotional gratification (Coltrane 2004).

However, living in a two-parent family does not guarantee children a happy childhood. Children whose parents argue constantly, abuse them, or are alcoholics have a worse family experience than do children in a single-parent family where there is a supportive environment. Women (and men) who are employed full-time and are lone-parents probably have the greatest burden of all. These women (and men) must fulfill their paid employment duties and meet the needs of their children and the household, often with little help from ex-partners or relatives.

How prevalent are lone-parent households? The past two decades have seen a significant increase in lone-parent households due to divorce, death of a parent, and births outside of marriage. In 2011, lone-parent families made up 16.3 percent of the total number of families in Canada (see Table 11.1). Who heads most one-parent households? Today, 80 percent of all one-parent families

are headed by single mothers, while men are heads of about 19 percent of one-parent families.

What effect does a one-parent household have on children? According to some studies, children growing up with only one biological parent are at risk of serious problems, including poor academic achievement, dropping out of school, drug and alcohol abuse, teen pregnancy, early marriage, and divorce. Obviously, living in a one-parent family does not necessarily cause these problems. Factors such as poverty, discrimination, unsafe neighbourhoods, parenting styles (see below), and high crime rates must also be considered. Lone-parent families are definitely poorer than others. Figure 11.5 shows that whereas 8.2 percent of people under 18 years of age in two-parent families are below the low income cut-off after tax (LICO-AT), 21.8 percent of those under 18 years in female lone-parent families are below the cut-off.

On the other hand, some researchers have found some benefits to growing up in a one-parent family (Lauer and Lauer 1991). For example, children in one-parent families are often less pressured to conform to rigid gender roles. Rather than having chores assigned by gender, as is common in two-parent families, single-parent children typically take on a wider variety of tasks and activities. Many single-parent children also show high levels of maturity and self-sufficiency earlier because they have to help out at a younger age than do children in other families (Lauer and Lauer 1991).

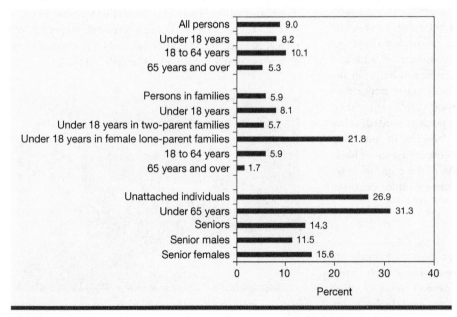

Figure 11.5   Incidence of Low Income using the After Tax Low Income Cut-off (LICO-AT), 2010.

Source: Statistics Canada, 2010, Income in Canada. Retrieved May 13, 2013 (http://www.statcan.gc.ca/pub/75-202-x/2010000/c-g/ct006-eng.htm).

What about the fathers of children in one-parent households headed by women? Although some fathers remain involved in their children's lives, others only occasionally take their children out for recreational activities or buy them presents on birthdays and holidays. Personal choice, workplace demands on time and energy, location of the ex-wife's residence, and limitations placed on visitation by custody arrangements are all factors that affect how often absentee fathers visit their children. Increasingly, parents are receiving joint custody of their children, and it appears that joint custody can minimize the disruption of divorce in a child's life if the ex-spouses cooperate with each other and live in relatively close geographical proximity. However, ex-spouses who constantly argue or live far away from each other can create serious problems for "commuter" children.

The transition from a two-parent family to a one-parent family is only one of many child-related family issues that many people today must deal with, as we discuss in the next section.

CHILD-RELATED FAMILY ISSUES
Reproductive Freedom, Contraception, and Abortion

One of the major issues facing many individuals and families today is reproductive freedom, a term that implies both the desire *to have* and the desire *not to have* a child. Reproductive freedom has been a controversial issue throughout much of Canadian history. In 1869, the Canadian government banned abortion. It was not until 100 years later that a bill was passed making it possible for a woman to get an abortion, with the judgment of three doctors in a hospital that a woman's life or health was in danger. That bill, introduced in 1967 by then Justice Minister and future Prime Minister Pierre Elliott Trudeau with the famous expression "The state has no business in the bedrooms of the nation!" also legalized homosexuality and contraception. Earlier in the 1960s, the "pill" was introduced, and public opinion about women's reproductive freedom began to change. By 1971, the pill was the most popular form of contraception in Canada (Bélanger 1998:17). Many women spend about 90 percent of their fertile years trying to avoid pregnancy, and it is estimated that almost 100 percent of women who have ever had sexual intercourse have used one or more contraceptive methods.

Over the past years, the methods of contraception have changed greatly. According to the General Social Survey of 1995, the use of contraceptive sterilization doubled in that time. Since 1976, there has also been a decline in the use of the pill and an increase in the use of condoms. This may be because of the cost, or perhaps men are willing to take more responsibility for contraception and are more concerned about

For a number of decades, there have been intense public confrontations between abortion rights advocates and members of the anti-abortion movement. Demonstrators are a familiar sight outside abortion clinics, hospitals, and government buildings.
Fred Chartrand/CP Images

the spread of sexually transmitted diseases (Bélanger 1998:19).

Although the 1967 law permitted abortion, it was not always easy to obtain one. Some provinces were not sympathetic to abortions, and some hospitals did not set up committees to judge the situations. Because he felt that women had a basic right to abortions, Dr. Henry Morgentaler started to perform abortions in a clinic in Montreal. Since he was breaking the law, he was tried three times, but no jury would convict him. He took his case to the Supreme Court of Canada and won. The law permitting abortions under strict circumstances was declared unconstitutional in 1988. The next year, the federal government tried once again to pass an abortion bill, but it was defeated in the Senate. No provincial government has tried to pass a bill on abortion since that time, and opportunities for abortion increased in the 1990s. To provide direct and immediate help, Morgentaler set up clinics in several Canadian cities, but not without a struggle: in 1992, his clinic in Toronto was bombed.

Opposition to abortion was strong into the mid-1990s. In 1994, a doctor who performed abortions, Garson Romalis, was shot in Vancouver. Two other anti-abortion shootings took place, one in Ontario in 1995, and one in Manitoba in 1997. While protesting at clinics has continued, no further serious attacks have occurred in Canada. This may be due to a decline in the number of abortions being performed. In 2005, 96 615 abortions were performed for Canadian women, a decrease of 3.2 percent from 2004. Now there are fewer than three abortions for every 10 live births in Canada (Statistics Canada 2008d). At the microlevel, abortion is a solution for some pregnant women and their families, but a problem for others, particularly when they face religious or family opposition. At the macrolevel, abortion is both a problem and solution when activists try to influence the making and enforcement of laws pertaining to women's reproductive rights and the control of new reproductive technologies.

Infertility and New Reproductive Technologies

Infertility is defined as an inability to conceive after a year of unprotected sexual relations. In 40 percent of cases, the woman is infertile, and in another 40 percent, the man is infertile; 20 percent of the time, the cause is impossible to determine (Gabriel 1996).

Sexually transmitted diseases are a leading cause of infertility: each year, many women become infertile as a result of a sexually transmitted disease that develops into pelvic inflammatory disease (Gold and Richards 1994). There are also some women—both married and unmarried—who would like to have a child but cannot because of disabilities. Some analysts point out that a growing number of prospective parents delay childbearing into their 30s and 40s, by which time it may be more difficult for them to conceive.

About 50 percent of infertile couples who seek treatment can be helped by conventional, low-tech treatments such as fertility drugs, artificial insemination, and surgery to unblock fallopian tubes. The other 50 percent require advanced technology, sometimes called assisted reproductive technology (ART). Many middle- and upper-income couples, for example, receive in vitro fertilization (IVF), which, according to the Infertility Awareness Association of Canada, costs a minimum of $7000 and up to $10 000 (with travel and drugs) per attempt (see Table 11.2). Despite the popularity of such treatments and the growth of fertility clinics (from 30 slightly over a decade ago to more than 300 today), only one in five couples who receive ART actually become parents (Gabriel 1996). As of 2015, the Ontario Hospital Insurance Plan (OHIP) will help pay for one cycle of IVF for all infertile people. Infertility Awareness Association of Canada has a wide variety of resources for those contemplating this procedure, such as clinics, adoption services, counsellors, embryo donation, attorneys, and support groups.

Because IVF does not get much financial support and is not always successful, some women have many embryos implanted, and a new situation of more multiple births is occurring. In Canada in 2007, one woman gave birth to six children of whom four survived, and in the United States in 2009, a woman known as "Octomom" gave birth to eight children.

Adoption

Adoption is a legal process through which the rights and duties of parenting are transferred from a child's biological and/or legal parents to new legal parents. The adopted child has all the rights of a biological child. In long past adoptions, a new birth certificate was issued, and the child had no further contact with the biological parents, although more recently agencies have been arranging for people to meet their biological parents or children with mutual consent. Now some provincial acts have made disclosure a right. For example, as of June 2009, in Ontario it is possible to unseal birth records if either a birth parent or adult adoptee requests it, unless a veto has been signed. Five other provinces in Canada have equivalent legislation, beginning 10 years ago with British Columbia.

TABLE 11.2 Forms of Assisted Reproductive Technology

Name	Description
In vitro fertilization (IVF)	Eggs that were produced as a result of administering fertility drugs are removed from the woman's body and fertilized by sperm in a laboratory dish. The embryos that result from this process are transferred to the woman's uterus.
Gamete intrafallopian transfer (GIFT)	The woman is given hormones to simulate the production of multiple eggs. Unfertilized eggs and sperm are placed into the woman's fallopian tube(s) using laproscopy, a microsurgical procedure. Fertilization occurs in the fallopian tubes before the embryo implants in the uterine wall.
Zygote intrafallopian transfer (ZIFT) and tubal embryo transfer (TET)	Eggs are removed from the woman and fertilized in a lab before being transferred by laproscopy to the fallopian tube rather than the uterus.
Intracytoplasmic sperm injection (ICSI)	A single sperm is injected directly into a mature egg. The embryo is then transferred to the woman's uterus or fallopian tube.

Matching children who are available for adoption with prospective adoptive parents can be difficult. The children often have specific needs, and prospective parents often specify the kind of children they want to adopt. Because many prospective parents do not want to adopt children who are non-White (most prospective parents are White), older, or have disabilities or diseases, many children available for adoption are not chosen, and instead move from foster home to foster home.

Prospective parents frequently want infants, but fewer infants are available for adoption than in the past because contraception and abortion are more readily available, and more unmarried teenage parents are deciding to keep their babies. Some teenagers, however, believe that adoption is the best way to solve the problem of early childbearing.

Because fewer infants are available for adoption, some Canadians are adopting through a private agency or from a foreign country (e.g., China, Russia, Haiti, and Ethiopia have been prominent in the recent past). Another option for couples waiting to adopt is to submit a profile of themselves and hope that they are chosen by the birth mother. Since 2006, Adoption Profiles has been instrumental in helping over 100 childless couples match with birth mothers. With an online presence, and a free waiting-families registry, Adoption Profiles is the first service of its kind in Canada.

Parenting Style

Besides the influence of factors such as low income and family structure, other factors, including the way parents treat their children, affect children's development. To study the effect of parenting styles on child development, a massive study was begun in 1994. The National Longitudinal Survey of Children and Youth (NLSCY) is a study of 23 000 families that is investigating a wide variety of variables, including income, family structure, and parenting style, on child development. Parenting style is based on responses to questions about being the following:

- rational (e.g., How often do you think that the kind of punishment you give him/her depends on your mood?);
- responsive (e.g., How often do you praise?);
- reasoning (e.g., When your child breaks the rules . . . do you: (a) calmly discuss the matter? And (b) describe alternative ways of behaving . . . ?); and
- firm (e.g., When you give him/her a command to do something, what proportion of the time do you make sure that he/she has done it?).

Based on answers to questions such as these, the parents are divided into four groups ranging from positive (warm and nurturing) to ineffective (very intolerant and erratic). Among the first findings the researchers made was that parenting style had more effect on behavioural problems than family structure or income. Children living with two parents with poor parenting skills were five times more likely to have such developmental problems as aggression, hyperactivity, and depression than children living with a single but effective parent were; this is also a wider gap than one due to income differences (Statistics Canada 1998).

However, if the parenting environment changed from punitive to non-punitive over the ages 2–3 to 8–9 years, then aggressive behaviour will decline (Statistics

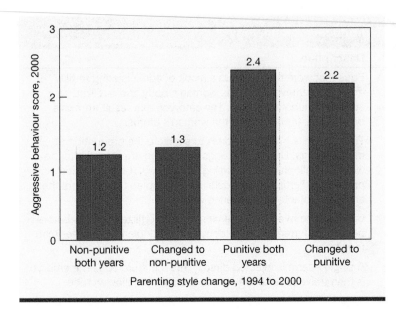

Figure 11.6   Children's Aggressive Behaviour Linked with Current Punitive Parenting.

Source: *Statistics Canada, 2004, "Parenting Style and Children's Aggressive Behaviour, 1994 to 2000,"* The Daily (October 25), Catalogue no. 11-001.

Canada 2004). Figure 11.6 shows children's behaviour changes to the level of the children in the non-punitive environment if the parent's punitive behaviour changes to non-punitive. Note that the reverse is possible too. Why do you think this occurs?

Another kind of parenting style was very much in the news in 2011 when *Revenge of the Tiger Mother* was published. Box 11.2 introduces the topic and presents a longitudinal study of whether demanding and controlling parents lead to children becoming superstars.

Teen Pregnancies and Unmarried Motherhood

The birth rate among teenagers has declined substantially over the past few decades. From the early 1970s to the 1990s, the proportion of births to teenagers declined from 11 to 6 percent of all births (Milan 2000:7). And more recently, teenagers' (age 15–19 years) age-specific fertility rates have dropped from 14.0 in 2007 to 12.6 in 2011 (Statistics Canada 2013e).

According to social analysts, the outcome of teen pregnancies is problematic because teenage mothers are typically unskilled at parenting, are likely to drop out of school, and have no social support other than relatives (Chase-Lansdale et al. 1992). Family support is extremely important to unmarried pregnant teens because emotional and financial support from the fathers of their children is often lacking (Nath et al. 1991). Without this support, teen mothers rely on their own parents and grandparents to help with child rearing. The picture for the children of teenage mothers without

parental support is especially bleak because few of these mothers have adequate parenting skills or knowledge of child development. Children of unwed teenage mothers tend to have severely limited educational and employment opportunities and a high likelihood of living in poverty. Teenagers are not the only ones having children without getting married. The birth rate for older single (never married) women is high. Of those aged 20 to 24, 46.1 percent of babies were born to single (never married) women. Of those aged 25 to 29, 29.0 percent were born to single (never married) women. And for the next four age categories 30 to 34, 35 to 39, 40 to 44 and 45 to 49 the percentages of babies born to single (never married) women were 18.8, 14.4, 14.0, and 13 respectively (Statistics Canada 2013e). According to demographer analysts, these percentages reflect the declining importance of marriage as a social prerequisite for reproduction. With less of a social stigma attached to unmarried pregnancy, fewer women seem to be seeking abortion and are deciding instead to raise the child themselves, whether the pregnancy was planned or not.

So, overall, how well are children doing in Canada? Recent information from UNICEF, suggests that we are doing only average among high-income countries (see Box 11.3).

DIVORCE AND REMARRIAGE

Divorce is the legal process of dissolving a marriage, which allows former spouses to remarry if they so choose. Have you heard such statements as "Almost one

Box 11.2

Tiger Mothers Do not Always Produce Superstars

In 2011, Amy Chua's book, *Revenge of the Tiger Mother,* about the value of being tough and demanding of her children to produce superstars, caused controversy in the media. One of her daughters got to both Carnegie Hall (playing violin) and Harvard. But Amy Chua was roundly criticized for not being more supportive.

Does any data exist to support or refute this approach? Su Yeong Kim, an associate professor of human development and family sciences at the University of Texas, had data for this. Kim had been following Asian-American families for a decade. She had wondered if Asian parents were very strict and whether that was related to the high performance of Asian students. In a three-wave longitudinal design spanning eight years, from early adolescence to emerging adulthood, adolescents, fathers, and mothers from 444 Chinese-American families reported on eight parenting dimensions (e.g., warmth and shaming) and six developmental outcomes (e.g., GPA and academic pressure). Most of the parents were foreign born and most of the children were born in the United States. The researcher controlled for birth order and socioeconomic status.

Children and parents were asked about parents' behaviour. Warmth, reasoning, monitoring, and democratic parenting were considered positive attributes, while hostility, psychological control, shaming, and punitive measures were considered negative. These characterizations were then combined to determine Kim's four parenting profiles:

- "supportive" parents scored high on the positive dimensions;
- "easygoing" parents scoring low on the negative dimensions;
- "harsh" parents scored high on negative attributes and low on positive ones; and
- "tiger" parents scored high on both positive and negative dimensions.

Despite the popular image of Chinese-American parenting that Chua's book bolstered as being widespread,

fewer "tiger" parents emerged from Kim's analysis than did "supportive" parents. "Easygoing" were similar in number as "tigers," and the fewest parents were deemed "harsh."

Supportive parents had the best developmental outcomes, as measured by academic achievement, educational attainment, family obligation (considered positive outcomes), academic pressure, depressive symptoms, and parent–child alienation (considered negative). Academic achievement and attainment were purely data-driven, while information on the other four outcomes came from different assessments developed by academics over the years, which are somewhat subjective. Children of easygoing parents were second in outcomes, while tiger moms produced kids who felt more alienated from their parents and who experienced higher instances of depressive symptoms. They also had lower GPAs, despite feeling more academic pressure. Tiger children's GPAs and depressive symptoms were similar to those whose parents were very harsh.

Kim and colleagues concluded that contrary to the common perception, tiger parenting is not the most typical parenting profile in Chinese-American families, nor does it lead to great performances among Chinese-American adolescents. Moreover, Chinese parents are not that different from American parents of European origin (Kim et al. 2013).

Questions for Consideration

1. Think of the parenting styles that you have observed. Do you notice any similarities or difference in the children's behaviour that might be due to these styles?
2. Think of how you were parented. How do you think this affected you as an adult?
3. Will you follow the approach of your parents when you become a parent? What would you do differently and why?

out of every two marriages ends in divorce"? Statistics might initially appear to bear out this statement, but consider the following: most sociologists use a statistic called the *refined divorce rate* to calculate the incidence of divorce. The number of divorces in a year is divided by the total number of marriages in that year. In Canada, marriages and divorces have plateaued since 2002 (see Figure 11.3). However, it is misleading to compare the

number of marriages with the number of divorces from year to year and say that the divorce rate is 50 percent, because couples who divorce in any given year are very unlikely to have come from the group that married that year. Also, some people go through several marriages and divorces, which skews the divorce rate because the likelihood of divorce goes up with each subsequent marriage. As Figure 11.7 shows, about 6 percent of the Canadian

Social Problems in Global Perspective

Box 11.3

Canadian Children in Global Perspective

In early 2013, UNICEF released a report card, *Child Well-Being in Affluent Countries A Comparative Overview* indicating that relative to 29 other affluent countries, Canada ranks only in the middle (17th out of 29), a position it has maintained since the last survey 10 years ago. This comprehensive report measures over two dozen variables under five major concepts: material well-being, health and safety, education, behaviours and risks, and housing and environment. While this position is lower than we might have expected, data from other studies in this text (e.g., the Conference Board's Report Card (Chapters 2, 8, 10, and Chapter 12) and the 2007 OSDUHS survey of students in Grades 7–12 (Chapters 8 and 12) support the authors' claim.

On the bright side, Canadian children (some data comes from studies of students in their late teens) are:

- above average in educational achievement, eating fruits, exercising, not smoking, and living in low levels of air pollution;
- average in the child poverty gap, low family affluence, low birth weight of newborns, eating breakfast daily, teenage births, alcohol use, and fighting; and
- below average in relative child poverty, infant mortality, the percentage without immunization, NEET (percentage not in employment, education or training), being overweight, cannabis use, bullying, national homicides, children's life satisfaction, and participation in further education.

Canada has made progress in some behaviours like educational achievement, reducing smoking, cannabis, and alcohol use, but has lost ground in being overweight and children's life satisfaction. Actually, children's life satisfaction was at a very low level: Canada ranked 24th of

29 countries on that measure. In support of that finding, the 2007 OSDUHS (see Chapter 8) study found that students in Grades 7–12 feel a large amount of stress, feel depressed, and lose self-confidence and sleep (2007:10).

Another major problem where Canadian children are disadvantaged relative to the children in other countries is spanking. Many states around the world have enacted laws to eliminate corporal punishment of children. The Global Initiative to End all Corporal Punishment of Children website identifies ways of tackling the problem and lists 33 countries that have outlawed corporal punishment (2012). These include predictable nations, such as the Scandinavian countries; continental European countries, including Spain, Germany, Greece, and the Netherlands; and a variety of others, such as Costa Rica, New Zealand, Ukraine, and Israel. In Canada in 2004, the Supreme Court of Canada limited but upheld the right of parents to physically punish their children. Thus we will not be signing this treaty soon.

Questions for Consideration

1. What should we do about the relative low performance of Canada in the UNICEF report card?

2. Are there other programs we can implement for problems where we are below average, especially programs to increase children's life satisfaction and reduce the stress in their lives?

3. Should we be conducting more regular studies on our nation's children?

4. Do you believe in a parent's right to spank a child? What kind of laws should we enact to protect children?

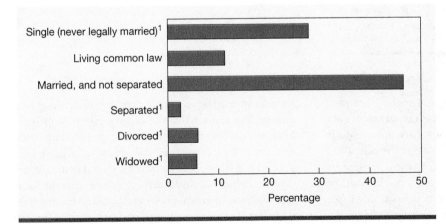

Figure 11.7   Marital Status of Canadians, 2011.

Source: *Statistics Canada*, 2011 Census of Population. *Retrieved June 18, 2013* (*http://www.statcan.gc.ca/pub/12-581-x/2013000/pop-eng.htm#c02*).

population 15 and older are divorced and not living with anyone. Thus it does not seem to be a pattern that engulfs half the population.

Why does divorce occur? A number of factors contribute to a couple's statistical likelihood of becoming divorced, including

- getting married during the teenage years;
- getting married after only a short acquaintanceship;
- having relatives and friends disapprove of the marriage;
- having limited economic resources and earning low wages;
- both partners having a high school education or less;
- having parents who were divorced or who had unhappy marriages; and
- having children present at the beginning of the marriage.

Because these factors are interrelated with such other factors as class, racialization, and age, determining the likelihood of divorce is very complicated. For example, age is intertwined with economic resources, and people from low-income families typically marry earlier than do people from more affluent families; but if divorce occurs, which factor—age or economic resources—is more closely associated with it?

Religion may affect the divorce rate of some. People who attend religious services weekly are much more likely to want to keep the family together and place more importance on home life than do non-attenders, according to the 1995 General Social Survey (GSS) (Clark 1998).

Divorce laws in Canada once required the partner seeking the divorce to prove misconduct on the part of the other spouse. Under today's no-fault divorce laws, however, proof of blameworthiness is no longer necessary. As a result, most divorces are granted on the grounds of irreconcilable differences, which means that a breakdown has occurred in the marital relationship and neither partner is to be specifically blamed.

With or without blame, divorce usually has a dramatic economic and emotional impact on family members. An estimated 60 percent of divorcing couples have one or more children. Indeed, some children experience more than one divorce during their childhood because one or both of their parents may remarry and subsequently divorce again. Although we do not know how many Canadians have experienced multiple divorces, we do know about multiple disruptions (including death and/or remarriage of a parent) of the family and their effects on childhood happiness. The 1995 GSS asked about family disruptions and their effects on children's feelings of well-being and closeness

to parents. According to Statistics Canada analyst Cara Williams (2001:3), 8 percent of Canadians (1.9 million people) aged 15 and older experienced one change in parental structure, 800 000 Canadians experienced two, and 200 000 experienced three or more. Disruptions do affect childhood happiness. Whereas 92 percent of those without disruptions reported having a happy childhood, only 50 percent of those with three or more disruptions reported having happiness (Williams 2001:4). Those with one or more disruptions also reported being less close to their mother and father than those without disruptions (Williams 2001:4). Although the effects can be overstated, disruptions do tend to have negative effects on childhood happiness and on relationships with parents.

Divorce changes relationships not only for the couple and children involved, but also for other relatives. Some grandparents feel that they are the big losers. Grandparents who wish to see their grandchildren have to keep in touch with the parent who has custody; but if the grandparents are in-laws, they are less likely to be welcomed and may be seen as taking the "other side" simply because they are the parents of the ex-spouse. Recently, some grandparents have sued for custody of minor grandchildren. For the most part, these suits have not been successful, except when there has been some question about the emotional stability of the biological parents or the suitability of a foster-care arrangement.

In 2006, most people who divorced intended not to remarry, but many do remarry and men are more likely to remarry than women are (Statistics Canada 2008g). Most divorced people marry others who have been divorced (London and Wilson 1988), though remarriage rates vary by gender and age. Among women, the older a woman is at the time of divorce, the lower her likelihood of remarrying (Wallerstein and Blakeslee 1989). Women who have not graduated from high school and have young children tend to remarry relatively quickly. Women with a college or university degree and without children are less likely to remarry (Glick and Lin 1986).

Divorce followed by remarriage often creates complex family relationships. A **blended family** or **step-family consists of a married couple, children from previous marriages, and children (if any) from the new marriage.** At least initially, stress in blended families may be fairly high because of scheduling of activities and visits for other spouses, rivalry among the children, and hostilities directed toward step-parents or babies born into the family. The 2011 census found that 12.6 percent of families were blended and they came in two types: one child of both parents as well as one child of one parent (5.2 percent), or all children of one of the parents (Globe and Mail 2012:A10–11). The children from blended families were more likely than children from intact families to say they lacked emotional support from their parents and to report difficulties in getting along with siblings and parents. In some cases, when parents divorce and marry other partners, the children become part of a binuclear family, living with one biological parent and a step-parent part of the time and with the other biological parent and another step-parent the rest of the time.

As Cherlin (1992) points out, the norms governing divorce and remarriage are ambiguous, so people must make decisions about family life (such as who should be invited to a birthday celebration or a wedding) on the basis of their own feelings about the people involved. But in spite of the problems, many blended families succeed.

DOMESTIC VIOLENCE

The term *domestic violence* obscures the fact that most victims of domestic violence are women and children. Women are more likely to be assaulted, injured, or raped by their male partners than by any other type of assailant. Children are extremely vulnerable to abuse and violence because of their age and economic and social dependence on their parents or other adult caregivers.

Child Abuse

In 2001, Nico Trocmé and his colleagues published the first Canadian Incidence Study of Reported Child Abuse and Neglect (CIS), a nation-wide study to examine the incidence of reported child maltreatment and the characteristics of children and families investigated by Canadian child welfare services. When we hear the words *child abuse,* most of us think in terms of physical injury or sexual abuse. However, the most frequent form of child maltreatment, according to the CIS, is child neglect—not meeting a child's basic needs for emotional warmth and security, adequate shelter, food, health care, education, clothing, and protection (Trocmé et al. 2001:xv). In 2005, Trocmé and his associates published the second nation-wide study. In 2010, Trocmé et al. published their third study.

In the past, children in Canada were considered the property of their parents and could be punished or ignored as the parents wished. Now, despite legislation protecting children through child welfare services in the provinces and territories, many physical injuries to children are intentionally inflicted by parents and other caregivers (see Trocmé et al. 2001:4–5). Parental violence can, in fact, lead to the *battered child syndrome,* a psychological disorder in which a child experiences low self-esteem and sometimes clinical depression associated with former or current abuse by a biological or custodial parent (Kempe et al. 1962).

The first CIS identified four kinds of maltreatment: physical abuse, sexual abuse, neglect, and emotional maltreatment. In 1998, the researchers tracked 7672 cases (excluding Quebec), of which 9 percent were substantiated. In 2003, the researchers tracked 14 200 cases in a representative sample of 63 jurisdictions, of which 47 percent of the cases were substantiated. This is a much higher rate than that substantiated in the first study. This study found 21.71 substantiated cases of abuse per 1000 children. A much higher rate of substantiated exposure to domestic violence and emotional maltreatment accounted for this rise. Regarding the kinds of maltreatment discovered in the 2003 study (excluding Quebec):

- 24 percent were physical abuse;
- 3 percent were sexual abuse;
- 30 percent were neglect;
- 15 percent were emotional maltreatment; and
- 28 percent were exposure to intimate partner violence. (Trocmé et al. 2005:1–2)

In 2008, the third study tracked 15 980 child maltreatment investigations conducted in a representative sample of 112 child welfare service organizations. This study found 36 percent of the investigations were substantiated, or 14.19 substantiated cases of abuse per 1000 children. Regarding the kinds of maltreatment discovered in this study:

- 20 percent were physical abuse;
- 3 percent were sexual abuse;
- 34 percent were neglect;
- 9 percent were emotional maltreatment; and
- 34 percent were exposure to intimate partner violence. (Trocmé et al. 2010:4)

A substantial decline appears to have taken place in the percent of substantiated cases. But in a further 8 percent of investigations, while there was insufficient evidence to substantiate maltreatment, maltreatment was suspected by the intake worker (2010:4). So it is possible that no decline occurred. Over the five years, little change was found in the percentage distribution, except for slight increases in neglect and exposure to domestic violence. A very small percent of sexual abuse was found in each study, but unfortunately, this may be because there is a lack of consensus on how to define *sexual abuse*. In the study, *sexual abuse* was defined in terms of seven categories: sexual activity attempted, sexual activity completed, touching/fondling genitals, adult exposing genitals, sexual exploitation (e.g., prostitution), sexual harassment, and voyeurism (Trocmé et al. 2001:33).

The various kinds of abuse of children in Canada are a serious social problem that remains largely hidden. Some researchers have found that children are most likely to be assaulted in their own homes if their parents were abused, neglected, or deprived as children, and if their parents are socially isolated as adults. Parents who lack a support network and suddenly face a crisis tend to make their children the targets of their frustration and sometimes their aggression (Kempe and Kempe 1978). Other researchers have found that abusive parents characteristically feel unloved and unworthy and totally unprepared to cope with their circumstances (Tower 1996).

In fact, reporting of suspected child abuse has improved significantly in recent years because of increased training, awareness, and legislation, which established that reports of suspected abuse would be investigated promptly and fully. In the past, even when physicians suspected abuse, they often chose to treat the child but not to report the incident, believing that abuse would be too difficult to prove (Tower 1996).

More comprehensive data on victimization of youth in comparison with adults reported to police are now available. Table 11.3 shows children and youth under the age of 18 are less likely than the adult population to be violently victimized. In 2010, about 74 000 children and teenagers were victims of violent crime, corresponding to a rate of 1080 victims per 100 000 under the age of 18. This is 10 percent lower than the violent crime rate recorded for adults (1199 victims per 100 000). Despite the lower rate of violent victimization, children and teenagers are more at risk of sexual-based crimes, as noted above. Children and teenagers are five times more likely than adults to become a victim of sexual offences (212 versus 41 per 100 000), with Level 1 sexual assaults accounting for three-quarters of these sex crimes. Another 22 percent of sexual offences committed against children and teenagers are child-specific, including sexual interference, invitation to sexual touching, luring a child via a computer, and corrupting children.

In a dramatic example of child sexual abuse, Jeannie Hilton went public with her story about her father, champion boxer Dave Hilton, Jr., and his abuse of her and her sister. In the fall of 2004, Jeannie Hilton published a book detailing the five years of abuse suffered by her and her sister, Anne Marie. Originally written in French, the book was entitled *Le Coeur au buerre noir (The Heart with a Black Eye).* The father, Dave Hilton, Jr., was convicted in 2001 of sex-related charges and received a seven-year sentence. According to an article in the *Globe and Mail,* he had begun molesting his daughters at age 11, first forcing them to perform oral sex and then taking their virginity through intercourse (Ha 2004:A9). Jeannie Hilton is quoted as saying, "I never had a chance to be young. . . . In high school when they were saying, 'Let's move to first base and kiss boys,' I was doing things with my father." But also affirming, "You have to talk about it. If you don't, it'll eat at you. . . . There is no way out of it" (Ha 2004:A9).

The vast majority (93 percent) of the perpetrators of maltreatment are parents and relatives (Trocmé et al. 2001:49). The alleged perpetrators of physical abuse are almost evenly divided between biological mothers (47 percent) and fathers (42 percent), and the perpetrators of sexual abuse are mostly male—both biological fathers (15 percent) and other relatives (28 percent) (Trocmé et al. 2001:49).

A usually less severe form of punishment, used by many parents, is spanking. Some people consider this abuse. Box 11.3 includes a note about spanking, because Canada is one of the few high-income countries to permit it. In their chapter "Should Johnny Be Spanked?," Tepperman and Blain (2006:36–37) identify some of the negative consequences of corporal punishment—from immediate depression, anxiety, lower grades, and slower physical development, to crime, racism, and violence as adults—while acknowledging that though a majority of people are spanked, only a minority become abusive or criminal. They conclude that to reduce misbehaviour, reasoning with or withholding rewards from the child are more successful than spanking if consistency is maintained.

Another kind of abuse that deserves attention is parental abuse. This is not elder abuse (see Chapter 5), but rather abuse of middle-aged people by their teenaged offspring. Types of parental abuse include physical, psychological, and financial (stealing or damaging the home or possessions). Some children who abuse may have a disorder or condition such as ADHD. Mothers are the most frequent victims of parental abuse, but fathers are susceptible too. Although this abuse can occur in any class or family structure, abused mothers are often lone-parents (Cottrell 2001).

TABLE 11.3 Adult and Child and Youth Victims Violent Crime in Canada, 2010

Type of offence	Adult victims (18 years and older)		Children and youth victims (0–17 years)	
	number	rate[1]	number	rate[2]
Homicide/attempted murder	**1014**	**4**	**115**	**2**
Murder, manslaughter, infanticide	358	1	47	1
Criminal negligence causing death	67	0	17	0
Other related offences causing death	1	0	1	0
Attempted murder/conspire to commit murder	588	2	50	1
Sexual offences	**10 912**	**41**	**14 508**	**212**
Sexual assault (Level 3)—aggravated	135	1	39	1
Sexual assault (Level 2)—weapon or causing bodily harm	268	1	114	2
Sexual assault (Level 1)	10 206	38	10 810	158
Sexual interference	…	…	2335	34
Invitation to sexual touching	…	…	503	7
Luring a child via a computer	…	…	288	4
Incest	50	0	163	2
Sexual exploitation	11	0	111	2
Voyeurism	229	1	79	1
Corrupting children	…	…	47	1
Anal intercourse	13	0	18	0
Bestiality—commit, compel, incite a person	0	0	1	0
Assaults	**201 172**	**751**	**39 046**	**571**
Assault (Level 3)—aggravated	2919	11	338	5
Assauilt (Level 2)—weapon or causing bodily harm	41 896	156	8032	117
Assault (Level 1)	138 903	518	29 702	434
Pointing a firearm	479	2	147	2
Unlawfully causing badily harm	411	2	92	1
Criminal negligence causing badily harm	167	1	73	1
Using firearm or imitation firearm in commission of offence	129	0	29	0
Discharge firearm with intent	167	1	54	1
Trap likely to or causing badily harm	1	0	0	0
Other assaults[3]	16 100	60	579	8
Deprivation of freedom	**3454**	**13**	**1044**	**15**
Kidnapping and forcible confinement	3454	13	623	9
Abduction/removal of child from Canada	…	…	421	6
Other violent offences	**104 804**	**391**	**19 170**	**280**
Criminal harassment	17 011	63	2122	31
Uttering threats	47 720	178	8628	126
Indecent or harassing phone calls	17 119	64	1295	19
Trafficking in persons	22	0	3	0
Other[3]	22 932	86	7122	104
Total	**321 356**	**1199**	**73 883**	**1080**

… not applicable

1. Rates are calculated on the basis of 100 000 populations. Population based upon July 1 estimates from Statistics Canada, Demography Division.
2. Includes assaults against police and other peace officers, as well as other types of assaults such as administering noxious thing.
3. Other violent offences include robbery, extortion, arson—disregard for human life, intimidation of a justice system participant or journalist, intimidation of a non-justice participant, and other violent violations.

Note: Excludes incidents where the sex and/or age of victim was unknown and where the relationship between the victim and the accused was unknown. Excludes spousal victims under the age of 15 years.

Source: *Statistics Canada, "Family Violence in Canada: A statistical profile, 2010,"* Juristat. *Retrieved June 10, 2013* (http://www.statcan.gc.ca/pub/85-002-x/2012001/article/11643/tbl/tbl3-1-eng.htm).

Intimate Partner Violence

In past editions, we spoke of spousal violence. We are expanding this section to include violence by dating partners. From the days of early Rome to current times, intimate partner violence has been acknowledged to exist, but until recently, it was largely ignored or tolerated. Fortunately, the rates of abuse seem to be declining in step with the decline of crime generally (see Figure 9.1). According to the 2010 edition of the report *Family Violence in Canada: A Statistical Profile* (Statistics Canada 2012c), female and male victim rates for homicide dropped for the past 12 years (1998 to 2010), but there are still generally three or more times as many female as male victims (see Table 11.4).

The suffering and other painful consequences such as needing medication are experienced much more strongly by women victims. Unfortunately, some of these abused women end up victims of homicide. As noted above in the section on the feminist perspective, women are more than seven times as likely as men to be killed by their spouses or intimate partners. Fortunately, a substantial decline in intimate partner homicide is occurring for both sexes.

Social Responses to Intimate Partner Violence

Although every few months we read or hear about extreme domestic violence, such as murder (of a woman) and suicide (by a man), many people who are aware of domestic abuse don't do anything about it, feeling that they do not want to become involved in a "private matter."

Historically, in Canada, an ideology of non-intervention—a strong reluctance on the part of outsiders to interfere in family matters—has led people and police officers to ignore or tolerate domestic violence (Lauer 1995). Unfortunately, the pattern of violence that ultimately results in a homicide is eerily similar in many cases of domestic abuse, and in most of those cases, death might have been prevented by earlier intervention. Positive changes in how law enforcement officials handle domestic violence calls are now being made—changes that are long overdue.

One other major change is the growth of shelters for abused women. In Canada, 593 shelters admitted 64 500 women and children between April 1, 2009 and March 31, 2010. On April 15, 2010, a census was taken in the shelters. On that day, 4645 women were present. Nearly 80 percent of these women and children were attempting to flee an abusive situation. Emotional abuse and physical abuse were most often cited as reasons for seeking shelter. Three-quarters of the women reported abuse by a spouse or former spouse. In terms of child abuse, one of the types was witnessing domestic violence; 25 percent of the women sought shelter so their children would not witness violence against their mother. About 90 percent of women who left the shelter did not return to their spouses (Statistics Canada 2011a).

FAMILY-RELATED PROBLEMS IN THE 21ST CENTURY

As we have seen, families and intimate relationships changed dramatically during the 20th century. Because of these changes, some people believe that the family as we know it is doomed; others think that returning to traditional family values can save this important social institution and create a more stable society. Another point of view, however, comes from sociologist Lillian Rubin (1994), who suggests that clinging to a traditional image of families is hypocritical in light of our society's failure to support the family, whether through family allowances or decent public-sponsored child-care facilities. Some laws even hurt children whose families do not fit the traditional model. Welfare cuts, like those made by the Progressive Conservative government in Ontario in 1995, for example, affect children as well as the adults who are trying to provide for them. Interestingly, the federal Conservative Party of Canada recently introduced child benefits and fitness and arts income tax credits for people bringing up children under 18 years.

WHAT CAN YOU DO?

- Investigate if any shelters for women could use help in your community. Volunteer at the shelter; help is always needed.

- Analyze who does what unpaid domestic labour in your household, or suggest that a tutorial be devoted to discussing who should do what unpaid domestic labour in a relationship.

- Find out what family concerns feminist groups on campus have and help them to address those concerns.

- Look further into the topic of Canadian parenting styles by studying recommendations of parenting magazines and websites and thinking of new variables or situations for this research topic.

TABLE 11.4 Victims of Violent Crime by Partners in Canada, 2010

| | Victims of intimate partner violence[1] | | | | | |
| | Female victims | | Male victims | | Total | |
Type of offence	number	percent	number	percent	number	percent
Homicide/attempts	146	0.2	53	0.3	199	0.2
Sexual assault[3]	2309	3	60	0	2369	2
Physical assault	57 989	71	16 304	79	74 293	72
Major assault (Levels 2 and 3)[4]	8506	10	3809	19	12 315	12
Common assault (Level 1)[5]	46 685	57	11 764	57	58 449	57
Other assaults[6]	2798	3	731	4	3529	3
Criminal harassment	7075	9	1057	5	8132	8
Indecent/harassing phone calls	4022	5	1316	6	5338	5
Uttering threats	7820	10	1580	8	9400	9
Robbery	257	0	49	0	306	0
Other violent offences[7]	2550	3	126	1	2676	3
Total offences	**82 168**	**100**	**20 545**	**100**	**102 713**	**100**

1. Intimate partner violence refers to violence committed by legally married, separated, divorced, common-law partners, dating partners (current and previous), and other intimate partners. The intimate partner category is based on victims aged 15 to 89.
2. Non-intimate partner violence refers to violence committed by other family members (parent, child, sibling, and extended family), friends, acquaintances, business, relationships, criminal relationships, authority figures, and strangers. The non-intimate partner category is based on victims aged 0 to 89.
3. Includes sexual assault, classified as one of three levels according to the seriousness of the incidents. Level 1 sexual assault is the category of least physical injury to the victim; Level 2 includes sexual assault with a weapon, threats to use a weapon, or causing bodily harm; and Level 3 includes aggravated sexual assault which wounds, maims, disfigures, or endangers the life of the victim. Also includes other sexual crimes such as sexual intereference, invitation to sexual touching, sexual exploitation, incest, corrupting children, luring a child via a computer, and voyeurism.
4. Level 2 assault is defined as assault with a weapon or causing bodily harm and Level 3 assault is defined as assault that wounds, maims, disfigures or endangers the life of the victim.
5. Level 1 assault is the least serious form of assault and includes pushing, slapping, punching, and face-to-face verbal threats.
6. Other assaults include unlawfully causing bodily harm, discharge firearm with intent, assault against peace-public officer, and other assaults.
7. Includes abduction, kidnapping, hostage-taking, arson, and other violent violations.

Note: Percentages may not add up to 100% due to rounding. Excludes incidents where the sex and/or age of victim was unknown and where the relationship between the victim and the accused was unknown.

Source: Statistics Canada, 2012c, Canadian Centre for Justice Statistics. Retrieved May 11, 2013 (http://www.statcan.gc.ca/pub/85-002-x/2012001/article/11643/tbl/tbl2-4-eng.htm).

SUMMARY

What Is a Family?

A family is a relationship in which people live with commitment, form an economic unit, care for any young, and consider the group critical to their identity. This definition modifies the traditional definition to account for today's greater diversity in living arrangements and relationships in families.

Are Canadian Families in Decline?

Not at all, say analysts who take a social change perspective. Families are becoming more complex (e.g., common-law, lone-parent, living apart together, blended or stepfamilies, and same-sex), adapting to other changes in society. For one thing, marriage is no longer a cultural imperative; for another, many people reaffirm their belief in the institution through serial monogamy—a succession of marriages over a lifetime.

What Are the Sociological Perspectives on Family-Related Problems?

Functionalists believe that the family provides social order and economic stability; the family is the solution to many societal problems, and dysfunctional families threaten the well-being of individuals and the whole of society.

Conflict theorists see the family as a problem in society, not a solution; they believe that the family is a major source of inequality in society brought on by capitalism.

Feminist theorists see women's subordination as rooted in the patriarchal system, coming long before capitalism.

Interactionists view the family first in terms of socialization. Some speak of the shared reality of marriage; some view family problems in terms of the subjective meanings that people give to their everyday lives; and some cite partners' unrealistic expectations about love and marriage.

What Characterizes Singlehood in Canada Today?

The proportion of Canadian households that have a single occupant has risen to 30 percent. Some people remain single by choice, others by necessity; many working-class young people cannot afford to marry and set up a household.

Why Do Young People Postpone Marriage Today?

Four factors are important: changing job structures in Canada lead to economic uncertainty; more women are in the labour force; sexual relationships outside of marriage are more socially acceptable than before; and young people observing the rising divorce rate may be cautious about jumping into marriage.

Does Common-Law Living or Cohabitation Usually Lead to a Successful Marriage?

According to one recent study, only about 50 percent of cohabiting couples marry, and evidence on the success of those marriages is mixed. Some studies show little or no effect; others show that partners who cohabit are more likely to divorce than partners who do not.

Living Apart Together Families

Currently some families (in Canada about 7 percent of couples) are not living together for various reasons, such as jobs, benefits, etc.

What Does Research Show about Dual-Earner Marriages?

More than 60 percent of all marriages in Canada are dual-earner marriages; that is, marriages in which both spouses are in the labour force. Many women in these marriages do much of the domestic work at home after completing their workday jobs, though there is a gradual trend toward a more egalitarian division of labour.

Is a Two-Parent Family Always Preferable to a One-Parent Family?

If the parents argue constantly, abuse the children, or are alcoholics, a supportive single-parent family would be preferable. However, a child growing up in a single-parent household faces serious risks that are complicated by other factors, such as poverty, discrimination, unsafe neighbourhoods, and high crime rates.

Why Is Reproductive Freedom Such a Controversial Issue?

Reproductive freedom implies the option to have or not to have a child. The roles that religious organizations, physicians, and society (through the legal system) should (and should not) play in controlling a woman's fertility continue to be debated. Contraception, abortion, and new reproductive technologies all raise personal and societal issues.

Which Is More Important, Parenting Style or Income?

A Canadian national study has found that parenting styles ranging from positive to ineffective had more influence on behavioural problems than family income or structure. An American study suggests "tiger mothers" do not always produce superstars.

Are Non-Marital Pregnancies Increasing or Declining?

Births to teenagers, as a percentage of all births, have decreased over the past 30 years, but the birth rate is higher for unmarried teenagers than in the past, perhaps because those who became pregnant were "forced" to marry. In addition, the proportion of births to unmarried women aged 25 to 34 has greatly increased.

Who Gets Divorced? Do Most People Remarry?

Many factors affect who gets divorced (e.g., marrying during the teen years or having limited economic resources), and these factors are interrelated with class, racialization, and age, so it is very difficult to determine any kind of statistical likelihood of divorce. Most people do remarry, and divorce followed by remarriage leads to complex family relationships, such as blended or stepfamilies.

Domestic Violence

Child abuse is substantial and appears in a wide variety of forms. The percentage of substantiated cases of abuse appears to be constant from 2003–08, as do the types of abuse identified. While the rate of violence toward children is lower than the rate toward adults, children and youth are more likely to be victims of sexual offences. Intimate partner violence seems to be on the decline, but women are still three or more times as likely to be victims as males are.

KEY TERMS

blended family, p. 245
cohabitation, p. 236
common-law, p. 236
dual-earner marriages, p. 237

extended family, p. 229
family, p. 229
kinship, p. 229
monogamy, p. 231

nuclear family, p. 230
second shift, p. 237
stepfamily, p. 245

QUESTIONS FOR CRITICAL THINKING

1. Sociologist Andrew Cherlin says that the family is a highly adaptable social institution, but we can minimize the costs of change in the family unit by modifying other social institutions of daily life such as the economy and workplace. What specific suggestions can you give for modifications in work–family arrangements?

2. What do you think of Margaret Mead's proposal of a two-stage marriage? What problems, such as reducing "starter marriages," might it forestall? Would it create any new problems?

3. What suggestions can you offer to help offset the potentially detrimental effects of single-parent households, especially when the parent is a woman who is employed full-time?

4. Do you think lesbian and gay couples will be having more children in the future? Why or why not?

AL Harvey/Slide Farm

12

Problems in Education

Canada and other industrialized nations highly value *education*—**the social institution responsible for transmitting knowledge, skills, and cultural values in a formally organized structure.** But a wide gap exists between the ideals of Canadian education and the realities of daily life in many schools. As a result, business and political leaders, parents, teachers, and the general public tend to complain about the state of education in this country, even as many parents report feeling relatively positive about the schools their children attend.

In this chapter you will learn about the problems of how well Canada is doing in education relative to other high-income countries regarding low-level literacy; opportunities for both high school completion and post-secondary education; performance on math, science, and reading tests, socio-economic backgrounds, racialized/ethnic backgrounds, gender, and regions; bullying, school violence, and cyber-bullying; residential schools for Indigenous children; increased tuition costs, the commercialization of post-secondary education, the emergence of MOOCs (Massive Open Online Courses), and the economic advantage of post-secondary education; overall learning and the future of education; and what you can do about them.

First, the sociological perspectives—functionalist, conflict, interactionist, and feminist—on education will be outlined to help us understand the problems and to show how educational problems are often intertwined with other issues.

PERSPECTIVES ON EDUCATION

The way a sociologist studies education depends on the theoretical perspective he or she takes. Functionalists, for example, believe that schools should promote good citizenship and upward mobility, and that problems in education are related to social disorganization, rapid social change, and the organizational structure of schools. Conflict theorists believe that schools perpetuate inequality and that problems in education are the result of bias based on racialization, class, and gender. Meanwhile, interactionists focus on microlevel problems in schools, such as how communication and teachers' expectations affect students' levels of achievement and dropout rates. Lastly, feminist theorists focus on the differences of male and female performance in, and responses to, the educational system.

Functionalist Perspectives

Functionalists believe that education is one of the most important social institutions because it contributes to the smooth functioning of society and provides individuals with opportunities for personal fulfillment and upward social mobility. According to functionalists, when problems occur, they can usually be traced to the failure of educational institutions—schools, universities, colleges—to fulfill one of their manifest functions. *Manifest functions* **are open, stated, and intended goals or consequences of activities within an organization or institution.** While the most obvious manifest function of education is the teaching of academic subjects (reading, writing, mathematics, science, and history), education has at least five major manifest functions in society:

1. *Socialization:* From kindergarten through college/university, schools teach students the student role, specific academic subjects, and political socialization. In kindergarten, children learn the attitudes and behaviour generally considered appropriate for a student (Ballentine and Hammack 2009). In primary and secondary schools, ideally, students are taught specific subject matter that is appropriate to their age, skill level, and previous educational experience. At the college/university level, students expand their knowledge and seek out new areas of study. Throughout, students learn the democratic process.
2. *Transmission of culture:* Schools transmit cultural norms and values to each new generation and play a major role in *assimilation*, the process whereby recent immigrants learn dominant cultural values, attitudes, and behaviour so that they can be productive members of society.
3. *Social control:* Although controversy exists over whose values should be taught, schools are responsible for teaching values such as discipline, respect, obedience, punctuality, and perseverance. Schools

teach conformity by encouraging young people to be good students, conscientious future workers, and law-abiding citizens.

4. *Social placement:* Schools are responsible for identifying the most qualified people to fill available positions in society. Students are often channelled into programs on the basis of their perceived individual ability and academic achievement. Graduates receive credentials generally required for entering the paid labour force.

5. *Change and innovation:* Schools are a source of change and innovation. To meet the needs of student populations at particular times, new programs—such as HIV/AIDS education, computer education, and multicultural studies—are created. In addition, new sustainability teacher education programs are created to promote an inclusive, responsible society that cares about the future. The sixth annual survey (2009) of post-secondary schools found that among teacher education schools, the Ontario Institute for Studies in Education (OISE) had the highest score for these criteria, followed by the education schools of the universities of British Columbia, Saskatchewan, and Alberta (Corporate Knights 2009:48). University faculty members are expected to conduct research and publish new knowledge that benefits the overall society. A major goal of change and innovation in education is to reduce social problems.

In addition to these manifest functions, education fulfills a number of *latent functions*—**hidden, unstated, and sometimes unintended consequences of activities in an organization or institution.** Consider, for example, these latent functions of education: compulsory school attendance keeps children and teenagers off the streets (and, by implication, out of trouble) and out of the full-time job market for a number of years (controlling the flow of workers). High schools, colleges, and universities serve as matchmaking institutions where people often meet future marriage partners. By bringing people of similar ages, racialized/ethnic groups, and social-class backgrounds together, schools establish social networks.

Functionalists acknowledge many *dysfunctions* in education, but to many, one seems overriding: our public schools at all levels were once not adequately preparing students for jobs and global competition. In comparative rankings of students across countries on standardized reading, mathematics, and science tests, Canadian students were lagging until a decade ago. In the most recent international assessment, Canadian students did very well on math and reading tests. In fact, the Report Card from the Conference Board of Canada comparing Canada to other high-income countries on a wide variety of criteria showed Canada to be in second place (out of 16) (see Box 12.1). If these scores are maintained in future tests, this will show that significant change can occur in the educational system.

Other dysfunctions include the fact that our schools are not preparing students for their political responsibilities as citizens of a democracy (to think and question and be well informed).

Conflict Perspectives

Sociologists using a conflict framework for analyzing problems in education believe that schools—which are supposed to reduce social inequalities in society—actually perpetuate inequalities based on class, racialization, and gender. In fact, conflict theorists such as French sociologist Pierre Bourdieu argue that education *reproduces* existing class relationships (see Bourdieu and Passeron 1990). According to Bourdieu, students have differing amounts of *cultural capital* that they learn at home and bring with them to the classroom (see Chapter 2). Children from middle- and upper-income homes have considerable cultural capital because their parents have taught them about books, art, music, and other forms of culture. According to Bourdieu, children from low-income and poverty-level families have not had the same opportunities to acquire cultural capital. Some social analysts believe it is students' cultural capital—rather than their "natural" intelligence or aptitude—that is measured on the standardized tests used for tracking. Thus, test results may unfairly limit some students' academic choices and career opportunities (Oakes 1985).

Other sociologists using the conflict framework focus on problems associated with the hidden curriculum, a term coined by sociologist John C. Holt (1964) in his study of why children fail. The **hidden curriculum refers to how certain cultural values and attitudes, such as conformity and obedience to authority, are transmitted through implied demands in the everyday rules and routines of schools** (Snyder 1971). These conflict theorists, such as sociologists Samuel Bowles and Herbert Gintis (1976), suggest that elites use a hidden curriculum that teaches students to be obedient and patriotic—values that uphold the status quo in society and turn students into compliant workers—to manipulate the masses and maintain the elite's power in society. An update by Bowles and Gintis (2002) showing that genetic inheritance of cognitive skill explains only a small part of the persistence of status levels among families further supports this finding.

Although students from all social classes experience the hidden curriculum to some degree, working-class

Social Problems in Global Perspective

Box 12.1

Canada's Education and Skills Report Card

Canada's performance in `some sectors of society may leave something to be desired, but in education, Canada is performing very well on criteria chosen by the Conference Board of Canada. Table 12.1 shows that Canada places second of 16 high-income countries in education and skills.

Twenty criteria were set and Canada's relative performance was determined on each one. Canada's grade on 20 education and skills criteria are a standing of A or B for:

- high school, college, and university completion;
- low percentages of students with low-level skills in reading, math, and science skills (and high percentages of students with high-level skills);
- performance of disadvantaged schools (difference in reading scores between the advantaged and disadvantaged schools);
- equity in learning outcomes (performance of immigrant students relative to others);
- foreign student index (share of foreign tertiary students); and
- gender gap (very small) in tertiary education and return on investment in tertiary education for women (in dollars).

(Note that in December 2013, the 2012 results of the Programme for International Student Assessment (PISA) math test showed that Canada had a slightly lower score than in 2009. Since Canada was still above the OECD average score, this decline is unlikely to substantially affect its overall score.)

Canada received a grade of C or D in:

- PhD completion, and percentage of students in math and sciences courses;
- adult participation in education; and
- return on investment in tertiary education for men (though the return received is higher than for women).

Questions for Consideration

1. Should Canada be faulted for not producing more PhDs when there are too many PhDs now for positions available?

2. Young men can get a good salary in the energy sector without tertiary education. How might these men be attracted to tertiary education so that they are not dependent on semi-skilled jobs?
3. How might adult education be made more attractive to adults?

TABLE 12.1 Canada's Education and Skills Report Card

	REPORT CARD	
Education and Skills		
1	Finland	A
2	Canada	A
3	Japan	B
4	Australia	B
5	Switzerland	B
6	Sweden	C
7	Germany	C
8	U.K.	C
9	Netherlands	C
10	Norway	C
11	U.S.	C
12	Belgium	D
13	Ireland	D
14	Austria	D
15	Denmark	D
16	France	D

Source: Conference Board of Canada, 2013, Education and Skills. Retrieved June 20, 2013 (http://www.conferenceboard.ca/hcp/details/education.aspx).

and poverty-level students are the most adversely affected (Ballantine and Hammack 2009). When middle-class teachers teach students from lower-class backgrounds, for example, the classrooms are very structured and the teachers have low expectations about the students'

academic achievement (Alexander et al. 1987). In one study of five elementary schools with students from different class backgrounds, researchers found significant differences in how knowledge was transmitted despite similar curricula (Anyon 1980). Schools for working-class students emphasize rules and rote memorization without much decision making, choice, or explanation of why something is done a particular way. In contrast, schools for middle-class students stress the processes that are involved in getting the right answer. Elite schools develop students' analytical powers and critical-thinking skills, teaching them how to apply abstract principles to problem solving.

The limitations on what and how these students in lower-track schools are taught mean that many of them do not get any higher education and therefore never receive the credentials to enter high-paying professions (Bowles and Gintis 1976). Our society emphasizes *credentialism*—a process of increasing demands for higher levels of education for a particular position. And credentials are more important than ever. According to a report on post-secondary education by the (now disbanded) Canadian Council on Learning, between 1990 and 2007, the number of jobs requiring post-secondary graduates almost doubled. Only half as many jobs were available for those who had not completed high school (2009b:11). Credentialism is closely related to *meritocracy*—a social system in which status is acquired through individual ability and effort (Young 1994). People who acquire the appropriate credentials for a job are assumed to have gained the position through what they know, not who they are or whom they know. According to conflict theorists, however, the hidden curriculum determines in advance that credentials, at least at the higher levels, will stay in the hands of the elites. Therefore Canada is not a meritocracy, even if it calls itself one.

Interactionist Perspectives

Whereas functionalists examine the relationship between the functions of education and problems in schools, and conflict theorists focus on how education perpetuates inequality, interactionists study classroom dynamics and how practices such as labelling affect students' self-concept and aspirations.

Interactionists believe that education is an integral part of the socialization process. Through the formal structure of schools and interpersonal relationships with peers and teachers, students develop a concept of self that lasts long beyond their schooling. Overall, social interactions in school can be either positive or negative. When students learn, develop, and function effectively, their experience is positive. For many students, however, the school environment and peer group interactions leave them discouraged and unhappy. When students who might do better with some assistance from teachers and peers are instead labelled "losers," they may come to view themselves as losers and thus set the stage for self-fulfilling prophecies. As noted in Chapter 1, *a self-fulfilling prophecy* occurs when a false definition of a situation evokes a new behaviour that makes the original false conception come true.

According to interactionists, labels such as *learning disabled* stigmatize students and *marginalize* them—put them at the lower or outer limits of a group—in their interactions with parents, teachers, and other students. Such labelling leads to self-fulfilling prophecies (Carrier 1986; Coles 1987). To counteract this possibility, many of these students have been reintegrated into regular classes over the past decade.

At the opposite end of the spectrum, labelling students *gifted* and *talented* may also result in self-fulfilling prophecies. Students who are identified as having above-average intellectual ability, academic aptitude, creative or productive thinking, or leadership skills may achieve at a higher level because of the label. However, this is not always the case. Girls who are identified as gifted may deny their intelligence because of cultural norms about the proper roles of women and men (see Eder 1985; Eder and Parker 1987). Afraid that their academic achievement will make them unpopular, high-achieving girls, and sometimes boys, can become victims of *anti-intellectualism*—hostility toward people who are assumed to have great mental ability or toward subject matter that is thought to require significant intellectual ability or knowledge. White students are overrepresented in gifted and talented programs, whereas visible minority students are underrepresented.

The interactionist perspective, emphasizing that society is the sum of interactions of individuals and groups, would also stress the importance of the influence of excellent teachers, the development of special programs to help students overcome barriers to learning, and initiatives of parents to determine which is the best school for their children.

An example of an exceptional teacher is Ainsworth Morgan, a former vice principal with Nelson Mandela Park Public School in Toronto and consultant to Pathways to Education. He is actually a graduate of the inner-city school where he now teaches, the first graduate to return to teach there in the school's 150 years. He says that his inspiration comes from his mother, who created, first, an atmosphere of respect at home, believing that "love comes later." With this inspiration, hard work, and considerable athletic ability, he obtained his bachelor's degree in the United States on an athletic scholarship. He returned to Canada to play wide receiver for the Toronto Argonauts and Saskatchewan Roughriders. Realizing his true calling was teaching, he then took teacher training at the University of Toronto and obtained a job teaching science and core Grades 7 and 8 at his "alma mater." He thinks it's important that those who leave the community should return to be a role model. He works closely with the students, frequently staying until six o'clock to help them with projects. (When one of the authors (EGT) visited his class at the end of the school day, he saw a student preparing to storm out of the class. After Ainsworth's quiet request for an explanation for leaving and an expression of interest in her, she returned and was still working when the author left.)

An example of a program specially designed to help students with math is the JUMP (Junior Undiscovered Math Prodigies) program. JUMP Math's mission is to "enhance the potential in children by encouraging an understanding and a love of math in students and educators". This Toronto-based charitable program was founded in 1998 by mathematician and writer John Mighton and eight volunteers. JUMP Math is primarily intended to be used by teachers in the classroom. The program offers a complete package of resources intended to cover the curricula for Grades 1 to 8. Professional development is also offered to teachers wishing to add to their teaching credentials. While JUMP Math has developed into a mainstream set of curriculum-based resources, it is intended to be flexible and can be used as a support in after-school tutoring by schools and community organizations, as well as by parents at home.

The JUMP Math program has been adopted by many classroom teachers in Toronto, Vancouver, Edmonton, Winnipeg, and elsewhere in Canada, as well as internationally. Supporting the findings of accumulating research in early childhood education, JUMP believes that children, with very few exceptions, are born capable of learning anything, and that when any student fails a test, it should be seen as a failure of the education system. With its innovative teaching program and one-on-one approach, JUMP is adding to the evidence. Summaries of the research showing its effectiveness can be found on the program's website.

An example of parents taking initiative in choosing a school for their children is their use of a website called School Information Finder, set up by the Ontario Ministry of Education in 2009. This website allows people to see reading and math student achievement and background characteristics of students in prospective schools. Whether this innovation constitutes increasing transparency or creates polarization of classes is uncertain (see Box 12.2).

Feminist Perspectives

Feminist theorists and researchers traditionally emphasized the extent to which girls and women were disadvantaged by receiving less attention than boys and men in mathematics and science classes (see Chapter 4). Recent work has shown that it is no longer easy to show

---

Social Problems and Social Policy

Box 12.2

The School Information Finder

To help parents choose an elementary/secondary school for their children, in April 2009, the Ontario Ministry of Education created a website that provides data about students' academic performance on math and reading tests and demographic characteristics, including family income, parents' education status, and immigration status. These scores can be compared with provincial averages on the variables. Parents at first could compare three schools at a time, but now they can view only one school at a time to prevent invidious comparisons. Some groups, such as People for Education, still object to the presentation of these characteristics. Annie Kidder, spokesperson for People for Education, has expressed concern about the social polarization that could occur when parents are seeking for their children to be with other students like them. The Ministry of Education claims that the website is about transparency and providing information to parents. Parents have indicated that they wish to know more about

schools. This information (much from Statistics Canada that is already available) is now available on one website. The ministry also expects that this kind of information will encourage schools that have low scores to work harder to increase their scores. Visit the website (the URL is provided in the References) and look up your local school's characteristics and compare them with neighbouring schools.

Questions for Consideration

1. Do you think this website is a good way to promote transparency and improve math and reading scores?
2. Do you think it will encourage the polarization of children in Ontario?
3. Are there other variables you would like to see on this website?

that women are disadvantaged given their performance in all levels and in all subjects except STEM (Science, Technology, Engineering, and Mathematics) courses. In fact, a recent study from Third Way, a Washington research group, shows that boys and men are disadvantaged regarding the qualities necessary for a knowledge economy, an economy that requires brains not brawn. For example, studies in elementary schools show that boys are less attentive, less well-behaved, less independent, and less persistent than girls. Regarding these qualities, 48 percent of girls get scores of A and B while 31 percent of boys get these scores, and this sex difference is greater than that for class (DiPrete and Buchmann 2014). Especially since the recession, men who formerly had blue-collar jobs have been having great difficulty in returning to the economy. Feminists have traditionally been concerned with those at a disadvantage by gender, racialization, disability, etc. In the future, we may find them not looking at men as the opposition, but rather conducting programs and research to help anyone at a disadvantage in school and later in the economy.

PROBLEMS IN PRIMARY AND SECONDARY EDUCATION

Although we have already identified a variety of problems in education, other issues must be addressed in planning for the future of this country. These issues include the performance of Canadian students in math, science, and reading; adult literacy; post-secondary school completion rates; racialized, class, and gender inequalities in educational opportunities; growing concerns about bullying, violence, and cyber-bullying in schools; and the continuing problems due to residential schools for Indigenous peoples.

What Can Be Done about Educational Performance?

Regarding performance at the primary and secondary levels, Box 12.1 shows that Canadian students do very well (scoring As and Bs) on a wide variety of performance variables relative to students of other high-income countries. Though more could be accomplished, this is one area that is not as problematic as others.

Educational Opportunities and Ascribed Statuses in Education

We have long known that ascribed statuses—such as people's gender, age, or racialized/ethnic status, and the geographic region where they live—have a significant

Volunteers and trained professionals are an important link in reducing adult illiteracy. How can we make it easier for people to learn to read without experiencing embarrassment?
Bill Bachman/Alamy

effect on educational outcomes. Regarding primary and secondary education, the Report Card on Education and Skills also shows disadvantage is removed substantially as a factor in some scores. Disadvantage has to do with the influence of ascribed statuses like gender, socio-economic background, and ethnicity. First, regarding gender, both boys and girls do very well. In addition, children and youth from disadvantaged schools perform very well relative to children and youth from advantaged schools. The difference in reading scores between the advantaged and disadvantaged schools is very low (about 10 months, where the high-income country average is two years). As a result, Canada gets an A rating, ranking third of 16 high-income countries. Disadvantaged schools are ones where the socio-economic background of families is below the national average. This is measured by the educational background of mothers. Disadvantaged schools are those with a high proportion of students who have mothers with less than high school education. Advantaged schools are those with a high proportion of students whose mothers have tertiary education. While opportunities might be more equitable in an ideal world, ascribed statuses appear to have less influence in Canada than elsewhere.

Bullying, School Violence, and Cyber-bullying

In the past dozen years, a number of dramatic bullying incidents have been reported, some of which led to suicide. Most recently the reporting was about the cyber-bullying of Amanda Todd in October 2012 and Rehtaeh Parsons in April 2013, which caused each to commit suicide. An example from the United States also gained widespread attention, though the victim did not commit suicide. In Steubenville, Ohio, a picture of two high school football players carrying a naked girl who appeared to be unconscious was posted on Instagram. The two high school boys were later convicted of raping the girl. Because of incidents like these, bullying and cyber-bullying have continued to be a very prominent social problem.

As a result of its prominence, questions about bullying—defined as "when one or more people tease, hurt, or upset a weaker person on purpose. It is also bullying when someone is left out on purpose"—were added by drug use researchers Angela Paglia-Boak and colleagues (2012:46) to their continuing survey of older students in Ontario. This study is one of the continuing biennial (since 1977) surveys of Ontario students' drug use by the Centre for Addiction and Mental Health. Previous waves of this study of drug use had asked students in Grades 7, 9, 11, and OAC about committing assault and carrying weapons. In 2001, 31.8 percent of students in Grades 7 through OAC (Grade 13, now abolished) reported bullying others at school and 24.6 percent reported being bullied. The replication of that study in 2007 indicated that a slightly reduced percentage of students, 24.7 percent, reported bullying others, but an increased percentage, 29.9 percent, reported being bullied (Adlaf et al. 2007:vi). In 2011, 21 percent reported bullying (about 208 000 students in Ontario) and 29 percent reported being bullied (about 288 000 students in Ontario). Girls are more likely to report being bullied than boys, and they primarily report being verbally bullied (Paglia-Boak et al. 2012:15). It seems that there continues to be a consistent amount of bullying and being bullied.

Adlaf and colleagues (2002:43) found that 12.3 percent of the students surveyed had assaulted someone in the past year, and 10.4 percent admitted carrying a weapon at school. In both cases, a higher percentage of males reported the offence, but no significant grade or age differences occurred. In 2007, the percentage of students reporting they carried a weapon was lower, at 8.7 percent, and the percentage who reported fighting (a slightly different question from assault) at school was 15.8 percent (2007:vi). In 2011, students were asked whether they fought on school property (12 percent did) and whether they were threatened by a weapon (7 percent were) (Paglia-Boak et al. 2012:14). Again, the figures show a consistent amount of violence over time.

Cyber-bullying is a particularly devastating kind of bullying because it can occur around the clock, on a variety of devices and sites, and it can possibly be forwarded to a large number of people while the bully remains hidden. Determining how much cyber-bullying exists is not easy because many methods can be included (e.g., text message bullying, picture/video-clip bullying via mobile phone cameras, phone call bullying via mobile phone, email bullying, chat room bullying, and bullying through instant messaging (IM)), and different researchers use different questions and different time periods. For example, the Ontario Student Drug Use and Health Survey (OSDUHS) asks: In the last 12 months how many times did people pick on you through the Internet (Paglia-Boak et al. 2012:23). In their General Social Survey of Canadians in 2009, Statistics Canada used the question: (If you) had ever previously received threatening or aggressive messages; been the target of hate comments spread through emails, instant messages, or postings on Internet sites; or threatening emails sent using the victim's identity (Statistics Canada 2013j). Finally, Mishna and colleagues used a shorter time period (three months) but included more in the definition, like spreading rumours and sexual messaging (2010:364).

In 2011, students were asked by OSDUHS for the first time if they were bullied over the Internet. The survey found that 21.6 percent of students reported being victims of cyber-bullying (Paglia-Boak et al. 2012:17), but they were not asked if they had committed cyber-bullying. Statistics Canada found in 2009 that 17 percent of 18 to 24-year-olds had experienced cyber-bullying, and among parents 9 percent reported that at least one child was cyber-bullied (Statistics Canada 2013j). Mishna and colleagues surveyed 2186 students in 33 schools in the Greater Toronto Area. In the previous three months, half reported being bullied online, mostly by friends, and 35 percent reported having bullied other kids online, mostly attempting to make them feel bad (Mishna et al. 2010:368). This figure is higher than found in other studies. The authors suggest that this difference occurs because questions about specific acts occur before the term cyber-bullying was mentioned in the questionnaire. Thus, depending on how widely it is defined, a fifth to a third of all teenagers experience cyber-bullying.

In the fall of 2014, the federal government passed the Protecting Citizens from Online Crime Act C-13. It made the non-consensual distribution of intimate images a new crime and includes an amendment allowing officials to remove such pictures from the Internet. This legislation contains powers for the police for surveillance, tracking, and gathering information. Though the Bill was not aimed at terrorists, it could be used for tracking them also. What kind of measures, if any, would you consider appropriate for this kind of bullying?

Most educational analysts acknowledge that technology—for example, metal detectors—alone will not rid schools of violence and crime. In Canada, a wide variety of programs have been developed—from zero tolerance of violence in Toronto schools, to Alberta's Safe and Caring School Project, to a website created by the B.C. government to help parents and children who may be dealing with cyber bullying, to the creation of the Canadian Safe Schools Network (CSSN)—a grassroots organization dedicated to reducing youth violence and making schools and communities safer. Years ago, the CSSN launched the Empowered Student Partnerships (EPS) program to empower students to plan, organize, and execute safe-school programs in the Toronto area. Organizations involved include the Toronto Police Service, city council, ProAction (a concerned business association), and the Toronto District School Board. The CSSN has also created a CD-ROM of six bullying incidents and interventions, which can be viewed from the perspective of the victim, perpetrator, and bystander. Another website devoted to promoting relationships and eliminating violence is PREVNET. This site has a host of resources for dealing with violence, bullying, and cyber bullying.

Residential Schools

In June 2008, Prime Minister Harper made a formal apology in the House of Commons to former students of residential schools operated by churches and government. Compensation of $4 billion (in April 2013, that figure was considered too low because the number who have applied for compensation has climbed to 37 716 (*Globe and Mail* 2013:A4) was offered and an Indian Residential Schools Truth and Reconciliation Commission was established, with $60 million in funding, to hear from the students and their families, communities, and churches, and to educate all Canadians on the residential schools system. This report was presented in June 2015 and clearly indicted the residential schools as agents of cultural genocide. The churches had already begun their Remember the Children campaign in March 2008 (Munnik 2008).

Residential schools were created to assimilate Indigenous children to mainstream culture. The idea of assimilation by force began in the late 18th century, and by 1920 attendance was compulsory for children 7 to 15 years of age. Children were forcibly taken from their families by priests, Indian agents, and police officers. By 1930, 80 residential schools were operating in Canada. The high point of attendance occurred in 1948 with 9368 students in 21 schools. Overall, about 150 000 Indigenous students attended these schools.

The schools began to decline in numbers and students decreased, so that in 1979 there were 12 residential schools with 1899 students (Assembly of First Nations 2008).

In the 1980s, students began to disclose forms of abuse at the residential schools. Generally, the Indigenous students experienced more misery than benefit from poor facilities, poor teaching methods, and frequent physical and sexual abuse. In addition, Indigenous languages were forbidden in the school, Indigenous ways were disparaged, and Euro-Canadian values were considered superior (Miller 2002). Indigenous people began to organize, and the last school was closed in 1996. Various reports, class action lawsuits, apologies by the churches and governments, and offers of compensation occurred before the federal government's 2008 offer.

In an article on Indigenous peoples' experiences in residential schools,

- Janice Acoose, associate English professor, First Nations University of Canada reported that her belongings were taken away from her and she was given a number for identification;
- Darwin Blind, family support worker, Gordon Wellness and Therapy Centre, George Gordon First Nation, Saskatchewan reported that many children like him suffered physical, mental, emotional, and sexual abuse at night in a big crowded room;
- Alex Janvier, artist, reported that fear was instilled in him but that art replaced his loss;
- Chief Frank Johnson, Wuikinuxv First Nation, B.C. reported that his supervisor locked him in a locker for fighting; and
- Judge Alfred Scow, retired provincial court judge, and first Indigenous person to graduate from law school and be called to the bar in British Columbia, reported that if Indigenous children spoke in their own language, they were punished. (Stueck and Boesveld 2008:A8–9)

Another revelation in October 2008 was that many of the thousands of children who went missing from the schools were buried in unmarked or anonymous graves (Curry 2008). The Truth and Reconciliation Commission was asked to undertake to discover how many residential students died and who they were, what they died from (possibly from tuberculosis but also neglect), and where they were buried. Researchers now estimate that 3000 children died while in attendance at the residential schools, the primary killer was TB, and the Spanish flu of 1918–19 was also devastating (Perkel 2013).

Some have suggested that the schools were not entirely bad. For example, Jim Miller, Canada Research

Chair in Native Newcomer Relations at the University of Saskatchewan, said, "From the very early days in the 1990s, the story got framed as a story of abuse. I can understand how that would happen, but it's had an effect of oversimplifying the story." Mr. Wagamsese, a column writer with the *Calgary Herald* and author of several books, said that he did not discount the pain and suffering endured by many who attended residential schools, but "I can't possibly believe that every one of those people functioning as missionaries and clergy were predators" (Stueck and Boesveld 2008:A8).

Another ominous consequence of residential schools is their long-term effect. A survey of off-reserve Indigenous people in 2006 found that, according to the reports of parents who saw report cards and had knowledge of their work, 7 of 10 children 6 to 14 years of age were doing well or very well. But off-reserve Indigenous children whose parents had attended residential schools were less likely to do as well or very well than those whose parents had not. About 12 percent of off-reserve Indigenous children had parents (one or both) who indicated that they had been students in the residential school system that operated across Canada between 1830 and the 1990s (Statistics Canada 2009a). Thus, living in residential schools was a problem not only for attenders, but also for future generations.

PROBLEMS IN POST-SECONDARY EDUCATION

Increased Costs and Inadequate Governmental Support

It is well known that governments have been cutting back on school budgets. Although support for post-secondary education in Canada is among the highest in the high-income countries, and has been increasing at a rate higher than inflation for the last decade, this is still not considered enough to support increased costs.

In order to make up the shortfall, universities and colleges have increased tuition substantially during the past two decades. As a result, an almost four-fold increase in non-specialty undergraduate fees and expenses has occurred, on average from $1464 in 1990–1991 to $5581 in 2012–2013 Most recently, a 5 percent increase in fees occurred between 2011–12 and 2012–13, as shown in Table 12.2, while inflation was under 2 percent during those years.

The student fees in Quebec are very low relative to the fees elsewhere. In June 2012, the Quebec Liberal government decided to progressively increase fees ($325/year for five years). In response the students rioted and shut down the city centres of Montreal and Quebec City.

TABLE 12.2 Undergraduate Tuition Fees for Full-time Canadian Students, 2010–2013

	2010/2011	2011/2012	2012/2013[1]
		average ($)	
Canada	**5146**	**5313**	**5581**
Newfoundland and Labrador	2649	2649	2649
Prince Edward Island	5131	5258	5470
Nova Scotia	5497	5722	5934
New Brunswick	5647	5728	5917
Quebec	2411	2520	2774
Ontario	6316	6815	7180
Manitoba	3593	3638	3729
Saskatchewan	5431	5734	6017
Alberta	5505	5663	5883
British Columbia	4758	4919	5015

Note: Provincial average tuition fees have been weighted by the number of students enrolled in 2008.

1. Estimated.

Source: *Statistics Canada, 2013, Canada at a Glance. Retrieved June 20, 2013 (http://www.statcan.gc.ca/pub/ 12-581-x/2013000/edu-eng.htm).*

The figure was reduced to $219/year for seven years, however, the students continued their demonstrations. The Liberals lost the election late that year to the Parti Québécois. The new government compromised further and raised tuition by only 3 percent. And even in 2014–15, undergraduate tuition in Quebec was far below other provinces at $2743 (Statistics Canada 2015).

Since costs of educating students in professional faculties are much higher than educating students in arts and sciences, and since incomes of these graduates are quite high, tuition for professional programs has increased greatly. In 2012/2013, undergraduate students in dentistry paid the highest average undergraduate fees ($16 910). They were followed by students in medicine ($11 891) and pharmacy ($10 297). At the graduate level, the most expensive programs remained the executive master of business administration (EMBA) with tuition fees of $38 508, and the regular MBA program, at $23 757. Students enrolled in a graduate program paid an average of $5695 in tuition fees in 2012/2013, up 4.5 percent, following a 3.7 percent increase a year earlier (Statistics Canada 2012d).

High tuition has major consequences for student debt, especially with poor job prospects at graduation. According to the *Financial Post*, in 2012 a student left university with an average debt of $28 000, and the average payback time is 14 years (Lagerquist 2012). The state of Oregon suggested in June 2013 that instead of leaving students with a high debt upon graduation, education should be paid for with a 3 percent tax on students' salaries for 24 years. Students with more remunerative jobs would pay more tax, and money collected after the debt is "paid off" would be a kind of interest. Would you be willing to accept these terms to be debt free at the end of your undergraduate years? In addition to the costs of schools, many other factors determine which school to attend (see Box 12.3).

Commercialization of Post-Secondary Education

Another important aspect of school financing is commercialization. The commercialization of universities and colleges takes many forms—for example, the obvious increase in corporate advertisements in washrooms and corridors and the greater numbers of soft-drink machines (see Box 10.2 about taxing soft drinks) and fast-food franchises, such as Tim Hortons. The machines are on almost every floor, and the franchises are in almost every building with classrooms on campus. Another form of commercialization is the opportunity for corporations to name buildings and classrooms. Individual bricks are available for the names of donors. As a speaker at a retirement party for a university

president suggested, "Only the doorknobs remain." As a result, the fundraising arm of universities—called by a succession of euphemisms, such as external relations, advancement, and development—has gained in importance and its vice-president is sometimes the highest-paid official at the university. These forms of commercialization are found at both colleges and universities, but a third form of commercialization is more problematic for universities.

Universities are being encouraged to form partnerships with corporations. These relationships are intended to provide research facilities and funding as government funding declines. From the access to university researchers, businesses feel they can be at the cutting-edge of their industry. The university can enhance its image if it can contribute innovative products—from drugs to software. For example, the University of Waterloo is well known for its innovative contributions to computer technology and creating of companies like OpenText and Blackberry (formerly Research In Motion). Finally, students can gain because the collaborations can help them find co-op assignments and future employment.

On the other hand, in their book *No Place to Learn: Why Universities Aren't Working*, political scientists Tom Pocklington and Allan Tupper (2002:148) discuss the close links between universities and corporations and conclude that universities and corporations may become linked in financing a project or testing a new product in such a way that the corporation asks for more control over the process or outcome than is appropriate for scientific study or the independence of universities.

Educational Opportunities and Gender, Ethnicity, and Indigenous Status

The most recent data on this topic comes from the 2011 National Household Survey (NHS), which replaced the cancelled long-form of the 2011 census. It was sent to about one-third of Canadian households, and after much follow-up, gained a response rate of 68.6 percent. This approach, unlike the census, has been criticized severely for overlooking small areas and isolated Canadians. In its defence, the directors state that its response rate is similar to other voluntary Statistics Canada surveys.

Figure 12.1 shows that among older people (55–64 years), a higher percentage of men than women have all kinds of degrees. However, among younger people, a higher percentage of women than men earn bachelor's degrees (59.1 versus 40.9 percent). This difference has been well known for some time. But now, a higher percentage of women are earning medical degrees (e.g., medicine, dentistry, pharmacy, and optometry) than young men (62.2 versus 37.8 percent), and a higher percentage of

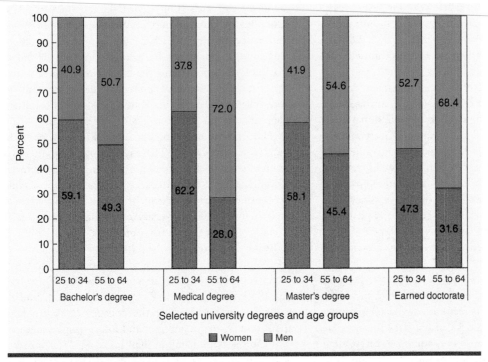

Figure 12.1   Type of University Degree by Sex and Age Group in Canada, 2011.

Source: *Statistics Canada, 2013*, 2011 National Household Survey. *Retrieved June 27, 2013* (*http://www12.statcan.gc.ca/nhs-enm/ 2011/as-sa/99-012-x/2011001/c-g/c-g01-eng.cfm*).

master's degrees (58.1 versus 49.1 percent). Finally, women are very close to equality with men regarding earned doctorates. On the other hand, women have not moved into the trades in the same numbers. Only 20 percent of trades apprentice certificates were held by women.

Recent data about gender and STEM (Science and technology, Engineering, and Mathematics) degrees can be found in Figure 12.2. While women are taking science and technology degrees, (e.g., biology), they are not taking engineering and mathematics degrees.

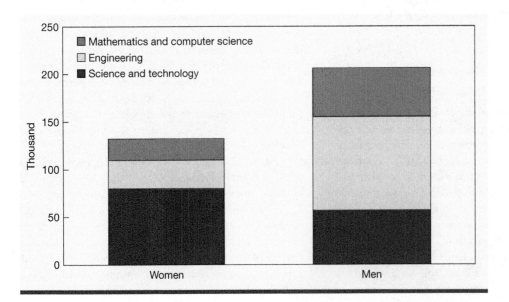

Figure 12.2   Number of STEM University Graduates by Sex, 2011.

Source: *Darcy Hango, Gender differences in STEM programs at university,* The Daily. *Retrieved December 18, 2013* (*http://www.statcan.gc.ca/ pub/75-006-x/2013001/ article/11874-eng.htm*).

Critical Thinking and You

Box 12.3

International reputation or student satisfaction: How does one choose a university to attend?

One major distinction among universities is size: large, medium, and small. Advantages exist for all kinds of universities. The traditional view is that large universities can offer a great variety of programs, some with international recognition and some at the forefront of innovation in particular fields, but they pay little attention to the undergraduate student experience. Small and medium universities can offer worthwhile personal experiences and teacher-student interactions, but perhaps they are not doing the most innovative research and do not have the reputation to guarantee going on to do graduate work at a top international university. The evidence bears this out. In the four major world surveys of universities (Times Higher Education, QS World University, Shanghai Jiao Tong University, and National Taiwan University rankings), the University of Toronto almost always ranks first in Canada (the University of British Columbia and McGill University rank second and third respectively). U of T also does very well in comparison with other major universities in the world, ranging from 7th to 27th in the four surveys. No other Canadian university ranks in the top 30 in all surveys. These comprehensive surveys review two dozen subject areas at each university (*U of T Magazine* 2013:14).

However, when university students in Canada were surveyed by the *Globe and Mail* and *Maclean's*, these major universities usually rank far down the list on student satisfaction. The 2013 *Globe and Mail*'s annual national survey, *Canadian University Report*, consists of about 100 questions put to 31 000 undergraduate students. A mean score was obtained for each question for each institution, and institutions were assigned a grade from D for a score below 5.0 to A+ for a score greater than 8.2 out of 9.0 (Tustin 2013:4). Universities were divided into large (enrollment over 22 000 students), medium (enrollment 10 000–22 000), small (enrollment 4000–10 000), and very small (enrollment under 4000). For overall student satisfaction, the U of T and U of British Columbia, received Bs and McGill received a B+. Few of the universities in the large, medium, and small categories received an A, but in the very small category, 11 of 15 universities received an A. Regarding other questions about campus atmosphere, student-faculty interaction, academic counselling, and work/play balance, the *Canadian University Report* found the same differences. On instructors' teaching style, none

of the large universities received an A, but 10 of 15 of the very small ones did (2013:48–49). In terms of class size, all the very small universities received an A and none of the largest universities did (2013:68) The large universities received high scores regarding building and facilities, recreation and athletics, and libraries, but the very small universities did also. Maclean's *2013 Canadian Universities Guidebook* also provides the results of a survey of undergraduates. The first-year and senior-year students were asked to evaluate their entire educational experience at their institution. Once again, students gave high rankings to small universities. Whereas universities like Huron, Bishop's, and Mount Allison received excellent rankings from 56 to 72 percent of the senior students, U of T, U of British Columbia, and McGill received excellent rankings from less than a third (25–32 percent) of the senior students.

Finally, a third criterion for consideration is employability of students after graduation. A major survey of graduates around the world placed U of T first in Canada and 14th in the world. The third annual Global Employability Survey, released October 2013, used 2300 international executives and 2700 recruiters in 30 and 20 countries respectively to create a profile of the ideal university graduate and the ideal university for producing such a potential employee among 150 universities around the world (*U of T News* 2013).

Questions for Consideration

1. How would you advise a secondary school student who approached you about how to choose a college or university?

2. Do the advantages of international status, innovative potential, and employability outweigh student satisfaction?

Independent Research

1. Develop some questions to test students' appreciation of high world standing and survey students about the value, if any, to them of high world ranking.

2. Using your sociological imagination, what could you suggest large universities do to enhance student experience?

Regarding ethnicity, especially visible minority status, while not explicitly measured, immigrant status could serve as a proxy measure since so few of our immigrants come from high-income countries. In 2011, while immigrant adults aged 25 to 64 represented just under one-quarter of Canada's total adult population, they represented over one-third (34.3 percent) of adults with a university degree. About half (50.9 percent) of all STEM degrees were held by immigrants, including both those who have lived in Canada for many years and newcomers (Statistics Canada 2013k).

Another important variable to consider is Indigenous status. A substantial improvement in the percentage of Indigenous people with post-secondary qualifications has occurred. Almost half (48.4 percent) of the Indigenous population aged 25 to 64 had a post-secondary qualification in 2011, and a higher percentage of young men and women had post-secondary qualifications than older ones (Statistics Canada 2013q). In comparison, almost two-thirds (64.7 percent) of the non-Indigenous population aged 25 to 64 had a post-secondary qualification, though a few decades ago only about 50 percent of Canadians had a post-secondary degree or diploma.

Online Education: MOOCs (Massive Open Online Courses)

Online education in various forms has been available since the early life of the Internet. Some schools have combined class and Web components, and some, like Athabasca University, have courses and programs that are entirely online. Now something revolutionary has been created in online education. Perhaps somewhat influenced by the wildly popular Khan Academy, which was developed to provide short tutorials on topics like math, science, humanities, etc., the most revolutionary innovation is called MOOCs (massive open online courses). They first emerged in Stanford University where a professor's popular course was oversubscribed and he decided to put it on the Web. Within a short time there were 160 000 followers. Other professors followed the example and Coursera, an organization to coordinate this activity, was created. As of July 5, 2013, over 4 million students were enrolled in 370 courses from 69 partners in this organization. It was just a short time before rivals emerged. For example, Harvard, Berkeley, and MIT collaborated to create their own program, edX. Besides giving students living anywhere a chance to learn a topic, it is expected that this approach would allow universities to save money by reducing the size of some faculties, given the decline of public funding for them, and reduce the cost of tuition for students. University of Toronto was the first Canadian university to join Coursera and it has also joined edX. U of T offered three computer science courses, one in social work and one in Aboriginal studies from the Ontario Institute for Studies in Education (OISE) on Aboriginal Studies, in 2013. The university offered 15 courses in 2015.

As popular as the online courses are likely to be, they are also likely to create problems, such as:

1. A high percentage of students will drop out.
2. A small percentage of professors could become superstars, leaving other professors whose institutions use these courses wondering what kinds of jobs and status they will have. Will this be another winner-take-all development and will a two-tiered university system emerge like that the professional sports' system? Are minor leagues with much lower pay in the offing for some professors, like with athletes? Or will there be jobs at all, since teaching assistants could monitor a MOOC and deal with questions, tests, etc. Philosophy professor Michael Sandel's lectures at Harvard are supposed to have had 20 million views, including from China and Korea. On April 29, 2013, the philosophy department of San Jose State University, in the California system, published an open letter to Prof. Sandel about their concerns, including how a video lecture from Prof. Sandel at Harvard University with Harvard students' comments is an improvement on the often criticized lecture as being pontification or spouting off, and how providing the same course to every student in the country would harm diversity of thought. (The URL for full letter can be found in the References.) Prof. Sandel responded that he made a resource available and the receiving departments should use it as they see fit, and that he does not want his "lectures to be used to undermine faculty colleagues at other universities" (Sandel 2013). A small percentage of the students will want credit for their work. How should they be graded? One solution is to have exam sites where students would assemble as they do now in universities at the end of terms. For students a great distance away, some kind of monitoring via Skype might be possible.
3. How will essays be marked for students in humanities courses? edX has developed a program using artificial intelligence to grade essays. Although responses have been considered good and speedy, they are not those created by a knowledgeable grader who may also know the student and therefore better understand the student's response. In addition, professors have been able to fool the program with nonsense essays.

4. How will students rate their educational experience participating in a MOOC? Interestingly, in Canada, the only online university, Athabasca, gets higher ratings from both first year and fourth year students than dozens of universities like Toronto, Calgary, and Sherbrooke, according to *The Canadian Universities Guidebook* (*Maclean's* 2013:236).

5. Some observers make a distinction between technical and practical understanding. Obviously it is possible to teach technical skills online, like some engineering and computer programming skills, but will students develop the ability to work in a complex world without the practical understanding that working with others inside and outside classes at a complex institution like a university? Will people develop resilience or emotional self-awareness online? There are obviously many questions that will have to be dealt with.

The Economic Benefit of Post-Secondary Education

Given the high cost of university education, and the perhaps many years required to pay off debt, is it worth it? Should those who are not at the top of their class go straight to an apprenticeship program? There are three ways of answering this question related to employment outcomes. (Tertiary education could also be worthwhile for personal growth.) What is the difference in employment rates for university and non-university graduates; what is the difference in their incomes; and what is the overall economic benefit to the student and society? First, data from the NHS show that in 2011, in general, the employment rate increased with education level (Statistics Canada 2014). The employment rate for those with university credentials was 81.6 percent, compared with 55.8 percent for those who had no certificate, diploma, or degree. Second, Figure 12.3 shows that university graduates, especially females, have much higher wages than secondary school graduates, though the difference is narrowing.

Third, the Education and Skills Report Card (see Box 12.1) noted that Canada gets grades of only B and C in the return on investment for tertiary education for women and men respectively. The return on investment is measured by adding private benefits (e.g., salary) minus private costs (e.g., tuition) and public benefits (e.g., increased taxes) minus public costs (e.g., spending on education). In 2008 (the latest available year of data), this amounted to $220 000 for men and $158 000 for women. However, women and men have practically the same ranking (9th and 10th respectively among 15 high-income countries (Conference Board 2013).

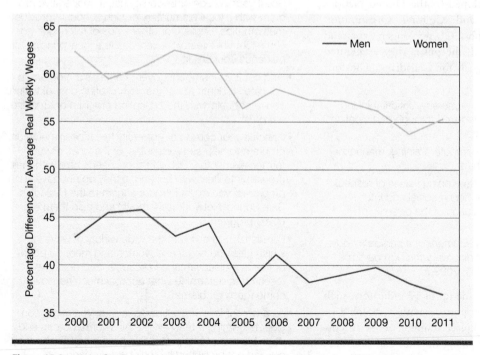

Figure 12.3   Wage Gap Between University Graduates and High School Graduates, 2000–2011.

Source: *Statistics Canada, 2013q*, Economic Insights. *Retrieved June 20, 2013* (*http://www.statcan.gc.ca/pub/11-626-x/2012008/c-g/c-g03-eng.htm*).

EDUCATIONAL GOALS FOR THE 21ST CENTURY

The Conference Board Report Card gave Canada a C in adult participation in education (see Box 12.1), placing us 10th of 15 countries. Our position is due to the relatively few hours of non-formal job instruction that Canadian workers receive. Not only do Canadians aged 25 to 64 years participate less in non-formal job-related education than their peers in other high-income countries, they also receive, on average, far fewer hours of instruction. Canadian adults received about 49 hours of job-related non-formal education in 2008, less than half the hours of instruction received by adults in Denmark (105). Younger workers receive more than older workers, but we are in the middle of the group of countries on both measures (Conference Board 2013).

Now that we are in a society of continuous change, we have come to recognize that learning cannot stop with a degree or diploma—we must promote learning outside school. Lifelong learning is crucial. How are Canada and communities within Canada faring regarding overall learning? Although measuring learning is much more difficult than measuring the percentage of people with degrees or even literacy, the Canadian Council on Learning (CCL) attempted to do so in 2006. It devised the Composite Learning Index (CLI) based on four learning pillars, developed by the United Nations Educational, Scientific, and Cultural Organization (UNESCO). Although the CCL no longer exists and the CLI is no longer used, the pillars they established are still a worthy set of goals for Canadians. The four pillars are

- *Learning to know:* literacy, numeracy, critical thinking, and general knowledge, acquired through participation in post-secondary education;
- *Learning to do:* skills like computer training, managerial training, and apprenticeships;
- *Learning to live together:* developing values of respect and concern for others, fostering social and interpersonal skills and appreciation of the diversity of Canadians; and
- *Learning to be, or the development of a person's body, mind, and spirit:* personal discovery through participation in arts and sports. (CCL 2009a)

The four pillars are made up of 17 indicators, such as youth literacy skills, proportion with a diploma or degree, availability of workplace training, access to cultural resources, and participating in clubs and organizations. These indicators have 25 (in total) measures of the indicators. Data were obtained from Statistics Canada and other sources for over 4700 cities and communities in Canada. Top city scores in 2009 went to Calgary (89), Victoria (88), Guelph (85), and Ottawa (84). Toronto (80), Montreal (68), and Vancouver (77) were in the middle of the pack (CCL 2009b). From 2006 to 2008, Canada's overall score rose slightly to 77. In 2009, the overall score declined to 75. The CCL reported that the decline was not related to the recent economic downturn, since many of the measures came from late 2007 and early 2008, but rather to substantial decreases in the "learning to be" pillar, somewhat offset by increases in the "learning to do" pillar. Given the difficulties we are facing in this continuing slow economic recovery, we need to remember the importance of maintaining or increasing all forms of learning to weather this storm and prepare for those in the future. Governmental support is also crucial for support not only of teachers and educational institutions, but also of cultural workers, including curators, actors, musicians, and institutions such as museums, art galleries, theatres, and concert halls. We should try to promote adult participation in education of all kinds, and make it possible for Canadians to increase their score in this educational measure in the future.

WHAT CAN YOU DO?

- See if your college or university has a cooperative program with a local elementary or high school to provide mathematics, English, or other kinds of tutoring. If not, you might volunteer your services to a local principal or guidance counsellor.
- Find out if your student government has a program to educate students about the skyrocketing cost of tuition. You might help with the education program or organize a protest.
- Check if your college or university has a peer-mediator program to help settle disputes, or if a local, or your former, elementary or high school needs help with their programs to deal with bullying. If they do not have such programs, you might introduce them to the Canadian Safe School Network (see above) and help them organize a program.
- Familiarize yourself with the wide variety of ways in which girls and boys, and women and men, do poorly or feel at a disadvantage in schools, and do some research to determine what approach can help overcome these problems.
- As a way of following all perspectives, you might consider becoming a teacher, like Ainsworth Morgan and John Mighton, to help students have a say in who they are and not be limited by their backgrounds.

SUMMARY

What Is Education?
Education is the social institution responsible for transmitting knowledge, skills, and cultural values in a formally organized structure.

What Is the Functionalist Perspective on Education?
Functionalists believe that education contributes to the smooth functioning of society when it fulfills its manifest functions. Education has at least five major manifest functions: socialization, transmission of culture, social control, social placement, and change and innovation. Schools also fulfill a number of latent functions—hidden, unstated, and sometimes unintended consequences of its activities—like matchmaking and networking.

What Is the Conflict Perspective on Education?
Conflict theorists believe that schools, which are supposed to reduce inequality in society, actually perpetuate inequalities based on class, racialization, and gender. The sociologist Pierre Bourdieu, for example, says that children from low-income and poverty-level families come to school with less cultural capital (values, beliefs, attitudes, and competencies in language and culture) than middle- and upper-income children do. Conflict theorists also think that elites manipulate the masses and maintain their power in society through a hidden curriculum that teaches students to be obedient and patriotic and thus perpetuates the status quo in society.

What Is the Interactionist Perspective on Education?
Interactionists study classroom dynamics and the ways in which practices such as labelling affect students' self-concept and aspirations. If students are labelled "learning disabled," for example, the label may become a self-fulfilling prophecy—that is, an unsubstantiated or erroneous belief that results in behaviour that makes the false belief come true. A student who is erroneously labelled "learning disabled" may stop trying, and teachers may lower their expectations, with the result that the student doesn't succeed in the long run. Interactionists also stress the importance of significant individuals and programs.

What Is the Feminist Perspective on Education?
Feminists were traditionally concerned that girls were not getting equal attention in class with boys, especially for such courses as science and mathematics. Now, girls are performing almost as well as boys on international science and mathematics tests at the secondary level, and women are surpassing men in academic attainment at university, except for STEM and doctoral programs. As a result, some feminists are concerned that boys are at a disadvantage, with higher levels of learning disabilities, lower reading scores on the same international tests, and lower high school completion rates than achieved by girls.

How Does Canada's Performance in Education and Skills Compare Worldwide?
Canadian students are doing well in measures of performance in relation to other high-income countries (placing 2nd of 17 countries) according to the Report Card of the Conference Board of Canada.

How Do Ascribed Statuses like Ethnicity, Gender, and Indigenous Status Affect Educational Opportunities in Secondary and Post-Secondary Schools?
In Canada schools do a good job of removing disadvantage due to ethnicity, gender, and Indigenous status, according to the Education and Skills Report Card. In post-secondary schools females are narrowing the gap and in some cases have overtaken males in obtaining degrees, and immigrant students are doing very well in the STEM subjects. Indigenous people are attending post-secondary schools in much greater numbers than earlier.

How Have Bullying, Violence, and Cyber-bullying Affected Our Schools?
Suicides of students who were bullied have highlighted cyber-bullying as a significant factor at school. Among Grade 7 to Grade 12 students in Ontario, a quarter report being bullied, and almost a third report bullying someone in the past year. Although assault and weapon carrying seem to be declining, the levels are still unacceptably high. In Ontario, between a fifth and a third of students report being cyber-bullied, depending on the definition, due to an increased use of social media.

What Are the Consequences of Residential Schools?
Residential schools continue to be a dreadful example of the oppression (e.g., cultural, physical, and sexual abuse) of Indigenous children. An apology of by Prime Minister Harper, a commission, and compensation are helpful. But the consequences of this attempt at assimilation will likely be with us for a long time.

What Is the Crisis in School Financing?
Most educational funds for elementary and secondary education come from provincial and local taxes. The per-student grant is lower relative to costs now than in the mid-1990s. In 2012–2013, undergraduate education averaged $5531. Since fees for professional and graduate schools have been deregulated, some fees have skyrocketed. As a result of past increases, some students have high levels of debt. With poor employment prospects, some students have had to default on their loans. Still, there is an economic benefit from completing post-secondary education.

Will Online Education MOOCs (Massive Open, Online Courses) be a Prominent Form of Post-secondary Education?
These courses provide an opportunity for anyone with the Internet to access prominent courses from major universities. Some feel these courses could reduce the costs of university tuition. Some problems include dropouts, creating a few superstar professors, gaining credit, and missing intangible outcomes of dynamic class experiences.

What Educational Goals Should We Set for the 21st Century?

To deal with continuous learning, Canada must pursue a policy of providing young and older people with a high-quality education and opportunities for overall, lifelong learning, including workplace training, volunteer opportunities, and access to cultural programs. The CLI, a measure of this learning, was in a slight decline and our performance in the Report Card was mediocre. We should try to make it possible for Canadians to increase their lifelong learning in the future.

KEY TERMS

education, p. 254
hidden curriculum, p. 255
latent functions, p. 255
manifest functions, p. 254

QUESTIONS FOR CRITICAL THINKING

1. How might the costs of post-secondary education be reduced?

2. How might cyber-bullying be reduced?

3. What are your learning goals for after graduation? How do you plan to be a lifelong learner?

4. How would you rate your university or college in comparison with others? Should the provincial governments create a website for post-secondary education like School Information Finder for primary and secondary education? What characteristics would you like to see compared to help others make the best choice?

Kevin Frayer/CP Images

SUMMARY

P
erhaps nothing better illustrates the close interaction of politics and the economy in Canada today than discussions about pipelines to move oil from the Alberta oil sands to the world. Since Alberta is land-locked, the oil companies must arrange for a method to transport it to ports. Pipelines are the cheapest and safest means to transport oil. Movement by rail is possible, but the tanker cars that exploded and killed 47 people at Lac-Mégantic in 2013 show that pipelines are safer. Protests by environmentalists are causing delays and rethinking about pipelines. TransCanada Corp. had planned a pipeline, called Keystone XL, to transport oil south through the United States to the Gulf of Mexico in 2008 and expected it to be finished by 2013. However, protesters, including prominent Democratic Party supporters, ultimately led President Obama to veto the plan supported by the U.S. Congress in early 2015.

Meanwhile the Canadian government is now seeking other ways of transporting oil to ports by going west and east through Canada. Northern Gateway is the name of the proposed pipeline, going west through British Columbia to Kitimat or another port proposed by Enbridge Inc. This pipeline, too, seems to have enormous political forces opposed to it. First the government's own study by the Joint Review Panel suggested that 209 conditions must be met before proceeding. Then the B.C. government wanted revenues from the oil, along with other conditions, before permitting the pipeline to cross its province. Many Indigenous groups were either outright opposed to the pipeline, or wanted very extensive protection from any spill that would harm their ancestral lands along the 1200-kilometre pipeline route. The pipeline running east will cross the ancestral lands of dozens of Indigenous peoples. In June 2014, the Supreme Court of Canada ruled that Indigenous peoples should have greater control over ancestral lands. They must not only be consulted, but they must also give consent to how those lands will be used. These pipeline negotiations certainly show how closely politics and the economy are tied together—which we will examine in this chapter.

Politics **refers to the social institution through which power is acquired and exercised by certain individuals and groups.** Although political decisions typically are made on a nation-by-nation basis, many of these decisions affect the lives and economic status of people in other nations as well, such as the American delay with the Keystone decision affecting the Canadian economy. The *economy* **is the social institution that ensures that a society will be maintained through its production, distribution, and consumption of goods and services.** Because of the extent to which politics and the economy are related in high-income, industrialized nations such as Canada, some sociologists believe that it is more accurate to refer to the "political economy" as one entity—a combined social institution where the players, rules, and games often overlap. The *political economy* **refers to the interdependent workings and interests of political and economic systems.** To gain a better understanding of how the political economy works, it is important to take a closer look at various types of economic systems, the global economy, and the role of governments and corporations in shaping economic conditions around the world.

MODERN ECONOMIC SYSTEMS AND THE UNDERGROUND ECONOMY

There are three major modern "legitimate" economic systems—capitalism, socialism, and mixed economies—along with an "illegal" system called the underground economy. The Canadian economy is a form of *capitalism*, **which is characterized by private ownership of the means of production, from which personal profits can be derived through market competition and without government intervention.** The four distinctive features of "ideal" capitalism include: private ownership of the means of production, pursuit of personal profit, competition, and lack of government intervention. First, capitalism is based on the right of individuals to own various kinds of property, including those that produce income (e.g., factories and businesses). Second, capitalism is based on the belief that people should be able to maximize their individual gain through personal profit, which is supposed to benefit everyone, not just capitalists. Third, capitalism is based on competition, which is supposed to prevent excessive profits. For example, when companies are competing for customers, they must offer innovative goods and services at competitive prices. The need to do this, it is argued, prevents the market pricing of goods from spiralling out of reach of the consumer. Finally, capitalism is based on a lack of government intervention in the marketplace. According to this *laissez-faire* (meaning "leave alone") policy, also called *free enterprise*, competition in a free marketplace—not the government—should be the force that regulates prices and establishes workers' wages.

Socialism is characterized by public ownership of the means of production, the pursuit of collective goals, and centralized decision making. Under socialism, there are governmental limits on the right of individuals and corporations to own productive property. In a truly socialist economy, the means of production are owned and controlled by a collectivity or by the state, not by private individuals or corporations. Unlike capitalist economies, in which the primary motivation for economic activity is personal profit, the primary motivation in a socialist economy is supposed to be the collective good of all citizens. Although socialist economies typically have less economic inequality than in Canada or the United States, there has been a move in many socialist nations toward *privatization*, a process in which resources are converted from state ownership to private ownership, and the government maintains an active role in developing, recognizing, and protecting private property rights. Privatization continues today in formerly socialist countries such as the Republic of Turkey, where the nation's iron and steel industry has been privatized so that it can compete with similar businesses in the rest of the world. Through privatization of the steel maker, political leaders hoped to realize a profit that would help pay down the country's budget deficit and attract foreign investors (Presidency of the Republic of Turkey 2010). As socialist countries continue to develop a capitalist model of economic production and distribution, it is important to reflect on how Karl Marx viewed socialism as an answer to the problems produced by capitalism.

Unlike capitalist economies, in which the primary motivation for economic activity is personal profit, the primary motivation in a socialist economy is the collective good of all citizens. For Karl Marx, socialism was only an intermediate stage to an ideal communist society in which the means of production and all goods would

be owned by everyone. Under communism, Marx said, people would contribute according to their abilities and receive according to their needs. Moreover, government would no longer be necessary, since it existed only to serve the interests of the capitalist class.

No economy is purely capitalist or purely socialist; most are mixtures of both. A *mixed economy* **combines elements of both capitalism (a market economy) and socialism (a command economy).** In one type of mixed economy, *state capitalism*, the government is involved in the dealings of privately owned companies, including having a strong role in setting the rules, policies, and objectives of the businesses. Countries such as Japan and Singapore in Asia and Saudi Arabia in the Middle East are examples of state capitalism; however, the outcomes are quite different. In Asia, greater government involvement may have resulted in greater good for more individuals, but in Saudi Arabia, it appears to have only made a few people extremely wealthy.

Some Western European nations, including Sweden, Great Britain, and France, have an economic and political system known as *democratic socialism*, in which private ownership of some of the means of production is combined with governmental distribution of some essential goods and services and free elections. Although most industry in mixed economies is privately owned, there is considerable government involvement in setting rules, policies, and objectives. The government is also heavily involved in providing services such as health care, child care, and transportation. Debates about problems in the Canadian economy often involve comparisons of capitalism with other types of economic systems.

As compared to the legitimate economy in which taxes are paid on income and people have licences or credentials that allow them to perform the work they do, the *underground economy* is made up of money-making activities that people do not report to the government and for jobs they do not have licences or credentials to perform. Sometimes referred to as the "informal" or "shadow economy," one segment of the underground economy is made of workers who are paid "off the books," which means they are paid in cash, their earnings are not reported, and no taxes are paid. Lawful jobs like nannies, construction workers, and repair workers are often part of the shadow economy because workers and bosses make under-the-counter deals where bosses pay lower wages and workers do not pay taxes. This economy also involves trade in lawful goods that are sold "off the books" so that no taxes are paid, and unlawful goods, such as counterfeit "designer" merchandise. The discussion of organized crime in Chapter 9 mentions that the total value of the global black market products and services in 2013 was estimated at US$1.79 trillion (Havocscope 2013a), about the same as Canada's Gross Domestic Product (GDP). For some individuals, the underground economy offers the only means for purchasing certain goods and services or overcoming unemployment for low-income people or illegal immigrants. A news item from 2014 suggested the European Union wanted prostitution and drugs to be included in the GDP of countries. Italy would gain the biggest increase in GDP if this occurred.

In a recent article, Nils Gilman writes of the growth of the underground economy, which he calls the "criminal insurgency," due in part to the growth of the "plutocratic insurgency," the growth of the very rich discussed later under inequality. Since less opportunity exists for former labouring classes, they have become entrepreneurs in the underground economy and even benefactors to the poor, who are getting reduced government help because the rich are paying less tax. The growth of these two groups could be devastating to the middle classes who would face a choice of reduced services or likely joining the criminal insurgency (Gilman 2014).

PROBLEMS IN THE GLOBAL ECONOMY

The global financial crisis of 2008–2010 demonstrated how closely connected problems in the Canadian economy are with those of other nations. When Canadian and U.S. financial institutions are in crisis, the economic well-being of many other nations is also in question because it has been widely assumed that high-income nations with advanced economic development will continue to set the pace of global economies. Not all nations are at the same stage of economic development, however, and this creates a widely stratified global economy in which some countries are very wealthy, some are much less wealthy, and still others are very poor. As we discussed in Chapter 2, nations are referred to as high-income, upper and lower middle-income, and low-income. How these nations are classified is related to their level of economic development and the amount of national and personal income in the country. This development can be traced to the economic organization of societies in the past.

Inequality Based on Uneven Economic Development

Depending on the major type of economic production, a society can be classified as having a preindustrial, industrial, or postindustrial economy. In preindustrial economies, most workers engage in *primary sector production*—the extraction of raw materials and natural resources from the environment. In this type of economy, materials and resources are used without much processing. Today, extracting diamonds in the Canadian Arctic and oil in Alberta are examples of primary sector production.

In comparison with preindustrial economies, most workers in industrial economies are engaged in *secondary-sector production*—the processing of raw materials (from the primary sector) into finished products. Work in industrial economies is much more specialized, repetitious, and bureaucratically organized than in preindustrial economies. Assembly-line work, now done on a global basis, is an example.

Although computers and other technologies have changed the nature of the production process, factory work is still often specialized, repetitious, heavily supervised, and full of rules for workers to follow, whether these assembly plants are located in Canada, China, or other nations in today's global economy.

Unlike preindustrial and industrial economies, postindustrial economies are characterized by *tertiary sector production*, where workers provide services rather than goods as *their primary source of livelihood*. Tertiary sector production includes work in such areas as fast-food service, transportation, communication, education, real estate, advertising, sports, and entertainment. Inequality typically increases in postindustrial economies where people in high-tech, high-wage jobs often thrive financially and have business connections throughout the world, while workers in low-tech, low-wage jobs in the service sector (such as fast-food servers or hotel cleaning personnel) may have a hard time paying their basic bills and may feel very isolated from the economic mainstream of their own society.

Although Canada still has primary and manufacturing sectors, the service sector has been the one that has grown the most rapidly in recent decades. For this reason, sociologists refer to Canada as an *advanced industrial society*, which is characterized by greater dependence on an international division of labour (Hodson and Sullivan 2008). In Canada, corporations rely on workers throughout the world to produce goods and services for consumers in this country and elsewhere.

Twenty-five years ago, about one-third of the world's workers lived in countries with *centrally planned economies*—economies in which the government decides what goods will be produced and in what quantities—and another third lived in countries only weakly linked to international commerce because of protective barriers to trade and investment. Today, however, it is possible that fewer than 10 percent of the world's workers live in countries that are largely disconnected from world markets—even North Korea and Cuba are somewhat connected, and Cuba will be much more so with diplomatic recognition by the United States. While the breakdown in trade barriers and the turn to economies based on the demands of the marketplace have brought new goods, capital, and ideals to many, they have also brought new fears.

Rapid change is never easy. In rich and poor countries alike there are fears of rising insecurity, as technological change, expanding international interactions, and the decline of traditional community structures threaten jobs, wages, and support for the elderly. Nor have economic growth and rising integration solved the problem of world poverty and deprivation. The bulk of the more than a billion individuals living on a dollar or less a day depend on pitifully low returns to hard work. In many countries workers lack representation and work in unhealthy, dangerous, or demeaning conditions.

In the wake of the latest recession, these numbers have increased. The rapid changes in economies, and the roles that transnational corporations are playing in those changes, have raised serious concerns about the accountability of corporations.

Transnational Corporations and Canada

Today, the most important corporate structure is the **transnational corporation (TNC)—a large-scale business organization that is headquartered in one country but operates in many countries, which has the legal power (separate from individual owners or shareholders) to enter into contracts, buy and sell property, and engage in other business activity.** Transnational corporations—by design, truly global entities—prosper by serving global markets in an increasingly economically borderless world. They have advanced global capitalism in unprecedented ways. Some transnational corporations constitute a type of international monopoly capitalism that transcends the boundaries and legal controls of any one nation. Of the 100 largest economies in the world, 52 percent are private corporations and not national economies (Andersson and Schemberg 2003). The largest transnationals are headquartered in the United States, China, Japan, Korea, Great Britain, and Germany. Transnationals dominate in petrochemicals, motor vehicles, consumer electronics, pharmaceuticals, tobacco, soft drinks, fast food, financial consulting, and luxury hotels. Canadian transnational corporations deal predominantly in resources, gold, and other minerals, such as nickel and copper, and oil, as well as in gas, and banks.

Because transnational corporations are large and powerful entities, they play a significant role in the economies and governments of many countries. At the same time, by their very nature, they are not accountable to any government or any regulatory agency. Corporate executives often own a great number of shares in a transnational company. The shareholders in transnational corporations live throughout the world. These people have little control over where plants are located, how much money employees are paid, or how the environment is protected. As transnational corporations gain power, they increasingly determine what will be defined as news, which university departments will receive funding, what technology will be developed, and which political parties will be supported. Because transnationals do not depend on any one country for labour, capital, or technology, they can locate their operations in countries where political and business leaders accept their practices and where few other employment opportunities exist for resident workers. For example, when Nike workers went on strike in Indonesia, Nike subcontracted to Korean entrepreneurs operating assembly plants in Vietnam. Although many workers in low-income nations earn less than a living wage from transnational corporations and they often work in very dangerous places—for example, in 2012 in Dhaka, Bangladesh, over 110 garment factory workers died in a fire in a building that had no emergency exits—the products they make are often sold for hundreds of times the cost of raw materials and labour. According to media coverage, managers of these plants are often also physically abusive to the women workers, and union and other human rights organizing are strongly deterred. Designer clothing, athletic shoes, and children's toys are examples of products that are made under exploitative conditions.

Still another concern is that transnational corporations aggressively promote global consumerism. Global consumerism inevitably and dramatically changes local cultures and encourages a "shop till you drop" mentality through advertising and the strategic placement of their business operations around the world. The golden arches of McDonald's and Coca-Cola's signs can be seen from Confederation Square in Ottawa to Red Square in Moscow, and the malls in China could be easily mistaken for the malls in Canada, except that in China they tend to be larger—for example, the US$400 million South China Mall is currently the world's largest shopping mall, covering more than 7.1 million square feet and providing shopping and entertainment for millions of consumers annually. Both McDonald's and Coca-Cola are conquering other nations as aggressively as they have Canada. Today, Coca-Cola sells products in more than

195 countries, distributing 37 percent of total gallons sold in the Unites States; 43 percent in Mexico, Brazil, Japan, and China; and the remaining 20 percent throughout the rest of the world (Coca-Cola Company 2005). Canada is host to many transnational corporations, like General Motors, McDonald's, Walmart, and Coca-Cola, primarily from the United States, with some from Asian countries, like Toyota and Honda.

PROBLEMS IN THE CANADIAN ECONOMY

Despite a period of strong economic growth through the late 1990s and into the late 2000s, Canadians, like so many others from all high-income countries, entered a recession in 2008. The impacts of the recession have been and will continue to be felt in many years to come, as we struggle to rebuild the economy with growing national deficits and debt, growing consumer debt, and rising unemployment. How well Canada's economy is doing now can be seen in part in Box 13.1, Canada's Economic Report Card.

Though our economy has performed quite well since the recession, other problems have emerged like the concentration of wealth, corporate welfare, national and consumer debt, and unemployment.

Concentration of Wealth

Through the economic boom of the late 20th and early 21st centuries, corporate wealth became increasingly concentrated in Canada and in many parts of the world. *Economic concentration* **refers to the extent to which a few individuals or corporations control the vast majority of all economic resources in a country.** Concentration of wealth is a social problem when it works to ensure that elected representatives enact legislation supporting the growth of corporations and preventing their regulation.

The concentration of wealth in Canada has gone through many stages. In the earliest stage, most investment capital was individually owned. Families tended to control all the major trade and financial organizations. Canadian families like the Seagrams and the Irvings controlled whole segments of the Canadian economy.

In early monopoly capitalism, ownership and control of capital shifted from individuals to corporations. As monopoly capitalism grew, a few corporations gained control over major Canadian industries. A *monopoly* **exists when a single firm controls an industry and accounts for all sales in a specific market.** Monopolies in Canada have ranged from Canadian telephone and power-generating monopolies to the many marketing boards that cover dairy products, poultry, fruit, and wheat and other grains, as well as Canada Post's monopoly over first-class mail delivery.

In advanced monopoly capitalism (between 1940 and the present), ownership and control of major industrial and business sectors became increasingly concentrated. After World War II, there was a dramatic increase in *oligopoly*—**a situation in which a small number of companies or suppliers control an entire industry or service.** These large corporations use their economic resources, through campaign contributions, to lobby and influence the outcome of government decisions that affect their operations. Smaller corporations have only limited power and resources to bring about political change or keep the largest corporations from dominating the economy.

Today, mergers often occur *across* industries. In this way, corporations gain near-monopoly control over all aspects of the production and distribution of a product because they acquire both the companies that supply the raw materials and the companies that are the outlets for the product. For example, an oil company may hold leases on the land where the oil is pumped out of the ground, own the refineries that convert the oil into gasoline, and own the individual gasoline stations that sell the product to the public. Corporations that have control both within and across industries and are formed by a series of mergers and acquisitions across industries are referred to as *conglomerates*—combinations of businesses in different commercial areas, all of which are owned by one holding company. Media ownership is one case in point (see Chapter 14).

Further complicating corporate structures are *interlocking corporate directorates*—**members of the board of directors of one corporation who also sit on the board of one or more other corporations.** The problem with such interlocking directorates is that they diminish competition by producing interdependence. People serving on multiple boards are in a position to forge cooperative arrangements that benefit their corporations but not necessarily the general public. When several corporations are controlled by the same financial interests, they are more likely to cooperate (e.g., price fixing) than compete with one another.

The concentration of individual wealth in Canada has also been increasing over the last 20 years. There are two major ways of measuring concentration of wealth among individuals, income and overall wealth. Regarding income, as Figure 13.1 shows, the Gini Index in Canada (a measure of inequality where 1.0 represents perfect inequality and 0 represents perfect equality) was

Social Problems In Global Perspective

Box 13.1

Canada's Economic Report Card

Relative to other high-income countries, Canada is doing quite well six years after the recession, ranking sixth of 16 countries with a grade of a low B (see Table 13.1). This overall grade is based on performance on eight variables: income per capita, GDP growth, labour productivity growth, inflation, unemployment rate, employment growth, inward foreign direct investment, and outward foreign direct investment.

TABLE 13.1 Canada's Economic Report Card

REPORT CARD

Economy

1	Norway	A
2	Australia	A
3	Belgium	B
4	U.S.	B
5	Austria	B
6	**Canada**	**B**
7	Sweden	C
8	Switzerland	C
9	Denmark	C
10	Germany	C
11	Japan	C
12	Finland	D
13	Netherlands	D
14	U.K.	D
15	France	D
16	Ireland	D

Source: *Conference Board, 2014,* Economy. *Retrieved June 23, 2013 (http://www. conferenceboard.ca/hcp/details/economy.aspx).*

Canada's best performance, with a grade of A, was for keeping inflation low. Letting inflation occur would decrease the amount of goods we could produce with the same money.

Canada got a B grade in GDP growth (which enhances one's standard of living), labour productivity growth (which shows we are being more efficient producing the same amount of goods and services with fewer workers), employment growth (which shows the ability of the economy to absorb more workers—a crucial variable for university graduates' prospects), and unemployment rate, which is a problem also discussed in Chapter 2 and later in this chapter.

Canada did not do well in the other variables, getting a grade of C in income per capita (which reflects our ability to maintain living standards) and outward foreign direct investment (which shows our access to foreign markets and how closely we are tied to the global economy). Building pipelines and shipping oil to more countries, as mentioned at the beginning of the chapter, would help us integrate more with the global economy.

Finally, Canada did poorly in inward foreign direct investment, earning a grade of D. This variable shows our ability to attract foreign direct investment into our economy. With more direct investment, our companies gain technologies and knowledge from larger international companies and improve their productivity.

Relative to many other high-income countries, our economy is doing quite well. We frequently compare ourselves to other G7 countries, especially the United States. Of the G7 countries, only the United Sates is ahead of us on the report card.

Questions for Consideration

1. While we need foreign investment, should we seek it from companies that are state-controlled by non-democratic governments like China?

2. How much should we work at improving labour productivity when it usually means laying off workers?

3. Should interest rates be kept low, when it leads to much borrowing and possibly another financial bubble, which if it burst would cause another recession?

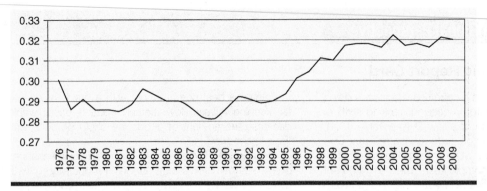

Figure 13.1   Income Inequality in Canada, 1976–2009.

Source: *Conference Board of Canada, 2009,* Canadian Income Inequality. *Retrieved May 18, 2014* (http://www.conferenceboard.ca/hcp/hot-topics/caninequality.aspx).

quite low from the 1970s to the early 1990s, but began to rise in the mid-1990s.

Figure 13.2 shows that the wealthiest quintile of earners has increased its share of total income from 36 to 39 percent in the last 20 years. The poorest and middle groups have lost some of their share.

But those who have really benefitted are the richest 1, 0.1, and 0.01 percent of Canadians. The richest 1 percent of earners earned about $200 000 in 2010 in comparison with $147 000 in 1982. The richest 0.1 percent earned $685 000 in 2010 in comparison with $368 586 in 1982. Finally, the richest 0.01 percent earned $2.5 million in 2010 in comparison with $1.1 million in 1982 (Grant and McFarland 2013).

The unequal compensation becomes even more pronounced when the very top paid executive salaries from 2012 are compared with the average wage of Canadians in 2012 of $46 634 (McKenzie 2014:4). While the base salaries might be reasonable, the huge amounts they receive in bonuses and stock options increase their compensation by 10 times, as shown in Table 13.2.

Turning to overall wealth, as opposed to income, Canada has 384 000 households (2.9 percent of our households) with millionaire status. The United States has the highest number of millionaire households at over 7 million, and Qatar has the highest percent of millionaire households at 17.5 percent (Blackwell 2014).

Corporate Welfare

***Corporate welfare* occurs when government helps industries and private corporations in their economic pursuits.** Corporate welfare has occurred since the beginning of Canada and the building of the Canadian Pacific Railway. During the last recession, the Canadian and Ontario governments gave General Motors $10.6 billion during their bankruptcy protection, and even as recently as 2013 gave automotive companies and their suppliers $250 million to keep jobs in secondary-sector production. Statistics Canada has totalled the amount of corporate welfare subsides given by governments between April 1, 1980 and March 31, 2009. Three levels of government gave $683.9 billion in subsidies to private

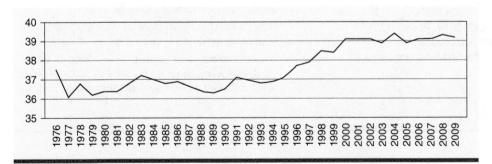

Figure 13.2   Share of National Income of Richest 20 Percent of Canadians.

Source: *Conference Board of Canada, 2009,* Canadian Income Inequality. *Retrieved May 18, 2014* (http://www.conferenceboard.ca/hcp/hot-topics/caninequality.aspx).

TABLE 13.2 Top CEO Salaries in Canada, 2013

Bank	Name	Company	Base Salary	Bonus	Shares	Options	Pension	Other	Total
1	E. Hunter Harrison	Canadian Pacific Railway Ltd.	1 045 069	1 319 688	1 776 539	10 017 735	17 062	34 974 972	49 151 065
2	James C. Smith	Thomson Reuters Corp.	1 549 566	2 855 084	7 813 127	1 936 996	4 600 711	49 566	18 805 050
3	John A. Manzoni	Talisman Energy Inc.	947 000		4 050 001	1 349 991	852 200	11 471 766	18 670 958
4	Paul N. Wright	Eldorado Gold Corp.	1 456 000	3 166 800	2 184 000	2 184 000	9 671 140		18 661 940
5	Donald J. Walker	Magna International Inc.	324 909	8 057 163	5 371 436	2 721 238		376 305	16 851 051
6	Mark Barrenechea	OpenText Corp.	309 628	239 947	3 418 928	10 741 061		106 893	14 816 457
7	Gordon M. Nixon	Royal Bank of Canada	1 500 000	2 850 000	6 600 000	1 650 000	1 087 000	44 877	13 731 877
8	Gerald W. Schwartz	Onex Corp.	1 299 636	11 996 640					13 296 276
9	Mark Thierer	Catamaran Corp.	874 755	1 649 538	8 997 480	1 332 627		37 989	12 892 389
10	Al Monaco	Enbridge Inc.	804 167	1 033 550	771 256	5 237 400	4 251 000	69 099	12 166 472

Source: *Hugh McKenzie, 2014, "All in a day's work. CEO pay in Canada,"* Centre for Policy Alternatives. *Retrieved May 19, 2014 (https:// www.policyalternatives.ca/sites/default/files/uploads/publications/National%20Office/2014/01/All_in_a_Days_Work_CEO_%20Pay.pdf).*

sector business, government business enterprises, and consumers (though consumers may not be aware that, to use one example, subsidies were applied to their electricity and heating bills, reducing the amounts payable to something less than the market rates) (Milke 2014:iii).

The National Deficit and Debt

In mid-2014, the Canadian government was predicting a revenue surplus for 2014–15, but with the steep decline in the price of oil it looked like the government would have another deficit. A *deficit* **refers to the situation when a government's spending on initiatives and programs, along with the interest charges on its outstanding debts, exceeds its revenues in a given year.** When governments run a deficit in any given year, they borrow money, with interest, which becomes a national *debt*—**the amount of money borrowed by the government to offset its deficits.** In an era of welfare state retrenchment, governments typically lay the blame on social and other normal program spending, urging individuals to do what they can to "tighten their belts" and deal with the "necessary" cuts as best they can. While normal program spending continues to be blamed, an analysis of the deficit from just after the beginning of the recession in 2008 by TD Bank's chief economist presents a different picture:

- The 2 percent cut to the GST led to a $12 billion decrease in federal revenue (a $6 billion annual loss for each percentage cut).
- Corporate tax revenues decreased by $10 billion.
- EI payouts increased by $3 billion to $5.5 billion.
- The Canadian auto industry received a $10 billion bailout.

- New infrastructure programs for job creation received $10 billion. (Clancy 2009; Department of Finance 2009)

After the Great Recession, the federal budget deficit in 2009–10 was $55.6 billion. Since then, the federal government has been able to project a reduction in this deficit, using increased revenues and reduced spending. In 2015–16, the government plans to have a surplus of $1.4 billion, with plans to continue to have a surplus to 2019–20. While revenues are increasing, most of this increase comes from taxing citizens. While in the 1960s, Canadian citizens and business contributed 50–50 to tax

Unemployment is a growing problem in Canada.
Michael de Adder/Artizans

revenues collected, today Canadian citizens account for over 92 percent of all tax revenues. Business contributes only 8 percent. As business has withdrawn its tax contribution, the Canadian government has fallen further and further into debt, as have governments all over the world. Like the federal government, many individuals and families in this country are deeply in debt.

Consumer Debt

Canada boasts the eleventh-largest economy on the planet, with a GDP of $1.7 trillion (in 2012) (*The Economist* 2014). However, few think their incomes have grown over the past 30 years. Why, following a period of strong economic growth, would this be the case? For many people, a heavy debt load is the culprit. Consumer debt is rising, and, according to a study reported in the *Financial Post* in early 2014, it is now more than $1.422 trillion. Two factors contribute to high rates of consumer debt. The first is the instability of economic life in modern society; unemployment and underemployment are commonplace. The second factor is the availability of credit (interest rates are very low) and the extent to which credit card companies and other lenders extend credit beyond people's ability to repay. It is typical today for many people to use credit (loans, lines of credit, or credit cards) as a means of getting by or even increasing their standard of living. Many people run up credit card charges that are greatly out of proportion to their income; others cannot pay off the charges they initially believed they could afford when their income is interrupted or drops due to a sudden layoff or decreased work hours.

Is this sight a familiar one to you? In stores throughout the world, consumers are increasingly using their credit cards to make purchases of basic necessities such as food and clothing. What are the risks of excessive credit card debt? What are some risks associated with a high national debt and staggering amounts of consumer debt?

Erik Isakson/Blend Images / Alamy

Having a high level of consumer debt is a personal problem for people, but it is also a public issue—particularly when credit card issuers negligently give fifth, sixth, or seventh credit cards to people who are already so far in debt that they cannot pay the interest, much less the principal, on their other cards.

Unemployment

There are three major types of unemployment—cyclical, seasonal, and structural. *Cyclical unemployment* occurs as a result of lower rates of production during recessions in the business cycles. A *recession* is a decline in an economy's total production that lasts at least six months. Although massive layoffs occur at first, some of the workers will be eventually rehired, largely dependent on the length and severity of the recession. *Seasonal unemployment* results from shifts in the demand for workers based on conditions such as weather (in agriculture, construction, and tourism) or the season (holidays and summer vacations). Both of these types of unemployment tend to be temporary.

By contrast, *structural unemployment* arises because the skills demanded by employers do not match the skills of the unemployed, or because the unemployed do not live where jobs are located. This occurs when a number of plants in the same industry are closed or when new technology makes certain jobs obsolete. Structural unemployment often results from capital flight—the investment of capital in foreign facilities, as previously discussed. Today many workers fear losing their jobs, exhausting their unemployment benefits (if any), and still not being able to find another job.

The **unemployment rate is the percentage of unemployed persons in the labour force seeking employment.** The second decade of the 21st century has seen a large increase in unemployment (6.6 percent in Canada in early 2015). (Statistics Canada's Home Page provides up-to-date unemployment rate.) But some groups are more affected than others. Young people, especially those with little education, are particularly hard hit.

PROBLEMS IN POLITICAL PARTICIPATION AROUND THE WORLD

Social scientists distinguish between politics and government. *Politics*, as previously defined, is the social institution through which power is acquired and exercised by some people and groups. The essential component of politics is *power*—the ability of people to achieve their goals despite opposition from others. People who hold positions of power achieve their goals because they have control over other people; those who lack power carry out the wishes of others. Powerful people get others to acquiesce to their demands by using persuasion, authority, or force.

In contemporary societies, the primary political system is *government*—**a formal organization that has legal and political authority to regulate relationships among people in a society and between the society and others outside its borders**. The government (sometimes called the state) includes all levels of bureaucratized political activity, such as executive, central, and local administrations; the legislature; the courts; and the armed forces and police.

Political participation varies widely because political freedom and other factors that contribute to the quality of our democracy are uneven worldwide. Although people in Canada might take elections, health care, and gender opportunity as givens and decide not to participate even when they have the freedom to do so, people in many other nations do not have the opportunity to participate in free and fair elections and opportunities for all. Box 13.2 provides a ranking of countries according to freedoms and opportunities.

PROBLEMS IN CANADIAN POLITICS

Before looking at our problems, take a moment to consider your own personal political orientation (see Box 13.3). Do you think your orientation will affect how you view our problems? Although Canada has a very high ranking of 13th for the Quality of Democracy 2013 Ranking, issues pertaining to political participation and the quality of our democracy remain a concern both in Canada and around the world. For example, we still have problems with voter apathy and confidence in parliament.

Voter Apathy

Since we live in a democracy, we might assume that people would take every opportunity to participate in political decision making. One of the easiest ways to participate is by voting, since it takes only a few minutes once or twice a year (depending on the number of elections for federal, provincial/terrirorial, and municipal legislators). But as the Conference Board of Canada points out, not only do we have a low rate of voter turnout for federal elections, but the percentage turnout for provincial and municipal elections is usually even lower (54 percent of adult Canadians voted in the last federal election in 2011, and 52 percent voted in the last Ontario election in June 2014). A more extreme example occurred in four federal by-elections held in June 2014. Voter turnout in the two Ontario elections was a

weak 29.4 percent in Scarborough-Agincourt and 31.6 percent in Trinity-Spadina. A much more disappointing voter turnout occurred in Alberta, where 19.6 percent turned out in Macleod and 15.2 percent turned out in Fort McMurray-Athabasca. This is thought to be a record low for voter turnout in Canada (Curry 2014:A1).

We also have low participation rates relative to other high-income democracies. Canada scores a C and ranks 14th out of 17 peer countries in terms of voter turnout (Conference Board 2013). People have generally explained the low percentages by pointing to the lower turnout of young people. Some observers have suggested that we should make voting compulsory, like in Australia. Do you think this is a good idea? Why or why not?

Confidence in Parliament

Another important feature of a stable democracy is confidence in one's parliament. If confidence is high, this might compensate for a comparatively low voter turnout. Canada earned a C rating and ranks 6th among 16 high-income countries according to the Conference Board of Canada (2013). In this case, confidence in parliament is measured as the proportion of respondents in each country who answered "a great deal" or "quite a lot" to the following question in the World Values Survey which took place in 2005–07: "Could you tell me how much confidence you have in parliament: is it a great deal of confidence, quite a lot of confidence, not very much confidence, or none at all?" Thirty-eight percent of Canadians reported having a great deal or quite a lot of confidence in parliament. Not only does Canada have a mediocre ranking among other high-income countries, but this rating has also declined over time. Although a decline of about 5 percent occurred between the 1980s and 2000s, the drop is not as dramatic as that for the United States, which dropped from over 50 percent to 30 percent in the same time period.

Many reasons could explain the decline, such as

- Increased educational levels of the population could be encouraging a more critical approach to all institutions of authority, including parliament;
- Increased claim of busyness by people;
- Leisure activities encouraging cocooning rather than social engagement;
- Discouragement by the apparent influence of major corporations and their lobbies; and
- Feeling that government will not be able to fulfill people's needs regarding education, health care, pensions, transit, environment, etc.

How confident do you feel about our parliament? How might parliament improve this feeling of confidence?

The Democracy Ranking of the Quality of Democracy 2013

Democracies have been measured in many different ways, including

- Freedom House's set of freedoms and a multi-party system (http://www.freedomhouse.org/) (where Canada ranks as more free);
- *The Economist's* Democracy Index for 2012, where Canada's score was 9.08/10 and ranked eighth after most of the Scandinavian countries and above the United States (*The Economist* 2014:39); and
- The Democracy Ranking of the Quality of Democracy 2013 Vienna: Democracy Ranking (see Figure 13.3) that tries to measure such features of democracy as

electoral process and pluralism, civil liberties, the functioning of government, and freedoms, plus concerns with justice topics like opportunities for women, health (e.g., life expectancy), and environment. The Quality of Democracy 2013 Ranking includes the political dimension and five other ones: socio-economic and educational gender equality, economic strength, knowledge (including being an information society), health status and system, and environmental sustainability. Each country is given a score ranging from 1 to 100 (high) and the scores are combined to rank all the countries. The highest and lowest ranked countries are shown in the map in Map 13.1. Canada had a rank of 13, and the

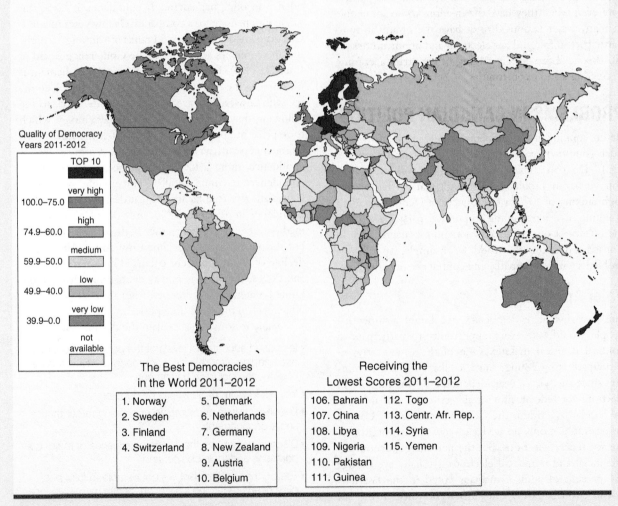

Quality of Democracy Years 2011-2012

TOP 10	
very high	100.0–75.0
high	74.9–60.0
medium	59.9–50.0
low	49.9–40.0
very low	39.9–0.0
not available	

The Best Democracies in the World 2011–2012

1. Norway
2. Sweden
3. Finland
4. Switzerland
5. Denmark
6. Netherlands
7. Germany
8. New Zealand
9. Austria
10. Belgium

Receiving the Lowest Scores 2011–2012

106. Bahrain
107. China
108. Libya
109. Nigeria
110. Pakistan
111. Guinea
112. Togo
113. Centr. Afr. Rep.
114. Syria
115. Yemen

Figure 13.3 The Democracy Ranking of the Quality of Democracy, 2013.

Source: Democracy Ranking, 2013. *Retrieved June 16, 2014 (http://democracyranking.org/wordpress/?page_id=738). Copyright by Democracy Ranking, Vienna, 2013.*

Social Problems in Global Perspective

Box 13.2 continued

United States had a rank of 15. This expanded ranking permits a fuller estimation of how much people are able to participate in their countries.

Questions for Consideration

1. How complex should we allow a term like democracy to become? Can you see a disadvantage of the term becoming too complex?

2. Do you have suggestions for criteria that should be added to or subtracted from the criteria of this ranking?

3. Why do small countries have an easier time than big countries achieving a high ranking?

Critical Thinking and You

Box 13.3

Are You a Conservative or a Liberal? The Language of the Political Economy

The *Gage Canadian Dictionary* defines *conservatism* and *liberalism* as follows:

Conservatism

1. The inclination to keep things as they are, opposed to change.
2. The principles and practices of a conservative political party. (1983:250)

A conservative is one who favours traditional views and values. A conservative is a supporter of political conservatism.

Liberalism

1. The inclination to be generous, broadminded, and progressive.
2. A political party usually having progressive policies. (1983:664)

A liberal is one who is open to new ideas for progress, favours proposals for reform, and is tolerant of the ideas and behaviour of others.

This sounds simple enough, doesn't it? However, politicians, scholars, and everyday people constantly argue about the meaning of these words as they seek to determine where individuals fit on the political spectrum, a continuum that represents the wide range of political attitudes. Linguistics scholar George Lakoff (2002) raises a number of interesting points that might assist us in our critical thinking about our views on the political economy. According to Lakoff, conservatives and liberals not only choose different topics on which to focus their attention, but they also use different words to discuss these topics.

For example, the following words and phrases are used over and over in conservative discourse: character, virtue, discipline, tough it out, get tough, tough love, strong, self-reliance, individual responsibility, backbone, standards, authority, heritage, competition, earn, hard work, enterprise, property rights, rewards, freedom, intrusion, interference, meddling, punishment, human nature, traditional, common sense, dependency, self-indulgent, elite, quotas, breakdown, corrupt, decay, rot, degenerate, deviant, lifestyle.

Lakoff asks us to think about the following questions: What unifies this collection of words? Why do conservatives choose the words they do? What do these words mean to conservatives? Now, let's look at Lakoff's list of words that are favourites among liberals.

Liberals talk about: social forces, social responsibility, free expression, human rights, equal rights, concern, care, help, health, safety, nutrition, basic human dignity, oppression, diversity, deprivation, alienation, big corporations, corporate welfare, ecology, ecosystem, biodiversity, pollution, and so on.

Obviously, we cannot easily sort everyone into either the conservative or liberal school of thought based on their choice of words. In fact, people move around somewhat on the political spectrum: individuals may have more liberal attitudes on some social issues and more conservative attitudes on others.

Questions for Consideration

1. Do you most often use the language of liberalism or of conservatism? Are you a middle-of-the-road type of person when it comes to political issues? What words do you most often use in discussing political and economic issues?

Box 13.3 continued

2. Think about your attitudes on the following topics and state what, if anything, you believe the government should do about the following: abortion; death penalty; government funds for victims of floods, earthquakes, fires, and other natural disasters; health care as a commodity; health care as a right; increasing/decreasing budgets for the military, prisons, and Canadian security; increasing/decreasing spending for regulatory agencies that control businesses or seek to protect the environment; and welfare for individuals who are chronically poor and homeless.

Independent Research

Listen to local, provincial/territorial, and national political leaders. What language do they use? Do their actions reveal attitudes that are conservative, liberal, or somewhere in between as they confront social problems and seek to reduce or eliminate them?

PERSPECTIVES ON THE POLITICAL ECONOMY

The economy is so intertwined with politics in Canada that many sociologists speak of the two as a single entity, the *political economy*. At issue for most sociologists is whether political and economic power are concentrated in the hands of the few or distributed among the many in this country. Functionalists adopt a pluralistic model of power, while conflict theorists adopt an elitist model. Symbolic interactionists focus on the microlevel patterns of people's relationships with one another, and feminists adopt a holistic analysis of power inequalities in society.

The Functionalist Perspective

Pluralism is rooted in the functionalist perspective, which assumes that people generally agree on the most important societal concerns—freedom and security—and that government fulfills important functions in these two regards that no other institution can. According to the early functionalists, government serves to socialize people to be good citizens, to regulate the economy so that it operates effectively, and to provide necessary services for citizens (Durkheim 1893/1933). Contemporary functionalists identify four similar functions: a government maintains law and order, plans society and coordinates other institutions, meets social needs, and handles international relations, including warfare.

But what happens when people do not agree on specific issues or concerns? Functionalists say that divergent viewpoints lead to political pluralism; that is, when competing interests or viewpoints arise, government arbitrates. Thus, according to the *pluralist model*, **power is widely dispersed throughout many competing interest groups in our political system** (Dahl 1961). In the pluralist model, (1) political leaders make decisions on behalf of the people through a process of bargaining, accommodation, and compromise; (2) leadership groups (such as business, labour, law, and consumer organizations) serve as watchdogs to protect ordinary people from the abuses of any one group; (3) ordinary people influence public policy through voting and participating in special interest or lobby groups; (4) power is widely dispersed in society (the same groups aren't equally influential in all arenas); and (5) public policy reflects a balance among competing interest groups, not the majority group's view (Dye, Zeigler, and Schubert 2012).

How might a social analyst who uses a functionalist framework address problems in the globalized economy? Such an analyst might begin by saying that since dysfunctions are inevitable in any social institution, it is important to sort out and remedy the specific elements of the system that create the problems. It should not be necessary to restructure or replace the entire system. Consider, for example, government regulations: some regulations are considered to be good, and some are considered to be bad. The trick, functionalists say, is to keep the good ones and get rid of the bad. Too often, the Canadian government is seen as moving between two extremes: overregulation of business and society, or seeking to end most, if not all, regulation. This perspective is based on the belief that a certain amount of government intervention in the economy is appropriate but that too much—or the wrong kind—is detrimental.

The Conflict Perspective

Most conflict theorists believe democracy is an ideal, not a reality, in our society today. This is because the government primarily benefits the wealthy and the politically powerful, especially business elites. In fact, according to conflict theorists, economic and political elites use the powers of the government to impose their will on the masses. According to the *elite model*, **power in political systems is concentrated in the hands of a small group, whereas the masses are relatively powerless.** In the elite model, (1) elites possess the greatest wealth, education, status, and other resources and make the most important decisions in society; (2) elites generally agree on the basic values and goals for the society; (3) power is highly concentrated at the top of a pyramid-shaped social hierarchy, and those at the top set public policy for everyone; (4) public policy reflects the values and preferences of the elite, not of ordinary people; and (5) elites use the media to shape the political attitudes of ordinary people (Dye, Zeigler, and Schubert 2012).

According to sociologist C. Wright Mills (1959a), there is a hierarchical structure of power. The rulers are the *power elite*, **which at the top is composed of business leaders, the executive branch of the federal government, and the "top brass" of the military.** The corporate rich—the highest-paid CEOs of major corporations—are the most powerful because they have the unique ability to parlay their vast economic resources into political power. The next most powerful level is occupied by members of parliament, special interest groups, and local opinion leaders. The lowest (and widest) level of the pyramid is occupied by ordinary people, the unorganized masses who are relatively powerless and vulnerable to economic and political exploitation.

Individuals who comprise the power elite have similar class backgrounds and interests and interact on a regular basis. Through a revolving door of influence, they tend to shift back and forth between and among the business, government, and military sectors. For example, it is not unusual for people who have served in the prime minister's cabinet to later become directors of major corporations that do business with the government, for powerful businesspeople to serve in parliament, or for former military leaders to become important business-people. Through such political and economic alliances, people in the power elite can influence many important decisions, including how federal tax money will be spent and to whom lucrative subsidies and government contracts are awarded.

In his analysis of the political economy, sociologist G. William Domhoff (1978) speaks of a *ruling class*, which is made up of the **corporate rich—a relatively fixed group of privileged people who wield power over political processes and serve capitalist interests.** The corporate rich influence the political process in three ways: (1) by financing campaigns of candidates who favour their causes; (2) by using loophole contributions to obtain favours, tax breaks, and favourable regulatory rulings; and (3) by gaining appointment to governmental advisory committees, national commissions, and other governmental positions. For example, some members of the ruling class influence international politics through their involvement in banking, business services, and law firms that have a strong interest in overseas sales, investments, or raw materials extraction (Domhoff 1990).

Some analysts who take a conflict perspective say that the only way to overcome problems in politics and the economy is to change the entire system. Our present system exploits poor people, people of colour, women, LGBT individuals, people with disabilities, and all others who are disenfranchised from the political and economic mainstream of society.

Other conflict theorists think that we can solve many problems by curbing the abuses of capitalism and the market economy and thereby reduce the power of political and economic elites. Political scientist Benjamin R. Barber (1996:242) believes that we cannot rely on the capitalist (market) economy to look after common interests. We must do what markets will not/cannot do like education and social services and we must control market abuses.

The Symbolic Interactionist Perspective

Symbolic interactionism focuses on the micro, or small-scale, interactions that occur between individuals in specific settings. This perspective views society as a dynamic process that is continually being created through human interaction and negotiation. As a result, humans develop subjective interpretations of the physical world at the same time that they are socialized to integrate into society. Symbolic interactionism is particularly interested in how members of society socialize one another and how people use shared symbols—objects, words, sounds, and events—to construct social reality and express their experiences of it.

With a focus on the subjective meanings that people attach to their own and other people's behaviour and the processes people engage in to construct and agree upon various definitions of reality, researchers ask very specific questions about human activity. In terms of the political economy, people using this perspective will want to study the interactions that occur between people within democratic processes and business negotiations. How do people experience and interpret laws, fiscal priorities, and budget cuts? How do these societal activities influence people's relationship to and involvement in the democratic process? How do people reach agreements about the role politicians should take in addressing the issues of dissatisfied constituents, and what should citizens do if they are not satisfied with what is happening in their communities? Clearly, it is important to consider the opinions of a diverse range of people in order to build a complete picture of society. People from different racialized/ethnic, gender, and social-class groups, and of different sexual orientations, to name just a few variables, experience the world in dramatically different ways. Their perspectives are essential to the project of understanding the microlevel patterns of human interactions in society.

One question that symbolic interactionists like to ask is, "What happens when a network of people comes together to challenge the status quo?" This explains the fascination with the forces that shaped the "Battle in Seattle" (a popular media phrase for the 1999 anti-WTO protests in Seattle), the G20 protest in Toronto, and the Occupy Wall Street (OWS) movement. Why did anti-corporate-globalization protestors gather in Seattle, Toronto, and in the case of OWS, a great many cities? Why did people develop and use the protest strategies they did during the marches? Why did politicians react to the protest in the heavy-handed manner they did? What shaped the interactions between police and civilians during the protests? While the meaning each individual and small group attributes to the experience is important, so too are the ways in which symbols are used. Symbolic interactionists may focus their attention on ways that mainstream media reporters framed the protestors as dangerous and "anarchistic." They may also do a comparative analysis of the contents of protestors' accounts of police confrontations and the official reports of the same incidents given by police chiefs and elected officials.

Feminist Perspectives

"Black women, be ready. White women, get ready. Red women, stay ready . . ." (Honey, in Brodribb 1999:13). Feminist theoretical perspectives are as diverse as the women who develop them. While feminism as a whole has advanced women's rights and institutional accountability in Canada, a wealth of diverse approaches are responsible for these successes. A close-up look at feminist engagements with the political economy show that liberal, materialist, multicultural, radical, and ecological feminists are among those most concerned with addressing issues of the political economy.

Liberal feminists, for example, work to ensure that women have the rights and abilities to participate fully in political and economic spheres of social life. Securing women's right to vote in Canada; pushing for pay equity, equal opportunity legislation, and universal day care; and supporting women in business are some of the liberal-feminist initiatives. Their work from the 1960s to the present dramatically increased the rights of and opportunities available to women in Canada.

Materialist feminists are concerned with class inequity and the widening gaps between different groups' control over resources, participation in the production of knowledge, and control of power globally. Central commitments are to analyze, challenge, and work to change business practices, globalization initiatives, and development programs that continue to exploit women's productive and reproductive labour.

Multicultural feminists maintain that global survival depends on meaningful exchanges of knowledge, understanding, and solidarity between peoples across the globe. Multicultural feminists focus on the experiences of African, Asian, Middle Eastern, Latin American, and Caribbean women in Canada and around the world. Institutional, interpersonal, and internalized racism and their impacts on the lives of people such as foreign domestic and sweatshop factory workers and immigrant and refugee women and their communities are a primary concern for these feminists.

Radical feminists see women's personal experiences as political, and focus on developing strategies of resistance (Elliott and Mandell 2001:34). This perspective critiques patriarchal and masculinist practices that construct women as passive and submissive. Radical feminists engage in actions such as the fight for the rights and freedoms of women and children who are trafficked in the global sex trade (Kempadoo 1998; see Chapter 7).

Anarcha-feminists analyze the role patriarchy plays in subjugating women and believe that the state is inherently oppressive and should be abolished. Anarcha-feminists view the struggle against patriarchy and the state as the same struggle, with patriarchy being but one of many of the state's tools, as well as being critical in its creation and maintenance (Infoshop 2009).

Ecological feminists draw feminist, ecological, and materialist perspectives together to build an understanding of how political and economic activities such as free trade agreements, transnational corporations, and war impact women, the natural environment, and the quality of life of people, animals, and the earth (Sturgeon 1997). The concerns of this perspective are captured by internationally renowned physicist Vandana Shiva, reflecting on the consequences of the multinational presence in poorer nations. Shiva suggests that much of the world is being controlled by the forces of free trade and large transnational companies, and women in India have done much to oppose this, from being the first tree huggers to being the seed keepers to prevent the emergence of crop monocultures (Shiva 2000) (see also Chapter 15).

These feminists represent perspectives that, when brought together, can be used to build a holistic understanding of the matrices of oppression that shape our current historical moment. Feminists have impacted theoretical and practical approaches to the political economy in many significant ways in Canada. While women today have many rights and freedoms that women in Preconfederation Canada did not, feminists point out that some of the advances women have made are still legally tenuous and in times of backlash are slowly revoked. It comes as no surprise, then, that today, Canadian women and children are still the poorest of the nation's citizens (see Chapter 2).

PROBLEMS IN THE POLITICAL ECONOMY IN THE 21ST CENTURY

What will the Canadian political economy be like as we progress through the 21st century? There is no single vision, of course, but many social analysts think that *digital democracy*—the use of information technologies such as the Internet and the World Wide Web—will dramatically change not only economic relationships, but also the way in which politics and government are conducted. For example, digital democracy can inform people about political candidates and issues. Volunteers use email and websites to encourage people to go to the polls and vote for their particular candidate. These tools can also be used to send messages to voters who indicate an interest in a specific topic, and Canadian voters may soon be exercising their democratic rights via the Internet.

The World Wide Web, cable access channels, and other new information technologies have radically democratized access to political information. However, critics point out that there are some major problems with trying to maintain a pluralist democracy through digital democracy. For example, Fineman is concerned that the political leadership, if too close to voters, will become just the sum of our "whims and misinformation" (1997:52).

Is it possible that the Canadian economy and democratic politics will become inconsequential in the face of the global economy and digitized democracy? Despite digital democracy and the transnational nature of politics and the economy, scholars argue that individual nations will remain the primary locus of identity for most people. Regardless of whom their employers are and what they do for a living, individuals pay taxes to a specific government, are subject to its laws, serve in its armed forces, and can travel internationally only by having its passport. Therefore, as new challenges arise, most people in democracies still turn to their own governments and demand solutions.

WHAT CAN YOU DO?

There are many things that individuals can do on their own and in groups to address the important economic and political issues we face as Canadians in a global economy:

- Remember that your consumer habits are a way of registering votes in the global economy—make informed decisions.
- Learn more about globalization and how it affects you.
- Find out what these are—NAFTA, WTO, FTAA, GATT, NORAD, NATO, and OAS—and how their mandates are impacting you in your daily life.
- Find out about anti-sweatshop campaigns and make informed consumer decisions that reflect your knowledge.
- Organize a non-sweatshop fashion show or "anti-fashion" show or another kind of awareness-raising event at your university or in your community.
- If you invest, or know people who do, research companies that invest in things that reflect your politics.
- Explore what kinds of alternative actions you can take if your concerns and priorities are not being addressed.

SUMMARY

What Kind of Economic System Does Canada Have?
Canada has a capitalist economy. Ideally, capitalism is characterized by private ownership of the means of production, pursuit of personal profit, competition, and lack of government intervention.

How are Societies Classified by their Predominant Type of Work?
Societies are classified as preindustrial (extracting resources from the environment and industrial-processing of raw materials) or postindustrial (providing services rather than goods).

What Are Transnational Corporations, and Why Do They Pose Social Problems?
Transnational corporations are large-scale business organizations headquartered in one country but operating in many countries. Many transnationals lack accountability to any government or regulatory agency. They are not dependent on any one country for labour, capital, or technology. They can play important roles in the economies and governments of countries that need them as employers and accept their practices.

What Is Concentration of Wealth?
Concentration of wealth refers to the extent to which a few individuals or corporations control the vast majority of all economic resources in a country. Concentration of wealth is a social problem when it works to society's detriment, particularly when people are unable to use the democratic process to control the actions of the corporations and governments.

Why Is the National Debt a Serious Problem? How Is Consumer Debt a Public Issue?
When we increase the national debt (85 percent of GDP in 2014), we are borrowing from future generations, leaving them with a social debt of higher taxes, fewer benefits, and a lower rate of economic growth. Consumer debt becomes a public issue when people cannot repay their credit cards and other loans.

What Is Corporate Welfare?
Corporate welfare occurs when the government helps industries and private corporations in their economic pursuits. Many subsidies that were originally put in place to help stabilize the economy continue unnecessarily because of lobbying by special interest groups and business campaign contributions.

What are Voter Apathy and Confidence in Parliament?
Voter apathy allows the interests of only a few to be represented in parliament. Confidence in parliament is measured here as the proportion of respondents who answered "a great deal" or "quite a lot" to the following question "Could you tell me how much confidence you have in parliament: is it a great deal of confidence, quite a lot of confidence, not very much confidence, or none at all?" It is another measure of how well parliament represents the whole population and not just special interests.

What Is the Functionalist–Pluralist Model of the Political Economy?
The functionalists use a pluralist model, believing that power is widely dispersed through many competing interest groups in our political system. Functionalists therefore believe that problems can be solved by identifying dysfunctional elements and correcting them.

What Do Conflict Theorists Say about Power Elites?
Conflict theorists use an elite model, believing that power in political systems is concentrated in the hands of a small group, whereas the masses are relatively powerless. Sociologist C. Wright Mills used the term *power elite* to describe this small group composed of business leaders, the executive branch of the federal government, and the "top brass" of the military.

What Aspect of the Political Economy Do Symbolic Interactionists Focus on?
Symbolic interactionists focus on the micro, or small-scale, interactions that occur between individuals in specific settings. They want to know how humans are socialized, how we develop subjective interpretations of the political economy, and how we find ways to function within it. Specific attention is paid to how people use shared symbols—objects, words, sounds, and events—to build, challenge, and change political and economic activities.

What Are Feminist Approaches to the Global Economy?
Feminists are concerned with political, economic, gendered, racialized/ethnic, and sexual power inequalities in the world. Global capitalism is seen as a force that threatens the health and well-being of people and the planet. Feminists are theoretically and socially committed to protecting and improving the rights, freedoms, and opportunities of all people across the globe.

KEY TERMS

capitalism, p. 272
corporate rich, p. 285
corporate welfare, p. 278
debt, p. 279

deficit, p. 279
economic concentration, p. 276
economy, p. 272
elite model, p. 285

government, p. 281
interlocking corporate directorates, p. 276
mixed economy, p. 273

monopoly, p. 276
oligopoly, p. 276
pluralist model, p. 284
political economy, p. 272

politics, p. 272
power elite, p. 285
socialism, p. 273

**transnational corporation
(TNC),** p. 275
unemployment rate, p. 280

QUESTIONS FOR CRITICAL THINKING

1. How would you respond to this Canadian Gallup Poll survey question: "Do you think that the government is run by a few big interests looking out for themselves or that it is run for the benefit of all the people?" Please explain your answer.

2. Do you favour or oppose the government taking a role in restraining credit card companies? What do you think about the idea of limiting profit and restricting incentives for accepting new credit cards? What would you propose as other means of reducing consumer debt?

3. How do you think globalization will affect democratic practices in Canada in the next 10 years?

4. How would you reduce voter apathy?

5. What roles do you think the Internet has played and will play in future in the political economy?

CHAPTER

14

Problems in the Media

Andrew Vaughan/CP Images

M
edia play a vital role in the daily lives of Canadians. Whether we applaud their existence or try to ignore their influence, most of us are constantly inundated with a variety of media. In this chapter we will look at the role media play in contemporary society. In particular, we explore the convergence of media in Canada, global and Canadian media issues, and the potential effects of media on audiences.

THE IMPORTANCE OF THE MEDIA IN COMTEMPORARY LIFE

What constitutes media? Canadian sociologists Bruce Ravelli and Michelle Webber (2010:443–444) make a helpful distinction between mass communication and mass media: mass *communication* refers to "the transmission of messages by a person or group through a device to a large audience," whereas *mass media* refers to "any medium designed to communicate messages to a mass audience." *Media* is the plural of *medium*, which refers to any instrument that transmits a message. *Media* therefore includes newspapers, radio, magazines, television, movies, and the internet, among other things. When sociologists refer to the media (or mass media), however, they are usually speaking of the **media industries—major businesses that own, or own interests in, radio and television production and broadcasting; cellphones and other personal digital assistants (PDAs); motion pictures, movie theatres, and music companies; newspaper, periodical (magazine), and book publishing; and Internet services and content providers, and those that influence people and cultures worldwide.** To understand how pervasive media industries are in our daily lives, consider one typical day's activities in the life of university or college students (possibly yourself): in the morning they awaken to the sound of an AM/FM adult-contemporary radio station owned by a media conglomerate (e.g., Bell or Rogers; see Table 14.1); during their day and evening they watch one of the TV stations owned and delivered by a media conglomerate (e.g., Rogers or Bell); they read part of the *Globe and Mail* or another paper owned by a conglomerate (e.g., Torstar or Postmedia); they check their email several times on a smart phone provided by Rogers or Bell; and they read texts by Pearson (a British international conglomerate). During the course of the day, students are exposed to numerous forms of media provided by a few media conglomerates.

Recent estimates show that the average person in North America spends more than one-half of her or his waking hours in some media-related activity. Indeed, today, many people spend more time in media-related activities than they do in any other single endeavour, including sleeping, working, eating, or talking with friends and family (Biagi 2012). Consider, for example, that in the last quarter of 2013 (see Figure 14.1), the average Canadian 18+ years of age spent about 10 hours/day watching TV, listening to radio, surfing the Internet, etc. (Munoz et al. 2014:12).

Is this time well spent? Most analysts and media scholars agree that the media industries that emerged in the 20th and 21st centuries are some of the most significant social institutions at work in Canada and in many other nations. The media facilitate human communication and provide news, information, products, entertainment, and social networking to their consumers. Therefore, the corporations that own and control media content and distribution have a powerful influence on all the social institutions, including education, health care delivery, religion, families, and politics. Some aspects of this influence are positive, but other aspects may be negative. Some critics who are concerned about possible negative influences note that we are experiencing a media glut and increased commercialization of all aspects of life (Biagi 2012). For example, commercialization of the Internet and the rise of the World Wide Web in the 1990s have magnified the amount of media messages and products that confront people who use computers and online services. In our current Canadian cultural context, democracy, consumption, and media have become inextricably linked. Today, radio, television, newspapers, and the Internet are the main sources of news and entertainment for most people. As a result, it is important to know who owns these media in order to assess the quality of the information that is being disseminated through them, and to understand the roles media play in shaping (and creating) public opinion.

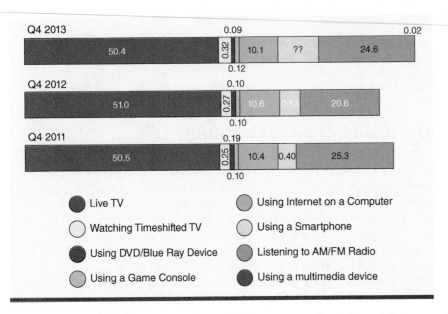

Figure 14.1   Time Spent in Media-related Activity in Hours per Day in the Fourth Quarters, 2011–2013.

Source: *Claudio Munoz, Joe Lee, and Lucas Armstrong, 2014, Digital Transition: Canadian Media Experiments in 2014*, MaRS Market Insights. *Retrieved June 11, 2014 (http://www.marsdd.com/app/uploads/2014/04/Digital-Transition-Canadian-Media-Experiments-in-2014.pdf).*

THE POLITICAL ECONOMY OF MEDIA INDUSTRIES

Over the past few decades, media ownership has become increasingly concentrated. Today, just a handful of companies own a large percentage of television and radio stations, film studios, and publishing houses. In 2013, fewer than 10 U.S. corporations (e.g., Time Warner, Disney, NBCUniversal, Viacom, News Corporation, CBS, and Cox Corporation) controlled most of the publishing, recording, television, film, and theme park business in the high-income nations of the world. Of course, they are also very influential in Canada.

These few companies and their monopolistic control over media content, production, and distribution are known as Big Media. Many factors have led to the development of Big Media—in the main, the evolution of media-related technology. Technology, in the form of motion pictures, radio, and television, increased competition and broadened media markets throughout the 20th century and the Internet in the 21st century. Before that, newspapers and books had been the primary means of disseminating information and entertainment to large numbers of people simultaneously. The companies involved in producing these forms of media were usually small and focused on a single output. For example, newspapers were produced by companies whose only business was newspaper production, and books were published by companies that dealt just in books (Biagi 2012). However, at least two factors limited market demands for the information and entertainment provided by the newspaper and publishing industries: the length of time it took to get the product to consumers and consumers' literacy. Radio, by contrast, offered consumers, from coast to coast, immediate access to information and entertainment. In Canada, the first broadcasting licence was issued in 1919, and by 1922, radio had become a competitor to the newspaper and publishing industries. Simply by turning a knob, consumers could listen to the latest news (sometimes even as it happened!), hear the latest song, laugh with their favourite comedian (e.g., Red Skelton), or thrill to the adventures of their favourite detective (e.g., Dick Tracy). Consumers and corporate executives alike felt that radio's dominance in the media industries could not be shaken. In 1952, however, a new cable television technology took hold in Canada. By 1958, the Canadian Broadcasting Corporation's (CBC) microwave network extended from Victoria, B.C., to Sydney, Nova Scotia, making it the longest television network in the world (Canadian Museum of Civilization 2003). Television's domination in the media world had begun: it had all the advantages of radio plus one more: *moving images*. Now consumers could not only listen to the world around them, they could watch it unfold. Then, the World Wide Web became available to people in 1995, and a huge number of information, entertainment, and networking sites from various parts of the world became available, as did the ability to disseminate information to various parts of the world to all who had access.

Media Ownership and Control

Just as technology has played a significant role in the development of media industries, it has played a significant role in the changes that have occurred within these industries.

Consider, for a moment, the effects that fibre-optic cable, broadcast satellites, and computers, cellphones, and tablets have had on media industries. The introduction of cable television, for example, brought about a significant shift in media ownership. The development of more sophisticated space satellites in the 1970s made it possible for cable television systems to become interconnected throughout North America and contributed to the success in Canada of cable networks such as Shaw Cable, Rogers Communications, Quebecor, and Bell, to which customers pay a monthly subscription fee. Having a variety of cable channels to watch increased the number of cable TV subscribers, resulted in more broadcast stations being built, and inspired the creation of additional cable channels. At the same time, the dramatic increase in cable television viewers drastically reduced the audience share previously held by the original television networks.

This type of corporate convergence in the media industry has led to media concentration. **Media concentration refers to the tendency of the media industries to cluster together in groups with the goal of enhancing profitability** (Biagi 2012). Media ownership is more highly concentrated in Canada than almost anywhere else in the industrialized world. Since 2005, almost all private Canadian television stations have been owned by national media conglomerates. And, because of increasing cross-ownership, many of our newspapers are owned by the same corporations that own television and radio stations (Anderson 2009).

As the definition of media concentration suggests, profit is the driving force. According to media scholar Shirley Biagi (2012), media are owned by people whose interest is in making money. Since profits in this sector are high compared with profits in the manufacturing sector, businesspeople view investments in the media industries positively. Thus far, corporate megamergers have led to the following changes in the media industries (based on Biagi 2012):

1. *Concentration of ownership within one industry:* e.g., Torstar and Postmedia Network
2. *Cross-media ownership:* e.g., Quebecor and Rogers Communications
3. *Conglomerate ownership:* e.g., Bell Media and Rogers Communications
4. *Vertical integration:* e.g., Shaw Communications and Rogers Communications

Table 14.1 shows the small number of major media industries currently in Canada and the wide variety of activities they have brought together through mergers.

In addition to these media conglomerates, a number of smaller ones also exist, like Cogeco, Maritime Broadcasting, and Brunswick News/Acadia Broadcasting, along with publicly funded networks like CBC/Radio Canada, TVO, TFO, and APFN.

Supporters of convergence believe that much can be gained by these corporate strategies—they speak of synergy. The term *synergy* is often used to describe the process used in capitalizing on a product to make all the profit possible. Media analysts believe that synergy is created, for example, when a corporation acquires ownership of both a production studio and a television network. This synergy allows for the programs and products generated by one branch of the company to be promoted through others in an efficient and cost-effective manner.

Problems Associated with Convergence

Concentration and conglomeration are profitable for investors and media executives. These processes don't only involve the amalgamation of businesses, they also involve initiatives designed to streamline media systems. Strategies to increase profits include asking journalists to report on several separate stories each day as opposed to developing one or two well-researched stories. These stories are then distributed throughout the same conglomerate's different media outlets. Many people watching these trends are concerned about the effects this is having on the quality and integrity of journalism in Canada (Lill 2001). For example, analysts indicate that convergence has reduced the amount of *message pluralism*, the "broad and diverse representation of opinion and culture," available to the Canadian public (Biagi 2012). This is also a concern when the bias of the small community of media owners influences the nation's media content. As one media scholar has noted, as a result of convergence:

> media fare is even more closely linked to the needs and concerns of a handful of enormous and powerful corporations, with annual revenues approaching the [GDP] of a small nation. These firms are run by wealthy managers and billionaires with clear stakes in the outcome of the most fundamental political issues, and their interests are often distinct from those of the vast majority of humanity. By any known theory of democracy, such a concentration of economic, cultural, and political power into so few hands—and mostly unaccountable hands at that—is absurd and unacceptable. On the other hand, media fare is subjected to an ever-greater commercialization as the dominant firms use their market power to squeeze the greatest possible profit from their products. (McChesney 1999:29–30)

TABLE 14.1 Media Concentration

Company	Media Outlets	Other Interests
Astral (As of July 2012, part of BCE)	• 25+ TV • 80+ radio • 100+ websites	• Out-of-home advertising division
Bell Canada Enterprises http://www.bce.ca/aboutbce/ bceoverview/?Locale=en_US	• 55+ TV • 30 radio • *Globe and Mail* • Numerous websites for TV, radio, and *Globe and Mail*	• TV, home phone, mobile and wireless provider • Television production company • Music publisher
Postmedia Network Canada Corporation http://www.postmedia .com/company/	• 15+ newspapers • 4 magazines • 10+ websites	• News agency • Software
Quebecor http://www.quebecor .com/en	• 40+ daily newspapers • 100+ magazines and weekly newspapers • 15+ TV	• TV, home phone, mobile and wireless service provider • Book publishing • Music publishing
Rogers Communications http:// www.rogers.com/web/ir/overview	• 25+ TV • 60+ magazines • 50+ radio • 10+ websites	• TV, home phone, mobile and wireless service provider • Television production company • Toronto Blue Jays, and Rogers Centre
Shaw http://www.shaw.ca/ Corporate/About-Shaw/ Shaw-Companies/	• Global TV and 19 specialty channels	• TV, home phone, mobile and wireless service provider • Cable and satellite TV
Telus http://about.telus.com/ community/english/news_centre/ company_overview/telus_at_a_ glance	• TV, entertainment, and video products	• TV, home phone, mobile and wireless provider • Internet
Torstar http://www.torstar.com/ html/our-business/index.cfm	• 4 newspapers including *Toronto Star,* Canada's largest daily newspaper • 100 community papers and 3 daily newspapers through Metroland Media Group • Many websites for papers	• Book publishing • Many websites and applications • Torstar Media Group Television

NOTE: The number of websites includes independent online publishing efforts, not the websites associated with the company's other media outlets.)

Sources: *derived from Dillan Theckedath and Terrence J. Thomas, 2012, "Media ownership and convergence in Canada."* Library of Parliament Research Publications. *Retrieved May 24, 2014 (http://www.parl.gc.ca/content/ lop/researchpublications/2012-17-e.htm).*

Commercialization and branding have already found their way to the Internet, which, even as it is hailed as a newer source of news and entertainment that is relatively free from corporate constraints, has experienced criticism similar to that levelled at longer-established forms of media.

Among the problems that analysts believe have been brought about by convergence are (1) the decline of journalism as a public service profession; (2) constant pressure for all journalistic endeavours to be immediately profitable; (3) a significant decrease in the quantity and quality of international news available to Canadian audiences; (4) the quashing of public debate about the power of the media industries and how they deal with important social issues; and (5) a dramatic increase in the influence of powerful lobbyists who represent the interests of the media conglomerates. Because the reach of the media industries is worldwide, these concerns are not limited to Canada.

On the other hand, sites on the Internet, like blogs and *Huffington Post*, make it possible to obtain news 24/7, while sites like Netflix make it possible to get and stream movies on demand, allowing people to bypass the dominant players some of the time.

GLOBAL AND CANADIAN MEDIA ISSUES

Although a number of global media concerns are significant in the 2010s, the central issues are (1) the role that large media conglomerates play in disseminating information and entertainment worldwide; (2) the role that state-run media and/or government censorship play in distorting or repressing news and information in nations such as Cuba, North Korea, and Iraq; and (3) the role of a smaller country's public broadcasting system, like our CBC, that competes with American media conglomerates.

In the past, information travelled slowly in many regions of the world, but globalization and the technological revolution have changed that in many nations. The proliferation of cellphones, satellite television, and Internet access has increased instant communications and access to information, particularly among middle- and upper-income persons in many regions. The Internet and social media have provided people with more opportunities to speak out, giving their opinions about what is happening in their nation and around the world. In high-income nations, access to newer information technologies has increased dramatically in a relatively short time. However, in low-income, less-developed nations, the process has been much slower, and it is nonexistent in some countries.

Perhaps it should not be surprising that advertising by transnational corporations has fuelled the rise of commercial television—and consequently, the profitability of media conglomerates—around the world. As international agreements over trade, such as NAFTA (the North American Free Trade Agreement) and GATT (the General Agreement on Tariffs and Trade) have come into effect, companies in fields such as oil production, aerospace engineering, and agribusiness have used transnational media corporations to improve their communication base and extend their international operations (Schiller 1996). All in all, the global economy has proved profitable for media conglomerates. These conglomerates can create other problems in the race to be first with

sensational details. For example, Box 14.1 discusses the problem of journalistic ethics that brought disrepute to News Corp.

A second important media issue is the effect of state-run media and/or government control on information in some nations. Government-controlled media refers to media that operate in a government-controlled environment. Some of the most dominant forms of government-controlled media have existed in nations where the media are controlled and directed by the Communist Party. However, the strength of this kind of censorship or propaganda has been diminished somewhat over the past two decades with the introduction of the Internet and social media, which have made it more difficult, but not impossible, for governmental authorities to maintain control over information that is disseminated in, and about, their country (e.g., China has great control over the Internet that its citizens see). China's state-run media are a contemporary example of the influence of the Communist Party on news. The *People's Daily* newspaper, which includes People's Daily Online Co., Ltd., is published by the Community Party and has largely published information at the pleasure of the party in the past. Cuba and North Korea are two other countries in which the media are closely controlled by government.

While global media industries obviously provide news and entertainment to people who otherwise might not know what is going on in the world, according to media critic Robert McChesney (1999), they also contribute to the development of "neoliberal" democracies in those nations in which people have the formal right to vote but where the wealthy actually hold political and economic power.

Many critics also worry that the North American-based media giants undermine traditional cultural values and beliefs in other nations, replacing them with American values—particularly those that support materialism and consumerism. Some call this *media imperialism,* which occurs when one society's media dominates another country's culture (Knight 1998:110). U.S. media critic Jean Kilbourne (1999:55) states, "Today we export a popular culture that promotes escapism, consumerism, violence and greed." The countries that import media portrayals of Western culture do not always have the means to depict values, activities, or perspectives indigenous to their own country in a way that rivals the ability of the United States in particular. The Canadian Radio-Television and Telecommunications Commission (CRTC) regulates the media industries that broadcast programming and demands Canadian content (CanCon) in the broadcasting schedule. The CBC was set up and

Journalism Ethics 101: The Media and the People They Cover

The Guardian, London, July 2011:

"Milly Dowler Phone Hacking: Family Shocked by New Revelations"

Washington Post, July 2011:

"Tabloid Accused of Hacking Slain Teen's Phone"

As simple as these headlines sound, these accusations of phone hacking were the beginning of an international uproar regarding the journalism ethics of the worldwide news media. Especially in the spotlight were the actions of Andy Coulson, Chief Press Officer, and Rebekah Brooks, Chief Executive, of News of the World, a subsidiary of News Corp., under the ownership of Rupert Murdoch, the world's most powerful media mogul. Accusations had been made for more than a decade that Britain's top Sunday tabloid was hacking the phones of celebrities, politicians, British royalty, and members of parliament. But these accusations became headline news only when the British parliament held hearings. The hearings revealed that the tabloid often hired "investigators" to hack into other people's voicemails so that the tabloid could use information gathered for its own enrichment. This is an example of a journalistic endeavour intended to be immediately profitable (see above problems of media convergence). In the case of Milly Dowler, a teenaged girl reported missing in 2002 and found murdered six months later, News of the World officials admitted that their "investigators" had hacked her voicemail repeatedly during the period that she was listed as "missing." Little did law enforcement officials or her family know that her voicemail was being hacked by investigators who were deleting some messages, including ones left by family members, to free up additional space for new messages. The tabloid wanted to "scoop" other media in its coverage of the Dowler case and listen to the parents' desperate pleas to their daughter. However, in addition to the privacy issue, the tabloid's actions could have jeopardized the police investigation by making authorities believe that the victim was alive. When the hackers deleted messages from Dowler's voicemail, her family was also given false hope that she was listening to her phone messages, but this was not the case. Had this been the only case, it might not have received so much attention. But it was soon learned that numerous cases of hacking by News Corp. personnel had allegedly occurred, including one in which News of the World had offered to pay New York police officers to hack into the phone messages of victims of the September 11, 2001, terrorist attacks in the United States.

Several key questions emerged as a result of the media hacking cases: What has happened to ethics in journalism? What about the international concept of breach of privacy—intrusion into the personal life of another individual, without just cause, that gives the person whose privacy has been invaded a right to bring a lawsuit for damages against the person or entity that intruded? According to law professor Richard T. Karcher, journalists have an "ethical obligation to 'seek the truth,' avoid sensationalism and trivia, and protect individual privacy interests" (Karcher 2009:781). In the case of media coverage of sensationalized crime stories or of stories about celebrities, sports figures, and other high-profile individuals, the media's ethical obligations are routinely discounted. Because members of the media are largely self-regulating in regard to journalism ethics, when violations do occur, few external enforcement mechanisms exist apart from judgments in lawsuits filed by aggrieved individuals (Karcher 2009). Whether in Great Britain, the United States, or other nations, the issue of privacy is a key concern in journalism ethics. Now, more than ever, many communications devices and software technologies exist for "hacking" and providing other illegitimate access to supposedly private information. Email, voicemail, social media sites such as Facebook and Twitter, and smartphones containing vast amounts of personal data and individual preferences are all potentially available to hackers who desire to use our personal information in ways we have not approved.

The *News of the World* was shut down after the scandal surfaced. On June 24, 2014, Andy Coulson was found guilty of conspiring to intercept messages to break news about royalty, celebrities, and victims of crime, and Rebekah Brooks was found not guilty of interfering with a police investigation into the phone-hacking scandal. Will the conviction change anything? In the aftermath of the 2011 scandal, Rupert Murdoch promised to usher in a new era of ethics in journalism by issuing an updated and revised code of behaviour for all News Corp. employees. He still retains his position as chairman of News Corp. It seems like most alleged changes occur after a scandal. Is this just a smoke screen? Will updates of the journalism code of ethics make a difference in news and social media industries, or will the need to be sensational trump these concerns? Only time will tell, of course, but in the meantime, it remains for each of us to be vigilant in separating out the "tabloidization" of life from what is actually newsworthy information we need to know. It is also important to identify valid journalistic methods and sources of information as opposed to relying on tidbits picked up by hackers and those who spy through illegal and/or unethical "keyholes" to see what unsavory information they can gather about people for their own financial gain. Since so much of what is presented by the media is in the form of "infotainment"—providing information in an entertaining way—there is a problem with determining the truth.

After the scandal broke in England, the (British) Conservative government set up an investigation called the Levenson Inquiry, which became, in the words of Doug Saunders, a *Globe and Mail* journalist, "a barrage against all journalistic invasions of privacy" (2014:A11). Saunders believes that all good journalism is an invasion of privacy, and gives an example of exposing the evidence used to launch the Iraq war. The Inquiry recommended that an agency be created to monitor and police the media. However, Saunders believes that such an agency could "stifle important investigations" (2014:A11).

Questions for Consideration

1. What limits should be placed on the news media in terms of how journalists and other media employees go about gathering information about supposedly newsworthy individuals and topics?

2. Is a government agency the best way to deal with this?

3. Will it be possible to protect the privacy of individuals in the future, given rapid advances in information technologies (such as in medical environments) and the proliferation of handheld communications devices such as iPads and cellphones?

Independent Research

If you would like to know more about the issue of journalism ethics, visit various media websites and compare the organizations' policies on this issue. Here are a couple of suggestions to get you started:

Globe and Mail Editorial Code, March 2013
Society of Professional Journalists' Code of Ethics

supported by the federal government to reflect and promote Canadian culture and values, but also to counter American media. But what happens when the government, which for decades has supported the network, substantially reduces its support (see Box 14.2)?

As Kilbourne and other media scholars point out, for the first time in history, people are hearing most stories about life, not from their parents, schools, churches, or friends, but from transnational media conglomerates that have something to sell. If it is true that the media are a crucial influence in shaping and creating global cultural perceptions, then all of us must give careful consideration to the images and information offered to us. Of particular significance is how the news is framed. **Framing refers to how news content and the accompanying visual images are linked together to create certain audience perceptions and give specific impressions to viewers and readers.** When framing occurs in a news story, some analysts use the term "spin," because the process often involves "spinning" information to present it from a particular (and different) angle or point of view. Critics point out that once a frame is established, journalists must adhere to it. The danger is that media coverage falling outside of the frame is not covered by mainstream media. In Canada, media bias is a growing concern for professional journalists.

Media bias, in the form of *structural media bias,* refers to the areas of life and work that are not covered in the media. This distorts how people view the world and can significantly influence the priorities people develop. For example, in the 1990s, the face of national news changed in Canada. Hollinger Press, owned then by Conrad Black, changed its reporting priorities and cut regular columns on the environment, social affairs, education, and health issues and replaced them with entire sections on business affairs. This structural bias resulted in media coverage that suggested to Canadians that national and international business interests were now the most pressing concerns of the 21st century, while other issues, such as the environment or culture, being only intermittently important.

POTENTIAL MEDIA EFFECTS ON AUDIENCES

As previously mentioned, global media industries today are the primary source of news and entertainment for many people. Although these industries may have greater influence over some people than over others, media analysts suggest that all of us are more profoundly influenced by media messages than we realize. The portrayal of violence is one example of a negative media influence.

Violence and the Media

Should we be concerned about how—and the extent to which—media depict violence? A number of media

Should Canadians Have Substantial Public Broadcasting Services and Should There Be a Substantial Number of Hours of Canadian Content?

The CBC is a public service that was created to inform, educate, and entertain, and to reflect and promote Canadian culture to Canadians. The first radio stations went on air in the 1920s: the CBC News Service began in 1941; and the first television stations emerged in the 1950s. For over 70 years, the CBC has been supported by the federal government to provide news, current affairs programming, and entertainment that was worthwhile for Canadians (e.g., *Street Legal, Little Mosque on the Prairies, Murdoch Mysteries,* and dozens of documentaries), as opposed to providing programs to please advertisers like private commercial stations and networks. The CBC receives about 1.34 billion dollars yearly from the federal government (Rowland 2014:A9). But relative to other high-income countries, especially the Scandinavian countries, the government contributes a very small amount per capita to public broadcasting. During the last few years, the federal government has reduced revenues to the CBC. According to a Nordicity report, the CBC received $33/capita in 2011, and this was expected to decline to $29/capita in 2014/15 (2013:2). In comparison, the average for the 17 high-income countries is about $82/capita. At the extremes, Norway spends $180/capita and the United States spends $3/capita.

In June 2014, the CBC released a plan to greatly reduce spending by shifting primarily from broadcast to digital services; reducing in-house production except for news, current affairs, and radio; in the process eliminating up to 1500 creative positions by 2020 in addition to a staffing cut of 657 in April 2014; selling off real estate; and reducing suppertime news programs from 90 to 30 minutes. Wade Rowland, a professor of communication studies, has expressed concern that traditional broadcasting brings people together, while Internet broadcasting promotes the individual and his/her interests (2013), contributing to the fragmenting of our society. Rowland also suggested that this move is because advertising revenue is shifting to the Internet, and the government wants the CBC to earn more advertising revenue (2013). In 2011, commercial revenue was 34 percent of total revenue (Nordicity 2013:3). But what will the orientation of the CBC become if it requires a larger amount of commercial revenue to survive?

Regarding Canadian content, in March 2015 the CRTC suggested new guidelines for Canadian TV. Among the recommendations are that although prime-time TV must have a Cancon (Canadian content) quota, the daytime Cancon quota could be reduced to zero; big budget shows that are about Canadian novels or novels written by Canadians would be labelled Canadian content if some Canadians are leading the show; and ways be found to permit Canadians to find Canadian shows as people find shows on Netflix. These recommendations will likely mean fewer industry jobs, perhaps more choice for the consumer, but certainly less Canadian work for Canadians to see.

Questions for Consideration

1. How often do you watch CBC TV and/or listen to CBC Radio in comparison to private stations (Canadian and American)?

2. Do you think the CBC is fulfilling its mandate of reflecting and promoting Canadian values, and will this be true if the new guidelines are implemented?

3. Do you think the CBC should be a public system like Medicare and the school system and receive sufficient support to serve Canada, or should it become a private network?

---

analysts assert that the need of media industries to capture public interest and thus increase the size of their markets has contributed to the use of violence as a means of selling newspapers, television programs, movies, music, and other media-related commodities. A Canadian study reports that television violence affects children of varying age groups differently, and with children between the ages of 10 and 17 spending the majority of their time engaged with media, the overall impacts must be considered (Children Now 1999). According to an extensive study that was conducted by the Center for Communications and Social Policy at the University of California at Santa Barbara, violent television shows made up 60 percent of all television programming during the three years of the study. Moreover, that percentage continued to increase over the course of the study (Stern, 1998). Today, the amount of violence shown, and the severity of violence, is even greater if we primarily look at portrayals of crime, terrorism, and criminal investigations. To capture younger, male audiences, many shows focus on the depiction of brutal crimes, horrendous crime scenes, and violent encounters among ordinary citizens, criminals, and law enforcement officials. Aggression and violence are more often found in programming on cable channels and subscription movie channels such as HBO and Showtime.

Some analysts have suggested that violent programs are intricately related to commercial broadcasting because bloody, violent encounters and sex are what sells. Although some television executives claim that their programs reflect audience desires, it is also true that high ratings encourage corporations to spend millions on advertising their products. Not all highly rated series have violence, particularly in the age of reality television, but franchises such as CSI, NCIS, Criminal Minds, and their successors are rooted in a culture of aggression and violence.

What effect does the depiction of violence have on audiences? There is no definitive answer to this question. Most media scholars do not believe that media portrayals alone cause aggressive behaviour in people. Some studies have shown a relationship between at least short-term aggressive behaviour and media depictions of violence. Other studies have found that the media may prevent acts of violence by providing people with an outlet for pent-up feelings and emotions. According to the *cathartic effect hypothesis*, the media offer people a vicarious outlet for feelings of aggression and may reduce violence by the media consumer. However, other analysts argue that the cathartic effect hypothesis has been disproven, meaning that continual depictions of violence actually desensitize viewers and create attitudes that contribute to aggressive behaviour and reinforce feelings of fear and frustration (Gerbner, 1995). Over time, as people become more desensitized to portrayals of violence, it is necessary for films and television series to become even more violent in order to attract the audience's attention. This theory might help explain the popularity of animal documentaries showing "kill sequences" and blood fights among animals, such as on Animal Planet and the Discovery Channel, as opposed to earlier programming that focused on topics such as cute puppies and how animals seek to communicate with humans. See Chapter 1 (Secondary Analysis of Existing Data) for an analysis of the effects of TV violence on young people.

In sum, at a minimum, constant exposure to violence-laden media content might contribute to an individual's feelings of fear and a need for greater security and protection in everyday life. However, studies of the relations between violence and the media are not being conducted at the same rate as they were in the latter part of the last century. We would hope that researchers will once again pursue this topic so we will learn more about the causes and consequences of extensive media violence in society.

Racial and Ethnic Stereotyping

The Conference Board of Canada reported that Canadians have a grade of A for acceptance of diversity—a higher percentage of people (over 80 percent) answered "yes" to the question of whether their community was accepting of people from different racial, ethnic, and cultural groups than in any other high-income country (see Figure 3.4). But such a high score in acceptance does not always eliminate stereotyping in many parts of life, such as the media.

Stereotyping can involve one or more of the following:

1. Perpetuating images that appear to be positive in nature and thus flattering to members of a specific racialized group;
2. Exaggerating the physical appearance of subordinate-group members;
3. Creating racialized or ethnic characters who have undesirable attributes;
4. Using statements and visual images that link subordinate racialized groups to illegal actions such as terrorism, crime, and drug dealing; and
5. Under-representing people relative to their percentage in the population.

A recent study by Baumann and Ho of 244 commercials about food and dining (so they could be easily compared) that aired in prime time on CBC, Global, and CTV found that stereotyping did take place. When the racialized groups appearing in commercials were analyzed, 84 percent of the primary characters were White, 9 percent Black, 1 percent East or South East Asian, 3 percent South Asian, and less than 1 percent were Latino, Arab, or Indigenous. While the proportion of White is not far off the percentage in the population (80 percent), South Asians are underrepresented (3 vs. 7 percent of the population), as are Arabs and Indigenous (both less than 1 vs. 3 percent of the population). Moreover, White characters were more likely to be associated with nostalgia and a more high-status lifestyle. Black people were more frequently shown in working-class occupations, and Asians were often shown as "technocrats." The authors concluded that advertising as media content influences the way we understand the world around us. It is easy to pick up stereotypes and they communicate easily to audiences (Baumann and Ho 2014).

Gender Stereotyping

According to scholars who have conducted studies of gender stereotypes in the contemporary media, such stereotyping may result, at least in part, from the under-representation of women as producers, directors, and executives in the largest media industries. Regardless of the cause, some studies of television and film have shown the following gender stereotypes of women.

1. The intertwining of gender and age bias as it uniquely affects women: Gender-specific age bias is apparent in the casting of many female characters. Older men and significantly younger women are often cast in leading roles in films, causing some women actors to ask "where are the roles for older women in Hollywood?" A few older women are cast in leading roles, like Judi Dench, Helen Mirren, and Meryl Streep.

2. The perpetuation of traditional roles for women and the maintenance of cultural stereotypes about the importance of beauty, thinness, and femininity for getting and keeping a man: Female characters who do not live up to the gendered expectations associated with femininity are overtly or subtly punished for their conduct.

3. Impulsive conduct by women holding professional positions: When television shows portray professional women, the women are often shown as engaging in compulsive behaviour such as constantly purchasing very expensive designer shoes, smoking or drinking alcohol excessively, and having other bizarre habits. Men are not exempted from such portrayals, but they are more likely to be shown as displaying professional competence in the workplace.

4. Women in positions of power abusing their positions: Prior to the 1990s, most female characters were depicted in lower-status occupations or in roles that were clearly subordinate to those of men. Although more female characters on prime-time television shows and in film today are lawyers or judges than in the past, these characters are often shown as "seducers, harassers, and wimps in black robes" (Goodman 1999:AR 47). When female characters are not seducing men, they are often depicted as "bitches" or "bimbos." On *Judge Judy*, Judy Sheindlin, a former family court judge in New York, berates and demeans people appearing in her court (Goodman 1999).

5. Women overwhelmed by their work or seemingly having few job responsibilities even when they are employed full time: The imbalance between the portrayal of female characters as either having so much work to do that they cannot complete it all or the depiction of them as having an important occupation but spending little time actually doing the work tends to convey the message that women are less than adequate in many careers and occupations. Examples include *Grey's Anatomy*, where

female surgical interns are more often shown in romantic liaisons than in hospital work, and attorney and police shows where female characters primarily focus on interpersonal relationships, especially with men, rather than getting their job done. A counter-example occurs in *Murdoch Mysteries*, where, at least in the early few years of episodes, Dr. Julia Ogden, the pathologist, was frequently shown doing autopsies and giving reports to the police. In more recent episodes she has been supporting women candidates for political office.

Although the depiction of women characters in television programs, films, and other forms of media has improved significantly in recent decades, much remains to be done if women are to be shown in the wide diversity of occupations and endeavours in which real-life women participate on a daily basis.

It should be noted that, although the nature of male stereotypes is somewhat different, men have not been exempt from gender stereotyping in the media. Among the most frequently employed stereotypes of male characters are men depicted primarily as jokers, jocks, strong silent types, big shots, action heroes, or buffoons. For example, working-class men frequently are portrayed as buffoons who are dumb, immature, irresponsible, or lacking in common sense. These male characters are the object of jokes and are often shown as being sloppy in appearance, ignorant, and sometimes racist (Kendall 2011) (see Feminist Perspectives below).

PERSPECTIVES ON MEDIA-RELATED PROBLEMS

Just as they do in regard to other social issues, interactionist, functionalist, conflict, and feminist approaches to media-related problems start with differing assumptions about these problems.

The Interactionist Perspective

Perhaps the earliest interactionist theory concerning the media's effect on individuals and groups was the *hypodermic needle theory*, which suggested that audiences were made up of passive individuals who were injected with the message and directly affected by the message as people are by a drug. However, a World War II study of military personnel who were shown movies designed to portray the enemy as evil and to increase morale among soldiers concluded that most of the subjects showed little change in their morale level, although the movies did influence their views of the "enemies" as "evil." Based on these findings, researchers suggested an alternative explanation: the theory of limited effects. The ***theory of limited effects*** **states that the media have a minimal effect on the attitudes and perceptions of individuals.** According to this theory, people may not always be selective about what they watch or read, but they gather different messages from the media, and many people carefully evaluate the information they gain. This theory notes that when people are interested and informed about an issue, they are less likely to be influenced by what members of the media report. Those who are poorly informed or have no personal information about a particular topic or issue are more likely to be affected by what other people, including reporters and journalists, say about the social concern.

A similar theory, known as *use and gratification theory,* suggests that people are active audience participants who make conscious decisions about what they will watch, listen to, read, and surf on the Internet. However, this theory assumes that people using different media have specific wishes or desires and will choose media sources that gratify their desires. In other words, people use the media to entertain and inform themselves but are aware of the limitations the media have in their coverage of topics and the forms of entertainment.

Another interactionist theory, mentioned elsewhere in the book, is ***social learning theory,*** **which is based on the assumption that people are likely to act out the behaviour they see in role models and media sources.** To support this theory, social psychologist Albert Bandura (1977) conducted a series of experiments on aggression in children. For the experiment, children were divided into four groups. One group watched a film of a man attacking and beating a large, inflatable doll and being rewarded for his behaviour. The second group saw a similar film, except in this version the man was punished for attacking the doll. The third group was shown a version in which the man was neither rewarded nor punished for his behaviour. The final group was not shown any film. Prior to the experiment, researchers believed that the children who saw the man rewarded for hitting the doll would be the most likely to show aggressive behaviour toward the doll. However, this did not prove to be true. Regardless of which version of the film they saw, children who were prone to aggression before the film tended to act aggressively toward the doll but other children did not. As a result, the researchers concluded that many factors other than the media influenced aggressive behaviour in children, including their relationship with their parents, how much formal education their parents possessed, and the personality of the children.

More recent theories have sought to explain the effects of media on individuals by emphasizing the part that viewers, listeners, and readers play in shaping the media. According to the *audience relations approach,* people use their own cultural understandings to interpret what they hear and see in the media. Factors involved in the audience relations approach include how much previous knowledge individuals have about a topic and the availability of other sources of information. This viewpoint is somewhat in keeping with functionalist approaches, which highlight the important contemporary functions of the media.

The Functionalist Perspective

Functionalist approaches to examining the media often focus on the functional—and sometimes dysfunctional—effects the media have on society. Functionalists point out that the media serve several important functions in contemporary societies:

- First, the media provide news and information, including warnings about potential disasters, such as an approaching hurricane.
- Second, the media facilitate public discourse regarding social issues and policies, such as welfare reform.
- Third, the media pass on cultural traditions and historical perspectives, particularly to recent immigrants and children (Lasswell 1969).
- Fourth, the media are a source of entertainment, providing people with leisure-time activities (Biagi 2012).
- Fifth, the media confer status on individuals and organizations by frequently reporting on their actions or showing their faces and mentioning their names. According to sociologist Joshua Gamson (1994:186), becoming a media celebrity is a means of gaining power, privilege, and mobility: "Audiences recognize this when they seek brushes with it and when they fantasize about the freedom of fame and its riches and about the distinction of popularity and attention."
- Finally, with the emergence of social media people can now express themselves and disseminate their opinions and ideas.

As Gamson notes, some people become celebrities *because* the media confers that status on them. In other words, as the popular saying goes, "Some people are famous for being famous." As a Canadian example, a Torontonian became possibly the most well-known lawyer in North America for a short while when he sued Starbucks Coffee Company for $1.5 million because of damage to his penis—an injury he received from getting it caught in a toilet seat in the washroom of one of Starbucks' coffee shops. Reporters and producers from across North America deluged the man with requests for interviews. In Toronto, the media focused so heavily on this story that only the WTO talks and protests that year were covered more heavily (Associated Press 1999; Hackett et al. 2000).

Although the media are a source of entertainment for many, functionalist theorists state that the media are dysfunctional when they contribute to a reduction in social stability or weaken other social institutions, such as the family, education, politics, law, and religion. For example, television has brought about significant changes in family interaction patterns, as one media scholar explains:

> The most pervasive effect of television—aside from its content—may be its very existence, its readily available, commanding, and often addictive presence in our homes, its ability to reduce hundreds of millions of citizens to passive spectators for major portions of their waking hours. Television minimizes interactions between persons within families and communities. One writer I know only half-jokingly claims, "I watch television as a way of getting to know my husband and children." Another associate, who spent years in Western agrarian regions, relates how a farmer once told her: "Folks used to get together a lot. Now with television, we see less of each other." (Parenti 1998:188)

Several dysfunctions of media include perpetuation of misinformation, like the weapons of mass destruction (WMD) that contributed to the war in Iraq, loss of privacy, as shown in Box 14.1, and cyber bulling (see Chapter 12). While the media have changed how people interact with one another, they may have also profoundly influenced the ways in which individuals react to events in their personal and community-based lives. There are other functionalist approaches, however, which suggest that individuals and families are responsible for social change in regard to the media. Analysts who favour this approach believe that rather than changing the nature of television programming, parents should monitor their children's television-watching habits and schools should offer media education for parents and children to make them aware of the classic persuasion and propaganda techniques often used in programming and advertising (Minow and LaMay 1999).

The Conflict Perspective

Conflict theorists typically link the media industries with the capitalist economy. From this approach, members of the capitalist class own and control the media, which, along with other dominant social institutions, instruct people in the values, beliefs, and attitudes that

they should have (Curran et al. 1982). All of these efforts to maintain the status quo and the privileged position of the power elites within it are achieved through **hegemony—the use of the media and other cultural institutions to represent the interests, values, and understandings of the capitalist class and other powerful groups as natural and universal** (Knight and Greenberg 2008:108). According to this perspective, the *process of legitimization* takes place as media consumers are continually provided with information that supports the validity of existing class relations. As a result, members of the working class are lulled into a sense of complacency in which they focus more on entertainment and consumption than on questioning existing economic and social relations. This perspective is sometimes referred to as **hegemony theory—the view that the media are instruments of social control and are used by members of the ruling classes to create "false consciousness" in the working classes.** Edward S. Herman and Noam Chomsky, in their book *Manufacturing Consent* (1988) and the 1993 National Film Board film of the same title, discuss this concept at length. One of the major points in this work is that people from the ruling classes need not be involved together in any kind of conspiracy to hoodwink the masses. Rather, the fact that their interests are the same dictates that they act in a manner similar to one another.

Although there are various conflict approaches, most view ownership and economic control of the media as a key factor in determining what kinds of messages are disseminated around the globe. Media analysts such as Michael Parenti believe that media bias is inevitable as transnational media industries become concentrated in the hands of a few megacorporations:

> Media bias usually does not occur in random fashion; rather, it moves in the same overall direction again and again, favouring management over labour, corporations over corporate critics, affluent whites over inner-city poor, officialdom over protestors, the two-party monopoly over leftist third parties, privatization and free-market "reforms" over public-sector development . . . domination of the Third World over revolutionary or populist social change, investor globalization over nation-state democracy, national security policy over critics of that policy, and conservative commentators and columnists . . . over progressive or populist ones. (1998:149)

According to Parenti, the built-in biases of the media reflect the dominant ideology that supports the privileged position of members of the capitalist class.

There are a number of ways in which media manipulation can occur: (1) sponsors control broadcasting decisions; (2) information may be suppressed by omitting certain details of a story or the entire story, particularly if the story may have a negative effect on a person or organization to whom members of the media feel beholden; (3) a story may be attacked or the reporting may not present a balanced view of the diverse viewpoints involved; (4) negative labels that stereotype groups of people, for example, "Islamic terrorists," "inner-city gangs," or "welfare cheats," may be used; and (5) stories may be framed to convey positive or negative connotations through the use of visual effects, placement, and other means. Like other conflict theorists, Parenti (1998:157) believes that the media tell people what to think before they have had a chance to think about an issue for themselves: "When we understand that news selectivity is likely to favour those who have power, position, and wealth, we move from a liberal complaint about the press's sloppy performance to a radical analysis of how the media serve the ruling circles all too well with much skill and craft." Viewing media activities in Canada from these perspectives inspires one to learn more about the relationship between media, social control, and the economy in the new millennium.

In an era marked by increased concentration of all forms of media, including the Internet, conflict perspectives on media ownership and control raise important questions. Although people engaged in political critique and social activism, such as members of environmental or women's groups, have sometimes been able to marshall the media on their behalf, the media often implicitly support the status quo because of their corporate interests and their need to maintain and enhance advertising revenues.

Feminist Perspectives

Beginning in the late 1960s, second wave feminist media scholarship focused on the role of visual representation in women's oppression. Studying media texts that range from television and movies to radio, feminists have critiqued male domination in the media and its role in reinforcing gender stereotypes that sustain socially endorsed and oppressive views of gender.

Second wave feminists radicalized Canadians' understanding of the problem of women's devaluation (be it individualistic, psychological, sociocultural, biologistic, or economic) and the ways traditional relationships between men and women are used to normalize such things as violence against women in the media. Both feminists and conflict theorists are concerned about the role media have in shaping people's values, beliefs, and attitudes. They are also critical of the role the mass media play in supporting and perpetuating hierarchies of oppression. One dramatic example of this is the concept of the *gaze*. Originally used by Jacques Lacan to describe the understanding that one can be viewed, the concept has been developed by Laura Mulvey to show how males oppress females in film, portraying them as sexual objects, or at least passive to males, because they control the film. But, according to Mulvey, there is also a female gaze which describes women viewing other women as men would. Mulvey notes that this pattern could change as more radical filmmakers free the look of the camera and audience to encourage questioning and dialectics (Mulvey 1999:844).

Feminists maintain that meaning is mediated, and therefore they examine both media texts and the ways in which they are produced. As a result, how media present women's roles in both the "public" and "private" spheres of life and the discords that exist between represented and lived experiences are important. Viewing women as agents, feminists also study the ways in which women and girls are receptive to (or rejecting of) the media and the ways these individuals interpret and consume media images. The goal is to challenge male dominance in the media and the devalued status of women in media and society. To this end, women involved in alternative feminist media (i.e., feminist film, documentaries, publishing houses, and art) use the media as a political tool by articulating their own perspectives and demands and representing and re-representing themselves. In the 22 years that the women's arm of the Canadian National Film Board, Studio D, was in operation, it actively supported the creation of 125 films by, for, and about women.

Today, feminist analysis of the media is made more complex by the work of postmodern and post-structural feminists, multicultural feminists, queer feminists, Marxist feminists, anti-racist feminists, "Third World" feminists, and other third wave feminists. Feminists today understand that the matrices of oppression are interconnected and, therefore, theory and lived experience cannot be separated (see Chapters 2 and 3 for more discussion). Now, feminists study the impact of gender along with class, racialization/ethnicity, sexual orientation, age, national origin, and physical and mental ability in their analysis of the roles mass media play in shaping the life conditions and life choices of people in media texts and in real life. They also look at the role media play in the construction and deconstruction of identities, nations, and borders, to name but a few, and likewise the role we all play in constructing media.

Around the globe, U.S. media conglomerates influence local cultures through continual marketing of films, television programming, and other media. These Harry Potter fans in Tokyo wait excitedly in line for tickets to the Japanese premiere of *Harry Potter and the Order of the Phoenix*. According to media sources, the film was a gigantic box-office success in Tokyo and other cities worldwide.

AP Photo/Shizuo Kambayashi/CP Images

Theoretically and methodologically, feminists of all persuasions analyze the activities and impacts of the mass media at the institutional, organizational, and individual levels (Valdivia 1995). Institutional analysis is concerned with studying the norms and values that govern the media as an institution and subsequently the smaller institutional entities, such as the press, that comprise the whole. Analysis on an organizational level is concerned with studying the conventions and practices that govern each institution. Finally, individual-level analysis is concerned with the ways in which individuals participate in accepting, challenging, and reproducing societal norms and values. The activities of individuals within the media institution and the ways they function within established practices that are shaped by institutional norms and values are studied. Constructions of "race," class, age, sexual orientation, and ability and the impacts of these constructions on all of us, as well as the constructions of femininity and masculinity and the impacts of the media specifically on men, women, and trans people, are considered important because all groups are negatively affected by gendered discourse in the media.

Regardless of which theoretical perspective on the media industries most closely resembles our own thinking, each of us should take a closer look at the ideas, images, and advertisements that bombard us daily. We can learn a great deal from reflecting upon the ways images are produced and the role media play in maintaining oppressive hierarchies that are all too readily accepted as a satisfactory status quo. While most of us may believe that we are not affected by the constant stream of advertisements we encounter, we should realize that much of advertising's power comes from the belief that advertising does not affect us. Although individuals alone cannot solve the problems associated with the media industries, they can become more aware of the pervasive impact of television, films, newspapers, the Internet, and other forms of mass communication.

MEDIA IN THE 21ST CENTURY

Problems associated with the media will continue well into this century, and many of the issues will probably become even more complex. For example, it has been suggested that the Internet and e-commerce will affect all aspects of life, particularly in high-income nations such as Canada. Some analysts have suggested that Canadian cities will lose more of their tax base to untaxed Internet commerce, bringing about a need to restructure relations between cities, provinces, and the federal government (Friedman 2000). Indeed, the ability of a single government to control the activities of transnational media industries may be weakened as globalization continues to occur. Thus, according to journalist Thomas L. Friedman (2000:A31), a world of global communications means that many issues that were once considered the domain of individual nations and governments will have to be viewed from a new perspective. In the years to come, new communication technologies will undoubtedly continue to change our lives and bring emergent issues to our attention (see Box 14.3). While new forms of media offer many potential benefits, they also raise serious concerns about social life as many of us know it.

WHAT CAN YOU DO?

- Become media literate by learning about who owns your local media and identifying their political and economic interests.
- Critically analyze advertisements and think about how they affect you, your family members, and your friends.
- Think critically about everything you see, hear, or read (including this text) in the media.
- Find out about current events by accessing both alternative and mainstream media sources in order to see the spin different media give an issue and if the issue is even covered.
- Contact your local, provincial, and national newspapers and state that you want journalists to dig deeper and to seek out more diverse viewpoints before they write—insist that their employers support this type of journalism.

Net Neutrality: The Beginning of a Two-tiered System?

Since the Internet became a viable entity, network providers in Canada and the United States have operated under a principle of *net neutrality*, **meaning that they do not** *discriminate against,* **by degrading, blocking, or slowing access to, or** *discriminate for,* **by prioritizing and speeding up access to certain content, services, or applications based on their source, ownership, or destination.** A Canadian organization that emerged to protect net neutrality is called Open Media (openmedia.ca) (formerly Democratic Media). It wishes to engage Internet users to protect their online rights. However, because the Canadian Radio-Television and Telecommunications Commission (CRTC) has taken a hands-off approach to Internet service provision, many Internet service providers are now claiming they have the right to determine how customers receive programming. Today, however, Canada's largest cable and telephone companies want to decide the pace of certain web activity. This means that content providers who cannot pay the equivalent of a new "toll" (e.g., community organizations, Wikipedia, and fund-raising activities) could see their sites slowed to a crawl, which ultimately will result in a loss of viewers or customers.

Open Media stands for the following principles:

- expression cannot be censored;
- everyone should have access to fast and affordable networks; and
- the Internet should be open to free communication, to protect the freedom of entrepreneurs to create new work (e.g., apps for the Internet), and to protect people's privacy so that users can control how their data is used. (Open Media 2014)

Net neutrality permits beginning and less famous artists to gain quicker connection to their audiences because they can have access to an audience in a regular queue. Without net neutrality, they could be sent to a slower service because an artist in greater demand, and thus more profitable to the media company, would have priority.

In May 2014, the U.S. Federal Communications Commission (FCC) put forward a draft rule to permit broadband providers to sell faster use of their infrastructure to content companies. In Canada, Internet service providers are not treated as a special group; they are just like traditional telecommunications carriers. In Canada, telecommunications carriers cannot easily create a multi-tiered system. However, we have little regulatory influence in the World Wide Web since so much traffic goes through the United States. If fast lanes are permitted, then those who will not or cannot pay will be regulated to the slow lanes—possibly at the speed of dial-up connections. In late February 2015, the FCC voted for tough guidelines to prevent broadband providers from setting up fast lanes and slowing or blocking Internet traffic.

Questions for Consideration

1. How should Canada try to follow the standard of the FCC?
2. How might you feel the impact of a two-tiered system?
3. Would you be willing to pay more for faster Internet service?

- Actively learn about the impacts of "cross-ownership" of broadcast and newspaper holdings (where one company owns both radio or television stations and newspapers) and media concentration on your life.
- Insist on diversity in the media you consume, so that media owners, journalists, reporters, and stories reflect the diversity of your community and province.

- Email (or call) the customer relations departments of media you engage with and tell them when you feel they are getting something right (or wrong).
- Check out alternative Canadian media activist associations that might be of interest to you.

SUMMARY

What Are the Media Industries? How Much Time Do Individuals Spend in Media-Related Activities?

According to social scientists, the media industries are media businesses that influence people and cultures worldwide and own interests in radio and television production and broadcasting; motion pictures, movie theatres, and music companies; newspaper, periodical (magazine), and book publishing; and Internet services and content providers. Today, many people spend more time in media-related activities than they do in any other single endeavour, including sleeping, working, eating, or talking with friends and family; therefore, some analysts believe the media have a major influence on how people think, feel, and act.

What Part Does Technology Play in How Various Media Industries Change Over Time?

For many years, newspapers were the primary source of news. However, new technologies brought about radio as the media phenomenon of the 1920s and television as the phenomenon of the 1950s. With the introduction of new communications technologies such as computers, fibre-optic cable, and broadcast satellites, the media industries continue to change rapidly. For example, it is now possible for individuals to communicate with people all over the world.

How Has Media Ownership Changed?

Although there once were a variety of independent companies that produced books, records, television programs, and films, there are now large corporate conglomerates that own more than one form of the media business.

What Is Convergence? How Does It Relate to Media Concentration?

Convergence refers to a melding of the communications, computer, and electronics industries that gives a few huge corporations control over an increasing proportion of all media sources. Convergence contributes to greater concentration in the media. Media concentration refers to the tendency of the media industries to cluster together in groups.

What Forms May Media Concentration Take?

Media concentration may take place in several forms: (1) within one industry (such as newspaper chains); (2) cross-media ownership, in which media companies own more than one type of media property (such as newspaper chains and television stations); (3) conglomerate ownership, in which corporations own media properties but also own other businesses; and (4) vertical integration, in which the corporations that make the media content also control the distribution channels (such as film and television production companies, television networks, and movie theatres).

Why Do Some People Favour Media Convergence Whereas Others Do Not?

Supporters believe that much can be gained from the synergy created by media convergence because it makes it possible to take a media brand and capitalize on it. This process is clearly profitable for investors and media executives; however, media critics believe convergence limits the news and entertainment that the public receives by reducing message pluralism. Other problems include: (1) the decline of journalism as a public service profession; (2) constant pressure for all journalistic endeavours to be immediately profitable; (3) a significant decrease in the quantity and quality of international news available to North American audiences; (4) the quashing of public debate about the power of the media industries and how they deal with important social issues; and (5) a dramatic increase in the influence of powerful lobbyists representing the interests of the media giants.

What Potential Problems Are Associated with Global Media Concentration?

A few large media conglomerates are rapidly gaining control over most of the publishing, recording, television, film, and theme park business worldwide. One major problem is the extent to which a few media giants have almost complete control over the world's information. Some people in other nations have been critical of how the media conglomerates depict nations around the globe and the influence, often negative, that they have on the politics and culture of other nations.

What Is Framing, and How Does It Affect Media Coverage?

Framing refers to how news content and its accompanying visual images are linked together to create certain audience perceptions and give specific impressions to viewers and readers. This process of "spinning" information provides audiences with a particular angle, which usually is favourable to the media owners and the interests they favour while minimizing or eliminating coverage of other issues and concerns.

Why Are Some Media Critics Concerned about Depictions of Violence in the Media?

Although most scholars do not believe that the media *cause* aggressive behaviour in people, a number of media analysts assert that the media's need to capture public interest has contributed to the gratuitous use of violence as a means of selling newspapers, television programming, movie tickets, music, and other media-related commodities.

What is a Stereotype and How Can the Media Perpetuate Stereotypes about Racial and Ethnic Groups?

A stereotype is an overgeneralization about the appearance, behaviour, or other characteristics of all members of a group. The media can perpetuate stereotypes by over- or under-representing groups (according to population) in various programs and advertisements. Other media stereotyping includes exaggerating people's physical appearance, suggesting that all people in a specific category look or behave alike, creating racial or ethnic characters who have undesirable attributes, and using statements and visual images that continually link subordinate racial or ethnic group members to illegal actions.

■ **Why is Gender Stereotyping Pervasive in the Media? What Major Forms Does This Problem Take?**

Under-representation of women among producers, directors, and executives in the largest media industries might be a factor in the more limited range of roles available to women in television programs and films. First, gender-specific age bias is apparent in the casting of many female characters. Second, television shows and films often perpetuate traditional roles for women and maintain cultural stereotypes of femininity.

■ **How Do Interactionists Explain the Influence of the Media on Individuals?**

According to the theory of limited effects, the media have a minimal effect on individuals' attitudes and perceptions. The use and gratification theory suggests that people are active audience participants who make conscious decisions about what they will watch, listen to, read, and surf on the Internet. However, social learning theory is based on the assumption that people are likely to act out the behaviour they see in role models and media sources. The audience relations approach states that people interpret what they hear and see in the media by using their own cultural understandings as a mental filtering device.

■ **How Do Functionalist and Conflict Perspectives on the Media Differ?**

According to some functionalist analysts, the media fulfill several important functions in contemporary societies, including providing news and information, facilitating public discourse on social issues and policies, passing on cultural traditions and historical perspectives, entertaining people, and now via the Internet, providing the opportunity to communicate with people. Some media also fulfill dysfunctions of providing misinformation, e.g., about unproven climate change, lack of privacy, and cyber-bullying. In contrast, conflict theorists assert that members of the capitalist class (either intentionally or unintentionally) use the media to provide information that supports the validity of existing class relations. Hegemony theory states that the media are an instrument of social control that is used by members of the ruling classes to create false consciousness in the working classes.

■ **What Does the Feminist Perspective Say about the Relationship between Textual or Visual Representations of Women's Lives in Media and the Lived Experiences of Women?**

Mass media in Canada have consistently represented women and men in traditional gender roles and relationships of power inequity that undermine efforts to challenge and change oppressive values, beliefs, and attitudes, as exemplified by "the gaze." Contemporary feminists are particularly articulate in their criticism of the discords between reality presented in the media and lived reality. These theorists and activists understand how gender, class, racialization, ethnicity, sexual orientation, age, national origin, and physical ability act together to shape the life conditions and life choices of people in media texts and in real life—realities that are seldom depicted with accuracy in the mass media.

KEY TERMS

framing, p. 297
hegemony, p. 302
hegemony theory, p. 302

media concentration, p. 293
media industries, p. 291
net neutrality, p. 305

social learning theory, p. 301
theory of limited effects, p. 301

QUESTIONS FOR CRITICAL THINKING

1. Why might media concentration be a potentially greater social problem than concentration in other industries?

2. Sociologist Graham Knight (1998:108) has said, "In order to be successful, hegemony must incorporate a range of different viewpoints." Explain why this might be so.

3. Is continued consolidation in the media a serious threat to democracy? Explain.

4. Do media "manufacture consent"?

5. Should we be concerned about the ability of some companies to "buy" political influence? Why or why not?

CHAPTER
15

Population, Urbanization, and the Environmental Crisis

Dick Hemingway

G lobal population control and environmental policies are the subject of international controversy. Although some people believe that government policies are essential for curbing overpopulation and protecting the environment, others argue that they are a means by which dominant group members decide the composition of the population regarding gender, racialization, and class, or whether resources will go towards protecting the environment.

In this chapter, you will learn about the causes of population growth; fertility, mortality, and migration; the impact of population growth and the consequences for world hunger; suggestions for controlling population growth; immigration and its consequences; problems of Canadian cities; environmental problems including air and water pollution, global warming, soil erosion, deforestation, and solid and toxic/hazardous wastes; and how sociologists study these problems using the functionalist, conflict, interactionist, and feminist perspectives. We will also discuss what the earth's population and the environment will be like in the future, and what you can do about it.

GLOBAL POPULATION PROBLEMS

During the past 60 years, the world's population has more than doubled, growing from 2.5 billion in the 1950s to over 7.3 billion today. And it is projected to go above 9.5 billion by mid-century. Although many hundreds of millions have gained middle-income status, more than 1 billion of the world's people do not have enough food and lack basic health care. Will the earth's resources be able to support such a population? This is an urgent question and one for which we need answers.

Population Growth

Growth rates vary among nations: high-income nations (for example, Canada and the United States) have a lower population growth rate than low-income nations, especially those in Africa, Asia, and Latin America. A *population* is all the people living in a specified geographic area. In some nations, the population growth rate is negative; that is, fewer people are added to the population through birth and immigration than are lost through death and emigration. Population projections suggest that countries such as Italy, Romania, Russia, and Spain will shrink in population over the next 50 years. Table 15.1 shows some of Canada's population figures, including the fact that in 2012 our population was over 34.9 million people.

Demography is the study of the size, composition, and distribution of populations. Global population changes are important because they have a powerful influence on social, economic, and political structures both within societies and between societies. For example, the population growth imbalance between high-income and middle- and low-income nations is a potential source of global conflict,

TABLE 15.1 Demographic Indicators

Population

Number (in millions)[1]	35.2
Total growth rate 2012/2013 (per 1000)	11.6
Median age[1] (in years)	40.2
Proportion aged 0 to 14 years (%)[1]	16.1
Proportion aged 65 years and over (%)[1]	15.3

Fertility (2011)

Total fertility rate	1.61
Average age of birth (in years)	30.2

Mortality (2011)

Life expectancy at birth (in years) 2009/2011	
Males	79.3
Females	83.6
Infant mortality rate (per 1000 births)	4.8

Immigration (2011)[2]

Number of immigrants	248 747
Immigration rate (per 1000)	7.2

1. As of July 1, 2013.

2. Data available as of November 2012.

Source: *Statistics Canada, 2013o,* Report on the Demographic Situation in Canada. *Retrieved March 18, 2015 (http://www.statcan.gc.ca/pub/91-209-x/ 91-209-x2013001-eng.htm).*

particularly if world hunger and environmental destruction increase. Three primary factors affect the rate of population growth in any nation or area: fertility (births), mortality (deaths), and migration (movement between geographic areas). We'll look at each in turn.

Fertility

Fertility **refers to the number of children born to an individual or a population.** The most basic measure of fertility is the number of live births per female. Table 15.1 showed that in 2011, women in Canada gave birth to about 1.61 children. This low number indicates that the Canadian population is not replacing itself. The fertility rate that allows a population to replace itself is about 2.1. So Canadian women would have to have at least 2.1 babies for our population to replace itself. We have already seen one of the consequences of a low fertility rate in Chapter 5, Inequality Based on Age. Many observers are worried that too few babies are being born

to become workers to support the rising number of seniors who are also living longer (see the next section, "Mortality").

The level of fertility in a society is associated with social as well as biological factors. For example, countries that have high rates of infant and child mortality often have high birth rates. By having many children, parents in these nations are more likely to see a few of them survive to adulthood. In nations without social security systems to provide old-age insurance, parents may view children as an "insurance plan" for their old age. In patriarchal societies, having many children—especially sons—is proof of manliness. Finally, in cultures in which religion dictates that children are God-given and family planning is forbidden because it "interferes with God's will," many more children are usually born. On the other hand, high-income countries have low fertility, partly because of occupational opportunities for women, effective birth control, and the cost of raising children.

Although men are obviously important in the reproductive process, the measure of fertility focuses on women because pregnancy and childbirth are more easily quantified than biological fatherhood. Biological factors that affect fertility include the general health and nutrition level of women of childbearing age. However, on the basis of biological capability alone, most women could produce 20 or more children during their childbearing years. In industrialized nations, therefore, many people limit their biological capabilities by practising abstinence, refraining from sexual intercourse before a certain age, using contraceptives, being sterilized, or having one or more abortions over the course of their reproductive years. Fertility rates also are affected by the number of partners available for sex and/or marriage, the number of women of childbearing age in the workforce, and government policies regarding families.

Mortality

Births are one factor in population growth; another is a decline in *mortality*—**the number of deaths that occur in a specific population.** Table 15.1 shows that life expectancy is now 83.6 for females and 79.3 for males, and we have already seen how the population 65+ years is rising relative to the population of 0 to 14 year olds in Chapter 5. In many high-income nations, mortality has declined dramatically as diseases such as malaria, polio, cholera, tetanus, typhoid, and measles have been virtually eliminated by vaccinations and improved sanitation and personal hygiene (Weeks 2012).

In addition to measuring deaths, demographers often measure the *infant mortality rate*—the number of deaths of infants under 1 year of age per 1000 live births in a given year. In general, infant mortality has declined worldwide over the past two decades because many major childhood and communicable diseases are now under control. Still, infant mortality rates vary widely among nations. In a high-income nation like Canada, the infant mortality rate is quite low, 4.8 in 2011 (see Table 15.1). In low-income countries like those of sub-Saharan Africa, the infant mortality rate can be over 100 per 1000 live births.

In any nation, the infant mortality rate is an important reflection of a society's level of preventive (prenatal) medical care, maternal nutrition, childbirth procedures, and neonatal care for infants. In Canada, differential levels of access to these services are reflected in the gap between infant mortality rates for Indigenous and non-Indigenous people. While we do not have the exact rates for Indigenous people, we do have rates for the Northwest Territories and Nunavut where they are found in greatest proportion. The infant mortality rates for the Northwest Territories and Nunavut were 15.5 and 14.8 respectively in 2009, about three times the rate of Canada overall (Statistics Canada 2013l).

Migration

Migration **is the movement of people from one geographic area to another for the purpose of changing residency.** Migration takes two forms: *immigration*—the movement of people *into* a geographic area to take up residency—and *emigration*—the movement of people *out of* a geographic area to take up residency elsewhere. Most migration occurs from south (low-income) countries to north (high-income) countries. But a large proportion also migrates from south to south and north to north countries, and an increasing percentage is moving from north to south for jobs or retirement.

Table 15.1 shows Canada received 248 747 immigrants in 2011. This is a large number of people for a country the size of Canada. The number is about twice the size of the natural increase (births minus deaths) in the country. However, it should be noted that official immigration statistics do not reflect the actual number of immigrants who arrive in this country. Canadian immigration authorities record only legal immigration based on entry visas and change-of-immigration-status forms. Some people who enter the country as temporary visitors, coming for pleasure or business, as students, or as temporary workers or trainees, do not leave when their stated purpose has been achieved and their permits expire.

Approximately 14 500 refugees were also admitted to Canada in 2012 as permanent residents (Statistics Canada 2013m). According to the 1951 United Nations Convention on Refugees, the term *refugee* applies solely to those who leave their countries because of persecution for reasons of racialization, religion, nationality, membership in a particular social group, or political opinion. People who leave home to escape famine or to improve their economic position, for example, do not officially qualify as refugees.

Although some immigrants enter illegally, it is impossible to estimate their number or how many are still in Canada, since many come to Canada to gain access into the United States. Occasionally we learn of large numbers of illegal immigrants because of problems with the boats that were transporting them.

To determine the effects of immigration and emigration, demographers compute the *net migration*—the net number of migrants (total immigrants minus total emigrants) in a given year.

The Impact of Population Composition and Growth

What is the effect of population composition on a society? Population growth affects **population composition—the biological and social characteristics of a population, including such attributes as age, sex, racialization, marital status, education, occupation, income, and size of household.** In Canada, for example, the age distribution of the population is associated with the demand for community resources such as elementary and secondary schools, libraries, health care, recreational facilities, employment opportunities, and age-appropriate housing. Figure 15.1 shows how the population composition has changed over the last 50 years and how it will change in the future. Table 15.1 shows that the proportion of our population 0–14 years of age is 16.1 percent, just a little above those 65+ years of age at 15.3 percent. What consequences do you think this will have for our governments?

What are the consequences of global population growth? Not all social analysts agree on the answer to this question. As you will discover in the sections that follow, some analysts warn that the earth is a finite system that cannot support its rapidly growing population. Others believe that capitalism—if freed from government intervention—could develop innovative solutions to such problems as hunger and pollution. Still others argue that capitalism is part of the problem, not part of the solution.

The Malthusian Perspective

Rapid population growth and overpopulation are not new problems. Causes and solutions have been debated for over two centuries. In 1798, for example, Thomas Malthus, an English clergyman and economist, published

An Essay on Population. Malthus (1798/1965) argued that the global population, if left unchecked, would exceed the available food supply. The population would increase in a geometric (exponential) progression (2, 4, 8, 16, …), but the food supply would increase only by an arithmetic progression (1, 2, 3, 4, …). Thus, the population would surpass the food supply, ending population growth and perhaps eliminating the world population (Weeks 2012). Disaster, according to Malthus, could be averted only by positive checks (e.g., famine, disease, and war) or preventive checks (e.g., sexual abstinence before marriage and postponement of marriage for as long as possible) to limit people's fertility.

The Neo-Malthusian Perspective

In the late 1960s, *neo-Malthusians* (or "new Malthusians") spoke of the "population explosion" and "population bomb" to emphasize the urgent need to reduce global population growth. More recently *The Population Bomb Revisited* (Ehrlich and Ehrlich 2009) continues to state this dire prediction. To neo-Malthusians, the earth is a dying planet with too many people in relation to the available food supply. Overpopulation and rapid population growth exacerbate global environmental problems, ranging from global warming and rainforest destruction to famine and epidemics such as HIV/AIDS. Neo-Malthusians have encouraged people to be part of the solution to the problem of overpopulation by having fewer children. In reality, people in most parts of the world *are* having fewer children (Weeks 2012).

Demographic Transition Theory

According to *demographic transition theory*, **societies move from high birth and death rates to relatively low birth and death rates as a result of technological development.** The demographic transition takes place in four stages. The *preindustrial stage* is characterized by little population growth: high birth rates are offset by high death rates. This period is followed by the *transitional* or *early industrial stage,* which is characterized by significant population growth as the birth rate remains high but the death rate declines because of new technologies that improve health, sanitation, and nutrition. Today, large parts of Africa, Asia, and Latin America are in this second stage. The third stage is *advanced industrialization and urbanization*: the birth rate declines as people control their fertility with various forms of contraception, and the death rate declines as medicine and other health care technologies control acute and chronic diseases. Finally, in the *postindustrial stage*, the population grows very slowly, if at all. In this stage, a decreasing birth rate is coupled with a stable death rate.

Proponents of demographic transition theory believe that technology can overcome the dire predictions of Malthus and the neo-Malthusians. Critics point out that not all nations go through all the stages or in the manner outlined. They think that demographic transition theory explains development in Western societies, but not necessarily in others.

World Hunger and Malnutrition

Food shortages, chronic hunger, and malnutrition are the consequences of rapid population growth, particularly in low-income nations. The United Nations Food and Agriculture Organization estimates that nearly 870 million people, or one in eight people in the world, were suffering from chronic undernourishment from 2010 to 2012. Almost all the hungry people, 852 million, live in low-income countries, representing 15 percent of the population of these counties. There are 16 million people undernourished in high-income countries also (World Hunger Education Service 2013). Chronic undernourishment contributes to childhood health problems such as anemia (a blood condition that produces weakness and a lack of energy and can result in child mortality or impaired mental functioning), stunting (impaired physical growth or development), and being underweight. In pregnant women, malnutrition increases the risk of anemia, infection, birth complications, and lack of breast milk. In contrast, improvements in nutrition significantly reduce health risks and the spread of some communicable illnesses.

What efforts are being made to reduce global food shortages and world hunger? Organizations such as the United Nations, the World Health Organization, and the International Red Cross have programs in place, but the most far-reaching initiatives are known as the green revolution and the biotechnological revolution.

The Green Revolution

The *green revolution* refers to dramatic increases in agricultural production that have been made possible by high-yield "miracle" crops, pesticides, fertilizers, and good farm management. In the 1940s, researchers at the International Maize and Wheat Improvement Center started the green revolution by developing high-yield varieties of wheat, which increased world grain production. The new dwarf-type wheat, which produces more stalks, has dramatically increased the wheat yield in countries such as India and Pakistan since the 1960s. Researchers have also developed a high-yield dwarf rice with twice as many grains per plant, greatly improving the rice output in India, Pakistan, the Philippines, Indonesia, and Vietnam (Weeks 2012). Table 15.2 shows that irrigated areas increased fivefold in the last century.

TABLE 15.2 The Measure of the 20th Century

Item	Increase Factor, 1890s to 1990s
World population	4
Urban proportion of world population	3
Total world urban population	13
World economy	14
Industrial output	40
Energy use	16
Coal production	7
Air pollution	~5
Carbon dioxide emissions	17
Sulphur dioxide emissions	13
Lead emissions to the atmosphere	~8
Water use	9
Marine fish catch	35
Cattle population	4
Pig population	9
Horse population	1.1
Blue whale population (Southern Ocean only	0.0025 (99.75 percent decrease)
Fin whale population	0.03 (97 percent decrease)
Bird and mammal species	0.99 (1 percent decrease)
Irrigated area	5
Forest area	0.8 (20 percent decrease)
Cropland	2

Note: Some of the numbers are more trustworthy than others. Comments on their reliability appear in the source from which they are drawn.

Source: *J.R. McNeill,* Something New Under the Sun. *Copyright © 2000 by J.R. McNeill. Used by permission of W.W. Norton & Company, Inc.*

How successful has the green revolution been in reducing world hunger? During the 1970s, the green revolution helped to increase the global food supply at a somewhat faster pace than the global population grew; but in the 1980s and 1990s, agricultural production slowed considerably. There are several reasons why food production has not increased at the rate advocates predicted in the 21st century. For one thing, the fertilizers, pesticides, and irrigation systems needed to produce these new crops are very costly and beyond the budgets of most middle- and low-income nations. Furthermore, the fertilizers and pesticides often constitute health hazards

and become a source of surface water and groundwater pollution (Weeks 2012). Moreover, for the green revolution to eliminate hunger and malnutrition, the social organization of life in many middle- and low-income nations would have to change significantly. People would have to adopt the Western methods of farming on which the green revolution was built, and they would have to be willing to produce a single crop in very high volume. But reliance on a single crop can lead to nutritional deficiencies if other varieties of food are not available. Even with these drawbacks, however, the green revolution continues. Researchers recently developed high-yield sorghum, yams, and other crops that can be grown successfully in the nations of Africa where some of the greatest food shortages exist (Weeks 2012).

The Biotechnological Revolution

A second approach to reducing global food shortages, known as the *biotechnological revolution,* encompasses any technique for improving plants or animals or using micro-organisms in innovative ways. Developing pest-resistant crops, thus reducing the need for pesticides, is one technique. Using growth hormone to increase milk output in cows is another technique. Scientists are also exploring ways to genetically alter the reproductive cells of fish, poultry, sheep, and pigs to speed up conventional breeding times. Scientists have already genetically altered micro-organisms in several ways. Soon, for example, it should be possible to spray frost-sensitive plants, such as strawberries, with a strain of bacteria that will protect the plants against up to 80 percent of frost damage.

Some scientists believe that the biotechnological revolution can close the gap between worldwide food production and rapid population growth, but the new technology is not without problems. First, giving growth hormones to animals can make their meat unfit for human consumption. Hogs that get growth hormones are prone to gastric ulcers, arthritis, dermatitis, and other diseases. Second, the cost of biotechnological innovations is beyond the budgets of most middle- and low-income nations. Third, the new biotechnologies are developed for use with conventional (Western) farming methods. Fourth, genetic erosion (by breeding or gene manipulation) may eventually make the people of the world reliant on only a few varieties of plants and animals for their entire food supply, and thus vulnerable to famine as the result of a single pest or disease. Finally, environmental accidents, such as the unintentional release of genetically manipulated micro-organisms, pose a potential hazard.

Increasing the food supply is one way of coping with a rapidly growing world population, but hardly the only way. Some people believe that we can forestall the problem by controlling fertility.

CONTROLLING FERTILITY

The global population increase in the 20th century has been unprecedented. As Table 15.2 shows, the global population has increased by a factor of four.

Although demographers know that limiting fertility is the best way to slow down population growth, they also know that the issue is fraught with controversy. Consider the three preconditions that demographer Ansley Coale (1973) believes are necessary before there can be a sustained decline in a society's fertility:

1. *People must accept calculated choice as a valid element in marital fertility.* If people believe a supernatural power controls human reproduction, it is unlikely that they will risk offending that deity by trying to limit fertility. On the other hand, the more worldly wise people are, the more likely they are to believe they have the right to control reproduction.
2. *People must see advantages to reduced fertility.* People must have some reason to want to limit fertility. In some places, children become workers for the family and support parents in their old age. Without incentives to reduce fertility, natural attraction could lead to unprotected sexual intercourse and perhaps numerous children.
3. *People must know about and master effective techniques of birth control.* The means for limiting family size must be available, and people must know how to use them successfully.

Although Coale believes that all three preconditions must be met to limit fertility effectively, most government policies in the developing world focus only on the third: family planning measures (Weeks 2012).

Family Planning

Family planning programs in the developing world provide birth control information, contraceptive devices, sometimes sterilization and abortion procedures, and health services. The earliest programs were based on the assumption that women have large families because they do not know how to prevent pregnancy or they lack access to birth control devices. Though we know today that women may have large families for many other reasons, most programs are still based on this assumption. Such programs do little, for example, to reduce a couple's desire to have children, and they ignore the reality that, in some middle- and low-income nations, women are not free to make their own decisions about reproduction.

But now the United Nations Population Fund is taking a new strategy. The publication, *Choices not Chance: the UNFPA Family Planning Strategy 2012–2020,* which outlines the human-rights based approach, is intended to help the hundreds of millions of women, particularly in low-income countries, who want to delay or avoid a pregnancy but do not have access to or are not using an effective method of family planning. For example, about 222 million women in low-income countries want to avoid pregnancy but are not using modern contraceptives (UNFPA 2015:1–2). The strategy focuses on expanding access to information and services, as well as supplies, improving the quality of care, and supporting nations to create health systems that offer women and men access to contraception. There is also an emphasis on meeting the needs of marginalized populations (UNFPA 2015:iii).

Zero Population Growth

With *zero population growth*, **there is a totally stable population, one that neither grows nor decreases from year to year because births, deaths, and migration are in perfect balance** (Weeks 2012). For example, the population growth rate would be zero if a nation had no immigration or emigration and the birth rate and the death rate were the same (Ehrlich and Ehrlich 1991).

Canada is nearing zero population growth because of several factors.

1. A high proportion of women and men in the labour force find satisfaction and rewards outside of family life.
2. Birth control is inexpensive and readily available.
3. The trend is toward later marriage (see Chapter 11).
4. The cost of raising a child from birth to adulthood is rising rapidly.
5. Schools and public service campaigns make teenagers more aware of how to control fertility.

Near-zero population growth is one characteristic of the Canadian population; another is a rapidly changing population.

IMMIGRATION AND ITS CONSEQUENCES

High rates of immigration, primarily of visible minorities like Chinese, South Asian, and West Asian, are changing the composition of the Canadian population. Figure 15.1 shows the total number of immigrants admitted each year and the immigration rate from 1900 to 2011. The rate is 7.2 per 1000 population for 2011. This rate is higher than that of all high-income countries except Norway and Australia. According to the National Household Survey, about one in five Canadians is foreign-born. This is the highest percentage of immigrants in the Canadian population since the early part of the 20th century.

What are the consequences of today's high rate of immigration to Canada as a whole? Not all social analysts agree on the answer to this question. Some believe that immigrants cost taxpayers millions of dollars each year in adjustment and education costs (e.g., teaching English

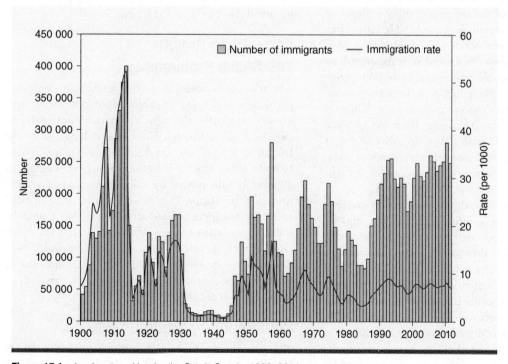

Figure 15.1   Immigrants and Immigration Rate in Canada, 1900–2011.

Source: *Statistics Canada, 2013,* Migration: International, 2010 and 2011. *Retrieved September 25, 2013* (http://www.statcan.gc.ca/pub/91-209-x/2013001/article/11787/fig/fig1-eng.htm).

or French as a second language). But we also know that immigrants contribute as workers, consumers, and taxpayers to the economy and society. Other observers are also concerned about large numbers of unassimilated immigrants, wondering whether these large numbers from very different countries will affect cultural cohesion.

Richard Florida (2002:T8), director of the Martin Prosperity Institute at the University of Toronto, claims that Canada's economic future depends on highly educated immigration, which helps to create and nourish a "creative class." Some examples of the extraordinary contributions immigrants are making to Canada are found in the Top 25 Canadian Immigrants awards sponsored by *Canadian Immigrant* magazine and the Royal Bank (RBC). The 2014 winners included a Federal Court judge, the president of Western University, a doctor, the executive director of We Day Global, and the artistic director of Les Grands Ballet Canadiens de Montréal. The stories of these and other award winners are available at the *Canadian Immigrant* website (*Canadian Immigrant* 2015).

Regarding concerns about cultural cohesion, ethnocultural diversity is an important consequence of present-day immigration. Statistics Canada projects that over the next two decades, diversity will increase substantially. In 2031, about 3 in 10 Canadians will be a visible minority (totalling 11 to 14 million people). Diversity will also increase among the Canadian-born population because of the different fertility patterns of immigrants already settled in Canada. The two largest groups of visible minorities will be what exist now, South Asian and Chinese. Arabs and West Asians will be the fastest growing visible minorities. Since immigrants tend to settle in cities, three in five in Toronto (primarily South Asian) and Vancouver (primarily Chinese) will be visible minorities (Demosim Team 2013). Since immigrants seek to live with people like themselves, at least at the beginning, will we have large groups of unassimilated immigrants because they can access resources in their original language? Some, like the Parti Quebecois (PQ) government in 2013, think that some characteristics of immigrants, such as burqas and face coverings for women and turbans and other head coverings for men, are challenging basic values of secularism and gender equality and, thus, cultural cohesion. In the fall of 2013, the PQ introduced a Charter of Values ("Charter affirming the values of State secularism and religious neutrality and the equality between women and men, and providing a framework for accommodation requests") which, if implemented, would have forbidden the wearing of religious or national symbols by those people employed by the government and in private businesses that do business with the government. Although the government stated that they were promoting basic values, the other political parties in Quebec, two former leaders of the PQ, Jacques Parizeau and Lucien Bouchard, and people of the rest of Canada spoke out against this Charter, and were willing to allow religious freedom for immigrants. The bill died when an election was called in 2014. Do you think that Islam or other non-Western religions, or even fundamentalist Christianity, is a threat to the cultural cohesion of our society?

CHANGES IN CANADIAN CITIES

Cities are obviously important to Canada. But over the past couple of decades, the increased services our cities have had to provide—as a result of provincial downloading of hundreds of millions of dollars in new responsibilities with no increase in taxing powers—have put overwhelming strains on their capacity to provide support for Canada's new economy. Can Canadian cities recover from this situation?

Urban problems in Canada are closely associated with the profound socio-economic, political, and spatial changes that have taken place since the Industrial Revolution. Over 100 years ago, many people (about two-thirds of Canadians) lived in rural areas. In the 21st century, about 80 percent of the Canadian population lives in urban areas (see Map 15.1), and many live in cities that did not exist 200 years ago.

Early Urban Growth and Social Problems

According to sociologists, a *city* is a relatively dense and permanent settlement of people who secure their livelihoods primarily through non-agricultural activities (Weeks 2012). Although cities existed long before the Industrial Revolution, the birth of the factory system brought about rapid *urbanization,* which we defined in Chapter 1 as the process by which an increasing proportion of a population lives in cities rather than in rural areas. Canada industrialized after World War I, and the shift toward urban living is shown in home-ownership rates. About two-thirds of Canadian households own their homes. In 1931, although over three-quarters of rural families owned their own home, less than half of urban families did (Kremarik 2000:18).

Contemporary Urban Growth

The growth of suburbs and outlying areas after World War II changed the nature of city life in this country for the next 50 years. Suburban areas existed immediately adjacent to many central cities in the 1920s, but after the

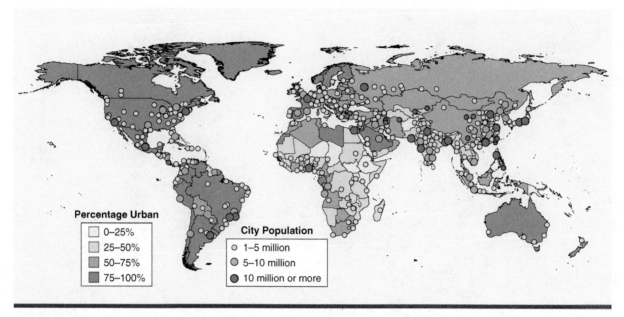

Map 15.1   Percentage of Urban Population by City Size.

Source: *United Nations, Department of Economic and Social Affairs, Population Division,* World Urbanization Prospects, the 2011 Revision. *Retrieved December 31, 2013* (*http://esa.un.org/unup/Maps/maps_urban_2011.htm*).

late 1940s, these communities began to grow in earnest because of the automobile and families wanting homes to raise what is now called the "baby boom" generation. They were referred to as "bedroom communities" because most of the residents were there on nights and weekends but went into the central city for jobs, entertainment, and major shopping. Most suburban dwellers drove to work each day, except where public transit was convenient, establishing a pattern that would result, decades later, in traffic congestion and air pollution, problems that have drastically worsened in the past decade.

To reduce the housing shortage, the federal government subsidized what became a mass exodus from the central city to outlying suburbs. The federal government established the Central (now Canada) Mortgage and Housing Corporation to grant and insure mortgages. Between 1945 and 1951, the CMHC was responsible for the construction of half a million houses (Kremarik 2000:19). Other factors also contributed to the postwar suburban boom, including the availability of inexpensive land, low-cost mass construction methods for building tract houses, new federally and provincially financed highway systems, inexpensive gasoline, and consumers' pent-up demands, after the Depression and war, for single-family homes on individually owned lots. Although some people lost their homes in the 2008 bursting of the housing bubble, the foreclosures in Canada were not as widespread as those in the United States.

Early suburbanization provided many families with affordable housing, good schools and parks, and other amenities not found in the central city; however, the shift away from central cities set up an economic division of interests between cities and suburbs that remains in place even today. While many people in the suburbs still rely on the central city for employment, entertainment, or other services, they pay taxes to their local governments and school districts. As a result, suburban police and fire departments, schools, libraries, and recreational facilities are usually well funded and well staffed, with up-to-date equipment. Suburbs also have newer infrastructures (such as roads, sewers, and water treatment plants) and money to maintain them.

Now in the 2010s, this pattern seems to be reversing itself with young people and empty-nesters moving from the suburbs to the city centres to be near work and/or leisure activities and to avoid the costs (e.g., a second car) and frustrations of driving. This is especially noticeable in Toronto and Vancouver. In July 2013, 55 000 new condominium units were under construction in Toronto (Austin 2013). In his book *Country of Cities,* New York architect and university professor Vishaan Chakrabarti argues that cities are the means to reduce environmental degradation with an end to sprawl, (they have a lower carbon footprint than suburbs do), to make us more prosperous and upwardly mobile, and even to make us happier (Chakrabarti 2013).

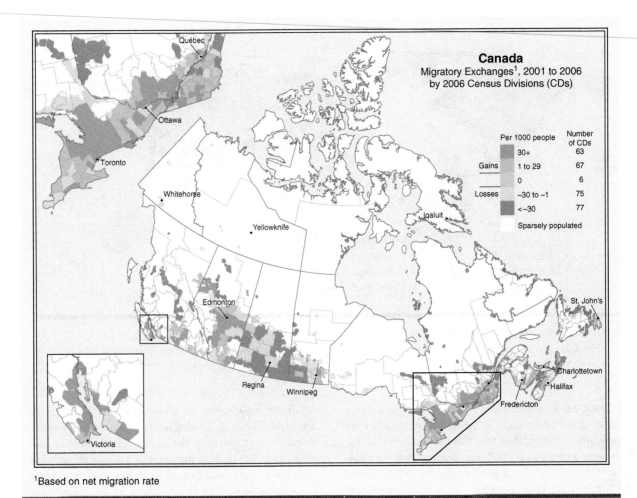

Canada
Migratory Exchanges[1], 2001 to 2006
by 2006 Census Divisions (CDs)

	Per 1000 people	Number of CDs
Gains	30+	63
	1 to 29	67
	0	6
Losses	−30 to −1	75
	<−30	77
	Sparsely populated	

[1]Based on net migration rate

Map 15.2 Migratory Exchanges, Canada, 2001 to 2006.
Source: *Statistics Canada, 2008,* Canada Migratory Exchanges 2001–2006.

Even if this belief is an exaggeration, the move downtown is substantial and permanent. In Toronto, some observers are talking about a new problem, called *hyperdensity*: too many people for services like public transit, roads, and parks.

Thirty years ago, edge cities were springing up beyond the central cities and existing suburbs. An **edge city is a middle- to upper-middle-class area that has complete living, working, shopping, and leisure activities so that it is not dependent on the central city or other suburbs** (Garreau 1991). Map 15.2 presents the Canadian population migratory exchanges between the 2001 and 2006 censuses. It shows the development of edge cities around Toronto, Montreal, and Vancouver, and from Calgary to Edmonton.

Edge cities begin as residential areas; then retail establishments and office parks move into the adjacent area, creating an unincorporated edge city. Automobiles are the primary source of transportation in many edge cities, and pedestrian traffic is discouraged—and even dangerous—because streets are laid out to facilitate high-volume automobile traffic, not walkers or cyclists. Edge cities may not have a governing body, so they drain taxes from central cities and older suburbs. Many businesses and industries move their physical plants—and tax dollars—to these areas because land is cheaper, workers are better educated, and utility rates and property taxes are lower than those in the city.

Over time, large-scale metropolitan growth produces a *megalopolis*—**a continuous concentration of two or more cities and their suburbs that have grown until they form an interconnected urban area.** The East Coast of the United States, for example, is a megalopolis, with Boston, Providence, Hartford, and their suburbs merging into New York City and its suburbs, which in turn merge southward into Newark, Philadelphia, Baltimore, and Washington, D.C., and their suburbs. It is almost impossible to tell where one metropolitan area ends and another begins. When metropolitan areas merge into a megalopolis, there are big population changes that can bring about or exacerbate social problems and inequalities based on racialization, class, and gender. In Map 15.2, the beginning of megalopolises can be seen in the west, Surrey-Delta-Vancouver; and in the centre, Hamilton-Toronto-Oshawa. In the future, that concentration could extend to Montreal and beyond.

URBAN PROBLEMS IN CANADA

While we traditionally thought that Canadian cities did not have the magnitude of the problems of poverty, crime, racism, homelessness, drug abuse, and inadequate school systems that cities in the United States experience because of years of neglect and deterioration, periodic fiscal crises are of major concern to mayors of Canadian cities.

Fiscal Crisis in Cities

It has traditionally been thought that Canadian cities were in better fiscal shape than U.S. cities. No major Canadian city has gone into bankruptcy like Detroit has or has threatened bankruptcy like many others did in the United States in 2013 after the recession (e.g., Washington, D.C., New York, and Honolulu). Nor did our cities experience as great a flight to the suburbs. Major U.S. cities have had to deal with major *deindustrialization*—**the process by which capital is diverted from investment in basic industries (in the form of economic resources, plants, and equipment) to business practices such as mergers and acquisitions and foreign investment.** This process left many blighted areas in the centres of U.S. cities. Still, federal and provincial government cutbacks have left Canadian cities, with their limited sources of revenue—primarily property taxes—in desperate financial straits. Cities have recently received more support, such as revenue from the federal government from a GST rebate and gas taxes. For example, the Gas Tax Fund was first announced in the 2005 federal budget. It provides $2 billion annually to municipalities across the country—a stable and predictable source of funding to support their investments in sustainable infrastructure (City of Toronto 2013). From 2005 to 2014, the Gas Tax Fund contributed over $1 billion to help in funding public transit, including the purchase of buses

and subway cars in Toronto (City of Toronto 2103). In September 2013, the federal finance minister offered to contribute $660 million dollars to help build an extension on Toronto's subway.

One plan to help the cities is to build homes and condominiums on sites of abandoned factories and the waterfront. In Toronto, Massey-Ferguson, a major maker of farm machinery, and Inglis, a maker of stoves, closed their factories and left land vacant for a decade. This was an early example of in-fill, and there are a dozen condominium complexes and hundreds of houses on these properties, home to over 5000 people. City planners say that this community, called King West Village, is a good example of the kind of redevelopment they want to promote. Another large-scale plan is under way in the south-central part of Toronto. In *Re: Our New Blue Edge,* are introductions to a number of waterfront developments, many of which are for housing (e.g., the West Don Lands, the Lower Don Lands, and the East Bayfront). Each area will include housing, recreation, and some businesses.

The Crisis in Urban Health Care

Since about 80 percent of the population lives in cities, most of our social problems are urban problems. This is also true for health care. However, other issues may be at play, particularly with disadvantaged populations. We know from Chapter 10 that disadvantaged people have greater rates of disease, disability, and death. A study of hospital use in a downtown neighbourhood in Toronto showed that while those from poor neighbourhoods were not discriminated against regarding admission, they had high admission and re-admission rates (Glazier et al. 2000). As a result, the costs of care are about a third greater for poor than for wealthy neighbourhoods. Figure 10.8 shows that the people in the lowest income quintile receive more dollars in health care than do those in the highest quintile ($4200 versus $3400). These added costs put greater burdens on hospital emergency, admitting, and discharge departments (Glazier et al. 2000:272). The authors conclude that "Canadian policy makers should take account of the income levels of the neighbourhood when deciding on resource allocation for public health, ambulatory care, community services and hospitals" (2000:272). If hospitals in downtown neighbourhoods do not get additional resources, they will not be able to continue to provide appropriate help to the often disadvantaged people they serve. Perhaps this is one of the reasons that downtown hospitals place lower in the CBC program Rate My Hospital list than do suburban hospitals (see Chapter 10).

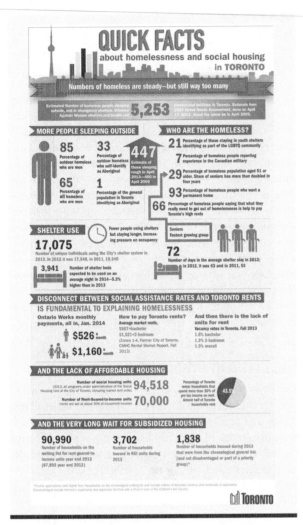

Figure 15.2   Homelessness and Social Housing in Toronto, 2013.

Source: *City of Toronto, 2013,* Quick facts about homelessness and social housing in Toronto. *Retrieved September 23, 2013* (http://www.toronto.ca/housing/pdf/quickfacts.pdf).

Housing Problems

Many regions in Canada lack affordable housing for low-income individuals and families (see Chapter 2). Over the past 15 years, there has been an increase in homelessness, especially among families with children (see Figure 15.2). Each year, we are made aware of the plight of homeless people through extensive media coverage during the Christmas holiday season and after winter deaths on the streets. During the rest of the year, many people view the homeless with less compassion.

The Shortage of Affordable Housing

When people speak of the "housing shortage," they are referring to the availability of relatively low-cost housing.

Affordable housing, particularly in very expensive housing markets like most cities in Canada (certainly Toronto and Vancouver) is never enough to fulfill the demand. For example in Toronto, as Figure 15.2 shows, the number of social housing units in Toronto in 2013 was 94 520 and the number of units with rent geared to 30 percent of the household's income was 70 000. Regarding demand, the number of households on the active waiting list for social housing (third quarter 2012) was 86 892. However, the number of households placed in the third quarter was a tiny 986. Moreover, the annual cost of Toronto social housing in 2011 was $656.9 million (City of Toronto 2011). Clearly, the creation of a sufficient amount of social housing is a major challenge that would be extraordinarily difficult and expensive to overcome. Since the 1970s, some middle- and upper-middle-class families and developers have re-entered central city areas and gentrified properties. **Gentrification is the process by which people renovate or restore properties in central cities.** Some people view gentrification as the way to revitalize the central city. Others think that it further depletes the stock of affordable housing for the poor and pushes low-income people out of an area where they previously lived.

Homelessness

The worst outcome of the housing shortage has been a significant increase in the number of homeless people in Canada. Accurate data about the actual number of homeless people are unavailable. It is extremely difficult to count the number of homeless people because many avoid interviews with census-takers and social scientists, and many are not readily found. The 2001 census did try to identify one group of homeless people by counting those in shelters for persons lacking a fixed address. On May 14, 2001, 14 145 people were counted in such shelters (Statistics Canada 2002a). This count does not identify all the homeless people, since many others may have been in other accommodations or on the street. A more comprehensive study of the number of homeless people in a major metropolitan area, Toronto, was conducted on the night of April 17, 2013. Results are based on more than 2000 completed surveys. This is more completed surveys than in the previous Street Needs Assessment conducted on April 19, 2009. At 13 questions, this survey was also the longest survey of the homeless. Key findings include: the estimated homeless population of Toronto was 5219 people, of which 450 lived outdoors; the average length of homelessness was 3 years (almost identical to 2009); more than one-third of the outdoor homeless population identified themselves as Indigenous; almost 20 percent of homeless youth identified themselves as a part of the LGBTQ community; almost 10 percent of the homeless population were seniors (61+ years) (almost double that in 2009); and almost half of the homeless population was on a waiting list for subsidized housing (City of Toronto 2013).

Although Canadian cities do not have the blighted neighbourhoods and abandoned buildings found in the centre of U.S. cities, they do have pockets of poverty. And for these pockets, social housing is badly needed. Figure 15.2 shows that in Toronto, the number of social housing units was 94 000, the number of households on the waiting list was 86 000, and the number housed in Q3 2012 was just 986. Governments in recent years have again realized the importance of social housing. For example, Toronto plans to compensate for this with its Housing Opportunities Toronto (HOT) project. HOT contains actions to be undertaken by the City of Toronto and the federal and provincial governments, including new investment of $484 million annually for the years 2010 to 2020 to help 257 700 households with high housing costs or inadequate accommodation (City of Toronto 2013).

Although little high-rise social housing has been built in Canada, St. James Town, in Toronto, is a similar high-rise project to some American projects (such as the Pruitt-Igoe project in St. Louis, which proved to be a failure and was demolished). It was developed in the 1960s by the private sector and consists of 18 high-rise apartment buildings with 7000 units for 12 000 people. It is one of the most densely populated residential areas in Canada (Hulchanski 1990:16). While it is still fully occupied, this development never became the model neighbourhood its proponents claimed it would.

But another large development *has* become a neighbourhood. The St. Lawrence neighbourhood in downtown Toronto is a good example of a large development that is socially mixed. This neighbourhood was conceived in the mid-1970s, with first occupancy in mid-1979. Although it is a large development of 3500 units, it has become a neighbourhood because people who wanted to live there were involved in the planning. St. Lawrence was begun, planned, and implemented by the municipal government (the former City of Toronto) in cooperation with other levels of government, the private sector, and community organizations (such as housing cooperatives and non-profit societies; Hulchanski 1990:4). The neighbourhood is

- socially mixed, including people of different ages, income, and household size (Hulchanski 1990:13);
- tenure mixed, including 39 percent condominium apartments, 30 percent non-profit cooperatives and non-profit rentals, 27 percent municipal non-profit rental,

and 4 percent ownership of townhouses (Hulchanski 1990:15); and
- 57 percent non-market, or social, housing (Hulchanski 1990:3): "St. Lawrence demonstrates that public planning of large development projects in an open and democratic fashion can be successful and that desirable high density socially mixed neighbourhoods can be developed by a municipality" (Hulchanski 1990:17).

It has worked so well that unlike other social housing developments like the original Regent Park, no problems are ever heard about it. In a recent article in praise of this development, Daniel LeBlanc identified three guiding principles of this development: first, the surrounding streets would extend into the site; second, the buildings would be similar to those on neighbouring streets (e.g., doors facing the streets, the opposite of the Regent Park); and third, there would be both market and social housing (LeBlanc 2013:G4).

Because of the lack of affordable housing in major Canadian cities, homeless people rely on homeless shelters for food and protection at night, or resort to constructing their own form of shelter in unused city lots or buildings.

Michael Wheatley / Glow images

The original Regent Park was developed in Toronto in the late 1940s and was the first and possibly the largest social housing development in Canada. The developers thought that people would want low-rise buildings that turned inward into a courtyard without streets to encourage communication. It was ultimately a failure. It was a magnet for drug dealers and other criminals who could hide easily in the shadows from the police because having no streets made it difficult for the police to enter and apprehend the criminals. Now, however, Regent Park is being redeveloped according to the St. Lawrence template of mixed-income, with streets and businesses. This area will have the same number of social housing units, but twice the population of the former development (about 7500 versus 12 000–17 000 people). More information about the revitalization of Regent Park can be found at their website. Toronto has several other developments that mix and add sustainability to their purpose (e.g., West Don Lands and Lower Don Lands).

Spatial Separation of the Poor and Visible Minorities

Although it is generally acknowledged that Canada does not have the permanent segregation of poor—especially racialized poor—and non-poor found in the United States, the increasing immigration of racialized/ethnic minorities to our cities leaves open the possibility that the U.S. segregation problems could occur here. Residential segregation in the United States, according to sociologists Douglas S. Massey and Nancy Denton (1992), is associated with many other problems.

Pockets of poverty, measured by the low-income cut-off, do exist in cities. For example, pockets are found in the City of Toronto. While some are in the south-central part, most are in the periphery of the city.

Since the vast majority of recent immigrants have been from East and South Asia, and since they migrate to cities, a big increase in the percentage of visible minorities has occurred in Canadian cities. For example, the visible minority population in 2006 was 42.9 percent in Toronto and 41.7 percent in Vancouver (Statistics Canada 2009). By 2031, the percentage of visible minorities in both cities will be 60 percent (see Immigration and its Consequences earlier in this chapter). However, the proportion of visible minorities in a census metropolitan area (CMA) does not indicate the extent of segregation in that area. The concentration of visible minorities seems greater in Montreal than in Toronto or Vancouver, where they are more evenly distributed.

To determine the extent of spatial separation of visible minorities in Canada, Hou and Picot studied the extent to which minority group members are exposed only to one another (isolation index) in their neighbourhoods (census tracts in Toronto, Montreal, and Vancouver) from the 1981 to 2001 censuses. In tracing the composition of the population over the 20 years, they discovered that the mass immigration of visible minorities has created more visible minority neighbourhoods. The number of visible minority neighbourhoods increased in these cities from 6 in 1981 to 254 in 2001. The majority of these neighbourhoods were Chinese (60 percent), followed by South Asian (about 33 percent) (Hou and Picot 2004:11). Few (13) Black neighbourhoods existed, perhaps because Blacks have been in Canada for many generations and come from several places. Toronto and Vancouver have many more visible minority neighbourhoods (135 and 111, respectively) than Montreal has (8) (Hou and Picot 2004:11). Far fewer visible minority immigrants go to Montreal than to the other two cities. Whether the increase in visible minority neighbourhoods is a good or bad thing is debatable. On the plus side, these neighbourhoods can provide a wide variety of support and services for immigrants and help promote ethnic identity. On the negative side, immigrants may become socially isolated and be slow to learn the host area language and take advantage of available educational and occupational opportunities. These neighbourhoods also have the tendency to have high unemployment and low-income rates. This is probably because a third of the population are recent immigrants, and recent immigrants do less well than earlier immigrants upon arrival (see Kazemipur and Halli 2001).

Not only do Canadian cities have problems with growth, but global cities, especially those in low-income countries, are also growing at a great rate (see Box 15.1).

PERSPECTIVES ON URBAN PROBLEMS

Throughout the 20th century, sociologists analyzed urban problems to determine the causes and consequences of rapid industrialization and urbanization for people's daily lives and the structure of society. The conclusions they reached about the underlying problems and possible solutions depended on the framework they applied.

The Functionalist Perspective

In examining urban problems, most functionalists focus on three processes that have contributed to social disorganization and the disruption of social institutions. First, mass migration from rural areas to urban areas

Social Problems in Global Perspective

Box 15.1

Global Cities

Although people have lived in cities for thousands of years, more people worldwide now live in or near a city than in rural areas. In 1900, only 1 person out of 10 lived in a city; now, 1 person out of 2 worldwide lives in a city. Map 15.1 shows the extent to which certain countries, and not just high-income countries, have become highly urbanized. This map also shows the locations of the cities in Table 15.3.

Global cities can be classified in several ways. The first and most simple is by population. In 1950, New York was the only mega-city with 10 million or more inhabitants. Today, Tokyo is the world's largest city (see Table 15.3). No Canadian city is such a huge agglomeration as these cities. Toronto, with 5 million people, does not appear on the list of the top 30 cities. When cultural, political, and economic activity are criteria for the ranking, New York and London rank first and second, while Toronto ranks 16th of 66 global cities in 2012 (A.T. Kearney 2012). For another ranking of North American cities for creativity (Bohemian Index), see the Interactionist Perspective section below.

Rapid global urbanization is producing a wide variety of problems, including overcrowding, environmental pollution, and the disappearance of farmland. In fact, many cities in middle- and low-income nations are quickly reaching the point at which food, housing, and basic public services are available to only a limited segment of the population. Cities such as Cairo, Beijing, and São Paulo are likely to soon have acute water shortages, while Mexico City is already experiencing a chronic water shortage. Natural increases in population (higher birth rates than death rates) account for two-thirds of new urban growth, and rural-to-urban migration accounts for the rest. While many problems of slum development, such as malnutrition and the spreading of disease, occur, industrializing cities grow so big and so fast precisely because they generate vast economic advantages that do not exist in the countryside.

Another way of ranking cities is in terms of the position of their nation in the world economic system. Immanuel Wallerstein (1984) tried to do this by first identifying three kinds of nations:

- *Core nations* **are dominant capitalist centres characterized by high levels of industrialization** (e.g., New York, Tokyo, and London).
- *Peripheral nations* **are dependent on core nations' centres and characterized by having exploited resources** (e.g., sub-Saharan and Caribbean cities).
- *Semi-peripheral nations* **fit between core and peripheral nations** (e.g., São Paulo and Singapore).

But this classification subordinates the city to its nation and cannot account for cities that are major hubs but are not in core nations, such as Seoul, Brussels, Singapore, and Mexico City.

TABLE 15.3 Population of the World's Largest Cities, 2012

	Pop. (millions)
City, Country	2012
Tokyo, Japan	34.4
Guangzhou, China	25.6
Seoul, S. Korea	25.3
Shanghai, China	25.1
Mexico City, Mexico	23.1
Delhi, India	22.9
New York, United States	22.0
São Paulo, Brazil	21.0
Mumbai, India	20.7
Manila, Philippines	20.5
Jakarta, Indonesia	18.8
Los Angeles, United States	18.1
Karachi, Pakistan	17.2
Osaka, Japan	16.8
Beijing, China	16.3
Moscow, Russia	16.1

Source: *Encyclopedia Britannica, 2013,* Populations. *Time Almanac: Chicago.*

Questions for Consideration

1. Can you think of other interesting ways of ranking cities?
2. What would be the problems with slow or negative growth in cities in countries like Russia with a declining population?
3. What are the problems with identifying cities as being from only three kinds of countries, as Wallerstein did?

during the industrializing of Canada contributed to social disorganization by weakening personal ties in family, religion, education, and other institutions. Second, large-scale immigration in the late 19th and early 20th centuries was more than most cities could absorb, and many individuals were never fully assimilated into the cultural mainstream. With larger numbers of strangers living close together in central cities, symptoms of social disorganization, such as high rates of crime, mental illness, and suicide, grew more pronounced. So far the high levels of immigration in the late 20th and early 21st century have not caused severe problems, but according to Durkheim (1933/1893), urban life changes people's relationships. Rural areas are characterized by *mechanical solidarity*—**social bonds based on shared religious beliefs and a simple division of labour**—but these bonds are changed with urbanization. Urban areas are characterized by *organic solidarity*—**social bonds based on interdependence and an elaborate division of labour (specialization).** Although Durkheim was optimistic that urbanization could be positive, he also thought that some things were lost in the process.

Third, mass suburbanization created additional social disorganization, and many central cities in the United States, though less so in Canada, have been unable to reach an equilibrium since the mass exodus to the suburbs following World War II. According to urban ecologist Amos Hawley (1950; 1981), new technologies, such as commuter railways and automobiles, have led to the decentralization of city life and the movement of industry from the central city to the suburbs, with disastrous results for some people. Although urbanization, mass immigration, and suburbanization have had functional consequences—including citizenship, job opportunities, and home ownership—they have also created problems for many people, particularly for people who are left behind in declining parts of central cities and people who experience discrimination.

Besides emphasizing processes, functionalists also emphasize systems. Sociologist Talcott Parsons (1966:28) identified four systems that interact with one another in urban areas: the cultural system, the social system, the personality system, and the behavioural organism. William Michelson (1976:24) has drawn attention to a

Overcrowded living conditions are a way of life for people residing in this area of Mumbai. How will rapid population growth in the future affect urban areas in global cities?

Guy Erwood/Shutterstock

fifth system, the environmental system, in particular the human-made physical, or built, environment, most fully illustrated by the urban environment. He suggested that the effects of the phenomena in the built environment on the other systems, and vice versa, should be studied. Michelson also developed the concept of *congruence* to indicate that some states of variables in one system may better coexist with some states of variables in another system than with others. Mismatches of states of variables constitute incongruence. An example of incongruence is the building of economically efficient high-rise subsidized housing for families with small children, like the Pruitt-Igoe project in St. Louis, a project famous for crime, inadequate maintenance, and poor management; mothers living in such projects are not able to follow their children to other floors and ground level to supervise or protect them (Michelson 1976:26). High-rise public housing has also had problems with property damage and bullying because of lack of supervision.

The Conflict Perspective

Conflict analysts do not believe that cities grow or decline by chance. Members of the capitalist class and political elites make far-reaching decisions about land use and urban development that benefit some people at the expense of others (Castells 1977; Feagin and Parker 1990). According to conflict theorists, the upper classes have successfully maintained class-based and sometimes racialized segregation (in the United States) through political control and legal strategies such as municipal incorporation, defensive annexation, restrictive covenants, and zoning regulations. But where do these practices leave everyone else? Marx suggested that cities are the arenas in which the intertwined processes of class conflict and capital accumulation take place; class consciousness and worker revolt are more likely to develop when workers are concentrated in urban areas (Flanagan 1995).

Contemporary conflict theorists Joe R. Feagin and Robert Parker (1990) speak of a *political economy model,* believing that both economic and political factors affect patterns of urban growth and decline. Urban growth, they say, is influenced by capital investment decisions, power and resource inequality, class and class conflict, and government subsidy programs. Members of the capitalist class choose corporate locations, decide on sites for shopping centres and factories, and spread the population that can afford to purchase homes into sprawling suburbs located exactly where the capitalists think they should be located (Feagin and Parker 1990). In this view, a few hundred financial institutions and developers finance and construct most major and many smaller urban development projects, including skyscrapers, shopping malls,

and suburban housing projects. These decision makers can make housing more affordable or totally unaffordable for many people. Ultimately, their motivation rests not in benefitting the community, but rather in making a profit, and the cities they produce reflect this mindset (Feagin and Parker 1990).

The concept of *uneven development*—the tendency of some neighbourhoods, cities, or regions to grow and prosper while others stagnate and decline—is a by-product of the political economy model of urban development (Perry and Watkins 1977). Conflict theorists argue that uneven development reflects inequalities of wealth and power in society. Uneven development not only affects areas in decline, but also produces external costs that are paid by the entire community. Among these costs are increased pollution, traffic congestion, and rising rates of crime and violence. According to sociologist Mark Gottdiener (1985:214), these costs are "intrinsic to the very core of capitalism, and those who profit the most from development are not called upon to remedy its side effects." One advantage of the political economy framework is that it can be used to study cities in middle- and low-income nations, as well as high-income nations (see Jaffee 1990; Knox and Taylor 1995; Wilson 1997).

Uneven development does not occur in the same way in Canadian cities as it does in U.S. cities. Canadian city governments are more actively involved in land-use management and are committed more strongly than U.S. city governments to public services, including transit, parks, and libraries. Canadian cities are also characterized by more equal distribution of public services than the more politically fragmented U.S. cities (Ley and Bourne 1993). Thus, the land and property values in the Canadian central city remain highly competitive despite a substantial rate of suburban development, and more so now with the move to the city core.

The Interactionist Perspective

Interactionists examine urban problems from the standpoint of people's *experience* of urban life and how they subjectively define the reality of city living. How does city life affect the people who live in a city? According to early German sociologist Georg Simmel (1950), urban life is so highly stimulating that people have no choice but to become somewhat insensitive to events and individuals around them. Urban residents generally avoid emotional involvement with one another and try to ignore the events—including, possibly, violence and crime—that take place nearby. They are wary of other people, looking at others as strangers; some people act reserved to cloak deeper feelings of distrust or dislike toward others. At the same time, Simmel thought that urban living could be liberating because it gives people opportunities for individualism and autonomy.

On the basis of Simmel's observations of social relations in the city, early University of Chicago sociologist Louis Wirth (1938) suggested that urbanism is a "way of life" that increases the incidence of both social and personality disorders in individuals. *Urbanism* refers to the distinctive social and psychological patterns of life that are typically found in the city. According to Wirth, the size, density, and heterogeneity of urban populations result in an elaborate division of labour and in spatial segregation of people by racialization/ethnicity, social class, religion, and/or lifestyle. The division of labour and spatial segregation produce feelings of alienation, powerlessness, and loneliness.

In contrast to Wirth's gloomy analysis of urban life, sociologist Herbert Gans (1962/1982) believed that not everyone experiences the city in the same way. On the basis of research in the West End of Boston in the late 1950s, Gans concluded that many residents develop strong loyalties and a sense of community in central city areas that outsiders often view negatively. According to Gans, in large urban areas, personal behaviour is shaped by the type of neighbourhood a person lives in. For example, *cosmopolites*—students, artists, writers, musicians, entertainers, and professionals—view the city as a place where they can be close to cultural facilities and people with whom they share common interests. *Unmarried people* and *childless couples* live in the city because they want to be close to work and entertainment. *Ethnic villagers* live in ethnically segregated neighbourhoods because they feel most comfortable within their own group. The *deprived* and the *trapped* live in the city because they believe they have no other alternatives. Gans concluded that the city is a pleasure and a challenge for some urban dwellers and an urban nightmare for others.

According to interactionists, the deprived and the trapped contribute to a social construction of reality that stereotypes some city dwellers as poor, down-and-out, and sometimes dangerous, whereas almost all city dwellers are not this way. Because of U.S. movies and television shows seen by Canadians, and particularly because of extensive media coverage of crime or racialized unrest in the largest metropolitan areas of the United States, which presents a very negative image of cities, an anti-urban bias remains strong among many non-urban dwellers. Even urban dwellers can have negative stereotypes of parts of cities. The note about Regent Park shows that social housing for poor people can change over several decades to become an object of media vilification, but when new plans are developed to improve the area, strong sentiments about the area can change, as shown by people's willingness to move into the new buildings.

On the other hand, Richard Florida, like Gans, believes that cities can be pleasurable and tolerant, and thus attract the kind of creative people (what he calls the creative class) who will hold the key to Canada's economic future. Florida has developed a Bohemian Index which makes use of data from Statistics Canada and the U.S. Census Bureau to rank cities on creativity. The Index, published in 2010 for North American cities, found that Los Angeles was first; New York was second; then came Vancouver and Toronto; and Montreal was tenth (Florida 2010). Interactionists believe that the city can be experienced in many ways, and the more creative cities can help individuals and the country to flourish. As noted above, Vishaan Charkrabarti is also suggesting that cities would help the environment and make people more prosperous, healthier, and happier (2013).

Finally, cities are also known for problems of loneliness and alienation. Some interactionists propose that people who live in large metropolitan areas develop subcultural ties to help them feel a sense of community and identity. A *subculture* **is a group of people who share a distinctive set of cultural beliefs and behaviours that set them apart from the larger society.** Joining an interest group—from bowling with friends from the office to volunteering in a literacy program—is one way of feeling connected. Ethnic neighbourhoods are an example of subcultures; some are tightly knit, whereas others have little influence on residents' daily lives. Interactionists note that members of subcultures, especially those based on racialization, ethnicity, or religion, sometimes come into conflict with one another. These conflicts can result in verbal exchanges, hate crimes, or other physical violence, or they can cause the individuals to withdraw almost entirely from the larger community and become more intensely involved with the subculture.

Feminist Perspectives

In the same way that great social policy issues are urban policy issues, feminist analyses are germane to virtually every aspect of city life. Many of these analyses have been dealt with in other chapters; here are just a couple of examples of feminism's application to urban problems. Some feminist theorists emphasize the occupational opportunities, freedom, convenience, and stimulation for women present in cities but not available in smaller centres or suburbs—Betty Freidan (1963) and, then, Margrit Eichler (1995) have been very critical of the lack of stimulation and the oppressiveness of women's lives in low-density suburbs. In cities, women have the chance to participate in a variety of occupations, and they are very well represented in the (usually low-paid) jobs that are part of the Bohemian Index (e.g., artists and entertainers). Moreover, in cities, women do not have to worry about what the neighbours will think of their behaviour. They can choose to interact with their neighbours or not. Lastly, women who live in a city instead of a suburb and have the dual roles of worker and mother will usually have a shorter commute to their jobs and more locally available services. Thus, they may feel less stress in fulfilling their responsibilities and have more time for themselves. On the other hand, some feminists have been so concerned about the threats to women at night in cities that they have organized "Take Back the Night" marches in most major centres. Some feminists have also taken exception to the suggestion by police and others that they should be more restrained in what they wear. In consequence, they have organized "SlutWalks" in many cities. The first one was held in Toronto in 2011.

URBAN PROBLEMS IN THE FUTURE

In a best-case scenario, Canada would convert to regional governments to provide water, wastewater (sewage), transportation, schools, parks, hospitals, and other public services. In this scenario, revenues would be shared among central cities, affluent suburbs, and edge cities, since everyone would benefit from the improved quality of life. Cities would get a permanent source of taxation, besides property taxes, and they would create a tolerant and creative climate. Meanwhile, as we wait and hope for solutions to the problems of urbanization at the macro-level, we can—as citizens, neighbours, tenants, property owners, workers, employers, and users of public and private services throughout the city—exercise some degree of control over the quality of life in our own communities. There is increasing impetus to take control because one thing is certain: as the world population continues to grow in this century, urban problems will intensify, and this will affect us all.

ENVIRONMENTAL PROBLEMS

The environment provides us with the means to survive and thrive. Although it is popularly believed that most environmental problems arise from rapid growth in middle- and low-income nations, this is not entirely the case. Many scientists believe that high-income nations present a much greater threat to the earth's ecosystems, as energy use and general consumption are greater (Ehrlich and Ehrlich 1991). An *ecosystem* is "all the populations of plants and animal species that live and interact in a given area at a particular time, as well as the chemical and physical factors that make up the nonliving environment" (Cable and Cable 1995:124). Thus, an ocean is an

ecosystem; a tropical rainforest is an ecosystem; and, on a much smaller scale, a house on a lot is an ecosystem. When all of the earth's ecosystems are put together, they make up the *biosphere*.

Ecosystems do not have an infinite ability to support either population growth or environmental depletion or destruction. In fact, some scientists believe that many of the world's ecosystems have already exceeded their *carrying capacity*—the maximum population that an ecosystem can support without eventually being degraded or destroyed. According to Ehrlich and Ehrlich (1991), a baby born in a country like the United States, and to a lesser extent Canada, will have two times the destructive impact on the earth's ecosystems and services as a baby born in Sweden; 140 times the impact of a baby born in Bangladesh or Kenya; and over 280 times the impact of a baby born in Chad, Rwanda, Haiti, or Nepal. Thus the size of the population, its level of affluence, and the harmful technology available in the society are major contributing factors to **environmental degradation—disruptions to the environment that have negative consequences for ecosystems** (Cable and Cable 1995). Environmental degradation involves both removing natural resources from the environment and adding to environmental problems through pollution.

In Canada, environmental degradation increases as people try to maintain the high levels of wealth and material comfort to which they have become accustomed. They consume the earth's resources and pollute its environment with automobiles, airplanes, speedboats, computers, television sets and DVD players, year-round air conditioning and heating, and other amenities that are far beyond the grasp of most of the world's people. Although these products are made possible by high levels of industrial production and economic growth, economic growth often depletes and destroys the environment.

Economic Growth and Environmental Degradation

During most of the 20th century, economic growth in Canada and the world was based on increased output in the manufacturing sector (see Table 15.2 for the increase in the world's industrial output in the 20th century). The environment is affected at all phases of the manufacturing process, from mining and transportation to manufacturing and waste disposal. Industrial production involves extracting raw materials—natural resources—from the environment, usually through mining. Mining depletes mineral resources and fossil fuel reserves—coal, oil, and natural gas. Mining also disturbs ecosystems; this is particularly true of surface mining, which strips bare the land, destroying natural vegetation and wildlife habitats. Other problems typically follow, including erosion of the land by wind and water and runoff of acids, silt, and toxic substances into nearby surface water and groundwater; this leads to the pollution of rivers and streams with toxic compounds that kill fish and other aquatic life.

Table 15.2 provides some indication of the enormous effects humanity's activity has had on our planet during the 20th century. This chart ignores huge expansions that took place after 1900, like automobiles—in Canada, from zero to 14 million by the end of the century—and huge declines of natural resources of special interest to Canadians, such as the 99 percent decrease in the cod fishery, which has not returned and may never return to 1980s levels despite a continuing moratorium on fishing.

The environmental impact of mining doesn't stop when the raw materials have been mined. Now the raw materials must be transported to a plant or factory, where workers will transform them into manufactured products. Transporting requires the use of energy—particularly the burning of fossil fuels—which contributes to air pollution because motor vehicles produce carbon monoxide, nitrogen oxides, and photochemical pollutants. Each of these pollutants is associated with various illnesses, including heart and respiratory disease and cancer. The manufacturing process further depletes the supply of fossil fuels and contributes to air pollution. (See Table 15.2 for the amount of various kinds of pollution produced in the 20th century.) People who work in or live near facilities that pollute the environment are often harmed by the solid or toxic/hazardous wastes resulting from the manufacturing process.

Many analysts believe that we cannot continue this pattern of environmental degradation. They believe future economic development—in Canada and globally—will require drastic changes in the structure of industry, especially in the energy, transportation, chemical, and agricultural sectors of the economy. If we don't make changes, environmental degradation—of our air, water, soil, and forests—constitutes a major threat to the well-being of all human beings and ecosystems on the earth. On the other hand, not all types of industries are harmful. Green industries, like wind turbines, solar power, and industrial water purification projects, could provide future sources of economic development and jobs.

How well is Canada doing regarding protecting the environment? The Conference Board of Canada compared Canada to other high-income countries and produced a Report Card on the Environment (see Table 15.4). Canada does not do well, receiving a grade of C on environmental performance and ranking 15th of 17 countries. This overall grade is based on performance in more than a dozen measures regarding air pollution,

TABLE 15.4 Canada's Overall Environmental Performance

REPORT CARD

Environment

1	France	A
2	Norway	A
3	Sweden	A
4	U.K.	A
5	Ireland	A
6	Switzerland	A
7	Japan	A
8	Italy	A
9	Austria	A
10	Denmark	A
11	Germany	B
12	Finland	B
13	Belgium	B
14	Netherlands	B
15	Canada	C
16	U.S.	D
17	Australia	D

Source: *Conference Board of Canada, 2013, Environment. Retrieved June 21, 2013 (http://www.conferenceboard.ca/hcp/details/environment.aspx).*

waste and water treatment, greenhouse gas (GHG) emissions, and so on. Supporting this position, Canada ranked among the OECD and BRIC (Brazil, Russia, India, and China) countries in a more comprehensive score for sustainability. In a *Corporate Knights* survey, Canada ranked 15th of 39 countries (Hamilton 2013:26).

In the Winter 2015 edition of *Corporate Knights,* another ranking was created of the 100 most sustainable corporations in the world based on eight factors like energy productivity, waste productivity, CEO-to-average worker pay, and, as we showed in Chapter 4, the percentage of women on the board of directors. Canada had 12 companies among the 100, with Tim Hortons (taken over by Burger King in late 2014) the highest ranking firm in 11th place. Many of our financial institutions were also well placed. The United States had 20 companies in this list (Runnalls 2015). However, Canada's individual companies will have to do much better to make this list. Next we will outline some major environment problems, and then give Canada's grade if it is included in the Report Card.

Air Pollution and Smog

Nature performs many *ecosystem services*—valuable, practical functions that help to preserve ecosystems. For example, if the atmosphere is not overburdened, it can maintain a proper balance between carbon dioxide and oxygen, as well as provide ozone for protection against ultraviolet radiation. However, air pollution interferes with many ecosystem services. The carbon dioxide that pollutes the air we breathe keeps the sun's heat from radiating back into space, thereby causing the earth to heat up (the greenhouse effect, discussed in the next section).

The huge amount of air pollution that has accumulated during the 20th and first part of the 21st century has placed a great burden on the atmosphere's ecosystem. Beginning with the Industrial Revolution in the late 19th and early 20th centuries, more and more pollutants have been emitted into the atmosphere by households, industries, and automobile traffic. Though these three sources have become more fuel-efficient in Western countries, constantly increasing amounts of carbon dioxide, carbon monoxide, nitrogen oxide, and sulphur oxide, as well as such heavy metals as lead, zinc, and copper, still pollute our air, coming from low-income countries like India and China. The Conference Board of Canada has identified four pollutants: nitrogen oxides emissions; sulphur oxides emissions; volatile organic chemicals (VOC) emissions (vehicle emissions, chemical manufacturing, the evaporation of automotive fuels and other petroleum-based products, and chemical solvents); and pm10 (particulate matter that can cause many respiratory and other problems). Canada's grade on controlling all four of these air pollutants is uneven, with grades of D, B, D, and B respectively. The good news is that Canada has reduced these air pollutants by at least a third from 1990 to 2009 (Conference Board of Canada 2013).

Air pollution affects all life and ecosystems on the planet. Air pollution in the form of acid rain destroys forests, streams and lakes, and other ecosystems. **Acid rain is rainfall containing large concentrations of sulphuric and nitric acids (primarily from the burning of fuel and car and truck exhausts)**. Canadian efforts to reduce acid rain from the United States have been blocked by the automobile industry; companies that mine, haul, and sell high-sulphur coal; and coal miners. Fortunately, new industries are less dependent on burning coal than are older factories in the industrial areas. Both the United States and Canada have reduced their coal use and plan to reduce it further in the near future.

To monitor air pollution in Ontario, the Air Quality Index (AQI) was devised to measure ground-level ozone, nitrogen dioxide, carbon monoxide, sulphur dioxide, sulphur compounds, and fine suspended particles. An AQI of 50+ may cause eye irritation, breathing difficulties, and even lung damage to those who are physically active. Ontario's air quality has improved steadily since 1988. Ontario has good air quality approximately 90 percent of the time (Ontario Ministry of Environment 2013).

In the past, air pollution in middle- and low-income nations was attributed primarily to the fight for survival and economic development, whereas most air pollution in high-income nations was attributed to relatively luxurious lifestyles. However, distinctions between air pollution in high-income and middle- and low-income nations are growing weaker; automobile ownership is greatly increasing in places like Mexico, Brazil, and China. Cities such as Mumbai, Shanghai, and Jakarta have also seen a significant increase in the number of automobiles, bringing a corresponding rise in air pollution and traffic problems. In 2009, China surpassed the United States in carbon dioxide emissions. Still, Western

Air pollution is a pressing problem in many nations, but nowhere more so than in Mexico City, where daylight hours often look like they do in this photo. How is air pollution related to people's health and life expectancy?
Kitch Bain/Shutterstock

industrial nations account for about two-thirds of the carbon dioxide in the atmosphere.

The Greenhouse Effect

Emissions from traffic and industry not only add to general air pollution, but also contribute to the enhanced *greenhouse effect*—**an environmental condition caused by excessive quantities of carbon dioxide, methane, and nitrous oxide or greenhouse gases (GHG) in the atmosphere.** When carbon dioxide (CO_2) molecules build up in the earth's atmosphere, they act like the glass roof of a greenhouse, allowing sunlight to reach the earth's surface but preventing the escape of infrared radiation back into space. The radiation that cannot escape is reradiated as heat, causing the earth's surface temperature to rise (Weiner 1990). Once again Canada does poorly on the Conference Board of Canada Report Card, with a grade of D. Canada's GHG emissions were 20.3 tonnes per capita, higher than any of the high-income countries average of 12.5 tonnes. The primary reason is growth in production and export of energy resources (especially the oil sands). Not only does it take a lot of energy to separate the oil from the sand, but large amounts of water are used and large areas of forests are cut down. Greenpeace, a famous environmental advocacy group, has labelled the oil sands as the fifth most serious climate threat in the world (Greenpeace 2013). Also contributing to this level is the need for protection from the cold and the great distances we drive. As a result of increased GHG emissions here and elsewhere, over the past half century, average temperatures in Canada have been trending up one degree Celsius, as shown in Figure 15.3. Scientists believe that the earth will have a temperature increase of 1.5 to as much as 5 degrees over the next 100 years. In fact, if current rates of emission into the atmosphere remain unchanged,

temperature increases might eventually bring about catastrophic consequences. In early 2015, it was reported that 2014 was the hottest overall year on record.

One consequence of increased emissions could be significant changes in weather patterns and climate. Changes in weather patterns could bring increased evaporation, creating new deserts and decreasing regional water reserves. Changes in air circulation and climatic conditions could also result in more frequent and intense storms, hurricanes, flooding, and droughts. Vegetation zones could shift, and forests in the northern hemisphere might be infested with new insects or die off. Map 15.3 gives a sample scenario about how Canada's winters might become warmer from 2041 to 2070 in comparison to 1961 to 1990. If this occurs, Hudson's Bay and the Arctic will be much warmer, and no place will be colder.

Global warming is beneficial to some areas: Greenland is now benefitting from warming by growing vegetables and exploring for minerals in areas once covered by ice.

Over 90 percent of climactic scientists believe in the existence of global warming and its influence on many things, including Arctic Sea ice. In summer 2013, many commentators made disparaging remarks about global warming when the area of ice grew from 2012 to 2013. However, the 2012 limit was the smallest ever recorded and the 2013 limit was still below average. A short video about this topic is available from *Slate*, the online magazine. Among other items, it shows a graph about sea ice trending downward, like the temperatures trending upward in Figure 15.3 (Plait 2013). What we should do about this problem is considered in Box 15.2.

Depletion of the Ozone Layer

The ozone layer is the thin atmospheric band that protects the earth and its inhabitants from the sun's harmful ultraviolet rays. There is much evidence that the ozone

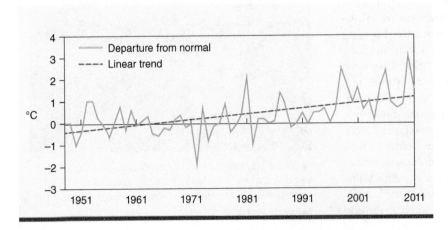

Figure 15.3   Mean Temperatures in Canada, 1951–2011.

Source: *Statistics Canada, 2013, Environment, Canada at a Glance. Retrieved June 21, 2013 (http://www.statcan.gc.ca/pub/12-581-x/2013000/envi-eng.htm).*

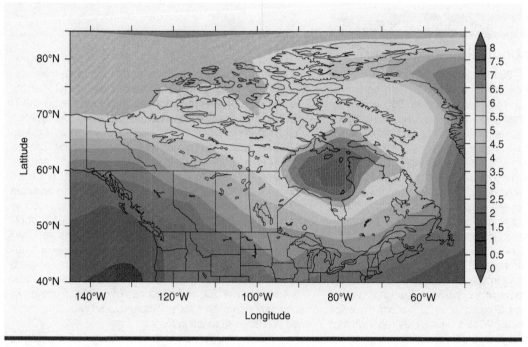

Map 15.3   Sample Scenario: Significantly Warmer Winters, 2014–2070.

Source: *Environment Canada, 2013, Significantly Warmer Winters*, The Canadian Climate Change Scenarios Network. *Retrieved October 2, 2013* (*http://www.ec.gc.ca/sc-cs/default.asp?lang=En&n=FE6B6E6B-1*).

layer of the atmosphere has been endangered by air pollution. In 1992, a hole the size of North America was reported in the ozone layer over Antarctica, and scientists concluded that the ozone layer was thinning out at a rate of 6 percent a year in the 1990s (Hauchler and Kennedy 1994). A thinning ozone layer increases risk of skin cancer, damages marine life, and lowers crop yields. It is important to note that the ozone shrinkage that scientists are currently measuring is the result of emissions in the early 1980s. Thus, the emissions we produce today will exert their destructive effects in the future (Hauchler and Kennedy 1994). Many countries, hoping to control damage to this delicate ecosystem in the future, are now phasing out products that contain CFCs, which damage the ozone layer and do not break down quickly. In 1987, 49 countries signed the Montreal Protocol to cut CFC production and consumption. Although the ozone hole has been decreasing due to the Montreal Protocol's influence, in September 2013, the hole was larger than in 2012 and larger than average for the last few years. In 2014, it was a little smaller (Ozone Hole 2015).

Problems with Water, Soil, and Forests

Water, soil, and forests (vegetation) are interdependent, crucial resources that face increasing degradation or destruction because of pollution. As a result of climate changes, waste, pollution, and rapid depletion, the earth's drinking water is endangered and its fertile land is being lost.

Water Shortages and Pollution

Water depletion and pollution are serious problems. A shocking example occurred in 2000 in the small town of Walkerton in southern Ontario. Seven people died and about 2300 became ill as a result of *E. coli* contamination in the water. The primary source of the contamination was manure that had been spread on a farm near a major well. This well had not been monitored appropriately by the water utility operators. In the end, Ontario Premier Mike Harris was forced to admit that he and his government were, in part, responsible for the tragedy: despite ongoing strong public support for environmental protection, they had slashed funding for environmental programs (along with funding for welfare, education, and health). At the same time, they had devolved responsibility in many areas—including water testing and manure management—to the municipalities, which had neither the money nor the knowledge needed to handle these responsibilities. Fortunately there have been no other similar examples in Canada since that time.

Social Problems and Social Policy

Box 15.2

What to Do about Global Warming?

In late September 2013, the Intergovernmental Panel on Climate Change (IPCC) published its fifth and most comprehensive report yet involving over 250 scientists. The report stated that global warming is occurring with a 95 percent probability (equivalent to the probability of cigarette smoking and illness), and humans are causing it—even if the last few years have been stable. They agreed (among many findings) that warming of the climate is definitely happening, causing the atmosphere and the oceans to become warmer; sea levels have risen as a result of snow and sea ice diminishing; the increase in warmth in the last three decades is unprecedented; the Greenland and Antarctic ice sheets are contracting and the seas are rising; concentrations of carbon dioxide, methane, and nitrous oxide have increased by 40 percent since the Industrial Revolution began; and climate change is caused by humans (Working Group 2013:10). If more evidence was needed, in January 2015 it was widely reported that 2014 was the hottest year in recorded time.

In 1997, in an attempt to reduce GHG emissions, 150 nations met in Kyoto, Japan and agreed to a plan, called the Kyoto Protocol, to reduce the amount of emissions expected in the year 2012 by 20 to 30 percent. The Canadian Liberal government ratified the Kyoto Protocol in 2002. But, in 2006, after Prime Minister Harper acknowledged that Canada would not meet its GHG emissions target on time, the Conservative government took a different approach. In October 2006, they introduced the *Clean Air Act,* which called for a reduction in intensity of emissions over a long period of time, not an absolute reduction in emissions, and made no mention of the Kyoto Protocol. The Act's long range goals included:

- reducing GHG emissions 17 percent below 2005 levels by 2020;
- capping GHG emissions through national targets for smog and ozone levels by 2025; and
- reducing GHG emissions from 2003 levels by 45 to 65 percent by 2050. (Curry 2006:A4)

Canada did not meet its Kyoto targets, and now it appears that it will not meet the Conservative government's targets, according to Environment Canada. In 1990, Canada emitted less than 600 million tonnes of carbon; in 2005, Canada emitted 750 million tonnes; and the best scenario is that Canada will emit 720 million tonnes in 2020 (Environment Canada 2012)—not even close to the 17 percent reduction promised. In the Speech from the Throne in September 2013, the government promised to do something to reduce GHG emissions in that session, but was not more specific.

Although Canada has not met its Kyoto or other targets, it has reduced its GHG intensity level. GHG intensity is a ratio of GHG in megatonnes emitted to the growth in GDP in billions of dollars. This GHG intensity has declined by 21 percent since 1990, meaning it's now taking less GHG emissions to produce more GDP. However, Canada receives a grade of D from the Conference Board of Canada for intensity. In 2009, Canada used 0.25 tonnes per US$1000 of GDP, much more than the average of 0.15 tonnes per US$1000 for the other high-income countries (Conference Board of Canada 2013). In addition, a few provinces, especially Ontario, have reduced their emissions by less use of coal and more use of natural gas and renewables. But Alberta, with its use of great quantities of natural gas to produce oil from the oil sands, is emitting over 200 million tonnes of carbon. If growth of consumption of oil sands oil increases as expected, there is no chance of meeting targets.

How should we deal with this problem? First, scaring and shaming people does not work well. It did not work well to reduce cigarette smoking, and it is not working well to reduce obesity. Many think that a "carbon tax," where people pay a tax on the fossil fuels they consume, is a good idea, since taxes usually produce less of whatever is taxed. The latter approach was supported by former Liberal leader Stéphane Dion, Premier Gordon Campbell of British Columbia, former President Bill Clinton, and James Henson, a pioneer in the campaign against GHG. In 2008, British Columbia instituted a carbon tax, and it is expected to drop emissions by one-third by 2020. The tax was designed to be revenue neutral—increased carbon taxes meant lower income taxes. It is working: consumption is down by almost 20 percent. It does not cover every problem, such as gas flaring by drilling, but it is simple to administer. Quebec and Alberta have a similar kind of tax, but the federal government has not created one, nor has the U.S. government created one.

Another approach is to use more of a cleaner fuel (than coal) (e.g., shale gas obtained by fracking). Fracking is the horizontal drilling through shale and other permeable rocks using hydraulic fracturing (with high pressure liquids) to release the natural gas. This process is widespread in the United States and is causing the price of natural gas to plummet. Natural gas emits 45 percent less carbon dioxide than coal. By switching from coal to shale gas, the United States has reduced it emissions by 500 million tonnes (Lomborg 2013). And shale gas is becoming cheaper than other fossil fuels. At this time, renewable sources of energy (e.g., solar and wind) are so expensive that their operations must be subsidized. Shifting to the use of more shale gas might give us time to create more

Social Problems and Social Policy
Box 15.2 continued

effective processes for obtaining energy from renewables. If that were possible, then every nation would change voluntarily. On the other hand, locals are protesting fracking, claiming that it could affect ground water with contaminated water and add methane to the atmosphere. In the fall of 2013, Indigenous and non-Indigenous people in New Brunswick protested the development of fracking and the lack of consultation. In 2015, oil decreased greatly in price, so some of the wells became idle and President Obama vetoed the Keystone XL pipeline, so less oil will likely come from the oil sands.

Questions for Consideration

1. Given the alternatives and the various problems associated with each approach for reducing GHG emissions, what would you suggest that governments do?
2. Nuclear power does not contribute to global warming. Should we use more nuclear power?
3. Many parts of Canada would become warmer with global warming. Would that be an overall good thing for this country?

Obviously, such problems are not limited to Canada. Although approximately 70 percent of the earth's surface is covered by water, most water is not drinkable: 97 percent is saltwater, 2 percent is in ice caps and glaciers, and most of the remaining 1 percent is so far underground that it is beyond human reach (Petersen 1994). The primary sources of water for use and consumption are rainfall, streams, lakes, rivers, and aquifers (accessible underground water supplies). Canada is often thought to be a source of limitless fresh water, but we have only 7 percent of the world's renewable, or flowing, fresh water, as opposed to the stationary fresh water in lakes; moreover, 60 percent of our fresh water runs north.

Because of the current rate of world population growth and existing climatic conditions, water scarcity is increasing throughout the world. According to the WHO, water scarcity affects one in three people on every continent of the globe. The situation is getting worse as the need for water increases along with population growth, urbanization, and increased household and industrial uses (WHO 2013).

According to the Conference Board of Canada's Report Card, Canada's record on water quality and quantity is uneven. Canada does well in water quality, earning a grade of A (4th of 16 countries) and below average in water withdrawals, earning a grade of C (15th of 16 countries). Although Canada's water quality is threatened by poorly treated municipal waste, industrial effluent, and fertilizer runoff from agriculture, overall treatment is extensive. On the other hand, regarding water withdrawals, since we believe we have so much fresh water, safeguards about use are not carefully followed (Conference Board of Canada 2013).

Where does the water go? The largest amount (about 70 percent) is used for crop irrigation; in some African and Asian countries, as much as 85 percent of the available water is used in agriculture. The second largest use of water is in industry (23 to 25 percent). Industrial use of water depends on the level of development in a country and the structure of its economy. For example, high-income nations use as much as 60 percent of their water for industry, whereas a middle- or low-income nation may use less than 10 percent. (In Canada, industry uses about 70 percent of the water and agriculture 12 percent.) A mere 8 percent of all available water is used for domestic or private household use. Over the past century, water withdrawals have been increasing at a greater rate than population increases, with affluent people in high-income nations using far more water than do families living in African villages, where water must often be carried several kilometres (about 2 to 5 litres is the physical minimum needed per person per day). The

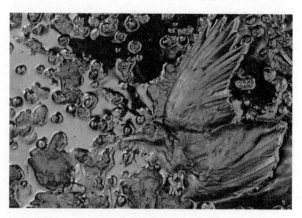

In our delicate ecosystem, water pollution has a disastrous effect on all forms of life—not just on human life. What measures might we implement to reduce water pollution like this?

forest badger/Shutterstock

UN Water website has a wide variety of statistics about how water is used around the world. For example, part of the current pressure on water resources comes from increasing demands for animal feed. Meat production requires 8 to 10 times more water than cereal production, and water withdrawals are predicted to increase by 50 percent by 2025 in developing countries and 18 percent in developed countries (UN Water 2013). Thus, the future will see increased pressure on water resources, and this pressure will be aggravated by climate change and population growth.

Soil Depletion, Forests, and Desertification

Over many decades, Canada's prairies have experienced much soil erosion. It was very pronounced in the 1930s and 1980s. But various programs have been developed to conserve it. A study was undertaken to examine long-term trends in dust emissions on the Canadian prairies and to determine whether the efforts of soil conservation have had a measurable impact on dust frequency. The researchers examined records of airborne dust frequency from seven weather stations from 1961 to 2006. The dramatic reduction of dust from 1990 appears to be a region-wide threshold crossing, where the effects of soil conservation efforts began to occur. Overall, the results show a substantial reduction in dust frequency from 1991 to 2006, which can be attributed to changes in farm management practices in the late 1980s. This finding was also supported by the reduction in dust that occurred in the droughts of 2001–2002 (Fox et al. 2012).

About 11 percent of the earth's surface is used for growing crops, 31 percent is forest, and 24 percent is used to graze animals. Each year, however, many acres of usable land are lost through erosion and contamination. *Deforestation*—excessive removal of trees—usually results in serious erosion. Since the 1992 Earth Summit in Rio de Janeiro, high-income nations have made an effort to protect forests. Unfortunately, prior industrialization in Canada and other high-income nations has already taken a serious toll on forests, and the pattern is continuing in some middle- and low-income nations as they become more industrialized. In Canada, especially in the Pacific Northwest, logging is an issue. Environmentalists say that logging destroys old-growth forests, and increases landslides, floods, and changes in rivers and streams, which devastate fish stocks. However, Canada changed its approach after the international campaign to prevent cutting of the old-growth forest in British Columbia's Clayoquot Sound in 1992 and the international boycotts of our forest products led by Greenpeace. The

Conference Board of Canada of Canada gives Canada a grade of A in use of forest resources and we rank second among high-income countries because now the rate of harvesting is at or below the rate of replacement or regrowth (Conference Board of Canada 2013).

Today, many regions are losing an increasing amount of usable land as a result of *desertification*—**the process by which usable land is turned into desert because of overgrazing, harmful agricultural practices, or deforestation.** It is estimated that desertification destroys as many as 6 million hectares (15 million acres) of land a year. An additional 20 million hectares (50 million acres) of crop and pasture land become inefficient each year because of excessive application of herbicides and pesticides, insufficient crop rotation, and intensified agricultural production.

Although desertification takes place in high-income and middle- and low-income nations, its effects are particularly devastating in middle- and low-income nations. When a country is already hard hit by rapid population growth, virtually any loss of land or crops is potentially devastating to large numbers of people. The United Nations and other international organizations have therefore tried to make protection of the environment an integral part of all economic development policy. However, environmental protection specialists say that to translate policy into action, conservation programs must be supported by the people, and the major sources of the problem—population and poverty—must also be addressed. As part of their conservation program, the United Nations developed a campaign to plant 7 billion trees by the end of 2009. As of early August 2009, they had planted over 4 billion trees. This plan was handed over to Plant for the Planet, and by June 2015 they had planted over 14 billion trees toward their new goal of planting 1000 billion trees by 2020.

Solid, Toxic/Hazardous, and Nuclear Wastes

Even with a rapidly growing world population and ongoing economic development in industrialized nations, the planet might be able to sustain life for a long time if it weren't for all the solid and toxic chemical waste that is dumped into the environment.

Solid Waste

In Canada and some other high-income nations, people consume a vast array of products and—in these *disposable societies*—throw away huge quantities of paper, plastic, metal, and other materials. *Solid waste* is any and all unwanted and discarded materials that are not liquids

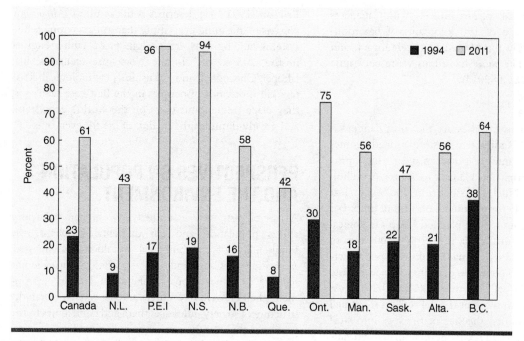

Figure 15.4   Participation in Composting in Canada, 1994 and 2011.

Source: *Statistics Canada, Environment Accounts and Statistics Division,* Households and the Environment Survey (survey number 3881), 1994 and 2011. *Retrieved October 2, 2013 (http://www.statcan.gc.ca/pub/16-002-x/2013001/article/11848-eng.htm).*

or gases. Canada receives another grade of D from the Conference Board of Canada for so little recycling of its waste. For example, in 2008, 34 million tonnes of waste was generated, and 26 million tones went to landfill and incinerators (Conference Board of Canada of Canada 2013). Most of the information about Canadians recycling and resource conservation is about five or more years old. So in the fall of 2013, Canada conducted a comprehensive Households and the Environment Survey (HES) to measure the environmental behaviours of Canadian households relating to the condition of our air, water, and soils. The objective of the HES is to provide data to enable the development and improvement of three key environmental indicators: air quality, water quality, and greenhouse gas emissions.

Figure 15.4 provides information about participation in composting activity in Canada. Over half of Canadian households (61 percent) participated in some form of composting activity in 2011, more than double the rate in 1994. Overall, 45 percent of all households reported composting kitchen waste using curbside collection and 68 percent of households with a lawn or garden reported composting yard waste (Statistics Canada 2013n).

Toxic/Hazardous Waste

At the same time that technology has brought about improvements in the quality and length of life, it has created the potential for new disasters. One source of a potential disaster is *toxic/hazardous waste,* the hazardous chemical by-products of industrial processes. Perhaps the most widely known U.S. case of toxic/hazardous waste is Love Canal. In the late 1970s, residents of Niagara Falls, New York, learned that their children were attending a school that had been built on top of a toxic landfill (Gibbs 1982). After large numbers of children became ill and the smell and appearance of the chemicals permeated the entire area, many people mobilized against Hooker Chemical Company, which had dumped tons of chemicals there (Gibbs 1982). Eventually, the federal government bought many of the houses, moved the residents out, and removed as much of the toxic waste as possible. A lesser-known Canadian example of chemical discharge, by Uniroyal Chemical, permanently contaminated the water supply in Elmira, Ontario, with a "toxic soup of cancer-causing chemicals." In 1989, the Ontario Ministry of the Environment ordered Uniroyal to cease the discharge and clean up the local environment (Cameron 1995:298).

The Organisation for Economic Co-operation and Development (OECD) ranks Canada relative to other OECD countries regarding the production of hazardous waste. Canada's ranking among OECD nations is very poor. Among the 27 OECD nations for which reliable data are available, though nothing more recent than

1991, Canada ranks 24th of 27 countries, with Canadians producing an average of 190 kilograms of hazardous waste annually. Only the United States, Hungary, and Luxembourg generate more hazardous waste per capita than Canadians (OECD 2013).

Nuclear Waste

Nuclear, or radioactive, wastes are the most dangerous of all toxic wastes. Radioactive waste in Canada comes primarily from 22 nuclear power plants, which provide enough electricity in Canada to power 6 million homes (Canadian Nuclear Association 2002). Nuclear waste remains deadly for prolonged periods of time. For example, the estimate for the planned Deep Geological Repository (DGR) in Canada is over 400 000 years of storage (Wilkins 2105:64). Canada ranks very poorly relative to other OECD countries in terms of nuclear waste disposal, ranking 28th of 28 countries (OECD 2013). As of mid-2015, the plan is to put the 2.4 million spent fuel bundles (48 000 tonnes) the size of fire logs into steel containers and then into a DGR. Several small town candidates are vying to be the site (Wilkins 2015). Although there are many problems with nuclear power, some environmentalists are reconsidering its value, because it does have the advantage of not producing CO_2 emissions.

Technological Disasters

Technological disasters have increased global awareness of the problems associated with massive oil spills, explosions, gas leaks, and radioactive waste. A number of these types of disasters have caused death and destruction around the world, such as:

- Lac Mégantic's derailment and explosion of oil tanker cars in 2013, which killed 47 people and demolished about half the town;
- Fukushima Daiichi's nuclear plant disaster in 2011 after the tsunami—radiation deaths have not been reported, but the tsunami and earthquake killed over 18 000 people;
- Deepwater Horizon Gulf of Mexico's oil spill in 2010, which caused great damage to wildlife and the environment;
- Chernobyl's nuclear plant's 1986 meltdown and radiation leak in Ukraine, which caused over 50 immediate deaths, exposed hundreds of thousands to radiation, and likely precipitated thousands of cancer deaths; and
- Bhopal, India's leakage of lethal gases at the pesticide plant, which killed over 3000 people in 1984.

Sociologist Kai T. Erikson sees the world facing a new species of trouble today. He notes how humans pollute things rather than increase wreckage, and create fears, as the above disasters did. The chaos that Erikson (1991:141) describes is the result of *technological disasters*—"meaning everything that can go wrong when systems fail, humans err, designs prove faulty, engines misfire, and so on." In the worst-case scenarios, like Bhopal, Chernobyl, and Fukushima, technological disasters kill thousands of people; in the best-case scenarios, they place tremendous stress on the world's ecosystems and greatly diminish the quality of life for everyone.

PERSPECTIVES ON POPULATION AND THE ENVIRONMENT

As sociologists have examined how human behaviour affects population and environmental problems, the subdiscipline of environmental sociology has emerged. According to Cable and Cable (1995:5), "*environmental sociology* examines people's beliefs about their environment, their behaviour toward it, and the ways in which the structure of society influences them and contributes to the persistent abuse of the environment." Like all sociologists, environmental sociologists—as well as demographers—approach their study from one or another perspective.

The Functionalist Perspective

Some functionalists focus on the relationship between social structure, technological change, and environmental problems. On the one hand, they say, technological innovation serves important functions in society. For example, automation and mass production have made a wide array of goods—from automobiles and computers to McDonald's burgers—available to many people. On the other hand, technological innovation has latent dysfunctions; automation and mass production, for example, create air pollution, overuse and depletion of natural resources, and excessive solid waste. From this point of view, some environmental problems are the price a society pays for technological progress. If this is true, the best way to alleviate the problem is to develop new technologies. This is what happened, some functionalists note, when the catalytic converter and other antipollution devices were developed for automobiles.

Other functionalists take a neo-Malthusian perspective and believe that to reduce food shortages and environmental problems, population must be controlled. In other words, the more people there are alive, the greater are the overuse of finite resources and degradation of soil, water, and land.

No matter which view functionalist environmental sociologists take, they believe that solutions to overpopulation and environmental degradation lie in social institutions such as education, the government, and business.

Educators can encourage population control by teaching people about the limits to agriculture and the difficulty of feeding rapidly increasing populations. Government leaders and international organizations such as the United Nations can cooperate to find far-reaching and innovative solutions and develop understandings about more equitable use of the world's resources (Ehrlich and Ehrlich 1991). Business can be helpful by becoming "greener"—applying environmentally friendly principles to its buildings and operations, putting gardens on factory roofs, using alternative energy sources to coal and oil, sequestering greenhouse gases in underground storage, and cutting waste. Business can also develop environmentally friendly products such as cars powered by a hybrid of gasoline-powered engines and electric motors (e.g., the Toyota Prius, Honda Insight, and Ford Escape) and solar- and wind-powered devices.

To show the extent to which countries are protecting their environment, the Yale Center for Environmental Law and Policy, the Center for International Earth Science Information Network at Columbia University, and the World Economic Forum have devised an index to rank countries' efforts to meet two objectives: to reduce environmental stress on human health and to promote ecosystem vitality and sound resource management.

In total, 25 indicators of these two objectives were selected, ranging from reducing air pollution and increasing water safety to protecting critical habitats, reducing climate change, and improving management of fisheries, agriculture, and forestry. Map 15.4 shows the different levels of effort of countries. Comparisons with the 2008 Index show that Europe and the Americas have improved their performance, and Russia and some West Asian countries worsened their performance. Switzerland, Norway, Sweden, Finland, and Costa Rica have scores over 90. On this scale, Canada ranks 12th with a score of 86, and the United States ranks 39th with a score of 81. While our score can provide some comfort, we are still very deficient in reducing greenhouse gases.

Within Canada, some variation exists among provinces for their climate change plans, according to the *Corporate Knights'* Green Provincial Report Card. This score card consists of six major environmental variables (very similar to those of the Conference Board of Canada), with data from 2008 to 2011. Whereas British Columbia, Ontario, and Quebec rank high in their performance,

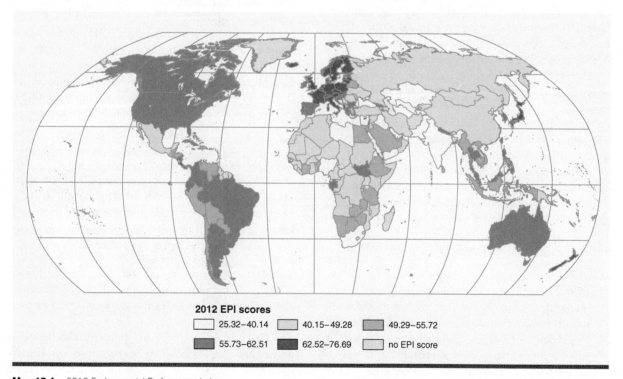

Map 15.4   2012 Environmental Performance Index.

Source: *Yale Center for Environmental Law and Policy (YCELP)/Yale University, Center for International Earth Science Information Network (CIESIN)/Columbia University, World Economic Forum (WEF), Joint Research Centre (JRC)/European Commission, 2012, 2012 Environmental Performance Index and Pilot Trend Environmental Performance Index. Palisades, NY: NASA Socioeconomic Data and Applications Center (SEDAC). Retrieved September 24, 2013 (http://sedac.ciesin.columbia.edu/data/set/epi-environmental-performance-index-pilot-trend-2012).*

earning grades of A, Alberta, Saskatchewan, Manitoba, New Brunswick, and Newfoundland and Labrador earn grades of C (Marchington 2012:44–48). Turning to cities, *Corporate Knights* has also evaluated Canadian cities on sustainability, consisting of six variables comprising ecological integrity, but also governance and social well-being. It ranks Toronto and Edmonton first and second among large cities, Vancouver and Mississauga among medium cities, and Victoria and Saskatoon among small cities (Marchington 2011:32).

The Conflict Perspective

Analysts using a conflict framework believe that population and environmental problems have less to do with overpopulation and shortages of resources than with power differentials in societies and in the larger global economy. For example, early conflict theorists, such as Karl Marx and Friedrich Engels (1848/1976), did not think that the food supply was threatened by overpopulation because agricultural technology (even in their era) could meet the food needs of the growing world population, if it were not for poverty. According to Marx and Engels (1848/1976), poverty exists because workers are exploited by capitalists. They argued, for example, that poverty existed in England because the capitalists skimmed off some of the workers' wages as profits. Thus, the labour of the working classes was used by capitalists to earn profits, which, in turn, were used to purchase machinery that could replace the workers rather than supply food. From this classical Marxist point of view, population growth is encouraged by capitalists who use unemployed workers (the industrial reserve army) to keep other workers from demanding higher wages or better working conditions.

According to contemporary conflict theorists, corporations and the government are the two main power institutions in society. As a result, when economic decisions made by members of the capitalist class and elite political leaders lead to environmental problems, the costs are externalized, or passed along to the people (Cable and Cable 1995:13):

> [The externalization of environmental costs of production] . . . means that the costs of production's negative impact on the environment (for example, the expense of cleaning polluted water to make it suitable for drinking) are not included in the price of the product. The company neither pays for the privilege of polluting the water nor cleans it; it saves the cost of proper waste disposal and makes environmentally conscious competition impossible. Not even the consumer of the product pays the

environmental costs of production directly. Rather, the public at large essentially subsidizes the company, by either paying for the cleanup of the environment or enduring degraded environmental quality.

Another conflict approach uses an *environmental justice framework,* examining how class affects the struggle for scarce environmental resources. Of particular interest to these theorists is what we call **environmental classism, which occurs when a disproportionate number of hazardous facilities are present in areas with large proportions of poor people (measured by low-income cut-offs).** Hazardous facilities include waste disposal and treatment plants and chemical plants (Schneider 1993). PollutionWatch (2008) combined maps of poverty areas and air pollutants in Toronto from 2005 data. Areas with poverty rates above the national average of 11.8 show a disproportionate number of sources of air pollution from the National Pollutant Release Inventory (NPRI).

The Interactionist Perspective

Since interactionists take a microlevel approach, viewing society as the sum of all people's interactions, they look at environmental problems in terms of individuals' social construction of reality.

According to sociologist John A. Hannigan (1995), environmental claims-makers assemble, present, and contest the claims they make about various environmental problems. To gain public attention and support, the claims must be newsworthy, have scientific credibility, and get past various interests. It is helpful to have:

- supporters who span science and media, such as David Suzuki, the award-winning scientist (the UN Environmental Medal and many honorary degrees), host of the CBC program *The Nature of Things*, and author of many books concerned with the environment;
- incentives for change, such as better health; and
- sustaining support by major international organizations, such as the United Nations. (Hannigan 1995)

Having institutional support can lead to the creation of international protocols, like the Kyoto Protocol for global warming, though it cannot guarantee full international cooperation.

The social construction approach also helps us understand people's labelling of the estimation of environmental risk and their response to different kinds of communication. A dramatic example of this is Greenpeace's labelling of the oil sands. Greenpeace has labelled them the "tar sands," and ranked them as the fifth worst example of pollution on earth after coal expansion in China, Australia, the United States, and oil exploration in the Arctic (Greenpeace 2013).

Feminist Perspectives

Two strands of feminist theorizing in population and the environment are *women's agency* and *ecofeminism*. Regarding overpopulation, the relationship between women's literacy and fertility is well established. Higher-educated women have fewer children, not only in developed countries, but also in developing countries. While the fertility rate in India is over 3.0, the rate in Kerala, a state in which women are well educated and participate in the labour force, is below replacement level at 1.7 (Sen 1999:199). Thus, encouraging women's education and participation in the labour force would contribute to both women's well-being and the reduction of fertility rates.

The term *ecofeminism* was coined by French writer Françoise d'Eaubonne, who thought that men's oppression of women and of the environment were two components of the same phenomenon (Eckersley 2001). Ecofeminists believe that women are more nurturing, cooperative, and conservation-minded than men, and point to the term "Mother Nature" to support the general acceptance of women as being closer to nature. The viewpoint that women have a unique capacity to construct a new approach to the environment is combined with activism (Mies and Shiva 1993).

An example of ecofeminism was the 1993 protest against clear-cutting a temperate rainforest at Clayoquot Sound on Vancouver Island, British Columbia. It was organized by women and ranks as the second largest example of civil disobedience in Canada. News of the protest spread worldwide, and cutting was stopped. Since that time, members of environmental groups and Indigenous groups have worked with logging companies, including the Indigenous-run Iisaak Forest Resources. It has produced positive results according to the high grade in the Conference Board of Canada's Report Card (see above).

POPULATION AND THE ENVIRONMENT IN THE FUTURE

The problems we have considered in this section include some of the greatest challenges that humans face in the 21st century. Global overpopulation and environmental depletion and devastation have irreversible consequences, and actions taken—or not taken—today will be with us far into the future. Futurists believe that we must use a wide-angle lens to examine population and environmental concerns (Petersen 1994). We must see the world and our role in it in a much different way than we

did in the past. We must understand that environmental issues are *security* issues—as much as a terrorist threat or a missile or bomb (Petersen 1994). Once we understand that, we will think of environmental problems in a completely different light. For example, to eliminate the global threats posed by overpopulation and environmental degradation, all societies can make the following changes (based on Petersen 1994:109).

- Reduce the use of energy.
- Shift from fossil fuels to solar-based energy systems or other energy-efficient systems such as water power, wind power, or geothermal energy.
- Develop new transportation networks and city designs that reduce automobile use.
- Push for equality between women and men in all nations, emphasizing literacy training, educational opportunities, and health care (including reproduction and contraception information) for women.
- Effect a rapid transition to smaller families.
- Cooperate internationally to reduce the consumption of resources by wealthy nations and bring higher living standards to poorer nations.

Are these changes likely to occur? Not if people in high- and middle-income nations adhere to their current belief systems. Some social analysts think that it will take a threatening event—a drastic change in the earth's weather patterns or a sudden increase in natural disasters—to capture the attention of enough of the earth's people and convince political leaders that a serious change in direction is required if the planet is to continue to support human life. We can only hope that people will not wait until it's too late.

WHAT CAN YOU DO?

For this cause, there is no shortage of opportunities to do something. Here are a few places to start for the environment:

- Visit the Biosphere, Environment Museum which highlights a great many activities: Spaceship Earth, Arctic, the Turning Point, Biokits, etc. for various kinds of projects. The education site is under review. But this site can be visited http://ec.gc.ca/biosphere/default. asp?lang=En&n=3C2E8507-1
- Lobby members of parliament, by yourself or with others, to encourage them to take action to protect the environment.
- Join with others to change energy use (e.g., urge people to stop idling their cars).

Here are some things you can do for cities:

- If you live in a city, you might join your local residents' association. These associations are always looking for volunteer help for committees, to undertake liaison with the police, to have representatives for every street in the area, to keep track of problems like drug dealing and prostitution, and to undertake social projects. Be aware that some of the members of some of these groups are more concerned with enhancing the value of their properties than with solving social problems in the area and may seek to reduce local shelters and social agencies.

• If you are searching for a place to live and like the idea of working with your neighbours, try cooperative housing. You will gain a great experience working with others.

• Join a group lobbying for the homeless. Public interest research groups are found on many university and college campuses, and some, like the Ontario Public Interest Research Group in Toronto, support action to help the homeless.

• Participate in regular programs to plant trees or clean up your neighbourhood.

• Sit in on a city council meeting so you can learn more about the activities and governance of a city, meet other interested citizens, and lobby your councillor or mayor.

SUMMARY

What Is the Global Population? Why Is Population Growth a Problem?

The world's population is more than 7 billion now; it doubled in the past 50 years and, if this trend continues, could increase by 50 percent in the next 50 years. Can the earth's resources support this rapid population growth?

What Are the Primary Factors that Affect Population Growth?

Three factors affect population growth: fertility, the actual number of children born to an individual or population; mortality, the number of deaths that occur in a specific population; and migration, the movement of people from one geographic area to another for the purpose of changing residency.

How Does Population Growth Affect a Society?

Population growth affects population composition—the biological and social characteristics of a population, including such attributes as age, sex, racialization, marital status, education, occupation, income, and size of household. In Canada, for example, the age distribution of the population affects the need for schools, employment opportunities, health care, and age-appropriate housing.

What Are the Major Theoretical Perspectives on Overpopulation?

According to the Malthusian perspective, population expands geometrically while the food supply increases arithmetically; disaster can be averted through positive checks (e.g., famine, disease, war) or preventive checks (e.g., sexual abstinence, delayed marriage). The neo-Malthusians believe that the earth is a ticking bomb because population problems exacerbate environmental problems. The third perspective is more hopeful. According to demographic transition theory, societies move from high birth and death rates to low birth and death rates as a result of technological development. However, critics say that demographic transition theory applies chiefly to Western societies.

What Solutions Do We Have to World Hunger?

Two of the most far-reaching initiatives are the green revolution (the growing of high-yield "miracle" crops) and the

biotechnological revolution, which involves "improving" plants or animals or using micro-organisms in innovative ways. However, some social analysts believe that the solution is not to produce more food, but rather to control fertility.

How Is Immigration Changing the Population Composition of Canada?

Today, the proportion of immigrants in the Canadian population is about 20 percent and most new immigrants are visible minorities. If immigration continues at the present rate, visible minorities will account for 60 percent of the major cities by 2031. (Canada is otherwise below zero population growth—a stable population.) Immigration could lead to higher taxes and problems of cultural cohesion, but it also brings substantial economic and cultural benefits.

How Did Urbanization Come About?

Urbanization—the process by which an increasing proportion of a population lives in cities rather than rural areas—began with industrialization. Before the Industrial Revolution, most people lived in sparsely populated rural areas, where they farmed. Industrialization led to the growth of cities, and urbanization brought about profound changes in societies and spawned new social problems, such as housing shortages, overcrowding, unsanitary conditions, environmental pollution, and crime.

How Did Mass Suburbanization Occur? What Were the Results?

Mass suburbanization began with government efforts to correct the housing shortage that followed World War II. The Central (now Canada) Mortgage and Housing Corporation contributed to the building of half a million homes between 1946 and 1951 by granting mortgages. Other factors included the availability of inexpensive land, low-cost mass construction methods, new federally financed highway systems, inexpensive gasoline, and consumer demand for single-family homes on individually owned lots. Mass suburbanization brought about a dramatic shift in the distribution of the Canadian population and set up an ongoing economic division of interests between cities and suburbs. The movement appears to be reversing now, with people filling downtown condominiums to be closer to work and/or leisure activities.

Why Are Many Cities in Fiscal Crisis?

Cities do not have regular sources of income such as income or sales taxes. They have taxes on property values, which can vary widely over time; levies, such as service fees; and a portion of gas taxes. They have a wide variety of services to provide, from social services to transportation. Many middle- and upper-income people have moved back into the central cities, but this does not compensate for increased needs. Moreover, suburbanites who regularly use city services do not pay taxes to the city to keep up these services.

Why Is There a Housing Shortage in Canada? What Is Being Done about It?

A major reason for the housing shortage is that Canada has yet to find a way to provide safe, livable, low-income housing. In addition, as part of governmental cutbacks in the mid-1990s, the federal and provincial governments stopped building social housing. Now they have increased the building of social housing, but it is never enough. Some nongovernmental groups have been doing good work. Among the most successful initiatives for creating affordable housing are developments like St. Lawrence and Regent Park in Toronto.

How Great a Problem Is Homelessness? Are There Any Solutions?

Accurate data on the actual number of the homeless are extremely difficult to get because homeless people typically avoid interviews with census-takers and social researchers. A recent study in Toronto puts its homeless population at over 5000 people. Most experts agree that any long-term, successful solution to homelessness must take structural factors into account, especially low-income housing and mental-health care.

Does Residential Racialized or Ethnic Segregation Exist?

Spatial separation of the poor and non-poor is greater than separation of racialized/ethnic groups. While, in contrast to U.S. cities, there are no extensive areas of blight, decay, or abandoned housing in Canadian cities, pockets of poor racialized/ethnic groups coexist beside upscale neighbourhoods.

What Are the Major Problems in Global Cities?

In 2013, one out of every two people in the world lived in a city. Increasing population accounts for two-thirds of the new urban growth, and rural-to-urban migration accounts for the rest. Rapid urban growth brings a wide variety of problems, including overcrowding, environmental pollution, and the disappearance of farmland.

What Is the Functionalist Perspective on Urban Problems?

Functionalists believe that today's urban problems are the result of mass migration from rural areas during the Industrial Revolution, large-scale immigration in the 20th

and early 21st centuries, and mass suburbanization though now that appears to be reversing. One solution is to create regional governments.

What Is the Conflict Perspective on Urban Problems?

Conflict theorists believe that cities grow or decline according to decisions made by capitalists and the political elite. In other words, these theorists use a political economy model. Urban problems can be reduced through political activism and organized resistance to oppressive conditions.

What Is the Interactionist Perspective on Urban Problems?

Interactionists look at how people subjectively experience urban life. According to German sociologist Georg Simmel, urban life is so stimulating that people have no choice but to become somewhat insensitive to people and events around them. On the other hand, urban living gives people opportunities for individualism and autonomy. Sociologist Louis Wirth expanded on Simmel's ideas, saying that urbanism produces feelings of alienation and powerlessness. Herbert Gans concluded from his research that city life is a pleasure for some and a nightmare for others. Commenting on Toronto and Vancouver, Richard Florida states these cities have a high rate of Creative Class people because of the stimulation and tolerance in these cities and are a key to a bright economic future. A way to avoid the nightmare of alienation is to develop subcultural ties.

What Is the Feminist Perspective on Urban Problems?

Feminist theorists emphasize the occupational opportunities, freedom from scrutiny, and convenience of short distances between work and home that allow fulfillment of multiple roles for women.

What Is Environmental Degradation? What Are Its Causes?

Environmental degradation is caused by disruptions to the environment that have negative consequences for ecosystems. Human beings, particularly as they pursue economic development and growth, cause environmental degradation.

What Are the Major Sources of Air Pollution? What Are Its Effects?

The major sources of fossil fuel pollution are transportation and industry. One of the most serious consequences of air pollution is the greenhouse effect, an environmental condition caused by excessive quantities of carbon dioxide, methane, and nitrous oxide in the atmosphere, leading to global warming. Another is depletion of the ozone layer, the part of the earth's atmosphere that absorbs dangerous ultraviolet radiation from the sun. Although the great reductions in the use of CFCs may prevent serious depletion, the already present CFCs will continue to adversely affect the ozone layer.

What Water, Soil, and Forest Problems Do We Face?

Water is increasingly scarce throughout parts of the world, and water pollution further diminishes the available water supply. However, desertification is greatest in middle- and low-income nations.

Why Are Solid, Toxic/Hazardous, and Nuclear Wastes a Problem?

High-income nations are running out of space for the amount of solid waste produced by their "disposable societies." Toxic/hazardous waste (hazardous chemical by-products of industry) causes death and disease if it is not disposed of properly. Nuclear, or radioactive, waste is a problem because of the length of time it remains deadly.

What Is the Functionalist Perspective on Population and the Environment?

Functionalists say that the latent dysfunctions of technology cause environmental problems, but that new technologies can solve these problems. Most functionalists take a neo-Malthusian perspective on population but believe that social institutions, especially education and the government, can cooperate to solve population and environmental problems.

What Is the Conflict Perspective on Population and the Environment?

In the classical Marxist view, there would be enough food for all people if poverty were alleviated; poverty exists because capitalists skim workers' wages for profits. Contemporary conflict theorists believe that the two main power institutions in society—corporations and the government—make economic decisions that result in environmental problems.

What Is the Interactionist Perspective on Population and Environment?

Interactionists see population and environmental problems in microlevel—individual—terms. Social constructionists show how environmental claims-makers assemble, present, and contest the claims they make about various environmental problems. Sometimes scary scenarios are created, and those who challenge this definition of reality are dismissed as wishful thinkers. Social contructionists can also help us understand people's estimation of environmental risk.

What Is the Feminist Perspective on Population and the Environment?

Feminists emphasize the importance of promoting women's literacy and participation in the labour force to help control fertility. Ecofeminism emphasizes that patriarchy is the root cause of the oppression of women and of nature. Living off the backs of others and living beyond ecological means are both unsupportable.

KEY TERMS

acid rain, p. 329
core nations, p. 323
deindustrialization, p. 319
demographic transition theory, p. 312
demography, p. 309
desertification, p. 334
edge city, p. 318

environmental classism, p. 338
environmental degradation, p. 327
fertility, p. 310
gentrification, p. 320
greenhouse effect, p. 330
mechanical solidarity, p. 324
megalopolis, p. 318
migration, p. 311

mortality, p. 310
organic solidarity, p. 324
peripheral nations, p. 323
population composition, p. 311
semi-peripheral nations, p. 323
subculture, p. 326
zero population growth, p. 315

QUESTIONS FOR CRITICAL THINKING

1. Which perspective on population growth do you favour—neo-Malthusian or demographic transition theory—and why?

2. Where do you live—in a core central city, an edge city, a suburb, or a megalopolis? What examples from your everyday life can you give that relate to the problems described in this chapter? Which sociological perspective do you think best explains the urban problems you observe?

3. The government has so far failed to eliminate homelessness. What new initiatives can you suggest?

4. The 2011 census releases include tables on various characteristics of cities, including age and sex distribution, family structures, and income percentages. You can download data from your city from Statistics Canada's website. Using various demographic variables, write a social study of your area.

5. If you had to focus on a single aspect of environmental degradation—air pollution; water, soil, or forest problems; or solid, toxic, or nuclear waste disposal—which would it be, and why? What would you do to make people aware of the seriousness of the problem? What new solutions could you propose?

6. Is it possible to have development without environmental degradation?

Dev Carr/Getty Images

Global Social Problems: War and Terrorism

With the collapse of the former Soviet Union and the end of the Cold War between the United States and the former Soviet bloc in the 1980s, prospects for world peace were bright. This hope was challenged in 2001 by the attacks on the twin towers in New York and the Pentagon and by the United States' declaration of sustained war against nations that harbour terrorists. The war was mandated to expand anywhere in the world, beginning with Afghanistan, and has been fought with the participation of several other allied nations, including Canada. In 2003, Iraq was invaded by the United States, which maintained that the Iraqi government, with its supposed *weapons of mass destruction (WMD)*—**nuclear, biological, chemical, or radiological weapons that can kill thousands of people and destroy vast amounts of property at one time**—and potential for terrorist activity, posed a threat to the world. In spite of extensive searches for the so-called weapons of mass destruction, the U.S. government was forced to concede that these weapons did not exist and that Saddam Hussein did not in fact have links to al-Qaeda (McQuaig 2006). Canada did not participate in that war, but it did send troops to Afghanistan. The U.S. fighting against terror is still very active in the Middle East, though it is continually taking on new forms and directions. The United States and Canada have withdrawn most fighting troops from Afghanistan, but the United States had retained about 10 000 troops by the end of 2014, and continues to attack targets using drones (see Military Technology below).

In August 2014, with the victories the Islamic State (IS) in Iraq (also called ISIS—Islamic State of Iraq and Syria, and sometimes called ISIL—Islamic State of Iraq and the Levant), a Sunni terrorist group that wishes to create a caliphate in Iraq and Syria, the United States sent advisors back to Iraq. With Canada's and other nations' help, the United States began bombing IS targets to help the Kurds and Iraqis to (in President Obama's words) "degrade and defeat IS." The United States also plans to supply arms to Lebanon. In early 2015, Canada indicated that it would extend its original six-month mission, and it is now uncertain how long this war will last.

WAR AS A SOCIAL PROBLEM

What is war? *War* **is organized, armed conflict between nations or distinct political factions.** Most people think of war as armed conflict between two countries or two factions within a country, such as the U.S. invasion of the St. Lawrence region of Quebec in 1775, the German invasion of Poland in 1939, or the Korean War of 1950. But social scientists define *war* more broadly, including not only *declared* wars between nations or parties, but also *undeclared* wars, civil and guerrilla wars, covert operations, and some forms of terrorism. To social scientists, *general warfare* refers to violent armed conflict between nations, whereas *regional warfare* refers to conflict between rival factions located within a specific geographic area.

According to these definitions, a large number of wars and insurgencies are currently taking place throughout much of the world. Various continents have many countries, and within them militias, guerrillas, separatist groups, and anarchic groups, involved in war. For example, as of 2014:

- Africa has 24 wars and 146 insurgencies respectively;
- Asia has 15 and 127 respectively;
- Europe has 8 and 70 respectively;
- Middle East has 8 and 168 respectively; and
- Americas have 5 and 25 (including drug cartels) respectively.

The result is a total of 61 wars and 537 other conflicts between militias–guerrillas, separatist groups, and anarchic groups (Wars in the World 2014).

Social scientists also say that societies that are prepared at all times for war possess a *war system*—**components of social institutions (e.g., the economy, government, and education) and cultural beliefs and practices that promote the development of warriors, weapons, and war as a normal part of the society and its foreign policy** (Cancian and Gibson 1990).

The 20th century saw the development of advanced technologies that provided new potential for wars that could be far more deadly than those in the past, and this development continues into the 21st century. While the stockpile of nuclear weapons from the arms race between the former Soviet Union and the West has been reduced, the remaining warheads, including those from other countries (such as Israel, India, and Pakistan, and, perhaps soon, Iran), vastly increase the potential for waging war on a massive scale.

This chapter will examine some of the characteristics of war and terrorism and look at Canada's role in past and upcoming conflicts. We will examine some of the consequences of war and terrorism and look at possible explanations for seeing war and terrorism as a solution to global conflicts. Finally, we will look at resistance and prospects for peace and discuss the roles and effectiveness of citizens' groups in opposing war and terrorism in the 21st century.

How, then, do social scientists define *peace*? Sociologists Francesca M. Cancian and James William Gibson (1990) believe that peace is a less clearly defined concept than war. Cancian and Gibson note that people generally agree that peace is highly desirable, but they often have different ideas of what constitutes peace. Some equate peace with harmonious relations in a world where there is no bloodshed between groups; but sometimes nations equate peace with prevailing in battle (Gibson and Cancian 1990). Despite the problems associated with distinguishing between war and peace, we can conclude that both consist of actions and beliefs held by people like ourselves, and that these actions and beliefs have serious consequences for individuals, groups, and nations.

THE CHARACTERISTICS OF WAR

First and foremost, war is an institution that involves *violence*—behaviour intended to bring pain, physical injury, psychological stress, and/or death to people or to harm or destroy property. Violence occurs on both micro and macro levels. As we have seen, violence is a component of many social problems, including violent crime and sexual assault. Both of these are forms of *interpersonal violence* and typically involve a relatively small number of people who are responding to a particular situation or who are pursuing their own personal goals. In contrast, war is a form of **collective violence that involves organized violence by people seeking to promote their cause or resist social policies or practices that they consider harmful, oppressive, and unjust.**

War is an abstract concept for many Canadians. It is less abstract for those who have experienced combat, or who are friends and family members of people who have experienced it, or who are survivors of war. Early in Canada's history, during the fighting of civil wars and rebellions, war was much less abstract: it took place at home or close to home. But in the 20th and 21st centuries, military action was transformed: wars were now fought on foreign soil and vastly more Canadian military personnel were sent into combat. In World War I, for example, Canada, with a population of 8 million people, sent 418 000 of them overseas to fight. In World War II, Canada entered the war with an entirely Canadian command and forces. At that time, Canada had a population of 12 million people, and 1.1 million of them were in uniform. Of these people, 45 000 people gave their lives and another 55 000 were wounded (Veterans Affairs Canada 2014).

The two world wars were different from each other in a very significant way. In World War I, killing civilians was considered unduly violent, but in World War II civilians were killed intentionally. The targeting of civilians during World War II using air power added a new dimension (Hynes 1997). In 2001, terrorists with ties to al-Qaeda used a different form of "air power"—hijacking commercial airplanes and destroying the New York twin towers and part of the Pentagon—to bring war and terror to the United States, intentionally killing over 2000 people in the process. But the subsequent wars in Afghanistan and Iraq took place on foreign soil.

Following World War II, Canada emerged as a leading "middle power"—assuming the role of peacekeeper and negotiator in international disputes. This was a natural extension for Canada, as the protocol from 1909 to 1946 was that the prime minister also served as the Canadian Secretary of State for External Affairs. Canadian prime ministers have maintained that tradition and have endeavoured to remain prominent in international affairs, taking part in visits from foreign heads of state, world tours, treaty negotiations, and other activities. Until recently, some viewed Canada as a "moral superpower"—one that exercised a "soft power" when it came to world affairs. Since 1956, Canada has sent peacekeeping forces into operations around the world. Soldiers, police, and civilians have all played prominent roles in separating armies and in the resolution of conflicts in places such as Cypress, the Middle East, Haiti, Bosnia, Cambodia, El Salvador, and Angola, almost three dozen in total. However, more than 160 Canadians have been killed while on peacekeeping duties around the world in 2007, and operations in Somalia and Rwanda led to a crisis of confidence in the Canadian military's peacekeeping efforts. In Somalia in 1993, as part of a United Nations humanitarian effort, members of Canada's elite Airborne Regiment brutally and fatally tortured a Somali teen, 16-year-old Shidane Arone, who they had taken captive. They documented the hours-long torture with photos, marring the international reputation of Canadian soldiers as peacekeepers. Two other unarmed Somali teens were shot in the back by the regiment just days before that murder. The whistleblower was a physician, Major Barry Armstrong. The Airborne Regiment was disbanded after an official inquiry in 1995 (CBC Digital Archives 2009; O'Reilly 1998).

At approximately the same time, UN peacekeeping forces were also stationed in Rwanda, under the leadership of Canadian Brigadier General Romeo Dallaire. The 1993–1994 mission to Rwanda has been nearly unanimously described as "doomed" and as a "failure" of humanity to support the United Nations (Barris 2009). UN peacekeepers managed to save tens of thousands of lives, but could only stand by as 1 million more were massacred in the violent civil war. Dallaire had requested 5000 additional soldiers from the UN, but instead had forces cut to 450: "The explosion of genocide could have been prevented. If the political will had been there and if we had been better skilled. . . it could have been prevented" (Veterans Affairs Canada 2009; Barris 2009:26).

Canada's role in armed conflicts seems to have been shifting over the past two decades. From 1956 to 1992, Canada was usually the single largest contributor to UN peace missions. For example, in 1991, approximately 1150 Canadian soldiers were involved in UN peacekeeping missions. However, by the fall of 2006, only 55 of the 100 000 UN peacekeepers were Canadian (LaBerge 2008). Recently Canada has ranked 57th, giving only 11 military personnel and 16 police officers to peacekeeping efforts (Byers 2014). Canada's state of peace relative to the other countries of the world is discussed in The Global Peace Index (Box 16.1).

According to Ehrenreich (1997), the end of World War II was marked by the U.S. government's declaration of itself as the "leader of the free world." The ideology supporting this pronouncement gave the nation's political and economic leaders the impetus to perpetuate the United States' position as a world military superpower. Since that time, the American Congress has established defence spending as a national priority, and the U.S. *military–industrial complex*—**a term referring to the interdependence of the military establishment and private military contractors**—that emerged during World War II has become a massive industrial infrastructure that today produces an array of war-related goods, such as uniforms, tanks, airplanes, and warships. This military–industrial complex flourished during the 1950s, when the international arms race brought about what became known as the *Cold War*—a conflict between nations based on military preparedness and the threat of war but not actual warfare. Between 1950 and the mid-1990s, the U.S. government responded to the perceived "Soviet threat" by spending approximately US$10.2 trillion for its arms buildup. Now, at $645.7 billion, the U.S. defence budget is still the largest in the world, equal to more than the next dozen countries' defence budgets combined (*The Economist* 2014:102).

THE CONSEQUENCES OF WAR

The primary direct effects of war are loss of human life and serious physical and psychological harm to survivors. It is impossible to determine how many human lives have been lost in wars throughout human history. Were we to attempt to do so, we would need a more precise definition of what constitutes war, and we would have to

Brigadier General Romeo Dallaire
Patrick Robert/Sygma/Corbis

Social Problems in Global Perspective

Box 16.1

The Global Peace Index (GPI)

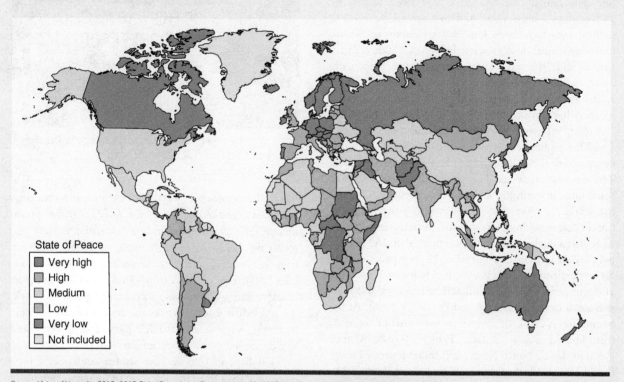

State of Peace
- Very high
- High
- Medium
- Low
- Very low
- Not included

Source: *Vision of Humanity, 2015, 2015 Global Peace Index.* Retrieved June 28, 2015 (http://www.visionofhumanity.org/#/page/our-gpi-findings).

The GPI measures peace in 162 countries according to 22 qualitative and quantitative indicators of the absence of violence and fear of violence, e.g., percentage of GDP devoted to military expenditure, homicides/100 000 population, access to small weapons, number of security officers and police/100 000 population, and proportion of population in jail. Since 2008, the world has become less peaceful. For example, 78 countries have become less peaceful (e.g., Libya and Ukraine) and 81 countries have become more peaceful (e.g., Guinea Bissau, Cote d'Ivoire, Egypt, and Benin). Europe is the most peaceful region, with small, stable democracies like Iceland and Denmark the most peaceful. Canada ranks very high, placing 7th of 162 countries. The United States ranks in the middle, placing 94th of 162 countries. The bottom three countries are Iraq, Afghanistan, and Syria. It is estimated that the total economic impact of containing violence is equivalent to 13.4 percent of global GDP, or US$14.3 trillion.

Questions for Consideration

1. Russia and China are pressuring areas outside their borders like Ukraine (where Russia has annexed Crimea) and South China Sea (where China is building islands to take advantage of the 200 mile limit in water for sovereignty. What should Western countries do about this, if anything?

2. Can the West do anything about the internal conflict in Syria, which is creating a huge number of refugees, when it supports neither a brutal dictator (Assad) nor the insurgents supported by Hamas and Iran? How can the United States contribute to the degrading and defeating of IS without putting "boots on the ground"?

3. With so many countries having nuclear weapons, is there any point in advocating a nuclear weapon free world, or even zones?

assume that there would always be survivors available to count the dead (Hynes 1997).

Despite these difficulties, social analyst Ruth Sivard (1991; 1993) has tackled the problem in a limited way. She determined that 589 wars have been fought by 142 countries since 1500, and that approximately 142 million lives have been lost. But according to Sivard, more lives were lost in wars during the 20th century than in all of the other centuries combined. Since early 2002, when the Canadian military was deployed to Afghanistan, 158 Canadian soldiers, a diplomat, and aid workers have been killed (Staff 2014:Day of Honour). But many thousands of Afghanis were also killed.

The consequences of all these wars pale when compared to the consequences of an all-out nuclear war. The devastation would be beyond description. Today, some nuclear warheads held by governments throughout the world are more than 4000 times as powerful as the bombs that were dropped on Japan. In fact, scientists estimate that a nuclear war would kill more than 160 million people outright, and that more than 1 billion people would die in the first few hours as a result of radiation poisoning, environmental contamination and destruction, and massive social unrest (Friedman and Friedman 1996). At the beginning of 2014, those nations with nuclear weapons (the United States, Britain, France, Russia, China, Pakistan, Israel, North Korea, and India) possessed more than 17 000 nuclear warheads (Ploughshares Fund 2014).

Even though an international treaty bans underground nuclear tests, it is believed that a number of nations are developing and stockpiling nuclear weapons. The idea that "others" may be secretly building and stockpiling weapons and the inability to substantiate such claims reliably provided the rationale for the 2003 U.S.-led invasion of Iraq. At that time, the Bush Administration claimed that the regime of Iraqi President Saddam Hussein was in possession of weapons of mass destruction and had to be overthrown as a preemptive measure to protect the United States and other nations. When no weapons of mass destruction were found in Iraq, extensive public debate occurred and much criticism of the Bush Administration followed for having inaccurately represented the scope and immediacy of the threat posed (Moeller 2004).

Civilians are not the only ones adversely affected by war. Veterans Affairs Canada provides benefits to veterans who served in wars in which Canada has been involved. Many of these veterans are totally disabled, and not all injuries sustained in wars are physical. We have no accurate count of the soldiers and civilians—of all nations—who experience psychological trauma that affects them the remainder of their lives. One psychological disorder

What justifications are sufficient to support a war in which the final death toll is almost certain to include millions of children?

Jeff Malet Photography/Newscom

that has been getting a great deal of attention in recent years is known as *post-traumatic stress disorder* (PTSD). Symptoms include difficulty sleeping and concentrating, anxiety, and recurring flashbacks or nightmares, many of which are triggered by loud, sudden noises such as thunder, automobiles backfiring, or other things that sound like gunshots or explosions. When some stimulus triggers a flashback, the individual re-experiences the horror of some deeply traumatic wartime event. High rates of drug abuse and suicide among war veterans are attributed to PTSD.

Civilians in Canada have shown evidence of high levels of PTSD from participating in military operations; for example, medical staff and war correspondents suffer from the effects of witnessing death and destruction. Many of the artists commissioned to paint the World War I and II canvasses also suffered deep depression and other emotional side-effects upon returning from the wars (Abbott 2000). PTSD, however, is most documented among war vets and peacekeepers. In Canada, 20 percent of peacekeeping troops are believed to have the symptoms. Consider, for example, the psychological effects experienced by General Romeo Dallaire, the UN commander in Rwanda, who left that country shaken and went on indefinite sick leave. He reported not being able to cope for a couple of years, unable to sleep, and sometimes wished that he had lost a limb instead of having PTSD because it is easier to explain and gain the support needed. He even suggested he was becoming suicidal. He also encouraged those with this problem to get help because they could become a danger to themselves and others (CBC TV 1999).

While we cannot put a price tag on loss of life, physical disability, or psychological trauma associated with war, we know that the direct economic costs of war are astronomical. The cost to Canada of the Afghanistan war has been estimated at $28 billion (Howell 2011). (It is interesting to consider that that amount of money would provide four years of tuition for about one million Canadians.) Stiglitz and Bilmes (2008) report the total budgetary cost of the Iraq War (operations plus veterans' benefits and other military expenses) is realistically estimated to be US$2.655 trillion. In 2012, Canada's military spending budget was $22.5 billion, about 15th on the list of military spending.

War on Ecology

Ecological and human health is an important aspect of military activity. Landscapes and human bodies reveal a great deal about the long-term effects of violence, toxicity, and invasions. As images of ecological devastation and human suffering around the world are depicted in mainstream media, it is becoming more and more difficult to ignore these issues. People are also recognizing that, in this global era, citizens and their economies, health, and environments are interconnected. In a brief to the International Peace Bureau (IPB) in Geneva, Disarmament Coordinator for the Bureau David Hay-Edie advised that military activities place a number of stresses on the physical environment, but their contribution to overall environmental deterioration has not received its share of attention (2002:2).

To illustrate Hay-Edie's concerns, consider that the world's military forces are responsible for more than two-thirds of the chlorofluorocarbon-113 released into the ozone layer. If the Iraq War was ranked as a nation in terms of emissions, it would emit more CO_2 annually than 139 nations—the equivalent of 25 million more cars on the road in the United States in one year (Reisch and Kretzmann 2008). How much CO_2 was produced during the war? At the outset of the Iraq War in March 2003, the U.S. Army estimated it would need more than 40 million gallons of gasoline for three weeks of combat, exceeding the total quantity used by all Allied forces in the four years of WWII. Among the army's weapons, the 2000M-1 Abram's tanks burn 250 gallons of fuel per hour. The U.S. Air Force is the single largest consumer of jet fuel in the world:

- The F-4 Phantom Fighter burns more than 1600 gallons of jet fuel per hour and peaks at 14 400 gallons per hour at supersonic speeds.
- The B-52 Stratocruiser, with eight jet engines, consumes 500 gallons per minute, and 10 minutes of flight uses as much fuel as the average driver does in one year of driving.

A quarter of the world's jet fuel powers the U.S. fleet of jets; in 2006, they consumed as much fuel as U.S.

planes did during the Second World War (1941–1945), an astounding 2.6 billion gallons (Hynes 2011). Between 2003 and 2007, the war produced at least 141 million metric tons of carbon dioxide equivalent (CO_2e), more each year of the war than 139 of the world's countries release annually (Hynes 2011).

Other kinds of warfare include chemical and biological warfare. The use of chemical and biological warfare—such as scorched-earth tactics, "Agent Orange," and other toxic materials believed to be linked to the disorder called Gulf War syndrome—are all examples of the long-term impacts these weapons have. In Vietnam, for example, about one-third of the country was rendered a wasteland by military activity. It will take many generations to repair these agricultural areas. In the Gulf War, 4 to 8 million barrels of oil spilled into the sea, damaging 740 kilometres of coastline—creating an inestimable loss for generations to come. Air attacks in Kuwait and during the NATO military action in Kosovo and the Federal Republic of Yugoslavia have destroyed oil refineries and caused the leakage of oil products and chemicals into lands, rivers, lakes, and oceans (Hay-Edie 2002). The U.S.-led attack on Iraq damaged their water and sewage systems as well as the nation's fragile desert ecosystem. Additionally, oil well fires spewed smoke across the countryside (Institute for Policy Studies and Foreign Policy in Focus 2004). These actions have devastated the integrity of drinking water, arable land, yards, school grounds, and public parks, as well as natural habitats and ecological reserves.

As humans and the earth are connected, toxic attacks on the earth are equally damaging to humans. One particularly potent hazard to human and ecological health is depleted uranium—a waste product that arises during the production of enriched uranium for nuclear weapons and reactors. This very dense material has the capability

War can have disastrous ecological effects.
Yahya Ahmed/AP Images

of slicing through heavily armoured vehicles. Seventy percent of the uranium burns on impact, turning into a fine ceramic dust of depleted uranium oxide particles that get distributed across great distances by wind and water activity. One of the most devastating aspects about this compound is that it has a radioactive half-life of 4.5 billion years. Environmental educator Guy Dauncey (2003:1) states this means that the cities, battlefields, and locations where depleted uranium is used will remain radioactive for the next 4.5 billion years, which is as long as the earth has existed.

Depleted uranium was used by the U.S. army in Iraq, in Kosovo, and in Afghanistan. Even though the United Nations wants a worldwide ban on it, reports indicate that the United States used it in its war against Iraq: "U.S.-fired depleted uranium weapons have contributed to pollution of Iraq's land and water, with inevitable spillover effects in other countries" like Iraq, Iran, and Kuwait (Dauncey 2003:1; Institute for Policy Studies and Foreign Policy in Focus 2004).

While it is obvious how war can harm the environment, it is likely true that changes in the environment could contribute to the emergence of conflict and war. For example, the drought of the second decade of the 21st century in the Middle East, one of the worst droughts in decades, was devastating to crops in Syria and Iraq (Holthaus 2014). Global warming due to the general increase in CO_2 and the extra CO_2 from the conduct of the war is likely having severe consequences for droughts, crop failure, and movement of farmers to the cities in places like Syria and Iraq, and contributing to their destabilization. While it is difficult to blame the emergence of IS directly on global warming, IS is certainly making matters worse by threatening the water supply now that it controls a dam on Mosul (Holthaus 2014). Thus one could expect a vicious cycle of war contributing to global warming, which in turn causes droughts and other problems that bring about political instability and conflict.

Military Technology and War

War is conducted on the basis of the technology that is available in given societies at a specific point in time. However, wars are not necessarily won or lost on the basis of military technology alone. In the Vietnam War, for example, many factors contributed to the inability of the United States to declare a victory. Similarly, efforts to declare victory when the George W. Bush administration ordered U.S. troops to Iraq to find weapons of mass destruction and remove Saddam Hussein from power were slowed by frequent bombings, assassinations, and a resurgence in violence by various militias.

The most significant military technology is referred to as the **weapons system**, **which comprise a weapons platform (e.g., a ship, aircraft, or tank), a weapon (e.g., a gun, missile, or torpedo), and the means of command and communication** (Kaldor 1981). The importance of the weapons system is pointed out by George Friedman and Meredith Friedman (1996:25): "The rise and fall of strategically significant weapons systems is the history of the rise and fall of nations and epochs. The strategically significant weapon is the one that brings force to bear in such a way that it decisively erodes the war-making capability of the enemy." According to Friedman and Friedman (1996:25–26), the use of strategically significant weapons determines the "winners" and "losers" in war:

> Let us assume that the greatest threat presented by the enemy is the ability to move weapons platforms around quickly, and that by destroying his petrochemical production facilities we could impede his mobility. Strategically significant weapons would be those that would destroy petrochemical plants. So, in World War II, bombers with the range to reach these targets were such weapons. In Vietnam, the enemy's war-making ability could not be decisively crippled by the same sort of long-range bombers. There, the strategic weapon was North Vietnamese infantry, able to move stealthily and impose a rate of attrition on American troops that was politically unacceptable to the United States. The failure to recognize strategically decisive weapons is catastrophic.

In other words, though factors other than military technology may determine a nation's ability to win or lose a war, military technology is a dominant factor.

For example, in the 14th century, Europeans used a simple new technology—black powder, an explosive made from charcoal, sulfur, and saltpeter—to overwhelm larger armies. Black powder could destroy the enemy's walls and other fortifications. When it was discovered that black powder could be exploded at the base of a metal tube and propel a projectile to a target, the gun became the basis of European and Western military power. Gunpowder made it possible for a small number of troops to overwhelm a much larger army that had only non-explosive weapons (Friedman and Friedman 1996).

Although black powder weapons remained the primary type of weaponry for many years, the platform that was used for carrying the weapons changed over time. With the development of such weapons platforms as coal-powered ships, petroleum-driven ships, and railroad locomotives, it became possible to move explosive-based technology virtually anywhere to destroy enemy forces. From the early 1900s to the end of World War II, the battleship, the tank, and the bomber were the primary weapons platforms. Today, the battleship has been replaced by the aircraft carrier, but the tank and the bomber continue to be important sources of weapons transportation.

As the U.S. military sought to enhance traditional weapons platforms to deal with enemy threats, new precision-guided munitions were developed, rendering many of the older ideologies and technologies obsolete, including the concept of the battlefield. No longer do foot soldiers have to engage in skirmishes for war to take place; missiles can be fired from sites located 16 000 kilometres from the target (Friedman and Friedman 1996). Unfortunately, the same technology that makes possible the expanded battlefield brings with it a new system of intelligence that makes global warfare possible. According to Friedman and Friedman (1996:37–38), sensors, guidance systems, satellite communications, and other technologies that make it possible to hit a target 16 000 kilometres away also make it possible for weapons fired from one continent to guide themselves to targets on other continents very quickly and relatively inexpensively:

> The hyperintelligent, hypersonic, long-range projectile. . . . will destroy the old way of making war, while securing the new geopolitical system for generations. Where guns were inaccurate, these projectiles are extraordinarily precise. Where guns must travel to within miles of a target before firing, precision munitions can devastate an enemy from any distance. Where gun/petrochemical technology requires total commitment of resources and mass production, precision munitions require technical skill. The new weaponry places inherent limits on war, both in terms of scope and in terms of damage to unintended targets. The age of total war is at an end and a more limited type of war is at hand.

Clearly, the nature of warfare has changed dramatically over the past century as older technologies have become obsolete, and newer weaponry, such as hyperintelligent projectiles with extraordinary precision, has been introduced. As the nature of warfare continues to evolve in the 21st century, even-newer technologies, such as unmanned aerial vehicles (UAVs) or drones—pilotless aircraft operated by remote control—have been increasingly employed by the U.S. government to track down suspected militants and terrorists in remote, unreachable areas, as well as to strike enemy leaders, troops, and infrastructure. Some drones are unarmed and used primarily for surveillance; others are armed predator drones

that hunt down a target. Drones have a unique ability to fly lower and get better visibility on targets than other kinds of aircraft, and they are uniquely suited for use in high-density, urban areas. UAVs have been employed in nations such as Iraq, Afghanistan, Pakistan, Yemen, Somalia, and Libya.

As drone technology becomes more affordable and accessible, the popularity of drones will probably increase because of their stealth nature, the lack of need for human pilots who may be injured or killed, and the drone's unique ability to stalk an enemy and bring it down before the enemy knows what has happened. For example, the high-flying Global Hawk jet, which is designed to slip through the air at over 18 000 metres and carry cameras and eavesdropping gear, costs a whopping $218 million for each plane, compared with $28 million for the Reaper, the U.S. Air Force's largest armed drone (Drew 2011). The Reaper will also be replacing the older U-2 spy planes that were created in the 1950s to monitor nuclear sites in what was then the Soviet Union. Some of these planes are still used for surveillance in North Korea and Iran from outside the borders of those nations (Drew 2011).

Although drones are changing the nature of warfare because they can be remotely piloted, they are not without their critics. Some analysts believe that drones have the potential to invade people's privacy, including citizens who might be observed without being aware that they are under surveillance. A second major criticism involves the deadly effects of armed, predator drones, which may kill only militants and terrorists, but which also produce extensive "collateral damage," a term that refers to civilian casualties and destruction of non-combat-related locations such as private homes, hospitals, schools, and other public property.

According to some experts, the "drone race" is just starting, with about 50 countries using surveillance drones. However, few countries are using armed drones in the same way that the United States does. The involvement of other nations in the drone buildup opens up a new world for warfare and potential terrorism. Many countries have developed and deployed various kinds of unmanned aerial vehicles. In the future, drones will be even more accessible to various nations because the components are now more available than they have been in the past. If we look at recent technology that we use daily, such as smart phones, laptops, and tablets, we can see how many components for equipment used in surveillance and warfare may be no farther away than the local electronics store. This creates new concerns because it places potentially dangerous technology in the hands of terrorists or others who operate outside of the control of any governmental regulatory body, or in the hands of governmental officials in a nation whose interests do not mesh with those of the United States.

Although high-technology weaponry used in warfare has been the topic of widespread political debate and extensive media coverage, less attention has been paid to the potential significance of poison gas manufacturing and the use of chemical and biological toxic agents by domestic and international terrorists.

GLOBAL TERRORISM

Terrorism **is the use of calculated, unlawful physical force or threats of violence against a government, organization, or individual to gain some political, religious, economic, or social objective.** Terrorists, however, are often difficult to conclusively identify, because those who are perceived as terrorists in one country may be perceived as freedom fighters by another. Some groups, like Arabs, have often been inappropriately stereotyped as terrorists. There are some things that are relatively easy to agree upon however, such as identification and assessment of terrorist tactics. Typically, these include bombing, kidnapping, hostage taking, hijacking, assassination, and extortion. Although terrorists sometimes attack government officials and members of the military, they more often target civilians as a way of pressuring the government.

As collective violence, terrorism shares certain commonalities with war. Both terrorism and war pose major threats to world stability and domestic safety. Terrorism and war also extract a massive toll on individuals and societies by producing rampant fear, breakdown of families, widespread loss of human life, and extensive destruction of property and the environment.

One form of terrorism—political terrorism—is actually considered a form of unconventional warfare. *Political terrorism* uses intimidation, coercion, threats of harm, and other violent attempts to bring about a significant change in or overthrow an existing government. There are three types of political terrorism: revolutionary terrorism, repressive terrorism, and state-sponsored terrorism.

Revolutionary terrorism **refers to acts of violence against civilians that are carried out by internal enemies of the government who want to bring about political change.** Some groups believe that if they perpetrate enough random terrorist acts, they will achieve a political goal. Modern terrorism is not always based in a single country, as we have learned from efforts to apprehend Osama bin Laden and the al-Qaeda network, who have been accused of planning the September 11, 2001, attacks on the United States and attacks at other times and sites associated with U.S. interests and citizens.

After being America's most wanted man for a decade, bin Laden was found in Pakistan and killed in May 2011.

How do officials find terrorists? Money usually is a crucial ingredient in terrorism, and following the so-called money trail has been a key way in which law enforcement agencies have sought to apprehend those accused of violent terrorist attacks and of financing terrorism. In some circumstances, revolutionary terrorists receive economic help from other governments that support their objectives.

Unlike revolutionary terrorism, *repressive terrorism* **is conducted by a government against its own citizens for the purpose of protecting an existing political order.** Repressive terrorism has taken place in many countries around the world, including Haiti, the People's Republic of China, and Cambodia. Recent examples include most of the countries involved with the "Arab Spring," like Egypt, Libya, Syria, and Tunisia.

In the third type of political terrorism, *state-sponsored terrorism*, **a government provides financial resources, weapons, and training for terrorists who conduct their activities in other nations.** Nations that use terrorism as a means of political expression have been of concern for many years. Throughout the first two decades of the 21st century, countries such as Iran, Iraq, Syria, Libya, Cuba, North Korea, and Sudan have been considered to be state sponsors of terrorism. In the past, Libyan dictator, Muammar Qaddafi, provided money and training for terrorist groups such as the Arab National Youth Organization. This group was responsible for skyjacking a Lufthansa airplane over Turkey and forcing the Bonn government to free the surviving members of Black September, a terrorist group that was responsible for killing Israeli Olympic athletes in the 1970s. Qaddafi had been accused of many acts of state-sponsored terrorism, particularly in recent years in the North African country of Misrata. In 2011, the United Nations sanctioned Qaddafi and the United States recognized the Transitional National Council as the legitimate government of Libya, not Muammar Qaddafi. Since that time, Qaddafi was killed. In the 2010s, state-sponsored terrorism is a concern around the world. India has demanded that Pakistan not allow territory under its control to be used for terrorism directed against India. Similar concerns are shared by other nations, including the United States, which alleged that Pakistan had been harbouring Osama bin Laden for several years prior to his death in 2011.

Cyber attacks have also been officially recognized as a new form of state-sponsored terrorism. Cyber attacks target computer networks, information systems, and many individual computers to commit theft, obtain secret knowledge, or destroy systems. Canada's Department of National Defence, like similar departments of our allies, is examining how we can best respond to future cyber attacks. Further contributing to the possibility of state-sponsored terrorism in the form of cyber hacking is the era of cloud computing, in which important information is stored on servers that are accessible to a wider array of invaders. Cyberterrorism is possible when hackers are able to steal government files. Although analysts state that many governments are involved in cyberespionage, how these governments use the data is a pressing social problem because it could affect human life, national security, and the nation's infrastructure. A major problem is how difficult it is to track hacking back to its source, since intermediary computers could be used for the hacking. However, it is important that nations persist in identifying the persons and countries responsible. One of the cyberattacks that awakened security experts to the dangers of cyberterrorism was the 2010 Stuxnet computer worm that allegedly attacked and damaged an Iranian nuclear facility.

Protestors marching against the "War on Terror".
Joel Stuthman / Alamy

A final kind of terrorist attack is one that has not yet occurred, a *biogenic attack*. We do not know what research is taking place in bioscience and bioengineering in many places in the world, making it difficult to predict what might happen. Moreover, the raw materials for biogenic attacks are now cheaper and easier to produce, conceal, and deliver.

How widespread is terrorism? While terrorist attacks have varied greatly over the last 30 years, a U.S. State Department report found that there was a 43 percent increase in such attacks from 2012 to 2013. Most of these were local attacks, not international like the 9/11 attacks. The major decline in security in Iraq, the civil war in Syria, and terrorism in Pakistan and Afghanistan contributed to a significant growth in total terrorist attacks in 2013. The largest number of attacks was by the Taliban. They were responsible for over 2000 deaths in over 600 attacks. Al-Qaeda attacks were lower in number because of isolated former al-Qaeda groups acting on their own (Ackerman 2014).

Although many terrorist attacks in recent years have been attributed to people from other nations, our country also has a history of domestic terrorism.

TERRORISM IN CANADA

Terrorism also occurs intra-nationally. Domestic terrorism is sometimes referred to as "home-grown terrorism" by the media because the perpetrator is usually a resident of the country in which the incident occurs or has other strong ties to the country, such as relatives or acquaintances who live there. Like international terrorism, domestic terrorism typically is used to reach some political goal. The most famous example of Canadian domestic terrorism involves the Front de Liberation du Quebec (FLQ), which sought to turn Quebec into an independent state. In the late 1960s, the group set off several bombs, and in the 1970s, they kidnapped British Trade Commissioner James Cross and Quebec's Labour and Immigration minister, Pierre Laporte. Prime Minister Pierre Trudeau invoked the *War Measures Act* in response to the kidnappings. The night after the *War Measures Act* was proclaimed, Laporte's body was found in the trunk of an abandoned car. Eventually, Cross was freed by his captors, who were given free passage to Cuba in exchange for his life (NFB 1973).

In 1985, a bomb exploded on an Air India flight flying from Canada to Britain, killing 329 people. Marc Lapine's killing of 14 women in 1989 and wounding of another 10 women and 4 men could also be considered a terrorist attack since he had grievances against women in engineering. Other mass killings might not have a political agenda, like the killing of eight in Edmonton in 2014, and the police prevention of the killing of many people in a shopping mall in Halifax in 2014, but they are very similar to terrorist attacks.

Between 2008 and 2009, the EnCana natural gas pipeline in northeastern British Columbia was the target of several explosions. The first occurred just shortly after EnCana received a letter demanding it cease operations in the area. Then, in July 2009, a local newspaper received a second letter addressed to EnCana, alerting the company and the RCMP Anti-Terrorism Unit—the Integrated National Security Enforcement Team—that the company would be given a three-month reprieve to formulate plans to withdraw from the area. The letters' authors also recommended that EnCana shift its focus to green alternative fuels (Stolte 2009). No one was injured in the blasts, and apparently there was no danger to the public or to the environment from the leaks caused by them. No one has been convicted in connection with the explosions. However, the reward for information leading to conviction, in what the RCMP is calling "domestic terrorism," was increased to $1 million by EnCana (Stolte 2009).

In mid-October 2014, Canadians experienced two shocking terrorist attacks. First, Martin Couture-Rouleau ran down two soldiers in uniform, killing one, in Saint-Jean-sur-Richelieu, Quebec before he was killed. Second, Michael Zehaf-Bibeau shot and killed a soldier standing guard at the National War Memorial in Ottawa and then went to the Centre Block of the parliament buildings with a rifle. After shots were fired, confusion and panic followed since no one knew the scope of the attack. He was killed by the sergeant-at-arms, a former RCMP officer. It turned out that Zehaf-Bibeau, like Couture-Rouleau, were "lone-wolf" terrorists, not members of terrorist organizations. The world has experienced many of these lone-wolf terrorists, such as Anders Breivik in Norway; Theodore Kaczynski, the Unabomber, and Timothy McVeigh in the United States; and Medho Nemmouche in Belgium. The two Canadians appeared to be following Islamist terrorist ideas of revenge on the Internet, and a video released in March 2015 confirmed Zehaf-Bibeau's terrorist orientation. They appeared to have been cyber-radicalized. It is a very complex question about what to do about people like them, even if they are known to the police, as Zehaf-Bibeau was. Foreigners suspected of being likely to commit terrorist acts can be imprisoned, and Canadians who are similarly suspected can be monitored and prohibited from getting weapons. But Zehaf-Bibeau was under surveillance, yet still managed to get a rifle. What do you think should be done by authorities when they have people like Zehaf-Bibeau under surveillance and, according to the RCMP commissioner, 90 others?

In early 2015, the federal government brought forth an anti-terrorism bill (C-51). This bill proposes making advocating terrorism a crime, putting terror suspects on a no-fly list, permitting security agencies to communicate with each other, and giving new powers to CSIS to stop any activity that undermines the "sovereignty, security or territorial integrity of Canada." It is clear that we need to protect critical infrastructure, like EnCana's pipelines (see above). But do we want to give CSIS the power to investigate those advocating Quebec's separation or Indigenous peoples' opposition to pipelines? What limits should be placed on CSIS?

A new concern has emerged with the growth and victories of IS. Many young citizens of Western countries, including Canada, have joined this organization and other similar organizations. For example, Canadians were among those who attacked a gas plant in Algeria in 2013, killing 40 workers. It is impossible to estimate either the numbers of Westerners or the number of Canadians who think of themselves as jihadis. What could happen when these citizens return home? Canada can charge terror tourists and they can be imprisoned. But should Canada become more punitive by taking away their citizenship and banishing them from our country? (See Box 16.2 for more information on this topic.)

CANADIAN POLITICS AND TERRORISM

Canada was quick to show its support to the United States in the form of infrastructural, citizen, and military support; freezing the assets of suspected terrorists; and working with the United States to improve security along the 8850-kilometre Canada–U.S. border (Council on Foreign Relations 2003). Canada also supported the NATO decision to invoke Article V of the NATO charter, which declares an armed attack against any member of the council is considered "an attack against them all." In October 2001, former Canadian Prime Minister Jean Chrétien committed Canadian forces to the U.S.–led war in Afghanistan (Ljunngren 2003). And after the fall of the Taliban regime in late 2001, Canadian involvement in Afghanistan increased steadily for 10 years, although it ended as of March 12, 2014. According to CBC figures, this mission cost 162 Canadian and thousands of civilian lives and about $18 billion (not counting future liabilities for problems like PTSD, etc.) (CBC 2014).

Sociologists critically analyze the motives and actions of people and their governments in times of war or anticipated war. They ask questions such as, "Why is Canada participating in the 'war on terror' in the ways it is, and how are these actions affecting people in Canada?"

Historically, wars and periods of national crisis have resulted in serious and unjustified losses of civil rights for many, especially for immigrants, refugees, and people of colour. This is because war is not simply a fight for justice; rather, war is an institution that shapes the economic, environmental, civic, ideological, and political activities and practices of civilians and governments. For example, almost immediately after the September 11 attack in New York, the Canadian federal government passed Bill C-36, an *Anti-Terrorism Act*. Bill C-36 is a key component of the government of Canada's anti-terrorism plan and gives wide-ranging powers to the government, presumably to deal with the threat of terrorism. The controversial December 2001 omnibus bill has four objectives.

1. Stop terrorists from getting into Canada and protect Canadians from terrorist acts.
2. Bring forward tools to identify, prosecute, convict, and punish terrorists.
3. Prevent the Canada–U.S. border from being held hostage by terrorists and impacting on the Canadian economy.
4. Work with the international community to bring terrorists to justice and address the root causes of such hatred. (Department of Justice 2001)

The bill was passed in haste and within a panicked civic environment. It comes under the *Criminal Code* and is linked to at least 12 UN Anti-Terrorism Conventions. Unlike the *War Measures Act,* Bill C-36 is not emergency legislation. It changed, forever, laws and conduct under the *Criminal Code,* the *Official Secrets Act,* the *Privacy Act,* and the *Canada Evidence Act.*

The government maintained that this act ensured that Canadian values of respect and fairness are preserved and "rigorous safeguards ensure that the fundamental rights and freedoms of Canadians are upheld" (Department of Justice 2001). Generally speaking, Bill C-36 was criticized because many Canadians believed that many of its features were incompatible with our existing Charter of Rights and Freedoms. Some provisions of the bill regarding preventative arrest and investigative hearings expired in March 2007, despite the urgings of the Conservative government to renew them.

There have been two convictions of people who broke this law. In 2010, Zakaria Amara, mastermind of the "Toronto 18," was sentenced to life imprisonment for conspiring to blow up buildings in Toronto, like the Toronto Stock Exchange, to kill people and hurt the economy. Another member of the "Toronto 18," Saad Gaya, was convicted of a lesser charge and sentenced to 12 years in prison.

Bill C-36, similar to the U.S. *Patriot Act,* passed at the same time, is not the only controversial bill. Other bills that were ratified around the same time included the new *Citizenship of Canada Act* (Bill C-18—replacing the 1977 *Citizenship Act*), the *Immigration and Refugee Protection Act* (Bill C-11), and the *Public Safety Act* (Bill C-42).

Bill C-42 raises anxieties about the need to balance fundamental rights with security interests. Of particular concern is a provision that allows the minister of defence to declare certain areas—even in major cities—security zones, thereby curtailing the right of peaceful assembly and protest (Canadian Human Rights Commission 2003). Given the extent of legitimate and peaceful protest against the G-20 and various trade acts, many people see this bill as being more about unfettered access to trade than about citizen "security" per se. The Ontario Council of Agencies Serving Immigrants (OCASI) is concerned that Bill C-18 will create a two-tiered approach to citizenship in Canada—the implications of which are immensely disturbing. For example, a child born outside of Canada to a first-generation Canadian (even if the mother has lived all but the first couple of months of her life in Canada) does not have the right to citizenship and may even become stateless. There are no citizenship restrictions faced by a Canadian-born mother who lives outside of the country but gives birth in Canada (Casipullai 2003). The bill also gives broad powers to Cabinet to refuse citizenship to a person who has "demonstrated a flagrant and serious disregard for the principles and values underlying a free and democratic society" (in Casipullai 2003). The Act does not clearly outline the aforementioned "principles" and "values," but rather leaves it up to the interpretation of cabinet ministers and other individuals in a given historical moment. The possibility of an abuse of power and a decision to refuse citizenship within this framework is real. The revocation of citizenship is yet another potential for the violation of human rights, as is the policy that evidence used against an individual in an immigration process may not be disclosed to the person in question, giving a person no way of addressing, or even knowing about, allegations against them (in Casipullai 2003).

The impact of these bills is already being felt by many people—most significantly, those involved in immigration processes, those who belong to "visible minorities," and those who are the victims of racialized or ethnic profiling. Some critics say that these are all cases of *scapegoating*—a process where people blame visible and generally marginalized "others" for a perceived threat. The implementation of tighter immigration laws, legislation such as that discussed above, and cases of civilian hostility against people most easily identified as immigrants and refugees are all aspects of this larger movement of "nationalist protectionism." Many point out, however, that these attitudes are not new. Rather, feelings of vulnerability to attack lead people to create a hostile climate where underlying attitudes of suspicion, discrimination, and intolerance gain strength and even become institutionalized as new legislation and policies (Choudry 2001). Recalling the internment of Japanese-Canadians and German-Canadians during World War II provides easy examples.

Ethnic or racialized profiling is a controversial policing technique that involves identifying and pursuing suspects on the basis of their ethnicity or racialization. It is becoming increasingly common practice among Canada–U.S. immigration officers in a post-9/11 world. While proponents of ethnic/racialized profiling say that it can provide a government with a tool for risk analysis, they acknowledge that it inevitably involves injustices (Gillis 2001). The result is that a person fitting the profile for a "high-risk" group—these days, a person from any of Afghanistan, Algeria, Bahrain, Djibouti, Egypt, Eritrea, Indonesia, Iran, Iraq, Jordan, Kuwait, Lebanon, Libya, Malaysia, Morocco, Oman, Pakistan, Qatar, Saudi Arabia, Somalia, Sudan, Syria, Tunisia, Turkey, the United Arab Emirates, and Yemen—may be searched, fingerprinted, photographed, registered, detained, and even deported without real evidence of wrongdoing. As the criterion for this invasive treatment is a person's ethnicity or racialization, authorities assume that all people from certain ethnic/racialized groups have the potential to be affiliated with terrorists from their country (or region) of origin—or of ancestral origin—and could therefore pose a threat to national security. An example of this is the case of one of Canada's most celebrated writers, Indian-born Canadian Rohinton Mistry. Mistry was given such humiliating and traumatic treatment by U.S. border officials while on a U.S. book release tour that he cancelled the second half of the tour (Gillis 2001).

The Canada Race Relations Foundation (CRRF) has tried to put current legislative activities into a historical context. It has drawn the country's attention to the injustices suffered by the Japanese-Canadian community during World War II and attempted to draw parallels to the current "backlash" being visited today upon Muslim and Arab Canadians in a post-9/11 world. "We have witnessed grave injustices that befell a community and, from this, have a clearer understanding of what can arise in response to increased security concerns in a society that has not yet stripped itself of racism" (CRRF 2001). Indeed, Indigenous people and other non-White Canadian citizens have always faced, and continue to face, "racial" profiling, not only in war times, but also in everyday life. "Racial" profiling accompanies racist attitudes and structures. This is not a new phenomenon, although a broader awareness does seem new. In this current historical moment, Canadians are actively engaged in shaping the face of Canadian politics. In this global age, people understand that all things are connected—including the causes and effects of war and terrorism on national and international levels.

In 2012, Parliament began debate on a bill to renew two measures of the original anti-terrorism bill that lapsed in 2007 because of a five year sunset clause. The first measure was to compel a suspect believed to have information relating to a terrorist offence to undergo an investigative hearing before a judge, without being charged with any offence. The second measure was to allow an individual to be arrested without charge and then placed on recognizance, in which he or she would have to agree to certain conditions for up to 12 months. The bill was introduced in the Senate first and was called S-7. As part of S-7, the government has also introduced four new terrorism offences to the Criminal Code, all of which have to do with leaving or attempting to leave Canada to commit several of the existing terrorism offences in the Code. The bill was passed in the Senate and then passed in the House of Commons as Bill C-24 in April 2013. Bill C-51, introduced after the Ottawa attacks (mentioned above), makes several actions easier, including:

- the transfer of information among federal agencies;
- the prevention of someone boarding a plane;
- preventative arrests; and
- the protection of classified information regarding immigration.

Despite criticism of the bill, since the Conservatives have a majority it passed in May 2015.

Social Problems and Social Policy

Box 16.2

To Banish or Not To Banish Citizens for Treason or Terrorism

In June 2014, the federal government was considering amendments to the *Citizenship Act* to remove the citizenship of someone who was an immigrant or someone born in Canada but holding dual citizenship, for causes of terrorism, treason, and spying for the enemy. Of course, it is often difficult to know if people accused of these crimes are guilty. The case of Maher Arar shows what could happen to a person who is banished without the opportunity to defend himself. In September 2002, Arar, a Syrian-born Canadian engineer, on his way home to Montreal from Zurich after a family vacation, landed at Kennedy Airport in New York. U.S. authorities suspected ties to al-Qaeda and deported him to Syria without consulting Canadian officials. When Canada's Foreign Affairs Department learned of the deportation, they protested it, saying there was no information that the man posed a security threat, but to no avail (Arar 2009; *Migration News* 2002). While he was imprisoned, Arar was beaten, tortured, refused contact with family or a lawyer, and forced to make a false confession (Arar 2009). He was finally released in October 2003 and returned home to Canada. In September 2006, Arar was cleared of all terrorism allegations, based on the fact that there was "no evidence to indicate that Mr. Arar has committed any offence or that his activities constitute a threat to the security of Canada" (Arar 2009).

On the other hand, when people become Canadian citizens they vow to "faithfully observe the laws of Canada and fulfill the duties as a Canadian citizen." Should people who have broken their vow by joining jihadi movements and conducting terrorist activities against Canada or the West generally be charged with terrorism or treason, and if found guilty banished from a state they vowed to support? People who break this vow performing other crimes, even homicide, do not have their citizenship revoked. We know of cases where young people have gone overseas to be jihadis. With the training they get overseas, they would be able to attract more young people to terrorism when they return or cause considerable destruction. In June 2014, Canadians discovered that a Calgarian, Salman Ashrafi, became a suicide bomber for IS in November 2013. Other Canadians, such as some in the "Toronto18," were arrested in 2006 for devising two plots to bomb the Toronto Stock Exchange and to drive Canadians out of Afghanistan. Additionally, two people from London, Ontario have been identified in the jihadi struggles in Algeria (Zekulin 2014). If those who go overseas to fight in jihadi movements were to have their citizenship revoked and then be banished, it would likely be more difficult to attract other Canadians to these movements. Some observers suggest that it might be possible to distinguish between those who could be dangerous and those who are disillusioned with jihad by interviewing them. After all, many Canadians have chosen to go to foreign wars like the Spanish Civil War and the Vietnam War without becoming terrorists at home when they returned. Others argue that citizenship is a right and once gained without fraud, it should not be possible to be taken away.

Questions for Consideration

1. Can you conceive of any instance when a person's citizenship should be revoked besides gaining it by fraud, or do you think it is a basic right?
2. Totalitarian countries, such as the Soviet Union, banish dissidents. Should democratic governments do this also when citizens participate in jihadi movements that attack Western interests?
3. What can be done to prevent the recruitment of Canadians to jihadi movements?

PERSPECTIVES ON WAR AND TERRORISM

What causes collective violence such as war and terrorism? Can war and acts of terrorism be reduced? Despite centuries of war and terrorism, we know little about the origins of violence or how to reduce such acts (Turpin and Kurtz 1997). We will now examine four sociological approaches to violence as they relate to war and terrorism.

The Functionalist Perspective

Some functionalist explanations focus on the relationship between social disorganization and warfare or terrorism. According to these explanations, disorganization in social institutions, such as the government, contributes to overall political instability. Militia members believe that governments no longer serve the purposes for which they were intended—namely, to protect the individual's rights and freedom. In their eyes, governments have become dysfunctional. Some militia groups engage in acts of terrorism to undermine a particular government in the hope that it will change radically or be abolished.

Other functionalists focus on the functions that war serves. Looked at from this perspective, war can settle disputes between nations. However, in the age of nuclear weaponry, many nations seek other means to deal with their disagreements. Among these means are *economic sanctions,* or cutting off all trade. Thus, in the past Canada has imposed economic sanctions rather than engaging in war or military action against countries engaging in terrorism, environmental violations, abuse of workers' rights, regional strife, drug trafficking, human and political rights abuses, and nuclear proliferation (Myers 1997). In 2014, Canada imposed economic sanctions against Russia for its destabilizing actions against Ukraine. However, some political analysts argue that Canada is cutting off its nose to spite its face when it imposes economic sanctions against other governments. This is because economic sanctions are dysfunctional for another social institution—the economy. Also, even though Canada has used sanctions against other nations from its earliest days, corporations are concerned that the sanctions deny them access to the world's markets and the profits in those markets (Myers 1997).

Some functionalists believe we will always have wars because of other important functions that they serve in societies. First, war demonstrates that one nation or group has power over another. Historically, conquering forces acquire the "spoils of war," including more territory and material possessions. Second, war functions as a means of punishment in much the same manner that the Canadian government uses sanctions to force other nations to comply with our viewpoint on certain issues. Third, war is a way to disseminate ideologies, usually political or religious. For example, under the slogan "making the world safe for democracy," the United States has fought its largest wars in defence of a democratic form of government (Crossette 1997). Canada explains its involvement in contemporary conflicts partly using the same ideological commitment to the protection and strengthening of democracy in the world. But as we saw in Chapter 13, democracy is not a form of government that is just present or absent. Box 13.2 shows that countries have a range of scores to show the quality of their democracy. Since 2008, some countries have become more democratic, e.g., Georgia, Thailand, and Tunisia, and some less democratic, e.g., Paraguay, Sri Lanka, and Venezuela (Democracy Ranking 2013).

Finally, many functionalists point out the economic function of war: war benefits society because it stimulates the economy through increased war-related production and provides jobs for civilians who otherwise might not be able to find employment. In 2012, Canada ranked 13th in arms exports valued at US$276 million (*The Economist* 2014:103). Conflict analysts also see an economic side to war, but they are not so optimistic.

Conflict and Interactionist Perspectives

Conflict theorists view war from the standpoint of how militarism and aggressive preparedness for war contribute to the economic well-being of some, but not all, people in a society. According to sociologist Cynthia Enloe (1987:527), people who consider capitalism the moving force behind the military's influence "believe that government officials enhance the status, resources, and authority of the military in order to protect the interests of private enterprises at home and overseas." In other words, the origins of war can be traced to corporate boardrooms, not to governmental war rooms. Those who view war from this standpoint note that workers and business owners alike come to rely on military spending for jobs.

A second conflict explanation focuses on the role of the nation and its inclination toward coercion in response to perceived threats. From this perspective, nations inevitably use force to ensure compliance within their societies and to protect themselves from outside attacks.

A third conflict explanation is based on patriarchy and the relationship between militarism and masculinity. Across cultures and over time, the military has been a male institution, and the "meanings attached to masculinity appear to be so firmly linked to compliance with military roles that it is often impossible to disentangle the two" (Enloe 1987:531).

Interactionists would call this last perspective the *social construction of masculinity*. That is, certain assumptions, teachings, and expectations that serve as the standard for appropriate male behaviour—in this case, values of dominance, power, aggression, and violence—are created and re-created, presumably through gender socialization, and particularly in military training. Historically, the development of manhood and male superiority has been linked to militarism and combat—the ultimate test of a man's masculinity (Cock 1994; Enloe 1987). This is also a perspective held by some feminists who have focused a great deal of attention on the relationships between patriarchy and military violence.

Feminist Perspectives

Feminist scholarship on war has proliferated since the late 1980s. Women are the targets of massacres in wars, the victims of systematic rape during warfare, and the largest percentage of the population that is forced to flee war-torn areas. Women are also increasingly participating as soldiers in the military and are continuing to work together internationally for peace (Goldstein 2001:1). While war and gender are connected, feminists take many theoretical and political approaches to understanding issues of women and war. As a result, a cohesive "feminist theory" of war does not exist; rather, a chorus of female voices constitutes current scholarship and political debate about women and war (J. Elshtain in Goldstein 2001:2).

Most feminists share a concern with changing "masculinism" in both scholarship and political–military practice, where *masculinism* is defined as an ideology justifying male domination. Within this framework, women are seen as a disadvantaged class, unjustly dominated and exploited by men. In addition to their substantive objections to arguments of biological determinism, some feminists challenge the methods of knowledge generation that they see as based on masculine qualities—such as objectivity, control, and theoretical parsimony (especially binary dualisms)—at the expense of detailed knowledge about complex social relationships (Goldstein 2001).

Liberal feminists, with their emphasis of classical individual rights to full participation in all social and political roles, maintain that women should also be able to assume war roles without facing discrimination. They argue that women equal men in ability and that the gendering of war reflects male discrimination against women (i.e., sexism). Furthermore, the exclusion of women from positions of power in international relations is unfair and prevents women from contributing fully to society (Goldstein 2001). Liberal feminist scholars often include women as subjects of study—female state leaders, female soldiers, and other women operating outside the traditional gender roles in international relations. This brand of feminism pays homage to women who succeed in non-traditional positions despite the obstacles they face in a sexist society (Goldstein 2001).

Materialist feminists draw upon a Marxist approach to class differences and their role in the perpetuation of power inequalities in and between societies. To this end, materialist feminists have studied the construction of productive and reproductive roles of women and men beginning in horticultural societies and progressing through to post-capitalist economies (Mies 1986). By paying particular attention to the links between economies and warfare, these feminists have come to challenge the construction of gender roles in general, and those concerning violence and aggression in particular. Research by materialist feminists shows that the claims that gender roles are genetically determined, natural, difficult to change, and adaptive in an evolutionary sense are easily proven

false (Goldstein 2001; Mies 1986). While war has existed perhaps as long as humans have, an explanation for the roots of war is often sought. Anthropologists, for example, have turned to an evolutionary model to explain the origins of war. Such scholars have tended to argue, for example, that in early societies, man-the-hunter used his tools to protect woman-the-gatherer. With the advent of agricultural economies, men began to engage in larger-scale conflicts in order to protect accumulated wealth, land, and community and, finally, in capitalist societies, men engaged in large, often international modes of warfare (Mies 1986). The underlying argument is that males have an evolutionary predisposition to wage war. Materialist feminists show that man-the-hunter actually used violence to control his own communities and that warfare across the ages is more often linked to battles for control over resources and power than it is about adaptive protection and preservation tactics (Meis 1986).

Multicultural feminism theorizes about war and peace from the perspective of "Third World" and Indigenous women. It is a perspective that shows how globalization and colonization remain rooted together. It also demonstrates that there will be no true and sustainable social justice, no anti-racism, feminist emancipation, or liberation of any kind for anybody until Indigenous people have self-determination and the fundamental divide between the South and the North, between low-income people and high-income people, is ended (Thobani 2001a).

Ecofeminism brings together theories of feminism, environmentalism, and movements for social justice and equality under one theoretical perspective. Ecofeminists begin with critiques of the 17th-century philosopher of science, Francis Bacon, who cast nature as female and used explicit sexual metaphors to demonstrate the requisite relations of domination and seduction that were to replace an earlier attitude of wonder and contemplation (Merchant 1983; Sturgeon 1997). Ecofeminists argue that all forms of oppression are deeply connected, although they pay particular attention to the types of violence that are created by patriarchal systems of rule and anthropocentrism, which permit people to exploit the natural world based on an ideology of human supremacy.

War is seen as an extension of the aggressive and exploitative relationships embodied in sexism, racism, and the "rape" of the environment. Ecofeminism influenced the character of women's peace movements in the 1980s and 1990s, and of the Green political parties in Europe (Goldstein 2001; Mies 1986; Sturgeon 1997). These feminists trace war to an "ideology of control" that gives rise to various forms of oppression; ecofeminism sees the problem of war in very broad terms, connecting peace to a deep restructuring of society (Goldstein 2001).

OVERCOMING WAR AND TERRORISM IN THE 21ST CENTURY

What will happen during this new century? How will nations deal with the proliferation of arms and nuclear weapons? What should be done with the masses of nuclear waste being produced? How can people be protected from terrorists? How can we best deal with the inevitable consequences of war to humans, animals and our planet? No easy answers are forthcoming, as Ehrenreich explains, war is a "formidable adversary," a "tonic for political malaise" (e.g., Putin's attacks on Ukraine are supported by most Russians), and a diversion from more serious threats like climate change (1997:239).

Ehrenreich, like most other social analysts, is not totally pessimistic about the future. She believes that human resistance to war can provide a means to spare this nation and the world from future calamities.

The anti-war movements of the late 20th and early 21st centuries show that "the passions we bring to war can be brought just as well to the struggle *against* war" (Ehrenreich 1997). But, she notes, people must be willing to educate, inspire, and rally others to the cause. As with other forms of warfare, the people struggling for peace must be willing to continue that struggle even when the odds seem hopeless. Ehrenreich's point is supported by Gibson and Cancian (1990:9), who believe that making peace can be more difficult than making war since it involves confronting powerful forces, participating in political decision making, and not automatically thinking that another group is our enemy.

Why do we end our discussion of social problems with war and terrorism? They are the ultimate category of social problems. When class, racialization, ethnicity, or any of the other dominant/subordinate categories discussed in this text escalate to a level of "doing something about it" regardless of the consequences, terrorism or war may be the result. Redressing inequality is an admirable goal, but saying "no" to war should also be our goal.

The international society—the community of all the nations of the world—must work to alleviate inequalities and create a better—more peaceful—world for future generations. What role will you play during the 21st century? Will you work toward a better world for all? Will you be part of the solution? The answers to these questions are up to all of us: each of us individually and all of us collectively.

WHAT CAN YOU DO?

- Check in with your local pro-peace or anti-war action groups to see what rallies and actions are happening in your area. Participate in them!
- Call, fax, or email your MLAs, MPs, and senators DAILY—several time a day if possible—to express your opposition to current military activities, including sanctions, questionable peacekeeping missions, anti-terrorist initiatives, and invasions.
- Write a letter to the editor of your local newspaper saying why you oppose a particular military initiative.
- Email a friend and ask her or him to join you in supporting peace. Send this list of things you can do to stop war to a friend along with a copy of information about current conflicts you wish to oppose.
- Distribute flyers about why people should stop war before it starts. Good, heavily trafficked locations include bus stops, subway stations, grocery stores, college and university campuses, libraries, and churches, among other sites. Look for sample flyers on the Internet.
- Organize a weekly vigil against current wars and conflicts at your parliament buildings, the office of an MLA or MP who supports the war, city hall, or another public place.
- Call a press conference where local community leaders, religious leaders, veterans, politicians, and others can speak out against war. Once you have some community leaders who are willing to speak out, determine the time and location of the press conference, send a news release to local media outlets, and then follow up with a phone call to tell editors and reporters what you are doing.
- Connect with the local peace group in your community and/or with an international peace organization. They will have many other ideas for how you can work to stop war.
- Speak out against racist and anti-immigrant attacks. Ensure that the needs of victims (and those at risk for attack) are front and centre.
- Circulate the criticisms of Bill C-42, Bill C-36, Bill C-18, and Bill C-11 that have been raised by many community groups. Find out about these bills and newer work from government, social justice organizations, and alternative media sources, and conduct your own critical analysis.
- Work with Canadian and U.S. immigrant and refugee-rights groups, such as the Canadian Council for Refugees (http://ccrweb.ca).
- Subscribe to local, regional, or national organizations that are addressing the effects of military activity on the health of humans and their environments.

SUMMARY

How Do Social Scientists Define War and Peace?

Social scientists define war broadly. The term *war* includes armed conflict between two countries, undeclared wars, civil and guerrilla wars, covert operations, and some forms of terrorism. War is a form of collective violence that involves organized violence by people seeking to promote their cause or resist social policies or practices that they consider oppressive. Peace seems less easy to define—while people generally agree that peace is desirable, they have different ideas about what it looks like. Some people equate peace with global harmony, while others define it as prevailing in battle.

What Are the Consequences of War?

The most direct effect of war is loss of human life. In World War I and before, it was mostly military personnel who lost their lives, but in World War II and thereafter, war was waged against civilians. If a nuclear war took place, the devastation would be beyond description. Other consequences for both military personnel and civilians are physical and psychological damage, including post-traumatic stress syndrome. Finally, the economic costs of war and war preparedness are astronomical.

How Does War Affect Human and Ecological Health?

The impacts of military activity in times of war and peace are often left out of mainstream debates about war. The effects, however, include both visible and invisible reminders of the impact military activity has on people and environments. Some examples of this are high CO_2 emission levels causing global warming, the effects of depleted uranium on human and ecological life, the loss of millions of lives through contaminated water and air, and post-traumatic stress disorder (PTSD). It is also possible that global warming is contributing to fighting by causing droughts, famine, and driving people to over-crowded cities.

How Important Is Military Technology to Winning a War?

Military technology is a dominant factor, as military history shows. In the 14th century, smaller European and Western armies defeated bigger armies by using the newly-discovered black powder. Today, precision-guided munitions render old technologies obsolete and global warfare possible. But wars can be won on the basis of factors other than military technology, too, as the U.S. experience in Vietnam shows. It is also possible to imagine the damage that could be done by biogenic and cyber attacks by small groups.

What Is Terrorism?

Terrorism is the use of calculated unlawful physical force or threats of violence against a government, organization, or individual to gain some political, religious, economic, or social objective. Tactics include bombing, kidnapping, hostage taking, hijacking, assassination, and extortion.

What Are the Prominent Possible Types of Terrorism?

Revolutionary terrorism involves acts of violence against civilians that are carried out by internal enemies of the government who want to bring about political change. Repressive terrorism is terrorism conducted by a government against its own citizens for the purpose of protecting an existing political order. In state-sponsored terrorism, a government provides financial resources, weapons, and training for terrorists who conduct their activities in other nations. Cyberattacks and biogenic attacks can also be types of terrorism.

What Forms of Terrorism Represent the Greatest Potential Threat to Canadian Citizens?

Some analysts identify the following as forms of terrorism that offer the greatest potential threat to Canadian citizens: (1) foreign-sponsored/influenced terrorism on Canadian soil such as the "Toronto 18" terrorist attacks; (2) domestic-sponsored terrorism with political or religious motivations such as violent protests against abortion clinics, for Quebec separatism, and against pipelines; (3) terrorism in other nations such as attacks at tourist sites or other public accommodations that are frequently visited by Canadians citizens like Bali (e.g., 2014 bomb blast); and (4) cyberterrorism or information terrorism—the destruction of computer systems and records or hacking into systems to gain valuable information and data.

What Is the Functionalist Perspective on War and Terrorism?

Some functionalists focus on the relationship between social disorganization and warfare or terrorism. Examining the growth of militias, they note that disorganization in social institutions contributes to overall political instability. Other functionalists say that war serves certain functions: war settles disputes, demonstrates that one nation or group has power over another, punishes, is one way to disseminate religious and political ideologies, and stimulates the economy.

What Are the Conflict and Interactionist Perspectives on War and Terrorism?

Some conflict theorists say that militarism and preparedness for war contribute to the economic well-being of some—not all—people. Another conflict perspective says that nations inevitably use force to ensure compliance within their society and to protect themselves from outside attacks. A third conflict perspective is based in patriarchy: across cultures and over time, the military has been a male institution; it is almost impossible to untangle masculinity from militarism. Interactionists call this last perspective the *social construction of masculinity*—the connection between manhood and militarism is historically created and re-created through gender socialization.

What Are Feminist Perspectives on War?

Feminist scholarship focuses on the links between war and gender. There is no such thing as a cohesive "feminist theory" of war. There are many thoughts that feminist scholars do agree upon, including constructions of masculinism, which is an ideology that justifies male domination. Liberal feminists focus on issues of women's equality with men and therefore work for women's rights to participate fully in all aspects of war. Materialist feminists analyze the relationship between economics, patriarchy, and power on a world scale and how this affects the life conditions of women in times of peace and conflict. Multicultural feminism theorizes from the perspective of "Third World" and Indigenous women and demonstrates how globalization and colonization remain rooted together. Ecofeminists take a holistic approach to war and maintain that ideologies of control over nature mirror patriarchal ideologies of men's control over women and anthropocentric attitudes of human's dominion over the earth.

KEY TERMS

collective violence, p. 345

military–industrial complex, p. 346

repressive terrorism, p. 352

revolutionary terrorism, p. 352

state-sponsored terrorism, p. 352

terrorism, p. 352

war, p. 344

war system, p. 344

weapons of mass destruction (WMD), p. 344

weapons system, p. 350

QUESTIONS FOR CRITICAL THINKING

1. How has war changed in the age of drones and computers from the World War II era where military personnel were directly involved in all aspects of warfare? Given the technology that is available, how can we safeguard service personnel and civilians alike?

2. What impacts do the U.S.-led anti-terrorist activities have on Canada and on the rest of the world today?

3. Given that our world will likely have multiple outbreaks of violence, how do we reconcile our beliefs in human rights and our interests, e.g., working with Iran to contain ISS and working with Russia to contain Iran's nuclear ambitions?

4. Consider the question posed in the last paragraph of this chapter: What can you yourself do to make the world a better—more peaceful—place in the 21st century?

Luc Novovitch / Alamy

How Can Social Problems Be Solved?

Review of Sociological Perspectives
New Possibilities and a Human Agenda

Y ou have now been introduced to a wide variety of social problems, from the status of women, to transnational crime, to global and local income inequality, to sustainable development, to peace and conflict, and many more. Can you think of any ways in which these problems can be reduced now? This final section will help you rethink the possibilities for change by reviewing the perspectives and providing a couple of examples of path-breaking work by young Canadians. It would also be helpful to revisit the section Social Change and Reducing Social Problems in Chapter 1.

Remember that, as social analysts have said, solving social problems is a far more complex undertaking than simply identifying them and pinpointing their social locations. Identifying social problems and calling for action are quite different matters from actually designing and implementing programs to solve them. Calling attention to the problem, for example, can often be accomplished relatively quickly and easily. Trying to actually carry out a solution, by contrast, involves "innumerable obstacles, delays, and frustrations," and demands "immense dedication and perseverance" (Weinberg et al. 1981:6).

Perhaps the first obstacle that we face in trying to solve social problems is the difference between ideal solutions and "do-able" solutions. As sociologists Martin S. Weinberg, Earl Rubington, and Sue Kiefer Hammersmith (1981:6) have stated, "There is usually considerable conflict between what the *ideal* solution would be and what a *workable* solution might be." Sometimes, for example, the ideal solution to a problem entails high costs that governments may be unwilling to pay. Sometimes there is little or no agreement about what the problem *is* and what efforts should be made to reduce or eliminate it. After all, the people and organizations involved in the problem-defining stage of a social problem generally are not the same people and organizations involved in the problem-solving stage. Social problems are often identified and defined by political or social activists, journalists, social scientists, and religious leaders. In contrast, the problem-solving stage usually involves elected officials and/or people working in agencies and governmental bureaucracies. Moreover, sometimes a proposed solution to a problem only gives rise to a whole new set of unforeseen problems (Weinberg et al. 1981). In this short epilogue, we will review several approaches for dealing with social problems and reiterate a pressing question: What are you willing to do to reduce or eliminate the social problems that you are concerned about?

Review of Sociological Perspectives

The underlying theoretical assumptions that we hold regarding social problems have a profound influence on what we feel may be the best solution for a specific problem. Do we believe society is based on stability, or conflict? Is conflict good or bad for society? Each of the four sociological perspectives summarized below suggests ways in which social problems may be reduced. In doing so, they produce divergent views on social changes that might reduce or eliminate social problems.

According to the functionalist perspective, a society is a stable, orderly system that is composed of a number of interrelated parts, each of which performs a function that contributes to the overall stability of the society. From the functionalist perspective, social problems arise when social institutions do not fulfill the functions they are supposed to or when dysfunctions (undesirable consequences of an activity or social process that inhibit a society's ability to adapt or adjust) occur. Dysfunctions create social disorganization, which in turn causes a breakdown in the traditional values and norms that serve as social control mechanisms. As shown in Table E.1, the social disorganization approach of functionalists traces the causes of social problems to any social change that leaves existing rules inadequate for current conditions. In societies undergoing social change—for example, retrenchment of social programs, high rates of immigration or emigration, rapid changes in technology, and increasingly complex patterns of social life—social disorganization can produce stress at the individual level and inefficiency and confusion at the institutional and societal levels (Weinberg et al. 1981). Thus, the functionalist approach to reducing social problems has as central factors the prevention of rapid social changes, the maintenance of the status quo, and the restoration of order.

TABLE E.1 Perceived Problems and Possible Solutions

Perspective	Causes	Possible Solutions
Functionalist		
Social disorganization	Social change; inadequacy of existing social rules	Development and implementation of social rules that are explicit, workable, and consistent
Conflict		
Value conflict	Conflict between different groups' values; economic, social, and cultural diversity	Group action involving confrontation of opponents for lasting changes in policy or legislation
Critical conflict (Marxist)	Relations of domination and subordination are reinforced by the global capitalist economy and political leaders who put other priorities ahead of the good of the people	Changing the nature of society, particularly inequalities that grow more pronounced as the wealthy grow richer and the poor worldwide become increasingly impoverished
Interactionist		
Deviant behaviour	Inappropriate socialization within primary groups	Resocialize or rehabilitate individuals so that they will conform
Labelling	How people label behaviour, how they respond to it, and the consequences of their responses	Changing the definitions through decriminalization; limit labelling
Feminist		
Interlocking oppressions	Patriarchy, capitalism, and other hierarchical systems that cause competition between groups and place value on one group over another	Consider the ways that oppressions are interconnected; educate oneself and others about inequities; change one's own behaviours; join with others to create models of change and visions of cooperative society; help to alleviate the suffering of individuals and groups who experience discrimination while simultaneously working to make broad-based and foundational social and political change

Source: *Based on Martin S. Weinberg, Earl Rubington, and Sue Kiefer Hammersmith, 1981,* The Solution of Social Problems: Five Perspectives *(2nd ed.), New York: Oxford University Press; and Joe R. Feagin and Claireece Booher Feagin, 2006,* Social Problems: A Critical-Conflict Perspective *(6th ed.), Upper Saddle River, NJ: Prentice Hall.*

In contrast, the conflict perspective assumes that conflict is natural and inevitable in society. Value conflict approaches focus on conflict between the values held by members of divergent groups. These approaches also highlight the ways in which cultural, economic, and social diversity may contribute to misunderstandings and problems. According to Marxist, or critical-conflict, theorists, groups are engaged in a continuous struggle for control of scarce resources. As a result of the unjust use of political, economic, or social power, certain groups of people are privileged while others are disadvantaged. Thus, for critical-conflict theorists,

social problems arise out of major contradictions that are inherent in the ways in which societies are organized. When this approach is used, the root causes of social problems—capitalism and spending priorities that place corporate tax breaks and military spending ahead of social services, for example—must be radically altered or eliminated altogether. Focusing on the political economy, one critical-conflict approach states that the capitalist economy, which is now global, maintains and reinforces domination and subordination in social relations. This approach also examines how political leaders and the economic elite may put their own interests ahead of any common good that might exist. Clearly, any solutions to social problems proposed by this approach would require radical changes in society and thus are not always viewed positively in societies in which economic prosperity based on individual attributes rather than collective activities is considered a mark of personal and social achievement. This is particularly problematic, conflict theorists point out, when elites maintain power through hegemony. Change can only be achieved, then, through counter-hegemonic means.

Operating at the microlevel, the interactionist perspective focuses on how people act toward one another and make sense of their daily lives. From this perspective, society is the sum of the interactions of individuals and groups. Thus, interactionists often study social problems by analyzing the process whereby a behaviour is defined as a social problem and how individuals and groups then come to engage in activities that a significant number of people view as major social concerns. Interactionist theories of deviance note that inadequate socialization or interacting with the "wrong" people may contribute to deviant behaviour and crime and, hence, to some social problems. Similarly, interactionists who use the labelling framework for their analysis of social problems study how people label behaviour, how they respond to people engaged in such behaviour, and the consequences of their responses (Weinberg et al. 1981).

Feminist theorists concentrate analyses at both macro and microlevels of interaction. Social problems are therefore examined on the basis of power in individual relations and in ideologies and structures, in particular looking at gender as a key component. Society is seen as a matrix of interlocking oppressions, organized according to specific relations of domination–subordination. Sexism, along with other forms of oppression, such as classism, homophobia, biphobia or transphobia, racism, and ableism, are examined in terms of the ways they privilege and disadvantage whole groups of people as well as the ways that these forms of oppression work in tandem to reinforce a paradigm of oppression, competition, and hierarchy. Feminist theorists who look at social problems look at the roles people play in resisting and/or perpetuating oppressions and at the locations or standpoints people come from. The inequalities and harm stemming from interlocking systems of oppression and domination are viewed as central to social problems. The solutions for reducing or eliminating social problems are therefore multifaceted: pivotal is the push for a paradigm shift that holds the values of co-operation, diversity, and power sharing in highest regard; also key is changing the unequal dynamics embedded in current racialized/

ethnic, class, and gender relations and in relationships between individuals that get played out within these and other contexts. Paradigm shifts require dramatic changes in the ways we view society and the ways we interact with one another individually and collectively. Further, paradigm shifts require us to retrain ourselves so that our behaviours fall into line with our new ways of thinking. This takes a great deal of commitment and hard work and is one of our challenges in the new millennium.

New Possibilities and a Human Agenda

The Internet has dramatically opened up new possibilities for activists to get information to those they would like to mobilize. Many sites serve as national and international mobilizing vehicles for groups seeking avenues to foster social change. Through news groups, bulletin boards, social networking sites, YouTube, and other similar vehicles, people are able to learn from one another and share information about social problems. They are also able to join in collective action or encourage others to take some specific action.

Do you follow the news about any social issues? If so, do you get your information primarily from television, radio, the Internet, or other sources? Based on the information you receive from various media sources, are you motivated to participate in organizations or actions that endeavour to bring about social change?

According to some analysts, we need to develop a human agenda that focuses on the needs of people and offsets the corporate agenda that is currently taking precedence over other issues and concerns. Social activists Jeremy Brecher and Tim Costello (1998) suggest that any proposed human agenda should:

- improve the lives of the great majority of the world's people;
- correspond to widely held common interests as well as integrate the interests of people worldwide;
- provide opportunities for action at a variety of levels;
- include elements that can be implemented independently, at least in part, but that are compatible or mutually reinforcing;
- make it easier to solve social problems such as environmental protection; and
- grow out of social movements and coalitions that have developed in response to the needs of diverse peoples.

But perhaps you would like us to take a step backward and ask a more fundamental question: Can social problems be solved? We believe wholeheartedly that they can; after all, what has been created can be re-created. So what is needed to re-create a more just world? Foundationally, we need social analysis, for as Swift,

Davies, Clarke, and Czerny (2003:202) state in their book *Getting Started on Social Analysis in Canada*, "the very activity of social analysis . . . helps to 'lift the fog' and overcome ideological confusion. . . . It can also lead directly into effective action." Take the quiz in Figure E.1 and evaluate your tendency toward social analysis.

We need some kind of shared vision and some shared values, without compromising the rich diversity that makes the world such a dynamic and joyful place. In their book on globalization and social problems, Peterson, Wunder, and Mueller (1999:414) provide an example of shared visioning and collective values using a statement derived from the 1993 Parliament of the World's Religions called *Toward a Global Ethic*. Some

of the values stated in this document include equality between men and women; the dignity and worth of all humans, regardless of ethnicity, gender, language, religion, ability, and so on; generosity, compassion, and caring for one another; economic and social justice; respect for the environment and human rights; truthfulness and honesty; moderation and modesty; loyalty; freedom, as long as it does not impose on others; safety; security; and so on. The ability to participate freely and fully in social life is at the core of these values, so, lastly, we need participation. Many of us feel paralyzed by the idea that social problems are big and we are small. Even small changes, however, can create critical mass, turning "seemingly impossible change into an inevitable

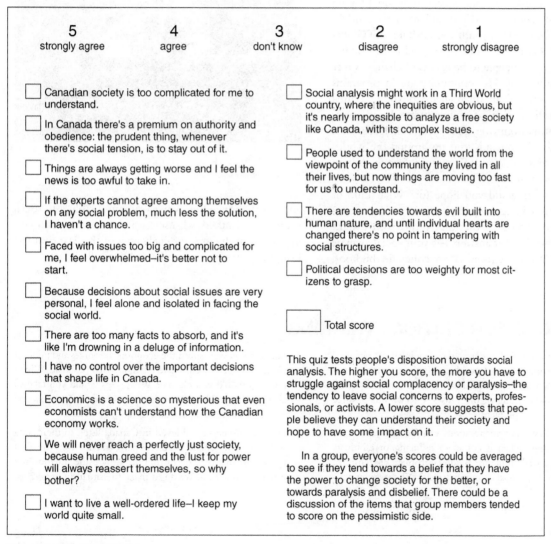

Figure E.1   Social Paralysis Quiz

Source: *Jamie Swift, Jacqueline M. Davies, Robert G Clarke, and Michael Czerny S.J., 2003,* Getting Started on Social Analysis in Canada, *4th ed., Toronto: Between the Lines, p. 8.*

one" (Swift et al. 2003:203). For a homegrown example of the difference small changes can make, look at what 12-year-old Craig Kielburger accomplished when he gathered together a small group of his Grade 7 classmates from Thornhill, Ontario in 1995 to try to put an end to child labour in Pakistan and other countries. Free The Children's mission was to create a world where all young people are free to achieve their fullest potential as agents of change. Today, Free The Children is an international charity, with more than 2.3 million youth involved in education and development programs. Since its inception, Free The Children has worked in more than 45 countries. Free The Children currently works in eight developing countries with its Adopt A Village program.

Two less well-known but equally influential young Canadians are Jennifer Corriero and Michael Furdyk, who in 1999 founded the youth website TakingITGlobal (TIG), which marries volunteers to good causes online to empower young people to be agents of change. Over 500 000 members of this community are in programs around the world, from micro-help to young entrepreneurs to nation-wide art competitions. In addition, 25 000 educators from over 4500 schools help connect with hundreds of thousands students around the world. Jennifer has won a World Economic Forum Young Global Leader award.

What kind of world you hope for? What kind of world are you willing to participate in to (re)create? What values do you hold that may propel you toward that participation? What answers has your social analysis brought you? What questions? As we conclude this book

Craig Kielburger
Tom Hanson/AP Images

and our time together, won't you join sociologists, social activists, and others who seek to use these tools to face up to one of the greatest challenges of the 21st century: bringing peace, justice, and equality to all?

QUESTIONS FOR CRITICAL THINKING

1. What is most useful about applying a sociological perspective to the study of social problems? Is there anything not useful in such an approach? How can you contribute to a better understanding of the causes, effects, and possible solutions to social problems?

2. Do you believe that corporations can be trusted to "do the right thing" when it comes to reducing or eliminating existing social problems? Is good corporate citizenship a possibility in the global economy today? Why or why not?

3. Suppose you were given the economic resources and political clout to reduce or eliminate a major social problem. Which problem would you choose? What steps would you take to alleviate this problem? How would you measure your success or failure in reducing or eliminating the problem?

4. Do governments at all levels in Canada listen to their constituents about social issues? What evidence can you find to support that they do or do not? Why is the situation the way it is? What can we do to make the situation better?

Glossary

ableism   prejudice and discrimination against people because of a physical or mental disability.

absolute poverty   a condition that exists when people do not have the means to secure the most basic necessities of life (food, clothing, and shelter).

acid rain   rainfall containing large concentrations of sulphuric and nitric acids (primarily from the burning of fuel and car and truck exhausts).

acute diseases   illnesses that strike suddenly and cause dramatic incapacitation and sometimes death.

ageism   prejudice and discrimination against people on the basis of age.

amalgamation   a process in which the cultural attributes of diverse racialized or ethnic groups are blended together to form a new society incorporating the unique contributions of each group.

androcentricity   putting males at the centre.

Anglo-conformity model   a pattern of assimilation whereby members of subordinate racialized/ethnic groups are expected to conform to the culture of the dominant (White) Anglo-Saxon population.

anti-Semitism   prejudice and discriminatory behaviour directed at Jews.

assimilation   the process by which members of subordinate racialized and ethnic groups become absorbed into the dominant culture.

biphobia   fear and intolerance of bisexuality.

blaming the victim   a practice suggesting that the cause of a social problem emanates from within the individual or group that exhibits the problem, by virtue of some inherent lack or flaw on the part of the individual or group.

blended family   a family that consists of a husband and wife or a same-sex couple, children from previous marriages, and children (if any) from the new marriage.

capitalism   an economic system characterized by private ownership of the means of production, from which personal profits can be derived through market competition and without government intervention.

chronic diseases   illnesses that are long term or lifelong and that develop gradually or are present from birth.

civil disobedience   non-violent action that seeks to change a policy or law by refusing to comply with it.

codependency   a reciprocal relationship between the alcoholic and one or more non-alcoholics who unwittingly aid and abet the alcoholic's excessive drinking and resulting behaviour.

cohabitation   two adults living together in a sexual relationship without being legally married.

collective behaviour   voluntary, often spontaneous activity that is engaged in by a large number of people and typically violates dominant group norms and values.

collective violence   organized violence by people seeking to promote their cause or resist social policies or practices that they consider harmful, oppressive, and unjust.

common law   two adults living together in a sexual relationship without being legally married.

compulsory heterosexism   a belief system that offers no options other than heterosexual behaviour and feelings and denies, denigrates, and stigmatizes gay, lesbian, or bisexual behaviour, identity, relationships, and community.

conflict perspective   a framework for viewing society that is based on the assumption that groups in society are engaged in a continuous power struggle for control of scarce resources.

core nations   dominant capitalist centres characterized by high levels of industrialization and urbanization.

corporate crime   illegal acts committed by corporate employees on behalf of the corporation and with its support.

corporate rich   a relatively fixed group of privileged people who wield power over political processes and serve capitalist interests.

corporate welfare   a situation in which the government helps industries and private corporations in their economic pursuits.

crime   a behaviour that violates criminal law and is punishable by fine, jail term, or other negative sanctions.

criminal justice system   the network of organizations, including the police, courts, criminal prosecutions, and corrections, involved in law enforcement and the administration of justice.

cultural capital   social assets, such as values, beliefs, attitudes, and competencies in language and culture, that are learned at home and required for success and social advancement.

date rape   forcible sexual activity that meets the legal definition of sexual assault and involves people who first meet in a social setting.

debt   the amount of money borrowed by the government to offset its deficits.

deficit   the situation when a government's spending on initiatives and programs, along with the interest charges on its outstanding debts, exceeds its revenues in a given year.

deindustrialization   the process by which capital is diverted from investment in basic industries (in the form of economic resources, plants, and equipment) to business practices such as mergers and acquisitions and foreign investment.

deinstitutionalization   the practice of discharging patients from mental hospitals into the community.

demographic transition theory   the theory that societies move from high birth and death rates to relatively low birth and death rates as a result of technological development.

demography   the study of the size, composition, and distribution of populations.

desertification   the process by which usable land is turned into desert because of overgrazing, harmful agricultural practices, or deforestation.

differential association theory   the belief that individuals have a greater tendency to deviate from societal norms when they frequently associate with people who tend toward deviance rather than conformity.

disability   a restricted or total lack of ability to perform certain activities as a result of physical or mental limitations or the interplay of these limitations, social responses, and the social environment.

discrimination   actions or practices of dominant group members (or their representatives) that have a harmful impact on members of subordinate groups.

dominant group   the group whose members are disproportionately at the top of the hierarchy, "with maximal access to society's power resources, particularly political authority and control of the means of economic production" (Marger 1999:273). See also **majority (or dominant) group**.

drug   any substance—other than food or water—that, when taken into the body, alters its functioning in some way.

drug addiction or drug dependency   a psychological and/or physiological need for a drug to maintain a sense of well-being and avoid withdrawal symptoms.

drug subculture   a group of people whose attitudes, beliefs, and behaviours pertaining to drug use differ significantly from those of most people in the larger society.

dual-earner marriages   marriages in which both spouses are in the labour force.

economic concentration   the extent to which a few individuals or corporations control the vast majority of all economic resources in a country.

economy   the social institution that ensures that a society will be maintained through its production, distribution, and consumption of goods and services.

edge city   a middle- to upper-middle-class area that has complete living, working, shopping, and leisure activities so that it is not dependent on the central city or other suburbs.

education   the social institution responsible for transmitting knowledge, skills, and cultural values in a formally organized structure.

elderly dependency ratio   the number of workers necessary to support those over age 64 or the ratio of seniors to 100 workers aged 20 to 64.

elite model   a view of society in which power in political systems is concentrated in the hands of a small group, whereas the masses are relatively powerless.

environmental classism   the belief that a disproportionate number of hazardous facilities are placed in areas with large proportions of poor people.

environmental degradation   disruptions to the environment that have negative consequences for ecosystems.

environmental tobacco smoke   the smoke in the air as a result of other people's tobacco smoking.

erotica   materials that depict consensual sexual activities that are sought by and pleasurable to all parties involved.

ethnic group   a category of people who are distinguished, by others or by themselves, on the basis of cultural or nationality characteristics. These can include language, country of origin, and adherence to culture.

ethnic pluralism   the coexistence of diverse racialized/ethnic groups with separate identities and cultures within a society.

ethnocentrism   the assumption that one's own group and way of life are superior to all others.

extended family   a family unit composed of relatives in addition to parents and children, all of whom live in the same household.

family   a relationship in which people live together with commitment, form an economic unit, care for any young, and consider the group critical to their identity.

feminization of poverty   the trend whereby women are disproportionately represented among individuals living in poverty.

fertility   the number of children born to an individual or a population.

fetal alcohol spectrum disorder (FASD)   an umbrella term used to describe the range of disabilities and diagnoses that result from drinking alcohol during pregnancy.

framing   how news content and the accompanying visual images are linked together to create certain audience perceptions and give specific impressions to viewers and readers.

functionalist perspective   a framework for viewing society as a stable, orderly system composed of a number of interrelated parts, each of which performs a function that contributes to the overall stability of society.

gender   socially constructed sets of attitudes that dictate what behaviours, thoughts, and emotions are appropriate for each sex—these are culturally specific, change over time, and are associated with notions of femininity or masculinity.

gender ideology   ideas of masculinity and femininity that are held to be valid in a given society at a specific historical time.

gendered division of labour   the process whereby productive tasks are separated on the basis on gender.

gendered racism   the interactive effect of racism and sexism in exploiting Indigenous women and women "of colour."

generalization   an idea held about a group of people that are open to revision or change and that can be rejected entirely at any time.

genocide   the deliberate, systematic killing of an entire people or nation.

gentrification   the process by which people renovate or restore properties in central cities.

glass ceiling   the invisible institutional barrier constructed by male management that prevents women from reaching top positions in major corporations and other large-scale organizations.

gonzo pornography   openly misogynist pornography with no pretensions of a plot.

government   a formal organization that has legal and political authority to regulate relationships among people in a society and between the society and others outside its borders.

grassroots groups   organizations started by ordinary people who work in concert to change a perceived problem in their neighbourhood, city, province or territory, or nation.

greenhouse effect   an environmental condition caused by excessive quantities of carbon dioxide, methane, and nitrous oxide in the atmosphere.

hate crime   an act of violence motivated by prejudice against people on the basis of racialized identity, ethnicity, religion, gender, or sexual orientation. This can include the dissemination of materials intended to incite hatred.

hegemony   the use of the media and other cultural institutions to represent the interests, values, and understandings of the capitalist class and other powerful groups as natural and universal.

hegemony theory   the view that the media are instruments of social control and are used by members of the ruling classes to create "false consciousness" in the working classes.

heteronormativity   a belief system that offers no acceptable options other than heterosexual behaviour and feelings and denies, denigrates, and stigmatizes gay, lesbian, or bisexual behaviour, identity, relationships, and community.

heterosexism   the belief that heterosexuality is the only normal, natural, and moral mode of relating, and hence is superior to homosexuality or bisexuality.

hidden curriculum   how certain cultural values and attitudes, such as conformity and obedience to authority, are transmitted through implied demands in the everyday rules and routines of schools.

homicide   the unlawful, intentional killing of one person by another.

homophobia   the irrational and excessive fear or intolerance of homosexuals and homosexuality.

hospice   an organization that provides a homelike facility or home-based care (or both) for people who are terminally ill.

iatrogenesis   problems caused by doctors and the health care system.

income   the economic gain derived from wages, salaries, and income transfers (governmental aid, such as income assistance [welfare], or ownership of property).

indictable offence   more serious crimes, such as murder or aggravated assault, that are punishable by more than a year's imprisonment.

individual discrimination   one-on-one acts by members of a dominant group that harm members of a subordinate group or their property.

industrialization   the process by which societies are transformed from a dependence on agriculture and handmade products to an emphasis on manufacturing and related industries.

infant mortality rate   the number of deaths of infants under one year of age per 1000 live births in a given year.

institutional discrimination   the day-to-day practices of organizations and institutions that have a harmful impact on members of subordinate groups.

interactionist perspective   a framework that views society as the sum of the interactions of individuals and groups.

interlocking corporate directorates   members of the board of directors of one corporation who also sit on the board of one or more other corporations.

internal colonialism   a process that occurs when members of a racialized/ethnic group are conquered or colonized and forcibly placed under the economic and political control of the dominant group.

internalized dominance   all the ways that White people learn they are normal, feel included, and do not think of themselves as "other" or "different."

intersectionality   when people experience oppression in more than one aspect of their lives (e.g., sexism plus racism plus homophobia), the resulting oppression is greater than the sum of these oppressions.

intersexed   having either unrecognizably male or female genitalia, or having both male and female genitalia.

kinship   a social network of people based on common ancestry, marriage, or adoption.

labelling theory   the proposition that delinquents and criminals are those people who have been successfully labelled as such by others.

latent functions   hidden, unstated, and sometimes unintended consequences of activities in an organization or institution.

life chances   the extent to which individuals have access to important societal resources such as food, clothing, shelter, education, and health care.

life expectancy   an estimate of the average lifetime of people born in a specific year.

lifestyle–routine activity approach   the belief that the patterns and timing of people's daily movements and activities as they go about obtaining the necessities of life—such as food, shelter, companionship, and entertainment—are the keys to understanding violent personal crimes and other types of crime in our society.

macrolevel analysis   focuses on social processes occurring at the societal level, especially in large-scale organizations and major social institutions such as politics, government, and the economy.

majority (or dominant) group   a group that is advantaged and has superior access to resources and rights in a society.

manifest functions   open, stated, and intended goals or consequences of activities within an organization or institution.

mass murder   the killing of four or more people at one time and in one place by the same person.

master status   the most significant status a person possesses, the one that most determines how the individual views him- or herself and how he or she is treated by others.

mechanical solidarity   social bonds based on shared religious beliefs and a simple division of labour.

media concentration   the tendency of the media industries to cluster together in groups with the goal of enhancing profitability.

media industries   major businesses that own, or own interests in, radio and television production and broadcasting; cellphones and other Personal Digital Assistants (PDAs); motion pictures, movie theatres, and music companies; newspaper, periodical (magazine), and book publishing; and Internet services and content providers; and that influence people and cultures worldwide.

medical–industrial complex   encompasses both local physicians and hospitals as well as global health-related industries such as the pharmaceutical and medical supply companies that deliver health care.

medicalization   the treating of a person's condition as an illness.

medicalization of crime   the converting of a criminal behaviour to a medical condition or disease.

megalopolis   a continuous concentration of two or more cities and their suburbs that have grown until they form an interconnected urban area.

meritocracy   a nation where the best person can rise to the top in any situation, despite his or her antecedents.

microlevel analysis   focuses on small-group relations and social interaction among individuals.

migration   the movement of people from one geographic area to another for the purpose of changing residency.

military–industrial complex   a term referring to the interdependence of the military establishment and private military contractors.

minority (or subordinate) group   a group whose members, because of supposed physical or cultural characteristics, are disadvantaged and subjected to negative discriminatory treatment by the majority group and regard themselves as objects of collective discrimination.

mixed economy   an economic system that combines elements of both capitalism (a market economy) and socialism (a command economy).

monogamy a marriage between any two adults.

monopoly a situation that exists when a single firm controls an industry and accounts for all sales in a specific market.

mortality the number of deaths that occur in a specific population.

multinational corporation (MNC) a complete corporate operation that is taken from its country of origin and integrated into its host country in order to successfully market its products in the local culture.

net neutrality the situation where net providers do not discriminate against or for website content, services, or applications based on the source, ownership, or destination.

norms established rules of behaviour or standards of conduct.

nuclear family a family unit composed of one or two parents and her/his/their dependent children who live apart from other relatives.

obscenity the legal term for all materials that are offensive by generally accepted standards of decency.

occupational (white-collar) crime illegal activities committed by people in the course of their employment or normal business activity.

oligopoly a situation in which a small number of companies or suppliers control an entire industry or service.

organic solidarity social bonds based on interdependence and an elaborate division of labour (specialization).

organized crime a business operation that supplies illegal goods and services for profit.

pansexuality people who are attracted to male, female, trans, androgynous, gender fluid, and non-gendered people.

patriarchy a hierarchical system of social organization in which cultural, political, and economic structures are controlled by men.

peripheral nations nations that depend on core nations for capital, have little or no industrialization (other than what may be brought in by core nations), and have uneven patterns of urbanization.

perspective an overall approach or viewpoint toward some subject.

plea bargaining a process whereby the Crown attorney negotiates a reduced sentence with a defence attorney in exchange for a guilty plea.

political economy the interdependent workings and interests of political and economic systems.

politics the social institution through which power is acquired and exercised by certain individuals and groups.

population composition the biological and social characteristics of a population, including such attributes as age, sex, racialization, marital status, education, occupation, income, and size of household.

power the ability of people to achieve their goals despite opposition from others.

power elite rulers of Canada, at the top is composed of business leaders, the executive branch of the federal government, and the "top brass" of the military.

prejudice a negative attitude about people based on such characteristics as racialization, gender, age, religion, or sexual orientation.

prestige the respect, esteem, or regard accorded to an individual or group by others.

primary deviance the initial act of rule breaking.

primary groups small, less-specialized groups (see **secondary groups**) in which members engage in face-to-face, emotion-based interactions over an extended period of time.

property crime the taking of money or property from another without force, the threat of force, or the destruction of property.

prostitution the sale of sexual services (of oneself or another) for money or goods and without emotional attachment.

punishment any action designed to deprive a person of things of value (including liberty) because of an offence the person is thought to have committed.

racialized group a category of people who have been singled out, by others or themselves, as inferior or superior, on the basis of subjectively selected physical characteristics such as skin colour, hair texture, and eye shape.

racism a set of attitudes, beliefs, and practices used to justify the superior treatment of one racialized or ethnic group and the inferior treatment of another racialized or ethnic group.

rape culture the pervasive system of cultural values, attitudes, and practices that supports and perpetuates sexualized violence against women.

relative poverty a condition that exists when people may be able to afford basic necessities, such as food, clothing, and shelter, but cannot maintain an average standard of living in comparison to that of other members of their society or group.

restorative justice the focus on repairing the harm caused by crime by holding moderated meetings of crime victims, offenders, and others affected by the crime; restorative justice practices can be used at different sites in the justice system.

revolutionary terrorism acts of violence against civilians that are carried out by internal enemies of the government who want to bring about political change.

secondary deviance the process that occurs when a person who has been labelled a deviant accepts that new identity and continues the deviant behaviour.

second shift the domestic work that many employed women perform at home after completing their workday on the job.

segregation the spatial and social separation of categories of people by racialization, ethnicity, class, gender, religion, or other social characteristics.

self-fulfilling prophecy the process by which a false definition of a situation results in new behaviour that makes the original false conception become true.

self-health management includes self-care practices, mutual aid, and membership in self-help groups.

semi-peripheral nations nations that are more developed than peripheral nations but less developed than core nations.

serial murder the killing of three or more people over more than a month by the same person.

sex the biological, physiological, hormonal, and chromosomal attributes of females, males, and intersex people.

sexism the subordination of one sex, female, based on the assumed superiority of the other sex, male.

sexual assault an act of violence in which sex is used as a weapon against a powerless victim.

sexual harassment a form of intentional, institutionalized gender discrimination that includes all unwelcome sexual attention affecting an employee's job conditions or creating a hostile work environment.

sexual orientation a preference for emotional–sexual relationships with individuals of the "same" sex (homosexuality), the "opposite" sex (heterosexuality), or both (bisexuality).

sexuality attitudes, beliefs, and practices related to sexual attraction and intimate relationships with others.

situational approach the belief that violence results from a specific interaction process, termed a "situational transaction."

social bond theory the proposition that criminal behaviour is most likely to occur when a person's ties to society are weakened or broken.

social change the alteration, modification, or transformation of public policy, culture, or social institutions over time.

social construct the classification of people based on social and political values—rather than a biological given.

social control the systematic practices developed by social groups to encourage conformity and discourage deviance.

social disorganization the conditions in society that undermine the ability of traditional social institutions to govern human behaviour.

social gerontology the study of the social (nonphysical) aspects of aging.

social learning theory based on the assumption that people are likely to act out the behaviour they see in role models and media sources.

socialism an economic system characterized by public ownership of the means of production, the pursuit of collective goals, and centralized decision making.

social movement an organized group that acts collectively to promote or resist change through collective action.

social problem a social condition (such as poverty) or a pattern of behaviour (such as violence against women) that people believe warrants public concern and collective action to bring about change.

social stratification the hierarchical arrangement of large social groups on the basis of their control over basic resources.

socialism an economic system characterized by public ownership of the means of production, the pursuit of collective goals, and centralized decision making.

society a large number of individuals who share the same geographical territory and are subject to the same political authority and dominant cultural expectations.

sociological imagination the ability to see the relationship between individual experiences and the larger society in which they are contextualized.

sociology the academic and scholarly discipline that engages in the systematic study of human society and social interactions.

state-sponsored terrorism political terrorism resulting from a government providing financial resources, weapons, and training for terrorists who conduct their activities in other nations.

stepfamily consists of a husband and wife or a same-sex couple, children from previous marriages, and children (if any) from the new marriage (see **blended family**).

stereotypes fixed and distorted generalizations about the appearance, behaviour, or other characteristics of all members of a particular group.

strain theory the proposition that people feel strain when they are exposed to cultural goals that they cannot reach because they do not have access to culturally approved means of achieving those goals.

subculture a group of people who share a distinctive set of cultural beliefs and behaviours that set them apart from the larger society.

subculture of violence hypothesis the hypothesis that violence is part of the normative expectations governing everyday behaviour among young males in the lower classes.

subordinate groups groups whose members, in relation to the dominant group (or groups), do not occupy positions of power. See also **minority group**.

summary conviction offences relatively minor crimes that are punishable by a fine or less than a year in jail.

terrorism the use of calculated, unlawful physical force or threats of violence against a government, organization, or individual to gain some political, religious, economic, or social objective.

theory a set of logically related statements that attempt to describe, explain, or predict social events.

theory of limited effects the media have a minimal effect on the attitudes and perceptions of individuals.

theory of racial formation a theory that states that the government substantially defines racialized and ethnic relations.

tolerance a condition that occurs when larger doses of a drug are required over time to produce the same physical or psychological effect that was originally achieved by a smaller dose.

total institution a place where people are isolated from the rest of society for a period of time and come under the complete control of the officials who run the institution.

transnational corporation (TNC) a large-scale business organization that is headquartered in one country but operates in many countries, which has the legal power (separate from individual owners or shareholders) to enter into contracts, buy and sell property, and engage in other business activities.

unemployment rate the percentage of unemployed persons in the labour force seeking employment.

urbanization the process by which an increasing proportion of a population lives in cities rather than in rural areas.

values collective ideas about what is right or wrong, good or bad, and desirable or undesirable in a specific society.

victimless crime a crime that many people believe has no real victim because it involves willing participants in an economic exchange.

violent crime actions involving force or the threat of force against others that includes homicide, attempted homicide, the three levels of assault and sexual assault, robbery, and other violent offences like criminal negligence causing death.

wage gap the disparity between women's and men's earnings.

war organized, armed conflict between nations or distinct political factions.

war system components of social institutions (e.g., the economy, government, and education) and cultural beliefs and practices that promote the development of warriors, weapons, and war as a normal part of the society and its foreign policy.

wealth the value of all economic assets, including income and savings, personal property, and income-producing property, minus one's liabilities or debts.

weapons of mass destruction (WMD) nuclear, biological, chemical, or radiological weapons that can kill thousands of people and destroy vast amounts of property at one time.

weapons system   a weapons platform (e.g., a ship, aircraft, or tank), a weapon (e.g., a gun, missile, or torpedo), and the means of command and communication.

welfare state   a nation in which the government intervenes in the welfare of its citizens through various social policies, programs, standards, and regulations.

withdrawal   a variety of physical and/or psychological symptoms that habitual drug users experience when they discontinue drug use.

youth crime   a violation of law or the commission of a status offence by a young person 12 to 17 years of age.

zero population growth   a situation in which a population is totally stable, neither growing nor decreasing from year to year because births, deaths, and migration are in perfect balance.

References

NOTE: References in red are new to the Fourth Edition.

Aalbers, Manuel B. 2005. "Big Sister Is Watching You: Gender Interaction and the Unwritten Rules of the Amsterdam Red-Light District." The Journal of Sex Research, 42:54–62.

Abbate, Gay. 1998. "Gangs Small But Growing Roots: Police Hope to Arrest Development." Globe and Mail (November 20):A10.

Abbott, Roberta. 2000. "From Shell Shock to Post-Traumatic Stress Disorder: What Are We Asking of Our Armed Forces Personnel?" Presented at the Third Annual Graduate Student Symposium Conference of Defence Associations Institute (November 3–4).

Abella, Irving. 1989. A Coat of Many Colours: Two Centuries of Jewish Life in Canada. Toronto: Lester and Orpen Dennys.

Abella, Irving, and Harold Troper. 1991. None Is Too Many: Canada and the Jews in Europe 1933–1948 (3rd ed.). Toronto: Lester and Orpen Dennys.

Ackerman, Spencer. 2014. "Global Terrorism Rose 43% in 2013 Despite Al-Qaida Splintering, US Report." theguardian (April 30). Retrieved June 11, 2014 (http://www.theguardian.com/world/2014/apr/30/global-terrorism-rose-despite-al-qaida-splintering).

Adams, Karen L., and Norma C. Ware. 1995. "Sexism and the English Language: The Linguistic Implications of Being a Woman." In Jo Freeman (Ed.), Women: A Feminist Perspective (5th ed.). Mountain View, CA: Mayfield, pp. 331–346.

Adams, Tom. 1991. Grass Roots: How Ordinary People Are Changing America. New York: Citadel Press.

Aday, David P., Jr. 1990. Social Control at the Margins: Toward a General Understanding of Deviance. Belmont, CA: Wadsworth.

Adlaf, Edward, and Angela Paglia-Boak. 2007. Drug Use among Ontario High School Students. Toronto: Centre for Addiction and Mental Health.

Adlaf, Edward, Angela Paglia-Boak, Joseph Beitchman, and David Wolfe. 2007. Mental Health and Well-Being of Ontario Students 1991–2007. Toronto: Centre for Addiction and Mental Health.

Alexander, Karl L., Doris Entwisle, and Maxine Thompson. 1987. "School Performance, Status Relations, and the Structure of Sentiment: Bringing the Teacher Back In." American Sociological Review, 52:665–682.

Alexander, Priscilla. 1987. "Prostitution: A Difficult Issue for Feminists?" In Frederique Delacoste and Priscilla Alexander (Eds.), Sex Work: Writings by Women in the Sex Industry. San Francisco: Cleis Press, pp. 184–214.

Allen, Mary, and Jillian Boyce. 2013. "Police-Reported Hate Crime in Canada, 2011." Canadian Centre for Justice Statistics. Juristat. Catalogue no. 85-002-x. ISSN: 1209-6393. Retrieved November 23, 2013 (http://www.statcan.gc.ca/pub/85-002-x/2013001/article/11822-eng.htm).

Allen, Paula Gunn. 1986. The Sacred Hoop: Recovering the Feminine in American Indian Traditions. Boston: Beacon Press.

Allman, Dan. 1999. M Is for Mutual, A Is for Acts: Male Sex Work and AIDS in Canada. Co-published with Health Canada; AIDS Vancouver; The HIV, Social, Behavioural, and Epidemiological Studies Unit, Faculty of Medicine, University of Toronto; and the Sex Workers Alliance of Vancouver. (http://www.walnet.org/members/dan_allman/mutualacts/index.html).

Almaguer, Tomás. 1995. "Chicano Men: A Cartography of Homosexual Identity and Behavior." In Michael S. Kimmel and Michael A. Messner (Eds.), Men's Lives (3rd ed.). Boston: Allyn and Bacon, pp. 418–431.

Alvi, Shahid, Walter DeKeseredy, and Desmond Ellis. 2000. Contemporary Social Problems in North American Society. Don Mills, ON: Addison-Wesley.

Alzheimer's Society. 2013. Dementia in Canada. Retrieved August 6, 2013 (http://www.alzheimer.ca/en/Get-involved/Raise-your-voice/Dementia-in-canada).

Amnesty International. 2014a. Kosovo: Amnesty International Calls on the Assembly to Guarantee the Rights of Victims of War Crimes of Sexual Violence. Retrieved March 19, 2014 (http://www.amnesty.org/en/library/asset/EUR70/007/2014/en/67068ac1-298e-4601-83f0-fae5b124074f/eur700072014en.pdf).

Amnesty International. 2014b. We Can't Endure Anymore: The Impact of Inter-Communal Violence on civilians in Central Darfur. Retrieved March 19, 2014 (http://www.amnesty.org/en/library/asset/AFR54/002/2014/en/8da5fe37-ab2b-445a-bf50-7ab84c28e5cb/afr540022014en.pdf).

Amott, Teresa, and Julie Matthaei. 1991. Race, Gender, and Work: A Multicultural Economic History of Women in the United States. Boston: South End Press.

Andersen, Margaret L., and Patricia Hill Collins (Eds.). 1997. Race, Class, and Gender: An Anthology (3rd ed.). Belmont, CA: Wadsworth.

Anderson, S. 2009. "Why Big Media Is Failing." The Tyee (March 11). Retrieved July 19, 2009 (http://thetyee.ca/Mediacheck/2009/03/11/MediaFailing).

Anderson, S.J., S.A. Glantz, and P.M. Ping. 2005. Emotions for Sale: Cigarette Advertising and Women's Psychosocial Needs. Tobacco Control, 14:127–135.

Anderssen, Erin. 2002. "Same-Sex Census Numbers Due Today." Globe and Mail (October 22):A9.

Andersson, Thomas, and Georgina Schemberg. 2003. Transnational Corporations and Export Competitiveness: A Summary and Comment. Retrieved February 8, 2009 (http://www.iked.org/pdf/UNCTAD.pdf).

Angus Reid. 2006. "Same-Sex Marriage Issue Settled, Say Canadians." Angus Reid

Global Monitor: Polls & Research (June 21). Retrieved October 4, 2006 (http://www.angus-reid.com/polls/index.cfm/fuseaction/viewItem/itemID/12288).

Angus Reid. 2009. "American Majority Opposes Same-Sex Marriage." Angus Reid Global Monitor: Polls & Research (January 5). Retrieved June 23, 2009 (http://www.angus-reid.com/polls/view/american_majority_opposes_same_sex_marriage).

Angus Reid. 2013. Canadians and Britons Would Allow Euthanasia Under Some Conditions. Retrieved June 13, 2013 (http://angusreid.org/canadians-and-britons-would-allow-euthanasia-under-some-conditions/).

Angus Reid Public Opinion Poll. 2013. "Americans More Morally Conservative Than Canadians or Britons." Retrieved November 23, 2013 (http://www.angusreidglobal.com/wp-content/uploads/2013/01/2013.01.31_Morality.pdf).

Anyon, Jean. 1980. "Social Class and the Hidden Curriculum of Work." Journal of Education, 162:67–92.

Arar, Maher. 2009. "Maher's Story in Brief." Maherarar.ca. Retrieved August 24, 2009 (http://www.maherarar.ca).

Assembly of First Nations. 2008. "Residential Schools." Retrieved November 29, 2008 (http://www.afn.ca/residentialschools/index.html).

Associated Press. 1999. "Crushed Cock Earns Cash." (December 2). (http://www.geocities.com/athens/thebes/9940/taboo/sexnews.html).

Associated Press. 2013. Study: Later Retirement May Help Prevent Dementia. Retrieved July 20, 2013 (http://news.yahoo.com/study-later-retirement-may-help-prevent-dementia-124022246.html).

Aulette, Judy Root. 1994. Changing Families. Belmont, CA: Wadsworth.

Austin, Ian. 2013. A Dizzying Condo Market in Toronto. New York Times (July 2). Retrieved October 11, 2013 (http://www.nytimes.com/2013/07/03/business/a-soaring-condo-market-in-toronto-ignites-fears-of-a-crash.html?_r=0).

Axinn, William G., and Arland Thornton. 1992. "The Relationship between Cohabitation and Divorce: Selectivity

or Casual Influence?" Demography, 29(3):357–374.

Baird, Vanessa. 2007. The No-Nonsense Guide to Sexual Diversity (updated ed.). Toronto: Between the Lines.

Bakanic, Von. 2009. Prejudice: Attitudes about Race, Class and Gender. Upper Saddle River, NJ: Pearson Prentice Hall.

Baker, G. Ross, Peter C. Norton, Virginia Flintoft et al. 2004. "The Canadian Adverse Effects Study: The Incidence of Adverse Effects in Canadian Hospitals." Canadian Medical Association Journal, 170 (11):1678–1686.

Baker, Jean M. 2001. How Homophobia Hurts Children: Nurturing Diversity at Home, at School, and in the Community. London: Harrington Park Press.

Baldwin, Margaret. 1984. "The Sexuality of Inequality." Law and Inequality 2:643.

Ballentine, Jeanne H., and Floyd M. Hammack. 2009. The Sociology of Education: A Systematic Analysis (6th ed.). Upper Saddle River, NJ: Pearson/Prentice Hall.

Bandura, Albert. 1973. Aggression: A Social Learning Analysis. Englewood Cliffs, NJ: Prentice-Hall.

Bannerji, Himani. 1995. Thinking Through: Essays on Feminism, Marxism and Anti-Racism. Toronto: Women's Press.

Barber, Benjamin R. 1996. Jihad vs. McWorld: How Globalism and Tribalism Are Reshaping the World. New York: Ballantine Books.

Barlow, Hugh D. 1996. Introduction to Criminology (7th ed.). New York: HarperCollins.

Barnett, Laura, and Julia Nichol. 2011/2012. "Background paper: Prostitution in Canada, International Obligations, Federal law and Provincial and Municipal Jurisdiction." Publication 2011-119-E, September 17, 2011, Revised April 30, 2012. Library of Parliament.

Barofsky, I. 1978. "Compliance, Adherence and the Therapeutic Alliance: Steps in the Development of Self-Care." Social Science and Medicine, 12:369–376.

Barrett, Stanley R. 1991. "White Supremists and Neo-Fascists: Laboratories for the Analysis of Racism in Wider Society." In Ormond McKague (Ed.), Racism in Canada. Saskatoon: Fifth House, pp. 85-99.

Barris, Ted. 2009. "Romeo Dallaire: Peacekeeping in the New Millennium." The

Memory Project: Stories of the Second World War. Retrieved August 24, 2009 (http://www.thememoryproject.com/Vol3Dallaire.pdf).

Barry, Kathleen. 1995. The Prostitution of Sexuality. New York: New York University Press.

Bauerlein, Monika. 1995. "The Borderless Bordello." Utne Reader (November–December):30–32.

Baumann, Shyon, and Loretta Ho. 2014. Cultural hemas for Racial Identity in Canadian Television Advertising. Canadian Review of Sociology. 51:152–169.

Bawer, Bruce. 1994. A Place at the Table: The Gay Individual in American Society. New York: Touchstone.

BBC News. 2013. Robot Astronaut Launched to ISS. Retrieved August 5, 2013 (http://www.bbc.co.uk/news/science-environment-23564924).

Beare, Margaret E. 1996. Criminal Conspiracies. Scarborough, ON: Nelson.

Becker, Howard S. 1963. Outsiders: Studies in the Sociology of Deviance. New York: Free Press.

Bélanger, Alain. 1998. "Trends in Contraceptive Sterilization." Canadian Social Trends (Autumn):16–19.

Belle, Marilyn, and Kevin McQuillan. 1994. "Births Outside Marriage: A Growing Alternative." Canadian Social Trends (Summer): 14–17.

Bem, S.L. 1974. "The Measurement of Psychological Androgyny." Journal of Consulting and Clinical Psychology, 42:155–162.

Benokraitis, Nijole V., and Joe R. Feagin. 1995. Modern Sexism: Blatant, Subtle, and Covert Discrimination. Englewood Cliffs, NJ: Prentice-Hall.

Berger, Peter. 1963. Invitation to Sociology: A Humanistic Perspective. New York: Anchor.

Berger, Peter, and Hansfried Kellner. 1964. "Marriage and the Construction of Reality." Diogenes, 46:1–32.

Berger, Peter, and Thomas Luckmann. 1967. The Social Construction of Reality: A Treatise in the Sociology of Knowledge. Garden City, NY: Anchor Books.

Berger, Ronald J., Patricia Searles, and Charles E. Cottle. 1991. "Feminism and Pornography." Praeger Publishers.

Bernard, Jessie. 1982. The Future of Marriage. New Haven, CT: Yale University Press.

Biagi, Shirley, 2012. Media Impact: An Introduction to Mass Media (10th ed.). Belmont, CA: Cengage/Wadsworth.

Bindel, Julie. 2013. "Meet the Middle-Aged, Middle-Class Women who are Britain's Female Sex Tourists." Mail Online. Retrieved March 19, 2014 (http://www.dailymail.co.uk/femail/article-2401788/Sex-tourism-Meet-middle-aged-middle-class-women-Britains-female-sex-tourists.html).

Blackwood, E. 1986. "Breaking the Mirror: The Social Construction of Lesbianism and the Anthropological Discourse on Homosexuality." In The Many Faces of Homosexuality: Anthropological Approaches to Homosexual Behavior. New York: Harrington Park Press, pp. 1–17.

Blackwell, Richard. 2014. "The 1 Percent Lead Charge as Wealth Grows, Canada Lags." The Globe and Mail. June 11:B1&B10.

Blasius, Mark. 2001a. "An Ethos of Lesbian and Gay Existence." In Mark Blasius (Ed.), Sexual Identities—Queer Politics. Princeton, NJ: Princeton University Press, pp. 143–177.

Blasius, Mark. 2001b. "Sexual Identities, Queer Politics, and the Status of Knowledge." In Mark Blasius (Ed.), Sexual Identities—Queer Politics. Princeton, NJ: Princeton University Press, pp. 3–19.

Bonacich, Edna. 1972. "A Theory of Ethnic Antagonism: The Split Labor Market." American Sociological Review, 37:547–549.

Bonacich, Edna. 1976. "Advanced Capitalism and Black–White Relations in the United States: A Split Labor Market Interpretation." American Sociological Review, 41:34–51.

Bonanno, George A. 2009. "Grief does not come in stages." Psychology Today (October 26).

Bonanno, George A. 2010. The Other side of Sadness: What the New Science of Bereavement Tells Us about Life after Loss. New York, NY: Basic Books.

Bonger, Willem. 1969. Criminality and Economic Conditions (abridged ed.). Bloomington: Indiana University Press (orig. published in 1916).

Bourdieu, Pierre, and Jean-Claude Passeron. 1990. Reproduction in Education, Society, and Culture. Newbury Park, CA: Sage.

Bourgeois, Philippe. 1995. In Search of Respect: Selling Crack in el Barrio. New York: Cambridge University Press.

Bowles, Samuel, and Herbert Gintis. 1976. Schooling in Capitalist America: Education and the Contradictions of Economic Life. New York: Basic Books.

Bowles, Samuel, and Herbert Gintis. 2002. "Schooling in Capitalist America Revisited." Sociology of Education, 75(1):1–18.

Boyd, Monica, and Doug Norris. 1999. "The Crowded Nest: Young Adults at Home." Canadian Social Trends (Spring):2–5.

Brannigan, Augustine, Louis Knafla, and Christopher Levy. 1989. Street Prostitution: Assessing the Impact of the Law—Calgary, Regina, Winnipeg. Ottawa: Department of Justice Canada.

Brecher, Jeremy, and Tim Costello. 1998. Global Village or Global Pillage: Economic Reconstruction from the Bottom Up (2nd ed.). Cambridge, MA: South End Press.

Brennan, Denise. 2004. "Women Work, Men Sponge and Everyone Gossips: Macho Men and Stiganmized/ing Women in a Sex Tourist Town." Anthropological Quarterly 77(4):705–733.

Brennan, Shannon. 2013. "Section 5 Family Violence Against Seniors." Statistics Canada. Retrieved August 20, 2013 (http://www.statcan.gc.ca/pub/85-002-x/2013001/article/11805/11805-5-eng.htm).

Brents, Barbara, and Kathryn Hausbeck, 2005. "Violence and Legalized Brothel Prostitution in Nevada: Examining Safety, Risk, and Prostitution Policy." Journal of Interpersonal Violence, 20(3):270–295.

British Columbia (B.C.) Ministry of Attorney General. 1996. Community Consultation on Prostitution in British Columbia: Overview of Results. Victoria, BC: Ministry of Attorney General, Government of British Columbia.

Brodribb, Somer. 1999. "Introduction." In Somer Brodribb (Ed.), Reclaiming the Future: Women's Strategies for the 21st Century. Charlottetown, PEI: Gynergy Books, pp. 13–22.

Browne, Jan, and Victor Minichiello. 1995. "The Social Meanings Behind Male Sex Work: Implications for Sexual

Interactions." British Journal of Sociology, 46(4):598–623.

Brownell, Kelly D., and Thomas R. Frieden. 2009. "Ounces of Prevention: The Public Policy Case for Taxes on Sugared Beverages." New England Journal of Medicine. Retrieved April 15, 2009 (http://content.nejm.org/cgi/content/full/NEJMp0902392?resourcetype=HWCIT).

Bullough, Vern, and Bonnie Bullough. 1987. Women and Prostitution: A Social History. Buffalo, NY: Prometheus.

Butler, Robert N. 1969. "Ageism: Another Form of Bigotry." The Gerontologist, 9:243–246.

Byers, Michael. 2014. After Afghanistan: Canada's Return to UN Peacekeeping. National Defense. Retrieved May 20, 2014 (http://www.journal.forces.gc.ca/vol13/no1/page33-eng.asp).

Cable, Sherry, and Charles Cable. 1995. Environmental Problems, Grassroots Solutions: The Politics of Grassroots Environmental Conflict. New York: St. Martin's Press.

Cameron, David. 1995. "The Making of a Polluter: A Social History of Uniroyal Chemical in Elmira." In Michael D. Mehta and Eric Ouellet (Eds.), Environmental Sociology Theory and Practice. North York, ON: Captus Press, pp. 297–320.

Campion-Smith, Bruce. 2104. "UN Urges Canada to Hold National Inquiry on Missing Aboriginal Women and Girls." TheStar.com (May 12). Retrieved January 1, 2015 (http://www.thestar.com/news/canada/2014/05/12/canada_needs_to_do_better_in_relations_with_first_nations_un_says.html).

Canadian Advisory Council on the Status of Women. 1984. Prostitution in Canada. Ottawa: Canadian Advisory Council on the Status of Women.

Canadian Association of Food Banks. 2005. Time for Action: Hungercount 2005. Toronto: Canadian Association of Food Banks.

Canadian Association of Retired People. 2011. CARP Elder Abuse Report. Retrieved November 18, 2013 (http://www.carp.ca/2011/03/10/carp-elder-abuse-report/).

Canadian Centre for Justice Statistics (CCSJ) (Ed.). 1999. The Juristat Reader: A Statistical Overview of the Canadian Justice System. Toronto: Thompson.

Canadian Centre for Policy Alternatives, BC Office. 2008. The Time Is Now: A Poverty Reduction Plan for BC (December). Vancouver: CCPA BC.

Canadian Centre for Policy Alternatives (CCPA). 2008. "Majority Want Leadership on Poverty: Poll" (October 27). Retrieved June 30, 2009 (www.policyalternatives.ca/news/2008/10/pressrelease1988).

Canadian Council on Learning. 2009a. Canadian Composite Learning Index. Retrieved June 13, 2009 (http://www.ccl-cca.ca/CCL/Reports/CLI/index.htm?Language=EN).

Canadian Council on Social Development (CCSD). 2009b. Economic Security: Poverty Fact Sheet. Retrieved June 30, 2009 (http://www.ccsd.ca/factsheets/economic_security/poverty/ccsd_es_poverty.pdf).

Canadian Human Rights Commission. 2003. Annual Report 2001: The Health of Human Rights in Canada. (http://www.chrc-ccdp.ca/ar-ra/RapportAnnuel2001/AR01RA/annualReport_1_rapportAnnuel.asp?l=e).

Canadian Human Rights Commission. 2013. Report on Equality Rights of Aboriginal People. Retrieved June 10, 2014 (http://www.chrc-ccdp.gc.ca/sites/default/files/equality_aboriginal_report.pdf).

Canadian Immigrant. Canada's Top 25 Immigrants 2013. Retrieved September 2, 2013 (http://canadianimmigrant.ca/canadas-top-25-immigrants/canadas-top-25-immigrants-2013).

Canadian Institute for Health Information. 2013. National Health Expenditure Trends 1975–2012. Retrieved August 20, 2013 (https://secure.cihi.ca/estore/productSeries.htm?pc=PCC52).

Canadian Institute for Health Information. 2013. National Health Expenditure Trends 1975–2013. Toronto. Retrieved July 7, 2015 (https://www.cihi.ca/en/nhex_exec_sum_2013_en.pdf).

Canadian Labour Congress. 2006. Report Card 2005: Is Your Work Working for You? Ottawa: Canadian Labour Congress. (http://www.canadianlabour.ca).

Canadian Museum of Civilization, 2003. (http://www.civilization.ca).

Canadian Nuclear Association. 2002. Retrieved July 30, 2002 (http://www.cna.ca).

Cancian, Francesca M. 1990. "The Feminization of Love." In C. Carlson (Ed.), Perspectives on the Family: History, Class, and Feminism. Belmont, CA: Wadsworth, pp. 171–185.

Cancian, Francesca M., and James William Gibson. 1990. Making War, Making Peace: The Social Foundations of Violent Conflict. Belmont, CA: Wadsworth.

Carmichael, Stokely, and Charles V. Hamilton. 1967. Black Power: The Politics of Liberation in America. New York: Vintage.

Carrier, James G. 1986. Social Class and the Construction of Inequality in American Education. New York: Greenwood Press.

Carriere, Yves, and Diane Galarneau. 2011. "Delayed Retirement: A New Trend." Statistics Canada. Retrieved August 19, 2013 (http://www.statcan.gc.ca/pub/75-001-x/2011004/article/11578-eng.htm).

Carroll, William K. 1997. "Social Movements and Counterhegemony: Canadian Contexts and Social Theories." In William K. Carroll (Ed.), Organizing Dissent: Contemporary Social Movements in Theory and Practice. Toronto: Garamond Press, pp. 3–38.

Casipullai, Amy. 2003. "Bill C-18 (Citizenship Bill)." Ontario Council of Agencies Serving Immigrants (OCASI). (www.ocasi.org/sys/anno_detail.asp?AnnoID=70).

Cass, Vivien C. 1984. "Homosexual Identity Formation: Testing a Theoretical Model." Journal of Sex Research, 20:143–167.

Castells, Manuel. 1977. The Urban Question. London: Edward Arnold.

Cavender, Gray. 1995. "Alternative Approaches: Labeling and Critical Perspectives." In Joseph F. Sheley (Ed.), Criminology: A Contemporary Handbook (2nd ed.). Belmont, CA: Wadsworth, pp. 349–367.

CBC. 2014. Canadian Military Involvement in Afghanistan Formally Ends (March 12). Retrieved June 5, 2014 (http://www.cbc.ca/news/world/canadian-military-involvement-in-afghanistan-formally-ends-1.2569162).

CBC Digital Archives. 2009. "The Somalia Affair, 1992–1997." Retrieved August 24, 2009 (http://archives.cbc.ca/war_conflict/peacekeeping/topics/723).

CBC TV. 1999. Peacekeeping: The Invisible Wounds.

Chakrabarti, Vishaan. 2013. A Country of Cities: A Manifesto for an Urban America. New York: SHoP Architects and Norman Foster.

Chandler, Michael, and Christopher Lalonde. 2004. "Transferring Whose Knowledge? Exchanging Whose Best Practices? On Knowing about Indigenous Knowledge and Aboriginal Suicide." In J. White, P. Maxim, and D. Beavon (Eds.), Aboriginal Policy Research: Setting the Agenda for Change, Vol. 2. Toronto: Althouse Press, pp. 111–123.

Chapkis, Wendy. 1997. Live Sex Acts: Women Performing Erotic Labour. New York: Routledge.

Chase-Lansdale, P. Lindsay, Jeanne Brooks-Gunn, and Roberta L. Palkoff. 1992. "Research and Programs for Adolescent Mothers: Missing Links and Future Promises." Family Relations, 40(4):396–403.

Cherlin, Andrew J. 1992. Marriage, Divorce, and Remarriage (rev. and enlarged ed.). Cambridge, MA: Harvard University Press.

Chidley, Joe. 1995. "Red Light District . . . From S & M to Bestiality, Porn Flourishes on the Internet." Maclean's (May 22):58.

Children Now. 1999. "Children Now Annual Report 1999 Highlights." (http://www.childrennow.org/annual-reports/annual-report-1999.htm).

Choudry, Aziz. 2001. "Canada's Dirty War Over Words." ZMag (November 21). (www.zmag.org/sustainers/content/2001-11/21choudry.cfm).

CIHI. 2013. Lifetime Distributional Effects of Publicly Financed Health Care in Canada. Retrieved August 21, 2013 (https://secure.cihi.ca/estore/product-Family.htm?locale=en&pf=PFC2192).

City of Toronto. 2011. Housing & Homelessness Services. Retrieved September 17, 2013 (http://www.toronto.ca/housing/pdf/quickfacts.pdf).

City of Toronto. 2013. Affordable Housing. Retrieved October 11, 2013 (http://www1.toronto.ca/wps/portal/contentonly?vgnextoid=05d407ceb6f8e310VgnVCM10000071d60f89RCRD&vgnextfmt=default).

City of Toronto. 2013. Federal Gas Tax Fund. Retrieved September 27, 2013 (http://www.toronto.ca/gastaxworks/).

City of Toronto. 2013. Street Needs Assessment. Retrieved September 18, 2013 (http://www.toronto.ca/housing/SNA2013interim_report.htm).

Clancy, J. 2009. "Lies about the Deficit." National Union of Public and General Employees (June 2). Retrieved July 12, 2009 (http://www.nupge.ca/node/2334).

Clark, Warren. 1998. "Religious Observance, Marriage and the Family." Canadian Social Trends (Autumn):2–7.

Clinard, Marshall B., and R.F. Meier. 1989. Sociology of Deviant Behavior (7th ed.). Fort Worth, TX: Holt, Rinehart and Winston.

Coalition for Lesbian and Gay Rights in Ontario (CLGRO). 1998. *Young People and Sex.* Pamphlet [online]. (May). (http://www.web.net/~clgro/consent/htm).

Cock, Jacklyn. 1994. "Women and the Military: Implications for Demilitarization in the 1990s in South Africa." Gender and Society, 8(2):152–169.

Cochrane, J., J. Durbin, and P. Goering. 1997. Best Practices in Mental Health Reform. Discussion paper prepared for the Federal/Provincial/Territorial Advisory Network on Mental Health. Ottawa: Health Canada.

Cohen, Lawrence E., and Marcus Felson. 1979. "Social Change and Crime Rate Trends: A Routine Activity Approach." American Sociological Review, 44:588–608.

Coleman, Eli. 1981/2. "Developmental Stages of the Coming Out Process." Journal of Homosexuality, 7:31–43.

Coles, Gerald. 1987. The Learning Mystique: A Critical Look at "Learning Disabilities." New York: Pantheon.

Collins, Patricia Hill. 1991. Black Feminist Thought: Knowledge, Consciousness, and the Politics of Empowerment. New York: Routledge.

Coltrane, Scott. 2004. "Fathering: Paradoxes, contradictions and dilemmas." In Marilyn Coleman and Lawrence Ganong (Eds.) *Handbook of Contemporary Families: Considering the Past, Contemplating the Future* (pp. 224–243). Thousand Oaks, CA: Sage.

Conference Board of Canada. 2013. Confidence in Parliament; Voter Turnout; Income Inequality; Economy. Retrieved May 20, 2014 (http://www.conferenceboard.ca/hcp/details/society/trust-in-parliament.aspx. http://www.conferenceboard.ca/hcp/details/society/voter-turnout.aspx; http://www.conferenceboard.ca/hcp/details/

society/income-inequality.aspx; http://www.conferenceboard.ca/hcp/details/economy.aspx).

Conference Board of Canada. 2013. Education and Skills. Retrieved June 20, 2013 (http://www.conferenceboard.ca/hcp/details/education.aspx).

Conference Board of Canada. 2013. Elderly Poverty. Retrieved June 20, 2013 (http://www.conferenceboard.ca/hcp/details/society/elderly-poverty.aspx).

Conference Board of Canada. 2014. Child Poverty. Retrieved September 5, 2014 (http://www.conferenceboard.ca/hcp/details/society/child-poverty.aspx)

Conference Board of Canada. 2014. Disabled Income. Retrieved September 5, 2014 (http://www.conferenceboard.ca/hcp/details/society/disabled-income.aspx).

Conference Board of Canada. 2014. Elderly Poverty. Retrieved September 5, 2014 (http://www.conferenceboard.ca/hcp/details/society/elderly-poverty.aspx).

Conference Board of Canada. 2014. Income Inequality. Retrieved September 6, 2014 (http://www.conferenceboard.ca/hcp/details/society/income-inequality.aspx).

Conference Board of Canada. 2014. Working-Age Poverty. Retrieved September 5, 2014 (http://www.conferenceboard.ca/hcp/details/society/working-age-poverty.aspx).

Conference Board of Canada. 2014. World Income Inequality. Retrieved September 6, 2014 (http://www.conferenceboard.ca/hcp/hot-topics/worldinequality.aspx).

Connell, Christopher. 1995. "Birth Rate for Unmarried Women Surges." Austin American-Statesman (June 7):A18.

Connell, Nadine, Kristen Miggans, and Jean Marie McGloin. 2008. "Can a community Policing Initiative Reduce Serious Crime? A Local Evaluation." Police Quarterly 11(2):127–150.

Cormack, Elizabeth. 1999. "New Possibilities for a Feminism 'in' Criminology." Canadian Journal of Criminology, 41(2):161–170.

Corr, Charles A., Clyde M. Nabe, and Donna M. Corr. 1994. Death and Dying, Life and Living. Pacific Grove, CA: Brooks/Cole.

Cottle, Charles E., Patricia Searles, Ronald J. Berger, and Beth Ann Pierce. 1989.

"Conflicting Ideologies and the Politics of Pornography." *Gender and Society,* 3:303–333.

Cottrell, Barbara. 2001. Parent Abuse: The Abuse of Parents by Their Teenage Children. Family Violence Prevention Unit, Ottawa: Health Canada. Cat. no. H72-21/180-2000E. Retrieved October 25, 2006 (http://www.phac-aspc.gc.ca/ncfv-cnivf/familyviolence/html/fvparentsabu_e.html).

Council of Canadians. 1999. "Trade and Investment Must Serve . . . "Retrieved March 7, 2003 (http://www.canadians.org/display_document.htm?COC_token=1@@465cb4da239ed216035817807630876d&id=332&isdoc=1&catid=133).

Council on Foreign Relations. 2003. "How Did Canada, Australia, and New Zealand Respond to September 11?" (February 22). (http://www.terrorismanswers.com/coalition/canada.html).

Cowley, Geoffrey. 1997. "Can Marijuana Be Medicine?" Newsweek (February 3):22–27.

Cox, Oliver C. 1948. Caste, Class, and Race. Garden City, NY: Doubleday.

Crossette, Barbara. 1997. "Democracies Love Peace, Don't They?" New York Times (June 1):E3.

Crowe, Cathy. 2007. Dying for a Home: Homeless Activists Speak Out. Toronto: Between the Lines.

Curatolo, Peter W., and David Robertson. 1983. "The Health Consequences of Caffeine." Annals of Internal Medicine, 98:641–653.

Currah, Paisley. 2001. "Queer Theory, Lesbian and Gay Rights, and Transsexual Marriages." In Mark Blasius (Ed.), Sexual Identities—Queer Politics. Princeton, NJ: Princeton University Press, pp. 178–199.

Curran, James, Michael Gurevitch, and Janet Woollacott. 1982. "The Study of the Media: Theoretical Approaches." In Michael Gurevitch, Tony Bennett, James Curran, and Janet Woollacott (Eds.), Culture, Society and the Media. London: Methuen, pp. 5–35.

Curry, Bill. 2008. "Hunt Begins for Long Missing Students." Globe and Mail (October 27):A1.

Curry, Bill. 2014. "7% Turnout: Enough to Win with Record Low Voter Turnout." The Globe and Mail. July 2: A1.

Dahl, Robert A. 1961. Who Governs? New Haven, CT: Yale University Press.

Daly, Kathleen, and Meda Chesney-Lind. 1988. "Feminism and Criminology." Justice Quarterly, 5:497–533.

Danziger, Sheldon, and Peter Gottschalk. 1995. America Unequal. Cambridge, MA: Harvard University Press.

Dauncey, Guy. 2003. "101 Ways to Stop the War on Iraq." (http://www.earthfuture.com).

Dauvergne, Mia, and Holly Johnson. 2001. "Children Witnessing Family Violence." Juristat, 21(6).

Dauvergne, Mia. 2013. "Adult Criminal Court Statistics in Canada, 2010/2011." Statistics Canada. Retrieved June 29, 2013 (http://www.statcan.gc.ca/pub/85-002-x/2012001/article/11646-eng.htm

Davidson, Julia O'Connell. 1996. "Sex Tourism in Cuba." Race and Class, 38(1):39–49.

Davis, Kingsley, and Wilbert E. Moore. 1945. "Some Principles of Stratification." American Sociological Review, 10:242–249.

Davis, Kingsley. 1937. "The Sociology of Prostitution." American Sociological Review, 2:744–755.

DeKeseredy, Walter S., and Ronald Hinch. 1991. Woman Abuse: Sociological Perspectives. Toronto: Thompson.

Demczuk, Irene, Michele Caron, Ruth Rose, and Lyne Bouchard. 2002. Recognition of Lesbian Couples: An Inalienable Right. Ottawa: Status of Women Canada.

Democracy Ranking. 2013. Retrieved June 16, 2014 (http://democracyranking.org/wordpress/?page_id=738).

Demosim Team. 2013. "Projections of the Diversity of the Canadian Population, 2006 to 2031." Statistic Canada. Retrieved September 25, 2013 (http://www.statcan.gc.ca/pub/91-551-x/91-551-x2010001-eng.htm).

Department of Finance Canada. 2009. Canada's Economic Outlook and Policy Framework. Retrieved July 7, 2009 (http://www.fin.gc.ca/activty/pubs/EPFrmwrk08_eng.asp).

Department of Justice, Canada. 2001. "The Royal Assent of Bill C-36, The Anti-Terrorism Act." NewsRoom (December 18).

Department of Justice, Canada. 2002. "Stronger Child Pornography Laws Receive Royal Assent" (June 10). Retrieved October 16, 2006 (http://canada.justice.gc.ca/en/news/nr/2002/doc_30529.html).

Department of Justice, Canada. 2006. "Criminal Code: Part XXII, Sentencing." Retrieved July 21, 2006 (http://laws.justice.gc.ca/en/c-46/268353.html).

Department of Justice, Canada. 2006a. "Highlights of Bill C-2 Amendments to Protect Children and Other Vulnerable Persons: Backgrounder." Newsroom (March 31).

Department of Justice, Canada. 2006b. Criminal Code: Part XXII, Sentencing. Retrieved July 21, 2006 (http://laws.justice.gc.ca/en/c-46/268353.html).

Department of Justice, Canada. 2006c. The Youth Criminal Justice Act: Summary and Background. Retrieved September 20, 2006 (http://www.justice.gc.ca/en/ps/yj/ycja/explan.html).

DePasquale, Katherine M. 1999. "The Effects of Prostitution." Retrieved December 3, 1999 (http://www.feminista.com/v1n5/depasquale.html).

Desilver, Drew. 2013. "A Global Snapshot of Same-Sex Marriage," Pew Research Center. Retrieved November 24, 2013 (http://www.pewresearch.org/fact-tank/2013/06/04/global-snapshot-sex-marriage/).

Devereaux, Anna. 1987. "Diary of a Prostitute." Cosmopolitan (October 1987): 164, 166.

Dews, Peter B. 1984. "Behavioral Effects of Caffeine." In Peter B. Dews (Ed.), Caffeine: Perspectives from Recent Research. Berlin: Springer-Verlag, pp. 86–103.

Diamond, Jared. 2000. "The Greening of Corporate America." New York Times (January 8):A31.

Diamond, Lisa. 2008. "Female Bisexuality from Adolescence to Adulthood: Results from a 10-year Longitudinal Study." Developmental Psychology, 44(1):5–14.

Diamond, Sara. 1988. "Pornography: Image and Reality." In Arlene Tigar McLaren (Ed.), Gender and Society: Creating a Canadian Women's Sociology. Mississauga, ON: Copp Clark Pitman, pp. 390–404.

Dickinson, Harley D. 2000. "Work and Unemployment as Social Issues." In B. Singh Bolaria (Ed.), Social Issues and Contradictions in Canadian Society (3rd ed.). Toronto: Harcourt Brace, pp. 26–50.

Dietz, P. 1986. "Mass, Serial and Sensational Homicide." Bulletin of the New England Medical Society, 62:477–491.

Dimmock, Gary. 2002. "The Secret Life of a Teenage Cyber Informant." Vancouver Sun (June 29):A1, A14.

Dines, Gail. 2010. Pornland: How Porn has Hijacked our Sexuality. Boston, MA: Beacon Press

Diplock, Jordan, Darryl Plecas, and Len Garis. 2013. Targeting Marihuana Growing Operations in British Columbia. Retrieved July 13, 2014 (https://www.ufv.ca/media/assets/criminal-justice-research/Targeting-Marihuana-Growing-Operations-in-BC-Aug-12-2013.pdf).

DiPrete, Thomas A., and Claudia Buchmann. 2014. The Secret Behind College Completion: Girls, Boys, and The Power of Eighth Grade Grades. Third Way. Retrieved May 1, 2014 (http://www.thirdway.org/report/the-secret-behind-college-completion-girls-boys-and-the-power-of-eighth-grade-grades).

Dobinson, Cheryl, 2004. "Everyday Acts of Survival and Unorganized Resistance: Gay, Lesbian and Bisexual Youth Respond to Oppression." In James McNinch and Mary Cronin (Eds.), I Could Not Speak My Heart: Education and Social Justice for Gay and Lesbian Youth. Regina, SK: Canadian Plains Research Centre, University of Regina, pp. 49–80.

Doezema, Jo. 1998. "Forced to Choose: Beyond the Voluntary v. Forced Prostitution Dichotomy." In Kamala Kempadoo and Jo Doezema (Eds.), Global Sex Workers: Rights, Resistance and Redefinition. New York: Routledge, pp. 34–50.

Domhoff, G. William. 1978. The Powers That Be: Processes of Ruling Class Domination in America. New York: Random House.

Domhoff, G. William. 1990. The Power Elite and the State: How Policy Is Made in America. New York: Aldine de Gruyter.

Donziger, Steven R. (Ed.). 1996. The Real War on Crime: The Report of the National Criminal Justice Commission. New York: HarperPerennial.

Doyle, James A. 1995. The Male Experience (3rd ed.). Madison, WI: Brown and Benchmark.

Drew, Christopher. 2011. "Under an Unblinking Eye: A Costly Drone Is Poised to Replace the U-2." New York Times. August 3:B1, B4.

Drummond, Don. 2012. "Growth Can't Save Ontario—Only Reform Can." The Globe and Mail. February 16:A17.

Dua, Enakshi. 1999. "Canadian Anti-Racist Feminist Thought: Scratching the Surface of Racism." In Enakshi Dua and Angela Robertson (Eds.), Scratching the Surface: Canadian Anti-Racist Feminist Thought. Toronto: Women's Press, pp. 7–31.

Duggan, Maeve, and Aaron Smith. (2013). Social Media Update 2013. Pew Research Center. Retrieved November 24, 2013 (http://www.pewinternet.org/2013/12/30/social-media-update-2013/).

Dunlap, David W. 1996. "Role of Openly Gay Episcopalians Causes a Rift in the Church." New York Times (March 21):A8.

Durkheim, Emile. 1933. Division of Labor in Society. George Simpson (Trans.). New York: Free Press (orig. published in 1893).

Durkheim, Emile. 1964. The Rules of Sociological Method. Sarah A. Solovay and John H. Mueller. (Trans.). New York: Free Press (orig. published in 1895).

Dworkin, Andrea. 1988. Letters to a War Zone. New York: Dutton/New America Library.

Dye, Thomas R., Harmon Zeigler, and Louis Schubert. 2012. The Irony of Democracy; An Uncommon Introduction to American Politics. (15th ed.) Belmont, CA: Cengage.

Dynes, Wayne R. (Ed.). 1990. Encyclopedia of Homosexuality. New York: Garland.

Eckersley, Robyn. 2001. "Ecofeminism and Environmental Democracy: Exploring the Connections." Women & Environments International Magazine, 52/53 (Fall):23–26.

Eder, Donna. 1985. "The Cycle of Popularity: Interpersonal Relations among Female Adolescents." Sociology of Education, 58(July): 154–165.

Eder, Donna, and Stephen Parker. 1987. "The Cultural Production and Reproduction of Gender: The Effect of Extracurricular Activities on Peer Group Culture." Sociology of Education, 60:200–213.

EGALE. 2013. Canada Human Rights Trust. "Report Homophobic Violence." Retrieved November 24, 2013 (http://egale.ca/category/discrimination-and-hate-crimes/report-homophobic-violence-period/).

Ehrbar, Ned. 2009. "Golden Girl Says 'Yes' to Role." MetroNews (June 17):49.

Ehrenreich, Barbara. 1997. Blood Rites: Origins and History of the Passions of War. New York: Metropolitan Books.

Ehrlich, Paul R., and Anne H. Ehrlich. 1991. The Population Explosion. New York: Touchstone/Simon & Schuster.

Ehrlich, Paul, and Anne H. Ehrlich. 2009. "The Population Bomb Revisited." Electronic Journal of Sustainable Development. 1(3):63–71. Retrieved May 5, 2014 (http://www.docstoc.com/docs/12166078/Population-Bomb-Revisited).

Eichler, Margrit (Ed.). 1995. Change of Plans: Towards a Non-Sexist City. Toronto: Garamond Press.

Ellison, Marc. 2013. "Doctor Urges Toronto to Back Safe Injection Site." Toronto Star. (June 3):A4.

Encyclopedia Britannica. 2013. Populations. Chicago, IL: Time Almanac.

Engels, Friedrich. 1972. The Origin of the Family, Private Property and the State. New York: Pathfinder (orig. published in 1884).

Enloe, Cynthia. 1990. Bananas, Beaches, and Bases: Making Feminist Sense of International Politics. Berkeley: University of California Press.

Enloe, Cynthia H. 1987. "Feminists Thinking about War, Militarism, and Peace." In Beth Hess and Myra Marx Feree (Eds.), Analyzing Gender: A Handbook of Social Science Research. Newbury Park, CA: Sage, pp. 526–547.

Environment Canada. 2012. Canada's Emissions Trends 2012. Retrieved November 1, 2013 (http://www.ec.gc.ca/ges-ghg/default.asp?lang=En&n=022BADB5-1#Toc331765557).

Environment Canada. 2013. The Climate Change Scenarios Network. Retrieved October 2, 2013 (http://www.ec.gc.ca/sc-cs/default.asp?lang=En&n=FE6B6E6B-1).

Epstein, Cynthia Fuchs. 1988. Deceptive Distinctions: Sex, Gender, and the Social Order. New Haven, CT: Yale University Press.

Erickson, Patricia G., Jennifer Butters, Patti McGillicuddy, and Ase Hallgren. 2000. "Crack and Prostitution: Gender, Myths and Experiences." Journal of Drug Issues, 30(4):767–788.

Erikson, Kai T. 1962. "Notes on the Sociology of Deviance." Social Problems, 9:307–314.

Erikson, Kai T. 1991. "A New Species of Trouble." In Stephen Robert Crouch and J. Stephen Kroll-Smith (Eds.), Communities at Risk: Collective Responses to Technological Hazards. New York: Peter Land, pp. 11–29.

Essed, Philomena. 1990. Everyday Racism: Reports from Women of Two Cultures. Claremont, CA: Hunter House.

Essed, Philomena. 1991. Understanding Everyday Racism. Newbury Park, CA: Sage.

Farley, Melissa, and Jacqueline Lynne. 2004. "Prostitution in Vancouver: Pimping Women and the Colonization of First Nations." In Rebecca Whisnant and Christine Stark (Eds.), Not for Sale: Feminists Resisting Prostitution and Pornography. Melbourne, AU: Spinifex Press, pp. 106–130.

Feagin, Joe R. 1975. Subordinating the Poor: Welfare and American Beliefs. Englewood Cliffs, NJ: Prentice-Hall.

Feagin, Joe R., and Clairece Booher Feagin. 2011. Racial and Ethnic Relations (9th ed.). Upper Saddle River, NJ: Prentice Hall.

Feagin, Joe R., and Hernán Vera. 1995. White Racism: The Basics. New York: Routledge.

Feagin, Joe R., and Melvin P. Sikes. 1994. Living with Racism: The Black Middle-Class Experience. Boston: Beacon Press.

Feagin, Joe R., and Robert Parker. 1990. Building American Cities: The Urban Real Estate Game (2nd ed.). Englewood Cliffs, NJ: Prentice-Hall.

Fifth Estate. 2013. "Rate my Hospital." CBC News. Retrieved May 18, 2013 (http://www.cbc.ca/player/Shows/Shows/the+fifth+estate/Season+38/ID/2394118126/).

Findlay, Deborah A., and Leslie J. Miller. 2002. "Through Medical Eyes: The Medicalization of Women's Bodies." In B. Singh Bolaria and Harley D. Dickinson (Eds.), Health, Illness, and Health Care in Canada (3rd ed.). Scarborough, ON: Nelson.

Fineman, Howard. 1997. "Who Needs Washington?" Newsweek (January 27):50–52.

Firestone, Shulamith. 1970. The Dialectic of Sex. New York: Morrow.

Fisher, John. 1999. A report on lesbian, gay, and bi-sexual youth issues in Canada. Ottawa: EGALE.

Flanagan, William G. 1995. Urban Sociology: Images and Structure (2nd ed.). Boston: Allyn and Bacon.

Fleras, Augie. 2001. Social Problems in Canada: Conditions, Constructions, and Challenges (3rd ed.). Toronto: Prentice Hall.

Fleras, Augie. 2005. *Social Problems in Canada: Conditions, Constructions and Challenges.* (4ed.). Toronto: Pearson Prentice Hall

Fleras, Augie. 2010. Unequal Relations: An Introduction to Race, Ethnic, and Aboriginal Dynamics in Canada (6th ed.). Toronto: Pearson Canada.

Fleras, Augie, and Jean Leonard Elliott. 1996. Unequal Relations: An Introduction to Race, Ethnic and Aboriginal Dynamics in Canada. Scarborough, ON: Prentice Hall.

Fleras, Augie, and Jean Leonard Elliott. 1999. Unequal Relations: An Introduction to Race, Ethnic, and Aboriginal Dynamics in Canada (3rd ed.). Scarborough, ON: Prentice Hall/Allyn and Bacon.

Florida, Richard. 2002. "Toronto 2020." Globe and Mail(June 24):T8.

Florida, Richard. 2010. "The Bohemian Index." The Atlantic. Retrieved October 6, 2013 (http://www.theatlantic.com/national/archive/2010/06/bohemian-index/57658/).

Food Banks Canada. 2013. HungerCount 2013: A Comprehensive Report on Hunger and Food Bank Use in Canada. Retrieved September 9, 2014 (http://foodbankscanada.ca/getmedia/76907192-263c-4022-8561-73a16c06dd2f/HungerCount_2014_EN_HR.pdf.aspx).

Forbes. 2014. The Richest People on the Planet. Retrieved September 6, 2014 (http://www.forbes.com/billionaires/).

Fox, T.A., T.E. Barchyn, and C.H. Hugenholtz. 2012. "Successes of Soil Conservation in the Canadian Prairies Highlighted by a Historical Decline in Blowing Dust." Environmental Research Letters 7(1). Retrieved September 22, 2013 (http://iopscience.iop.org/1748-9326/7/1/014008/pdf/1748-9326_7_1_14008.pdf).

Fréchette, D., D. Hollenberg, A. Shrichand, C. Jacob, and I. Datta. 2013. What's Really Behind Canada's Unemployed Specialists? Too Many, Too Few Doctors? Findings from the Royal College's Employment Study. Ottawa, ON: The Royal College of Physicians and Surgeons of Canada. Retrieved October 22, 2013 (http://www.royalcollege.ca/portal/page/portal/rc/common/documents/policy/employment_report_executive_summary_2013_e.pdf).

Fraser Committee.1985. Online: http://www.justice.gc.ca/eng/rp-pr/cj-jp/yj-jj/rr01_13/p23.html#sec23

French, Dolores, with Linda Lee. 1988. Working: My Life as a Prostitute. New York: E.P. Dutton.

Freund, Matthew, Nancy Lee, and Terri Leonard. 1991. "Sexual Behavior of Clients with Street Prostitutes in Camden, New Jersey." Journal of Sex Research, 28(4) (November): 579–591.

Friedan, Betty. 1963. The Feminine Mystique. New York: Norton.

Friedman, Thomas L. 2000. "Boston E-Party." New York Times (January 1):A31.

Friedman, George, and Meredith Friedman. 1996. The Future of War. New York: St. Martin's Griffin.

Friend, Tim. 1996. "Teens and Drugs: Today's Youth Just Don't See the Dangers." USA Today (August 21):1A, 2A.

Fullilove, Mindy Thompson, E. Anne Lown, and Robert E. Fullilove. 1992. "Crack 'Hos and Skeezers: Traumatic Experiences of Women Crack Users." Journal of Sex Research, 29(2):275–288.

Gabriel, Trip. 1995. "Some On-Line Discoveries Give Gay Youths a Path to Themselves." New York Times (July 2): 1, 9.

Gabriel, Trip. 1996. "High-Tech Pregnancies Test Hope's Limit." New York Times (January 7):1, 10–11.

Gaetz, Stephen, Jesse Donaldson, Tim Richter, and Tanya Gulliver. 2013. The State of Homelessness in Canada 2013. The Homeless Hub. Retrieved September 29, 2014. (http://www.homelesshub.ca/SOHC2013#sthash.4MPA1kkW).

Gage. 1983. Gage Canadian Dictionary. Toronto, ON: Gage Educational Publishing Co.

Galabuzi, Grace-Edward. 2006. Canada's Economic Apartheid: The Social Exclusion of Racialized Groups in the New Century. Toronto: Canadian Scholars' Press.

Galt, Virginia. 2008. "Older Workers a Drain? Not a Chance, Study Finds." Globe and Mail (May 23):B5.

Gamson, Joshua. 1996. "Must Identity Movements Self-Destruct? A Queer Dilemma." In Steven Seidman (Ed.), Queer Theory/Sociology. Cambridge, MA: Blackwell, pp. 395–420.

Gamson, Joshua. 1994. Claims to Fame: Celebrity in Contemporary America.Berkeley: University of California Press.

Gans, Herbert. 1982. The Urban Villagers: Group and Class in the Life of Italian Americans (updated and expanded ed.). New York: Free Press (orig. published in 1962).

Gardner, Carol Brooks. 1995. Passing By: Gender and Public Harassment. Berkeley: University of California Press.

Gardner, Tracey A. 1994. "Racism in Pornography and the Women's Movement." In Alison M. Jaggar (Ed.), *Living with Contradictions: Controversies in Feminist Social Ethics.* Boulder, CO: Westview, pp. 171–176.

Garreau, Joel. 1991. Edge City: Life on the New Frontier. New York: Doubleday.

Gee, Ellen, and M. Kimball. 1987. Women and Aging. Toronto: Butterworths.

Gerbner, George. 1995. "Television Violence: The Power And The Peril" in Gail Dines and Jean M. Humez (eds.) Gender, Race and Class in Media: A Text-Reader. Thousand Oaks, CA: Sage:547–557.

Gerstel, Naomi, and Harriet Engel Gross. 1995. "Gender and Families in the United States: The Reality of Economic Dependence." In Jo Freeman (Ed.), Women: A Feminist Perspective (5th ed.). Mountain View, CA: Mayfield, pp. 92–127.

Gibbs, Lois Marie, as told to Murray Levine. 1982. Love Canal: My Story. Albany: State University of New York Press.

Gibson, James William, and Francesca M. Cancian. 1990. "Is War Inevitable?" In Francesca M. Cancian and James William Gibson (Eds.), Making War, Making Peace: The Social Foundations of Violent Conflict. Belmont, CA: Wadsworth, pp. 1–10.

Gil, Vincent E., Marco S. Wang, Allen F. Anderson, Guo Matthew Lin, and Zongjian Oliver Wu. 1996. "Prostitutes, Prostitution and STD/HIV Transmission in Mainland China." Social Science and Medicine, 42(1):141–153.

Gilbert, Richard J. 1986. Caffeine: The Most Popular Stimulant. New York: Chelsea House.

Gillis, Charlie. 2001. "Racial Profiling Inevitable: Courts Expected to Permit Practice at Points of Entry." National Post [online] (October 10). (http://www.geocities.com/CapitolHill/2381/CanadaCustomsandRevenueAgency/cdnracialprofilinevitable.html).

Gilman, Nils. 2014. "The Twin Insurgency." American Interest. Retrieved June 30, 2014 (http://www.the-american-interest.com/articles/2014/06/15/the-twin-insurgency).

Gilovich, Paula. 2002. "Invisible Sex." Seattle International Film Festival News (Feb 1). Retrieved October 23, 2006 (http://www.seattlefilm.org/news/detail.aspx?NID=14&year=2002).

Giobbe, Evelina. 1993. "Surviving Commercial Sexual Exploitation." In Diana E.H. Russell (Ed.), Making Violence Sexy: Feminist Views on Pornography. New York: Teachers College Press, pp. 37–41.

Giobbe, Evelina. 1994. "Confronting the Liberal Lies about Prostitution." In Alison M. Jaggar (Ed.), Living with Contradictions: Controversies in Feminist Social Ethics. Boulder, CO: Westview, pp. 120–136.

Gionet, Linda, and Shirin Roshanafshar. 2013. "Select Health Indicators of First Nations People Living Off Reserve, Métis and Inuit." Health at a Glance. Statistics Canada. Catalogue no. 82-624-x. Retrieved June 19, 2013 (http://www.statcan.gc.ca/pub/82-624-x/2013001/article/11763-eng.htm).

Glaser, Barney, and Anselm Strauss. 1968. Time for Dying. Chicago: Aldine.

Glazier, Richard H., Elizabeth M. Badley, Julie E. Gilbert, and Lorne Rothman. 2000. "The Nature of Increased Hospital Use in Poor Neighbourhoods: Findings from a Canadian Inner City." Canadian Journal of Public Health, 91(4): 268–273.

Gleick, Elizabeth. 1996. "The Children's Crusade." Time (June 3):30–35.

Glenny, Misha. 2008. McMafia: A Journey Through the Global Criminal Underworld. Toronto: House of Anansi Press.

Glick, Paul C., and Sung-Ling Lin. 1986. "More Young Adults Are Living with Their Parents: Who Are They?" Journal of Marriage and the Family, 48:107–112.

Global Age Watch. 2013. Global Age Watch Index 2013. Retrieved October 3, 2013 (http://www.helpage.org/global-agewatch).

Global Initiative to End all Corporal Punishment of Children. 2009. "End All Corporal Punishment of Children." Retrieved March 16, 2009 (http://www.endcorporalpunishment.org/).

GLSEN. 2011. The 2011 National School Climate Survey. Retrieved November 25, 2013 (http://www.glsen.org/sites/default/files/2011%20National%20School%20Climate%20Survey%20Executive%20Summary.pdf).

Goffman, Erving. 1961. Asylums: Essays on the Social Situation of Mental Patients and Other Inmates. Chicago: Aldine.

Gold, Rachel Benson, and Cory L. Richards. 1994. "Securing American Women's Reproductive Health." In Cynthia Costello and Anne J. Stone (Eds.), The American Woman, 1994–1995. New York: Norton, pp. 197–222.

Goldacre, Ben. 2013. Bad Pharma: How Drug Companies Mislead Doctors and Harm Patients. Toronto, ON: McClelland and Stewart/Signal.

Goldberg, Robert A. 1991. Grassroots Resistance: Social Movements in Twentieth Century America. Belmont, CA: Wadsworth.

Goldberg, Joshua. 1998. Personal correspondence to a friend. Author's Files. Victoria, BC.

Goldie, Terry (Ed). 2001. In a Queer Country: Gay and Lesbian Studies in the Canadian Context. Vancouver: Arsenal Pulp Press.

Goldstein, Joshua. 2001. War and Gender: How Gender Shapes the War System and Vice Versa. Cambridge, MA: Cambridge University Press.

Goode, William J. 1982. "Why Men Resist." In Barrie Thorne with Marilyn Yalom (Eds.), Rethinking the Family: Some Feminist Questions. New York: Longman, pp. 131–150.

Goodman, Emily Jane. 1999. Seducers, Harassers, and Wimps. New York Times. December 19: AR47, 51.

Gordon, Frances Linzee. 2000. Lonely Planet Guide to Ethiopia, Eritrea, and Djibouti (1st ed.). Victoria, Australia: Lonely Planet.

Gordon, Milton M. 1964. Assimilation in American Life: The Role of Race, Religion, and National Origins. New York: Oxford University Press.

Gottdiener, Mark. 1985. The Social Production of Urban Space. Austin: University of Texas Press.

Grant, Tavia. 2008. "When the Nest Egg Shatters, Keep at It." Globe and Mail (December 1):B10.

Grant, Tavia, and Janet McFarland. 2013. "How Globalization Has Benefitted the 1 Per Cent." The Globe and Mail. November 14:A12–13.

Graves, Frank. 2015. The EKOS Poll: Are Canadians Getting More Racist? Ipolitics. Retrieved March 14, 2015 (http://newcanadianmedia.ca/item/25197).

Green, K. 1985. "Identification of the Facets of Self-Health Management." Evaluation and the Health Professions, 8:323–338.

Greenpeace. 2013. Tar Sands Are the Fifth Largest Climate Threat in the World. Retrieved September 4, 2013 (http://www.greenpeace.org/canada/en/recent/Tar-sands-one-of-the-worlds-biggest-climate-threats/).

Grillo, Trina, and Stephanie M. Wildman. 1996. "Obscuring the Importance of Race: the Implication of Making Comparisons Between Racism and Sexism (or Other isms)." In Stephanie M. Wildman (Ed.), Privilege Revealed: How Invisible Preference Undermines America. New York: New York University Press, pp. 85–102.

Gross, Leonard. 1983. How Much Is Too Much: The Effects of Social Drinking. New York: Random House.

Ha, Tu Thanh. 2004. "Former Boxer's Daughter Breaks Silence on Incest." Globe and Mail (October 14):A9.

Hackett, Robert A, Richard Gruneau, Donald Gutstein, Timothy A. Gibson, and NewsWatch Canada. 2000. The Missing News: Filters and Blind Spots in Canada's Press. Aurora, ON: Canadian Centre for Policy Alternatives/Garamond Press.

Hallgrimsdottir, Helga K., Rachel Phillips, and Cecilia Benoit. 2006. "Fallen Women and Rescued Girls: Social Stigma and Media Narratives of the Sex Industry in Victoria, B.C., from 1980–2005." The Canadian Review of Sociology and Anthropology, 43(3):266–280.

Hamilton, Tyler. 2013. Sustainable Countries Scorecard. Corporate Knights 12(3):24–27.

Hango, Darcy. 2013. "Gender Differences in Science, Technology, Engineering, Mathematics and Computer Science (STEM) Programs At University." Statistics Canada. Retrieved December 18, 2013 (http://www.statcan.gc.ca/pub/75-006-x/2013001/article/11874-eng.htm).

Hannigan, John A. 1995. Environmental Sociology: A Social Constructionist Perspective. New York: Routledge.

Harrison, Susan. 1997. "Working with Women." In Susan Harrison and Virginia Carver (Eds.), Alcohol and Drug Problems: A Practical Guide for Counsellors. Toronto: Addiction Research Foundation, pp. 219–244.

Hartley, Nina. 1994. "Confessions of a Feminist Porno Star." In Alison M. Jaggar (Ed.), Living with Contradictions: Controversies in Feminist Social Ethics. Boulder, CO: Westview, pp. 176–178.

Hartmann, Heidi. 1981. "The Family as the Locus of Gender, Class, and Political Struggle: The Example of Housework." Signs, 6:366–394.

Hauchler, Ingomar, and Paul M. Kennedy (Eds.). 1994. Global Trends: The World Almanac of Development and Peace. New York: Continuum.

Havighurst, Robert J., Bernice L. Neugarten, and Sheldon S. Tobin. 1968. "Disengagement and Patterns of Aging." In Bernice L. Neugarten (Ed.), Middle Age and Aging. Chicago: University of Chicago Press, pp. 161–172.

Havocscope. 2013. Retrieved October 12, 2013 (http://www.havocscope.com/market-value/ Now the black market is worth more).

Havocscope. 2015a. Country Risk Ranking. Retrieved March 26, 2015 (http://www.havocscope.com/country-profile/).

Havocscope. 2015b. Gangs. Retrieved March 26, 2015 (http://www.havocscope.com/?s=gangs).

Hawley, Amos. 1950. Human Ecology. New York: Ronald Press.

Hawley, Amos. 1981. Urban Society (2nd ed.). New York: Wiley.

Hay, David I. 2009. Poverty Reduction Policies and Programs. Social Development Report Series. Ottawa: CCSD. Retrieved July 1, 2009 (http://www.ccsd.ca/SDR2009/Reports/Canada_Report_FINAL.pdf).

Hay-Edie, David. 2002. "The Military's Impact on the Environment: A Neglected Aspect of the Sustainable Development Debate." In A Briefing Paper for States and Non-Governmental Organisations (August). Geneva: International Peace Bureau.

Health Canada. 1993. Family Violence and Substance Abuse. Ottawa: National Clearinghouse on Family Violence.

Health Canada. 1998. Canada's Drug Strategy. Ottawa: Minister of Public Works and Government Services Canada.

Health Canada. 2012. CADMUS. Retrieved June 23, 2012 (http://www.hc-sc.gc.ca/hc-ps/drugs-drogues/stat/_2011/tables-tableaux-eng.php#t1).

Health Canada. 2012. Drug and Alcohol Use Statistics. Retrieved June 21, 2013 (http://www.hc-sc.gc.ca/hc-ps/drugs-drogues/stat/index-eng.php).

Health Canada. 2013. First Nations and Inuit Health. Retrieved September 2013 (http://www.hc-sc.gc.ca/fniah-spnia/promotion/mental/index-eng.php).

Health Canada. 2014. Extent of Impaired Driving. Retrieved April 29, 2014 (http://www.hc-sc.gc.ca/hc-ps/pubs/adp-apd/bp_treatment-mp_traitement/index-eng.php#a2.1).

Health Canada. 2014. Fetal Alcohol Syndrome and Fetal Alcohol Effects. Retrieved April 29, 2014 (http://www.hc-sc.gc.ca/fniah-spnia/famil/preg-gros/intro-eng.php).

Health Council of Canada. 2010. How Do Canadians Rate the Health Care System? Results from the 2010 Commonwealth Fund International Health Policy Survey. Canadian Health Care Matters, Bulletin 4. Toronto, ON: Health Council of Canada (www.healthcouncilcanada.ca).

Health Council of Canada. 2012. Fact Sheet: Progress Report 2012: Health Care Renewal in Canada. Retrieved October 22, 2013 (http://www.healthcouncilcanada.ca/rpt_det.php?id=487).

Health Council of Canada. 2013. Fact sheet: How Do Canadian Primary Care Physicians Rate the Health System? Retrieved October 22, 2013 (http://www.healthcouncilcanada.ca/rpt_det.php?id=447).

Health Council of Canada. 2013. Fact sheet: Progress Report 2013:Health Care Renewal in Canada. Retrieved October 22, 2013 (http://www.healthcouncilcanada.ca/rpt_det.php?id=487).

Hendriks, Aart, Rob Tielman, and Evert van der Veen. 1993. The Third Pink Book: A Global View of Lesbian and Gay Liberation and Oppression. Buffalo, NY: Prometheus.

Henry, Frances, Carol Tator, Winston Mattis, and Tim Rees. 2000. The Colour of Democracy: Racism in Canadian Society. (2nd ed.). Toronto: Harcourt Brace.

Herek, Gregory M. 1995. "Psychological Heterosexism and Anti-Gay Violence: The Social Psychology of Bigotry and Bashing." In Michael S. Kimmel and Michael A. Messner (Eds.), Men's Lives (3rd ed.). Boston: Allyn and Bacon, pp. 341–353.

Herman, Edward S., and Noam Chomsky. 1988. Manufacturing Consent: The Political Economy of the Mass Media. New York: Pantheon Books.

Hills, Stuart L. 1971. Crime, Power, and Morality. Scranton, PA: Chandler

Hirschi, Travis. 1969. Causes of Delinquency. Berkeley: University of California Press.

Hochschild, Arlie Russell, with Ann Machung. 1989. The Second Shift: Working Parents and the Revolution at Home. New York: Viking/Penguin.

Hodson, Randy, and Teresa A. Sullivan. 2008. The Social Organization of Work. Belmont, CA: Wadsworth.

Holmes, Robert M. 1988. Serial Murder. Beverly Hills, CA: Sage.

Holt, John C. 1964. How Children Fail. New York: Dell.

Holthaus, Eric. 2014. Is Climate Change Destabilizing Iraq? Slate. Retrieved June 27, 2014 (http://www.slate.com/articles/technology/future_tense/2014/06/isis_water_scarcity_is_climate_change_destabilizing_iraq.single.html).

Hooyman, Nancy, and H. Asuman Kiyak. 2008. Social Gerontology: A Multidisciplinary Perspective (8th ed.). Boston: Allyn and Bacon.

Horton Richard et al. 2012. "GBD 2010: Understanding Disease, Injury and Risk." Lancet 380(9859):2053–2054.

Hou, Feng and Garnett Picot. 2004. "Visible minority neighbourhoods in Toronto,

Montreal and Vancouver." *Canadian Social Trends.* (Spring 2004):8–13.

Howell, Alison. 2011. "Afghanistan's Price." Literary Review of Canada. Retrieved June 29, 2014 (http://reviewcanada.ca/magazine/2011/11/afghanistans-price/).

Huber, Manfred. 2005. Long-Term Care for Older People. Paris: Organisation for Economic Co-operation and Development.

Hughes, Donna (2004). "The use of new communication technologies for sexual exploitation of women and children," in Rebecca Whisnant and Christine Stark (Eds.), *Not for sale feminists: resisting prostitution and pornography*, North Melbourne, Victoria: Spinifex Press, pp. 38–55.

Hulchanski, J. David. 1990. "Planning New Urban Neighbourhoods: Lessons from Toronto's St. Lawrence Neighbourhood." In UBC Planning Papers. Vancouver: School of Community and Regional Planning, University of British Columbia

Hulko, Wendy. 2008. "The Time- and Context-Contingent Nature of Intersectionality and Interlocking Oppressions." Affilia: Journal of Women and Social Work, 24(1):44–55.

Hynes, H. Patricia. 2011. "The Military Assault on Global Climate." Truth Out. Retrieved June 29, 2014 (http://www.truth-out.org/news/item/3181:the-military-assault-on-global-climate).

Ibbitson, John. 2013. "Lost?" *The Globe and Mail* (April 6:F4).

ILGA. 2013. International Lesbian, Gay, Bisexual, Trans and Intersex Association. Retrieved November 24, 2013 (http://ilga.org/).

Illich, Ivan. 1975. Medical Nemesis. London: Calder and Brown.

Inciardi, James, Dorothy Lockwood, and Anne E. Pottieger. 1993. Women and Crack-Cocaine. New York: Macmillan.

Infographic. 2013. "It's Your Money: The New Caregivers." Toronto Star. Retrieved August 29, 2013 (http://www.thestar.com/life/modernmoney/2013/06/27/infographic-it-s-your-money-a-practical-guide-new-caregivers.html).

Infoshop. 2009. Anarcha-feminism. Retrieved July 7, 2009 (http://infoshop.org/page/Anarcha-feminism).

Institute for Policy Studies and Foreign Policy In Focus. 2004. "Foreign Policy in Focus." International Relations Center. Retrieved July 30, 2009 (http://www.fpif.org/papers/0406costsofwar.html).

International Lesbian and Gay Association. 2009. Retrieved April 5, 2009 (http://www.ilga.org/index.asp).

Jaffee, David. 1990. Levels of Socio-economic Development Theory. Westport, CT: Praeger.

Jankovic, Jovana. 2014. NFB/Blob Retrieved July 17, 2015 (http://blog.nfb.ca/blog/2014/03/05/international-womens-day-nfb/).

Janoff, Douglas Victor. 2005. Pink Blood: Homophobic Violence in Canada. Toronto: University of Toronto Press.

Jeffrey, Leslie Ann, and Gayle MacDonald. 2006a. "'It's the Money, Honey': The Economy of Sex Work in the Maritimes." Canadian Review of Sociology and Anthropology, 43(3):313–327.

Jeffrey, Leslie Ann, and Gayle MacDonald. 2006b. Sex Workers in the Maritimes Talk Back. Vancouver: UBC Press.

Jenkins, Philip. 2001. *Beyond Tolerance: Child Pornography on the Internet*. NY: New York University Press.

Jensen, Michael. 2007. "Ugly Betty Is Freaking Fabulous (and Gay)." Afterelton.com. Retrieved May 26, 2008 (http://www.afterelton.com/TV/2007/3/uglybetty).

Jewkes, Y. and C. Andrews. (2006). "The problem of child pornography on the internet: international responses," in Y. Jewkes (ed.) *Crime Online*, Cullompton: Willan.

Jhalli, Sut. (2007). *Dreamworlds 3: Desire, Sex & Power in Music Video* (film). Media Education Foundation. Retrieved July 20, 2015 (http://www.mediaed.org/cgi-bin/commerce.cgi?preadd=action&key=223).

Johnson, Allan G. 2006. Privilege, Power and Difference (2nd ed.). New York: McGraw-Hill.

Johnson, Bruce D., Paul J. Goldstein, Edward Preble, James Schmeidler, Douglas S. Lipton, Barry Spunt, and Thomas Miller. 1985. Taking Care of Business: The Economics of Crime by Heroin Abusers. Lexington, MA: Lexington Books.

Jolin, Annette. 1994. "On the Backs of Working Prostitutes: Feminist Theory and Prostitution Policy." Crime and Delinquency, 40(1):69–83.

Jones, Charles, Lorna Marsden, and Lorne Tepperman. 1990. Lives of Their Own: The Individualization of Women's Lives. Don Mills, ON: Oxford University Press.

Joyce, Greg. 2008. "Prostitutes to Open Brothel in Time for Vancouver 2010." TheStar.com (December 17). Retrieved January 31, 2009 (http://www.thestar.com/news/canada/article/555509).

Jung, John. 1994. Under the Influence: Alcohol and Human Behavior. Pacific Grove, CA: Brooks/Cole.

Justice Centre Constitutional Freedoms. 2013. JCCF Takes Government Health Care Monopoly to Court. Retrieved October 15, 2013 (http://www.jccf.ca/572/).

Kadie, Carl. 1993. *Computers and Academic Freedom* [online]. (http://www.eff.org. CAF/news/nov_28_1993).

Kaiser Family Foundation. 2003. "Key Facts: TV Violence." Retrieved June 17, 2014 (http://kaiserfamilyfoundation.files.wordpress.com/2013/01/key-facts-tv-violence.pdf).

Kaldor, Mary. 1981. The Baroque Arsenal. New York: Hill and Wang.

Kalish, Richard A. 1985. Death, Grief, and Caring Relationships (2nd ed.). Monterey, CA: Brooks/Cole.

Kaminer, Wendy. 1990. *A Fearful Freedom: Women's Flight from Equality*. Reading, MA: Addison-Wesley.

Karcher, Richard T. 2009. Tort Law and Journalism Ethics. Loyola University Law Journal. 40:781–845.

Katz, Stephen. 2000. "Busy Bodies: Activity, Aging, and the Management of Everyday Life." Journal of Aging Studies, 14(2):135–152.

Kazempur, Abdolmohammed, and Shiva S. Halli. 2001. "The Changing Colour of Poverty in Canada." Canadian Review of Sociology and Anthropology, 38(2):217–238.

Kearney, A.T. 2012. Global Cities Index. Retrieved September 2, 2013 (http://www.atkearney.com/gbpc/global-cities-index/full-report/-/asset_publisher/yAl1OgZpc1DO/content/2012-global-cities-index/10192).

Kempadoo, Kamala. 1998. "Introduction: Globalizing Sex Workers' Rights." In Kamala Kempadoo and Jo Doezema (Eds.), Global Sex Workers: Rights,

Resistance and Redefinition. New York: Routledge, pp. 1–28.

Kempadoo, Kamala. 2005. "Victims and Agents of Crime: The New Crusade against Trafficking." In Julia Sudbury (Ed.), Global Lockdown: Race, Gender, and the Prison-Industrial Complex. New York: Routledge, pp. 35–55.

Kempe, C. Henry, F. Silverman, B. Steele, W. Droegemueller, and H. Silver. 1962. "The Battered-Child Syndrome." Journal of the American Medical Association, 181:17–24.

Kempe, Ruth S., and C. Henry Kempe. 1978. Child Abuse. Cambridge, MA: Harvard University Press.

Kendall, Diana. 2000. Sociology in Our Times: The Essentials (2nd ed.). Belmont, CA: Wadsworth.

Kiel, Douglas P., David T. Felson, Marian T. Hanna, Jennifer J. Anderson, and Peter W.F. Wilson. 1990. "Caffeine and the Risk of Hip Fracture: The Framington Study." American Journal of Epidemiology, 132:675–684.

Kilbourne, Jean. 1999. Deadly Persuasion: Why Women and Girls Must Fight the Addictive Power of Advertising. New York: Free Press.

Kim, Su Yeong, Yijie Wang, Diana Orozco-Lapray, Yishan Shen, and Mohammed Murtuza. 2013. Does "tiger parenting" exist? Parenting profiles of Chinese Americans and adolescent development outcomes. Asian American Journal of Psychology, Vol. 4(1), Mar, 7–18.

Kimmel, Michael S. and Jacqueline Holler. 2011. The Gendered Society: Canadian Edition. Don Mills. Oxford University Press.

Kingsley, Cherry, and Melanie Mark. 2000. Sacred Lives: Canadian Aboriginal Children and Youth Speak Out about Sexual Exploitation. Vancouver: Save the Children Canada.

Kinnick, Katherine N. 2007. "Pushing the Envelope: The Role of the Mass Media in the Mainstreaming of Pornography," in Ann C. Hall and Mardia J. Bishop (Eds.), Pop-Porn: Pornography in American Culture. Westport, CT: Praeger Publishers, pp. 7–26.

Kinsman, Gary. 1996. The Regulation of Desire: Homo and Hetero Sexualities (2nd ed., rev.). Montreal: Black Rose Books.

Kipnis, Laura. 1996. Bound and Gagged: Pornography and the Politics of Fantasy in America. New York: Grove Press.

Kirsch, Max H. 2000. Queer Theory and Social Change. London: Routledge.

Kitzinger, Celia. 1987. The Social Construction of Lesbianism. London: Sage.

Kivel, Paul. 1996. Uprooting Racism: How White People Can Work for Racial Justice. Philadelphia: New Society Publishers.

Kivel, Paul. 2002. Uprooting Racism: How White People Can Work for Racial Justice (rev. ed.). Gabriola, BC: New Society Publishers.

Klockars, Carl B. 1979. "The Contemporary Crises of Marxist Criminology." Criminology, 16:477–515.

Knight, Graham. 1998. "The Mass Media." In Robert Brym (Ed.), New Society: Sociology for the 21st Century. Toronto: Harcourt Brace, pp.103–127.

Knight, Graham, and Josh Greenberg. 2008. "The Mass Media." In Robert J. Brym (Ed.), New Society (5th ed.). Toronto: Thomson Nelson, pp. 104–133.

Knox, Paul L., and Peter J. Taylor (Eds.). 1995. World Cities in a World-System. Cambridge, UK: Cambridge University Press.

Kremarik, Frances. 2000. "One Hundred Years of Urban Development." Canadian Social Trends (Winter):18–22.

Krohn, Marvin. 1995. "Control and Deterrence Theories of Criminality." In Joseph F. Sheley (Ed.), Criminology: A Contemporary Handbook (2nd ed.). Belmont, CA: Wadsworth, pp. 329–347.

Kübler-Ross, Elisabeth. 1969. On Death and Dying. New York: Macmillan.

Kurz, Demie. 1989. "Social Science Perspectives on Wife Abuse: Current Debates and Future Directions." Gender and Society, 3(4):489–505.

LaBerge, Roy. 2008. "May 2008: The Truth about Canada: Some Truly Appalling Things We Should Know about Our Country." Canadian Centre for Policy Alternatives. Retrieved July 26, 2009 (http://www.policyalternatives.ca/monitorissues/2008/05/monitorissue1934/?pa=BB736455).

Lagerquist, Jeff. 2012. "Student Debt: Average Payback Takes 14 Years." Financial Post. (September 4). Retrieved June 20 2013 (http://business.financialpost.com/2012/09/04/student-debt-average-payback-takes-14-years/).

Lakoff, George. 2002. Moral Politics: How Liberals and Conservatives Think. Chicago, IL: University of Chicago Press.

Lalonde, Marc. 1974. A New Perspective on the Health of Canadians. Ottawa: Minister of Supply and Services.

Lamanna, Marianne, and Agnes Riedmann. 1994. Marriages and Families: Making Choices and Facing Change (5th ed.). Belmont, CA: Wadsworth.

Lambert, Steve. 2013. "Canadian Dies in Assisted Suicide in Switzerland." Toronto Star. April 26: A4.

Langelan, Martha J. 1993. Back Off! How to Confront and Stop Sexual Harassment and Harassers. New York: Fireside/Simon & Schuster.

Laqueur, Thomas. 1992. Making Sex: Body and Gender from the Greeks to Freud. Cambridge, UK: Harvard University Press.

Lasswell, Harold D. 1969. "The Structure and Function of Communication in Society." In Wilbur Schramm (Ed.), Mass Communications. Urbana: University of Illinois Press, pp. 103–130.

Lauer, Robert H. 1995. Social Problems and the Quality of Life (6th ed.). Madison, WI: Brown.

Lauer, Robert H., and Jeannette C. Lauer. 1991. "The Long-Term Relational Consequences of Problematic Family Backgrounds." Family Relations, 40:286–290.

Lauer, Robert H., Jeanette C. Lauer, Zelda Abramson, and Jeanette A. Auger. 2006. Social Problems and the Quality of Life (Cdn. ed.). Toronto: McGraw-Hill Ryerson.

Leading Boards. 2014. Gender Diversity in Canadian Boardrooms. Retrieved October 20, 2014 (http://www.leadingboards.com/blog/gender-diversity-in-canadian-boardrooms/).

Leblanc, Dave. 2013. "35 years on St. Lawrence Is a Template for Urban Housing." The Globe and Mail February 8:G4.

Lee, Taylor. (2004), "In and Out: A Survivor's Memoir of Stripping," in Rebecca Whisnant and Christine Stark (Eds.), Not for sale feminists: resisting prostitution and pornography, North Melbourne, Victoria: Spinifex Press, pp. 56–63.

Lehmann, Jennifer M. 1994. Durkheim and Women. Lincoln: University of Nebraska Press.

Lehne, Gregory K. 1995. "Homophobia among Men: Supporting and Defining the Male Role." In Michael S. Kimmel and Michael A. Messner (Eds.), Men's Lives (3rd ed.). Boston: Allyn and Bacon, pp. 325–336.

Lehrer, Jonah. 2009. "Gambling Blows Your Mind." Times Online (February 20). Retrieved March 1, 2009 (http://entertainment.timesonline.co.uk/tol/arts_and_entertainment/books/non-fiction/article5772806.ece).

Lemert, Edwin. 1951. Social Pathology. New York: McGraw-Hill.

Lengermann, Patricia Madoo, and Jill Niebrugge-Brantley. 1992. "Contemporary Feminist Theory." In George Ritzer (Ed.), Contemporary Sociological Theory (3rd ed.). New York: McGraw-Hill, pp. 308–357.

Leong, Wai-Teng. 1991. "The Pornography 'Problem': Disciplining Women and Young Girls." Media, Culture, and Society, 13:91–117.

Leuchtag, A. 2003. "Human Rights, Sex Trafficking, and Prostitution." Humanist, 63(1):10–15.

Levine, Peter. 1992. Ellis Island to Ebbets Field: Sport and the American Jewish Experience. New York: Oxford University Press.

Levinthal, Charles F. 2011. Drugs, Behavior and Modern Society (7th edition). Upper Saddle River NJ: Pearson.

Lewis, Oscar. 1966. La Vida: A Puerto Rican Family in the Culture of Poverty—San Juan and New York. New York: Random House.

Lexchin, Joel. 2002. "Profits First: The Pharmaceutical Industry in Canada." In B. Singh Bolaria and Harley D. Dickinson (Eds.), Health, Illness, and Health Care in Canada (3rd ed.). Scarborough, ON: Nelson.

Ley, D.F., and L.S. Bourne. 1993. "Introduction: The Social Context and Diversity of Urban Canada." In L.S. Bourne and D.F. Ley (Eds.), The Changing Social Geography of Canadian Cities. Montreal: McGill-Queen's University Press, pp. 3–30.

Libin, Kevin. 2009. "Sentencing Circles for Aboriginals: Good Justice?" National Post (February 27). Retrieved July 14, 2014 (http://www.nationalpost.com/news/Sentencing+circles+aboriginals+Good+justice/1337495/story.html).

Lill, Wendy. 2001. "Media Chaos Reigns in Canada." Media Channel. Retrieved December 20, 2001 (http://www.mediachannel.org/ownership).

Lindell, Rebecca, and Rod Mickleburgh. 2010. "Gay Bashing on the Rise in Vancouver: Councillor." The Globe and Mail (July 30). Retrieved November 24, 2013 (http://www.theglobeandmail.com/news/british-columbia/gay-bashing-on-the-rise-in-vancouver-councillor/article563507/).

Lindsey, Linda L. 2005. Gender Roles: A Sociological Perspective (4th ed.). Upper Saddle River, NJ: Pearson Prentice Hall.

Lips, Hilary M. 1993. Sex and Gender: An Introduction (2nd ed.). Mountain View, CA: Mayfield.

Ljunggren, David. 2003. "Canada Sending Up to 2,000 Troops to Afghanistan." Reuters (February 13). (http://www.reuters.com).

Loftus, David. 2002. Watching Sex: How Men Really Respond to Pornography. New York, NY: Thunder's Mouth Press (div of Avalon Publishing Group Inc).

Logan, Ron. 2001. "Crime Statistics in Canada, 2000." Juristat, 21(8).

Lomborg, Bjorn. 2013. "Green Innovation Is Cheaper than Green Subsidies." The Globe and Mail July 16:A3.

London, Kathryn A. 1991. "Advance Data Number 194: Cohabitation, Marriage, Marital Dissolution, and Remarriage: United States 1988." U.S. Department of Health and Human Services. Vital and Health Statistics of the National Center, January 4.

London, Kathryn A., and Barbara Foley Wilson. 1988. "Divorce." American Demographics, 10(10):23–26.

Lorber, Judith. 1986. "Dismantling Noah's Ark." Sex Roles, 14(11–12):567–579.

Lorber, Judith. 1994. Paradoxes of Gender. New Haven, CT: Yale University Press.

Lottes, Ilsa. 1993. "Reactions to Pornography on a College Campus: For or Against?" Sex Roles: A Journal of Research, 29(1–2):69–90.

Lowman, John. 2000. "Violence and the Outlaw Status of (Street) Prostitution in Canada." Violence Against Women, 6(9):987–1011.

Lowman, John, and Chris Atchison. 2006. "Men Who Buy Sex: A Survey in the Greater Vancouver Regional District." Canadian Review of Sociology and Anthropology, 43(3): 282–296.

Lowman, John, Chris Atchison, and Laura Fraser. 1997. Sexuality in the 1990s: Survey Results—Men Who Buy Sex, Phase Two. Retrieved October 20, 2006 (http://users.uniserve.com/~lowman/ICSS/icss.htm).

Lowman, John, and Laura Fraser. 1995. Technical Report: Violence against Persons Who Prostitute: The Experience in British Columbia. Department of Justice Canada TR1996-14e, Research, Statistics and Evaluation Directorate Policy Sector. Retrieved October 20, 2006 (http://users.uniserve.com/~lowman/).

Luckenbill, David F. 1977. "Criminal Homicide as a Situated Transaction." Social Problems, 25:176–186.

Macionis, John J., and Linda M. Gerber. 2002. Sociology (4th Cdn. ed.). Toronto: Pearson.

Macionis, John J., and Linda M. Gerber. 2008. Sociology. Toronto, ON: Pearson Prentice Hall.

Mackenzie, Hugh. 2014. All in a Day's Work? CEO Pay in Canada. Centre for Policy Alternatives. Retrieved May 19, 2014 (https://www.policyalternatives.ca/sites/default/files/uploads/publications/National%20Office/2014/01/All_in_a_Days_Work_CEO_%20Pay.pdf).

MacKinnon, Catharine. 1987. Feminism Unmodified: Discourses on Life and Law. Cambridge, MA: Harvard University Press.

Maclean's. 2013. The Canadian Universities Guidebook. Maclean's 2013:236.

MacLeod, Jay. 1995. Ain't No Makin' It: Aspirations and Attainment in a Low-Income Neighborhood. Boulder, CO: Westview Press.

MacMillan, Craig S., and Myron G. Claridge. 1998. "Criminal Proceedings as a Response to Hate." Paper presented at the "Hatred in Canada" conference, University of Victoria, Victoria, BC (September).

Macy, Marianne. 1996. Working Sex: An Odyssey into Our Cultural Underworld. New York: Carroll & Graf.

Malarek, Victor. 2003. The Natashas: The New Global Sex Trade. Toronto: Viking Canada.

Malinowski, Bronislaw. 1964. "The Principle of Legitimacy: Parenthood, the Basis of Social Structure." In Rose Laub Coser (Ed.), The Family: Its Structure and Functions. New York: St Martin's Press.

Malthus, Thomas R. 1965. An Essay on Population. New York: Augustus Kelley, Bookseller (orig. published in 1798).

Mann, Patricia S. 1994. Micro-Politics: Agency in a Post-Feminist Era. Minneapolis: University of Minnesota Press.

Marchington, Erin. 2012. Green Provinces of Canada. Corporate Knights 11(1):40–48.

Marger, Martin. 1999. Social Inequality: Patterns and Processes. Toronto: Mayfield.

Marger, Martin N. 1994. Race and Ethnic Relations: American and Global Perspectives. Belmont, CA: Wadsworth.

Marlowe, Julian. 1997. "It's Different for Boys." In Jill Nagle (Ed.), Whores and Other Feminists. New York: Routledge.

Marshall, Barbara L. 2000. Configuring Gender: Explorations in Theory and Politics. Peterborough, ON: Broadview Press.

Marshall, Katherine. 2006. "Converging Gender Roles." Perspectives: 5–17. Statistics Canada Catalogue no. 75-001-XIE.

Marshall, Katherine. 2011. "Generational Change in Paid and Unpaid Work." Canadian Social Trends. No. 92 Catalogue No. 11-008:13–26.

Marshall, Victor W. 1980. Last Chapters: A Sociology of Aging and Dying. Monterey, CA: Brooks/Cole.

Marshall, Victor W., and Judith Levy. 1990. "Aging and Dying." In Robert H. Binstock and Linda George (Eds.), Handbook of Aging and the Social Sciences (3rd ed.). New York: Academic Press.

Martin, Patricia Yancy. 1992. "Gender, Interaction and Inequality in Organizations." In Cecilia Ridgeway (Ed.), Gender, Interaction and Inequality. New York: Springer-Verlag, pp. 208–231.

Marx, Karl, and Friedrich Engels. 1971. "The Communist Manifesto." In Dirk Struik (Ed.), The Birth of the Communist Manifesto. New York: International (orig. published in 1847).

Marx, Karl, and Friedrich Engels. 1976. The Communist Manifesto. New York: Pantheon (orig. published in 1848).

Mason, Gary. 2006. "Why Grieving Parents Forgave Reena's Killer." Globe and Mail (July 27):A3.

Massey, Douglas S., and Nancy A. Denton. 1992. American Apartheid: Segregation and the Making of the Underclass. Cambridge, MA: Harvard University Press.

Massey, James L., and Marvin D. Krohn. 1986. "A Longitudinal Examination of an Integrated Social Process Model of Deviant Behavior." Social Forces, 65:106–134.

Mastrofski, Stephen D. 1995. "The Police." In Joseph F. Sheley (Ed.), Criminology: A Contemporary Handbook (2nd ed.). Belmont, CA: Wadsworth, pp. 373–405.

Maticka-Tyndale, Eleanor, Jacqueline Lewis, and Megan Street. 2005. "Making a Place for Escort Work: A Case Study." Journal of Sex Research, 42(1):46–53.

Maxwell, Milton A. 1981. "Alcoholics Anonymous." In Martin S. Weinberg, Earl Rubington, and Sue Kiefer Hammersmith (Eds.), The Solution of Social Problems: Five Perspectives (2nd ed.). New York: Oxford University Press, pp. 152–156.

Mayall, Alice, and Diana E. H. Russell. 1993. "Racism in Pornography." In Diana E. H. Russell (Ed.), Making Violence Sexy: Feminist Views on Pornography. New York: Teachers College Press, pp. 167–177.

McCall, Nathan. 1994. Makes Me Wanna Holler: A Young Black Man in America. New York: Random House.

McChesney, Robert W. 1999. Rich Media, Poor Democracy: Communication Politics in Dubious Times. Urbana: University of Illinois Press.

McDonald, Lynn, Brooke Moore, and Natalya Timoshkina. 2000. Migrant Sex Workers from Eastern Europe and the Former Soviet Union: The Canadian Case. Ottawa: Research Directorate, Status of Women Canada.

McFetridge, John. 2008. "Pot of Gold." Driven (October):70–71.

McKenna, Barrie. 2014. "White-Collar Crime Hits More than a Third of Canadian Organizations." The Globe and Mail (February 24). Retrieved April 26, 2014 (http://www.theglobeandmail.com/report-on-business/white-collar-crime-rises-in-canada/article17058885/).

McKinlay, John B. 1994. "A Case for Refocusing Upstream: The Political Economy of Illness." In Peter Conrad and Rochelle Kern (Eds.), The Sociology of Health and Illness. New York: St. Martin's Press, pp. 509–530.

McMullan, John L. 1992. Beyond the Limits of the Law: Corporate Crime and Law and Order. Halifax: Fernwood.

McMullin, J.A., and Victor W. Marshall. 1996. "Family, Friends, Stress, and Well-Being: Does Childlessness Make a Difference?" Canadian Journal on Aging, 15(3):355–373.

McNamara, Robert P. 1994. The Times Square Hustler: Male Prostitution in New York City. Westport, CT: Praeger.

McPherson, Barry D., and Andrew Wister. 2008. Aging as a Social Process: Canadian Perspectives 5ed. Toronto, ON: Oxford University Press.

McQuaig, Linda. 2006. War, Big Oil, and the Fight for the Planet. Toronto: Doubleday Canada.

McWilliams, Peter. 1996. Ain't Nobody's Business If You Do: The Absurdity of Consensual Crimes in Our Free Country. Los Angeles: Prelude Press.

Mead, Margaret. 1966. "Marriage in Two Steps." Redbook, 127:48–49, 85–86.

Meadahl, Marianne. 2007. "Lack of Violence Among Off-Street Sex Workers." Simon Fraser News (June 28). Retrieved January 31, 2009 (http://www.sfu.ca/sfunews/print/Stories/sfunews06280710.html).

Merchant, Carolyn. 1983. The Death of Nature: Women, Ecology and the Scientific Revolution. San Francisco: Harper and Row.

Merton, Robert. 1938. "Social Structure and Anomie." American Sociological Review, 3(6):672–682.

Merton, Robert King. 1968. Social Theory and Social Structure(enlarged ed.). New York: Free Press.

Michael, Robert T., John H. Gagnon, Edward O. Laumann, and Gina Kolata. 1994. Sex in America: A Definitive Survey. New York: Warner Books.

Michelson, William H. 1976. Man and His Urban Environment: A Sociological Approach. Don Mills, ON: Addison-Wesley.

Mies, Maria. 1986. Patriarchy and Accumulation on a World Scale: Women in the International Division of Labour. UK: Zed Books.

Mies, Maria, and Vandana Shiva. 1993. Ecofeminism. Atlantic Highlands, NJ: Zed Books.

Migration News. 2002. "Canada: Immigration, Border." Migration News, 9(12, December).

Milan, Anne. 2000. "One Hundred Years of Families." Canadian Social Trends (Spring):2–12.

Milan, Anne. 2013. "Marital Status: Overview, 2011." Statistics Canada. Retrieved

September 25, 2013 (http://www.stat-can.gc.ca/pub/91-209-x/2013001/article/11788/fig/fig7-eng.htm).

Milke, Mark. 2014. Government Subsidies in Canada: A $684 Billion Price Tag. Fraser Institute (http://www.fraserinstitute.org).

Millar, Alison E. 2002. "Leaving the Trade: Exiting Experiences of Former Sex Trade Workers in the CRD." Unpublished master's thesis, University of Victoria, Department of Sociology, Victoria, BC.

Miller, Eleanor M. 1986. Street Woman. Philadelphia: Temple University Press.

Miller, J.R. 2002. "Residential Schools." The Canadian Encyclopedia. Retrieved October 20, 2002 (http://www.thecanadianencyclopedia.com/index.cfm?PgNm=TCE&TCE_Version=A&ArticleId=A0011547&MenuClosed=0).

Mills, C. Wright. 1959a. The Power Elite. Fair Lawn, NJ: Oxford University Press.

Mills, C. Wright. 1959b. The Sociological Imagination. London: Oxford University Press.

Minow, Newton N., and Craig L. LaMay. 1999. "Changing the Way We Think." In Robert M. Baird, William E. Loges, and Stuart E. Rosenbaum (Eds.), The Media and Morality. Amherst, NY: Promethus Books, pp. 309–330.

Mishna, Faye, Charlene Cook, Tahany Gadalla, Joanne Daciuk, and Steven Solomon. 2010. "Cyber Bullying Behaviors Among Middle and High School Students." American Journal of Orthopsychiatry 80(3):362–374.

Mitchell, Barbara A. 2009. Family Matters: An Introduction to Family Sociology in Canada. Toronto: Canadian Scholars' Press.

Moeller, Susan D. 2004. "Media Coverage of Weapons of Mass Destruction." Centre for International Security Studies at Maryland, University of Maryland, College Park (http://www.cissm.umd.edu/documents/WMDstudy_full.pdf).

Mooney, Linda A., David Knox, Caroline Schacht, and Adie Nelson. 2003. Understanding Social Problems (2nd Cdn. ed.). Scarborough, ON: Nelson Thomson Learning.

Morel, Sylvie. 2002. The Insertion Model or the Workfare Model? The Transformation of Social Assistance within Quebec and Canada. Ottawa: Research Directorate, Status of Women Canada.

Morgan, Robin. 1993. The Word of a Woman: Selected Prose 1968–1992. London: Virago Press.

Morrow, Doug. 2014. "The Global 1000." Corporate Knights. Winter:36–48.

Mulvey, Laura. 1999. "Visual Pleasure and Narrative Cinema." Film Theory and Criticism: Introductory Readings. Eds. Leo Braudy and Marshall Cohen. New York: Oxford UP:833–44.

Munnik, Katie. 2008. "First, Confess Then, Celebrate." Presbyterian Record (May):22–23.

Munoz, Sr, Claudio, Joe Lee, and Lucas Armstrong. 2014. Digital Transition: Canadian Media Experiments in 2014. Retrieved June 11, 2014 (http://www.marsdd.com/app/uploads/2014/04/Digital-Transition_-Canadian-Media-Experiments-in-2014.pdf).

Muszynski, Alicja. 2000. "The Social Construction/Deconstruction of Sex, Gender, Race and Class." In B. Singh Bolaria (Ed.), Social Issues and Contradictions in Canadian Society (3rd ed.). Toronto: Harcourt Brace, pp. 95–131.

Myers, Steven Lee. 1997. "Converting the Dollar into a Bludgeon." New York Times (April 20):E5.

Myles, John. 2000. "The Maturation of Canada's Retirement Income System: Income Levels, Income Inequality and Low Income among Older Persons." Canadian Journal on Aging,19(3):287–316.

Nath, Pamela S., John G. Borkowski, Thomas L. Whitman, and Cynthia J. Schellenbach. 1991. "Understanding Adolescent Parenting: The Dimensions and Functions of Social Support." Family Relations, 40:411–420.

Nathan, Debbie. 2007. Pornography. Toronto, ON: Groundwood Books/House of Anansi Press.

National Film Board of Canada (NFB). 1973. The October Crisis. Director Pierre Perrault.

National Television Violence Study. 1998. News Release. Retrieved June 17, 2014 (http://www.news.ucsb.edu/1998/011107/study-violence-remains-common-tv-programming).

National Victims Resource Center. 1991. Juvenile Prostitution: Fact Sheet. Rockville, MD: Victims Resource Center.

Nava, Michael, and Robert Dawidoff. 1994. Created Equal: Why Gay Rights Matter to America. New York: St. Martin's Press.

Nelson, Adie. 2006. Gender in Canada (3rd ed.). Toronto: Pearson Prentice Hall.

Nelson, Adie. 2010. Gender in Canada (4th ed.). Toronto: Pearson Education.

Newman, Zoe. 2001. "The Bisexuality Wars: The Perils of Identity as Marginality." In Terry Goldie (Ed.), In a Queer Country: Gay and Lesbian Studies in the Canadian Context. Vancouver: Arsenal Pulp Press, pp. 122–137.

Nordicity. 2013. Analysis of Government Support for Public Broadcasting and Other Culture in Canada. Retrieved June 29, 2014 (http://www.cbc.radio-canada.ca/_files/cbcrc/documents/latest-studies/nordicity-analysis-public-broadcasting-en.pdf).

Novak, Mark, and Lori Campbell. 2006. Aging and Society: A Canadian Perspective (5th ed.). Toronto: Nelson.

Novak, Mark, Lori Campbell, and Herbert C. Northcott. 2014. Aging and Society: A Canadian Perspective. Seventh Edition. Toronto: Thomson/Nelson.

O'Doherty, Tamara. 2011. "Victimization in Off-Street Sex Industry Work." Violence Against Women (July)17:944–963.

O'Reilly, Michael. 1998. "MD at Centre of Somalia Controversy Finds Peace in Northern Ontario." CMAJ,158:244–245. Retrieved August 24, 2009 (http://epe.lac-bac.gc.ca/100/201/300/cdn_medical_association/cmaj/vol-158/issue-2/0244.htm).

Oakes, Jeannie. 1985. Keeping Track: How Schools Structure Inequality. New Haven, CT: Yale University Press.

OECD. 2013. Environment at a Glance 2013. Retrieved October 16, 2013 (http://www.oecd.org/environment/indicators-modelling-outlooks/environment-at-a-glance-2013-9789264185715-en.htm). Ontario Ministry of the Environment. 2013. Air Quality Index. Retrieved October 6, 2013 (http://www.airquality-ontario.com/press/faq.php#1).

Ogrodnik, Lucie. 2010. "Towards the Development of a National Data Collection Framework to Measure Trafficking in Persons." Statistics Canada. Retrieved March 19, 2014 (http://www.statcan.gc.ca/pub/85-561-m/2010021/part-partie1-eng.htm).

Olsen, Gregg M. 2002. The Politics of the Welfare State: Canada, Sweden, and the United States. Don Mills, ON: Oxford University Press.

Olzak, Susan, Suzanne Shanahan, and Elizabeth H. McEneaney. 1996. "Poverty, Segregation, and Race Riots: 1960 to 1993." American Sociological Review, 61(August):590–613.

Omi, Michael, and Howard Winant. 1994. Racial Formation in the United States: From the 1960s to the 1990s (2nd ed.). New York: Routledge.

Open Media. 2014. Retrieved August 18, 2014 (https://openmedia.ca/).

Osberg, Lars. 2009. Canada's Declining Social Safety Net: The Case for EI Reform. Ottawa: Canadian Centre for PolicyAlternatives. Retrieved June 30, 2009 (http://www.policyalternatives.ca).

Otis, Leah. 1985. Prostitution in Medieval Society. Chicago: University of Chicago Press.

Overall, Christine. 2000. "Heterosexuality and Feminist Theory." In Barbara A. Crow and Lise Gotell (Eds.), Open Boundaries: A Canadian Women's Studies Reader. Toronto: Prentice Hall/Allyn and Bacon, pp. 262–269.

Ozone Hole. 2013. The Ozone Hole 2013. Retrieved September 21, 2013 (http://www.theozonehole.com/2013ozonehole.htm).

P.O.W.E.R.. 2013. FAQ. Retrieved October 1, 2013 (http://powerstudy.ca/).

Paglia-Boak, A., E.M. Adlaf, and R.E. Mann. 2011. Drug use Among Ontario Students, 1977–2011: Detailed OSDUHS Findings. CAMH Research Document Series No. 32. Toronto, ON: Centre for Addiction and Mental Health.

Paglia-Boak, A., E.M. Adlaf, H.A. Hamilton, J.H. Beitchman, D. Wolfe, and R.E. Mann. 2012. The Mental Health and Well-Being of Ontario Students, 1991–2011: OSDUHS Highlights. CAMH Research Document Series No. 35. Toronto, ON: Centre for Addiction and Mental Health.

Parenti, Michael. 1998. America Besieged. San Francisco: City Lights Books.

Parents and Friends of Lesbians and Gays. 2009. Home Page. Retrieved April 5, 2009 (http://www.pflagcanada.ca/en/index-e.asp).

Parrot, Andrea, and Nina Cummings. 2008. Sexual Enslavement of Girls and Women Worldwide. Westport, CT: Praeger.

Parsons, Talcott. 1951. The Social System. New York: Free Press.

Parsons, Talcott. 1955. "The American Family: Its Relations to Personality and to the Social Structure." In Talcott Parsons and Robert F. Bales (Eds.), Family, Socialization, and Interaction Process. Glencoe, IL: Free Press, pp. 3–33.

Parsons, Talcott. 1966. Societies: Evolutionary and Comparative Perspectives. Englewood Cliffs, NJ: Prentice Hall.

Pateman, Carole. 1994. "What's Wrong with Prostitution?" In Alison M. Jaggar (Ed.), Living with Contradictions: Controversies in Feminist Social Ethics. Boulder, CO: Westview, pp. 127–132.

Paul, Pamela. 2002. The Starter Marriage and the Future of Matrimony. New York: Random House.

Pearson, Caryn, Teresa Janz, and Jennifer Ali. 2013. "Mental and Substance Use Disorders in Canada." Statistics Canada. Catalogue no. 82-624-X. Retrieved September 18, 2013 (http://www.statcan.gc.ca/pub/82-624-x/2013001/article/11855-eng.htm).

Perkel, Colin. 2013. "At Least 3000 Native Children Died in Residential Schools: Research." The Globe and Mail (February 18). Retrieved February 20, 2013 (http://www.theglobeandmail.com/news/politics/at-least-3000-aboriginal-children-died-in-residential-schools-research-shows/article8786118/).

Perry, David C., and Alfred J. Watkins (Eds.). 1977. The Rise of the Sunbelt Cities. Beverly Hills, CA: Sage.

Perry-Jenkins, Maureen, and Ann C. Crouter. 1990. "Men's Provider Role Attitudes: Implications for Household Work and Marital Satisfaction." Journal of Family Issues, 11:136–156.

Petersen, John L. 1994. The Road to 2015: Profiles of the Future.Corte Madera, CA: Waite Group Press.

Peterson, R. Dean, Delores F. Wunder, and Harlan L. Mueller. 1999. Social Problems: Globalization in the Twenty-First Century. Upper Saddle River, NJ: Prentice Hall.

Peterson, V. Spike, and Anne Sisson Runyan. 1993. Global Gender Issues. Boulder, CO: Westview Press.

PFLAG. 2013. Parents, Families and Friends of Lesbians and Gays. Retrieved November 25, 2013 (http://community.pflag.org/page.aspx?pid=191).

Phillips, Rachel, and Cecilia Benoit. (2005). Social Determinants of Health Care Access Among Sex Industry Workers in Canada, in Jennie Jacobs Kronenfeld (ed.) Health Care Services, Racial and Ethnic Minorities and Underserved Populations: Patient and Provider Perspectives (Research in the Sociology of Health Care, Volume 23) Emerald Group Publishing Limited, pp.79–104.

Picard, Andre. 2005. "Cannabis Painkiller Approved." Globe and Mail. (April 20): A15.

Plait, Phil. 2013. What's Really Going On With Arctic Sea Ice? Slate. Retrieved September 20, 2013 (http://www.slate.com/blogs/bad_astronomy/2013/09/20/arctic_sea_ice_what_s_really_going_on.html).

Ploughshares Fund. 2014. World Nuclear Weapon Stockpile. Retrieved June18, 2014 (http://www.ploughshares.org/world-nuclear-stockpile-report).

Pocklington, Tom, and Allan Tupper. 2002. No Place to Learn: Why Universities Aren't Working. Vancouver: UBC Press.

PollutionWatch. 2008. "PollutionWatch Fact Sheet." Retrieved July7, 2009 (http://pollutionwatch.org/pressroom/factSheetData/PW_Toronto_Fact_Sheet.pdf).

Ponse, Barbara. 1978. Identities in the Lesbian World: The Social Construction of Self. Westport, CT: Greenwood Press.

Popenoe, David. 1996. Life without Father: Compelling New Evidence That Fatherhood and Marriage Are Indispensable for the Good of Children and Society. New York: Martin Kessler/Free Press.

Potterat, John J., Donald E. Woodhouse, John B. Muth, and Stephen Q. Muth. 1990. "Estimating the Prevalence and Career Longevity of Prostitute Women." Journal of Sex Research, 27(May):233–243.

Presidency of the Republic of Turkey. 2010. Business World Should Always Be Consolidated. Retrieved March 7, 2015 (http://www.tccb.gov.tr/news/397/77861/busineb-world-should-always-be-consolidated.html).

Princeton-Brookings. 2013. The Future of Children. Retrieved October 30, 2013 (http://www.princeton.edu/

futureofchildren/publications/figures-tables/figure_show.xml?fid=337).

Public Health Agency of Canada. 2013. HIV and AIDS in Canada: Surveillance Report to December 31st, 2013. Retrieved June 19, 2013 (http://www.phac-aspc.gc.ca/aids-sida/publication/survreport/2013/dec/index-eng.php).

Purvis, Andrew. 1996. "The Global Epidemic: AIDS Is Tightening Its Grip on the Developing World." Time (December 30):76–78.

Queen, Carol. 1997. Real Live Nude Girl: Chronicles of Sex-Positive Culture. Pittsburgh, PA: Cleis Press.

Rabinovich, Jannit, and Megan Lewis. 2001. The Story of PEERS: Prostitutes Empowerment, Education and Resource Society. Vancouver: Save the Children.

Ramlo, Andrew, and Ryan Berlin. 2010. Sustainability: British Columbia's Health Care System and Our Aging Population. Urban Futures Institute.

Raphael, Ray. 1988. The Men from the Boys: Rites of Passage in Male America. Lincoln: University of Nebraska Press.

Ravelli, Bruce, and Michelle Webber. 2010. Exploring Sociology: A Canadian Perspective. Toronto: Pearson Education Canada.

RCMP. 2006a. National Child Exploitation Coordination Centre (NCECC). Retrieved October 23, 2006 (http://www.rcmp.ca/factsheets/fact_ncecc_e.htm).

RCMP. 2006b. Virtual Global Taskforce. Retrieved October 23, 2006 (http://ncecc.ca/vgt_e.htm).

RCMP. 2013. Identity Theft and Identity Fraud. Retrieved October 21, 2013 (http://www.rcmp-grc.gc.ca/scams-fraudes/id-theft-vol-eng.htm).

RCMP. 2014. Serious and Organized Crime. Retrieved April 12, 2014 (http://www.rcmp-grc.gc.ca/soc-cgco/index-eng.htm).

Reckless, Walter C. 1967. The Crime Problem. New York: Meredith.

Rehm, Jurgen, William Gnam, Svetlana Popova, Dolly Baliunas, Serge Brochu, Benedikt Fischer, Jayadeep Patra, Anna Sarnocinska-Hart, and Benjamin Taylor. 2007. "The Costs of Alcohol, Illegal Drugs, and Tobacco in Canada, 2002." Journal of Studies on Alcohol and Drugs, 68(6). Retrieved July 18, 2013

(http://www.jsad.com/doi/abs/10.15288/jsad.2007.68.886).

Reisch, Nikki, and Steve Kretzmann. 2008. "A Climate of War: The War in Iraq and Global Warming." Oil Change International (March). Retrieved July 30, 2009 (http://priceofoil.org/wpcontent/uploads/2008/03/A%20Climate%20of%20War%20FINAL%20(March%2017%202008).pdf).

Renzetti, Claire M., and Daniel J. Curran. 1995. Women, Men, and Society (3rd ed.). Boston: Allyn and Bacon.

Reskin, Barbara F., and Irene Padavic. 1994. Women and Men at Work. Thousand Oaks, CA: Pine Forge.

Retrieved December 15, 2014 (http://www.tc.gc.ca/media/documents/roadsafety/TrafficCollisionStatisitcs_2011.pdf).

Revera. 2012. The Revera Report on Ageism. Retrieved March 6, 2015 (http://www.reveraliving.com/About-Revera/News/News-Releases/newsreleases/Age-Is-More-Release-FINAL.aspx).

Reynolds, Helen. 1986. The Economics of Prostitution. Springfield, IL: Charles C. Thomas.

Rich, Adrienne. 1984. "Compulsory Heterosexuality and Lesbian Existence." In Ann Snitnow, Christine Stansell, and Sharon Thompson (Eds.), Desire: The Politics of Sexuality. London: Virago Press, pp. 212–241.

Roberts, Nickie. 1992. Whores in History: Prostitution in Western Society. London: HarperCollins.

Robertson, Angela. 1999. "Continuing on the Ground: Feminists of Colour Discuss Organizing." In Enakshi Dua and Angela Robertson (Eds.), Scratching the Surface: Canadian Anti-Racist Feminist Thought. Toronto: Women's Press, pp. 309–329.

Robinson, David, Frank J. Porporino, William A. Millson, Shelley Trevethan, and Barry McKillop. 1999. "The One-Day Snapshot of Inmates in Canada's Adult Correctional Facilities." In Canadian Centre for Justice Statistics (Eds.), The Juristat Reader: A Statistical Overview of the Canadian Justice System. Toronto: Thompson, pp. 54–66.

Roos, Patricia A., and Barbara F. Reskin. 1992. "Occupational Desegregation in the 1970s: Integration and Economic Equity?" Sociological Perspectives, 35:69.

Ropers, Richard H. 1991. Persistent Poverty: The American Dream Turned Nightmare. New York: Plenum.

Rothenberg, Paula S. (Ed.). 2008. White Privilege: Essential Readings on the Other Side of Racism (3rd ed.). New York: Worth.

Rowland, Robyn, and Renate Klein. 1996. "Radical Feminism: History, Politics, Action." In Diane Bell and Renate Klein (Eds.), Radically Speaking: Feminism Reclaimed. London: Zed Books, pp. 9–36.

Rowland, Wade. 2014. The CBC's a Service not a Business. The Globe and Mail. June 27:A11.

Rubin, Lillian B. 1976. Worlds of Pain: Life in the Working-Class Family. New York: Basic Books.

Rubin, Lillian B. 1994. Families on the Fault Line. New York: HarperCollins.

Runnalls, Jeremy. 2015. "The Global 100 Most Sustainable Corporations." Corporate Knights. Winter 30-38.

Russell, Diana E. H. 1993. "Introduction." In Diana E. H. Russell (Ed.), Making Violence Sexy: Feminist Views on Pornography. New York: Teachers College Press, pp. 1–20.

Sacco, Vincent F., and Leslie W. Kennedy. 1998. The Criminal Event (2nd ed.). Scarborough, ON: Nelson.

Safilios-Rothschild, Constantina. 1969. "Family Sociology or Wives' Family Sociology? A Cross-Cultural Examination of Decision-Making." Journal of Marriage and the Family, 31(2): 290–301.

Sampson, Robert J. 1986. "Effects of Socioeconomic Context on Official Reactions to Juvenile Delinquency." American Sociological Review, 51(December): 876–885.

Sanday, Peggy Reeves. 1996. A Woman Scorned: Acquaintance Rape on Trial. New York: Doubleday.

Sandel. Michael. 2013. "Open Letter." The Chronicle of Higher Education. Retrieved April 12, 2013 (http://chronicle.com/article/The-Document-an-Open-Letter/138937/).

Sangera, Jyoti. 1997. "In the Belly of the Beast: Sex Trade, Prostitution and Globalization." Paper presented to the South Asia Regional Consultation on Prostitution, Bangkok, Thailand.

Satzewich, Vic, and Nikolaos Liodakis. 2007. "Race" and Ethnicity in Canada: A Critical Introduction. Don Mills, ON: Oxford University Press.

Saunders, Doug. 2014. "How Measures to Protect Privacy Stifle Good Journalism." The Globe and Mail. July 7:A11.

Sawyer, Janet. 1989. "Internalized Dominance." Quarterly Change, 1(4):16–23.

Schiller, Herbert I. 1996. Information Inequality: The Deepening Social Crisis in America. New York: Routledge.

Schneider, Keith. 1993. "The Regulatory Thickets of Environmental Racism." New York Times (December 19):E5.

Schur, Edwin M. 1965. Crimes without Victims: Deviant Behavior and Public Policy. Englewood Cliffs, NJ: Prentice-Hall.

Scott, James C. 1990. Domination and the Arts of Resistance: Hidden Transcripts. New Haven, CT: Yale University Press.

Severinson, Peter. 2008. "Red Light, Green Light: The Sex Industry in Vancouver." BC Business Magazine (http://www.bcbusiness.ca/careers/red-light-green-light-the-sex-industry-in-vancouver).

Seabrook, Jeremy. 2002. The No-Nonsense Guide to Class, Caste, and Hierarchies. Carlisle, UK: Carel Press.

Seager, Joni. 1997. The State of Women in the World Atlas (2nd ed.). London: Penguin.

Seager, Joni. 2003. The Penguin Atlas of Women of the World (rev. ed.). Brighton, UK: Penguin Books.

Segal, Lynn. 1990. "Pornography and Violence: What the 'Experts' Really Say." Feminist Review, 36:29–41.

Segall, Alexander, and Neena L. Chappell. 2000. Health and Health Care in Canada. Toronto: Prentice Hall.

Seidman, Steven. 1992. "An Investigation of Sex-Role Stereotyping in Music Videos." Journal of Broadcasting & Electronic Media (Spring):212.

Sen, Amartya. 1999. Development as Freedom. New York: Knopf.

Sexually Exploited Youth Committee of the Capital Regional District. 1997. Report of the Sexually Exploited Youth Committee of the Capital Regional District, Victoria, British Columbia. Victoria, BC: City of Victoria.

Shaver, Frances M., Jacqueline Lewis, and Eleanor Maticka-Tyndale. 2011. "Rising to the Challenge: Addressing Concerns of People Working in the Sex Industry."

Canadian Review of Sociology and Anthropology, Vol. 48, Issue 1, pp. 47–65.

Shelton, Beth Ann. 1992. Women, Men and Time: Gender Differences in Paid Work, Housework and Leisure. Westport, CT: Greenwood.

Sher, Kenneth J. 1991. Children of Alcoholics: A Critical Appraisal of Theory and Research. Chicago: University of Chicago Press.

Shiva, Vandana. 2000. Tomorrow's Biodiversity. London: Thames and Hudson.

Short, G. 1991. "Combating Anti-Semitism: A Dilemma for Antiracist Education." British Journal of Educational Studies, 39(1).

Shragge, Eric. 1997. "Workfare: An Overview." In Eric Shragge (Ed.), Workfare: Ideology for a New Under-Class. Toronto: Garamond Press, pp. 17–34.

Sidel, Ruth. 1996. Keeping Women and Children Last: America's War on the Poor. New York: Penguin.

Simmel, Georg. 1950. The Sociology of Georg Simmel. Kurt Wolff (Trans.). Glencoe, IL: Free Press (orig. written in 1902–1917).

Simon, Brenda M. 1999. "United States v. Hilton." Berkeley Technology Law Journal 14:385–403.

Single, Eric, Linda Robson, Xiadi Xie, and Jurgen Rehm. 1996. The Cost of Substance Abuse in Canada. Ottawa: Canadian Centre on Substance Abuse.

SIPRI Yearbook. 2103. Oxford University Press. Retrieved May 20, 2014 (http://www.sipri.org/yearbook/2013/files/sipri-yearbook-2013-chapter-3-section-2).

Sivard, Ruth L. 1991. World Military and Social Expenditures—1991. Washington, DC: World Priorities.

Sivard, Ruth L. 1993. World Military and Social Expenditures—1993. Washington, DC: World Priorities.

Skolnick, Arlene. 1991. Embattled Paradise: The American Family in an Age of Uncertainty. New York: HarperCollins.

Skolnick, Jerome H. 1975. Justice without Trial (2nd ed.). New York: Wiley.

Sleeter, Christine E. 1996. "White Silence, White Solidarity." In Noel Ignatiev and John Garvey (Eds.), Race Traitor. New York: Routledge, pp. 257–265.

Small, Shirley. 1978. "Canadian Narcotics Legislation, 1908–1923: A Conflict Model Interpretation." In William K. Greenaway and Stephen L. Brickey

(Eds.), Law and Social Control in Canada. Scarborough, ON: Prentice Hall.

Smith-Spark, Laura. 2014. "How Did Rape Become a Weapon of War?" BBC News (December). Retrieved March 19, 2014 (http://news.bbc.co.uk/2/hi/4078677.stm).

Snell, Cudore L. 1995. Young Men in the Street: Help-Seeking Behavior of Young Male Prostitutes. Westport, CT: Praeger.

Snitow, Ann Barr. 1994. "Mass Market Romance: Pornography for Women Is Different." In Alison M. Jaggar (Ed.), Living with Contradictions: Controversies in Feminist Social Ethics. Boulder, CO: Westview, pp. 181–188.

Snyder, Benson R. 1971. The Hidden Curriculum. New York: Knopf.

Soble, Alan. 1986. "Pornography in Capitalism: Powerlessness." In Alan Soble, Pornography: Marxism, Feminism and the Future of Sexuality. New Haven, CT: Yale University Press, pp. 78–84.

Solyom, Catherine. 2001. "Pigment Matters in Montreal: Survey." Gazette (October 26).

Special Committee on Pornography and Prostitution. 1985. Pornography and Prostitution in Canada: Report of the Special Committee on Pornography and Prostitution. Ottawa: Department of Justice Canada.

Speier, Suzu G. 1991. "Stereotypes Exercise." Anti-Racism and Community Development Train the Trainer Workshop Manual. Quesnel, BC: College of New Caledonia and 42nd Street Consulting.

Squires, Gregory D. 1994. Capital and Communities in Black and White: The Intersections of Race, Class, and Uneven Development. Albany: State University of New York Press.

Staff. 2014. "Day of Honour." The Globe and Mail (May 9):A10.

Stanley, Julia P. 1972. "Paradigmatic Woman: The Prostitute." Paper presented at South Atlantic Modern Language Association, Jacksonville, FL, cited in Jessie Bernard, The Female World. New York: Free Press, 1981.

Stasiulis, Daiva K. 1999. "Feminist Intersectional Theorizing." In Peter S. Li (Ed.), Race and Ethnic Relations in Canada (2nd ed.). Don Mills, ON: Oxford University Press, pp. 347–397.

Statistics Canada. 1999a. "Assets and Debts Held by Family Units, Canada and Provinces, 1999." Retrieved April 23, 2003 (http://www.statcan.ca/english/pgdb/famil99d.htm).

Statistics Canada. 2001. "How Healthy Are Canadians?" Health Reports, 12(3).

Statistics Canada. 2002. "Divorces." The Daily (December 2).

Statistics Canada. 2002a. "2001 Census: Collective Dwellings." Retrieved November 6, 2002 (http://www12.statcan.ca/english/census01/products/analytic/companion/coll/contents.cfm).

Statistics Canada. 2004. "Parenting Style and Children's Aggressive Behaviour." The Daily (October 25).

Statistics Canada. 2005. "Study: Exploring Crime Patterns in Canada." The Daily (June 29).

Statistics Canada. 2007c. "2006 Census: Families, Marital Status, Households and Dwelling Characteristics." The Daily (September 12). Retrieved February 24, 2009 (http://www.statcan.gc.ca/daily-quotidien/070912/dq070912aeng.htm).

Statistics Canada. 2008a. "Gay Pride . . . By the Numbers." (June 24). Retrieved February 24, 2009 (http://www42.statcan.ca/smr08/smr08_118-eng.htm).

Statistics Canada. 2008b. Gambling: Perspectives on Labour and Income. Retrieved February 24, 2009 (http://www.statcan.gc.ca/pub/75-001-x/2008109/topicssujets/gambling/5203656-eng.htm).

Statistics Canada, 2008c. "Canadian Community Health Survey." The Daily (June 18).

Statistics Canada. 2008d. Pregnancy Outcomes by Age Group (Live Births). Retrieved February 23, 2013 (http://www.statcan.gc.ca/tables-tableaux/sum-som/l01/cst01/hlth65b-eng.htm).

Statistics Canada. 2008e. More Than Half of Divorced Canadians Stated that they Do Not Intend to Remarry. Retrieved February 23, 2013 (http://www.statcan.gc.ca/pub/89-630-x/2008001/c-g/10659/5201038-eng.htm).

Statistics Canada. 2008f. "2006 Census Information on Same-Sex Common-Law and Married Couples." 2006 Census: Reference Material (October 15). Retrieved February 24, 2009 (http://www12.statcan.ca/census-recensement/2006/ref/info/same_sex-meme_sexe-eng.cfm).

Statistics Canada. 2008g. Divorces, by Province and Territory. Retrieved February

23, 2014 (http://www.statcan.gc.ca/tables-tableaux/sum-som/l01/cst01/famil02-eng.htm).

Statistics Canada. 2009. Visible Minority Population, By Census Metropolitan Areas (2006 Census). Retrieved October 11, 2013 (http://www.statcan.gc.ca/tables-tableaux/sum-som/l01/cst01/demo53c-eng.htm).

Statistics Canada. 2009a. "Aboriginal Peoples Survey: School Experiences of Children Aged 6 to 14 Living Off Reserve." The Daily (January 16).

Statistics Canada. 2010. Income in Canada, 2010. Retrieved May 6, 2013 (http://www.statcan.gc.ca/pub/75-202-x/2010000/c-g/ct006-eng.htm)..

Statistics Canada. 2011. "Aboriginal Identity." National Household Survey. Retrieved August 31, 2014 (http://www12.statcan.gc.ca/nhs-enm/2011/as-sa/99-011-x/2011001/tbl/tbl01-eng.cfm).

Statistics Canada. 2011a. "Shelters for Abused Women in Canada, 2010." Juristat. Retrieved May 3, 2013 (http://www.statcan.gc.ca/pub/85-002-x/2011001/article/11495-eng.htm#a12).

Statistics Canada. 2012a. "2011 Census of Population: Families, households, Marital Status, Structural Type Of Dwelling, Collectives." The Daily. Retrieved August 27 (http://www.statcan.gc.ca/daily-quotidien/120919/dq120919a-eng.htm).

Statistics Canada. 2012b. "Age-Standardized Mortality Rates for the 10 Leading Causes of Death, Canada, 2000 and 2009." Leading Causes of Death in Canada, 2009. Retrieved August 28, 2013 (http://www.statcan.gc.ca/pub/84-215-x/2012001/table-tableau/tbl007-eng.htm).

Statistics Canada. 2012c. "Family Violence in Canada: A Statistical Profile, 2010." Juristat. Retrieved May 3, 2013 (http://www.statcan.gc.ca/pub/85-002-x/2012001/article/11643/tbl/tbl3-1-eng.htm).

Statistics Canada. 2012d. "University Tuition Fees 2011/2012." The Daily. Retrieved June 20, 2103 (http://www.statcan.gc.ca/daily-quotidien/120912/dq120912aeng. htm).

Statistics Canada. 2012e. "Smoking, 2011." Health Fact Sheets. Retrieved June 21, 2013 (http://www.statcan.gc.ca/pub/82-625-x/2012001/article/11668-eng.htm).

Statistics Canada. 2012f. "Police-Reported Racially Motivated Hate Crimes 2010."

Juristat. Retrieved June 29, 2013 (http://www.statcan.gc.ca/pub/85-002-x/2012001/article/11635/c-g/desc/desc06-eng.htm).

Statistics Canada. 2012g. "Crime, 2011." Juristat. Retrieved June 28, 2013 (http://www.statcan.gc.ca/pub/85-005-x/2012001/article/11745-eng.htm).

Statistics Canada. 2012h. "Adult Correctional Services, 2010/2011." The Daily. Retrieved July 1, 2013 (http://www.statcan.gc.ca/daily-quotidien/121011/t121011c001-eng.htm).

Statistics Canada. 2013. Canada at a Glance 2013. Retrieved June 17, 2013 (http://www.statcan.gc.ca/pub/12-581-x/12-581-x2013000-eng.htm).

Statistics Canada. 2013a. "Admissions to Adult Correctional Services in Canada." Canadian Centre for Justice Statistics Adult Correctional Services Survey 2011/2012 and National Household Survey 2011. Retrieved September 20, 2014 (http://www.statcan.gc.ca/pub/85-002-x/2014001/article/11918-eng.htm).

Statistics Canada. 2013b. Violence Against Women, 2011. Retrieved September 15, 2014 (http://www.statcan.gc.ca/daily-quotidien/130225/dq130225a-eng.htm).

Statistics Canada. 2013c. "Number of Centenarians in Canada." Analytical Products. Retrieved August 19, 2013 (http://www12.statcan.gc.ca/census-recensement/2011/as-sa/98-311-x/2011003/fig/fi g3_1-1-eng.cfm).

Statistics Canada. 2013d. Study: Caregivers in Canada, 2012. Retrieved November 3, 2013 (http://www.statcan.gc.ca/dailyquotidien/130910/dq130910a-eng.htm).

Statistics Canada. 2013e. "Portrait of Families and Living Arrangements in Canada." 2011 Analytical Products. Retrieved May 3, 2013 (http://www12.statcan.gc.ca/census-recensement/2011/as-sa/98-312-x/2011001/tbl/tbl1-eng.cfm).

Statistics Canada. 2013f. 2011 Census of Canada: Topic-Based Tabulations. Retrieved November 23, 2013 (http://www12.statcan.gc.ca/census-recensement/2011/dp-pd/tbt-tt/Rp-eng.cfm?LANG=E&APATH=3&DETAIL=0&DIM=0&FL=A&FREE=0&GC=0&GID=0&GK=0&GRP=1&PID=102659&PRID=0&PTYPE=101955&S=0&SHOWALL=0&SUB=0&Temporal=2011&THEME=89&VID=0&VNAMEE=&VNAMEF=).

Statistics Canada. 2013g. An Overview of Issues - Mental Health and the Criminal Justice System. Retrieved September 9, 2013 (http://www.statcan.gc.ca/pub/85-561-m/2009016/section-a-eng.htm).

Statistics Canada. 2013h. "Fifty Years of Families in Canada: 1961to 2011." 2011 Analytical Products. Retrieved May 3, 2013 (http://www12.statcan.gc.ca/census-recensement/2011/as-sa/98-312-x/2011003/fig/fig3_1-1-eng.cfm).

Statistics Canada. 2013i. Study: Living Apart Together. Retrieved February 23, 2014 (http://www.statcan.gc.ca/daily-quotidien/130305/dq130305a-eng.htm).

Statistics Canada. 2013j. "Self-Reported Internet Victimization in Canada, 2009." Juristat. Retrieved November 25, 2013 (http://www.statcan.gc.ca/pub/85-002-x/2011001/article/11530-eng.htm).

Statistics Canada. 2013k. 2011 National Household Survey: Education in Canada: Attainment, Field of and Location of Study. Retrieved March 10, 2015 (http://www.statcan.gc.ca/daily-quotidien/130626/dq130626a-eng.htm).

Statistics Canada. 2013l. Infant Mortality Rates by Province and Territory. Retrieved September 17, 2013 (http://www.statcan.gc.ca/tables-tableaux/sum-som/l01/cst01/health21a-eng.htm).

Statistics Canada. 2013m. The Refugee System in Canada. Retrieved September 1, 2013 (http://www.cic.gc.ca/english/refugees/canada.asp).

Statistics Canada. 2013n. Study: Composting by Households in Canada. Retrieved September 22, 2013 (http://www.statcan.gc.ca/daily-quotidien/130710/dq130710a-eng.htm).

Statistics Canada. 2013o. Report on the Demographic Situation in Canada. Retrieved March 18, 2015 (http://www.statcan.gc.ca/pub/91-209-x/91-209-x2013001-eng.htm).

Statistics Canada. 2013p. Canadian Survey on Disability, 2012. Retrieved December 3, 2013 (http://www.statcan.gc.ca/pub/89-654-x/89-654-x2013002-eng.htm).

Statistics Canada. 2013q. "Wage gap Between Bachelor Degree Holders and High School Graduates, 2000 to 2011." Economic Insights. Retrieved June 20, 2013 (http://www.statcan.gc.ca/pub/11-626-x/2012008/c-g/c-g03-eng.htm).

Statistics Canada. 2013r. "Immigration and Ethnocultural Diversity in Canada." National Household Survey. Retrieved September 2, 2014 (http://www12.statcan.gc.ca/nhs-enm/2011/as-sa/99-010-x/2011001/tbl/tbl2-eng.cfm).

Statistics Canada. 2013s. "Trends in Economic Performance of Immigrants in Canada." Retrieved September. 9, 2014 (http://www.cic.gc.ca/english/resources/research/2012-migrant/sec05.asp).

Statistics Canada. 2013t. Incident-Based Crime Statistics, By Detailed Violations. CANSIM. Retrieved March 19, 2014 (http://www5.statcan.gc.ca/cansim/pick-choisir?lang=eng&p2=33 &id=2520051).

Statistics Canada. 2013u. Control and sale of alcoholic beverages, for the year ending March 31, 2012 (correction). Retrieved April 29, 2014 (http://www.statcan.gc.ca/daily-quotidien/130411/dq130411a-eng.htm).

Statistics Canada. 2013v. "Homicide in Canada, 2011." Juristat. Retrieved June 29, 2013 (http://www.statcan.gc.ca/pub/85-002-x/2012001/article/11738-eng.htm).

Statistics Canada. 2013w. "Measuring Violence Against Women." Juristat. Retrieved June 29, 2013 (http://www.statcan.gc.ca/pub/85-002-x/2013001/article/11766/11766-1-eng.htm).

Statistics Canada. 2013x. "Youth Crime, 2011." Juristat. Retrieved June 18, 2013 (http://www.statcan.gc.ca/pub/85-005-x/2012001/article/11749-eng.htm).

Statistics Canada. 2013y. "Select health Indicators of First Nations People Living Off Reserve, Métis and Inuit." Health at a Glance. Retrieved June 19, 2013 (http://www.statcan.gc.ca/pub/82-624-x/2013001/article/11763-eng.htm).

Statistics Canada. 2013z. "Self-Reported Victimization." Retrieved June 28, 2013 (http://www.statcan.gc.ca/pub/85-002-x/2010002/article/11340/tbl/tbl1-eng.htm).

Statistics Canada. 2014. "Median Total Income in 2005 by Aboriginal Identity." Aboriginal Statistics at a Glance. Retrieved September 22, 2014 (http://www.statcan.gc.ca/pub/89-645-x/2010001/c-g/c-g011-eng.htm).

Statistics Canada. 2014a. "Aboriginal Education and Work." Aboriginal Peoples Survey. Retrieved September 2, 2014 (http://www.statcan.gc.ca/pub/89-653-x/2013001/hl-fs-eng.htm).

Statistics Canada. 2014b. Labour Force Survey, August 2014. Retrieved September 16, 2014 (http://www.statcan.gc.ca/daily-quotidien/140905/dq140905a-eng.htm).

Stefanac, Suzanne. 1993. "Sex and the New Media." *New Media* (April):38–45.

Stern, Christopher. 1998. Researchers Shocked to Find—TV Violence. Variety (April20) 26:24.

Stewart, Charles T., Jr. 1995. Healthy, Wealthy, or Wise? Issues in American Health Care Policy. Armonk, NY: M.E. Sharpe.

Stiglitz, Joseph, and Linda Bilmes. 2008. The Three Trillion Dollar War: The True Cost of the Iraq Conflict. New York: W.W. Norton.

Stolte, Elise. 2009. "EnCana Ups Reward for Info on B.C. Pipeline Bomber." Edmonton Journal (July 30). Retrieved August 24, 2009 (http://www.globaltvedmonton.com/EnCana+bomber+reward/1845057/story.html).

Strueck, Wendy. 2014. "We Don't Need a National Inquiry." The Globe and Mail. (December 20):A6.

Stueck, Wendy, and Sarah Boesveld. 2008. "Schools Not Entirely Bad, Native Writer Contends." Globe and Mail (June 12):A8.

Sturgeon, Noel. 1997. Ecofeminist Natures: Race, Gender, Feminist Theory and Political Action. New York: Routledge.

Sulaimanova, Saltanat. 2006. "Trafficking in Women from the Former Soviet Union for the Purposes of Sexual Exploitation." In Karen Beeks and Delila Amir (Eds.), Trafficking and the Global Sex Industry. Oxford, UK: Lexington Books, pp. 61–76.

Sullivan, Harmony B., and Maureen C. McHugh. 2009. "The Critical Eye: Whose Fantasy Is This? Media Review of Dreamworlds 3: Desire, Sex and Power in Music Video." Sex Roles, 60(9–10):745–747.

Sutdhibhasilp, Noulmook. 2002. "Migrant Sex-Workers in Canada." In Susanne Thorbek and Bandana Pattanaik (Eds.), Transnational Prostitution: Changing Global Patterns. London: Zed Books, pp. 173–192

Sutherland, Edwin H. 1939. Principles of Criminology. Philadelphia: Lippincott.

Sutherland, Edwin H. 1949. White Collar Crime. New York: Dryden.

Swann, Maxine. 2013. "The Professor, the Bikini Model and the Suitcase Full of Trouble." New York Times Magazine (March 10). Retrieved March 10, 2013 (http://www.nytimes.com/2013/03/10/magazine/the-professor-the-bikini-model-and-the-suitcase-full-of-trouble.html).

Swanson, Jean. 1997. "Resisting Workfare." In Eric Shragge (Ed.), Workfare: Ideology for a New Under-Class. Toronto: Garamond Press, pp. 149–170.

Swanson, Jean. 2001. Poor-Bashing: The Politics of Exclusion. Toronto: Between the Lines.

Swift, Jamie, Jacqueline M. Davies, Robert G. Clarke, and Michael Czerny S.J. 2003. Getting Started on Social Analysis in Canada (4th ed.). Toronto: Between the Lines.

Swingewood, Alan. 2000. A Short History of Sociological Thought (3rd ed.). London: Macmillan Press.

Tannen, Deborah. 1990. You Just Don't Understand: Women and Men in Conversation. New York: William Morrow.

Taylor, Leanne. 2008. "Looking North: Exploring Multiracial Experiences in a Canadian Context." New Directions for Student Services,123(Fall). Published online by Wiley InterScience (http://www.interscience.wiley.com).

Taylor, M., Ethel Quayle, G. Holland. (2001). "Child Pornography, the Internet and Offending," The Canadian Journal of Policy Research (ISUMA), 2(2): 94–100.

Taylor, M. and E. Quayle. (2006). "Situational Perspectives of Sexual Offences against Children," Crime Prevention Studies Series (jointly published by Criminal Justice Press (US) and Willan Publishing (UK).

Teeple, Gary. 2000. "The Decline of the Canadian Welfare State: Policies and Implications of Retrenchment." In B. Singh Bolaria (Ed.), Social Issues and Contradictions in Canadian Society (3rd ed.). Toronto: Harcourt Brace, pp. 434–468. Wilson, William Julius. 1996. When Work Disappears: The World of the New Urban Poor. New York: Knopf.

Teotonio, Isabel. 2014. "Women Find Power in #BeenRapedNeverReported Hashtag." Toronto Star. Retrieved November 8, 2014 (http://www.thestar.com/life/2014/11/05/women_find_power_in_beenrapedneverreported_hashtag.html).

Tepperman, Lorne. 2009. Betting Their Lives: The Close Relations of Problem Gamblers. Don Mills, ON: Oxford University Press.

Tepperman, Lorne, and Jenny Blain. 2006. Think Twice! Sociology Looks at Current Social Issues (2nd ed.). Upper Saddle River, NJ: Prentice Hall.

Tepperman, Lorne, Patrizia Albanese, Sasha Stark, and Nadine Zahlan. 2013. The Dostoevsky Effect: Problem Gambling and the Origins of Addiction. Toronto, ON: Oxford University Press.

The Chilly Collective (Eds.). 1995. Breaking Anonymity: The Chilly Climate for Women Faculty. Ontario: Wilfred Laurier University Press.

The Coca-Cola Company. (2005). United States Securities and Exchange Commission: Form 10-K (December 31). Retrieved July 11, 2009 (http://www.sec.gov/Archives/Edgar/data/21344/000104746906002588/a2167326z10-k.htm).

The Economist. 2014. Pocket World Guide to Figures 2014. London, UK: Profile Books Ltd.

Theckedath, Dillan, and Terrence J. Thomas. 2012. Media Ownership and Convergence in Canada. Library of Parliament Research Publications. Retrieved May 24, 2014 (http://www.parl.gc.ca/content/lop/researchpublications/2012-17-e.htm).

Thobani, Sunera. 2001a. Speech at the "Women's Resistance: From Victimization to Criminalization" conference, October 1. Transcript provided by the Cable Public Affairs Channel (http://www.casac.ca/conference01/conf01_thobani.htm).

Thomas, Cal. 1996. "Overrule Same-Sex Marriage." Austin American-Statesman (December 6):A15.

Thomas, G. (2012). Analysis of Beverage Alcohol Sales in Canada. (Alcohol Price Policy Series: Report 2). Ottawa, ON: Canadian Centre on Substance Abuse.

Thomson, Elizabeth, and Ugo Colella. 1992. "Cohabitation and Marital Stability: Quality or Commitment?" Journal of Marriage and the Family, 54:259–267.

Thornton, Michael C., Linda M. Chatters, Robert Joseph Taylor, and Walter R. Allen. 1990. "Sociodemographic and Environmental Correlates of Racial Socialization by Black Parents." Child Development, 61:401–409.

Tierney, John. 1994. "Porn, the Low-Slung Engine of Progress." New York Times (January 9). Retrieved January 9, 1994 (http://www.nytimes.com/1994/01/09/arts/porn-the-low-slung-engine-of-progress.html?pagewanted=2).

Tierney, John. 2009. "Public Policy That Makes Test Subjects of Us All." New York Times (April 6). Retrieved April 15, 2009 (http://www.nytimes.com/2009/04/07/science/07tier.html).

Tjepkema, Michael. 2008. "Health Care Use Among Gay, Lesbian and Bisexual Canadians." Health Reports, Vol. 19, No. 1. Statistics Canada. Catalogue 82-003. Retrieved November 23, 2013 (http://www.statcan.gc.ca/pub/82-003-x/2008001/article/10532-eng.pdf).

Tjepkema, Michael, and Russell Wilkins. 2011. "Remaining Life Expectancy at Age 25 and Probability of Survival to Age 75, by Socio-Economic Status and Aboriginal Ancestry." Health Reports. Retrieved August 21, 2013(http://www.statcan.gc.ca/pub/82-003-x/2011004/article/11560-eng.htm).

Tjepkema, Michael, Russell Wilkins, and Andrea Lonh. 2013. "Cause-Specific Mortality by Income Adequacy in Canada: A 16-Year Follow-Up Study." Statistic Canada. Retrieved August 21, 2013 (http://www.statcan.gc.ca/pub/82-003-x/2013007/article/11852-eng.htm).

Tjepkema, Michael, Russell Wilkins, and Andrea Long. 2013. Cause-Specific Mortality by Income Adequacy in Canada. Statistics Canada. Retrieved July 17, 2013 http://www.statcan.gc.ca/pub/82-003-x/2013007/article/11852-eng.htm

Tovée, M.J., S.M. Mason, J.L. Emery, S.E. McCloskey, and E.M. Cohen-Tovee. 1997. "Supermodels: Stick Insects or Hourglasses." Lancet, 350(9089): 1474–1475.

Tower, Cynthia Crosson. 1996. Child Abuse and Neglect (3rd ed.). Boston: Allyn and Bacon.

Transcend Transgender Support and Education Society. 2001. Transforming Community: Resources for Trans People, Intersexed People and their Families. Victoria, BC: Transcend Transgender Support and Education Society.

Transport Canada. 2013. Canadian Motor Vehicle Traffic Collision Statistics 2011. Retrieved December 15, 2014 (http://www.tc.gc.ca/media/documents/road-safety/TrafficCollisionStatisitcs_2011.pdf).

Trocmé, Nico, Barbara Fallon, Bruce MacLaurin, Vandna Sinha, Tara Black, Elizabeth Fast, Caroline Felstiner, Sonia Hélie, Daniel Turcotte, Pamela Weightman, Janet Douglas, and Jill Holroyd. 2010. *2008 Canadian Incidence Study of Reported Child Abuse and Neglect*. Public Health Agency of Canada, Ottawa, ON.

Trocmé, Nico, Bruce MacLaurin, Barbara Fallon, Tara Black, and Jules Lajoie. 2005. "Child Abuse and Neglect Investigations in Canada: Comparing 1998 and 2003 Data." CECW Information, 26E. Retrieved May 12, 2009 (http://www.cecw-cepb.ca/sites/default/files/publications/en/CISComparisons26E.pdf).

Turcotte, Martin, and Grant Schellenberg, 2007. A Portrait of Seniors in Canada. Ottawa: Statistics Canada, Social and Aboriginal Statistics Division.

Turk, Austin T. 1966. "Conflict and Criminality." American Sociological Review, 31:338–352.

Turk, Austin T. 1971. Criminality and Legal Order. Chicago: Rand McNally.

Turpin, Jennifer, and Lester R. Kurtz. 1997. "Introduction: Violence: The Micro/Macro Link." In Jennifer Turpin and Lester R. Kurtz (Eds.), The Web of Violence: From Interpersonal to Global. Urbana and Chicago: University of Illinois, pp. 1–27.

Tustin, Steve. 2013. "Canadian University Report." The Globe and Mail. Retrieved July 8, 2013 http://www.theglobeandmail.com/news/national/education/canadian-university-report/canadian-university-report-2013-student-satisfaction-survey-results/article4631980/.

"Unionize Prostitutes, Nfld. Labour Leader Urges." 2004. CBC News (September 8). Retrieved October 16, 2006 (http://www.cbc.ca/canada/story/2004/09/06/prostitute040906.html).

Unitarian Universalist Association of Congregations. 2009. "Unitarian Universalists Support Freedom to Marry!" (March 2). Retrieved April 5, 2009 (http://www.uua.org/visitors/justicediversity/128897.shtml?cid=fm15&gclid=CLTvr5Kv25kCFRk_awodkx79XA).

United Nations. 2000. Protocol to Prevent, Suppress and Punish Trafficking in Persons, Especially Women and Children, Supplementing the United Nations Convention Against Transnational Organized Crime. Retrieved January 29, 2009 (http://www.uncjin.org/Documents/Conventions/dcatoc/final_documents_2/convention_%20traff_eng.pdf)

United Nations Department of Economic and Social Affairs. 2012. World Urbanization Prospects, the 2011 Revision. Retrieved December 31, 2013 (http://esa.un.org/wpp/ppt/CSIS/WUP_2011_CSIS_4.pdf).

United Nations Development Program. 2014. The Gender Inequality Index 2013. Retrieved September 15, 2014 (http://hdr.undp.org/en/content/table-4-gender-inequality-index).

United Nations Population Fund. 2015. Choices not Chance. Retrieved January 21, 2015 (http://www.unfpa.org/sites/default/files/pub-pdf/UNFPA%20CHOICES%20NOT%20CHANCE_final.pdf).

United Nations Water. 2013. Water Use. Retrieved September 22, 2013 (http://www.unwater.org/watercooperation-2013/water-cooperation/facts-and-figures/en/).

UNODC. 2012a. Global Report on Trafficking in Persons 2012. Retrieved March 19, 2014 (http://www.unodc.org/documents/data-and-analysis/glotip/Trafficking_in_Persons_2012_web.pdf).

UNODC. 2012b. Country Profiles – The Americas. Retrieved March 19, 2014 (http://www.unodc.org/documents/data-and-analysis/glotip/Country_Profiles_Americas.pdf).

UNODC. 2013. Global Study on Homicide 2013. Retrieved June 6, 2014 (http://www.unodc.org/documents/gsh/pdfs/2014_GLOBAL_HOMICIDE_BOOK_web.pdf).

Valdivia, Angharad N. 1995. Feminist Media Studies in a Global Setting: Beyond Binary Contradictions and Into Multicultural Spectrums in Feminism, Multiculturalisms, and the Media. Thousand Oaks, CA: Sage.

Valverde, Mariana. 1998. "Sexuality." In Robert J. Brym (Ed.), New Society: Sociology for the 21st Century (2nd ed.). Toronto: Harcourt Brace, pp. 74–102.

Valverde, Mariana. 2000. "Lesbianism: A Country That Has No Language" (1987). In Barbara A. Crow and Lise Gotell (Eds.), Open Boundaries: A Canadian Women's Studies Reader. Toronto: Prentice Hall/Allyn and Bacon, pp. 255–261.

Valverde, 1985

Van Brunschot, Erin Gibbs. 2003. "Community Policing and 'John Schools.'" Canadian Review of Sociology and Anthropology, 40(2):215–232.

Veterans Affairs Canada. 2014. Second World War. Retrieved June 18, 2014 (http://www.veterans.gc.ca/eng/remembrance/history/second-world-war).

Vision of Humanity. 2013. Global Peace Index. Retrieved May 16, 2014 (http://www.visionofhumanity.org/#/page/our-gpi-findings).

Vissing, Yvonne M. 1996. Out of Sight, Out of Mind: Homeless Children and Families in Small-Town America. Lexington: University of Kentucky Press,

Vito, Gennaro F., and Ronald M. Holmes. 1994. Criminology: Theory, Research and Policy. Belmont, CA: Wadsworth.

Waldron, I. 1997. "Changing Gender Roles in Health Behavior." In D. Gochman (Ed.), Handbook of Health Behavior Research I: Personal and Social Determinants. New York: Plenum, pp. 303–328.

Wallerstein, Immanuel. 1984. *The Politics of the World Economy*. Cambridge England: Cambridge University Press.

Wallerstein, Judith, and Sandra Blakeslee. 1989. Second Chances: Men, Women and Children a Decade after Divorce. New York: Ticknor & Field.

Ward, Martha, and Monica Edelstein. 2014. A World Full of Women (Sixth Edition). Upper Saddle River, NJ: Pearson.

Wars in the World. 2014. Retrieved May 20, 2014 (http://www.warsintheworld.com/?page=static1258254223).

Warshaw, Robin. 1994. I Never Called It Rape. New York: HarperPerennial.

Weedon, Chris. 1999. Feminism, Theory and the Politics of Difference. Oxford, UK: Blackwell.

Weeks, Carly. 2008. "Safe Injection May Save System $14 Million." Globe and Mail (November 18):L1.

Weeks, John. R. 2012. Population: An Introduction to Concepts and Issues. (11th ed.). Belmont, CA: Cengage/Wadsworth.

Weinberg, Martin S., and Colin Williams. 1975. Male Homosexuals. New York: Penguin.

Weinberg, Martin S., Colin J. Williams, and Douglas W. Pryor. 1994. Dual Attraction: Understanding Bisexuality. New York: Oxford University Press.

Weinberg, Martin S., Earl Rubington, and Sue Kiefer Hammersmith. 1981. The Solution of Social Problems: Five Perspectives (2nd ed.). New York: Oxford University Press.

Weiner, Jonathan. 1990. The Next One Hundred Years: Shaping the Fate of Our Living Earth. New York: Bantam.

Weitz, Rose. 1996. The Sociology of Health, Illness, and Health Care: A Critical Approach. Belmont, CA: Wadsworth.

Weitz, Rose. 2010. The Sociology of Health, Illness, and Health Care: a Critical Approach (5th ed.). Belmont, CA: Cengage/Wadsworth.

Weitzer, Ronald. 2005. "New Directions in Research on Prostitution." Crime, Law and Social Change, 43:211–235.

WHO. 2013. 10 Facts on Obesity. Retrieved August 21, 2013 (http://www.who.int/features/factfiles/obesity/facts/en/index1.html).

WHO. 2013. Climate Change and Health. Retrieved September 23, 2013 (http://www.who.int/mediacentre/factsheets/fs266/en/).

WHO. 2013. HIV/AIDS. Retrieved August 21, 2013 (http://www.who.int/mediacentre/factsheets/fs360/en/index.html).

Wiebe, J., P. Mun, and N. Kauffman. 2006. Gambling and Problem Gambling in Ontario, 2005. Guelph, ON: Ontario Problem Gambling Research Centre.

Wildman, Stephanie M., and Adrienne D. Davis. 2002. "Making Systems of Privilege Visible." In Paula S. Rothenberg (Ed.), White Privilege: Essential Readings on the Other Side of Racism. New York: Worth, pp. 89–96.

Wilkins, Charles. 2015. "The Deep." Report on Business. March:55–63.

Wilkinson, Sue, and Celia Kitzinger. 1996. "The Queer Backlash." In Diane Bell and Renate Klein (Eds.), Radically Speaking: Feminism Reclaimed. London: Zed Books, pp. 375–382.

Williams, Cara. 2001. "Family Disruptions and Childhood Happiness." Canadian Social Trends (Autumn): 2–4.

Williams, Cara. 2013. "Economic Well-Being." Statistics Canada. Retrieved September 1, 2014 (http://www.statcan.gc.ca/pub/89-503-x/2010001/article/11388-eng.htm).

Williams, Christine L. 1995. Still a Man's World: Men Who Do Women's Work. Berkeley, CA: University of California Press.

Williams, Linda. 2004. Porn Studies. Durham and London, UK: Duke University Press.

Williams, Robin M., Jr. 1970. American Society: A Sociological Interpretation (3rd ed.). New York: Knopf.

Williamson, Robert C., Alice Duffy Rinehart, and Thomas O. Blank. 1992. Early Retirement: Promises and Pitfalls. New York: Plenum.

Willis, Ellen. 1981. Beginning to See the Light. New York: Knopf.

Willis, Ellen. 1983. "Feminism, Moralism, and Pornography." In Ann Snitow, Christine Stansell, and Sharon Thompson (Eds.), Powers of Desire: The Politics of Sexuality. New York: Monthly Review Press, pp. 460–466.

Wilson, Dan, and David Macdonald. 2010. The Income Gap Between Aboriginal Peoples and the Rest of Canada. Canadian Centre for Policy Alternatives. Retrieved September 9, 2014 (http://www.policyalternatives.ca/sites/default/files/uploads/publications/reports/docs/Aboriginal%20Income%20Gap.pdf).

Wilson, David (Ed.). 1997. "Globalization and the Changing U.S. City." The Annals of the American Academy of Political and Social Science, 551(May). Special Issue. Thousand Oaks, CA: Sage.

Wilson, Susannah J. 2001. "Paid Work, Jobs and the Illusion of Economic Security." In Nancy Mandell (Ed.), Feminist Issues: Race, Class, and Sexuality (3rd ed.). Toronto: Pearson, pp. 219–241.

Wilton, Tamsin. 2000. Sexualities in Health and Social Care: A Textbook. Buckingham, UK: Open University Press.

Wilson, William Julius. 1996. When Work Disappears: The World of the New Urban Poor. New York: Knopf.

Winsa, Patty. 2013. "Police Board Takes Steps to Monitor 'Carding' of Young Men." thestar.com (April 26). Retrieved June 28, 2013 (http://www.thestar.com/news/gta/2012/04/05/police_board_takes_steps_to_monitor_carding_of_young_men.html).

Winsa, Patty. 2014. "Improper Police 'Carding' Continues in Jane-finch Area, Survey Finds." thestar.com (November 12) A1 and A11.

Wirth, Louis. 1938. "Urbanism as a Way of Life." American Journal of Sociology, 40:1–24.

Wolf, Robin. 1996. Marriages and Families in a Diverse Society. New York: HarperCollins.

Wolff, Lee, and Dorota Geissel. 2000. "Street Prostitution in Canada." In Canadian Social Trends, 3. Ottawa: Minister of Supply and Services Canada, and Toronto: Thompson, pp. 253–257.

Wolfgang, Marvin E., and Franco Ferracuti. 1967. The Subculture of Violence: Towards an Integrated Theory in Criminology. Beverly Hills, CA: Sage.

Women's International Network. 1995. "Sex Trade Flourishing in Japan." WIN News 21(Winter):42.

Working Group I Contribution to the IPCC Fifth Assessment Report. 2013. Climate Change 2013: The Physical Science Basis. Summary for Policymakers. Retrieved September 29, 2013 (http://www.climatechange2013.org/).

World Health Organization. 2011. Global Status Report on Alcohol and Health. Retrieved July 6, 2013 (http://www.who.int/substance_abuse/publications/global_alcohol_report/en/index.html).

World Hunger Education Service. 2013. 2013 World Hunger and Poverty Facts and Statistics. Retrieved September 1, 2013 (http://www.worldhunger.org/articles/Learn/world%20hunger%20facts%202002.htm)#Number_of_hungry_people_in_the_world).

Wren, Christopher. 1996. "Teen-Agers Find Drugs Easy to Obtain and Warnings Easy to Ignore." New York Times (October 10):A12.

Wright, Erik Olin. 1979. Class Structure and Income Determination. New York: Academic Press.

Wright, Erik Olin. 1985. Class. London: Verso.

Wright, Erik Olin. 1997. Class Counts: Comparative Studies in Class Analysis. Cambridge, UK: Cambridge University Press.

Yar, Majid. 2006. Cybercrime and Society. London, UK: Sage Publications Ltd.

Yinger, J. Milton. 1994. Ethnicity: Source of Strength, Source of Conflict? Albany, NY: SUNY Press.

Young, J.H. 1961. The Toadstool Millionaires: A Social History of Patent Medicine in America before Federal Regulation. Princeton, NJ: Princeton University Press.

Young, Michael Dunlap. 1994. The Rise of the Meritocracy. New Brunswick, NJ: Transaction.

Zekulin, Michael. 2014. "Homeward Bound: Made-in-Canada Terror." The Globe and Mail. June 11:A15.

Name Index

Note: Page numbers are annotated with b for boxes, t for tables, and f for figures, where appropriate.

Subject Index

Note: Page numbers are annotated with b for boxes, t for tables, and f for figures, where appropriate.